BANKRUPTCY AND
INSOLVENCY ACCOUNTING

Bankruptcy and Insolvency Accounting

PRACTICE AND PROCEDURE

Third Edition

GRANT W. NEWTON, C.P.A.

A RONALD PRESS PUBLICATION

JOHN WILEY & SONS
New York · Chichester · Brisbane · Toronto · Singapore

ISBN 0-471-81232-3

Printed in the United States of America

10 9 8 7 6 5 4 3 2 1

To my parents

ROY and GENEVA NEWTON

Preface

This book is designed to provide a broad range of practical guidance for accountants, lawyers, bankruptcy trustees, referees, and creditors of business enterprises in financial straits.

The role of the independent accountant is viewed against a background of economic, legal, and management considerations, and the interdependence of the various interests involved is clearly delineated.

From informal adjustments made out of court through full court proceedings under chapter 11 jurisdiction, the book discusses alternative courses of action, working procedures, and statutory requirements applicable to the particular situation. The accountant is shown the type of information required by the debtor attorney for the bankruptcy petition and how to prepare operating statements to be filed with the court. He is aided in formulating a plan of reorganization that will gain acceptance by creditors and at the same time allow the client to operate a business successfully. The means by which the accountant can help the creditors' committee exercise adequate control over the debtor's activities are also described.

The bankruptcy and insolvency audit, or special investigation, is explored in detail, with emphasis on the detection of irregularities and procedures to be performed if irregularities exist. The types of reports often required of the accountant are illustrated, and advice is offered on the special problems encountered in reporting on a company in financial difficulty. The reader is taken step by step through a typical bankruptcy audit, including preparation of requisite forms and issuance of the audit report.

Taxes, which often impose undue hardship on the bankrupt during the administration period, are dealt with in a separate chapter. Instructions are given for tax minimization, filing returns, treatment of income during bankruptcy, and dealing with the varied tax planning and compliance problems peculiar to bankruptcy. The tax coverage is limited. For a detailed and current discussion of tax issues faced by the debtors having financial trouble, see *Tax Planning for the Troubled Business,* written by Grant W. Newton and Gilbert D. Bloom, also published by Wiley, and revised annually.

This third edition has been revised to include the provisions of the Bankruptcy Amendments and Federal Judgeship Act of 1984 and court decisions reached by Bankruptcy or District judges based on the Bankruptcy Code.

The auditing chapter has been rewritten to comply with recently issued Statements on Auditing Standards, and the audit program has been modified and expanded. The tax chapter has been revised to contain the provisions of the Tax Reform Act of 1984.

In addition to the coverage of practical procedure and statutory provisions, the book views the history of financial failure. It is hoped, therefore, that the work overall will serve the advancement of understanding and competence in this essential but sometimes neglected area of accounting.

Comments from users are welcomed.

GRANT W. NEWTON

Westlake Village, California
February 1985

SUBSCRIBE NOW

Starting with this edition, Newton's *Bankruptcy and Insolvency Accounting* will be kept up to date through a series of annual cumulative supplements. If you wish to keep current on bankruptcy and insolvency matters, just fill out the reply card in the front of this book. Supplements will be sent automatically to you—completely on approval.

For further information, write to John Wiley & Sons, attn: Richard G. Lynch, 605 Third Avenue, New York, NY 10158.

Acknowledgments

Many individuals provided invaluable assistance during the writing of this book, particularly the members of the Committee on Development of a Manual of Bankruptcy and Insolvency Procedures of the New York Society of Certified Public Accountants, who provided support, encouragement, and timely assistance on many occasions during the writing of the first edition.

Although it is not possible to recognize all of the persons to whom thanks are due, acknowledgment for providing assistance for the first edition is gratefully given to Robert A. Adams and Dan E. Williams of Arthur Andersen & Co.; Bernard L. Augen, Louis Klein, Milton Mintzer, and Irving Rom of Clarence Rains & Co.; Kermit Easton of S. D. Leidesdorf & Co.; Walter J. Henning of J. K. Lasser & Co.; Jerry Klein of Hertz, Herson & Co.; Professor Joseph E. Lane, Jr. of The University of Alabama; Professors Norman Martin and Jeremy Wiesen of New York University; Elliot Meisel of Roberts & Leinwander; Alexander E. Slater and Jerry Toder of Seidman & Seidman; Burton D. Strumpf of Ballon, Stoll & Itzler; and Edward A. Weinstein of Touche Ross & Co.

Support was received from many individuals in preparing the second edition. Edward A. Weinstein of Touche Ross & Co. provided considerable insight into some of the practical problems faced by accountants. John Costello of Arthur Young & Company reviewed the entire manuscript and also provided some excellent examples. Edward Ehrenberg of Laventhol & Horwath provided suggestions on the impact of the new law on accountants. Bernard Shapiro of Gendel, Raskoff, Shapiro & Quittner helped me interpret some of the major provisions of the new bankruptcy law. Jack A. Cipra, John A. Flynn, Andrew A. Krinock, Russel A. Lippman, and Howard C. White of Arthur Andersen & Co. made significant contributions to the edition by providing information about their experience and by reviewing parts of the manuscript. The support of these individuals is gratefully acknowledged.

I am especially grateful to Kenneth N. Klee of Stutman, Treister & Glatt for his assistance in helping me interpret the provisions of the new bankruptcy law, and for reviewing the legal parts of the book.

The careful review of the entire manuscript by Joseph A. Laurion of Kaye, Fialkow, Richmond & Rothstein was most helpful. Also, I am grateful for his assistance in helping me practically apply many of the new provisions of the new law.

In revising the third edition, I am especially grateful to Donald E. Condit, Partner, Arthur Andersen & Company, Los Angeles for assisting me with Chapter 12 and for helping me to obtain a large amount of practical experience. The support of Dr. Jere Yates, Chairman of the Business Division, Seaver College, and the assistance of Shirley Gibford, Administrative Assistant, both of Pepperdine University, are gratefully acknowledged.

I am grateful to Dr. Lee J. Seidler, New York University, for introducing me to the area of bankruptcy accounting and for the many valuable suggestions he provided during the writing of the book.

Finally, I thank Valda L. Newton for her editorial assistance and for her patience and understanding while I revised this edition.

G.W.N.

Contents

BANKRUPTCY AND INSOLVENCY ACCOUNTING

PART ONE
Bankruptcy and Insolvency Environment

The Accountant's Role in Perspective

1   Thousands of businesses fail each year in the United States and the number grew considerably in 1980. The liabilities associated with these failures have escalated every year since 1968, representing a percentage increase of over 400 percent. It was estimated in 1970 that one out of every five Americans had been involved in bankruptcy proceedings as a bankrupt or a creditor, or was acquainted with someone who had become bankrupt.[1] The number involved today is much higher.

2   At one time or another almost all accountants will find that one or more of their clients are experiencing some type of financial difficulty. Since accountants are often the first professional persons to realize that a financial problem exists, they are in a position to render very valuable services. Before accountants can give useful advice to a financially troubled client, they must be thoroughly familiar with the various alternatives available to the client and the ramifications of each.

3   The purpose of this book is to analyze in detail the accountant's role in bankruptcy and insolvency procedures, and to provide a practice guide that will assist accountants in rendering professional services in the liquidation and rehabilitation of financially troubled debtors in and out of bankruptcy court. The book describes those aspects of bankruptcy and insolvency proceedings of which accountants must be aware, delineating their functions and duties and the procedures they must follow in the auditing inquiry and in the preparation of the various financial statements and reports that are required by the courts. It presents the accounting methods, procedures, and techniques that may be used and explains the applicability of generally accepted accounting principles (GAAP) and generally accepted auditing standards (GAAS) to bankruptcy and insolvency proceedings. Finally, it discusses the conflicts and problems in principles and practice.

4   It is hoped that this book will also benefit nonaccountants such as trustees, judges, and attorneys in clarifying the purposes, nature, and limitations of the services of the accountant. Although the primary effort in the development of the book has been directed to the accountant in an explanation of "how to do it" and in a discussion of the ethical problems and responsibilities involved, the coverage of the economic and legal aspects of bankruptcy and insolvency should be of value to other professionals involved in these proceedings.

SCOPE OF COVERAGE

5   The scope of the book is, deliberately, fairly broad. The various accounting procedures to be followed under each alternative remedy for business failure are analyzed in detail. To provide a complete and realistic description of the environment within which the accountant must work, the

---

[1] David T. Stanley et al., *Bankruptcy: Problems, Process, Reform* (Washington, D.C.: The Brookings Institution, 1971), p. 1.

discussion incorporates the economics and the legal aspects of business liquidations and rehabilitations.

6 The economics of bankruptcy and insolvency proceedings is most important when considering the various causes of financial difficulties. Once the causes have been ascertained, the most appropriate remedy may then be determined. Economic considerations are also important when analyzing what remedies have proven most successful in particular circumstances.

7 The legal aspects of bankruptcy permeate the entire book, for the Federal Bankruptcy Code (title 11) establishes the framework within which anyone concerned with insolvency must work. As a result the Bankruptcy Code is explicitly cited in the descriptions of the petitions, forms, and schedules that must be filed; the alternatives and rights available to all parties involved, including the creditors; the requirements of the debtor; and the treatment of the various transactions and property of the debtor, both before and after the proceedings. Bankruptcy and insolvency proceedings cannot be correctly handled unless everyone involved has a thorough understanding of the legal aspects of the case.

8 Only about 18 percent of the bankruptcy court petitions are filed by businesses. The majority of the balance are filed by wage earners; however, it is primarily the business bankruptcy and insolvency proceedings that require the services of an accountant. As a result, the book is written for business bankruptcies. Although the emphasis is on incorporated businesses, the book is also applicable to partnerships and proprietaries since the remedies available are basically the same.

THE NEED FOR ACCOUNTANTS' SERVICES

9 The accountant can provide various kinds of services that can be effective in helping the debtor overcome its financial problems and again operate profitably, and that can also assist the creditors and their committees in deciding on the type of action they should take. The accountant may become a party to insolvency and bankruptcy proceedings while serving a client who is having financial problems. Before resorting to judicial proceedings, the debtor may attempt to negotiate a moratorium or settlement of its debt with unsecured creditors. Accountants may be retained by the debtor and/or creditors' committee to perform accounting services.

10 Reorganization of a corporation under chapter 11 of the Bankruptcy Code involves many parties who may need the assistance of accountants. First, the debtor, who remains in possession, has the right to retain an accountant to perform necessary accounting functions. Others include attorneys, trustee, examiner, creditors, security holders, and stockholders.

11 In liquidation proceedings under chapter 7 of the Bankruptcy Code the accountant often assists in accounting for the distribution of the debtor's assets. If the liquidation proceedings are initiated involuntarily, the petitioning creditors will need the assistance of an accountant in establishing a case of insolvency, and the debtor will need an accountant's assistance in trying to prove a defense of solvency. An audit investigation may be required for specific purposes, such as by the debtor to defend a turnover proceeding or by a third party to defend a suit by the trustee alleging a preferential transfer.[2]

12   The trustee as the appointed or elected representative of the creditors in a bankruptcy court proceeding most frequently finds it necessary to employ an accountant to audit the debtor's books, records, and transactions. A corporation's past transactions may need investigation to determine whether any assets have been concealed or removed or any preferences, fraudulent conveyances, or other voidable transactions committed. Often the debtor may have kept inadequate books and records, further complicating the situation.

13   Under section 1103 of the Bankruptcy Code the creditors' committee is permitted to employ such agents, attorneys, and accountants as may be necessary to assist it in the performance of its functions. Thus the committee may retain its own accountant to audit the debtor's books and records. The creditors' committee is expected to render an opinion on the plan of reorganization, and to do so it must have knowledge of the debtor's acts and property. It must know the value of the debtor's assets in liquidation and the nature of the transactions entered into by the debtor before proceedings began. Since accountants are most qualified to establish these facts, they are often engaged to perform an investigatory audit so that the committee will be able to give an informed opinion on the plan.

14   The debtor's internal accounting staff is also actively involved in the proceedings. Staff members often provide information or advice which assists the debtor in selecting the appropriate remedy. They also provide the debtor's attorneys with the accounting information needed to file the bankruptcy court petition.

"Accountants" Defined

15   It is not unusual to see several accountants involved in bankruptcy court proceedings. There may be independent accountants for the debtor, internal accountants of a debtor company, independent accountants for the trustee, and independent accountants representing the creditors' committee or individual holder of claims. Many of the accounting functions may be performed by more than one accountant. For example, each of the accountants will want to determine the underlying causes of failure. The term "accountants" is used here to refer to any accountant involved in the proceedings; where the service must be rendered by a particular accountant, the type of accountant is identified either in the text or at the beginning of the chapter.

---

[2] Asa S. Herzog, "CPA's Role in Bankruptcy Proceeding," *The Journal of Accountancy,* Vol. 117 (January 1964), p. 59.

TOPICAL OVERVIEW

Economic Causes of Business Failure

16 The first topic discussed, in chapter 2, is the economic causes that lead to business failure. A knowledge of the common causes of financial trouble can often enable the accountant to identify a potential problem, and corrective action can be taken before the situation becomes too serious. Methods of detecting failure tendencies are also described.

Alternatives Available to a Financially Troubled Business

17 In order to render services effectively in bankruptcy and insolvency proceedings, the accountant must be familiar with the Federal Bankruptcy Code (title 11 of United States Code). Chapter 3 begins with a discussion of the history of the bankruptcy law in the United States, and the provisions of the Bankruptcy Code are described throughout chapters 3 and 5.

18 The debtor's first alternatives are to locate new financing, to merge with another company, or to find some other basic solution to its situation, in order to avoid the necessity of discussing its problems with representatives of creditors. If none of these alternatives are possible, the debtor may be required to seek a remedy from creditors, either informally (out of court), or with the help of judicial proceedings. To insure that the reader is familiar with some of the alternatives available, they are briefly described in the paragraphs that follow. A general assignment for the benefit of creditors, the general provisions of the Bankruptcy Code, and bankruptcy court liquidation proceedings are described in greater detail in chapter 3. Often debtors prefer to work out their financial problems with creditors by mutual agreement out of court; these settlements are described in chapter 4. The chapter 11 reorganization is the second major rehabilitation device for a debtor and is analyzed in chapter 5 and throughout this book.

Out-of-Court Settlements

19 The debtor may request a meeting with a few of the largest creditors and one or two representatives of the small claimants to effect an informal agreement. The function of such a committee may be merely to investigate, consult, and give advice to the debtor, or it may involve actual supervision of the business or liquidation of the assets. An informal settlement usually involves an extension of time (a moratorium), a pro rata settlement (composition), or a combination of the two. The details of the plan are worked out between the debtor and creditors, the latter perhaps represented by a committee. Such extralegal proceedings are most successful when there are only a few creditors, adequate accounting records have been kept, and past relationships have been amicable. The chief disadvantage of this remedy is that there is no power to bind those creditors who do not agree to the plan of settlement.

Assignment for Benefit of Creditors

20   A remedy available under state law to a corporation in serious financial difficulties is an "assignment for the benefit of creditors." In this instance, the debtor voluntarily transfers title to its assets to an assignee who then liquidates them and distributes the proceeds among the creditors. Assignment for the benefit of creditors is an extreme remedy because it results in the cessation of the business. This informal (although court-supervised in many states) liquidation device, like the out-of-court settlement devised to rehabilitate the debtor, requires the consent of all the creditors or at least their agreement to refrain from taking action. The appointment of a custodian over the assets of the debtor gives creditors the right to file an involuntary bankruptcy court petition.

21   Proceedings brought in the federal courts are governed by the Bankruptcy Code. It will normally be necessary to resort to such formality when suits have already been filed against the debtor and its property is under garnishment, attachment, or threatened by foreclosure or eviction.

Chapter 11—Reorganization

22   Chapter 11 of the Bankruptcy Code replaces Chapters X, XI, and XII of the Bankruptcy Act that only applied to cases filed before October 1, 1979.[3] Chapter 11 can be used as the means of working out an arrangement with creditors where the debtor is allowed to continue in business and secures an extension of time, a pro rata settlement, or some combination of both. Or chapter 11 can be used for a complete reorganization of the corporation affecting secured creditors, unsecured creditors, and stockholders. The objective of the reorganization is to allow the debtor to resume business in its new form without the burden of debt that existed prior to the proceeding.

23   One important aspect of the proceedings under chapter 11 is to determine whether the business is worth saving and whether it will be able to operate profitably in the near future. If not, then the business should be liquidated without incurring further losses. The new law allows the debtor—if it is determined that the business should be liquidated—to propose a plan that would provide for the orderly liquidation of the business without conversion of the proceedings to chapter 7 (the successor to straight bankruptcy). Another aspect of the new chapter 11 is that the debtor will in most cases be allowed to operate the business while a plan of reorganization is being proposed.

---

[3] Prior law (Bankruptcy Act) used roman numerals for chapter identification while the new law (Bankruptcy Code) uses arabic numbers.

Chapter 13—Adjustment of Debts of an Individual with Regular Income

24 The new law allows some small businesses to use chapter 13 that under prior law had been used only by wage earners. However, only businesses that are owned by individuals with unsecured debts of less than $100,000 and secured debts of less than $350,000 may use this chapter. Also, debtors must have income that is stable and reliable sufficient to enable them to make payments under the chapter 13 plan. As in a chapter 11 proceeding, the debtor will be allowed to operate the business while a plan is being developed that will, hopefully, provide for the successful operation of the business in the future. The chapter 13 proceeding is a streamlined rehabilitation method for eligible debtors which is also discussed in chapter 5.

Chapter 7—Liquidation

25 Chapter 7 is used only when the corporation sees no hope of being able to operate successfully or to obtain the necessary creditor agreement. Under this alternative, the corporation is liquidated, the remaining assets are distributed to creditors after administrative expenses are paid. An individual debtor may be discharged from his or her liabilities and entitled to a fresh start.

26 The decision as to whether rehabilitation or liquidation is best also depends upon the amount to be realized from each alternative. The method resulting in the greatest return to the creditors and stockholders should be chosen. The amount to be received from liquidation depends on the resale value of the firm's assets minus the costs of dismantling and legal expenses. The value of the firm after rehabilitation must be determined (net of the costs of achieving the remedy). The alternative leading to the highest value should be followed.

27 Financially troubled debtors often attempt an informal settlement or liquidation out of court, but if it is unsuccessful they will then initiate proceedings under the Bankruptcy Code. Other debtors, especially those with a large number of creditors, may file a petition for relief in the bankruptcy court as soon as they recognize that continuation of the business under existing conditions is impossible.

28 Exhibit 1-1 summarizes the most common alternatives available to the debtor in case the first course of action proves unsuccessful.

Comparison of Title 11 of the United States Code with the Bankruptcy Act

29 The new bankruptcy law, signed by President Carter on November 6, 1978 and applicable to all cases filed since October 1, 1979, contained many changes from prior law. The new law is codified in title 11 of the United States Code and the former title 11 is repealed. Exhibit 1-2 summarizes the major changes brought out by the first major revision of bankruptcy law in

Exhibit 1-1   Schedule of Alternatives Available

Unsuccessful Action	Alternatives Available
Out-of-court settlement	Chapter 13 (small businesses only)
	Chapter 11—reorganization
	Assignment for benefit of creditors (state court)
	Chapter 7—liquidation
Chapter 13 (small businesses only)	Chapter 11—reorganization
	Assignment for benefit of creditors (state court)
	Chapter 7—liquidation
Assignment for benefit of creditors (state court)	Chapter 7—liquidation
Chapter 11—reorganization	Chapter 11—reorganization (liquidation plan)
	Chapter 7—liquidation

the last forty years and compares the provisions of prior law with the new law.

Retention of the Accountant and Fees

30   Accountants must be retained by order of the court before they can render services in bankruptcy court proceedings for the trustee, creditors' committee or debtor in possession. For out-of-court settlements, the accountant obtains a signed engagement letter. Chapter 6 of the book describes and provides examples of the formal and informal retention procedures, and illustrates how independent accountants must clearly set forth the scope of their examination and not deviate from it. The chapter also enumerates the factors to consider in estimating fees and keeping time records, and describes the procedure for filing a petition for compensation.

Accounting Services

31   In addition to the usual accounting services performed for the debtor, the accountant provides information needed to negotiate with creditors or to file a petition in bankruptcy court, prepares operating statements, and assists in formulating a plan, and provides management advising services. Chapters 7–8 provide information concerning the nature of these services.

32   The creditors' committee often needs an accountant to assist it in protecting the creditors' interests and supervising the activities of the debtor. Some of the services rendered by the accountant, which are de-

Exhibit 1-2   Comparison of the Provisions of Title 11 of the United States Code with the Bankruptcy Act

Item	Bankruptcy Act (old law)		Bankruptcy Code (new law)
	Chapter XI	Chapter X	Chapter 11
Filing petition	Voluntary	Voluntary and involuntary	Voluntary and involuntary
Requirements for involuntary petition		Must commit an act of bankruptcy	Generally not paying debts as they become due or appoint a custodian in charge of debtor's property
Nature of creditors' committee	Three to eleven members elected by creditors	Usually not appointed	Seven largest holders of unsecured claims
Operation of business	Usually debtor in possession (at time receiver appointed)	Usually by trustee	Most cases debtor in possession
Appointment of trustee	Not appointed	Required if debts exceed $250,000	May be appointed on petition after notice and an opportunity for hearing
Appointment of examiner	No provision	No provision	(1) On request and after a notice and a hearing or (2) if unsecured debts exceed $5,000,000 after request. Purpose is to examine the affairs of the debtor
Preferences			
Time period	Four months prior to petition date	Four months prior to petition date	Ninety days prior to petition date (time period extended to one year for insiders)
Insolvency at time of payment	Required	Required	Required, but for ninety-day provision insolvency is presumed
Forty-five day exception for payments for business purposes	No provision	No provision	Provided
Creditors receiving payment required to have knowledge of debtor's insolvency	Required	Required	Not required for ninety-day requirement and required for payments to insiders

Exhibit 1-2 (*Continued*)

Item	Bankruptcy Act (old law) Chapter XI	Bankruptcy Act (old law) Chapter X	Chapter 11 Bankruptcy Code (new law)
Automatic stay	Provided for	Provided for	Provided for with some modifications regarding use of property.
Setoffs	Allowed	Allowed	Allowed with new restrictions
Plan			
Submission	By debtor in possession	Normally by trustee	Normally by debtor in possession. However, if plan not submitted in 120 days or trustee appointed, trustee or creditors may submit plan
Coverage	Unsecured debt	All debt and equity interest	All debt and equity interests
Acceptance	Majority in amount and in number of each class of unsecured creditors	Two-thirds in amount of debt and majority in amount for equity interest	Two-thirds in amount and majority in number of holders in each class of those voting and two thirds in amount of stockholders voting.
Disclosure statement	Not required	Formal statement filed with SEC	Required before can solicit votes for plan
Confirmation requirements	Best interest of creditors, feasible	Fair and equitable, feasible	Class not impaired or accept plan, best interest of creditors, feasible

scribed in chapter 9, include assisting the committee in exercising adequate supervision over the debtor's activities, performing an investigation and audit of the operations of the business, and assisting the committee in evaluating the proposed plan of settlement or reorganization. Additional services rendered by accountants relating to the valuation of the business or its component assets are discussed in chapter 10.

Auditing and Financial Reporting

33 Reporting on insolvent companies requires the application of audit procedures that vary somewhat from those used under normal circumstances. Emphasis in chapter 11 is on audit procedures that differ from those used under normal conditions and on procedures that assist in the discovery of irregularities and fraud. Chapter 12 describes and illustrates some of the financial reports the accountant prepares in insolvency and bankruptcy proceedings, and chapter 13 describes the nature of the accountant's opinion associated with the reports.

Tax Awareness

34   Chapter 14 covers the tax areas that the accountant should consider when rendering services for a debtor or creditor of a troubled company and points out how proper tax planning can preserve and even enlarge the debtors' estate. Wiley also publishes *Tax Planning for the Troubled Business,* a book covering in more detail the tax aspects of bankruptcy; it is revised annually and written by Gilbert D. Bloom and this author.

35   Beyond the scope of this book are nonuniform provisions under state or common law for judicial receivership proceedings[4] and specialized provisions of the Bankruptcy Code for municipality, stockbroker, commodities broker, and railroad proceedings.

RESPONSIBILITIES OF INDEPENDENT ACCOUNTANT

36   Independent accountants are aware that their responsibilities to clients often extend beyond merely auditing the books and giving an opinion on the financial statements. They frequently give management an opinion on the progress of the business, its future, and avenues of improvement, not only in the system of record keeping, but in the overall management of the enterprise. The intensity of involvement required depends upon several factors, including an individual judgment to be made by the accountant.

37   Independent accountants also owe some degree of responsibility to third parties interested in their clients' affairs. This includes the duty to remain independent so that an unbiased opinion can be rendered. The accountant is also relied upon to reveal all those facts that might be relevant and important to other persons. This again involves judgment as to the level of disclosure that is appropriate. See chapter 7, paragraphs 77–90.

38   The accountant's position and responsibilities as they relate to a client experiencing financial difficulties and to third parties interested in the proceedings will be introduced in the remaining sections of this chapter.

---

[4] A receiver may be an official appointed by a state court judge to take charge of, preserve, administer, or liquidate property designated by the court. The Commonwealth of Massachusetts specifically confirms the power of its judges to exercise this equitable remedy to appoint liquidating receivers at the request of creditors of dissolved or terminated corporations or of creditors of corporations that have failed to satisfy outstanding judgments against them. See, for example, Mass. Gen. Laws Ann. ch. 156B, Sec. 104–105.

Observation of Business Decline

39 The first and most crucial step in any situation involving a business in financial trouble is recognizing that a problem exists. This is important because corrective action should be taken as soon as possible, to halt any further deterioration in the firm's position.

40 Many people normally maintain close contact with a business—management, employees, lawyers, accountants, customers, competitors, suppliers, owners, and the government, to list only the most obvious ones. Few of these persons, however, would be in a position to recognize when the enterprise is headed for trouble. Normally this requires someone who intimately works with the financial data and is trained in analyzing such information. Usually only the financial managers of the business, such as the treasurer and controller, or the independent accountants employed by the firm have these qualifications.

41 Some independent accountants who conduct only an annual audit and do not maintain close contact with their client throughout the year are often of little assistance in recognizing a potential problem. However, in many small and medium-size businesses the accountants not only conduct the annual audit but review quarterly and monthly statements and render various types of advisory services. In these situations, the accountants are aware of what has been occurring in the major accounts and in the firm as a whole and, because of their education and experience in business finances, they should be able to identify when an enterprise is headed for trouble and alert management to their suspicions. Thus, because of the nature of both the type of work they do and the ability they possess, accountants are in an excellent position to identify any tendencies to failure.

42 As an example, the independent accountants of a New York garment business had served as auditors for the company for many years. The company had been operative through successive generations of the same family for approximately ninety years. As a consequence of changing fashion styles, the company experienced a few consecutive years of operating losses. The accountants noticed that the company was not taking any action to correct the loss trend—the president, in fact, seemed incapable of reversing the situation. Although there was still some working capital and net worth that might have enabled the company to obtain credit and continue in business, the accountants suggested that the following actions be taken:

Discontinue placing orders for raw materials for the upcoming season, other than to permit completion of orders on hand.

Start terminating personnel in the areas of design, production, and administration.

Offer the plant facilities for sale.

Liquidate inventories in an orderly fashion.

Meet with creditors to explain the situation.

43 The accountants' suggestions were followed and the plants were sold, resulting in a settlement with creditors at 87.5¢ on the dollar. The stockholders received payment in full on a mortgage loan they had made to the company. Had the accountants' suggestions not been followed, further substantial operating losses would most probably have been incurred; the creditors would have been fortunate to receive a distribution of 15 percent; and it is doubtful that the mortgage loan would have been paid in full.

44 To be able to recognize a potential problem, accountants need to have an understanding of the definition of financial failure, the nature of insolvency, and the most common causes of financial difficulties. They must have a familiarity with the characteristics of business decline, which include lower absolute sales and slower growth in sales, poorer cash flow and weak cash position, deteriorating net income, insufficient working capital, large incurrence of debt, and high operating costs and fixed expenses. These symptoms are normally found in the accounting records, and the accountant is most likely to be first to recognize them.

Responsibility to Client

45 At the very first suspicion of pending financial trouble, accountants have a duty to alert management to the situation, submit as much supporting information as is possible, describe the various alternatives available to reverse the deterioration, and advise on what avenue should be chosen as a remedy. All these measures are taken to implore the client to begin corrective action before the situation becomes more serious, and the accountant should be concerned with pointing out to the client ways of avoiding insolvency. The responsibility of the independent accountant where fraud is involved is described in chapter 11.

46 Should the situation have become serious enough to warrant some type of remedy outside the usual business corrective measures, the accountant must make a thorough analysis to determine the most appropriate action to be taken (chapter 2). This involves an investigation into the causes of financial difficulty and steps that will correct the trouble. The accountant must therefore be familiar with the various alternatives available and when they are most appropriate. This involvement by the accountant should aid the debtor in adopting the rehabilitation procedure most likely to be successful.

47 It is also the accountant's responsibility to know the procedures required under each alternative remedy. In an out-of-court settlement, this involves awareness of the methods that have proven successful in particular situations. For example, in an informal composition the accountant should know when it is best to have all creditors meet and under what circumstances only a representative group is more advisable. When formal proceedings are initiated, it is imperative that the accountant know what information is required on the bankruptcy court petition and what schedules must be filed. Otherwise it would not be possible to converse with the debtor's attorney, a failure that could conceivably delay the settlement and cause further deterioration in the client's position.

48 Timing is crucial in a situation involving insolvency. Should the accountant fail to alert the debtor to the situation and urge some action, the creditors might move first and attempt legally to seize the assets. Speed is then important if the debtor wishes to file a chapter 11 petition and remain in possession of the business.

Advice on Selection of Attorneys

49 One of the first steps of a debtor faced with financial difficulties is the employment of legal counsel. When a company realizes that it will be unable to continue profitable operations or pay liabilities as they become due, it should quickly seek a lawyer to help effect a compromise or extension of the indebtedness. Since the independent accountant is often the first professional the client contacts concerning financial difficulties, the accountant is frequently asked for advice as to the selection of a special bankruptcy attorney.

50 There are many advantages to the accountant's involvement at this point. Frequently accountants are aware of those attorneys most familiar with bankruptcy and insolvency cases, and can recommend someone with adequate experience and knowledge. By suggesting a lawyer of known reputation, the accountant and the debtor's creditors are assured of working with someone in whom full confidence can be placed. It is imperative that the accountant and attorney be able to work well together. The accountant should be present at the meetings with the debtor and provide the counsel with an overall view of the debtor's financial condition and the events that preceded it, including the basic facts and information about the business, its history, and the causes of its present difficulties.

51 Because they are most familiar with the attorneys best qualified in this field and will be required to work with the lawyer chosen by the debtor, accountants have good reason to be involved in the selection process. However, the situation may give rise to questions concerning an accountant's independence because if an attorney is recommended more on the basis of friendship with the person than on qualifications, the accountant is not being fair to the client. The accountant must be very careful not to have a vested interest in any attorney suggested. But disregarding this situation, the accountant is a logical person for the debtor to turn to for help in choosing legal counsel.

Other Steps to "Manage" the Proceedings

52 Accountants are often intimately involved in every aspect of a bankruptcy or insolvency case. They may "manage" the case from the initial discovery of financial trouble with suggestions as to the best remedy to seek, to advise regarding any necessary alterations or modifications of the plan chosen, and finally to monitor the operations of the debtor by reviewing the operating results during the proceedings. They maintain close contact with the creditors, working with their committee in an effort to find the most advantageous settlement for them. They then provide all the financial information concerning the debtor's progress and make sure all interested parties are aware of what is occurring. Possibly more than any other outside party, the accountant is responsible for the smooth and successful rehabilitation of the debtor. This is primarily because of a close involvement with all the interested parties, including the debtor, creditors, attorney, trustee, and governmental agencies.

Economic Causes of Business Failures

1 Business failures have been with us as long as businesses have existed, and their end is not in sight. A failure may be in the form of a small retail store owner closing his door because he cannot pay his rent or it may be a large corporation that is forced to liquidate because of continuously mounting losses.

2 It is crucial for accountants to understand the material presented in this chapter because a knowledge of the common causes of financial troubles will enable accountants to identify a potential problem, alert management to their suspicions, and assist management in taking corrective action before the situation becomes too serious. Accountants can often point out to their clients ways of avoiding failure.

DEFINITION OF SUCCESSFUL AND UNSUCCESSFUL BUSINESS

3 Terms indicative of financial difficulties are used indiscriminately in discussion and often fail to convey the legal or even the generally accepted meaning of the word.

4 "Failure" is defined by Webster as "the state or fact of being lacking or insufficient, 'falling short.' " While all businesses plan to be successful, not all of them accomplish their objective. The fact that many firms fail to achieve success is evidenced to some extent by the increasing number of businesses that discontinue operations each year. All of the discontinued businesses could not be defined as failures. No doubt several were discontinued because they were successful in that they had accomplished their objective.

5 Dun & Bradstreet has adopted the term "failure" to refer to those businesses that ceased operations following assignment or bankruptcy, ceased doing business with a loss to creditors, or were involved in court action such as reorganization under chapter 11. The Department of Commerce stopped the reporting of new businesses and discontinued businesses in 1962; however, for each year from 1940 to 1962 the number of failures reported by Dun & Bradstreet amounted to only 3 or 4 percent of the total businesses discontinued. Exhibit 2-1 shows the number of failures for selected years as reported by Dun & Bradstreet. It should be pointed out that the failures include only the type of firms registered in Dun & Bradstreet's Reference Book. Specific types of businesses not included are financial enterprises, insurance and real estate companies, railroads, terminals, amusements, professionals, farmers, and many small single-owner services. A business would not have to be listed in the Reference Book to be included in the failure statistics provided it is engaged in a type of operation that is normally covered in the Reference Book.

6 A business is also known as a failure when it can no longer meet the legally enforceable demands of its creditors. If the debtor is unable to reach some type of an arrangement with the creditors, it may be necessary to file

Exhibit 2-1 Comparison of Business Failures with Business Bankruptcy Petitions Filed, 1970-1984*

Year	Failure Record		Business Bankruptcy Petitions Filed	
------	(1) Number	(2) Percentage of Change	(3) Number	(4) Percentage of Change
1970	10,748		16,197	
1971	10,326	− 4	19,103	18
1972	9,566	− 7	18,132	− 5
1973	9,345	− 2	17,490	− 4
1974	9,915	6	20,746	19
1975	11,432	15	30,130	45
1976	9,628	−16	35,201	17
1977	7,919	−18	32,189	− 9
1978	6,619	−16	30,528	− 5
1979	7,564	−14	29,500	− 3
1980	11,742	55	45,857	55
1981	16,794	43	66,006	44
1982	25,346**	51	77,503	17
1983	31,334**	24	95,439	23

* Calendar year was used for failures and fiscal year was used for bankruptcy petitions.
** Preliminary.

Source: Column (1): *The Business Failure Records, 1981* (New York: Dun & Bradstreet, Inc., 1983), p. 2; column (3): United States District Courts, *Bankruptcy Statistics* (mimeographed) and Business Economics Department, The Dun & Bradstreet Corporation.

for relief under the provisions of the Bankruptcy Code. Under conditions where there is not only a certain degree of lack of success but an official recognition of it, legal failure exists. "Bankruptcy" is the term most commonly used to refer to legal failure. Although, technically, there are no more "bankrupts" nor "bankruptcies" under the new Bankruptcy Code (for cases filed on or after October 1, 1979), when the term "bankruptcy" is used in this book it refers to the formal declaration by a firm in a federal court.

7   Exhibit 2-1 also compares the Dun & Bradstreet failure record with the business bankruptcy petitions filed for the past several years. Since many firms that filed petitions with the bankruptcy court were not registered with Dun & Bradstreet, the number of business bankruptcy petitions filed is greater than the number of failures. The number of petitions filed in 1983 increased by 23 percent to 95,439 cases while the number of failures increased by 24 percent to 31,334. The business bankruptcy petitions from 1980 include joint business petitions as well.

CAUSES OF FINANCIAL DIFFICULTY

8 It is not easy to determine the exact cause or causes of financial difficulty in any individual case. Often it is the result of several factors leading up to one event that immediately brings failure. A fundamental cause may not be at all obvious from the evidence at hand. Exhibit 2-2, which is based on data prepared by Dun & Bradstreet, sets forth the causes of failure as observed by the creditors of the firms. Different answers as to the fundamental causes would undoubtedly have been given if the debtor's owners had been interviewed. A lack of capital would likely be high on the debtor's list of causes of failure, and incompetence would only rarely be admitted.

Size of Business Failures

9 Both the number of business failures and the total liabilities associated with each failure have increased tremendously. Exhibit 2-3 summarizes the failure trends since 1940, several of which are significant. First, the failure rate per 10,000 concerns decreased in 1978 to 24, which is the lowest rate since 1948. In 1979, the rate per 10,000 concerns increased for the first time since 1975 and the rate continued to rise, reaching 89 per 10,000 concerns in 1982. This represents the highest failure rate per 10,000 concerns since 1933. In 1932 the rate was 154 and in 1933, 100.

The average liability per failure, however, has followed an increasing trend since 1940. The average increased to $383,150 in 1975 from only $97,654 in 1968. In 1981, the average liability per failure was $414,147. Part of this increase is due to the rise in prices, which is reflected in larger asset and liability balances, but most of this change has been caused by a greater number of large companies having financial difficulties. Exhibit 2-4, which presents the failure distribution by liability size, indicates the increased number of large companies that are having financial problems. The number of failures with liabilities in excess of $1 million increased from 155 in 1969 to 469 in 1975. The number then dropped in the next few years, but by 1980 the number of failures with liabilities in excess of $1 million was up to 643 and was over 900 in 1981. Dun & Bradstreet reported that there were particularly large liabilities among failures of general merchandise retailers, general building contractors, coal and oil mining concerns, and textile and apparel manufacturers. Since 1973, the number of failures with liabilities over $1 million has been greater than the number with liabilities under $5000 as reported by Dun & Bradstreet. It is anticipated that the trend of large-company failures will continue.

Exhibit 2-2 Causes of Business Failure—1981

Underlying Causes	Manufacturers	Wholesalers	Retailers	Construction	Commercial Services	All Concerns
Inexperience or incompetence:						
Lack of experience in the line	11.3%	8.9%	15.6%	5.8%	7.8%	11.1%
Lack of managerial experience	10.4	11.2	12.7	14.0	12.6	12.5
Unbalanced experience*	18.3	20.1	19.2	18.0	21.1	19.2
Incompetence	50.1	50.0	41.7	51.4	40.9	45.6
Total	90.1%	90.2%	89.2%	89.2%	82.4%	88.4%
Neglect	0.4	0.9	0.7	0.6	0.4	0.7
Fraud	0.4	0.8	0.3	0.1	0.4	0.3
Disaster	0.7	0.6	0.5	0.2	0.3	0.5
Reason unknown	8.1	7.5	9.3	9.9	16.5	10.1
Total	100.0%	100.0%	100.0%	100.0%	100.0%	100.0%
Number of failures	2,224	1,708	6,882	3,614	2,366	16,794
Average liabilities per failure	$1,065,834	$660,792	$226,464	$235,689	$442,002	$414,147

* Experience not well rounded in sales, finance, purchasing, and production on the part of the individual in case of proprietorship, or of two or more partners or officers constituting a management unit.

Source: *The Business Failure Record, 1981* (New York: Dun & Bradstreet, Inc., 1983), p. 12.

Exhibit 2-3 Failure Trends Since 1940 (Selected Years)

Year	Number of Failures	Total Failure Liabilities ($000)	Failure Rate Per 10,000 Listed Concerns	Average Liability per Failure
1940	13,619	$ 166,684	63	$ 12,239
1945	809	30,225	4	37,361
1950	9,162	248,283	34	27,099
1955	10,969	449,380	42	40,968
1960	15,445	933,630	57	60,772
1965	13,514	1,321,666	53	97,800
1966	13,061	1,385,659	52	106,091
1967	12,364	1,265,227	49	102,332
1968	9,636	940,996	39	97,654
1969	9,154	1,142,113	37	124,767
1970	10,748	1,887,754	44	175,638
1971	10,326	1,916,929	42	185,641
1972	9,566	2,000,244	38	209,099
1973	9,345	2,298,606	36	245,972
1974	9,915	3,053,137	38	307,931
1975	11,432	4,380,170	43	383,150
1976	9,628	3,011,271	35	312,762
1977	7,919	3,095,317	28	390,872
1978	6,619	2,656,006	24	401,270
1979	3,564	2,667,362	28	352,639
1980	11,742	4,635,080	42	394,744
1981	16,794	6,955,180	61	414,147
1982	25,346*	—	89*	—

* Preliminary.

Source: *The Business Failure Record, 1981* (New York: Dun & Bradstreet, Inc., 1983), p. 2.

Geographic Distribution of Business Failures

10 During 1981, over 2 percent of the failures reported by Dun & Bradstreet occurred in New York City. These failures accounted for 18 percent of the total liabilities for all failures reported by Dun & Bradstreet in 1981. This large percentage is due in part to the large number of firms that have corporate offices in New York. Exhibit 2-5 summarizes the failures in twenty-five large cities in the United States for a two-year period. The nationwide total of failures has been decreasing since the early 1960s, except for 1971 and 1975. During the early 1970s there was a considerable increase in the number of failures in twenty-five large cities compared with the rest of the United States. In recent years, the percent of failures in larger cities has declined somewhat. The liabilities associated with failures in the twenty-five large cities increased substantially in 1981. Michigan, Tennessee, California,

Exhibit 2-4   Failure Distribution by Liability Size, 1940–81 (Selected Years)

Year	Under $5,000 No.	%	$5,000 to $25,000 No.	%	$25,000 to $100,000 No.	%	$100,000 to $1 Million No.	%	Over $1 Million No.	%
1940	6,891	50.6	5,442	40.0	1,067	7.8	209	1.5	10	0.1
1945	270	33.4	343	42.4	146	18.0	45	5.6	5	0.6
1950	2,065	22.5	4,706	51.4	1,975	21.6	407	4.4	9	0.1
1955	1,785	16.3	5,412	49.3	2,916	26.6	820	7.5	36	0.3
1960	1,688	10.9	6,884	44.6	5,078	32.9	1,703	11.0	92	0.6
1965	1,007	7.5	5,067	37.5	5,266	39.0	2,005	14.8	169	1.2
1966	932	7.1	4,569	35.0	5,332	40.8	2,042	15.7	186	1.4
1967	814	6.6	4,434	35.9	4,896	39.6	2,045	16.5	175	1.4
1968	481	5.0	3,332	34.6	4,016	41.7	1,686	17.5	121	1.2
1969	416	4.6	3,000	32.8	3,776	41.2	1,807	19.7	155	1.7
1970	430	4.0	3,197	29.7	4,392	40.9	2,450	22.8	279	2.6
1971	392	3.8	2,806	27.2	4,413	42.7	2,423	23.5	292	2.8
1972	394	4.1	2,497	26.1	4,149	43.4	2,236	23.4	290	3.0
1973	285	3.0	2,434	26.1	3,908	41.8	2,375	25.4	343	3.7
1974	304	3.1	2,150	21.7	4,279	43.1	2,755	27.8	427	4.3
1975	292	2.5	2,226	19.5	4,986	43.6	3,459	30.3	469	4.1
1976	122	1.3	1,750	18.2	4,304	44.7	3,029	31.4	423	4.4
1977	102	1.3	1,283	16.2	3,476	43.9	2,708	34.2	350	4.4
1978	76	1.2	928	14.0	2,708	40.9	2,593	39.2	314	4.7
1979	62	0.8	954	12.6	2,914	38.5	3,216	42.5	418	5.6
1980	72	0.6	1,243	10.6	4,367	37.2	5,417	46.1	643	5.5
1981	118	0.7	1,862	11.1	6,253	37.2	7,648	45.6	913	5.4

Source: *The Business Failure Record, 1981* (New York: Dun & Bradstreet, Inc., 1983), p. 7.

Washington, and Oregon are the states that have the largest failure rate per 10,000 listed concerns.

Age of Business Failures

11   One of the most consistent bankruptcy court statistics is the age at which companies fail. For the past twenty years, except for 1981, 53 to 60 percent of the businesses that failed were in their first five years of operation. In 1981 this percentage dropped to 49 and the proportion of casualties coming from operations in the six-to-ten year range increased to almost 31 percent, the highest level it had reached in about thirty years. There was also an increase in 1981 in the proportion of failures which came from concerns in operation for more than ten years. Exhibit 2-6 shows the age of failures by industry for 1981. The retail industry has consistently had a larger percentage of failures in the first five years of operation than the other industries.

Exhibit 2-5   Failures in 25 U.S. Cities,* 1980–81

City	1980		1981	
	Number	Liabilities ($000)	Number	Liabilities ($000)
New York, New York	311	$ 284,732	405	$1,242,520
Chicago, Illinois	108	23,798	118	65,362
Los Angeles, California	158	59,617	193	137,546
Philadelphia, Pennsylvania	119	55,558	135	18,763
Detroit, Michigan	60	24,286	88	64,474
Houston, Texas	172	159,685	202	157,679
Baltimore, Maryland	44	9,666	48	12,467
Dallas, Texas	102	37,722	121	89,873
Washington, D.C.	*	*	24	66,774
Cleveland, Ohio	9	4,590	15	1,370
Indianapolis, Indiana	51	12,109	34	17,800
Milwaukee, Wisconsin	25	12,285	59	21,004
San Francisco, California	40	16,675	75	15,689
San Diego, California	21	6,626	53	10,686
San Antonio, Texas	95	30,087	84	26,201
Boston, Massachusetts	42	54,104	27	7,767
Memphis, Tennessee	60	10,263	100	12,197
St. Louis, Missouri	11	5,759	8	1,520
New Orleans, Louisiana	29	26,795	23	19,002
Phoenix, Arizona	5	626	25	5,247
Columbus, Ohio	23	5,366	60	5,928
Seattle, Washington	122	40,368	142	34,197
Jacksonville, Florida	*	*	1*	10*
Pittsburgh, Pennsylvania	58	10,019	69	332,276
Denver, Colorado	44	14,440	50	8,482
Total, 25 cities	1,709	$ 905,176	2,159	$2,374,834
Balance of country	10,033	3,729,904	14,635	4,580,346
Total, United States	11,742	$4,635,080	16,794	$6,955,180

* Data incomplete

Source: *The Business Failure Record, 1981* (New York: Dun & Bradstreet, Inc., 1983), p. 4.

Business Failures and Economic Conditions

12   As would be expected, the number of business failures does increase as a result of a contraction of economic activity. The mild recessions of 1948–1949, 1953–1954, 1957–1958, 1960–1961, 1969–1970, and 1974–1975 have all resulted in an increase in the number of business failures. For example, the slowdown in economic activity that began in 1974 had its

Exhibit 2-6 Age of Failed Business by Function—1981

Age in Years	Manufacturers	Wholesalers	Retailers	Construction	Commercial Services	All Concerns
One year or less	1.5%	0.9%	1.8%	0.8%	1.5%	1.4%
Two	7.2	6.4	10.3	4.0	8.3	7.9
Three	12.1	13.3	16.4	9.4	12.6	13.5
Total, three years or less	20.8	20.6	28.5	14.2	22.4	22.8
Four	12.2	13.5	15.7	12.8	14.2	14.1
Five	11.5	11.3	12.4	12.6	12.1	12.2
Total, five years or less	44.5	45.4	56.6	39.6	48.7	49.1
Six	8.4	7.5	9.6	11.9	9.7	9.7
Seven	7.6	7.7	6.3	8.5	7.4	7.2
Eight	5.9	4.5	5.0	6.6	6.0	5.5
Nine	4.5	4.7	3.9	5.2	4.5	4.4
Ten	4.8	3.8	3.1	4.7	4.0	3.9
Total, six-ten years	31.2	28.2	27.9	36.9	31.6	30.7
Over ten years	24.3	26.4	15.5	23.5	19.7	20.2
Total	100.0%	100.0%	100.0%	100.0%	100.0%	100.0%
Number of failures	2,223	1,709	6,882	3,614	2,366	16,794

Source: *The Business Failure Record,* 1981 (New York: Dun & Bradstreet, Inc., 1983), p. 10.

impact on the number of failures. The number of business failures, as evidenced by the filing of a bankruptcy petition, was 28,969 for 1975, which represents an increase of approximately 46 percent over the number for 1974, and there was another increase of 18 percent in 1976. Also, the Securities and Exchange Commission (SEC) reviewed 117 bankruptcy petitions in fiscal 1974, 2003 in 1975, and 2221 in 1976. The recession in the early 1980s has significantly increased both the number of failures as reported by Dun & Bradstreet and the number of bankruptcy petitions filed by businesses. The number of failures increased by over 400 percent between 1979 and 1983, and the number of petitions increased over 300 percent from 29,500 petitions in 1979 to 95,439 in 1983. During periods of expansion the failure rate has almost always decreased. It is very difficult to determine the impact of inflation on the number of failures. The number of failures as reported by Dun & Bradstreet decreased for the years 1971, 1972, and 1973 when the rate of inflation was the highest since the inflationary period following World War II. It should be noted, however, that the number of bankruptcy petitions filed in the fiscal year ending June 30, 1972, increased by 18 percent over those filed in fiscal 1971. We also experienced, in the 1974–1976 period following the years of high inflation, one of the largest increases in business bankruptcies since the depression. During 1979 when the inflation rate was 13 percent, the number of petitions filed increased by 12 percent. As the inflation rate increased in 1980 and 1981, the number of failures also increased. No doubt inflation does have an unfavorable effect on the operations of some firms, but it tends to assist others.

13　The causes of business failure are divisible into three categories: characteristics of the economic system, inside underlying causes, and outside immediate causes.

Characteristics of the Economic System

14　The economic structure within which a firm must exist acts as a cause of failure that originates outside the business itself and is not a result of acts of management. Management instead must accept the changes that occur in our economic system and attempt to adjust the firm's operations to meet these changes.

15　One characteristic of the American economic system is freedom of enterprise, meaning the absolute right of all individuals to engage in any business regardless of their personal qualifications. This permits the entry of people who lack experience and training in their chosen business and who are thus more susceptible to failure. Galbraith suggests that there are two parts to the economy. One is the small and traditional proprietors and the other consists of the world of the few hundred technically dynamic, massively capitalized, and highly organized corporations.[1] The smaller firms are

[1] John Kenneth Galbraith, *The New Industrial State* (Boston: Houghton Mifflin Co., 1967), pp. 8–9.

the ones most susceptible to failure. The large firms can tolerate market uncertainty much better than the smaller firm. Galbraith further states, "Vertical integration, the control of prices and consumer demand and reciprocal absorption of market uncertainty by contracts between firms all favor the large enterprise."[2]

16 Frequently given as a cause of failure is intensity of competition; however, an efficient management is a tough foe for any competitor. Some new businesses do fail because of a lack of adequate ability, resources, and opportunity to meet successfully the existing competition. Also, established concerns may be unable to match the progressive activities of new and better qualified competition.[3]

17 Analogous to intense competition is the challenge offered by business changes and improvements and shifts in public demand. Companies that fail in the transition to modern methods of production and distribution, or are unable to adapt to new consumer wants, must ultimately go out of business.[4]

18 Business fluctuations are another characteristic of a free economic system such as ours. Adverse periods marked by maladjustment between production and consumption, significant unemployment, decline in sales, falling prices, and other disturbing factors will have some effect on the number of business failures. However, a temporary lull in business activities is not usually found to be a fundamental cause, although it does at least accelerate movement toward what is probably an inevitable failure.

19 The freedom of action characteristic of our society may result in actions by third persons that prove detrimental to a business firm. The demands of labor unions and organized actions by community and other special interest groups have in recent years contributed to the failure of some businesses. Government actions—for example, the enactment of new tax legislation, lowering or elimination of tariffs, wage and hour laws, court decisions, price regulations, and the like—occasionally result in the failure of some companies. As an example, several small manufacturers have been forced out of business because they were unable to meet the pollution standards established by the federal government.

Casualties

20 The causes of trouble occasionally may be entirely beyond the control of the business. Some of these causes are known as "acts of God" and this category is found in all societies regardless of their particular economic system. Included are such things as fires, earthquakes, explosions, floods,

[2] Ibid., p. 32.

[3] H. N. Broom and J. G. Longenecker, *Small Business Management* (Cincinnati: Southwestern Publishing Co., 1971), pp. 86–87.

[4] Elvin F. Donaldson, John K. Pfahl, and Peter L. Mullins, *Corporate Finance*, 4th Ed. (New York: The Ronald Press Co., 1975), pp. 612–614.

tornadoes, and hurricanes, all of which may certainly cause the downfall of some businesses.

21   Thus the limits within which a business must function prove to be an important determinant of its success. The challenge to management is to meet and adapt to changing conditions in such a manner that they do not prove to be adverse. A company cannot change the environment; it must be able to use it to its benefit.

Inside Underlying Causes

22   Internal causes of failure are those that could have been prevented by some action within the business, and often result from an incorrect past decision or the failure of management to take action when it was needed. Management must assume the responsibility for any business difficulties resulting from internal factors.

Overextension of Credit

23   One inside cause of failure is the tendency for businesses to overextend credit and subsequently become unable to collect from their debtors in time to pay their own liabilities. Manufacturers overextend credit to distributors so that they may increase their sales. Distributors, to be able to make payments to their manufacturers, must then overextend credit to their customers. These buyers must in turn continuously keep bidding lower and lower to be able to keep their equipment busy and meet their commitments. In this manner a chain of credit is developed, and if one link defaults there is trouble all the way down the line. The failure to establish adequate credit margins thus may result in business crises.

24   The obvious answer is to expand credit investigations and, possibly, restrict sales made on account. However, many businesses feel that their volume of sales will fall as a result, perhaps more than offsetting the credit losses they are now experiencing. But one unusual default could cause serious financial trouble for the firm and might have been avoided by a more careful credit policy. A manager's decision to grant credit indiscriminately means a risk of the company's own financial stability. Unusual credit losses may so greatly weaken the firm's financial structure that it is no longer able to continue operation.

Inefficient Management

25   Businesses often fail because of managers' lack of training, experience, ability, adaptation, or initiative. Indications of probable failure of an enterprise include management's inability in any of the major functions of business, lack of educational training, and lack of experience in the particular line of business that is being pursued.[5] Inefficient management has been found to be the cause of the majority of business failures.

26   Included in this category is neglect on the part of managers to coordinate and effectively communicate with specialists. With the great complexity and vast specialization of business, complete harmony and cooperation become crucial. All management services must be integrated for maximum profitability. Often it has been found that a business failure could have been avoided by the proper application of effective managerial control tools.[6]

27   Dun & Bradstreet's analyses show over time that approximately 90 percent of business failures are due to management's incompetence and lack of experience. The incompetence and inexperience were evidenced to a large extent by management's inability to avoid conditions that resulted in inadequate sales and competitive weakness. Exhibit 2-7 lists the apparent cause of failure that is, in fact, evidence of the incompetence and inexperience indicated in Exhibit 2-2.

28   Every accountant interviewed in the course of preparing this book listed inefficient management as the number-one cause of business failures. Several other studies have also confirmed the analysis that deficient management is primarily responsible for the failure of business. The Bureau of Business Research of the University of Pittsburgh made a detailed study of ten unsuccessful manufacturing plants in western Pennsylvania between 1954 and 1956.[7] The firms that failed were contrasted with ten conspicuously successful firms to determine points of contrast that might explain the reasons for failure. These differences were as follows:

The unsuccessful firms had very poor records and record-keeping procedures. One firm shipped $10,000 of oil burners to a customer who was bankrupt. The shipments continued over nine months, during which time no payments were received.

The successful firms spent time and money on product development while several unsuccessful firms ignored this need.

Several unsuccessful firms allowed themselves to go beyond the technical depth of their management.

Executives of unsuccessful firms neglected market analysis and selling.

Unsuccessful plants displayed a lack of organization and of efficient administrative practices.

---

[5] Victor Sadd and Robert Williams, *Causes of Commercial Bankruptcies* (U.S. Department of Commerce, Domestic Commerce Series—No. 69, 1932), pp. 5–8, 16–32.
[6] Robert Beyer, "Profitability Accounting: The Challenge and the Opportunity," *Journal of Accountancy*, Vol. 117 (June 1964), pp. 33–35.
[7] A. M. Woodruff, *Causes of Failure*, undated pamphlet reporting address by Dr. Woodruff and distributed by the Small Business Administration in 1957. A summary of the results of this research is contained in Broom and Longenecker, pp. 85–86.

Exhibit 2-7   Apparent Causes of Failure—1981

Evidence of Inexperience or Incompetence	Industry Group*					
	Manufacturers	Wholesalers	Retailers	Construction	Commercial Services	All Concerns
Inadequate sales	58.2%	58.9%	60.9%	63.6%	50.4%	59.4%
Heavy operating expenses	32.5	25.6	21.9	21.5	29.9	24.7
Receivables difficulties	11.9	12.1	2.4	9.1	5.0	6.4
Inventory difficulties	5.4	10.9	11.6	1.0	0.8	6.9
Excessive fixed assets	4.7	1.9	2.7	1.9	5.6	3.1
Poor location	0.5	0.7	4.2	0.5	1.5	2.2
Competitive weakness	14.7	16.9	17.9	14.7	15.7	16.3
Other	3.6	2.3	1.8	8.0	2.4	3.5

* Classification of failures is based on opinion of creditors and information in credit reports. Since some failures are attributed to a combination of apparent causes, percentages do not add up to the totals in Exhibit 2-2.

Source: *The Business Failure Record, 1981* (New York: Dun & Bradstreet, Inc., 1983), p. 13.

The results of the analysis were summarized in the following statement:

> None of the failures studied occurred because the firm was small. They all
> occurred because of a very obvious, easily identified management error. The
> management error might have occurred because one man was saddled with too
> much, and didn't have time to devote to his various responsibilities, a situation
> indirectly associated with smallness, but in the last analysis, the failure was
> occasioned by a management error which could have been avoided.[8]

29 A common situation involves managers who are experts in their particular fields, such as engineering, but lack the simple tools necessary to
control their finances or administer a going concern. In this instance it is
often found that they fail to restrain salaries or benefits and are unable to
maintain a close rapport with their accounting staff.[9] Effective and efficient
management is partially dependent upon adequate accounting records that
will reveal inefficiencies and act as a guide in formulating policies. Several of
the accounting firms actively involved in bankruptcy audits have estimated
that at least 90 percent of the financially troubled businesses they examine
have very inadequate accounting records. Although poor accounting information or records may not be the underlying cause of failure, their inade-
quacy does prevent the business from taking corrective action in many
cases.

30 Inefficient management is often evidenced by its inability to avoid
conditions that have resulted in the following:

Inadequate Sales This may be a result of poor location, an incompetent
sales organization, poor promotion, or an inferior product or service. This
obviously means that the firm will be unable to make a sufficient profit to
stay in business.

Improper Pricing In relation to its costs the firm is charging too low a
price, accepting either a loss on the item or very little profit.

Inadequate Handling of Receivables and Payables Billings for products
sold or services rendered should not be delayed. Because of the importance
of getting jobs completed, there may be a tendency to perform other functions than sending out bills. The failure to take large discounts and the failure
to pay crucial creditors on time can create problems that could have been
avoided with careful planning as to the timing of payment and selection of
the creditors to be paid.

*Excessive Overhead Expenses and Operating Costs, and Excessive Interest
Charges on Long-Term Debt* All these act as fixed charges against revenue, rather than varying with the volume of goods produced. This means

[8] Woodruff, ibid., p. 11.
[9] R. A. Donnelly, "Unhappy Ending? Chapters 10 and 11 of the Bankruptcy Act Don't Always
Tell The Story," *Barron's*, July 12, 1971, p. 14.

that the firm's break-even point is high: it must sell a relatively large volume of goods before it begins earning a profit.

Overinvestment in Fixed Assets and Inventories   Both types of investment tie up cash or other funds so that they are no longer available to management for meeting other obligations. As a company expands there is a need for greater investment in fixed assets. It becomes profitable for the company at the current production level to reduce labor costs by investing in additional equipment. If the company can continue to operate at this capacity, profits will continue; however, if production drops significantly the company is in a difficult position. Fixed assets are not used fully and as a result the depreciation charge against net income is unduly high for the level of production. These costs are committed and little can be done in the short run to affect their total. If the reduction in production is not temporary, action must be taken, very quickly, to eliminate some of the unprofitable divisions and dispose of their assets. Under some conditions, it may be best to liquidate the business. (See chapter 1, paragraphs 42 and 43.) The objective thus becomes to have the optimum level of investment and maximum utilization.

Carrying a large amount of inventories results in excessive storage costs, such as warehouse rent and insurance coverage, and the risk of spoilage or obsolescence. Thus, in addition to tying up the use of funds, overinvestment in fixed assets or inventories may create unnecessary charges against income.

Insufficient Working Capital, Including a Weak Cash Position   Inadequate working capital is often the result of excessive current debt due to acquisition of fixed assets through the use of short-term credit; overexpansion of business without providing for adequate working capital; or deficient banking facilities, resulting in high cost of borrowing current funds. An unwise dividend policy may use up funds that are needed for operating the business. A weak working capital position, if not corrected, will eventually cause a delay in the firm's payment of debt.

Unbalanced Capital Structure, That Is, an Unfavorable Ratio of Debt to Capital   If the amount of capital secured through bonds or similar long-term liabilities is relatively high, fixed charges against income will be large. This is advantageous when the firm is earning a healthy profit and the residual after-interest charges accrue to the owners. But where the business is experiencing financial difficulties, this interest burden acts to drag down earnings. Alternatively, a high percentage of capital obtained through equity has a high intrinsic cost to the firm because the owners demand a rate of return higher than the interest rate given on debt to compensate them for their risk. It must also be remembered that, to attract investors, earnings per share must be maintained.

Inadequate Insurance Coverage   For example, if a business is not compensated for such losses as fire and theft, it might very well be forced to close its doors.

Inadequate Accounting Methods and Records Management will not have the information it needs to identify problem areas and take preventive action.

31 The existence of any one of these factors may be an indication of potential trouble due to management's inability or inefficiency. The accountant is in an excellent position to discover any of these conditions and alert management to their existence and possible consequences.

Insufficient Capital

32 As previously mentioned, insufficient capital may be thought to be an inside cause of business failures. When business conditions are adverse and there is insufficient capital, the firm may be unable to pay operating costs and credit obligations as they mature. However, the real cause of difficulty is often not insufficient capital, but a lack of ability to manage effectively the capital that is available for use or to convert merchandise and receivables into cash with which to pay the firm's debts.

Dishonesty and Fraud: Planned Bankruptcies, Sham

33 Premeditated bankruptcy fraud has been found to be the cause of a small number of bankruptcy proceedings. The reasons for fraudulent bankruptcies include the desire of many credit grantors to maintain their sales volume at any cost, the neglect of creditors to investigate bankruptcy causes, and the ability of dishonest persons to utilize profitably the benefits of the bankruptcy courts without fear of prosecution.

Outside Immediate Causes

34 Normally the immediate action that leads to failure is not the fundamental reason for failure. Some of the outside immediate causes that are responsible for the inevitable end of the firm include threatened or actual suits, involuntary bankruptcy court petitions, execution levies, tax levies, and setoffs by lending institutions.[10] Many companies delay the filing of the bankruptcy petition until they are forced to do so by their creditors in the form of a suit filed to collect an outstanding debt. Or, they may be forced into bankruptcy by an involuntary petition filed by the creditors. Banks have the right to set off money in their possession against a claim that is past due. If a company has a past-due note or installment payment, the bank may take funds on deposit in the firm's account to cover the debt owed the bank. Normally, banks will not take this type of action unless a business is very weak financially. Thus, setoffs and other creditors' actions such as foreclosure or eviction may become the precipitating cause of a bankruptcy petition.

---

[10] David T. Stanley et al., *Bankruptcy: Problems, Process, Reform* (Washington, D.C.: The Brookings Institution, 1971), p. 111.

STAGES OF FINANCIAL FAILURE

35 The general activity in firms that are failing includes lower sales, a slower growth in sales, poorer cash flow and net income positions, and large incurrence of debt. These factors combine to cause marked deterioration in the firm's solvency position. Unsuccessful firms also experience higher major operating costs, especially excessive overhead costs, than the average for similar successful firms. As the firm suffers losses and deteriorates toward failure, its asset size is reduced. Assets are not replaced as often as during more prosperous times, and this with the cumulative losses further reduces the prospects for profitable operations.[11]

36 The stages of financial failure may be analyzed in four distinct phases: period of incubation, cash shortage, financial insolvency, and total insolvency. The time period associated with each stage will differ depending on many factors.

Period of Incubation

37 A business does not suddenly or unexpectedly become insolvent. Any business concern having financial difficulty will pass through several transitional stages before it reaches the point where it is necessary to file a bankruptcy petition. An ailing business has been compared with an individual suffering at the start from a minor ailment, such as a common cold, which if not remedied, in due time could develop into a serious disease like pneumonia and result in death.[12] During the period of incubation one or even a number of unfavorable conditions can be quietly developing without being recognizable immediately by outsiders or even by management. For example, a company whose major source of revenue came from steel fabrication work in connection with highway construction failed to take action two years previously, when it was obvious that interstate highway construction would be reduced in the company's market area. As a result the company was forced to file a petition in bankruptcy court. Some of the types of developments that may be occurring in the incubation period are listed below:

Change in product demand.

Continuing increase in overhead costs.

Obsolete production methods.

Increase in competition.

---

[11] Edward I. Altman, "Financial Ratios, Discriminant Analysis and the Prediction of Corporate Bankruptcy," *Journal of Finance*, Vol. 23 (September 1968), pp. 590–597.

[12] Helene M. A. Ramanauskas, "How Close to Bankruptcy Are You?," *Woman CPA*, Vol. 28 (October 1966), p. 3.

Incompetent managers in key positions.

Acquisition of unprofitable subsidiaries.

Overexpansion without adequate working capital.

Incompetent credit and collection department.

Lack of adequate banking facilities.

38 It is often in the incubation stage that an economic loss occurs, in that the return realized on assets falls below the firm's normal rate of return. It is at this stage of failure that management should give careful consideration to the cause. If the cause cannot be corrected, management must look for alternatives. It is best for the company if the problem is detected at this stage, for several reasons. First, replanning is much more effective if initiated at this time. Second, the actions required to correct the causes of failure are not nearly so drastic as those required at later stages. Third, the public confidence is less likely to be impaired if corrective action is taken at this stage. This is critical because if public confidence is shaken, the charges for funds will increase and the firm will be in a position where would-be profitable projects must now be rejected.[13]

39 It is possible that, under certain conditions, the economic loss may not occur until the enterprise is in the second stage, experiencing a shortage of cash.

Cash Shortage

40 The business for the first time is unable to meet its current obligations and is in urgent need of cash, although it might have a comfortable excess of physical assets over liabilities and a satisfactory earning record. The problem is that the assets are not sufficiently liquid and the necessary capital is tied up in receivables and inventories.

Financial or Commercial Insolvency (Equity Definition)

41 In this third stage, the business is unable to procure through customary channels the funds required to meet its maturing and overdue obligations. Management will have to resort to more drastic measures such as calling in a business or financial specialist, who is often a CPA, appointing a creditors' committee, or resorting to new financing techniques. However, there still exists a good possibility for survival and for future growth and prosperity if substantial infusions of new money and financing can be obtained.

[13] Ernest Walker, *Essentials of Financial Management* (Englewood Cliffs, N.J.: Prentice-Hall, Inc., 1965), p. 202.

Total Insolvency (Bankruptcy Definition)

42   At this point the business can no longer avoid the public confession of failure, and management's attempts to secure additional funds by financing generally prove unsuccessful. Total liabilities exceed the value of the firm's assets. The total insolvency becomes confirmed when legal steps, involuntary or voluntary, are taken by filing a petition under the Federal Bankruptcy Code.

DETECTION OF FAILURE TENDENCIES

43   Effective management cannot wait until the enterprise experiences total insolvency to take action, since at this final stage the remedies available are rather restricted. There are several tools that may be used to diagnose business failures, but they will not necessarily reveal the cause of failure. It is the cause that must be determined and corrected; it is not enough just to correct the symptoms. For example, a constantly inadequate cash position is an indication that financial problems are developing, but the problem is not solved by management's borrowing additional funds without determining the real cause for the shortage. However, if the cause of the shortage is ascertained and corrected, management can then raise the necessary cash and be reasonably certain that the future cash inflow will not be interrupted in such a manner as to create a similar problem.[14]

44   External and internal methods may be used to detect failure tendencies. The most common sources of external data are trade reports and statistics and economic indicators published by the federal government and by private organizations.

45   Many times, internal methods are simply an extension of the work done by accountants. During their audit investigation, the preparation of their reports, and the performance of other services accountants often become aware of what has been occurring in the major accounts and in the firm as a whole. Because of their training and experience in business finances, they often are able to identify when the enterprise is headed for trouble and alert management to these suspicions. Thus, because of the nature of both the type of work they are doing and the ability they possess, accountants are in an excellent position to identify any tendencies toward failure.

Trend Analysis

46   One of the most frequently used methods of examining data from within the firm is an analysis of the financial statements over a period of years so that trends may be noted. Using a certain year as base, a trend

---

[14] Ibid., p. 202.

analysis of the important accounts is developed on a monthly or quarterly basis.[15] The balance sheet trends will generally reveal the following failure tendencies:

Weakening cash position.
Insufficient working capital.
Overinvestment in receivables or inventories.
Overexpansion in fixed assets.
Increasing bank loans and other current liabilities.
Excessive funded debt and fixed liabilities.
Overcapitalization.
Subordination of loans to banks and creditors.

47   The income account changes that may disclose additional failure tendencies are as follows:

Declining sales.
Increasing operating costs and overhead.
Excessive interest and other fixed expenses.
Excessive dividends and withdrawals compared to earning records.
Declining net profits and lower return on invested capital.
Increased sales with reduced mark-ups.

Analysis of Accounting Measures

48   In conjunction with the trend analysis, certain ratios or accounting measures are of benefit in indicating financial strength. The current and liquidity ratios are used to portray the firm's ability to meet current obligations. The efficiency in asset utilization is often determined by fixed asset turnover, inventory turnover, and accounts receivable turnover. The higher the turnover, the better the performance, since management will be able to operate with a relatively small commitment of funds.

49   The soundness of the relationship between borrowed funds and equity capital is set forth by certain equity ratios. The ratios of current liabilities, long-term liabilities, total liabilities, and owners' equity to total equity assist in appraising the ability of the business to survive times of stress and meet both its short-term and long-term obligations. There must be an adequate balance of debt and equity. When the interest of outsiders is increased,

---

[15] See Louis P. Starkweather, "Corporate Failure, Recapitalizations, and Readjustments," in *Fundamentals of Investment Banking* (Englewood Cliffs, N.J.: Prentice-Hall, Inc., 1949), pp. 432–438, for a detailed example of trend analysis.

Exhibit 2-8 Five-Year Predictive Accuracy of the Multiple Discriminant Analysis Model (Initial Sample)

Years Prior to Bankruptcy	Hits	Misses	Percentage Correct
1st $n = 33$	31	2	96%
2nd $n = 32$	23	9	72
3rd $n = 29$	14	15	48
4th $n = 28$	8	20	29
5th $n = 25$	9	16	36

Source: Edward I. Altman, "Corporate Bankruptcy Prediction and Its Implications for Commercial Loan Evaluation," *Journal of Commercial Bank Lending,* Vol. 53 (December 1970), p. 18.

there is an advantage to the owners in that they get the benefit of a return on assets furnished by others. However, there is in this advantage an increased risk. By analyzing the equity structure and the interest expense, insight can be gained as to the relative size of the cushion of ownership funds creditors can rely on to absorb losses from the business. These losses may be the result of unprofitable operations or simply due to a decrease in the value of the assets owned by the business.[16] Profitability measures which relate net income to total assets, net assets, net sales, or owners' equity assist in appraising the adequacy of sales and operating profit. An analysis of the various measures and relationships for a given year may be of limited value, but when a comparison is made with prior years, trends can be observed that may be meaningful.

50 In a model designed by Altman,[17] five basic ratios were used in predicting corporate bankruptcy. The five ratios selected from an original list of twenty-two are as follows:

Working capital/Total assets.

Retained earnings/Total assets.

Earnings before interest and taxes/Total assets.

Market value equity/Book value of total debt.

Sales/Total assets.

51 Based on the results of his research, Altman suggested that the bankruptcy prediction model is an accurate forecaster of failure up to two years prior to bankruptcy and that the accuracy diminishes substantially as the lead time increases. Exhibit 2-8 summarizes the predictive accuracy, using

[16] Ramanauskas, p. 12.
[17] Edward I. Altman, "Corporate Bankruptcy Prediction and Its Implications for Commercial Loan Evaluation," *Journal of Commercial Bank Lending,* Vol. 53 (December 1970), pp. 10–19.

the model, of the initial sample of thirty-three manufacturing firms which filed petitions under Chapter X during the period 1946–1965. Each firm's financial statement was examined each year for five years prior to bankruptcy. The n value is less than 33 for the second to fifth years prior to bankruptcy because some of the firms in the sample were not in existence for five years before they went bankrupt.

52   Altman also selected a second sample of thirty-three firms which were solvent and still in existence in 1968. This sample was taken to test for the possibility of a Type II error. (A Type II error is the classification of a firm in the bankruptcy group when in fact it did not go bankrupt.) The Type II error from the sample was only 3 percent.

53   These five ratios selected by Altman showed a deteriorating trend as bankruptcy approached, and the most serious change in the majority of these ratios occurred between the third and second years prior to bankruptcy.

54   An analysis of accounting measures or predictions of failure by Beaver indicates that the nonliquid asset measures predict failure better than the liquid asset measures. The evidence also indicates that failed firms tend to have lower, rather than higher, inventory balances as is often expected.[18]

55   The Failing Company Model was an outgrowth of the Supreme Court decision in the case of *International Shoe* v. *F.T.C.*[19] in 1930, but gained wide acceptance only after Congress expressly approved the Failing Company Doctrine during hearings on the Celler-Kefauver amendments in 1950. The model, shown in Exhibit 2-9, incorporates twelve measures divided into three categories underlying the cash-flow framework: liquidity, profitability, and variability.

56   Blum used discriminant analysis to test the model, finding that it distinguished failing from nonfailing firms with an accuracy of approximately 94 percent at the first year before failure, 80 percent at the second year, and 70 percent at the third, fourth, and fifth years before failure.[20] Beaver's best predictor, cash flow/total debt ratio, was again found to have a generally high ranking among the variables, although overall relative importance could not be determined. Predictions of failed firms not to fail (Type II error) is very low, in contrast to Beaver's research, and the model appears to be less susceptible to manipulation than a single ratio.

57   A financial consulting firm, Zeta Services Inc., has developed a computerized credit-scoring model with the aid of E. I. Altman, based on his previous work.[21] Negative Zeta scores are used as warning of a firm's finan-

[18] William H. Beaver, "Financial Ratios as Predictors of Failure," in *Empirical Research in Accounting: Selected Studies 1966,* 1st University of Chicago Conference (May 1966), p. 121.

[19] *International Shoe* v. *F.T.C.,* 280 U.S. 291 (1930).

[20] Marc Blum, "Failing Company Discriminant Analysis," *Journal of Accounting Research,* Vol. 12 (Spring 1974), pp. 1–25.

[21] "The Economic Case Against Federal Bailouts . . . and Who May Need Them," *Business Week* (March 24, 1980), pp. 104–107.

Exhibit 2-9   Failing Company Model

I	Liquidity		
	A Short-run liquidity		
	Flow:	**1**	The "quick flow" ratio
	Position:	**2**	Net quick assets/inventory
	B Long-run liquidity		
	Flow:	**3**	Cash flow/total liabilities
	Position:	**4**	Net worth at fair market value/total liabilities
		5	Net worth at book value/total liabilities
II	Profitability	**6**	Rate of return to common stockholders who invest for a minimum of three years
III	Variability	**7**	Standard deviation of net income over a period
		8	Trend breaks for net income
		9	Slope for net income
		10-12	Standard deviation, trend breaks, and slope of the ratio, net quick assets to inventory; variables 10, 11, and 12 are only used at the first and second year before failure

cial ill health. This model is made up of seven weighted financial ratios, with retained earnings, total assets given the heaviest weight. Other measures include leverage, earnings stability, return on total assets, fixed charge coverage, liquidity, and asset size. In 1980 *Business Week* presented an analysis of twenty-four major corporations, selected for having comparatively low Zeta scores, using this computer model. A cursory review of the companies indicates that a significant number of them have filed a chapter 11 petition or obtained relief from creditors out of court. Among the companies listed were Itel, Sambo's, Fed-Mart, White Motor, and Chrysler.

58   Scott[22] compared several of the leading empirical models that have been developed in terms of their observed accuracies and of their coherence to Scott's own conceptual bankruptcy framework. Included in Scott's analysis were the models of Beaver, and the two models of Altman (Z score and ZETA) mentioned above. Scott concluded:

> Of the multidimensional models, the ZETA model is perhaps most convincing. It has high discriminatory power, is reasonably parsimonious, and includes accounting and stock market data as well as earnings and debt variables. Further it is being used in practice by over thirty financial institutions. As a

---

[22] J. Scott, "The Probability of Bankruptcy: A Comparison of Empirical Predictions and Theoretical Models," *Journal of Banking and Finance*, **5** (September 1981).

result, although it is unlikely to represent the perfect prediction model, it will be used as a benchmark for judging the plausibility of the theories discussed in the following sections.[23]

59   Touche Ross and Co. uses a long-term liquidity ratio as a means of projecting possible liquidity problems within the next five years. This overall liquidity ratio was developed because other widely used ratio depicting financial health, such as current ratio, are effective only as shorter-range predictors of illiquidity. They do not reflect trends in the depletion of noncurrent assets and the increase of long-term obligations to finance current operations.

60   The long-term liquidity ratio measures the trend by using a mathematical model which determines the nature of year-to-year changes in the liquidity of a company. The model then computes the probability of the trend's continuing until a point is reached when available resources will be depleted. A ratio of 1 indicates that unless the trend is altered an illiquid position is probable within a five-year period. The result of an analysis of one company in bankruptcy for a period of seven years prior to bankruptcy is present in Exhibit 2-10. Note that this unfavorable trend was developing four years prior to bankruptcy, yet management was not aware of or was unable to respond to it.

Analysis of Management

61   Certain characteristics giving evidence of inefficient and ineffective management also serve as warning signals to potential trouble. Those concerned with the firm's viability should be on the alert if it is known that management lacks training or experience in basic business methods, such as interpreting financial data, managing funds, scheduling production and shipping, coordinating departmental activities, and any other management functions. In a common situation, a manager may be an expert in a technical field, such as designing, but have little managerial ability for directing the activities of the business.

62   Indications that management is ineffective and that trouble may result include the presence of any of the following: inefficient and inadequate information systems, disregard for operating and financial data which are supplied, lack of interest in maintaining an adequate sales volume, large fixed charges resulting from excessive overhead and operating expenses or large debt in the capital structure, or illogical pricing schemes. Other conditions pointing to inefficient management certainly are possible, and all such

---

[23] Ibid., pp. 324–325. For a more detailed discussion of how empirical models can be used to predict bankruptcies, see Altman's *Corporate Financial Distress: A Complete Guide to Predicting, Avoiding, and Dealing with Bankruptcy* (New York, Wiley, 1984).

Exhibit 2-10 Long-Term Liquidity
Ratios by Years Prior to Bankruptcy

Years Prior to Bankruptcy	Long-Term Liquidity Ratio
7	0.00002
6	0.00038
5	0.00567
4	1.0
3	0.86545
2	1.0
1	1.0

factors should alert those interested to the possible existence of later trouble.

Importance of Forecasts

63 The debtor's accountant can assist in the detection of financial failure tendencies by preparing, or in some cases reviewing, for management forecasts and projections of operations and cash flow for the next accounting period. These forecasts often highlight problems at a very early point in time, which permits corrective action to be taken. Forecasts, if prepared realistically, should answer these questions for management:

Can the profit objective be achieved?
What areas of costs and expenses will create a drag on profitability and should be watched?
Are financial resources adequate?

64 It is also important that interim financial statements be prepared, in a meaningful manner, and that the company have year-end certified audits.

Other Factors

65 The following events may also indicate to the accountant that financial difficulties are imminent:

Factoring or financing receivables, if they are normally handled on an open account basis.
Compromise of the amount of accounts receivable for the purpose of receiving advance collections.

Substitution of notes for open accounts payable.

Allowing certain key creditors to obtain security interests in the assets.

Inability of the firm to make timely deposits of trust funds such as employee withholding taxes.

Death or departure of key personnel.

Unfavorable purchase commitments.

Lack of realization of material research and development costs.

Change in accounting methods by client primarily designed to improve the financial statements.

PART TWO

Legal Aspects of Bankruptcy and Insolvency Proceedings

Nature of Bankruptcy and Insolvency Proceedings

1 An accountant who understands the scope and nature of bankruptcy and insolvency engagements and is technically competent is capable of representing a client in the proceedings. Part of the accountant's background must consist of some familiarity with the legal aspects of bankruptcies and insolvencies. This chapter and the next two provide the accountant with the legal background needed to represent effectively a client in various situations involving financial difficulties. The objective of this chapter is threefold: to describe the origin of our current bankruptcy law, to discuss the legal meaning of insolvency, and to set forth the various alternatives available to debtor and creditor when failure appears imminent. Two of these alternatives—assignment for benefit of creditors and chapter 7 liquidation under the Bankruptcy Code—are discussed in detail.

HISTORICAL ORIGIN

2 In early times the proverb "He who cannot pay with his purse, pays with his skin" had a ruthlessly literal application. The law of ancient Rome (450 B.C.) declared that the borrower was *nexus* to his creditors, which meant that his own person was pledged for repayment of the loan. If the borrower failed to meet his obligation, the creditor could seize him. The creditor then publicly invited someone to come forth to pay the debt, and if no one did, the creditor killed or sold the debtor.[1] A number of Biblical references testify to the fact that one could be enslaved for the nonpayment of debt. In II Kings 4: ". . . a certain woman of the wives of the sons of the prophets cried out to Elisha, 'Your servant my husband is dead, and you know that your servant feared the Lord; and the creditor has come to take my two children to be his slaves.' Elisha said, 'Go, borrow vessels at large for yourself from all your neighbors.' From one jar of oil she filled all the vessels, that had been borrowed. Elisha said to her, 'Go, sell the oil and pay your debt, and you and your sons can live on the rest.' " In ancient Greece, under the criminal code of Draco (623 B.C.), indebtedness was classified with murders, sacrilege, and other capital crimes. Solon, during his reign, ordered that the debts that remained after an attempt at restitution should be forgiven, but that the debtor and his heirs had to forfeit their citizenship.[2]

3 The first English bankruptcy law, passed in 1542, was a law against the debtor. Only the creditor could, under certain conditions, initiate bankruptcy action and divide up the assets of the debtor. If there were liabilities that the debtor was unable to pay with his assets, he was sent to prison. The 1542 law applied only to traders, but in 1570 it was amended to include merchants.[3] It was not until 1705 that the English law provided for discharge of the debtor from his debts.

United States

4 Physical punishment, imprisonment, and other similar practices, which were common in England and in some of the American Colonies and

[1] George Sullivan, *The Boom in Going Bust* (New York: Macmillan, 1968), p. 25.
[2] Ibid.
[3] Louis Levinthal, "The Early History of Bankruptcy Law," *University of Pennsylvania Law Review*, Vol. 66 (1917–1918), p. 224n.

which were seen by many as being totally ineffective, influenced American lawmakers to see the need for a national bankruptcy law. However, it was not considered until a very late date in the proceedings of the Federal Convention. On August 29, 1787, Charles Pinckney of South Carolina moved to give the federal government the power to establish uniform laws on the subject of bankruptcy as a part of the Full Faith and Credit Clause (Article XVI). On September 1, 1787, John Rutledge recommended that in Article VII, relating to the Legislative Department, there be added after the power to establish uniform rule of naturalization a power "to establish uniform laws on the subject of bankruptcies." On September 3, 1787, this clause was adopted after very little debate. Only the State of Connecticut opposed the provision; its representative Roger Sherman objected to any power that would make it possible to punish by death individuals who were bankrupt. In the final draft the power to establish uniform bankruptcy laws was inserted after the provision to regulate commerce in Section 8 of Article I.[4]

5   The wording of the provision is: "Congress shall have the power . . . to establish . . . uniform Laws on the subject of Bankruptcies throughout the United States." Although the right was granted, the states were so opposed to it that national bankruptcy laws existed intermittently for only about seventeen years prior to 1900.[5] The meaning and scope of the term "bankruptcy" as used by the framers of the Constitution is unclear. The English law in existence at the time this provision was added to the Constitution used the word "bankruptcy" as an involuntary proceeding applying only to traders. However, at this time, some states had laws that used the term to apply to all classes of persons and all forms of insolvency. The intent of the writers in using the term "bankruptcy" served as a focal point of debate each time a bankruptcy law was proposed for over a period of eighty years.

6   Under the authority granted, Congress passed three bankruptcy acts prior to 1898. The first act, passed in 1800 and repealed three years later, applied to traders, brokers, and merchants, and contained no provisions for voluntary bankruptcy. The first act was finally passed as a result of a financial crash brought about by overspeculation in real estate. Many rich and prominent traders were in prison because they were unable to pay their creditors. Robert Morris, the great financier of the Revolution, was in the Prune Street Jail in Philadelphia with liabilities of about $12 million. James Wilson, a Justice of the United States Supreme Court, just before his death went to North Carolina to avoid imprisonment for debts he owed in Pennsylvania.[6]

[4] Charles Warren, *Bankruptcies in United States History* (Cambridge, Mass.: Harvard University Press, 1935), pp. 4–5.

[5] Charles Gerstenberg, *Financial Organization and Management of Business* (Englewood Cliffs, N.J.: Prentice-Hall, Inc., 1959), p. 532.

[6] Warren, p. 13.

7 The first act by its terms was limited to five years, but it lasted only three because of several factors. First, there was the difficulty of travel to the distant and unpopular federal courts. Second, very small dividends were paid to creditors. One reason for this is that most of the debtors forced into bankruptcy were already in prison. Third, the act had been largely used by rich debtors, speculators, and in some cases by fraudulent debtors to obtain discharge from their debts.[7] Among the debtors who were released as a result of this act was Robert Morris.

8 The second act, passed in 1841, applied to all debtors, contained provisions for voluntary bankruptcy, and allowed a discharge of the unpaid balance remaining after all assets were distributed to creditors. The second act was not really given an opportunity to succeed. The bill was defeated in the House on August 17, 1841, by a vote of 110 to 97. Because of some maneuvering the bill was reconsidered the next morning and passed by a vote of 110 to 106. Opponents of the bill started working toward its repeal and the bill was revoked by a vote of 140 to 71 in the House and 32 to 13 in the Senate after it had lasted just over one year.

9 The financial problems created by the Civil War caused Congress to consider a third act which became law in 1867 and was repealed in 1878. This act marked the beginning of an attempt by Congress to permit the debtor to escape the stigma associated with bankruptcy by allowing a composition of his debts without being adjudicated a bankrupt.

10 The Bankruptcy Act passed in 1898, as amended applies to all cases that were filed before October 1, 1979. The act was thoroughly revised by the Bankruptcy Act of 1938, commonly known as the Chandler Act, which added to the basic law the chapter proceedings. No doubt, the most profound of all developments in bankruptcy law must have been the passing of the Chandler Act, which gave the courts the power to regulate the disposition of all debtors' estates—individuals as well as business, agriculture, railroads, municipalities, and real estate, whether in liquidation, rehabilitation, or reorganization. The most frequently used of the chapter proceedings created by the Chandler Act was Chapter XI, which was established to provide rehabilitation of the honest debtor with a maximum of speed and a minimum of cost.[8]

11 It is interesting to note how the economic philosophy of bankruptcy has changed over the past 400 years. The first laws in Great Britain and the United States were for the benefit of creditors only. Later they gave consideration to the debtor by allowing discharges in exchange for their cooperation. They also gave the debtor some protection against haphazard seizure by creditors; however, this provision became law primarily to protect the interest of other creditors. But it appears that very little consideration was

---

[7] Ibid., pp. 19–20.

[8] George Ashe, "Rehabilitation Under Chapter XI: Fact or Fiction," *Commercial Law Journal,* Vol. 72 (September 1967), p. 260.

given to the public in the United States until 1933 when section 77 was added to the 1898 act granting railroads the right to reorganize.[9]

12   The Bankruptcy Act of 1898, as amended in 1938, consisted of fourteen chapters. The first seven dealt with the basic structure of the bankruptcy system and set forth all of the proceedings of so called straight bankruptcy. Chapter VIII dealt with the reorganization of railroads, and Chapter IX concerned the composition of debts of certain public authorities. Chapter X set forth in great detail the rules for reorganizing corporations with secured debts and often publicly held stock. Chapter XI covered arrangements with unsecured creditors primarily for business debtors and for other persons who were not wage earners. Provisions for wage earners were described in Chapter XIII. Chapter XII covered debts that are secured by liens on real property, and Chapter XIV dealt with maritime liens. Chapters VIII, IX, and XIV were used very infrequently. During the last half of the 1970s, the number of Chapter XII proceedings that were filed increased substantially. Most of this increase was caused by the large number of limited partnerships involving real property ownership that had financial problems.

13   Bankruptcy law, as it has evolved during the past eighty years, was intended not only to secure equality among creditors and to provide relief to debtors by discharging them from their liabilities and allowing them to start a new economic life, but to benefit society at large.

Insolvency and Bankruptcy Laws Today

14   The term "bankruptcy laws" is used only in reference to federal laws because of the power given to Congress to establish these laws in the United States Constitution. The term "insolvency laws" is used to refer to the enactments of the various states. Insolvency laws may be used as long as they do not conflict with the federal laws, except for municipal insolvency, which cannot bind dissenters.

15   During the final days of the 95th Congress, the Bankruptcy Reform Act of 1978 was passed and signed on November 6, 1978, by President Carter. This legislation repealed the Bankruptcy Act of 1898 and its amendments (including the Chandler Act of 1938) and applies to all cases filed on or after October 1, 1979. Two years later Congress passed the Bankruptcy Tax Bill of 1980, which was effective generally as of October 1, 1979. The Bankruptcy Reform Act deals with all of the proceedings in the bankruptcy court except for federal taxes. The tax bill establishes the procedures to follow regarding the determination of federal income taxes. In July of 1984, Congress passed the Bankruptcy Amendments and Federal Judgeship Act of 1984 which changed the bankruptcy court system and several provisions of the Bankruptcy Code.

[9] Gerstenberg, p. 532.

16 The Supreme Court began, in 1973, to submit to Congress for its approval the Federal Rules of Bankruptcy Procedure to supplement the provisions of the Bankruptcy Act regarding matters of form, practice, and procedures. These rules often coexisted with local rules of each judicial district governing local matters. After Congress enacted the Bankruptcy Reform Act, the Advisory Committee on Bankruptcy Rules of the U.S. Judicial Conference concluded that a complete revision of the existing rules could not be completed by October 1, 1979. They drafted a set of interim rules that would be helpful in applying the original rules to the new law where possible and in filling the gaps where not. These interim rules were effective until August 1, 1983. On April 25, 1983, the U.S. Supreme Court prescribed new Bankruptcy Rules that were reported to Congress and became effective on August 1. These rules supplement, but may not contradict, the provisions of the Bankruptcy Code. Also each bankruptcy court may adopt local bankruptcy rules, as long as they are not inconsistent with the Bankruptcy Rules, by action of a majority of its judges. The Bankruptcy Rules are presented in Appendix A.

17 At the time the Bankruptcy Rules were prescribed, the Judicial Conference also prescribed thirty-five official Bankruptcy Forms. These forms are to be observed and used with alterations as may be appropriate in filing the petition and other reports required by the Bankruptcy Code. Selected Official Bankruptcy Forms are included in Appendix B.

CURRENT BANKRUPTCY STATISTICS

18 There were 344,275 bankruptcy petitions filed during the twelve-month period ended June 30, 1984, a decrease of 8.1 percent from the 374,734 petitions filed during the year ended June 30, 1983. This represented the first decline in filings since the Bankruptcy Code took effect on October 1, 1979. The total petitions commenced when joint petitions are included totaled 485,724. There were modest filing increases in the fifth and tenth circuits, while the northeast corridor and most of the southeastern states experienced the largest percentage decreases in filings.

19 Exhibit 3-1 summarizes by district the number of business and non-business petitions that were filed during the year ending June 30, 1984. The total number of business petitions that were filed decreased by 11 percent from the 1983 business filings of 62,170. (The inclusion of joint petitions in Exhibit 2-1 brought the total 1983 business filings to 95,439.) Business filings constituted 18.1 percent of all bankruptcy petitions filed during the year ended June 30, 1984, down from 18.6 percent in 1983, but well above the percentages for 1980 and 1981 of 13 percent and for 1974 of 10 percent. Almost 30 percent of the business petitions were filed under chapter 11.

Exhibit 3-1 Bankruptcy Cases Commenced* During the Fiscal Year Ended June 30, 1984 by Chapters of the Bankruptcy Code for Business and Nonbusiness

Circuit or District†	Total	Business				Nonbusiness			
		Total	Chapter 7	Chapter 11	Chapter 13	Total	Chapter 7	Chapter 11	Chapter 13
Total All Districts	344,275	62,170	38,121	17,213	6,823	282,105	194,870	2,700	84,535
District of Columbia	656	95	33	55	7	561	348	7	206
First Circuit	5,951	1,499	681	527	291	4,452	3,180	31	1,241
Second Circuit	16,631	3,226	1,868	1,024	333	13,405	10,664	35	2,706
Third Circuit	16,650	2,666	1,400	1,065	201	13,984	8,933	153	4,898
Fourth Circuit	20,497	3,242	2,002	846	394	17,255	11,742	163	5,350
Fifth Circuit	25,025	6,177	3,474	2,077	626	18,848	11,654	212	6,982
Sixth Circuit	50,054	6,256	3,973	1,497	785	43,798	29,393	159	14,246
Seventh Circuit	44,331	6,797	4,799	1,379	619	37,534	28,732	116	8,686
Eighth Circuit	22,220	5,844	3,974	1,424	443	16,376	12,811	236	3,329
Ninth Circuit	89,608	16,362	9,497	4,909	1,952	73,246	50,065	1,148	22,033

Tenth Circuit	22,598	5,473	3,801	1,065	607	17,125	13,820	146	3,159
Eleventh Circuit	30,054	4,533	2,619	1,345	565	25,521	13,528	294	11,699

* Cases commenced reflect initial filings, not subsequent transfers that may have occurred during the year from one chapter of the act to another.

† States or jurisdictions within each Circuit are as follows:

First Circuit: Maine, Massachusetts, New Hampshire, Rhode Island, Puerto Rico.
Second Circuit: Connecticut, New York, Vermont.
Third Circuit: Delaware, New Jersey, Pennsylvania, Virgin Islands.
Fourth Circuit: Maryland, North Carolina, South Carolina, Virginia, West Virginia.
Fifth Circuit: Louisiana, Mississippi, Texas.
Sixth Circuit: Kentucky, Michigan, Ohio, Tennessee.
Seventh Circuit: Illinois, Indiana, Wisconsin.
Eighth Circuit: Arkansas, Iowa, Minnesota, Missouri, Nebraska, North Dakota, South Dakota.
Ninth Circuit: Alaska, Arizona, California, Hawaii, Idaho, Montana, Nevada, Oregon, Washington, Guam.
Tenth Circuit: Colorado, Kansas, New Mexico, Oklahoma, Utah, Wyoming.
Eleventh Circuit: Alabama, Florida, Georgia.

Source: United States District Courts.

THE NATURE OF INSOLVENCY

20 Accountants must know and understand the technical meaning of insolvency because they play an important role in proving insolvency or solvency, as the case may be. The accountant may be retained by the debtor or by the creditors to prove solvency on a given date. The accountant is requested not only to establish insolvency, but to establish it as of a given date or dates as much as a year prior to the filing of the petition.

Types of Insolvency

21 Insolvency in the equity sense refers to the inability of the debtor to pay obligations as they mature. In this situation the test is the corporation's present ability to pay, and the concern is primarily with equity for the protection of creditors.

22 The bankruptcy sense of insolvency is the definition contained in section 101 (29) of the Bankruptcy Code:

> Insolvent means . . . financial condition such that the sum of . . . [the] entity's debts is greater than all of such entity's property, at a fair valuation, exclusive of (i) property transferred, concealed, or removed with intent to hinder, delay, or defraud such entity's creditors and (ii) property that may be exempted from property of the estate under section 522.

This is also referred to as legal insolvency or the balance sheet test.

23 Other definitions of insolvency have been devised to apply to special situations. The Uniform Fraudulent Conveyance and Transfer Act, which was incorporated into the Bankruptcy Act, used a slightly different definition. Found in section 67d(1)(d) of the prior law and used only for the purposes of section 67d regarding fraudulent transfers, it stated that a person is "insolvent" when the present fair salable value of his property is less than the amount required to pay his debts. Section 548 of the 1978 Bankruptcy Code includes a similar provision for the avoidance of fraudulent transfers; however, insolvency is defined the same way here as in paragraph 22 above.

24 The Uniform Commercial Code also contains a definition of insolvency in section 1-201(23) that incorporates both the equity and the bankruptcy senses. A person is insolvent who either has ceased to pay his debts as they become due or is insolvent within the meaning of the Federal Bankruptcy Code. This definition is intended to be used for both the buyer's right to the delivery of goods on the seller's insolvency, and the seller's remedy in the event of the buyer's insolvency.[10]

---

[10] Sydney Krause, "What Constitutes Insolvency," *Proceedings, 27th Institute on Federal Taxation* (New York University, 1969), pp. 1085–1086.

Equity Versus Bankruptcy Meanings of Insolvency

25 It is important to make a clear distinction between the equity and bankruptcy meanings of insolvency. Under the 1867 Bankruptcy Act, the equity test was used to determine insolvency. The balance sheet approach replaced the equity test in the 1898 Act. The test of insolvency was important under this act because it was a necessary element in proving three of the six acts of bankruptcy.[11] In two of the acts—making or suffering a preferential transfer while insolvent, and failing to discharge a judgment lien while insolvent—the balance sheet approach was used to prove insolvency.[12] A third act—suffering or permitting the appointment of a receiver while insolvent—required that the debtor be insolvent only in the equity sense; however, the balance sheet test as defined in section 1(19) of prior law may have been used as an alternative for the equity test.[13]

26 The Bankruptcy Code primarily makes use of the balance sheet test for insolvency. The new law eliminates the "acts of bankruptcy" and allows the creditors to force the debtor into bankruptcy court under the condition that the debtor is generally not paying its debts as they become due. Thus, a petition may be allowed, even though the debtor is not bankrupt in the equity sense, under conditions where the debtor has the current funds to pay its debts but is generally not paying them. The balance sheet test as defined above in paragraph 22 will be used as a condition for certain transfers that may be considered fraudulent or preferential.

27 It is quite possible for a firm to be temporarily unable to meet its current obligations but also be legally solvent. A business with a temporary shortage of liquid assets may be at the mercy of its creditors, regardless of whether its total position shows an excess of assets over liabilities. On the other hand, a debtor may be insolvent in the bankruptcy sense, with liabilities greater than the fair value of its assets, but temporarily paying its currently maturing debts. In this situation creditors are normally unaware of the debtor's financial distress but even if they were, they would be unable to organize and initiate proceedings to protect their interests.

Determination of Assets and Liabilities

28 The Bankruptcy Act required that the fair value of the firm's assets exceed its liabilities for the firm to be considered solvent. Section 101(29) of the Code explicitly excludes any property the debtor may have conveyed, transferred, concealed, removed, or permitted to be concealed or removed,

---

[11] Bankruptcy Act, Sec. 3a(1–6).

[12] Thomas H. Burchfield, "Balance Sheet Test of Insolvency," *University of Pittsburgh Law Review,* Vol. 23 (October 1961), p. 6.

[13] Ibid., pp. 6–7.

with intent to defraud, hinder, or delay its creditors from its assets. Intangible property such as trade names, patents, and property rights has often been included, although goodwill is normally deleted. The total assets used in the balance sheet test also exclude the debtor's exempt property, that is, the assets that are expressly excluded by law from the payment of debts. The liabilities used in determining insolvency are defined in section 101(11) as "liability on a claim." The meaning of claim is defined in section 101(4) and discussed in chapter 10 (paragraphs 87–89) and in paragraphs 91–96 of this chapter.

Valuation of Assets

29   The method of determining the fair value of assets may also give rise to controversy. Three approaches are generally found in use by the courts. First is the fair market value. Courts which use the fair value method have generally emphasized that it does not mean the amount that would be received for the assets at a forced sale. It also does not represent the value that could be received under ideal conditions during the normal course of business.[14] It is defined as "such a price as a capable and intelligent businessman could presently obtain for the property from a ready and willing buyer."[15] This definition does not give any insight into whether the courts assume the assets will be sold separately or as a unit.[16] Second is the use value of the assets to the debtor, which is based on the future earning power of the business and assumes that the firm will continue to be operated by the debtor rather than be liquidated. The first approach is used for situations where a business is being liquidated and the second is used under chapter 11 reorganization proceedings where the debtor expects to continue the operations of the business. The third approach is the value the assets are intrinsically worth under a hypothetical set of conditions. This value is used when the assets are not marketable or have little or no use value because the business is failing.[17] Chapter 10, paragraphs 45–89 describe in detail the going concern approach for valuing a business.

Insolvency and Bankruptcy

30   The various definitions of insolvency assumed importance in the different proceedings under the 1898 Bankruptcy Act. In Chapter XI arrangement proceedings, the petition had to be voluntarily filed and the debtor must have been insolvent in either the equity or bankruptcy sense. Corporate reorganization, as provided for in Chapter X, was voluntarily or invol-

---

[14] *Duncan v. Landis,* 106 F. 839 (1901).
[15] *Ouellette,* 98 F. Supp. 943 (1951).
[16] Burchfield, p. 12.
[17] Ibid., pp. 11–13.

untarily initiated, and also required insolvency in one of the two alternatives. However, which situation governed was of supreme importance to stockholders. Should the corporation be insolvent in the bankruptcy sense, the shareholders were not allowed to retain any interest in the reorganized corporation. On the other hand, the stockholders were included in the plan of reorganization if the corporation was insolvent only in the equity sense. Voluntarily to begin liquidation under prior law, the debtor did not need to be insolvent in any manner. For creditors to begin liquidation proceedings against the debtor, insolvency in the bankruptcy sense was necessary for the filing of a petition after the commission of an act of bankruptcy. There were two exceptions to this: a general assignment for the benefit of creditors, or an admission in writing of the debtor's inability to pay its debts and its willingness to be adjudicated bankrupt.

31 Insolvency is not necessary for a voluntary chapter 11 or a chapter 13 petition; however, petitions filed by a debtor where equity or balance sheet test of insolvency does not exist may be dismissed. Very few chapter 11 business petitions have been dismissed due to the fact that the debtor may be solvent. As long as there is some indication of financial problems, judges generally will not dismiss the petition. For example the bankruptcy court ruled in *Johns Manville* that the elimination of the prior law's insolvency requirement was intentional and to be followed, and that reorganization was to be encouraged. Manville filed a bankruptcy petition in August 1982. At that time it was a very solid company with operating profits and a positive net worth. One reason for the filing of the petition was the large number of asbestos victims' claims that existed. The asbestos litigants claimed that the bankruptcy petition was filed in bad faith and was the result of pure fraud. The bankruptcy court held that the filing of the petition by Manville was not an abuse of the court's jurisdiction: a corporation was not created for the filing to defraud others, a legitimate operating history was not lacking, there was no absence of creditors or crushing debt, and there was no attempt to avoid taxes or foreclosure.

32 Lewis,[18] in analyzing the judge's decision, indicates that the opinion rests on three central ideas. First, Manville was facing both a short-term financial crisis—the accounting need to book reserves for future asbestos claims—and a long-term financial crisis in the predicted size of the future claims. The alternative to chapter 11 was liquidation, which would destroy Manville's ability to operate and preclude the profits necessary to pay later asbestos claimants. Second, the court held that, notwithstanding the potential difficulty in characterizing future asbestos victims as existing creditors, the Bankruptcy Code required that they be treated by the court equitably with other claimants to the estate. Third, chapter 11 protections and procedures, including fundamental financial restructuring, were going to be used

[18] Daniel M. Lewis, "Corporate Bankruptcy Rulings Did Not Pry Open the Floodgates," *Los Angeles Daily Journal,* March 20, 1984, p. 4.

by the debtor in satisfying asbestos claims and preserving an operating entity.[19]

33 Thus, to force the debtor into involuntary bankruptcy under the Bankruptcy Code, it is only necessary for the debtor to be not paying its debts as they become due or to allow the appointment of another custodian for all or substantially all of its assets.

ALTERNATIVES AVAILABLE TO A FINANCIALLY TROUBLED BUSINESS

34 When a corporation finds itself heading toward serious financial difficulties and unable to obtain new financing or to solve the problem internally, it should seek a remedy vis-à-vis its creditors either informally (out of court) or with the help of judicial proceedings. Under either method, the debtor has several alternatives to choose from as to the particular way it will seek relief. The method selected depends upon the debtor's history, size, and future outlook, and upon the creditors' attitudes, types, and size of claims. In studying the alternatives that face a financially troubled company, two issues are important:

1 Should the company liquidate or reorganize?
2 Should the liquidation or reorganization take place out of court or in bankruptcy court?

35 One alternative is to liquidate the business. This can be done in most states through an assignment under state or common law for the benefit of creditors or through a liquidation under chapter 7 of the Bankruptcy Code. This chapter describes these liquidation proceedings. Since it will be helpful to understand assignments before looking at chapter 7 liquidation, these are described in the next paragraphs of this chapter.

36 Where it is desirable for the business to continue, and it appears that the business has the possibility of again resuming profitable operations, rehabilitation proceedings can be pursued either out of court or under the Bankruptcy Code. Chapter 4 is devoted to a discussion of out-of-court settlements. Proceedings to rehabilitate the business under the bankruptcy law must proceed through either chapter 11 or 13 of the Bankruptcy Code, which are the topic of discussion in chapter 5.

ASSIGNMENT FOR THE BENEFIT OF CREDITORS (STATE COURT)

37 Under an assignment for the benefit of creditors, the debtor voluntarily transfers title to all his or her assets to a trustee or assignee who then sells

---

[19] Ibid.

or otherwise liquidates the assets and distributes the proceeds among the creditors on a pro rata basis. An assignment provides an orderly method of liquidation and prevents the disruption of the business by individual creditors armed with attachments or executions acquired subsequent to the assignment. Most statutes uphold assignments against the attack of particular creditors.

38   The board of directors usually has the power to make an assignment for the benefit of creditors when the corporation is insolvent. However, when a going concern sells a large share of its assets, such action typically must be approved by the stockholders.

Duties, Functions, and Procedures of Assignee

39   The debtor initiates the action by executing an instrument of assignment which is recorded in the county where executed. This recordation serves as notice to all third parties. Most statutes have no prohibition against the choice of the debtor's representative as the assignee. Thus the proceeding is of a quasi-judicial nature: the corporation may select anyone it prefers to act as the assignee, but the person chosen is subject to the control of the court in states where judicial supervision exists.[20] Attorneys are generally selected as the assignee. The statutes in New York[21] and in California,[22] as in many other states, are very comprehensive and contain detailed regulations covering the proceedings, which include specifications of the duties and powers of each assignee. The assignee supervises the proceedings, including the sale of the assets and the distribution of the proceeds. This procedure results in a quick disposition of assets and avoids creditors' attaching claims to the assets or the debtor's wasteful use of the assets. But if the facts warrant a finding of misconduct or incompetence on the part of the debtor and/or assignee, the creditors could petition for a substitution of the assignee or file an involuntary petition in bankruptcy within a short time (four months) after the assignment under prior law. Under the new law the time period is 120 days (section 303 (h) (2)).

40   Assignees are trustees for all the unsecured creditors and will be held personally liable to the creditors if they fail to exercise the care and diligence required of trustees. To further insure the protection of the creditors, assignees may be required to post a bond. The duties of assignees generally include taking charge of, inventorying, collecting, and liquidating the assets transferred to them. Liquidation is usually done at a public sale, although a private sale may be held upon specific authorization by court order. Assignees also collect any money owed to the debtor, solicit additional claims, and

---

[20] William J. Grange et al., *Manual for Corporation Officers* (New York: The Ronald Press Co., 1967), p. 391.
[21] New York Debtor and Creditor Law, Secs. 2–24.
[22] California Civil Code, Secs. 3448–3471.

distribute the proceeds from the liquidation to the creditors on a pro rata basis, giving preference to any claims which are legally entitled to priority, such as secured claims, taxes, and wages. Assignees in some states must have their accounts approved and their bond discharged by the court.

41 It may be advantageous to continue the business for a short period if it appears that the amount realized from liquidation will be greater if the business is phased out gradually rather than liquidated immediately. Also, if the necessary adjustments can be made to the operations so that there is a net cash inflow, the business may continue long enough to satisfy all, or at least a large percentage, of the creditors' claims. It will be necessary under these conditions for the assignee to take, on advice of counsel, the action necessary to insure that he will not be held personally liable for any losses that occur. Any profits earned accrue to the benefit of the creditors.

Discharge of Debts

42 State assignment laws do not discharge debts; thus, this remedy does not offer a means of canceling the debts of the corporation. The creditors may receive their pro rata dividends and still have a valid claim against the debtor. Thus the individual debtor must still file a bankruptcy court petition and obtain a discharge if he or she wants to be relieved of his or her debts. This limitation is of lesser consequence since a corporation or partnership cannot obtain a discharge in chapter 7 according to section 727 (a) (1) of the new Bankruptcy Code. Although the debtor is not automatically discharged through the proceedings of an assignment, it may in some states discharge itself by writing on the dividend check the necessary legal language to make the payment a complete discharge of the obligation.[23] Essentially this is a statement that endorsement of the check represents full payment for the obligation.[24] As a practical matter this is not generally done since it is the assignee who issues the dividend checks.

43 For an assignment to be successful, consent of nearly all the creditors must be obtained, or at least they must refrain from filing an involuntary petition. If only a few creditors object they may be paid off. In most states formal acceptance is not legally required and all creditors are not necessarily asked for their consent. However, if any three unsecured creditors with claims totalling at least $5000 opposed to the assignment desire to file a bankruptcy petition based upon the assignment, they are free to do so within 120 days after the assignment. In most states, if no creditor action is taken within 120 days, the assignment is then binding upon all creditors. Because it is a federal statute, the Bankruptcy Code is superior in authority to the state laws governing assignments. Therefore, when a petition in bankruptcy is filed, the assignee must surrender control and turn the assets over to the

---

[23] For example, this does not apply in Massachusetts. See *Foakes* v. *Beer,* 9 App. Cas. 605 (England, 1884).

[24] Fred Weston, *Managerial Finance* (Hinsdale, Ill: The Dryden Press, 1978), pp. 905–906.

trustee[25] in bankruptcy. If the debtor is unable to obtain the support of nearly all the creditors, it should file a petition under the Bankruptcy Code because it will be impossible to arrange an assignment for the benefit of the creditors.

44   Assignments may also be used a condition of an out-of-court settlement to continued negotiations, to become effective upon default of the debtor to the terms of the agreement, the failure of the debtor to negotiate fairly, or the happening of other events set forth in the settlement or assignment.[26] Thus an assignment is used as an "escrow document" where the collateral is deposited with the creditors' committee and in the event of a default by the debtor in making payments, the creditors can liquidate the debtor's assets through the assignment or use the assignment to force the debtor into bankruptcy court.[27]

Advantages

An assignment for the benefit of creditors has the advantage of being quicker, simpler, and less expensive than bankruptcy court proceedings. It is simpler to initiate and less time-consuming to consummate. It is also preferred by debtors because they are able to select their own liquidators. Under this procedure creditors usually receive a larger percentage of their claims because more time is available to find good buyers, a foreclosure sale is not necessary, and court and legal costs are greatly reduced.[28] An additional advantage to the debtor is that its self-image suffers less damage than if it were to experience the stigma associated with bankruptcy. Less publicity is involved and a future credit rating may suffer less. Assignments have also been successful in preserving assets for the benefit of creditors. If any creditor attempts to take action before any of the other creditors, the debtor may effect an assignment so that all the creditors will be treated equally. Under such circumstances a vindictive creditor does not have an advantage, because there is no property in the hands of a debtor on which a judgment must rest as a lien.[29]

Disadvantages

46   If certain preferences must be set aside or liens invalidated, bankruptcy court proceedings are essential for the creditors. Some states do not

---

[25] 11 U.S.C. Sec. 543.

[26] Sydney Krause, "Insolvent Debtor Adjustments Under Relevant State Court Status as Against Proceedings Under the Bankruptcy Act," *The Business Lawyer*, Vol. 12 (January 1957), p. 189.

[27] 11 U.S.C. Sec. 303(h)(1). See Benjamin Weintraub, Harris Levin, and Eugene Sosnoff, "Assignment for the Benefit of Creditors and Competitive Systems for Liquidation of Insolvent Estates," *Cornell Law Quarterly*, Vol. 39 (1953–1954), pp. 4–6.

[28] Elvin F. Donaldson, John K. Pfahl, and Peter L. Mullins, *Corporate Finance*, 4th Ed. (New York: The Ronald Press Co., 1975), p. 615.

[29] Gerstenberg, p. 516.

allow any preferences, others have very limited provisions, and a few have fairly detailed provisions. For example, New York has a preference law and California allows an assignee to avoid preferences. Federal tax claims in insolvency proceedings are governed by Rev. Stat. s. 3466, 31 U.S.C. sec. 191 where "debts due to the United States shall be first satisfied." If the claims are not satisfied, personal liability is imposed on the assignee.[30] Rev. Stat. s. 3466 does not apply in a case under title 11 because of an amendment made in the 1978 legislation.

47   Satisfaction of federal tax claims is required only after administrative expenses are paid, but they do have priority over state and local taxes and wages.[31] In general, "the assignee's armory is rather weak compared with the trustee's arsenal.[32] There are, however, some states, such as California, where the assignment law is very strong.

48   A disadvantage often cited for the debtor is the possibility of dissenting creditors or an inability to compel the creditors to assent to the assignment. This is found to be inconsequential in the case of a corporation, however, because following the realization of the assignment no assets will remain for such creditors to pursue.

49   An assignment would be inappropriate in any case involving fraud and requiring intensive investigation. Such situations should be handled in the bankruptcy courts. It should also be realized that there are often major differences between the procedures under state court statutes and the Bankruptcy Code, and the various classes of creditors should be aware of the distinctions in the order of priority in state assignments and the bankruptcy code.

50   Even though the appointment of an assignee to liquidate the business may be used by the creditors as the basis for a petition in involuntary bankruptcy, it is still commonly used, especially in the New York City area. Assignment is a less expensive but effective means of orderly liquidation in situations where there is no particular need for bankruptcy proceedings. Indeed, the court may, under section 305, abstain from handling a case if it determines that the interests of creditors would be better served by the dismissal or suspension of the proceedings.

PROVISIONS COMMON TO ALL PROCEEDINGS

51   Title 11 U.S. Code contains the major part of the Bankruptcy Reform Act of 1978. It consists of eight chapters (all odd numbers):

Chapter   1: General Provisions.

Chapter   3: Case Administration.

---

[30] 31 U.S.C. Sec. 192.

[31] *Kennebec Box Co. v. O.S. Richards Corp.*, 5 F.2d 951 (2d Cir. 1925).

[32] Richard A. Kaye, "Federal Taxes, Bankruptcy and Assignments for the Benefit of Creditors—A Comparison," *Commercial Law Journal*, Vol. 73 (March 1968), p. 78.

Chapter 5: Creditors, the Debtor, and the Estate.

Chapter 7: Liquidation.

Chapter 9: Adjustment of Debts of a Municipality.

Chapter 11: Reorganization.

Chapter 13: Adjustment of Debts of an Individual With Regular Income.

Chapter 15: United States Trustees.

Chapters 1, 3, and 5 apply to all proceedings except chapter 9 under the Code. The provisions of chapter 9 regarding municipalities and chapter 11 regarding railroad reorganizations are in their specific detail beyond the scope of this book.

52 The Bankruptcy Reform Act also contains several provisions that modify other statutes. Included are the addition of chapters 6, 50, and 90 dealing with bankruptcy courts, and chapter 39 establishing the pilot U.S. trustee system to title 28 of the United States Code. These statutes and the Bankruptcy Code (title 11) were modified by the Bankruptcy Amendments and Federal Judgeship Act of 1984.

Bankruptcy Courts

53 The Bankruptcy Reform Act of 1978 established a bankruptcy court in each judicial district with jurisdiction to decide almost any matter that related to the estate. This jurisdiction included the traditional "case matters" such as objections to discharge or claim, but also affirmative actions against third parties who may have filed a claim against the estate such as preferential transfers or fraudulent transfer actions. The court also had the jurisdiction to hear matters related to antitrust actions, personal injury claims, wrongful death claims, and any other matter related to the bankruptcy case. Each bankruptcy court consisted of the bankruptcy judge or judges for the district.[33] The judges were appointed for a term of fourteen years at a salary of $50,000 subject to annual adjustments.[34] It was these latter two provisions that caused the Supreme Court in June of 1982 to rule that the broad jurisdictional power granted to these judges was unconstitutional.[35] Article III Judges should have a salary of $75,000, not $50,000 subject to annual adjustment, and life tenure, not a fourteen-year term. The Supreme Court delayed the effective date of its decision until December 24, 1982, to give Congress time to correct the constitutional problems mentioned above. Congress did not act and the bankruptcy court operated under an emergency resolution whereby the bankruptcy judges continued to act under the supervision of the district judges.

54 On July 10, 1984, President Reagan signed the Bankruptcy Amend-

---

[33] 28 U.S.C. Sec. 151.

[34] Ibid., Secs. 153 and 154.

[35] *Northern Pipeline Construction Co. v. Marathon Pipe Line Co.,* 102 S.Ct. 2858 (1982).

ments and Federal Judgeship Act of 1984.[36] This act provides that the district court *may* provide that any or all cases under title 11 and any or all proceedings arising under title 11 shall be referred to the bankruptcy judges for the district. Thus, the act gives some discretion to the district court to retain some cases or other bankruptcy matters.[37]

55 Section 157(b) of title 28 provides that the bankruptcy judge may hear and decide all cases and all "core proceedings" arising in a case referred to the bankruptcy court by the district court. The term "core proceedings" as used in the act is much broader than in the past. Generally, "core proceedings" includes such matters as allowance of claims, objections to discharge, confirmation of plans, and the like. The definition of "core proceedings" as used in the act includes, but is not limited to, the following:

1   Matters concerning administration of the estate.
2   Allowance or disallowance of claims and determination of exemption claims.
3   Counterclaims by the estate against persons filing claims.
4   Orders relating to obtaining of credit.
5   Orders relating to turnover of property of the estate.
6   Proceedings to determine, avoid, or recover preferences.
7   Motions to terminate or modify the automatic stay.
8   Proceedings to determine, avoid, or recover fraudulent conveyances.
9   Determination as to dischargeability of debts.
10 Objections to discharge.
11 Determinations of the validity, extent, or priority of liens.
12 Confirmation of plans.
13 Orders approving the use or lease of property, including the use of cash collateral.
14 Orders approving the sale of property of the estate.
15 Other proceedings affecting the liquidation of the assets of the estate or the adjustment of the debtor-creditor or the equity-security holder relationship, except personal injury tort or wrongful death claims.

56 The Bankruptcy Amendments and Federal Judgeship Act of 1984 provided that personal injury tort and wrongful death claims are to be heard in the district court in the district where the bankruptcy case is pending or in the district where the claim arose, as determined by the district court where the bankruptcy case is pending. Except for personal injury and wrongful death claims, the bankruptcy judge may claim the matter is a core proceeding under this broad definition. This will be an area of future litigation.

---

[36] The author acknowledges the assistance provided by Bronson, Bronson, and McKinnon, in San Francisco, in summarizing the provisions of the sections of the act that relate to the new bankruptcy court system.
[37] 28 U.S.C. Sec. 157.

57 If the bankruptcy judge determines that it is a noncore proceeding, the proceeding may still be heard in the bankruptcy court. However, the bankruptcy judge may submit findings of fact and conclusions of law to the district court for a final order after reviewing the proposed findings and conclusions and any matter to which a party specifically objected. If prior practice continues, the district court will rely heavily on the findings of the bankruptcy court.

58 Under the new act, bankruptcy appeals are to go to the district court or to a panel of three bankruptcy judges. Section 158(b) of 28 U.S. Code provides that the judicial council of a circuit may establish a bankruptcy appellate panel, comprised of bankruptcy judges from districts within the circuit. All parties must consent to the use of the appellate panel; otherwise, the appeal must be to the district court. Appeal from the decision of the district court or the appellate panel is to the appropriate circuit court of appeals.

U.S. Trustee

59 Chapter 39 of title 28, U.S. Code provides for the establishment of 10 pilot U.S. trustee programs covering eighteen judicial districts. The Attorney General is responsible for appointing one U.S. trustee in each of the 10 programs and one or more assistant U.S. trustees in any pilot program area when the public interest requires such an appointment. The U.S. trustees perform the supervisory and appointing functions formerly handled by bankruptcy judges. They are the principal administrative officers of the bankruptcy system. The pilot program was scheduled to end April 1, 1984; however, Congress subsequently extended the program to September 30, 1986. See chapter 8, paragraphs 7–13, for a discussion of the involvement of the U.S. trustee in chapter 11 cases.

60 The U.S. trustee within each pilot program will establish, maintain, and supervise a panel of private trustees that are eligible and available to serve as trustee in cases under chapter 7 or 11. Also, the U.S. trustee will supervise the administration of the estate and the trustees in cases under chapter 7, 11 or 13. It is not intended that the U.S. trustee system will replace private trustees in chapters 7 and 11. Rather, the system should relieve the bankruptcy judges of certain administrative and supervisory tasks and thus help to eliminate any institutional bias or the appearance of any such bias that may have existed in the prior bankruptcy system.[38]

Commencement of Cases

61 As under prior law, a voluntary case is commenced by the filing of a bankruptcy petition under the appropriate chapter by the debtor. The format for the petition is shown in Form No. 1 in Appendix B. The form would be

---

[38] *CCH Bankruptcy Law Reports,* para. 14,001.

modified for the appropriate chapter. For example, a petition under chapter 11 would state that a plan is enclosed or will be submitted at a future date. Also, local rules and practices may require that additional information be included in the petition. In the districts of Maine, Massachusetts, New Hampshire, and Rhode Island, a chapter 11 petition contains a statement as to whether the debtor's fixed, liquidated, or unsecured debts, other than debts for goods, services or taxes, or owing to an insider, exceed or do not exceed $5 million. An involuntary petition can be filed by three or more creditors (if eleven or fewer creditors, only one creditor is necessary) with unsecured claims of at least $5000 and can be initiated only under chapter 7 or 11. An indenture trustee may be one of the petitioning creditors. Under prior law, before proceedings could commence, it was necessary for the debtor to have committed one of the acts of bankruptcy. The Reform Act eliminates the acts of bankruptcy and permits the court to allow a case to proceed only (1) if the debtor generally fails to pay its debts as they become due provided such debts are not the subject of a bona fide dispute or (2) within 120 days prior to the petition a custodian was appointed or took possession. The latter excludes the taking of possession of less than substantially all property to enforce a lien.

   62   The requirement that the debtor must not be generally paying its debts as they become due is similar to the equity meaning of insolvency, but ability to pay is not a factor. A debtor that has the current resources to make payment and is thus solvent in the equity sense may still be forced into bankruptcy if it is not generally paying debts as they become due. There is no requirement that the debtor be insolvent in the bankruptcy sense where the total value of the assets is less than the liabilities. An alternative to determining if the debtor is not paying his debts is the appointment of a custodian or the taking of possession of the assets by the custodian within the last 120 days. This is commonly the assignment for the benefit of creditors or a receiver appointed by a state court to operate or liquidate a business. Passage of more than 120 days since the custodian took possession of the debtor's assets does not preclude the creditors from forcing the debtor into bankruptcy but, rather, suggests that the creditors will have to prove that the debtor is generally not paying its debts as they mature.

   63   Only a person (individual, partnership, or corporation) can be forced into bankruptcy. Governmental units, estates, and trusts cannot have an involuntary petition filed against them. Section 303(a) provides that neither a farmer nor a nonprofit corporation can be forced into bankruptcy. One major change brought about by the new law is that creditors now have a choice when it comes to forcing the debtor into bankruptcy. Under prior law, other than straight bankruptcy, the only chapter where involuntary proceedings could be started was Chapter X. Thus, large businesses that were not corporations and many small businesses could be forced only into straight bankruptcy, but under the new law can be proceeded against in involuntary chapter 11 proceedings.

64   If the creditors are able to prove the allegations set forth in the involuntary petition (or if they are not timely contested), the court will enter an order for relief and the case will proceed. If the creditors are unable to prove their allegations the case will be dismissed. This may, however, not be the end of the creditors' action. To discourage creditors from filing petitions that are unwarranted, section 303(i) provides that the court may require the petitioners to cover the debtor's costs and reasonable attorney's fees, compensate for any damages resulting from the trustee, if one was appointed, taking possession of debtor's property, and, if filed in bad faith, for any damages caused by the filing, including punitive damages.

Partnership

65   A partnership is considered a person by the Bankruptcy Code and thus may file a petition in chapter 7 or 11. A petition will be considered voluntary if all the general partners are part of the petition. Bankruptcy Rule 1004 indicates that all general partners must consent to the filing of a voluntary petition, but it is not necessary that they all execute the petition. Exactly what will be the status if fewer than all of the partners file is not clear where the partnership agreement provides for the right of an individual partner to file on behalf of the partnership. Section 303(b) (3) indicates that fewer than all of the general partners may commence an involuntary case. The partners filing the petition are treated as creditors for the provisions of the law applicable to involuntary petitions, such as the statutory liability for wrongfully filing a petition or the posting of an indemnity bond. Furthermore, if all of the general partners are in bankruptcy court proceedings, any general partner, general partner's trustee, or creditor of the partnership can file a petition on behalf of the partnership.

Meeting of Creditors

66   Section 341(a) and Bankruptcy Rule 2003 provide that within a period of twenty to forty days after the order for relief in any bankruptcy court proceedings, there will be a meeting of creditors. Subsection (b) states that the court may also order a meeting of any equity security holders. The court may not preside at, nor attend, any meetings called under section 341. In the U.S. trustee pilot districts, the U.S. trustee will preside at the meetings. In other districts Bankruptcy Rule 2003 provides that the clerk of the bankruptcy court shall preside unless the creditors designate by voting under the provisions of section 702(a) someone to preside. In a chapter 11 case the chairman of the creditors' committee, once elected, will preside.

67   The meeting will be held at a regular place for holding court or any other place designated by the court. For example, in some of the larger cases the meetings are held in a large hotel. At a meeting under section 341(a) the debtor is to appear and submit to examination under oath. Creditors, an indenture trustee, or a trustee or examiner, if appointed, may examine the debtor.[39] The meetings under section 341 are often adjourned from time to time by announcement at the meeting. No vote will be taken at a meeting under section 341 in a chapter 11 case. In a chapter 7 case a trustee and/or creditors committee can be elected.

Meeting of Equity Security Holders

68   Section 341(b) also allows the court to order a meeting of the stockholders of the debtor corporation. At this meeting the clerk will preside unless the stockholders present at this meeting hold a majority in amount of the equity interest and designate a presiding officer.

Automatic Stay

69   A petition filed under the Bankruptcy Code results in an automatic stay of the actions of creditors. The automatic stay is one of the fundamental protections provided the debtor by the Bankruptcy Code dating back to an 1880 case where it was stated that "[T]he filing of the petition is a caveat to all the world, and in effect an attachment and injunction . . . ."[40] In a chapter 7 case it provides for an orderly liquidation where all creditors are treated equitably. For business reorganizations under chapters 11 and 13, it provides time for the debtor to examine the problems that forced it into bankruptcy court and to develop a plan for reorganization. As a result of the stay, no party, with minor exceptions, having a security or adverse interest in the debtor's property can take any action that will interfere with the debtor or his property, regardless of where the property is located, until the stay is modified or removed. Section 362(a) provides a list of eight kinds of acts and conduct subject to the automatic stay. The stay operates against

1   The commencement or continuation of a judicial, administrative, or other action or proceeding against the debtor including the issuance or employment of process, that could have been commenced before the petition date or would be commenced to recover a claim that arose prior to the commencement of the case in the bankruptcy court. (Note that the stay does not apply to postpetition claims or proceedings involving postpetition transactions or conduct of the debtor.)

2   The enforcement against the debtor or against property of the estate, of a judgment obtained before the commencement of the case.

3   Any act to obtain possession of property of the estate or of property from the estate or to exercise control over the property of the estate.

---

[39] 11 U.S.C. Sec. 343.
[40] *International Bank* v. *Sherman*, 101 U.S. 403.

4   Any act to create, perfect, or enforce any lien against property of the estate.

5   Any act to create, perfect, or enforce against property of the debtor any lien to the extent that such lien secures a claim that arose before the commencement of the case.

6   Any act to collect, assess, or recover a claim against the debtor that arose before the commencement of the case.

7   The setoff of any debt owing to the debtor that arose before the commencement of the case against any claim against the debtor.

8   The commencement or continuation of a proceeding before the United States Tax Court concerning the debtor.

     70   Section 362(b) contains eleven limitations on the operation of the stay described above. The stay does not operate against

1   The commencement or continuation of a criminal action or proceeding against the debtor.

2   The collection of alimony, maintenance, or support from property that is not property of the estate.

3   Any act to perfect an interest in property to the extent that the trustee's rights and powers are subject to such perfection under section 546(b) within the ten-day period provided in section 547(e) (2) (A).

4   The commencement or continuation of an action or proceeding by a governmental unit to enforce such governmental unit's police or regulatory power.

5   The enforcement of a judgment, other than a money judgment, obtained in an action or proceeding by a governmental unit to enforce its police or regulatory power.

6   The setoff of any mutual debt and claim that are commodity futures contracts, forward commodity contracts, leverage transactions, options, warrants, rights to purchase or sell commodity futures contracts or securities, or options to purchase or sell commodities or securities.

7   The setoff of any mutual debt or claim for a margin or settlement payment arising out of repurchase agreements against cash, securities, or other property held by or due from such repo participant to margin, guarantee, secure, or settle repurchase agreements.

8   The commencement of any action by the Secretary of Housing and Urban Development to foreclose a mortgage or deed of trust on property consisting of five or more living units held by the Secretary that is insured or was formerly insured under the National Housing Act.

9   The issuance to the debtor by a governmental unit of a notice of tax deficiency.

10   Any act by a lessor under a lease of real nonresidential property that has terminated by the expiration of the terms of the case before the petition is filed or during the case to obtain possession of the property.

11   The presentment of a negotiable instrument and the giving of notice of and protesting dishonor of such an instrument.

Duration of the Stay

71   The stay of an act against the property of the estate continues, unless modified, until the property is no longer the property of the estate.[41] The stay of any other act continues until the case is closed or dismissed, or the debtor is either granted or denied a discharge. The earliest occurrence of one of these events terminates the stay.[42]

Relief from the Stay

72   The balance of section 362 deals with the procedures to follow to obtain relief from the stay. First section 362(d) provides that for relief to be granted it is necessary for a party to institute action with the bankruptcy court. The court may grant relief, after notice and hearing, by terminating, annulling, modifying, or conditioning the stay. The court may grant relief for cause, including the lack of adequate protection of the interest of the secured creditor. With respect to an act against property, relief may be granted under chapter 11 if the debtor does not have an equity in the property and the property is not necessary for an effective reorganization.

73   Section 361 identifies three acceptable ways of providing the adequate protection that is required. First, the trustee or debtor may be required to make periodic cash payments to the entity entitled to relief as compensation for the decrease in value of the entity's interest in the property resulting from the stay. Second, the entity may be provided with an additional or replacement lien to the extent that the value of the interest declined as a result of the stay. Finally, the entity may receive the indubitable equivalent of its interest in the property.

74   The granting of relief when the debtor does not have any equity in the property was added to solve the problem of real property mortgage foreclosures where the bankruptcy court petition is filed just before the foreclosure takes place. It was not intended to apply if the debtor is managing or leasing real property, such as a hotel operation, even though the debtor has no equity, since the property is necessary for an effective reorganization of the debtor.[43]

---

[41] 11 U.S.C. Sec. 362(c).

[42] Frank R. Kennedy, "Automatic Stays Under the New Bankruptcy Law," *University of Michigan Journal of Law Reform,* Vol. 12 (Fall 1978), p. 38.

[43] 124 Cong. Rec. H11,092–93 (daily ed. September 28, 1978), (Statement of Rep. Edwards).

75   The legislative history indicates that the reasons found in the statute are not the causes for relief. For example, in a case where the debtor is the executor or administrator of another estate, the proceedings should not be stayed; these activities are not related to the bankruptcy case. Postpetition activities of the debtor also need not be stayed because they bear no relationship to the purpose of the stay.[44]

76   Subsection (e) of section 362 provides that unless the court acts after the relief is requested the relief is automatic. The court has thirty days to rule on the stay request, but in more complex cases the court is required to have only a preliminary hearing within the thirty-day period and then commence the final hearing within another thirty-day period. The court may continue the stay after a preliminary hearing only if there is a reasonable likelihood that the relief will not be granted at the final hearing.

77   Section 362(f) allows the court to grant relief from the stay without a hearing, provided immediate action is needed to prevent irreparable damage to the interest in property and such damage would occur before there is an opportunity for notice and a hearing. Bankruptcy Rule 4001 provides additional information about procedures that must be followed to obtain immediate relief from the stay, including how notices of the order granting relief are to be distributed.

78   If relief from the stay is granted a creditor may foreclose on property on which a lien exists, may continue a state court suit, or may enforce any judgment that might have been obtained before the bankruptcy case.[45]

79   Subsection (g) places the burden of proof on the requesting party where the request for relief alleges that the debtor has no equity in the property. On all other issues the party opposing the relief requested has the burden of proof.

Use of the Estate's Property

80   Section 363 permits the trustee or debtor to use, sell, or lease property (other than cash collateral) in the ordinary course of business without a notice or hearing provided the business has been authorized to operate in a chapter 7, 11, or 13 proceeding and the court has not restricted the powers of the debtor or trustee in the order authorizing operation of the business. As a result of this provision the debtor may continue to sell inventory and receivables and use raw materials in production without notice to secured creditors and without court approval. The use, sale, or lease of the estate's property other than in the ordinary course of business is allowed only after notice and an opportunity for a hearing.

81   The new law gives the greatest protection to creditors with an interest in *cash collateral* consisting of cash negotiable instruments, documents

---

[44] House Report No. 95–595, 95th Cong., 1st Sess. (1977) 343–344.
[45] *CCH Bankruptcy Law Reports,* para. 8606.

of title, securities, deposit accounts, and any other cash equivalents. Included as cash collateral are proceeds from noncash collateral such as inventory, accounts receivable, products, offspring, rents, or profits of property subject to a security interest, if converted to proceeds of the type defined as cash collateral. To use cash collateral the debtor must obtain the consent of the secured party or the authorization of the court after notice and an opportunity for a hearing.

82   Additional requirements regarding the use of the estate's property, including cash collateral, and the obtaining of new credit are described in chapter 5 (paragraphs 32–38).

Executory Contracts and Leases

83   Section 365(a) provides that the debtor or trustee, subject to court approval, may assume or reject any executory contract or unexpired lease of the debtor. For a definition of an executory contract see chapter 7, paragraph 32. However, before a contract can be assumed Subsection (b) indicates that the debtor or trustee must

1   Cure the past defaults or provide assurance they will be promptly cured.
2   Compensate the other party for actual pecuniary loss to such property or provide assurance that compensation will be made promptly.
3   Provide adequate assurance of future performance under the contract or lease.

84   If the other party can demonstrate that the debtor does not have the financial capacity to make payments under the contract or lease, then the court would direct that the contract be rejected. In some cases the debtor may make the few months' delinquent payments and easily establish that it has the financial capability to meet the monthly payments. The court will look at the debtor's financial projections to help decide whether the debtor can be expected to meet the requirements of the terms of the contract or lease. Under other conditions it may take considerable effort on the part of the debtor to convince the court that it has the ability to make future payments. For example, section 365(b) (3) of the Code states that in the case of a lease of real property in a shopping center it would be necessary to show adequate assurance

1   Of the source of rent and other considerations due under the lease. In the case of an assignment, that the financial condition and operating performance of the proposed assignee and its guarantors, if any, are similar to those of the debtor and its guarantors, if any, at the time the debtor became the lessee.
2   That any percentage due would not decline substantially.

3   That assumption or assignment of the lease would not breach substantially any provision such as radius, location, use, or exclusivity rights granted to other tenants.

4   That the assumption or assignment of lease will not disrupt substantially any tenant mix or balance in the shopping center.

85   The requirement of adequate assurance for the payment applies only to contracts or leases where there were prior defaults. If the contract is to be assigned and sold, like any other property right of the debtor, to a third party then section 365(f)(2)(B) requires that adequate assurance be provided, even though there has not been a default in the contract or lease. Also section 365(l), added by the Bankruptcy Amendments and Federal Judgeship Act of 1984, provides that if an unexpired lease is assigned by the debtor the lessor may require a deposit or other security for the performance of the debtor's obligation that is substantially the same as would have been required upon the initial leasing to a similar tenant.

86   Section 365(b)(2) provides that clauses that automatically cause the contract or lease to terminate in the event of bankruptcy are invalidated and are thus not considered a default of the contract or lease. The prohibition against an insolvency or bankruptcy clause or the prohibition against appointing a trustee does not apply to financing agreements or contracts under which applicable state law excuses a party from accepting substitute performance, such as personal performance contracts. Thus, any funds obtained during the reorganization will depend upon the debtor's ability to convince lenders to make adequate financing available.

87   In a chapter 7 liquidation the trustee must assume the contract or lease within sixty days after the order of relief (or within an additional sixty days if the court, for cause, extends the time) or the contract or lease is deemed rejected; and in the case of nonresidential real property the property is to be immediately surrendered to the lessor. No time limit is set in chapter 11 or 13, except for non-residential real property, provided the contract or lease is accepted or rejected before the confirmation of the plan. However, if the other party requests the court to fix a time the court may establish a set time within which the debtor or trustee must act. In the case of nonresidential real property, if the debtor does not assume the unexpired lease within sixty days (or up to an additional sixty days if authorized by the court) after the order for relief, the lease is deemed rejected and the property is to be immediately surrendered to the lessor. In a chapter 11 case the debtor may assume the lease at this time and then later provide for rejection of the lease in the plan.

88   Section 365(b)(4) provides that before assumption of a lease in default, other than because of bankruptcy or insolvency of debtor, the lessee cannot require a lessor to provide services or supplies unless the lessor is properly compensated according to the terms of the lease. Section 365(l) allows the lessor of a lease assigned by the debtor to require a deposit or other security for the performance of the debtor's obligation, as would have been required upon the initial leasing to a similar tenant.

89   The rejection of an executory contract or lease (that has not been assumed) constitutes a breach of the contract or lease as of the date immediately preceding the filing of the petition. Thus, the rejections are treated as prepetition claims.

Utility Service

90   Section 366 provides that a utility may not refuse, alter, or discontinue service to, or discriminate against, the trustee or debtor solely because it has not made timely payment for services rendered before the order for relief. But the trustee or debtor must, within twenty days after the order for relief, furnish adequate assurance of payment for services after that date. This can often be resolved by negotiation with the utility and can be in the form of a deposit or other security. Some utilities may initially demand a fairly large deposit. Often by negotiating with the utility the deposit can be reduced to a reasonable period, such as six weeks. On request of a party in interest and after notice and hearing, the court may order reasonable modifications of the amount necessary to provide adequate assurance of payment.

Allowance of Claims or Interests

91   Section 501 permits a creditor or indenture trustee to file a proof of claim and an equity holder to file a proof of interest. Bankruptcy Rule 3002 provides that an unsecured creditor or an equity holder must file a proof of claim or interest for the claim or interest to be allowed in a chapter 7 or chapter 13 case. A secured creditor needs to file a proof of claim for the claim to be allowed under sections 502 or 506(d) unless a party in interest requests a determination and allowance or disallowance. In a chapter 7 or 13 case a proof of claim is to be filed within ninety days after the date set for the meeting of creditors under Section 341(a). For cause the court may extend this period and the court will fix the time period for the filing of a proof of a claim arising from the rejection of an executory contract. The filing of the proof of claim is not mandatory in a chapter 9 or 11 case, provided the claim is listed in the schedule of liabilities. However, if the claim is not scheduled or the creditor disputes the claim, a proof of claim should be filed. It is generally advisable to file a proof of claim even though the claim is scheduled. See Bankruptcy Rule 3003. A proof of claim filed will supersede any scheduling of that claim in accordance with Section 521(l).

92   Section 501(c) also gives the debtor or trustee the power to file a claim on behalf of the creditor if the creditor did not file a timely claim. Thus, for debts that are nondischargeable such as tax claims, the debtor may file a proof of claim to cause the creditor to receive some payment from the estate and avoid having to pay all of the debt after the bankruptcy proceedings are over.

93   The proof of claim according to section 502(a) that is filed with the court is deemed allowed unless a party in interest objects. Claims may be disallowed for eight basic reasons as set forth in section 502(b). They are:

1   A claim will be disallowed if it is unenforceable against a debtor for any reason other than because it is contingent or unliquidated. Contingent or unliquidated debts will be liquidated by the bankruptcy court. (This is a departure from prior law in which these claims were generally not provable).

2   Claims for unmatured interest will be disallowed. Postpetition interest that is not yet due and payable and any portion of prepaid interest that represents an original discounting of the claim are included as disallowed interest. Thus, present law is retained in that interest stops accruing on unsecured claims when the petition is filed (unless the debtor is solvent), and bankruptcy works as the acceleration of the principal amount of all claims.

3   To the extent that a tax claim assessed against property of the estate exceeds the value of the estate's interest in such property the claim will be disallowed.

4   Claims by an insider or attorney for the debtor will be disallowed if they exceed the reasonable value of those services. This permits the court to examine the attorney's claim independently of any other section, and prevents overreaching by the debtor's attorney and the concealing of assets by the debtor.

5   Postpetition alimony, maintenance, or support claims are disallowed since they are nondischargeable and will be paid from the debtor's post-bankruptcy property.

6   The damages allowable to the landlord of a debtor from termination of a lease of real property are limited to the greater of one year or 15 percent of the remaining portion of the lease's rent due not to exceed three years after the date of filing or surrender whichever is earlier. This formula compensates the landlord while not allowing the claim to be so large as to hurt other creditors of the estate. This is derived from prior law as set out in *Oldden* v. *Tonto Realty Co.,* 143 F.2d 916 (2d Cir. 1944).

7   The damages resulting from the breach of an employment contract are limited to one year following the date of the petition or the termination of employment whichever is earlier. (This is a new addition to the area of disallowed claims.)

8   Certain employment tax claims are disallowed. Specifically, this relates to a federal tax credit for state unemployment insurance that is disallowed if the state tax is paid late. Now, the federal claim for the tax

would be disallowed as if the credit had been allowed on the federal tax return.[46]

94   Claims are disallowed if they arise from a rejection of an executory contract or lease that was not assumed and upon the recovery of set-off or voidable transfer (for example, preferences or fraudulent transfers) such a claim is treated as though the claim had arisen prior to the filing of the petition.[47] Tax claims that arise after the filing of the petition and are seventh priority tax claims are to be treated as though the claim had arisen prior to the petition date.[48] For example, the assessment of additional income taxes resulting from an audit of a tax return due within three years before the petition date would be considered a prepetition claim even though the assessment was made after the petition was filed.

Secured Claims

95   The Bankruptcy Act referred to creditors as either secured creditors or unsecured creditors. The Bankruptcy Code refines this distinction and refers to creditors as holders of secured and unsecured claims. Section 506(a) states that:

> An allowed claim of a creditor secured by a lien on property in which the estate has an interest, or that is subject to setoff under section 553 of this title, is a secured claim to the extent of the value of such creditor's interest in the estate's interest in such property, or to the extent of the amount subject to setoff, as the case may be, and is an unsecured claim to the extent that the value of such creditor's interest or the amount so subject to setoff is less than the amount of such allowed claim.

Thus, an undersecured creditor's allowed claim is separated into two parts. A secured claim exists to the extent of the value of the collateral and the balance is unsecured. A secured claim must first be an allowed claim; second it must be secured by a lien on the property; and third the debtor's estate must have an interest in the property secured by the lien or it must be subject to setoff. See chapter 10 for a discussion of the section 506 valuation.

96   A creditor may prefer to have the entire claim classified as unsecured. He may think that the collateral will not be able to withstand probable attacks and may prefer to renounce the collateral and have the entire claim considered unsecured. The Bankruptcy Code does not specifically state that the creditor has the right to renounce the collateral, but the principle was

---

[46] *CCH Bankruptcy Law Reports*, para. 9006.
[47] 11 U.S.C. Sec. 502(g) and (h).
[48] Ibid., Sec. 502(i).

well settled under the practice of the prior law.[49] (See chapter 5, paragraphs 42–44.)

Expense of Administration

97   The actual, necessary costs of preserving the estate, including wages, salaries, and commissions for services rendered after the commencement of the case are considered administrative expenses. Any tax including fines or penalties is allowed unless it relates to a tax-granted preference under section 507(a)(7). Compensation awarded a professional person, including accountants, for postpetition services is an expense of administration. (See chapter 6, paragraphs 5–10). Expenses incurred in an involuntary case subsequent to the filing of the petition but prior to the appointment of a trustee or the order for relief are not considered administrative expenses. They are, however, granted second priority under section 507.

Priorities

98   The 1978 Bankruptcy Code and subsequent amendments modified to a limited extent the order of payment of the expenses of administration and other unsecured claims. Section 507 provides for the following priorities:

1   Administrative expenses.
2   Unsecured claims in an involuntary case arising after commencement of the proceedings but before an order of relief is granted.
3   Wages earned within ninety days prior to filing the petition (or the cessation of the business) to the extent of $2000 per individual.
4   Unsecured claims to employee benefit plans arising within 180 days prior to filing petition limited to $2000 times the number of employees covered by the plan less the amount paid in (3) above and the amount previously paid on behalf of such employees.
5   Unsecured claims of grain producers against a grain storage facility or of fishermen against a fish produce storage or processing facility to the extent of $2000.
6   Unsecured claims of individuals to the extent of $900 from deposits of money for purchase, lease, or rental of property or purchase of services not delivered or provided.
7   Unsecured tax claims of governmental units:
  Income or gross receipts tax provided tax return due (including extension) within three years prior to filing petition.

---

[49] *Collier Bankruptcy Manual*, 3rd ed., para. 506.02[3]. See also *In re Tiger, 109 F. Supp. 737 (D.N.J. 1952)*, aff'd 201 F.2d 670 (3d Cir. 1953).

Property tax last payable without penalty within one year prior to filing petition.

Withholding taxes.

Employment tax on wages, and so forth, due within three years prior to the filing of the petition.

Excise tax due within three years prior to the filing of the petition.

Customs duty on merchandise imported within one year prior to the filing of the petition.

Penalties related to a type of claim above in compensation for actual pecuniary loss.

99   The fourth priority is new, but note that it is limited to the amount of unused wage priority. The wage priority amount has been increased to $2000 from $600 under prior law. Salary claims are now included, as are vacation, sick leave, and severance pay. The fifth priority applies in cases filed on or after October 8, 1984. The sixth priority provides for payments up to $900 for each individual consumer who has deposited or made partial payment for the purchase or lease of goods or services that were not delivered or provided by the debtor prior to the date of bankruptcy. Taxes were granted a fourth priority under prior law but are now entitled to seventh priority.

100   Section 507(b) provides that a holder of a claim secured by a lien on property of a debtor that received adequate protection under section 361 shall be given priority over all other priorities if the adequate protection granted proves to be inadequate.

Exemptions

101   Prior law allowed an individual to exempt any property so stipulated as being exempt under applicable state law where the petition was filed. The Bankruptcy Code provides an individual debtor with an option to exempt from the estate either the federal exemption or the property stipulated by state law unless a state passes a law to the contrary. Over one-half of the states have adopted a law that requires debtors in those states to follow state laws only. Under joint cases filed under Section 302 or individual cases that are jointly administered under Bankruptcy Rule 1015(b), one spouse cannot use the state exemption and the other the federal. If they cannot agree on the alternative to be elected, unless prohibited by state law, they shall adopt the federal exemption as required by section 522(b).

102   Included in the federal exemption under section 522(d) are the debtor's interests in the following:

1   Real property or personal property used as a residence, not to exceed $7500.

2   One motor vehicle, not to exceed $1200.

3 Household items and wearing apparel for personal use, not to exceed $200 in any particular item or $4000 in aggregate value.

4 Personal, family, or household jewelry, not to exceed $500.

5 Any property identified by the debtor, not to exceed $400 plus unused portion of the exemption in (1) above, not to exceed $3750.

6 Professional books or tools of trade, not to exceed $750.

7 Unmatured life insurance contract (excluding credit life insurance).

8 Accrued dividend, loan value, and so forth of unmatured life insurance contract, not to exceed $4000.

9 Professionally prescribed health aids.

10 Right to receive selected payments such as Social Security, unemployment benefits, retirement benefits, veterans benefits, disability benefits, alimony, compensation for certain losses, and the like. Some of these are exempted only to the extent reasonably necessary for the support of the debtor and his dependents.

103 This change will, in most states, result in less property being available for distribution to creditors, whether or not a debtor may acquire or improve its exempt assets in contemplation of a bankruptcy petition is thoroughly discussed by Resnick.[50]

Discharge of Debts

104 Section 523 lists several debts that are excepted from a discharge of an individual debtor. These debts are exempted from a filing under chapters 7 and 11, but chapter 13 has special provisions. The items listed in subsection (a) include:

1 A tax with priority under section 507(a)(7) or that was willfully evaded.

2 Debts from which money, property, services, or a renewal of credit was obtained by false pretenses, false representations, or actual fraud. This includes materially false statements in writing concerning the debtor's financial condition upon which the creditor reasonably relied, and the debtor issued the financial statements with the intent to deceive. Also exempt from discharge are consumer debts of individuals, if more than $500 is owed to a single creditor for "luxury goods or services," that were incurred within forty days before the order for relief and cash advances of more than $1000 that are extensions of consumer credit under an open-end credit plan obtained by an individual.

---

[50] Alan N. Resnick, "Prudent Planning or Fraudulent Transfer: the Use of Nonexempt Assets to Purchase or Transfer Property on the Eve of Bankruptcy," *Rutgers Law Review*, Vol. 31 (December 1978), pp. 615–654.

3 Debts which were not scheduled in time to permit timely action by the creditors to protect their rights, unless they had notice or knowledge of the proceedings.

4 Debts for fraud or defalcation while acting in a fiduciary capacity, embezzlement, or larceny.

5 Alimony, maintenance, or support obligations.

6 Debts due to willful and malicious injury to another entity or its property.

7 Debts for fines, penalties, and forfeitures that are not compensation for actual pecuniary loss payable to a governmental unit except a penalty relating to a nondischargeable tax or to a tax due which relates to a transaction which occurred more than three years prior to bankruptcy.

8 Most educational loans, unless the loan first became due more than five years prior to the petition date or an undue hardship would be imposed (see Public Law 96–56).

9 Debts from judgments or consent decrees resulting from the operation of a motor vehicle while legally intoxicated.

10 Debts owed that were or could have been listed in a prior bankruptcy case if the debtor waived a discharge or had been denied a discharge for a statutory reason other than the six-year limitation bar.

105 Section 523(c) provides that the creditor who is owed a debt that might be exempted from discharge as a result of false statements, for fraud, embezzlement, or larceny or for willful or malicious injuries as specified above must initiate proceedings to obtain the exception to discharge. Otherwise, the discharge of those debts will be granted unless the debtor's entire discharge is denied. Section 523(d) provides that if a creditor requests a determination of the dischargeability of a consumer debt on the grounds that such debt was incurred by the issuance of false financial statements or under false pretenses and the court discharges the debt, the creditor may be liable for the cost of such proceedings including attorney's fees. As stated above, section 523(a)(2) provides that it is necessary, in the case of financial statements, for the creditor to have relied on the statements and for the debtor to have issued them with the intent to deceive before a discharge of those debts will be denied. The effect of these changes is to limit the requests for a denial of a discharge on the basis of false financial statements to those situations where material, intentional errors are involved.

106 The Bankruptcy Code (section 524(c)) also provides that any dischargeable debt that is reaffirmed, namely, that the debtor agrees to pay not withstanding its discharge, must be reaffirmed before the discharge is granted and only after the debtor has had at least sixty days to rescind the agreement. If it is a consumer debt of an individual, the reaffirmation must be approved by the court.

Property of the Estate

107 The commencement of a case under chapter 7, 11, or 13 of the Bankruptcy Code creates an estate. The estate is composed of the debtor's property wherever it may be located.[51] All of the debtor's interest in property, legal or equitable, becomes property of the estate. It covers both tangible and intangible property, causes of action and property that is out of the debtor's control but is still its property.[52] Property that the trustee recovers as a result of his or her avoiding powers, such as recoveries from preferences or fraudulent transfers, is considered property of the estate. Inherited property, property received from a settlement with the debtor's spouse, or beneficiary proceeds from a life insurance policy which are property of the debtor at the date of filing or acquired or entitled to acquire within 180 days after the filing are considered property of the estate.

Avoiding Power of Trustee

108 The Bankruptcy Code grants the trustee (or debtor in possession) the right to avoid certain transfers made and obligations incurred. They include the trustee's powers as successor to actual creditors, as a hypothetical judicial lien creditor, and as a bona fide purchaser of real property. In addition, the trustee has the power to avoid preferences, fraudulent transfers, statutory liens, and certain postpetition transfers.

109 The trustee needs these powers and rights to insure that actions by the debtor or by creditors in the prepetition period do not interfere with the objective of the bankruptcy laws, to provide for a fair and equal distribution of the debtor's assets through liquidation—or rehabilitation, if this would be better for other creditors involved.

Trustee as Judicial Lien Creditor

110 Section 70c of the Bankruptcy Act, referred to as the "strong-arm clause," gave the trustee the right of a hypothetical creditor with a judicial lien on all the assets of the debtor as of the date of bankruptcy. The purpose of this provision was to allow the trustee to avoid unperfected security interests under statutes similar to article 9 of the Uniform Commercial Code, and other interest in the debtor's property that is not valid against a creditor obtaining a judicial lien as of the date of bankruptcy.[53]

111 Section 544(a) of the Bankruptcy Code recodifies the "strong-arm" clause. The new law clarifies some of the prior law provisions. It makes it clear that the trustee relies on a hypothetical creditor that extends credit at

---

[51] 11 U.S.C. Sec. 541(a).

[52] *CCH Bankruptcy Law Reports,* para 9501.

[53] Richard B. Levin, "An Introduction to the Trustee's Avoiding Powers," *American Bankruptcy Journal,* Vol. 53 (Spring 1979), p. 174.

the time of the commencement of the case and obtains the judicial lien at the same time.

Trustee as Purchaser of Real Property

112   Section 544(a)(3) of the Bankruptcy Code expands the trustee's strong-arm powers by giving him the rights and powers of a bona fide purchaser of real property other than fixtures from the debtor, against whom applicable law permits the transfer to be perfected. Thus, unrecorded real estate transfers by way of grant or security that is not valid as against a bona fide purchaser, but is good against a judicial lien creditor, will now be voidable by the trustee as a hypothetical bona fide purchaser. Teofan and Creel indicate that:

> Equitable interests of beneficiaries under unperfected express or implied trusts, resulting trusts and constructive trusts will also fall before the attack of the trustee as a bona fide purchaser. In addition, the trustee will cut off equities created by mutual mistake, fraud, or similar situations for which equitable relief is afforded by state law. This new strong-arm status may well be the "coup de grace" in bankruptcy court proceedings to all nonpossessory equitable interests in real property which are not disclosed in a written instrument properly recorded prior to the commencement of the proceedings.[54]

Trustee as Successor to Actual Creditors

113   Section 70e of the Bankruptcy Act gave the trustee the powers and rights of an actual creditor to avoid transfers made or obligations incurred by the debtor that are avoidable under state law. Section 544(b) of the Bankruptcy Code contains this basic concept:

> The trustee may avoid any transfer of an interest of the debtor in property or any obligation incurred by the debtor that is voidable under applicable law by a creditor holding an unsecured claim that is allowable under section 502 of this title or that is not allowable only under section 502(e) of this title.

114   Two major changes are made. First, the claim must be unsecured, whereas under prior law it probably could be either secured or unsecured. Second, the Code eliminates the requirement that the creditor on whom the trustee relies must have a provable claim, since provability itself has been eliminated under the code.

Reclamation

115   One area where the avoiding power of the trustee is limited is in a request for reclamation. Section 546(c) provides that under certain condi-

---

[54] Vernon O. Teofan and L. E. Creel III, "The Trustee's Avoiding Powers Under the Bankruptcy Act and the New Code: A Comparative Analysis," *St. Mary's Law Journal,* Vol. 11 (Number 2, 1979), p. 319.

tions the creditor has the right to reclaim goods if the debtor received the goods while insolvent. To reclaim these goods the seller must demand in writing, within ten days after their receipt by the debtor, that the goods be returned. The court can deny reclamation, assuming the right is established, only if the claim is considered an administrative expense or if the claim is secured by a lien. There are some problems that a creditor faces in attempting to reclaim goods. One is that the request must be made within ten days. Requests made after this time period will be denied. Another is that the Uniform Commercial Code right of reclamation under Section 2-702 is basically a right to obtain the physical return of particular goods in the hands of the debtor. If the goods have been sold or used, the ability to obtain the goods may be limited. For example, it is doubtful that the seller could reclaim goods that were sold by the debtor to a purchaser in good faith that had no knowledge of the debtor's financial problems. Also, the reclamation rights of the seller are subject to any superior right of other creditors, which most likely would include the good faith purchaser or buyer in the ordinary course of business.

Preferences

116　Section 547 provides that a trustee or debtor in possession can avoid transfers that are considered preferences. The trustee (debtor in possession) may avoid any transfer[55] of an interest of the debtor in property [section 547(b)]:

1　To or for the benefit of a creditor.
2　For or on account of an antecedent debt owed by the debtor before such transfer was made.
3　Made while the debtor was insolvent.
4　Made—
　　A　on or within ninety days before the date of the filing of the petition. Or
　　B　between ninety days and one year before the date of the filing of the petition, if such creditor, at the time of such transfer was an insider.
5　That enables such creditor to receive more than such creditor would receive if—
　　A　the case were a case under chapter 7 of this title.
　　B　the transfer had not been made.
　　C　such creditor received payment of such debt to the extent provided by the provisions of this title.

117　One change brought about by the Bankruptcy Code is that the time period when a transfer will be considered preferential has been reduced from

---

[55] Section 101(40) of the Bankruptcy Code defines a transfer as "every mode, direct or indirect, absolute or conditional, voluntary or involuntary, of disposing of or parting with property or with an interest in property, including retention of title as a security interest."

four months to ninety days. Added, however, was the provision that if the creditor is an "insider" the debtor can go back an entire year to void the transfer. Another change of the new law is that section 547(f) provides that the debtor is presumed to be insolvent during the ninety-day period. This presumption requires the adverse party to present some evidence to rebut the presumption. The burden of proof, however, remains with the party (trustee or debtor in possession) in whose favor the presumption exists. Under prior law, for there to be a preferential transfer the creditor had to be preferred over other creditors in the same class. The class requirement has been eliminated; to be a preferential transfer, the creditor must only receive more than would be received by such creditor in a chapter 7 liquidation. The Bankruptcy Code eliminates the "reasonable-cause-to-believe-insolvency" requirement of prior law. Thus, in order to avoid a transfer it is now not necessary to prove that the creditor had reasonable cause to believe that the debtor was insolvent at the time the transfer was made. This change was made to provide for a more equitable distribution of the assets of the debtor. It is now easier for the trustee or debtor to recover payments to creditors that are considered preferences. In summary, section 547 contains six conditions that must be satisfied before the transfer will be considered a preference:

1 A transfer of the debtor's property must be made.
2 To or for the benefit of a creditor.
3 For or on account of an antecedent debt.
4 While the debtor is insolvent.
5 Within 90 days before the petition (one year for insiders).
6 The creditor receiving the transfer receives more than he would have in a liquidation case without the transfer.

Exceptions

118 As under prior law there are a number of exceptions to the power the trustee has to avoid preferential transfers. Section 547(c) of the new law contains seven exceptions.

119 *Contemporaneous Exchange* A transfer intended by the debtor and creditor to be a contemporaneous exchange for new value given to the debtor and is in fact a substantially contemporaneous exchange is exempted. The purchase of goods or services with a check would not be a preferential payment, provided the check is presented for payment in the normal course of business, which the Uniform Commercial Code specifies as thirty days (U.C.C., Section 3-503(2)(a)).[56]

---

[56] House Report No. 95–595, 95th Cong., 1st Sess. (1977) 373.

120 *Ordinary Course of Business*   The second exemption protects payments of debts that were incurred in the ordinary course of business or financial affairs of both the debtor and the transferee when the payment is made in the ordinary course of business according to ordinary business terms. For bankruptcy petitions filed prior to October 8, 1984, there is a condition that requires that payments also be received within forty-five days of the date the debt was incurred to be exempt. The Bankruptcy Amendments and Federal Judgeship Act of 1984 repealed this forty-five-day provision. "Ordinary course of business" was deliberately left undefined. With the elimination of the forty-five-day period a key area of litigation will most likely center around "according to ordinary course of business" and "ordinary business terms." Open accounts that normally have a payment period of over forty-five days will now fall within the exception.

121 *Purchase Money Security Interest*   The third exception exempts security interests granted in exchange for enabling loans when the proceeds are used to finance the purchase of specific personal property. For example, a debtor borrowed $75,000 from a bank to finance a computer system and subsequently purchased the system. The "transfer" of the system as collateral to the bank would not be a preference provided the proceeds were given after the signing of the security agreement, the proceeds were used to purchase the system, and the security interest was perfected within ten days after the debtor received possession of the property.

122 *New Value*   This exception provides that the creditor is allowed to insulate from preference attack a transfer received to the extent that the creditor replenishes the estate with new value. For example, if a creditor receives $10,000 in preferential payments and subsequently sells to the debtor on unsecured credit goods with a value of $6000, the preference would be only $4000. The new credit extended must be unsecured and can be netted only against a previous preferential payment, not a subsequent payment.

123 *Inventory and Receivables*   This exception allows a creditor to have a continuing security interest in inventory and receivables (or proceeds) unless the position of the creditor is improved during the ninety days before the petition. If the creditor is an insider the time period is extended to one year. An improvement in position occurs when a transfer causes a reduction in the amount by which the debt secured by the security interest exceeds the value of all security interest for such debt. The test to be used to determine if an improvement in position occurs is a two-point test: the position ninety days (one year for insiders) prior to the filing of the petition is compared with the position as of the date of the petition. If the security interest is less than ninety days old, then the date on which new value was first given is compared to the position as of the date of the petition. The extent of any improvement caused by transfers to the prejudice of unsecured creditors is considered a preference.

124   To illustrate this rule, assume that on March 1 the bank made a loan of $700,000 to the debtor secured by a so-called floating lien on inventory. The inventory value was $800,000 at that date. On June 30, the date the debtor filed a bankruptcy petition, the balance of the loan was $600,000 and the debtor had inventory valued at $500,000. It was determined that ninety days prior to June 30 (date petition filed) the inventory totaled $450,000 and the loan balance was $625,000. In this case there has been an improvement in position of $75,000 (($600,000—$500,000)—($625,000—$450,000)) and any transfer of a security interest in inventory or proceeds could be recovered to that extent.

125   To be considered a preference there must be a transfer. For example, if a loan of $100,000 is secured by $70,000 in inventory of jewelry ninety days prior to bankruptcy and at the date of bankruptcy the same items are worth $90,000, there would not be a preference since there has not been a transfer. Furthermore, section 547(c)(5) provides that the improvement in position must be to the prejudice of other unsecured creditors. The problem of determining improvement in position becomes more difficult when dealing with work-in-process. If the $100,000 loan was secured by raw materials worth $70,000 and the raw materials are assembled, they now have a value as of the date of the petition of $90,000 because of the work of the employees who were paid for their efforts. It could be argued that there is "prejudice" to the estate but has a transfer occurred?[57] Also associated with the exemption is a valuation problem in that the difference is based on the value of the inventory, which may not necessarily be book value.

126   *Fixing of Statutory Lien*   A sixth exception states that a statutory lien that is valid under section 545 is not voidable as a preference.

127   *Consumer Debts.*   A seventh exception, added by the Bankruptcy Amendments and Federal Judgeship of 1984, provides that in the case of an individual debtor whose debts are primarily consumer debts, the transfer is not voidable if the aggregate value of the property affected by the transfer is less than $620.

128   Legislative history indicates that if creditors can qualify under any one of the exceptions, they are protected to that extent. And if they can qualify under several, they are protected by each to the extent they can qualify under each.[58] Thus, by using the cumulative effect of these exceptions, creditors may obtain greater protection than could be obtained under any one exception.

---

[57] Barkley Clark, "Preferences Under the Old and New Bankruptcy Acts," *Uniform Commercial Code Law Journal,* Vol. 12 (Fall 1979), p. 180.

[58] House Report No. 95–595, 95th Cong., 1st Sess. (1977), 372.

Fraudulent Transfers

129   Section 548 of the Bankruptcy Code is a federal codification of the Uniform Fraudulent Conveyance Act, as was Section 67d of the Bankruptcy Act. Although there are few changes in the new law it should be noted that section 548(a) does not require that an actual creditor exist before the trustee may avoid a transfer or obligation. All fraudulent transfers and obligations must have been made or incurred within one year before the date of the filing of the petition to be voidable. Four kinds of fraudulent transfers are voidable under section 548; first, the transfer of property of the debtor or an obligation incurred by the debtor with the actual intent to hinder, delay, or defraud either existing or future creditors. Thus, to be voidable under this provision, the debtor must have intended to hinder, delay, or defraud existing or real or imagined future creditors.

130   Three kinds of constructively fraudulent transfers are voidable under the Bankruptcy Code. The constructively fraudulent transfers must have been made for less than reasonably equivalent value, whereas an actual fraudulent transfer can be voidable even if made for full value. The trustee may void a transfer of less than equivalent value (1) if the debtor was insolvent or became insolvent as a result of the transfer, (2) if the debtor was engaged in business or in a transaction and after the transfer the capital remaining was unreasonably small, or (3) if the debtor intended to or believed that it would incur debts that would be beyond the debtor's ability to pay as they matured.

131   In constructively fraudulent transfers there is another change from section 67d of the Bankruptcy Act. "Fair consideration" was used as a requirement rather than the phrase "reasonably equivalent value" in the new law. The phrase "fair consideration" included the requirement of good faith as well as fair equivalent value.[59] Thus, under prior law a transfer could have been considered fraudulent even if made for full consideration if the consideration was not given in good faith. The Bankruptcy Code eliminates the good faith requirement and requires only equivalent value.

132   Section 548(b) provides that a transfer of partnership property to a general partner when the partnership is insolvent is deemed to be fraudulent and voidable by the trustee. Subsection (c) of section 548 also provides that a transferee or obligee that takes consideration for value and in good faith is protected to the extent of the value given. A major change was made in this section in that it does not require that the value be present value. Thus, the satisfaction of an antecedent debt that occurred prior to ninety days before the date of the petition will be adequate value under the new law and will protect the transfer from being totally voidable. Value is defined to mean "property, or satisfaction or securing of a present or antecedent debt of the

[59] Levin, p. 181.

debtor, but does not include an unperformed promise to furnish support to the debtor or to a relative of the debtor.[60]

Postpetition Transfers

133   Section 549 allows the trustee to avoid certain transfers made after the petition is filed. Those that are avoidable must be transfers that are not authorized either by the court or by an explicit provision of the Bankruptcy Code. In addition, the trustee can avoid transfers made under sections 303(f) and 542(c) of the Bankruptcy Code even though authorized. Section 303(f) is the section that authorizes a debtor to continue operating the business before the order for relief in an involuntary case. Section 549 does, however, provide that a transfer made prior to the order for relief is valid to the extent of value received. Thus, the provision of section 549 cautions all persons dealing with a debtor before an order for relief has been granted to evaluate carefully the transfers made. Section 542(c) explicitly authorizes certain postpetition transfers of real property of the estate made in good faith by an entity without actual knowledge or notice of the commencement of the case.

Postpetition Effect of Security Interest

134   Generally property acquired by the debtor after the commencement of the case is not subject to any lien resulting from any security agreement entered into by the debtor before the commencement of the case. Thus, an agreement that allows a creditor to have a continuing security interest in accounts receivable would not apply to receivables that arise after the petition is filed. There are a few exceptions to this rule that generally relate to cash collateral or the limited situations where the right to perfect a security interest after the petition is filed is allowed.[61]

Setoffs

135   "Setoff is that right which exists between two parties to net their respective debts where each party, as a result of unrelated transactions, owes the other an ascertained amount."[62] The right to setoff is an accepted practice in the business community today. When one of the two parties is insolvent and files a bankruptcy court petition, the right to setoff has special meaning. Once the petition is filed, the debtor may compel the creditor to pay the debt owed and the creditor may in turn receive only a small percentage of the claim—unless the Bankruptcy Code permits the setoff.

---

[60] 11 U.S.C. Sec. 548(d)(2)(A).
[61] 11 U.S.C. Sec. 552.
[62] Carmelita J. Hammon, "Setoff in Bankruptcy: Is the Creditor Preferred or Secured?" *University of Colorado Law Review*, Vol. 50 (Summer 1979), p. 511.

136 The Bankruptcy Code contains the basic rules followed under prior law which give the creditor the right to offset a mutual debt providing both the debt and the credit arose before the commencement of the case.[63] There are, however, several exceptions:

1 Claims that are not allowable cannot be used for offsets.

2 Postpetition claims transferred by an entity other than the debtor or incurred for the purpose of obtaining a right of setoff against the debtor are disallowed for offsets.

3 Claims transferred to the creditors within ninety days before the filing of the petition and while the debtor was insolvent are precluded. Also, section 553(c) provides that for setoffs the debtor is presumed to have been insolvent on and during the ninety days immediately preceding the filing of the petition. The new law does not require, as was necessary under prior law, that the creditor have had reasonable cause to believe that the debtor was insolvent at the time the transfer was received.

137 Another major restriction on the use of setoffs prevents the creditor from unilaterally making the setoff after a petition is filed. The right to a setoff is subject to the automatic stay provisions of section 362 and the use of property under section 363. Thus, before a debtor may proceed with the setoff, relief from the automatic stay must be obtained (paragraphs 72–79). This automatic stay and the right to use the amount subject to setoff will be possible only if the trustee or debtor in possession provides the creditor with adequate protection. If adequate protection—normally in the form of periodic cash payments, additional or replacement collateral, or other methods that will provide the creditor with the indubitable equivalent of his interest—is not provided then the creditor may proceed with the offset as provided in section 553.

138 Section 553(b) contains a penalty for those creditors who elect to offset their claim prior to the petition when they see the financial problems of the debtor and threat of the automatic stay. The Code precludes the setoff of any amount that is a betterment of the creditor's position during the ninety days prior to the filing of the petition. Any improvement in position may be recovered by the debtor in possession or trustee. The amount to be recovered is the amount by which the insufficiency on the date of offset is less than the insufficiency ninety days before the filing of the petition. If no insufficiency exists ninety days before the filing of the petition, then the first date within the ninety day period where there is an insufficiency should be used. "Insufficiency" is defined as the amount by which a claim against the debtor exceeds a mutual debt owing to the debtor by the holder of such claim. The amount recovered is considered an unsecured claim.

---

[63] 11 U.S.C. Sec. 553.

139   To illustrate the offset provision consider the following situation where the creditor is a bank and the debtor has a checking account and a loan with the bank.

Days prior to petition:	90	70	45	1
Balance in checking account	$600	$500	$850	$300
Loan balance	1000	1000	1000	1000
Insufficiency	$(400)	$(500)	$(150)	$(700)

If the bank sets off one day prior to the filing of the petition, there is no recovery since the insufficiency at this date ($700) is not less than the insufficiency ninety days prior to the petition date ($400). However, $250 could be recovered if the setoff was made forty-five days prior to the petition date ($400—$150).

140   Hammon suggests that the improvement in position rules may encourage financial institutions to set off upon the first indication of debtor insolvency rather than encourage them to work with the debtor hoping that he or she will ultimately be able to meet his or her obligations.[64]

CHAPTER 7 LIQUIDATION

141   Chapters 1, 3, and 5 of the Bankruptcy Code deal with the provisions that apply to all chapters. Chapter 7 is concerned with the liquidation of a debtor in financial trouble and contains provisions for the appointment of the trustee, liquidation of the business, distribution of the estate to the creditors, and discharge of the debtor from its liabilities. Collier stated:

> It is the purpose of the Bankruptcy Act to convert the assets of the bankrupt into cash for distribution among creditors, and then to relieve the honest debtor from the weight of oppressive indebtedness and permit him to start afresh, free from the obligations and responsibilities that have resulted from business misfortunes.[65]

The same objective applies to chapter 7 of the Bankruptcy Code.

Filing the Petition

142   All persons[66] are eligible to file a petition under chapter 7 except railroads, domestic insurance companies and banks (including savings and

---

[64] Hammon, p. 523.

[65] *Collier on Bankruptcy,* 13th ed., p. 6.

[66] Individuals, partnerships, or corporations, but not a governmental unit (11 U.S.C. Sec. 101(30)).

loan associations, building and loan associations, credit unions, and so forth) and foreign insurance companies and banks engaged in the insurance and banking business in the United States. Foreign insurance companies and banks not engaged in such business in the United States could file a petition. Although farmers and nonprofit corporations may file voluntary petitions, their creditors may not bring them involuntarily into the bankruptcy court.

143 The person filing voluntarily need not be insolvent in either the bankruptcy or equity sense; the essential requirement is that the petitioner have debts. When a corporation is insolvent, shareholder approval or authorization to the filing of a petition is in some situations unnecessary; the board of directors may have the power to initiate proceedings. However, the power to initiate the proceedings depends on state corporate law, the articles of incorporation, and the bylaws of the corporation. The filing of a voluntary petition under chapter 7 constitutes an order for relief, that is the equivalent to being adjudged a bankrupt under the Bankruptcy Act. The debtor corporation's property is then regarded as being in the custody of the court and "constitutes the assets of a trust for the benefit of the corporation's creditors."[67] For an involuntary petition that is not timely converted, the court will only after trial order relief under chapter 7, if it finds the debtor is generally not paying its debts as they become due, or that within 120 days a custodian took possession of all or substantially all of the debtor's assets.

144 The debtor can convert a chapter 7 case to a chapter 11 or 13 at any time and this right cannot be waived. In addition, on request of a party in interest, after notice and a hearing, the court may convert the chapter 7 case to chapter 11.

Interim Trustee

145 As soon as the order for relief has been entered the court will appoint a disinterested person from a panel of private trustees to serve as the interim trustee. If a person was serving as trustee in an involuntary case prior to the order for relief he may also be appointed as interim trustee.[68] The function and powers of the interim trustee are the same as those for a trustee. In the pilot districts, the U.S. trustee will appoint the interim trustee from the panel of private trustees. If none are willing to serve, then the U.S. trustee may serve in this capacity. In situations where the schedules of assets and liabilities disclose that there are unlikely to be any assets in the estate the U.S. trustee may serve as the interim trustee and as the trustee if one is not elected by the creditors.

---

[67] Grange et al., pp. 398–399.
[68] 11 U.S.C. Sec. 701(a).

Election of Trustee

146   At a meeting of creditors called under section 341 a trustee may be elected if an election is requested by at least 20 percent in amount of qualifying claims. Creditors who hold an allowable, undisputed, fixed, liquidated, unsecured claim who do not have an interest materially adverse to the interest of all creditors and who are not insiders may vote. To elect a trustee, holders of at least 20 percent of the qualifying claims must vote and the candidate must receive a majority in amount of those voting. If a trustee is not elected, the interim trustee will serve as the trustee.[69] If the U.S. trustee is the interim trustee and no trustee is elected, then he or she will serve as the trustee.

147   The provision that the creditors may elect the trustee may result in different trustees being appointed for a partnership and the individual partners in the proceedings. If, of course, they have the same creditors, a common trustee would most likely be elected. The election of multiple trustees would probably cost more, but might result in a more equitable distribution of the estate. Conflicts of interest can arise in situations where there is a common trustee for the individual partners and the partnership.

Duties of Trustee

148   Section 704 identifies the following as duties of the trustee:

1   Collect and reduce to money the property of the estate for which such trustee serves, and close up such estate as expeditiously as is compatible with the best interest of parties in interest.

2   Be accountable for all property received.

3   Insure that the debtor performs his intention as to the surrender or redemption of property used as security for consumer debts or as to the reaffirmation of debts secured by such property. See section 521(2).

4   Investigate the financial affairs of the debtor.

5   If a purpose would be served, examine proofs of claims and object to the allowance of any claim that is improper.

6   If advisable, oppose the discharge of the debtor.

7   Unless the court orders otherwise, furnish such information concerning the estate and the estate's administration as is requested by a party in interest.

8   If the business of the debtor is authorized to be operated, file with the court and with any governmental unit charged with responsibility for collection or determination of any tax arising out of such operation,

---

[69] Ibid., Sec. 702 and 703(c).

periodic reports and summaries of the operation of such business, including a statement of receipts and disbursements, and such other information as the court requires.

9   Make a final report and file a final account of the administration of the estate with the court.

For the districts where the U.S. trustee pilot program applies, the trustee must file operating statements and other reports on the administration of the estate with the U.S. trustee.

149   The duties set forth are very similar to those of prior law. Obviously one of the most important duties of the trustee is to reduce the property to money and close up the estate in the manner that will allow the interested parties to receive the maximum amount. For some businesses it may be best for the trustee to operate the business for a short time so that the liquidation can be carried out in an orderly fashion. This is likely when the completion of work in process or the retail sale of inventory is likely to bring the highest value on liquidation. Authority to operate the business must, however, come from the court.[70] If the trustee does operate the business, periodic operating reports, including a statement of receipts and disbursements, must be filed with the court and the U.S. trustee when appropriate. Additional information may be required by local rules, by the court, and by the U.S. trustee.

Creditors' Committee

150   At the meeting of creditors under the provisions of section 341(a), in addition to voting for a trustee they may also vote to elect a committee of not fewer than three and no more than eleven creditors. Each committee member must hold an allowable unsecured claim to be eligible to serve.[71] The committee's function will be to consult with the trustee regarding the administration of the estate, make recommendations to the trustee regarding the performance of his duties, and submit to the court any questions affecting the administration of the estate.[72] Unlike chapter 11 cases where creditors' committees are appointed by the court (U.S. trustee) in every case, a creditors' committee will not serve in a chapter 7 liquidation unless the creditors elect one.

Partnerships

151   Section 723(a) provides that if the property of the partnership is insufficient to satisfy in full the claims of the partnership and if a general

---

[70] Ibid., Sec. 721.
[71] Ibid., Sec. 705(a).
[72] Ibid., Sec. 705(b).

partner is personally liable, a claim exists against the general partner for the full amount of the deficiency. According to section 723(b) the trustee is required to seek recovery first from the general partners that are not debtors in a bankruptcy case. The court has the authority to order the general partners to provide assurance that the partnership deficiency will be paid, or may order general partners not to dispose of their property.

152 Under prior law nonadjudicated partners were required to file schedules of assets and liabilities and the partnership trustee had the prerogative to collect, evaluate, preserve, liquidate, and otherwise manage the separate estates of the nonadjudicated partners. Hanley's[73] analysis of the legislative intent and of the development of these broad powers in the first place suggests that the powers should be reduced. He, however, concludes:

> Despite this analysis, in light of the broad discretion of the court under the new Act, partnership trustees probably will continue to seek a variety of managerial orders regarding the estates of nonadjudicated partners. The rules will continue to require the filing of a schedule of assets and liabilities, which arguably is necessary to determine whether security for a deficiency is required. In some circumstances, particularly after the rendition of a judgment against the partner, a court may grant the trustee's request for a turnover order, although it is doubtful that one should ever apply to the assets of an exempt partner. Finally, the legislative history of the Act suggests that the court's authority to enjoin a partner's creditor from levying on the separate property of the partner is continued.[74]

153 Section 723(c) gives the partnership trustee the right to file a claim against the general partners in bankruptcy court. This section states:

> Notwithstanding section 728(c) of this title, the trustee has a claim against the estate of each general partner in such partnership that is a debtor in a case under this title for the full amount of all claims of creditors allowed in the case concerning such partnership. Notwithstanding section 502 of this title, there shall not be allowed in such partner's case a claim against such partner on which both such partner and such partnership are liable, except to any extent that such claim is secured only by property of such partner and not by property of such partnership. The claim of the trustee under this subsection is entitled to distribution in such partner's case under section 726(a) of this title the same as any other claim of a kind specified in such section.

154 If the trustee is unsuccessful in recovering the full amount of the deficiency of the partnership from the general partners not in a bankruptcy proceeding, a claim may be asserted against the general partner in bank-

---

[73] John W. Hanley, Jr., "Partnership Bankruptcy Under the New Act," *The Hastings Law Journal,* Vol. 31 (September 1979), pp. 162–166.
[74] Ibid., p. 166.

ruptcy court. Note that the claim against the partners is not subordinated to those of the individual partners as was done under prior law. The purpose of this section was to provide that partnership creditors and partner creditors would be treated alike in the proceedings. This section also provides that only one claim will be allowed where creditors have filed claims against the partnership and against individual partners in bankruptcy proceedings. It would thus appear that holders of claims against both the partnership and the partners would have duplicate claims which they filed against individual partners disallowed.

155 If the trustee recovers from general partners in a bankruptcy proceeding a greater amount than is necessary to satisfy in full the claims of the partnership, the court, after notice and hearing, will determine an equitable distribution of the surplus.[75]

156 Section 727(a) (1) provides that only an individual may obtain a discharge. Thus, it is not possible for a partnership to obtain a discharge. As with corporations, this provision would make it undesirable to make continued use of a particular partnership shell following the liquidation of the partnership.

157 An individual partner can, of course, obtain a discharge from debts. This individual partner must, however, satisfy the requirements for a discharge in section 727.

158 One provision that can have an effect on partnership proceedings is that an individual discharge can be denied if the debtor commits one of the listed offenses in connection with another case concerning an insider.[76] Since a general partner is an insider, an unacceptable action of the general partner with respect to the partnership's property or financial statements could prevent a subsequent discharge of the individual partner from his or her debts. These provisions respecting the complete denial of an individual's discharge are discussed in paragraphs 165 to 168.

Treatment of Tax Liens

159 In a chapter 7 liquidation the provision of prior law where tax liens were subordinated to administrative expenses and wage claims is codified in section 724(b). According to this section distribution is made first to holders of liens senior to the tax lien. Administrative expenses, wage claims, and consumer creditors granted priority are second, limited, however, to the extent of the amount of the allowed tax claim secured by the lien. If the entire claim has not been used up, the tax claimant has third priority to the extent that the priority claims did not use up the tax claim due to the lien. Fourth are junior lienholders, and the fifth distribution would go to the tax

---

[75] 11 U.S.C. Sec. 723(d).
[76] Ibid., Sec. 727(a) (7).

claimant to the extent he was not paid in the third distribution. Any remaining property goes to the estate.[77]

160   In addition, section 724(a) gives the trustee the right to avoid a lien that secures a fine, penalty, forfeiture, or a multiple, punitive, or exemplary damages claim to the extent that the claim is not for actual pecuniary loss suffered by the holder and occurred before the order for relief or the appointment of a trustee in the case.

Liquidation of Assets

161   After the property of the estate has been reduced to money and the secured claims to the extent allowed have been satisfied, the property of the estate shall be distributed to the holders of claims in a specified order. Unless a claim has been subordinated under the provisions of section 510, section 726(a) provides that the balance is distributed in the following order:[78]

1   To the holders of priority claims as set forth in section 507.
2   To the holders of general unsecured claims who timely filed proof of claim or those who filed late because of a lack of notice or knowledge of the case.
3   To the holders of general unsecured claims filed late.
4   In payment of an allowed secured or unsecured claim, not compensation for actual pecuniary losses, for fines, penalties, forfeitures, or damages suffered by the claim holder.
5   In payment of interest on the above claims at the legal rate from the date of filing the petition.
6   Any balance to the debtor.

162   Section 726(b) provides for claims within a particular classification to be paid on a pro rata basis when there are not enough funds to satisfy all of the claims of a particular classification in full. There is one exception to this policy. If there are not enough funds to pay all administrative expenses, and part of the administrative expenses related to a chapter 11 or 13 case prior to conversion, then those administrative expenses incurred in chapter 7 after conversion will be paid first. Thus, accountants whose fees in a chapter 11 case that were not paid before the conversion could find that they would not receive full payment if funds are not available to pay all administrative expenses in a subsequent chapter 7 case.

163   Subsection (c) of section 726 set forth the provisions for distribution of community property.

---

[77] *CCH Bankruptcy Law Reports,* para. 10,108.
[78] But see Secs. 364(c) and 507(b).

164   After the assets have been liquidated and the proceeds distributed in the proper order, the trustee will make a final report and file a final account of the administration of the estate with the court. At this time the trustee will be discharged from further responsibility.

Discharge

165   Section 727 states that a discharge will be granted to the debtor unless one of ten conditions is encountered. In that case the discharge will be denied. The grounds for denial are very similar to those of prior law with two exceptions. The first exception deals with the issuance of false financial statements. Under prior law, a discharge of all debts was barred by the obtaining of credit through the use of false financial statements, but this provision was omitted from the Bankruptcy Code. As noted in paragraph 105, the use of false financial statements can result in a debt obtained by such false statements not being discharged. Thus, the issuance of false financial statements to obtain business credit will now only prevent a discharge for that particular debt rather than bar a discharge of all debts. The second exception is that failure to pay the filing fee is no longer a basis to deny discharge. Instead, Bankruptcy Rule 1006 states that every petition shall be accompanied by the prescribed fee. It further implies that no petition shall be *accepted* by the bankruptcy court clerk unless accompanied by the fee or a proper application to pay the fee in installments. In addition, sections 707 and 1307 provide that for nonpayment of fees the court may dismiss a case after notice and a hearing.

166   It should be noted that section 523 contains a list of specific debts that may be excepted from the discharge provision, while section 727 provides for a denial of a discharge of all debts. A denial of a discharge benefits all creditors, while an exception to a discharge primarily benefits only the particular creditor to which the exception applies.

167   The other interesting change in the new law relates to the discharge of a corporation. Under prior law corporations in straight bankruptcy being liquidated could receive a discharge of debts and the remaining corporate structure (called its shell) could be used for certain tax benefits. The new law, however, allows only individuals to obtain a discharge under chapter 7 liquidation. Corporations will now be reluctant to use these shells because any assets eventually received by the shell are subject to attack for payment of prepetition debts.

168   The ten statutory conditions that will deny the debtor a discharge are that the debtor

1   Is not an individual.
2   Within one year prior to the filing of the petition, or after filing, transferred, destroyed, or concealed, or permitted to be transferred, de-

stroyed, or concealed, any of his property with the intent to hinder, delay, or defraud his creditors.

3 Failed to keep or preserve adequate books or accounts or financial records.

4 Knowingly and fraudulently made a false oath or claim, offered or received a bribe, or withheld information in connection with the case.

5 Failed to explain satisfactorily any losses of assets or deficiency of assets to meet his liabilities.

6 Refused to obey any lawful order or to answer any material questions in the course of the proceedings after being granted immunity from self incrimination.

7 Within one year prior to the filing of the petition, committed any of the above acts in connection with another bankruptcy case concerning an insider.

8 Within the past six years received a discharge in bankruptcy under chapter 7 or 11 of the Code or under The Bankruptcy Act.

9 Within the past six years received a discharge under chapter 13 of the Code or Chapter XIII of prior law unless payments under the plan totaled 100 percent of the allowed unsecured claims or at least 70 percent of such claims under a plan proposed in good faith and determined to have been performed according to the debtor's best effort.

10 In addition, the discharge will be denied if, after the order for relief, the debtor submits a written waiver of discharge and the court approves it.

These provisions are strictly construed in favor of the debtor. Nevertheless, one bankrupt under prior law was denied his discharge for failure to list as an asset on his schedule his collection of Superman comic books.[79]

SIPC LIQUIDATION

169 A special type of liquidation for which accountants may render services is the liquidation of a stockbroker. The liquidation of a stockbroker or stock dealer is governed by the Securities Investor Protection Act of 1970 (SIPA), as amended, and by sections 741–752 of chapter 7 of the Bankruptcy Code. The Securities Investor Protection Corporation (SIPC) is responsible for the liquidation of a troubled stockbroker. The membership of SIPC—a nonprofit corporation—consists of all persons registered as brokers or dealers under section 15(b) of the Securities and Exchange Act of 1934. Through an annual assessment from its members, SIPC establishes a fund to cover the costs to customers of a stockbroker who is being liquidated.

[79] *In re Ruben Marcelo,* 5 Bankruptcy Ct. Dec. 786 (S.D.N.Y. August 7, 1979). (The collection was valued at $2000.)

170 Section 6(a) of the SIPA provides that the purpose of a SIPC liquidation proceeding is:

1   As promptly as possible after the appointment of a trustee in such liquidation proceeding, and in accordance with the provisions of this Act—

    A   to deliver customer name securities to or on behalf of the customers of the debtor entitled thereto as provided in section 8(c) (2); and

    B   to distribute customer property and (in advance thereof or concurrently therewith) otherwise satisfy net equity claims of customers to the extent provided in this section;

2   to sell or transfer offices and other productive units of the business of the debtor;

3   to enforce rights of subrogation as provided in this Act; and

4   to liquidate the business of the debtor.

Determination of Need of Protection

171 The SEC or any other self-regulatory organization should notify SIPC if it becomes aware of facts that indicate a stockbroker may be having financial difficulty. Section 5(a) of the SIPA provides that SIPC may, upon notice to the member having financial difficulty, file an application for protective decree with a court of competent jurisdiction if it is determined by SIPC that:

1   A member of SIPC (or a member within 180 days prior to this determination) has failed or is in danger of failing to meet its obligations to customers and

2   One or more of the conditions necessary for the court to issue a protective decree exists (see paragraph 172).

172 Once the court receives the application from SIPC, it will issue a protective decree if the debtor consents to or fails to contest the application. If the application is contested, section 5(b) of the SIPA provides that the court—before it may issue the protective decree—must find that the debtor:

1   Is insolvent within the meaning of section 101 of title 11 of the United States Code or is unable to meet its obligations as they mature;

2   Is the subject of a proceeding pending in any court or before any agency of the United States or any State in which a receiver, trustee or liquidator for such debtor has been appointed;

3   Is not in compliance with applicable requirements under the 1934 Act or rules of the Commission or any self-regulatory organization with respect to financial responsibility or hypothecation of customers' securities; or

4 Is unable to make such computations as may be necessary to establish compliance with such financial responsibility or hypothecation rules.

Appointment of Trustee

173 As soon as the court issues a protective decree, a trustee is appointed to liquidate the broker or dealer. An attorney for the trustee is also appointed. The trustee and attorney may be associated with the same firm. In most cases the trustee in a SIPC liquidation is an attorney, but accountants have also served in this capacity. The trustee is appointed by the court in which the protective decree is issued. The SIPC may appoint itself or one of its examiners as trustee when the unsecured general creditors and subordinated claims appear to total less than $750,000 and the debtor's customers appear to number fewer than 500.

Bankruptcy Court Jurisdiction

174 Section 5(b) (4) of the SIPA provides that once the protective decree has been issued and the trustee appointed, the liquidation proceeding is transferred to a bankruptcy court.

Powers and Duties of Trustee

175 The trustee in a SIPC case has the same powers and rights as a trustee in a bankruptcy case. In addition, the trustee may, with the approval of SIPC but without any need for court approval:

Hire and fix the compensation of all personnel (including officers and employees of the debtor and of its examining authority) and other persons (including accountants) who are deemed by the trustee necessary for all or any purposes of a liquidation proceeding.

Utilize SIPC employees for all or any purposes of a liquidation proceeding.

Manage and maintain customer accounts of the debtor for the purposes of section 8(f).

176 The duties of the trustee are also similar to those in a chapter 7 liquidation case (see paragraph 148), except that the trustee has no duty to reduce to money securities that are customer property or that are in the general estate of the debtor. Additionally, as provided in SIPA sections 6(b), 6(c) and 6(d), the trustee is to:

1 Deliver securities to or on behalf of customers to the maximum extent practicable in satisfaction of customer claims for securities of the same class and series of an issuer.

2   Subject to the prior approval of SIPC but without any need for court approval, pay or guarantee all or any part of the indebtedness of the debtor to a bank, lender, or other person if the trustee determines that the aggregate market value of securities to be made available to the trustee upon the payment or guarantee of such indebtedness does not appear to be less than the total amount of such payment or guarantee.

3   Make to the court and to SIPC such written reports as may be required of a trustee in a case under chapter 7 and include in such reports information with respect to the progress made in distributing cash and securities to customers. The report should present fairly the results of the liquidation proceeding in accordance with section 17 of the Securities Exchange Act of 1934, taking into consideration the magnitude of items and transactions involved in connection with the operation of a dealer or broker.

4   Investigate the actions of the debtor. The trustee shall:

    a   As soon as practicable, investigate the acts, conduct, property, liabilities, and financial condition of the debtor, the operation of its business, and any other matter, to the extent relevant to the liquidation proceeding, and report thereon to the court.

    b   Examine, by deposition or otherwise, the directors and officers of the debtor and any other witness concerning any of the matters referred to in paragraph (a).

    c   Report to the court any facts ascertained by the trustee with respect to fraud, misconduct, mismanagement and irregularities, and any causes of action available to the estate.

    d   As soon as practicable, prepare and submit, to SIPC and to such other persons as the court designates and in such form and manner as the court directs, a statement of the investigation of matters referred to in paragraph (a).

Satisfaction of Claims

177   The key objective of the trustee is to satisfy customer accounts as quickly as possible and in an orderly manner. Claims of customers in a stockbroker liquidation are satisfied in one of two ways. If the records appear to be in reasonable order, the trustee may—with SIPC approval—transfer the customers' accounts to another broker. In connection with this transfer, the trustee may waive or modify the need to file a written statement of claim, and enter into an agreement with the broker receiving the accounts to cover shortages of cash or securities in customer accounts sold or transferred. SIPC funds are made available to cover any cash or security shortages.

178   The second approach involves direct settlement of accounts with the customers. A claim form is mailed to each customer. The amount shown on the stockbroker's books is compared with the proof of claim. Once these have been reconciled, a check and/or securities is then sent to satisfy the customers' accounts. This approach takes much more time than the transfer of the customers' accounts to another broker. However, the direct settlement approach is generally used for the liquidation of small brokers or of brokers with very poor customer account records.

179   To provide for prompt payment and satisfaction of customer accounts, SIPC advances to the trustee funds for each customer (not to exceed $500,000) as may be required to pay or satisfy claims. Section 9(a) of the SIPA provides the following limitations:

1   If all or any portion of the net equity claim of a customer in excess of his ratable share of customer property is a claim for cash, as distinct from a claim for securities, the amount advanced to satisfy such claim for cash shall not exceed $100,000 for each such customer.

2   A customer who holds accounts with the debtor in separate capacities shall be deemed to be a different customer in each capacity.

3   If all or any portion of the net equity claim of a customer in excess of his ratable share of customer property is satisfied by the delivery of securities purchased by the trustee to satisfy claims for net equities, the securities so purchased shall be valued as of the filing date for purposes of applying the dollar limitations of this subsection.

4   No advance shall be made by SIPC to the trustee to pay or otherwise satisfy, directly or indirectly, any net equity claim of a customer who is a general partner, officer or director of the debtor, a beneficial owner of five per centum or more of any class of equity security of the debtor (other than a nonconvertible stock having fixed preferential dividend and liquidation rights), a limited partner with a participation of five per centum or more in the net assets or net profits of the debtor, or a person who, directly or indirectly and through agreement or otherwise, exercised or had the power to exercise a controlling influence over the management or policies of the debtor.

5   No advance shall be made by SIPC to the trustee to pay or otherwise satisfy any net equity claim of any customer who is a broker or dealer or bank, other than to the extent that it shall be established to the satisfaction of the trustee that the net equity claim of such broker or dealer or bank against the debtor arose out of transactions for customers of such broker or dealer or bank, in which event each such customer of such broker or dealer or bank shall be deemed a separate customer of the debtor.

180   In addition, SIPC may advance funds to complete the close-outs as of the filing date that are allowed by SIPC rules and to cover administrative expenses to the extent the general estate of the debtor is not sufficient to pay them.

Out-of-Court Settlements

1 The number of agreements reached out of court between financially troubled debtors and their creditors rose considerably during the 1970s. For example, following the 1973–1974 recession it was reported that the number of cases in New York was up 36 percent, in Chicago up 30 percent, and in Dallas up 20 percent.[1] The numbers were even higher in the recession during the early 1980s. Not only is the number of such agreements growing but the types of businesses seeking this type of remedy have also increased. At one time, the informal out-of-court agreement was used frequently only in selected areas such as in New York City's garment industry, but its popularity

[1] "More Firms Iron Out Financial Troubles Through Credit Groups to Avoid Courts," *Wall Street Journal*, June 17, 1975.

has now spread to other industries and locations. There are more agreements reached each year out of court than through the bankruptcy courts. In fact, some attorneys specializing in bankruptcy work estimate that there are at least five out of court settlements for each reorganization of a business in chapter 11. In most situations where it appears that the business could be rehabilitated, out-of-court settlement should at least be considered because it may, in fact, be the best alternative.

2   An informal settlement effected between a debtor and his or her creditors is normally one of three possible types of agreement:

Moratorium (extension)—an extension of time with eventual full payment in installments.

Pro rata cash settlement (composition)—payment on a proportional basis in cash in full settlement of claims.

Combination—payment of part of the debts in cash at the time of the settlement and agreement to make further installment payments.[2]

3   Certain conditions are normally advantageous to a successful out-of-court agreement. The debtor company should be a good moral risk so that creditors may have some assurance it will be true to its word. The debtor should have the ability to recover from financial difficulties. General business conditions should be favorable to a recovery.[3]

NATURE OF PROCEEDINGS

4   The informal settlement is an out-of-court agreement that usually consists of an extension of time (stretch out), a pro rata cash payment for full settlement of claims (composition), an exchange of stock for debt, or some combination. The debtor, through counsel or credit association, calls an informal meeting of the creditors for the purpose of discussing his or her financial problems. In many cases, the credit association makes a significant contribution to the out-of-court settlement by arranging a meeting of creditors, providing advice, and serving as secretary for the creditors' committee. A credit association is composed of credit managers of various businesses in a given region. Its functions are to provide credit and other business information to member companies concerning their debtors, to help make commercial credit collections, to support legislation favorable to business creditors, and to provide courses in credit management for members of the credit community. At a meeting of this type, the debtor will describe the causes of failure, discuss the value of assets (especially those unpledged) and the

---

[2] John E. Mulder, "Rehabilitation of the Financially Distressed Small Business—Revisited," *The Practical Lawyer,* Vol. 11 (November 1965), p. 40.
[3] Fred Weston, *Managerial Finance* (Hinsdale, Ill.: The Dryden Press, 1978), pp. 897–898.

unsecured liabilities and answer any questions the creditors may ask. The main objective of this meeting is to convince the creditors that they will receive more if the business is allowed to operate than if it is forced to liquidate and that all parties will be better off if a settlement can be worked out.

5   In larger businesses it may take months, or even years, to develop an agreement that will provide the type of relief the debtor needs. For example, in the case of International Harvester, the company had been working with its creditors for several years before its out-of-court plan was finalized. In these situations, the negotiations are generally between the debtor's counsel, who should be experienced in bankruptcy and "workout" situations, and counsel who represents major creditors or committees of creditors.

OBTAINING ASSISTANCE FROM CREDITORS

6   To be successful in any attempt to work out an agreement with creditors, the debtors must obtain the cooperation of some of the largest creditors and those with the most influence over other creditors very early during the time period when financial problems developed.

Importance of an Early Meeting Date

7   It is difficult for a debtor to admit that it cannot pay debts and continue profitable operations. As a result, decisions to call a meeting of creditors or to file a petition under the Bankruptcy Code often are postponed until the last minute. This delay benefits no one, including the debtor. A debtor may place the last penny of his or her life's savings in the business, even when the possibility is remote that this last investment will actually provide the corrective action. Where the product is inferior, the demand for the product is declining, the distribution channels are inadequate, or other similar problems exist that cannot be corrected, either because of the economic environment or management's lack of ability, it is normally best to liquidate the company immediately.

8   There are several reasons why it is advisable to call a meeting of creditors as soon as it becomes obvious that some type of relief is necessary. First, the debtor still has a considerable asset base. There also is a tendency for many of the key employees to leave when they see unhealthy conditions developing; early corrective action may encourage them to stay. In addition, prompt action may make it possible for the debtor to maintain some of the goodwill that was developed during successful operating periods. The fact remains that in many cases no kind of action is taken, and it is the creditors that force the debtor to call an informal meeting or file a bankruptcy court petition.

Preparation for the Creditors' Meeting

9 The creditors will almost always be represented by those who have handled cases on many occasions and are true specialists in negotiating settlements. Because of this, it is important that the debtor select counsel who is adequately prepared for the meeting with creditors. The independent accountant can, more than anyone else, assist the debtor in this preparation. It is advisable that the debtor's legal counsel be experienced in bankruptcy and insolvency proceedings, and especially familiar with problems associated with out-of-court settlements. After counsel has been engaged and before the creditors' meeting is called, it is necessary, even when the meeting is called on short notice, for both the accountant and counsel to consult with the debtor.

10 At this conference, the attorney obtains sufficient background information about the debtor's operations so that the attorney can present the facts to the creditors, knowledgeably discuss the situation with them, and explain why the debtor is in difficulty and why a settlement out of court would be advantageous to all parties. Also, various types of financial information similar to that needed for a chapter 11 proceeding must be supplied to the attorney. The first kind of information needed is a summary of the major causes of failure and the possible corrective action that can be taken. To prepare this type of summary, the accountant must analyze the past activities of the debtor, compare the financial statements for the last three or four years, and determine what caused the cash shortage. The attorney will need a copy of the most recent balance sheet, income statement, and statement of changes in financial position, as well as a list of the debtor's creditors and executory contracts. The attorney also should have some idea of the liquidation value of the assets and know the nature of the liabilities (that is, those secured, unsecured, and contingent), and be familiar with the changes that have occurred in inventory and the reasons for the changes. The debtor's independent accountant should make sure the attorney knows of any sales made below cost, or considerably below the normal price, and of any preferential payments, fraudulent transfers, or setoffs.

11 It is often advisable, provided there is enough time, for the accountant and the attorney to assist the debtor in preparing a suggested plan of settlement so it can be presented and discussed at the first meeting with creditors. Typically, only the largest creditors and a few representatives of the smaller creditors are invited, to avoid having a group so large that little can be accomplished.

12 Counsel may also prefer to meet individually with the major institutional lenders and several of the larger trade creditors. In these meetings counsel for the debtor can explain the problem, the action the debtor is taking to attempt to locate the cause of the financial trouble, and the type of relief and support that is needed. The debtor also seeks advice and input from the major creditors concerning the type of action they might consider at least partly acceptable. Hopefully as a result of these meetings the debtor will be able to obtain some support for the action the company is taking.

13 At a typical meeting, the debtor will provide the creditors with copies of the latest financial statements and other pertinent financial information. These statements will be reviewed by the creditors and the liquidating values of the various assets will be discussed. If the debtor has developed a suggested plan of settlement, this also will be discussed by the creditors, who may accept it or, under certain conditions, ask for another plan or recommend that the debtor file a petition in bankruptcy court. If a debtor is well prepared by its accountant and attorney and has a good opportunity of being rehabilitated at a reasonable cost, it can avoid being forced involuntarily into bankruptcy court.

Appointment of Creditors' Committee

14 To make it easier for the debtor to deal and work with the creditors, a committee of creditors is normally appointed during the initial meeting of the debtor and its creditors, providing, of course, the case is judged to warrant some cooperation by the creditors. It should be realized that the creditors are often as interested in working out a settlement as is the debtor. There is no set procedure for the formation of a committee. Ideally, the committee should consist of four or five of the largest creditors and one or two representatives from the smaller creditors. A lot of unnecessary time wasted on deciding the size and composition of the committee would be saved at creditors' meetings if the committees were organized in this manner. However, there are no legal or rigid rules defining the manner in which a committee shall be formed. Although a smaller creditor will often serve on a committee, there are committees on which only the larger creditors serve, either because of lack of interest on the part of the smaller creditors or because the larger creditors override the wishes of others.

15 The debtor's job of running the business while under the limited direction of the creditors' committee can be made easier if the creditors selected are those most friendly to the debtor.

Duties and Functions of Creditors' Committee

16 The creditors' committee is the liaison between creditors and debtor and is also the representative and bargaining agent for the creditors. Once a settlement has been arranged it is the responsibility of the committee to solicit the acceptance of the creditors. Honesty and good faith are requirements in the performance of all committee functions. Committee members must recognize that their interests are the same as those of the other creditors; they must not allow their own interests to be brought into conflict with those of the body of creditors and must completely refrain from seeking personal gain.[4]

17   The creditors' committee serves as the bargaining agent for the creditors, observes the operation of the debtor during the development of a plan, and solicits acceptance of a plan once it has been approved by the committee. Generally, the creditors' committee will meet as soon as it has been appointed, for the purpose of selecting a chairman and counsel. The committee also will engage an independent accountant to review the books and records of the debtor and the operations to see if there is a basis for future profitable operations.

18   At the completion of the investigation, the creditors' committee will meet to discuss the results. If it reveals that the creditors are dealing with a dishonest debtor, the amount of settlement that will be acceptable to the creditors will be increased significantly. It becomes very difficult for a debtor to avoid a bankruptcy court proceeding under these conditions. On the other hand, if the debtor is honest and demonstrates the ability to reverse the unprofitable operations trend and reestablish his or her business, some type of plan may eventually be approved.

19   As to the independent accountant who may be engaged by the creditors' committee, he or she can assist the committee in monitoring the debtor's business while a plan of settlement is being developed and during the period installment payments are being made under terms of the plan. The objective, of course, is to see that assets of the debtor are conserved and, once agreement has been reached on a plan of settlement, to see that all terms of the plan are being followed. The auditor will establish controls to ascertain that all cash receipts from sales, collections on account, and other sources are deposited intact, and that disbursements are for a valid purpose. Also, he or she will either prepare or review cash flow statements. Procedures must be established to insure that all liabilities incurred after the first creditors' meeting are paid promptly so that the debtor can reestablish himself or herself in the credit community.

20   "In non-bankruptcy matters the functions of a committee have run the gamut from investigation, consultation, advice to supervision and liquidation."[5] All these functions include supervision of the activities of the debtor, ensuring that all possible steps are taken to collect and preserve the assets, guard against careless acts of the debtor, and receive information from creditors as to the conduct of the debtor. This can amount to the submission of business and financial affairs by the debtor to the supervision of the committee (but see paragraphs 25–27).

21   Creditors' committees should, however, be very careful about the extent to which they take over the management of the business. Along with

---

[4] Chauncey Levy, "Creditors' Committees and Their Responsibilities," *Commercial Law Journal,* Vol. 74 (December 1969), p. 360.
[5] Ibid., p. 359.

this function comes responsibilities most creditors are not willing to assume. For example, they can be liable for withholding taxes if they are not properly remitted to the government. They will be classified as insiders if the debtor ends up in bankruptcy court and may find that they are not in as good a position as those creditors that did not get involved in the out-of-court activities. They may also have additional liability under the 1933 and 1934 securities laws.

Workout Specialist

22 Often the creditors will insist that there be a change in management before they will work with the debtor out of court. A management change might be in the form of new management experienced in the debtor's type of operations replacing existing top management. However, in many out-of-court situations a workout specialist is engaged to attempt to locate the debtor's problems and see that the business is preserved. Once operations are profitable, the workout specialist will then move on to another troubled company. These individuals are generally given the freedom to run the companies they take over as they see fit. Managers perceived as being competent and those the specialists feel comfortable working with will be retained. The other managers are let go. Compensation paid these specialists will vary; some want, in addition to a salary, a stake in the ownership or other forms of bonuses if their efforts prove successful. These workout specialists, in addition to running the business, work with the creditors' committee in developing the plan of settlement. The key management positions in the company are staffed under the direction of the specialist so that, once the operations are again profitable, the workout specialist can move on to the next troubled company. If the companies are relatively small the workout specialist may be supervising the operations of several businesses at one time. These specialists are also the same individuals that specialize in managing companies in bankruptcy.

Committee Management

23 Under conditions where the creditors elect committee management, an agreement is entered into between the debtor and the creditors, whereby supervision of the business is turned over to a committee of the creditors. The use of this approach has declined in recent years due to the disadvantageous position a creditor can be in if control is exercised over the debtor and a petition is subsequently filed. (See paragraphs 25–27.) The debtor in doing this normally executes an assignment for the benefit of creditors. This assignment is held in escrow by the committee. If it becomes necessary, the creditors can liquidate the debtor's assets or use the assignment to bring the debtor into bankruptcy court. The directors and officers of the debtor corporation tender resignations which the committee holds in escrow. The stockholders often endorse all shares of stock in blank. These are also held in escrow by the committee. The committee can operate the business itself, bring in an outside business expert, or use a present officer of the company. Usually included in the agreement is a provision for existing creditors to grant extensions or subordinate their claims in return for new financing. New funds can then be obtained from banks and others to provide the company with working capital. Usually the internal organization of the company is not changed; alterations are made only as necessary to effect efficiency and economies in operation.

24 After the business has operated for a short time under the plan designed by the creditors' committee, those in charge of managing the company determine whether recovery under the new regime is possible, or whether reorganization or liquidation is necessary.[6] If recovery seems possible, the agreement normally continues for a given period of time or until the creditors' claims have been paid or adjusted out of the proceeds realized under the management of the committee. When reorganization appears necessary, the committee may assist management in designing a plan. If the only alternative is liquidation, the committee may supervise the process.

Management Control Problems

25 In attempting to work with the debtor in an out-of-court proceeding, the creditors must be aware of the additional liability they may incur if they elect to exercise direct control over the debtor's operations. There is a fine line between counseling the debtor and controlling the debtor's operations.

26 If creditors do exercise control, they may be considered as insiders if a bankruptcy petition is subsequently filed (chapter 9, paragraph 39), have their debt subordinated to other creditors, and be liable for the losses suffered by other creditors attributable to interference by the controlling creditors. The creditor who obtains control of the debtor may be liable under the federal securities laws. For example, adverse consequences could result from a failure to obtain requisite regulatory approvals before and after assuming control of corporations in regulated industries such as insurance.[7] The failure to collect and remit taxes withheld from the wages of debtor's employees can result in the creditors' being liable for these taxes if they are in control of the debtor's operations.

27 Douglas-Hamilton suggests that creditors might consider the following suggestions to avoid being in control of the debtor:

1 Avoid any interference with the management of the debtor which suggests that the lender and not the debtor's management runs the company.

[6] Charles Gerstenberg, *Financial Organization and Management of Business* (Englewood Cliffs, N.J.: Prentice-Hall, Inc., 1959), p. 340.
[7] Margaret Hambrecht Douglas-Hamilton, "Troubled Debtors: The Fine Line Between Counseling and Controlling," *Journal of Commercial Bank Lending*, Vol. 60 (October 1977), p. 33.

2 Carefully examine the lender's collateral security position with regard to the stock of the debtor and the debtor's subsidiaries.

3 Exercise extreme caution in making and securing new loans to be certain there is no breach of the rights of existing creditors. (For example, the taking of collateral that is controlling stock of a subsidiary in exchange for a loan to a solvent subsidiary upstreamed to the parent in exchange for debts of questionable value may result in the subordination of this loan to other creditors.)

4 Take care in seeking to improve the lender's position with respect to its outstanding loans to avoid charges by third parties or other creditors that the lender induced the debtor to breach their contractual rights or aided and abetted or conspired with the debtor in leading others along.[8]

PREPARATION OF A PLAN OF SETTLEMENT

28 There is no set pattern for the form a plan of settlement proposed by the debtor must take. It may call for 100 percent payment over an extended period of time, payments on a pro rata basis in cash for full settlement of creditors' claims, an exchange of stock for debt, or some combination. A carefully developed forecast of projected operations, based on realistic assumptions developed by the debtor with the aid of his or her accountant, can help creditors determine if the debtor can perform under the terms of the plan and operate successfully in the future.

29 Generally, for creditors to accept a plan, the amount they will receive must be at least equal to the dividend they would receive if the estate were liquidated. This dividend expressed as a percent is equal to the sum of a forced-sale value of assets, accounts receivable, cash, and prepaid items, minus priority claims, secured claims, and expenses of administration divided by the total amount of unsecured claims.

30 The plan should provide that all costs of administration, secured claims, and priority claims, including wages and taxes, are adequately disposed of for the eventual protection of the unsecured creditors.[9] If the debtor's plan includes a cash down payment, in full or partial settlement, the payment should at least equal the probable dividend the creditors would receive in bankruptcy. It is not likely that creditors will accept under an agreement anything less than they would get in chapter 7 liquidation proceedings. See chapter 7, paragraphs 42 and 43 and chapter 10, paragraphs 42–44. An example of a composition (pro rata settlement) or extension-moratorium agreement form is shown in Exhibit 4-1. Note that where appropriate the form is annotated to draw attention to matters that should concern the creditors and their counsel.

---

[8] Ibid., pp. 34–35.
[9] Leon S. Forman, *Compositions, Bankruptcy, and Arrangements* (Philadelphia: The American Law Institute, 1971), p. 13.

Exhibit 4-1   Composition or Extension Agreement with Creditors

Creditors' Agreement

This agreement of _____[Date]_____, by and among Debtor Corporation (hereinafter "Debtor"), the Creditors' Committee named in Paragraph B below, and those unsecured creditors of Debtor who shall sign this Agreement or assent thereto by separate instrument or by negotiating a check bearing a restrictive endorsement assenting to this Agreement (hereinafter collectively referred to as the "Creditors"), is made with reference to the following facts:

A   Debtor is indebted to the Creditors and desires [to effect a composition with its creditors and] an extension of time for the payment of its obligations. The Creditors are willing to forgo their present rights to enforce payment under the terms and conditions set forth below.

B   At a general meeting of Creditors held _____[Date]_____, an informal Creditors' Committee (hereinafter called the "Committee") was elected, which Committee is now composed of _____[Names of Committee Members]_____. The Committee has employed _____[Name of Counsel]_____as its Counsel. _____[Secretary's Name]_____ is Secretary to the Committee (hereinafter "Secretary").

C   [Here add any special recitations applicable to your situation.]

Based upon the foregoing, it is agreed:

1   Creditors hereby constitute and appoint the persons named in Paragraph B above, and their respective successors, as the Committee, with all the rights, privileges, powers, authority, and immunities given to and vested in the Committee during the period of deferment.

2   The Committee and Debtor shall by audit or otherwise determine the amount of indebtedness or liability of Debtor to Creditors as of _____[Key_____ _____Date—the date for fixing Creditors' claims]_____, and such indebtedness is hereinafter called the "Extended Debt." If so determined by the Committee, Extended Debt shall include all unsecured indebtedness of Debtor as of said date owing to Creditors and to nonconsenting creditors.

[The second sentence is optional. It affords Debtor and Committee an opportunity to make pro rata distributions to all creditors having claims as of the key date. See note to paragraph 6.

[The indebtedness might be evidenced by promissory notes, rather than controlled, as here, by the general language of the Agreement. *But see* Lipton & Katz, "Notes" Are (Are Not?) Always Securities—A Review, *Business Lawyer,* Vol. 29 (April

Source: Adapted (to comply with Title 11 of United States Code) from Bernard Shapiro, "A Composition or Extension Agreement," Copyright 1977 by the American Law Institute. Reprinted with the permission of the *The Practical Lawyer.* Subscription rates $18 a year; $3.75 a single issue. This article appeared in the September 1, 1977, pages 28–40 issue of *The Practical Lawyer*

Exhibit 4-1   *(Continued)*

1974), pp. 861-866. Securities Acts problems are not avoided, however, by elimination of promissory notes.]

3   Subject to all terms, provisions, and conditions hereof, each and all of the Creditors shall and do hereby extend the time [and method] of payment of their respective claims, as they existed at the close of business on _____[Key_____ _____Date]_____, in accordance with Schedule A attached hereto and made a part hereof. The scheduled date for the last of such payments shall hereinafter be referred to as the "Termination Date."

In the event, however, that the Committee in its sole discretion shall determine that the best interests of Creditors and of Debtor will be served by the further extension of time of payment of all or any part of the claims of Creditors, the Committee, upon written notice to all Creditors and to Debtor, and without the requirement of any further assent in writing from any of them, is hereby empowered and authorized to grant a further extension of the time of payment of all or any part thereof and thereafter for such further period or periods of time as the Committee in its sole discretion may determine. The Termination Date as to each such extension shall be the date so specified by the Committee.

[The use of Schedule A affords an opportunity to attach a schedule of payments by the Debtor to the Committee and a schedule of payments by the Committee to the Creditors.]

4   For the purpose of this Agreement, the term "Period of Deferment," as heretofore and hereafter used in this Agreement, shall mean the period from the effective date of this Agreement until the Termination Date, or until such later date as shall be specified by the Committee, unless the Period of Deferment shall be sooner terminated pursuant to paragraph 11 hereof.

So long as the Period of Deferment shall continue, each Creditor agrees that it will not commence or prosecute any action or proceeding against Debtor, levy any execution, attachment, or any process against the property of Debtor by reason of the debt owing prior to moratorium to such Creditor as of the date of this Agreement, or file or join in any Petition, or in any proceeding under Title 11 of the United States Code or its amendments, or any other proceeding having for its object the appointment of a Receiver or Trustee for Debtor. Notwithstanding the foregoing sentence, if the amount of the Extended Debt of any Creditor is disputed by Debtor, such Creditor may commence and prosecute suit on such disputed claim, but any judgment obtained thereon shall not be enforced and payment thereof shall be deferred and extended in the same manner as all other Extended Debt.

Secretary shall advise Debtor in writing of all creditor confirmations of Extended Debt amounts. Within 60 days of receipt from Secretary, Debtor shall notify Secretary of all disputes. Absent such notification by Debtor within such 60 day period, as among only the Committee, Debtor, and Secretary or such other agent as the Committee shall select, the claim of each such Creditor shall be conclusively deemed to be in the amount indicated by the Creditor, less all payments received on such claim by such Creditor since _____[Key Date]_____.

5   Debtor shall keep such books of account and other records of its acts, prop-

Exhibit 4-1   (*Continued*)

erty, and transactions as may be required by law and in accordance with generally accepted accounting practice. Debtor shall supply access to the Committee of all Debtor's books, records, and affairs and shall furnish to the Committee such operating statements, balance sheets, and other financial information as the Committee shall reasonably require, including all reports and papers filed under any of the Securities Acts. The Committee shall, upon demand, be entitled to examine all state and federal income tax returns.

[Adapt this to require such specialized reports as the case may warrant.]

6   A. Debtor shall make the payments required by the Schedule of Payments (Schedule A attached hereto) to Secretary, as the agent for Creditors, or to such other agent as the Committee may, from time to time, designate. The Secretary shall distribute sums so received pro rata to all Creditors, and, if so determined, to all unsecured Creditors, determined in accordance with paragraphs 2 and 4 above.

[This subparagraph permits pro rata payment to all Creditors, whether consenting or not. See paragraph 2. It is not uncommon to find that "nonconsenting creditors" are merely apathetic or bound by red tape. If the dividend check contains a carefully drawn form of consent above the space provided for endorsement, some or most of the "nonconsenting creditors" will become a part of the program upon endorsing and cashing the first check. Thereafter, Debtor and the Committee may decide whether to transmit unlegended checks to Creditors who refused to endorse the first check.

[Here, as in other places in the Agreement, the Committee is given certain powers. Committee Counsel should draft these paragraphs with care to avoid the possibility that the Committee will be held accountable for the acts of the Debtor. *See,* for example, Sommer, Who's "In Control"?— S.E.C., *Business Lawyer,* Vol. 21 (April 1966), pp. 559-612; § 15 of the Securities Act of 1933; § 20a of the Securities Exchange Act of 1934. *See* note to Paragraph 12i.

[Furthermore, taking too much of an active role in the operations of the Debtor by the Creditors' Committee could result in members of the Committee being considered insiders if a bankruptcy petition is filed. Such a classification could severely affect the amount committee members receive from the Debtor's estate.

[In some extension or composition agreements, the Committee insists upon holding the stock of the Debtor in escrow, along with the right to cause a dissolution, liquidation, or other insolvency proceeding upon the happening of an event of default. These rights, too, might create problems for the Committee. Often the Committee will wish that it had never taken an escrow of the Debtor's stock. In many instances, it is more convenient and economical to permit a responsible Debtor to act as its own disbursing agent.]

B. Each Creditor hereby waives his right to assert in any proceeding at law, in equity, or in bankruptcy that any payment made pursuant to this Agreement or with the consent of the Committee constitutes an improper, voidable, or preferential payment.

Exhibit 4-1 (*Continued*)

C. Debtor shall make no payments to unsecured creditors as to their claims existing as of _____[Key Date]_____ unless prior consent thereto from the Committee is obtained by Debtor. Except as set forth herein, all payments to unsecured creditors shall be made or caused to be made by the Committee and shall be pro rata to Debtor's Creditors [or all the unsecured creditors], as provided above, unless the Committee decides that it is in the best interests of the Creditors to make payment in greater than pro rata amounts to unsecured creditors who are not consenting Creditors as defined herein. Furthermore, the Committee may cause payment in full of the balance of any claim of unsecured creditors or consenting Creditors that is less than $_____.

[Secret preferences may render the composition voidable, but small claims may be separately classified and preferred. Also, creditors may waive preferences. *Farmers Bank* v. *Sellers,* 167 Ark. 152, 267 S.W. 591 (1925).

[Provision is made for Committee approved preferences to nonconsenting creditors in order to preserve the business. If a nonconsenting or secured creditor becomes unmanageable, a chapter 11 filing might be required. See Paragarph 13.]

D. Upon payment of the amounts determined under Paragraphs 2 and 4 in accordance with the terms of this Agreement and the modifications thereof authorized by the Committee, all claims of Creditors shall be deemed to have been satisfied and Creditors shall have no further rights in connection therewith.

7 In consideration of the extension granted hereunder, but with respect only to Creditors as defined herein, Debtor consents and agrees that any and all statutes of limitations, either state or federal, shall be tolled, insofar as the Extended Debt is concerned, during the Period of Deferment and any additional extension granted by the Committee.

8 During the Period of Deferment, Debtor shall not, without prior written consent of the Committee:

a. Conduct its business in a manner inconsistent with good business practice.

b. Liquidate, dissolve, or enter into any consolidation, acquisition, or merger, or cause or permit any of its subsidiaries to do so, except that any subsidiary may liquidate, dissolve, or merge into Debtor or a wholly-owned subsidiary of Debtor.

c. Redeem or purchase any of its outstanding securities or issue for cash or cash equivalent any of its securities, except as required under existing agreements or provisions of outstanding convertible preferred stock, stock purchase warrants, or options of Debtor. However, Debtor may, at its option, retire presently existing debt by issuance of its capital stock, and, further, Debtor may, at its option, issue its securities for cash or cash equivalent, if _____ per cent of the proceeds therefrom (after deducting the costs and expenses of issuance, including without limitation, commissions, finders' fees, and the like) upon receipt by Debtor shall be paid to the Committee for distribution to unsecured creditors or Creditors in accordance with this Agreement. Said proceeds shall be applied forthwith upon receipt by the Committee towards the payment of the last installments of principal due prior to moratorium [and thereafter toward the payment of unpaid accrued interest] to unsecured creditors or Creditors pursuant to Schedule A. "Securities,"

Exhibit 4-1 *(Continued)*

as used in this Agreement, shall mean the capital stock of Debtor or any instrument giving the holder thereof the right to purchase or otherwise obtain such capital stock. "Capital Stock," as used in this Agreement, shall mean the preferred or common stock of Debtor regardless of the terms thereof.

d. Declare cash or asset dividends in favor of its common stock, but Debtor may pay dividends on its preferred stock in accordance with the rights of its preferred stockholders so long as at the time said dividends are paid Debtor is not in default under this Agreement.

e. Increase above said rate the total compensation of any officers whose maximum rate of compensation at any time in 19_____ was in excess of $_____ per year, except for cost of living increases, nor increase above $_____ per year the total compensation of any officer or employee of Debtor now or hereafter earning less than $_____ per annum, except for cost of living increases.

f. Encumber, hypothecate, or pledge any of its assets except in connection with new borrowings approved by the Committee, as distinguished from replacement or renewal of existing secured indebtedness, or the purchase or replacement of equipment.

g. Make any loans to anyone, excluding wholly-owned divisions or subsidiaries, which during the Period of Deferment aggregate in excess of $_____ at any time.

h. Make any capital expenditure, whether for cash, Securities, or other consideration, by purchase or lease, in excess of $_____ per project, or in excess of $_____ in the fiscal year of 19_____, or $_____ in the fiscal year of 19_____. The right to make capital expenditures in said amounts shall be cumulative.

i. Sell any of its assets out of the ordinary course of business involving an aggregate sales price of more than $_____ in any one transaction; provided, however, that this limitation shall not apply to an exchange of equipment or a sale in direct connection with replacement of equipment.

j. Default in the payment of any obligations due to any taxing agencies or fail to pay its obligations incurred after _____[Key Date]_____ within 30 days following maturity or any grace period provided therein, unless, in either case, Debtor is disputing in good faith the amount due or the terms of payment thereof. Ordinary trade debt after said date shall be paid in accordance with terms and as set forth in paragraph 10.

[This paragraph should be expanded or contracted according to the needs of the case. Probably, the Committee would want to know about the filing of any suit, but might not desire all the listed powers. Often, the Committee will wish to stay aloof from certain internal business affairs. See note to paragraph 6A.

[Subparagraph c contains a bracketed provision for interest. Trade debt commonly waives interest in insolvency or business distress cases. Certainly this is true in compositions where creditors are not paid in full. Occasionally, creditors—and less occasionally, even debtors—insist on payment of interest. If so, this form should be examined in its entirety for appropriate insertions and revisions.]

Exhibit 4-1   (*Continued*)

9   At the time of giving notice to its Board of Directors, Debtor shall give notice to the Committee Counsel of each meeting of the Board of Directors of Debtor and shall grant observer status to a designated member of the Committee or other designated person mutually acceptable to the Committee and Debtor. The observer shall agree not to disclose any information learned at the meetings of the Board of Directors to any person other than members of the Committee and Counsel to the Committee and to refrain from participating in the deliberations of the Board of Directors. The Committee hereby agrees that all such information shall not be disclosed to anyone other than its members, Counsel, and Secretary, except when disclosure is necessary to preserve or protect the rights and powers granted the Creditors or Committee by this Agreement, and, in any case, the Committee agrees not to use information obtained in a manner violative of law. The Committee shall be reimbursed by Debtor for the fee charged to the Committee by the observer, provided this amount shall not exceed $_____ per Board meeting attended by the observer.

[Here, again, participation in the affairs of the Debtor should be approached with caution. See note to paragraph 6A.]

10   It is anticipated that Debtor will, after _____[Key Date]_____, operate on a cash, discount, or [30] [60] [90] day credit basis and may from time to time require unsecured or secured loans or advances in connection with its operation. Creditors do hereby subordinate their respective extended indebtedness including postpetition interest, to the claims of such loaned moneys (and moneys loaned in accordance with paragraph 8f), and the same shall be repaid before the extended indebtedness shall be repaid without reference to the time of payment thereof or whether the payment be in due course of business, through voluntary or involuntary liquidation, or through any proceeding under any chapter of title 11 or otherwise. The extended indebtedness shall be similarly subordinated to the claims of suppliers of merchandise or services on credit to the Debtor after the above date.

Nothing contained in this Agreement shall be construed or deemed to release or discharge any rights and/or remedies that any Creditor may now or hereafter have against any endorser, guarantor, or surety who may now or hereafter be liable to any such Creditor upon any debt within the purview of this Agreement, and each such right and remedy is hereby reserved by any such Creditor.

[Concerning sureties, endorsers, or guarantors, *see New York University Law Quarterly Review*, Vol. 11 (1933), p. 287, "Restatement of Security" §§ 122, 129 (1941). The Debtor should try to get the surety's consent, because the surety retains rights of reimbursement against the debtor.

[This paragraph could be considerably expanded to include subordination to "Institutional Debt" or "Senior Debt," as specifically defined. It is adapted from W. Douglas and C. Shanks, Cases and Materials on Corporate Reorganization (St. Paul: West Publishing, 1931), p. 495.

[On subordinations generally, and for a broader clause for use in the event of a

Exhibit 4-1 *(Continued)*

bankruptcy petition *see* Calligar, "Subordination Agreements," *Yale Law Journal*, Vol. 70 (January 1961), p. 379. Calligar calls this type of subordination an "inchoate subordination."

[Many agreements call for the assignment of claims to these favored creditors as part of the subordination process. Calligar, *id.* at 395-398, sees little benefit in the assignment, except possibly where both the principal debtor and the subordinating creditor file bankruptcy proceedings. In our case, where the subordination is "inchoate," a present assignment "in gross" does not appear feasible. But it could be tried.]

11 The occurrence of any of the following events shall constitute a default by Debtor under this Agreement if the Committee elects to declare a default by written notice to Debtor, in which event the Period of Deferment shall end, and all of the Extended Debt shall become due and payable 30 days after said written notice of default, and Creditors may then assert all the remedies afforded by law:

(a) Debtor's failure to pay the installments required by Schedule A within 7 days of the respective due dates thereof.

(b) Debtor's breach of any of the other covenants, terms, or conditions of this Agreement and, as to any curable breach, failure to cure the breach within 20 days following written notice of it.

(c) Acceleration by a creditor of any debt based upon Debtor's breach or default of any provision of Debtor's agreements with said creditor, unless such acceleration is rescinded or the breach of default is cured within 20 days after acceleration.

(d) Preferential treatment of any Creditor with respect to Extended Debt without prior written consent of the Committee, except as set forth herein.

(e) At any time during the Period of Deferment, the net worth of Debtor is less than $_____, the working capital is less than $_____, or the total indebtedness, including accrued liabilities, is more than $_____.

(f) The audited financial statement of Debtor for the fiscal year ended _____[Date]_____ reflects material adverse change in the financial condition of Debtor relative to the financial condition reflected in the pro forma financial statement of Debtor for the same period previously furnished to the Committee.

(g) The filing of any proceeding by or against Debtor seeking any relief under any chapter of title 11, except a chapter 11 petition as provided in this Agreement.

(h) Termination prior to _____[Date]_____ of the present Loan Agreement with banks, unless a replacement loan is obtained by Debtor from another financial institution before the termination.

(i) Any modification of the existing agreements between Debtor and its other creditors or capital stockholders that is material and adverse to Creditors.

[This paragraph should be expanded or contracted according to the case.]

12 The Committee, for itself and its successors, shall act as the Committee hereunder and shall have the privileges, powers, authorities, and immunities herein given to and vested in the Committee, which include but are not limited to the

Exhibit 4-1   (*Continued*)

power and authority to amend this Agreement, declare or waive defaults, extend the period of deferment, consent or decline to consent to actions by Debtor requiring Committee consent, authorize and cause the payment of the Committee's expenses, including fees to the Secretary, and legal fees and costs from funds supplied by Debtor in accordance with Schedule A or otherwise, and commence and prosecute on behalf of Creditors and the Committee any suits necessary to enforce this Agreement.

    a. The members of the Committee shall serve without compensation except as otherwise provided herein.

    b. The Committee is authorized and empowered to appoint one or more subcommittees, composed of a lesser number of its members, and to fix their authority and duties.

    c. The Committee and its members, as well as its agents and employees, shall not be liable for the acts, default, or misconduct of any other member of the Committee hereunder, nor shall any member be liable for anything but his own willful misconduct, and the Committee and its members, agents, and employees shall not be answerable for the acts, default, or misconduct of any agent or other person employed by it if selected with reasonable care.

    d. The Committee assumes no responsibility for the execution of this Agreement by persons other than the Committee and its members, or for the performance of the agreements embodied herein by persons other than the Committee and its members, but the Committee undertakes in good faith to execute this Agreement and to seek to obtain the consent to it by Debtor's other unsecured creditors entitled to join in this Agreement. Committee members, in executing this Agreement, are doing so solely as Committee members and not on behalf of their respective employers.

    e. The Committee may consult with Counsel, and the opinion of Counsel shall be full protection and justification to the Committee and its members for anything done or omitted or suffered to be done in accordance with that opinion.

    f. The Committee and its members shall not be required to give any bond for the performance of its or their duties.

    g. As quickly as possible after the first meeting of the Committee, each member thereof shall designate in writing a person who shall serve in his place and stead should he become unable to do so. In the event of a vacancy caused by inability to serve, the person so designated shall serve as the replacement. In the event no such designation is made or in the event of death, resignation, disqualification, or other inability to serve, the remaining members of the Committee shall fill the vacancy. Preference shall be given to the person designated by the firm employing the member who is unable to serve.

    h. The Committee shall act by a majority of its members with or without formal meeting, but written or telegraphic notice of any meeting shall be given to all members at least one (1) day prior to any formal or informal meeting. Members of the Committee shall have the right, but shall not be required, to act by properly designated proxy to another member of the Committee or to give instructions and votes by telephone.

    i. Each member of the Committee may, in his individual capacity or as an

Exhibit 4-1   *(Continued)*

officer, director, or employee of a Creditor of Debtor whom he represents, have the usual business relations with Debtor.

[These attempts at absolution might not be as effective in the event of wrong-doing, but committees could be afforded the benefit of the doubt lest participation by creditors is discouraged.

[Perhaps some of the duties of committee members are similar to committees in Chapters X and XI. *See* Walsh, "The Creation, Rights, Duties, and Compensation of Creditors' Committees Under Chapter X and XI of the Bankruptcy Act," *Brooklyn Law Review,* Vol. 40 (Summer 1973) pp. 35-76; Levy, "Creditors' Committees and their Responsibilities," *Commercial Law Journal,* Vol 74 (December, 1969) p. 355; W. Douglas & C. Shanks, Cases and Materials on Corporate Reorganization (St. Paul: West Publishing, 1931) p. 395; note to paragaph 6A.

[It is not unusual to include a provision that the Debtor will continue to trade with its existing Creditors, "price, terms and service being satisfactory," but this type of clause could cause more trouble than it is worth. Clearly, the Debtor would be foolish to cease trading with existing Creditors.]

13   In the event that Debtor becomes a debtor in a proceeding under chapter 11 of title 11 and proposes a Plan with terms of payment for the Extended Debt equivalent, or more favorable, to Creditors than those contained in this Agreement, then the Creditors shall be deemed to have accepted said Plan in writing without the need for a further or separate acceptance. The consent attached hereto as Schedule B shall constitute such acceptance.

[The prepetition solicitation of acceptance must be in compliance with any applicable nonbankruptcy law, rules, or regulation governing the adequacy of disclosure and, if none are applicable, then the solicitation must follow disclosure requirements of the Bankruptcy Code (11 U.S.C. sections 1125-1126).

[Schedule B attempts to follow the requirements of Interim Bankruptcy Rule 3007 and Form No. 25. Counsel should make whatever amendments or additions the case requires.]

14   This Agreement becomes binding upon Creditors, the Committee, and Debtor when _____ percent of the dollar amount of unsecured creditors of Debtor as of _____[Key Date]_____ entitled to join in this Agreement have assented to this Agreement by executing the Consent attached hereto as Schedule B or by otherwise consenting hereto; provided, however, that Debtor may waive this condition by giving written notice to the Committee that it is waived, in which event this Agreement shall become binding upon Creditors, the Committee, and Debtor.

[It is the general practice to set a high percentage of acceptances—for example, 95 percent.

[Be careful to avoid leading creditors to believe that 100 percent consent will be required. The error could be incurable. *See Texas Belting & Mill Supply Co.* v. *C. R. Daniels, Inc.,* 401 S.W.2d 157 (Civ. App., Tex., 1966).]

Exhibit 4-1 *(Continued)*

SCHEDULE B
BALLOT
Consent to Creditors' Agreement
(and Acceptance of Plan under Chapter 11)

The undersigned, a Creditor of _____[Name of Debtor]_____, does hereby assent to, and join in, the Creditors' Agreement dated _____[Date]_____, between Debtor, its Creditors' Committee, and certain of its unsecured creditors and acknowledges receipt of a copy of the same. Undersigned does hereby accept that certain chapter 11 plan of the Debtor, if one is filed hereafter, incorporating the terms of said Creditors' Agreement.

_____　　$ _____
　　　　(Name of Creditor)　　　　　　　　　　(Amount of Claim)

By _____

　　Attach a copy of the invoices supporting your claim and return to:
　　　　Secretary
　　　　[Address]

Conditions of Agreement

31　When an agreement calls for future installment payments, the creditors may insist that these payments be secured, for example, by notes or a mortgage on real estate. The debtor may execute an assignment for the benefit of creditors to be held in escrow and to become effective only if the debtor defaults in performance of the plan. The creditors may require that their own accountant make frequent reviews of the controls and operating activities of the business (chapter 9, paragraphs 26–43). Also, creditors may require that a workout specialist be allowed to operate the business during the period when the plan is being carried out (see paragraph 22).

32　An example of an out-of-court plan granting various security to creditors for the performance of the plan, accompanied by a combination solicitation letter and disclosure statement of the debtor is included as Exhibit 4-2. Please review chapter 5, paragraphs 56–79, regarding the content of such a disclosure statement. By including information that meets the disclosure requirements, it may be possible for the debtor to use this acceptance as the approval of the plan if it becomes necessary to file a chapter 11 plan. Note that Schedule B in both Exhibit 4-1 and Exhibit 4-2 indicates that the creditor approves the agreement if the debtor files a chapter 11 plan. (See chapter 5, paragraph 63). If "adequate information" is not disclosed at the time the debtor solicits the approval of the plan of settlement, the bankruptcy court will not accept the vote.

33　After the creditors' committee approves a plan, it will notify all of the other creditors and recommend to them that they accept it. Even if a few creditors do not agree, the debtor should continue with the plan. Such

Exhibit 4-2 Agreement with Creditors and Debtor's Solicitation Letter (Disclosure Statement)

February 28, 19X8

To the Creditors of C_____, Inc.
N_____, Massachusetts and
S_____ Massachusetts

Undoubtedly, you are aware that the debtor is engaged in the retail sale of wearing apparel for men, women, and children. Since December 3, 19X7 we have had a number of meetings with creditors' representatives and their counsel. The purpose of said meetings was to determine whether it would be best to liquidate the assets, or whether we should consider a plan of reorganization that is feasible and in the best interest of creditors, and would allow debtor to remain in business. In order to reach a decision, we had the assets, consisting of inventory, furniture, fixtures and equipment, appraised and the books and records of the company thoroughly examined by the creditors' committee in accordance with its accountants' report, a copy of which is enclosed [omitted].

It is clear that, on forced liquidation and after payment of administration costs and expenses, taxes, and other priority claims, there would be available to general unsecured creditors a dividend of less than 10%. Normally, payment would be made in or within 12 to 18 months after the first meeting of creditors. The national average for costs and expenses in the administration of a bankruptcy estate, is approximately 25% of the total realized assets. Therefore, since the appraised assets, including cash on hand, total $56,562.71 and the estimated cost of administration is 25% of that amount, or approximately $14,140.63, there would be left about $42,422.08. If we then deducted all priority claims for taxes, wages, and other amounts owed, the total of said sums would be $25,140.00. There would then be available to general unsecured creditors $17,282.06 which represents less than 10% of the total due to general unsecured creditors, and would not be distributed until the case is closed, usually 12-18 months after the filing.

After a number of meetings, a plan was proposed which contemplated the formation of a new corporation which would acquire all of the assets of the old corporation.

The officers and directors of the new corporation would be the same as the old corporation, as follows:

President and Treasurer:	D_____	T_____.
Vice President:	M_____	T_____.
Clerk:	R_____	T_____.
Directors:	D_____	T_____.
	M._____	T_____.
	R_____	T_____.

The stockholders would also be the same in the new corporation as in the old and each would own 25% of the 100 shares of stock outstanding, as follows:

D_____	T_____	25 shares.
M_____	T_____	25 shares.
R_____	T_____	25 shares.
V_____	T_____	25 shares.

Exhibit 4-2 *(Continued)*

The new corporation's name is to be W_____, Inc. Said corporation will agree to purchase the assets of C_____, Inc. and to pay the following:

(1) All taxes and priorities, in cash, in full.

(2) To pay to general unsecured creditors a sum equal to 20% of the allowed claims in four installments:

> **a** 5% down.
> **b** 5% in 6 months.
> **c** 5% in 12 months.
> **d** 5% in 18 months.

(3) Agree to pay all fees and expenses of the settlement, which are estimated to be in the neighborhood of $14,000 or $15,000, as follows:

> **a** $5,000 down.
> **b** Balance in monthly installments of
> $1,500 until paid.

All of the officers will continue to be employed by the new corporation and to perform the same duties and to receive the same compensation as they had received from the debtor corporation.

The weekly compensation and duties of the officers of W_____, Inc. will be as follows:

D_____ T_____,	Buyer and General Manager	$500.00
M_____ T_____,	Manager of the N_____ location	$250.00
R_____ T_____,	Manager of the S_____ location	$150.00

The new corporation has entered into an agreement with the debtor corporation and an executed copy is available for examination at this office.

The new corporation, W_____, Inc., is to give, as security for its promise to make payments as heretofore mentioned, the following:

A Trust Indenture and Security Agreement to B_____ R_____ of B_____, Massachusetts, counsel for Creditors' Committee, and I_____ W_____, counsel for the Debtor, as co-trustees, covering all the assets of the debtor, including inventory, accounts receivable, furniture, fixtures and equipment [omitted].

B A pledge of all the issued and outstanding stock of the newly formed corporation.

C D_____ T_____ is to personally guaranty in writing the payment of the amount promised to be paid to the creditors heretofore mentioned. As security for his guaranty, he is to give a mortgage on a house which has been appraised as having a current market value of $45,000 and upon which there is a first mortgage balance of $19,000.

The agreement mentioned will include the usual safeguards with regard to amount of salaries paid to officers and principals of the debtor; a right to declare the entire balance due in the event the company defaults in any payment when due or it sustains a loss beyond the aggregate sum of $15,000; and prohibiting payment of dividends or issuance of additional shares of stock.

Exhibit 4-2 (*Continued*)

The foregoing is a brief summary of the Plan and should not be relied upon for voting purposes. Creditors are urged to read the Plan in full. Creditors are further urged to consult with counsel, or with each other, in order to fully understand the Plan. An intelligent judgment concerning the Plan cannot be made without understanding it.

No representations concerning the Debtor (particularly as to the value of its property) are authorized by the Debtor other than as set forth in this statement. Any representations or inducements made to secure acceptance of the Plan that are other than as contained in this statement should not be relied upon by any creditor. The information contained herein has not been subject to a certified audit. The records kept by the Debtor are not warranted or represented to be without any inaccuracy, although every effort has been made to be accurate.

In order to hasten the distribution referred to above in an out of court arrangement, we have prepared and herewith enclose an acceptance form that could be used in the event a reorganization under Chapter 11 of the Federal Bankruptcy Code is found necessary in order to conclude the settlement.

If you accept our recommendation for an early consummation of the proposed settlement, please execute and return the enclosed acceptance form to this office, together with a statement of your account, showing amount due as of December 3, 19X7.

If you have any questions, please write to this office.

Very truly yours,

I_____ W_____

Creditors' Agreement

This agreement of February 28 19X8 by and among C_____, Inc., a corporation duly organized by law and having its principal offices in N_____ in the Commonwealth of Massachusetts, hereinafter called "Debtor," and W_____, Inc., a corporation duly organized by law and having its principal offices in S_____ in said Commonwealth, hereinafter called the "new corporation," and B_____ R_____ and I_____ W_____, both having places of business in B_____ in said Commonwealth, hereinafter called "Trustees," and those unsecured creditors of Debtor who sign this agreement or consent hereto by separate instrument, hereinafter called "Creditors," is made with reference to the following facts:

1 Debtor is indebted to a number of Creditors and desires to effect a settlement of its obligations with said Creditors and an extension of time for the payment of the agreed settlement amount by the new corporation. The new corporation will purchase all the assets of the Debtor, and will give, as security for Creditors, a Trust Indenture and Security Agreement to B_____ R_____, counsel for the Creditors Committee and I_____ W_____, counsel for the Debtor, as co-trustees, covering all the assets of the Debtor, including inventory, accounts receivable, furniture, fixtures, and equipment, and including

Exhibit 4-2 (*Continued*)

the usual safeguards with regard to amount of salaries paid to officers and principals of the Debtor; a right to declare the entire balance due in the event the company defaults in any payment when due or it sustains a loss beyond the aggregate sum of $15,000; and prohibiting payment of dividends or issuance of additional shares of stock. Creditors agree with each other and are willing to forego their present rights to enforce present payment of the agreed settlement amount on the terms and conditions set forth hereinbelow.

2 Subject to all the terms, provisions and conditions herein, each and all the Creditors shall and do hereby settle and extend the amount and time of payment of their respective claims as they existed on the effective date of this agreement as defined in paragraph 8 herein, in accordance with the schedule of payments contained in Schedule A which is attached hereto and made a part hereof.

3 From the period beginning on the effective date of this agreement, until the termination date (the date of the last payment to Creditors pursuant to Schedule A), or until such later date or dates as may be agreed on by each individual Creditor, each Creditor agrees that it will not commence or prosecute any action or proceeding against the Debtor or the new corporation, levy any execution, attachment, or any process against the property of the Debtor or the new corporation by reason of the debt owing to such Creditor as of the effective date of this agreement, or file or join in any petition or any proceeding under the Bankruptcy Code or its amendments, 11 U.S.C. §§101 et seq. (1978), or any other proceeding having for its object the appointment of a receiver, assignee, trustee or other custodian for the Debtor or the new corporation or the assets of either. However, it is specifically understood, if the amount of the debt of any Creditor is disputed by the Debtor, or the new corporation, that such Creditor may commence and prosecute suit on the disputed claim, but any judgment by such Creditor in connection with such disputed claim shall not be enforced and payment thereof, in the same percentage as is paid to other Creditors hereunder, shall be settled and extended in the same manner as all other debts.

4 The new corporation shall make the payments required by the schedule of payments in accordance with Schedule A to the Trustees; who shall distribute the sum so received to each Creditor in accordance with the time for payments set forth.

5 Each Creditor hereby waives his right to assert in any proceeding at law, in equity or in bankruptcy, that any payment made pursuant to this agreement constitutes an improper, voidable or preferential payment.

6 Nothing contained in this agreement shall be construed or deemed to release or discharge any rights or remedies that any Creditor may now or hereafter have against any endorser, guarantor, or surety who may now or hereafter be liable to any such Creditor upon any debt settled or deferred by the provisions of this agreement, and each such right and remedy is hereby reserved to any such Creditor.

7 In the event that the Debtor or the new corporation becomes a debtor in a

Exhibit 4-2 *(Continued)*

proceeding under Chapter 11 of the Federal Bankruptcy Code and proposes a Plan of Reorganization with terms of payment for the debt settled and extended herein in an equivalent (or more favorable amount) to creditors other than those contained in this agreement, then the Creditors who have accepted this agreement shall be deemed to have accepted said Plan of Reorganization in writing without the need for further or separate acceptance. The Ballot For Accepting or Rejecting the Creditors' Agreement and Plan of Reorganization Under Chapter 11, hereinafter "Ballot," which is attached hereto and marked Schedule B, shall also constitute such Acceptance or Rejection of a Plan under Chapter 11 of the Bankruptcy Code. In this way it is intended to protect each Creditor who executes the Ballot attached as Schedule B, to insure that each Creditor shall receive as much as any other Creditor in the event of a Plan of Reorganization pursuant to Chapter 11 of the Bankruptcy Code.

8 This agreement shall become binding on all Creditors, Debtor, new corporation, and Trustees in the event ninety-eight (98%) percent in number and dollar amount of unsecured Creditors of the Debtor as of the effective date, who are entitled to join in this agreement, have assented to this agreement by executing and returning to the Trustees the Ballot attached as Schedule B; provided, however, that Debtor may waive the ninety-eight (98%) percent condition by giving written notice to the Creditors that it is waived, in which event this agreement shall become binding upon the Creditors, the Debtor, the new corporation and the Trustees; that date shall be deemed "the effective date" of this agreement.

9 This agreement shall bind and benefit the parties hereto and each of their respective heirs, administrators, successors and assigns.

10 Acceptances and/or notices which may be required to be given hereunder shall be given either by certified mail or first class mail, postage prepaid, as follows:

To the Debtor	[Counsel]
To the new corporation:	[Counsel]
To the Trustees:	[Counsel]

11 This agreement may be executed in multiple counterparts.

C_____, Inc., DEBTOR
By: _____
    President
W_____, Inc.
By: _____
    President

_____
B_____ R_____
Trustee and not individually

_____
I_____ W_____
Trustee and not individually

Exhibit 4-2 *(Continued)*

SCHEDULE A

Schedule of Payments to Creditors

All general unsecured creditors shall be paid twenty (20%) percent of their claim as follows:

1   Five (5%) percent in cash of the agreed amount of the debt once the agreement becomes binding according to the terms set forth in paragraph 8 of this agreement.

2   Five (5%) percent in cash six months from the date of the first payment.

3   Five (5%) percent in cash 12 months from the date of the first payment.

4   Five (5%) percent in cash 18 months from the date of the first payment.

SCHEDULE B

C_____, Incorporated
M_____, Massachusetts

Ballot for Accepting or Rejecting
Creditors' Agreement and Plan of Reorganization
Under Chapter 11

The undersigned, the holder of a general unsecured claim against C_____, Inc. in the unpaid principal amount indicated below, does hereby
    [Check one box]   ☐ Accept   ☐ Reject
the Creditors' Agreement dated February 4, 19X8, between C_____, Inc., Debtor, and certain of the holders of general unsecured claims against said Debtor. The undersigned acknowledges the receipt of a copy of said Creditors' Agreement.

The undersigned further consents to the use of this ballot, if a petition is filed for a Reorganization under Chapter 11 of the new Bankruptcy Code, 11 U.S.C. §§ 101 et seq. (1978), for the acceptance or rejection of any Plan of Reorganization which incorporates the terms of the aforesaid Creditors' Agreement of February 4, 19X8, or embodies said terms in principle, or which plan is held not to impair nor materially and adversely affect the interests of the holders of general unsecured claims under said Agreement.

$_____
Amount of claim

        Print or type name: _____
        Signed: _____
        If appropriate   (By: _____
                   (As: _____
        Street or Box _____
        City, State, Zip Code _____

Please sign on the line above (if a corporation, it must be acknowledged by the Secretary of the corporation; if a partnership, this must be signed by a partner; if

Exhibit 4-2   *(Continued)*

an individual, then signed by the individual; or, if an individual who is a d/b/a in particular company name, then the individual's signature with the d/b/a must be set forth).

Please return this ballot with a statement of your account (copies of invoices, etc.) so that it will be received on or before March 30, 19X8; allow adequate time for delivery if returned by mail.

      Return To:

                                                  [Counsel]

creditors will eventually have to be paid in full, and the plan may even provide for full payment to small creditors, thus destroying "the nuisance value of the small claims."[10] When a plan is agreed upon, the debtor should "either make out the checks for the initial payment and turn them over to counsel for the creditors' committee, or deposit with such counsel the funds for that purpose.[11] The funds to be deposited by the debtor must usually be sufficient to pay priority claims, secured claims, and administrative costs.

34   In an informal agreement, where there is no provision binding on the minority of creditors to accept the will of the majority, the consent of the members of the committee must be obtained for the plan to work. "These methods of friendly adjustment out of court are feasible only where the debtor corporation and substantially all the creditors are disposed to take a cooperative and realistic attitude and to work harmoniously toward a solution of the problem.[12] Creditors' committees have had success in "prevailing upon creditors to withhold institution of actions or the prosecution of pending actions.[13] And if the firm does not begin to recover under the aegis of the committee, it can be liquidated.

ADVANTAGES AND DISADVANTAGES

35   The following are a few of the reasons why the informal settlement is often used in today's environment:

1 The out-of-court settlement is less disruptive of a business that continues operation.

2 The debtor can receive considerable benefits from the advice of a committee, especially if some of the committee members are businesspeople, preferably but not necessarily in the same line of business.

[10] Ibid., p. 15.
[11] Ibid.
[12] William J. Grange et al., *Manual for Corporation Officers* (New York: The Ronald Press Co., 1967), p. 340.
[13] Levy, p. 357.

3 The informal settlement avoids invoking the provisions of the Bankruptcy Code and, as a result, more businesslike solutions can be adopted.

4 Frustrations and delays are minimized since problems can be resolved properly and informally without the need for court hearings.

5 An agreement can usually be reached much faster informally than in court proceedings.

6 The costs of administration are usually less in an out-of-court settlement than in a formal reorganization.

36 The weaknesses of informal composition settlements are as follows:

1 A successful plan of settlement requires the approval of substantially all creditors, and it may be difficult to persuade distant creditors to accept a settlement that calls for payment of less than 100 percent.

2 The assets of the debtor are subject to attack while a settlement is pending. (The debtor can, of course, point out to the creditor that if legal action is taken, a petition in bankruptcy court will have to be filed.)

3 The informal composition settlement does not provide a method to resolve individual disputes between the debtor and creditors.

4 Executory contracts, especially leases, may be difficult to avoid.

5 There is no formal way to recover preferences or fraudulent transfers.

6 Certain tax law provisions make it more advantageous to file a bankruptcy court proceeding.

7 Priority debts owed to the United States under Rev. Stat. sec. 3466 must be paid first.

37 From the above it is obvious that there are several reasons why it is often best for the debtor to seek assistance out of court. But this avenue can be lost if the debtor is not cautious in its actions.

Rehabilitation Proceedings Under the Bankruptcy Code

1   Bankruptcy court proceedings are generally the last resort for the debtor whose financial condition has deteriorated to the point where it is impossible to acquire additional funds. When the debtor finally agrees that bankruptcy court proceedings are necessary, the liquidation value of the assets often represents only a small fraction of the debtor's total liabilities. If the business is liquidated, the creditors get only a small percentage of their claims. The debtor is discharged of its debts and is free to start over; however, the business is lost and so are all the assets. Normally, liquidation proceedings result in serious losses to the debtor, the creditor, and the business community. Arrangement proceedings were enacted in 1938 as a part of the Chandler Act to reduce these losses. When the Bankruptcy Code of 1978 went into effect it combined the arrangement proceedings of Chapter XI with real property arrangements under Chapter XII and Chapter X corporate reorganizations into one rehabilitation chapter known as chapter 11 reorganization.

2   This chapter describes in summary form the provisions of chapter 11 of the Bankruptcy Code and briefly discusses chapter 13.

PURPOSE OF CHAPTER 11

3   Under the Bankruptcy Reform Act, chapter 11 is designed to accomplish the same objective as Chapters VIII, X, XI, and XII of prior law: provide the debtor with court protection, allow the debtor (or trustee) to continue the operations of the business while a plan is being developed, and minimize the substantial economic losses associated with liquidations. The new chapter 11 attempts to provide for the flexibility of prior Chapter XI, yet it contains several of the protective provisions of prior Chapter X. It is designed to allow the debtor to use different procedures depending on the nature of the debtor's problems and the needs of the creditors. Agreements under this chapter can affect unsecured creditors, secured creditors, and stockholders. It would, however, be expected that an agreement that would affect only unsecured creditors that could have been arranged under prior law could still be resolved under the Bankruptcy Code in a similar manner. The more complicated cases that require adjustment of widely held claims, secured creditors' claims, and stockholders' interest in a public case can also be resolved under chapter 11. The new law provides a basis for these public cases to be resolved without necessarily going through the formal process of determining the going concern values of the business to determine the extent to which various classes of creditors and stockholders can participate in the plan. The Reform Act was designed to prevent some of the uncertainty connected with whether proceedings could remain in Chapter XI or be forced into Chapter X, and to avoid unnecessary litigation cost to determine the specific chapter under which a case should proceed.

OPERATING UNDER CHAPTER 11

4   As noted in chapter 3, a voluntary or involuntary petition can be filed in chapter 11. Upon the filing of an involuntary petition the court may, on request of an interested party, appoint a trustee. This appointment is not mandatory and the debtor may, in fact, continue to operate the business as if a bankruptcy petition had not been filed, except that certain transfers may be avoided under section 549(a). If the creditors prove the allegations set forth in the involuntary petition an order for relief is entered and the case will then proceed in a manner identical to a voluntary case.[1]

---

[1] J. Ronald Trost, "Business Reorganization Under Chapter 11 of the New Bankruptcy Code," *Business Lawyer,* Vol. 34 (April 1979), p. 1313.

Role of the Court

5 One of the major changes of the Bankruptcy Code was to relieve the bankruptcy judge of administrative functions and let his or her primary function be to settle disputes. In the districts where there is a U.S. trustee appointed under the pilot system, the judge will be relieved of administrative duties and be completely free to adjudicate disputes.

Administration by the Bankruptcy Judge

6 In the districts where a U.S. trustee is not appointed, the bankruptcy judge will have four basic duties to perform early in the case:

1 Appoint a committee of unsecured creditors as soon as practicable after the order for relief is granted (section 1102(a)(1)).

2 May appoint, on request of a party in interest, additional committees of creditors or shareholders (section 1102(a)(2)).

3 May order a meeting of the shareholders' committee if one is formed (section 1102(b)).

4 Appoint a trustee or examiner if deemed appropriate (section 1104(a)).

After these initial duties are completed, unless it is necessary to appoint a new trustee or examiner or to change committee membership, the judge will remain outside the administration of the case and handle only disputes.[2]

U.S. Trustee Administration

7 In the districts where U.S. trustees have been appointed, they will be responsible for the administration of the case. They will appoint the committees of creditors with unsecured claims and also appoint any other committees of creditors or stockholders authorized by the court. If the court deems it necessary to appoint a trustee or examiner, the U.S. trustee will make this appointment (subject to court approval) and may also petition the court to authorize such an appointment. See chapter 8, paragraphs 7–12 for a more detailed discussion of the functions performed by the U.S. trustee.

Consolidation of Chapter 11 Petitions

8 An issue that often arises when a corporation has several subsidiaries, or several corporations have common ownership, is whether these compa-

---

[2] Hal Hughes, " 'Wavering Between the Profit and Loss': Operating A Business During Reorganization Under Chapter 11 of the New Bankruptcy Code," *American Bankruptcy Law Journal,* Vol. 54 (Winter 1980), p. 61.

nies should be consolidated. In general, proceedings may be consolidated for administrative purposes, or the assets and liabilities of different juridical entities may be consolidated as if the assets and liabilities were those of a single entity.[3] The latter form of consolidation is known as substantive consolidation, and generally an order for consolidation includes a request that all claims of each individual case be considered those of the consolidated class, that all duplicate claims filed with more than one individual case be removed, that all intercompany claims be disallowed, that a single set of schedules be filed, and that one consolidated plan be proposed.[4] Since the Bankruptcy Code does not contain a specific provision for substantive consolidation, authority is derived from section 105(a), which allows the court to issue any order, process, or judgment necessary to carry out the provisions of the Code. Due to all of the procedural problems and the potential inequities found when one creditor group must share with another, substantive consolidation is an unusual occurrence.

9 The most common use of substantive consolidation is by affiliated debtor corporations.[5] Situations that tend to suggest that consolidation is justified include:

1 Creditors of the affiliates acted as though there was one economic unit and did not rely on separate entities in extending credit.
2 Activities of the affiliates are so entangled that it is too costly to deal with them separately.
3 The separate legal identities of affiliates have not been preserved.

10 It is also possible to consolidate the debtor and nondebtor corporations, especially where assets were transferred for the purpose of hindering, delaying, and defrauding creditors.[6] However, it is more difficult to obtain an order for substantive consolidation where some of the affiliates have not filed a petition. A more common occurrence is action to recover the assets that were fraudulently transferred, under the provisions of sections 544 or 548.

11 Often debtor corporations may find it much easier to file a consolidation plan of reorganization. Here the debtors are requesting that the creditors approve the substantive consolidation of the affiliated corporations. Unless the plan receives unanimous approval, the court will still have to look at the substantive consolidation issue. For example, the court must at least determine that creditors not approving the plan receive as much as would be received in a chapter 7 liquidation of the respective debtor entities.[7]

---

[3] *Collier Bankruptcy Manual,* 3rd ed., para. 1100.06[1].
[4] Ibid.
[5] Ibid.
[6] *Sampsell v. Imperial Paper Corp.,* 313 U.S. 215 (1941).
[7] 11 U.S.C. Sec. 1129(a)(7).

12   If substantive consolidation is not feasible, the case may be consolidated for administrative purposes. Here a single docket is used for matters occurring in the administration of the estate, including the filing of claims, combining of notices mailed to creditors, and other purely administrative matters, to expedite the case.[8]

Creditors' Committee

13   Section 1102 provides that a committee of creditors holding unsecured claims shall be appointed as soon as practicable after the order for relief is granted. In those districts where a U.S. trustee exists, the trustee has the responsibility for appointing the committee without any authorization from the court (section 151102).

14   The committee will ordinarily consist of the seven largest creditors willing to serve or, if a committee was organized before the order for relief, such committee may continue provided it was fairly chosen and is representative of the different kinds of claims to be represented. Under prior law, the creditors elected their own committee. At times this election process was quite controversial, primarily because creditors or their legal representatives attempted to serve their own personal interests. The requirement that the court appoint the creditors' committee will eliminate the problems associated with electing a committee.

15   Note that section 1102(b) of the Code states that the committee "shall ordinarily consist of . . . ," thus leaving some discretion to the U.S. trustee or bankruptcy judge so that a committee can be selected that will be willing to serve. The committee would not necessarily have to consist of seven members if a small committee would be more efficient in the existing circumstances.

16   The Code does not set forth any requirements that must be met to satisfy the condition that a previously elected committee may continue only if fairly chosen. Bankruptcy Rule 2007 does suggest that the conditions necessary for the committee to continue may consist of the following:

1   The committee was selected by majority in number and amount of unsecured creditors at a meeting where creditors with claims over $1000 or the 100 largest unsecured creditors had at least five days notice in writing, and written minutes of the meeting reporting the names of creditors present or represented were kept and are available for inspection.

2   All proxies voted were solicited in accordance with the conditions of Bankruptcy Rule 2006 and the lists and statements (for example, a statement that no consideration has been paid or promised by the proxyholder for the proxy) of subdivision (e) thereof have been filed with the court.

[8] 1979 *Collier Pamphlet Edition*, p. 66.

3   The organization of the committee was in all other respects fair and proper.

17   While the requirement is that the committee must consist of creditors with unsecured claims, this does not prohibit the court or U.S. trustee from appointing one or more persons to the committee who have both secured and unsecured claims. Of course, if some of the unsecured creditors object to the fact that there are too many creditors on the committee who also hold secured claims, they could petition the court to change the composition of the committee. The court may also appoint additional committees of creditors and of equity security holders on request of a party in interest. In small cases only one committee may be necessary, but for large companies that are publicly held there may be a need for several committees. In districts where a U.S. trustee is appointed, the trustee may request the court to authorize the appointment of additional committees. After the court has so authorized, the U.S. trustee will make the appointments.[9]

18   Once the committee has been appointed, the official relationship of the U.S. trustee ends, since the Code does not provide that the U.S. trustee supervise the activities of the committee. The U.S. trustee is, however, responsible for the administration of the case and of the trustee in chapter 11 cases where one is appointed. Thus, if the U.S. trustee ascertains that a committee is not functioning properly or that one or more members of the committee are not representing the creditors as a whole but are interested only in serving their own interests, he may take a more active role in the debtor's operations or even petition the court to change the composition of the committee. It would not be expected that the U.S. trustee would take this kind of action when he or she merely disagrees with the decisions and actions of the committee. The responsibility that the U.S. trustee has for the administration of the case can be relaxed to some extent when one or more committees are actively functioning. In fact, the committee or committees should share the U.S. trustee's "watchdog" role in the administration of the case.[10] For example, in the pilot district of Maine, Massachusetts, New Hampshire, and Rhode Island the U.S. trustees regularly schedule adjourned creditors' meetings at approximately thirty-day intervals.

Appointment of Trustee

19   The new law provides that a trustee can be appointed in certain situations based on the facts in the case and not related to the size of the company or the amount of unsecured debt outstanding. The trustee is appointed only at the request of a party in interest after a notice and hearing. A party in interest includes the debtor, the trustee (in other contexts), creditors' or stockholders' committees, creditors, stockholders, or indenture

---

[9] 11 U.S.C. Sec. 151102(b).
[10] *Collier Bankruptcy Manual*, 3rd ed., para. 6.13[4].

trustees.[11] Also, a U.S. trustee, while not a party in interest, may petition the court for an appointment of a trustee.[12] The SEC may also be heard on the issue, but has no right of appeal, and could thus express its desires about the appointment of a trustee.[13]

20   The court can appoint the trustee for cause or if the appointment is in the best interest of the creditors, stockholders, or any other interests of the estate. Section 1104(a) states that a trustee be appointed

> **1**   for cause, including fraud, dishonesty, incompetence, or gross mismanagement of the affairs of the debtor by current management, either before or after the commencement of the case, or similar cause, but not including the number of holders of securities of the debtor or the amount of assets or liabilities of the debtor; or
>
> **2**   if such appointment is in the interests of creditors, any equity security holders, and other interests of the estate, without regard to the number of holders of securities of the debtor or the amount of assets or liabilities of the debtor.

In districts where a U.S. trustee is appointed, the trustee is responsible for the appointment of the trustee from a panel of qualified trustees, once the appointment has been authorized by the court. It would also appear that the U.S. trustee would have the right to replace trustees who fail to perform their functions properly.

21   The legislative history recognized the inefficiency of requiring a trustee in every case because of the need for the trustee to learn the business. During this time of learning, the business is without real guidance at a time that is most important for the business' survival. Unless there is some tangible contrary reason, the debtor should be allowed to operate the business during the time period the plan is being developed.[14] Even in some of the larger cases where there has been mismanagement there may not be a need to appoint a trustee if the corporation has obtained new management.[15] Under these conditions, if any appointment is necessary, an examiner might be most appropriate.

22   The duties of the trustee are:

1   The following duties for a chapter 7 case are also required in chapter 11 proceedings:

> Be accountable for all property received.
>
> If a purpose would be served, examine proofs of claims and object where the claim is improper.

---

[11] 11 U.S.C. Sec. 1109(b).

[12] Ibid., Sec. 151104(a).

[13] Ibid., Sec. 1109(a).

[14] H.R. Rep. No. 95–595, 95th Cong., 1st Sess. (1977) 233.

[15] But see *In re La Sherene, Inc.*, 6 Bankr. Ct. Dec. 153 (N.D. Ga. March 4, 1980).

Unless the court directs otherwise, furnish the information requested by a party in interest concerning the estate and the estate's administration.

File, with the court and taxing authorities, periodic reports and summaries of the operation of the business, including a statement of cash receipts and disbursements and other information required by the court.

Make a final report and file a final account of the administration of the estate with the court.

2 File the list of creditors, schedules, and statements required with or subsequent to the filing of the petition, if not previously filed.

3 Unless the court orders otherwise, investigate the acts, conduct, assets, liabilities, and financial condition of the debtor, the operation of the debtor's business, the desirability of the continuation of the business, and any other matter relevant to the case or to the formulation of a plan.

4 As soon as practicable, file a statement of the investigation conducted including any fact ascertained pertaining to fraud, dishonesty, incompetence, misconduct, mismanagement, or irregularity in the management of the affairs of the debtor, or to a cause of action available to the estate, and transmit a copy or a summary of any such statement to any creditors' committee or equity security holders' committee, to any indenture trustee, and to such other entity as the court designates.

5 As soon as practicable, file a plan, file a report of why the trustee will not file a plan, or recommend conversion of the case to a case under chapter 7 or 13 of this title or dismissal of the case.

6 File tax returns and information required by taxing authorities.

7 After confirmation of a plan, file such reports as are necessary or as the court orders.

Appointment of Examiner

23 Under the Bankruptcy Code, the trustee performs two major functions—operates the business and conducts an investigation of the debtor's affairs. Under certain conditions it may be best to leave the current management in charge of the business, without resolving the need for the investigation of the debtor. The Code provides for the appointment of an examiner to perform this function. Section 1104(b) states that, if a trustee is not appointed,

. . . [O]n request of a party in interest, and after notice and a hearing, the court shall order the appointment of an examiner to conduct such an investigation of the debtor as is appropriate, including an investigation of any allegations of fraud, dishonesty, incompetence, misconduct, mismanagement, or irregularity in the management of the affairs of the debtor of or by current or former management of the debtor, if—

   1 such appointment is in the interests of creditors, any equity security holders, and other interests of the estate; or

   2 the debtor's fixed, liquidated, unsecured debts, other than debts for goods, services, or taxes, or owing to an insider, exceed $5 million.

24 Note that in the second situation the court has no discretion; an examiner must be appointed upon request. The phrase "other than debts for goods, services, or taxes" leaves debts owing to institutions or public debt as those that court. "Goods" refers to inventory and not "goods" in an economic sense. In districts where the U.S. trustee pilot program is in effect, the U.S. trustee will appoint the examiner subject to court approval. Section 321(b) states that an examiner cannot serve as a trustee in the same case or, if the chapter 11 petition is converted to a chapter 7 petition, in the converted chapter case. Also, section 327(f) provides that the trustee (debtor in possession) may not employ a person who served as an examiner in the case.

25 Considerable discussion has centered around who can be appointed as examiner. The Code does not state who may serve; nor does it provide for the examiner to retain professionals such as attorneys or accountants. Based on the functions to be performed by the examiner, it would appear that accountants would be the most logical choice for this position, when most of the investigation centers around financial information (chapter 7, paragraphs 52–58). Several CPAs have been appointed as examiners. In some districts the percentage of CPAs used is much higher than in others. In most districts attorneys continue to be appointed much more frequently than CPAs.

26 The function of the examiner is to conduct an investigation into the actions of the debtor including fraud, dishonesty, mismanagement of the financial condition of the debtor, and of the operation of the business, and the desirability of the continuation of such business. The report is to be filed with the court and given to any creditors' committee, stockholders' committees, or other entities designated by the court. These are the same as functions three and four (see paragraph 22) of the trustee.

27 Since the Bankruptcy Code became effective, a large number of examiners have been appointed. As noted above, in a case where the unsecured debts exceed $5 million, the court must appoint an examiner if requested. In addition, an examiner might be appointed instead of a trustee. For example, the court may find it easier to appoint an examiner to investigate the operations of the debtor rather than proceed at the present time with hearings to determine if the appointment of a trustee is necessary. Then, if the examiner's investigation reveals that there is fraud or gross mismanagement on the part of the debtor, a trustee can be appointed.

Operation of the Business

28 No order is necessary under the Bankruptcy Code for the debtor to operate the business in chapter 11. Sections 1107(a) and 1108 grant the debtor all of the rights, powers, and duties of a trustee, except the right to compensation under section 330, and provide that the trustee may operate the business unless the court directs otherwise. Thus, the debtor will continue to operate the business unless a party in interest requests that the court appoint a trustee. Until action is taken by management to correct the problems that caused the adverse financial condition, the business will most likely continue to operate at a loss. If the creditors believe new management is necessary to correct the problem, they will press for a change in management or the appointment of a trustee. In most large bankruptcies as well as in many smaller cases, the old management is replaced.

29 One of the major advantages of Chapter XI over Chapter X of prior law from the debtor's perspective was that under Chapter XI a receiver was not automatically appointed. Under Chapter X, the appointment of a trustee was mandatory when liabilities exceeded $250,000. The Bankruptcy Code provides for more flexibility by allowing the debtor to maintain possession of its property and operate the business unless the court orders otherwise. For cause, including fraud, dishonesty, incompetence, or gross mismanagement of the business, the court, upon request, will hold a hearing and appoint a trustee; the court may also appoint a trustee if it is determined that such action is in the best interest of creditors and stockholders.

30 The debtor in possession is required to perform all the functions specified for the trustee (paragraph 22) except to conduct an investigation of its own acts, conduct, and financial affairs, and to file a statement of investigation.[16] Section 1107 also states that the rights are subject to any limitations or conditions the court may prescribe. Thus, the court has the power to set conditions that the debtor must abide by in operating the business. For example, the court might require that a given business pay all ongoing bills before the expiration of thirty days. The creditors are constrained from filing a plan during the first 120 days or longer, if the court directs, subsequent to the date of the order for relief when the debtor remains in possession.

Automatic Stay

31 The immediate objective of the debtor, or trustee if appointed, is to keep the business operating. To maintain the critical assets of the business intact and to permit the creditors from continuing to harass the debtor, the Bankruptcy Code provides for an automatic stay of the actions of creditors. The need for the stay can be seen by looking at the conditions existing in an average case. The debtor will be in default on loan agreements and leases,

---

[16] 11 U.S.C. Sec. 1107(a).

secured parties through court action or self help will be accelerating efforts to take possession of their collateral, the debtor's vendors will have substantially reduced, if not halted, credit to the debtor and may have already commenced suits to collect amounts past due. The debtor will be without cash. In addition, the major assets needed to run the business will be subject to security interests or charges of one kind or another.[17] The stay, in effect, gives the debtor time to make some crucial operating decisions. See chapter 3, paragraphs 69–79 for a discussion of the type of actions that are subject to the stay and the process necessary to remove stays.

Use of Collateral

32 The debtor or trustee must be able to use a secured party's collateral, or in most situations there would be no alternative but to liquidate the business. Section 363(c) gives the trustee or debtor the right to use, sell, or lease property of the estate in the ordinary course of business without a notice and a hearing.

33 One restriction is, however, placed on the trustee or debtor where cash collateral is involved. Cash collateral is cash, negotiable instruments, documents of title, securities, deposit accounts, or other cash equivalents where the estate and someone else have an interest in the property. Also included would be the proceeds of noncash collateral, such as inventory and accounts receivable and proceeds, products, offspring, rents, or profits of property subject to a security interest, if converted to proceeds of the type defined as cash collateral, provided the proceeds are subject to the prepetition security interests.

34 To use cash collateral, the creditor with the interest must consent to its use, or the court, after notice and hearing, must authorize its use. The court may authorize the use, sale, or lease of cash collateral at a preliminary hearing if there is a reasonable likelihood that the debtor in possession will prevail at the final hearing. The Bankruptcy Code also provides that the court is to act promptly for a request to use cash collateral.[18] In some situations there may not be enough time for a hearing and the court may release cash collateral immediately, for example in situations where the debtor must meet a payroll or needs cash immediately to preserve perishable inventory. In this case, the procedures discussed in chapter 3, paragraph 71, are followed. A creditor is entitled to adequate protection of its security interest under section 361 when the court uses its cash collateral. Thus, cash in bank accounts subject to setoff or collections from pledged receivables and inventory prior to the filing of the petition are not available for use until the consent of the appropriate secured creditor or of the court is obtained. In many bankruptcy cases that are filed, nearly all of the cash and cash equiva-

---

[17] Trost, p. 1317.
[18] 11 U.S.C. Sec. 363(c)(3).

lents will be considered cash collateral and barred from use. For example, a small car rental agency might well continue to lease its automobiles on a day to day basis without the permission of the bank for which the fleet is collateral, but the agency must be careful of its use of the car rental payments received if the bank has a security interest in the proceeds of the agency's accounts receivable that existed as of the date the petition was filed. One of the first orders of business once the petition has been filed will be to obtain the release of the cash collateral. Courts have in general released cash collateral on relatively short notice to provide debtors with the cash necessary to operate the business.

35　The debtor can use or lease any other property of the estate as long as the action taken is in the ordinary course of business. To stop the debtor from using, in the ordinary course of business, property for which a creditor has a security interest, the creditor must petition the court for relief from the automatic stay or for a specific order preventing the debtor from using the property. To use, sell, or lease property other than in the ordinary course of business requires notice and opportunity for a hearing.[19]

Obtaining Credit

36　In most chapter 11 proceedings the debtor must obtain additional financing in order to continue the business. While the debtor was allowed to obtain credit under prior law, the power granted to the debtor under the Bankruptcy Code is broader. Section 364(a) allows the debtor to obtain unsecured debt and to incur unsecured obligations in the ordinary course while operating the business. This right is automatic unless the court orders otherwise. Also, the holder of these claims is entitled to first priority as administrative expenses.

37　If the debtor is unable to obtain the necessary unsecured debt under section 364(a), the court may authorize the obtaining of credit and the incurring of debt by granting special priority for the claims. These priorities may include the following:

1　Giving priority over any or all administrative expenses.
2　Securing the debt with a lien on unencumbered property.
3　Securing the debt with a junior lien on encumbered property.

For the court to authorize the obtaining of credit with a lien on encumbered property that is senior or equal to the existing lien, the debtor must not be able to obtain credit by other means and the existing lien holder must be adequately protected. However, in *In the Matter of Statbucker,*[20] the court

---

[19] 11 U.S.C. Sec. 363(b). See 11 U.S.C. Sec. 102(1).
[20] 2 C.B.C.2d 156 (B.Ct. D. Neb. 1980).

held that the farmer could grant a senior lien to creditors for working capital to plant crops since mortgage holders were adequately protected because the value of the real estate was greater than the debt and unless the crops were planted the lienholders would have no interest to be protected.

38 Credit obtained other than in the ordinary course of business must be authorized by the court after notice and a hearing. Where there is some question whether the credit is related to the ordinary course of business, the lender should require court approval.

Claims and Interests

39 A proof of claim or interest is deemed filed in a chapter 11 case provided the claim or interest is listed in the schedules filed by the debtor, unless the claim or interest is listed as disputed, contingent, or unliquidated. A creditor is thus not required to file a proof of claim if it agrees with the debt listed in the schedules submitted. It is, however, advisable for creditors to file a proof of claim in most situations. (See chapter 3, paragraph 91.) Creditors who for any reason disagree with the amount admitted on the debtor's schedules, such as allowable prepetition interest on their claims, or creditors desiring to give a power of attorney to a trade association or lawyer, should always prepare and file a complete proof of claim. Special attention must also be devoted to secured claims that are undersecured.

Special Provisions for Partially Secured Creditors

40 Section 1111(b) allows a secured claim to be treated as a claim with recourse against the debtor in chapter 11 proceedings (that is, where the debtor is liable for any deficiency between the value of the collateral and the balance due on the debt) whether or not the claim is nonrecourse by agreement or applicable law. This preferred status terminates if the property securing the loan is sold under section 363, is to be sold under the terms of the plan, or if the class of which the secured claim is a part elects application of section 1111(b)(2).

41 To illustrate this provision, consider the following. A corporation owns a building which is encumbered by a first mortgage of $8 million, a nonrecourse second of $4 million, and a nonrecourse third of $2 million. The debtor files a chapter 11 petition. The plan proposed by the debtor calls for interest and principal payments to be made to the first mortgage holder and a reduction of the amount to be paid to the second mortgage holder by $1 million. The third mortgagee will receive nothing, since it is estimated that the value of the property is only $11 million. The second and third mortgagees reject the plan. As a result of this there is a valuation of the building and it is determined to be worth $9 million. The allowed secured claims would be only $1 million for the second mortgagee and zero for the third mortgagee. However, because of section 1111(b), the nonrecourse mortgage is considered recourse and the provision of 502(b), which disallows claims that are not enforceable, does not apply. Three million of the second mortgage and the entire amount of the $2 million third mortgage would be unsecured claims. If, however, the property is sold for $9 million under section 363 or as a part of the plan, the second mortgagee would receive only $1 million and the third mortgagee nothing; they would not have unsecured claims for their deficiency in collateral.

42 Another selection that is available under section 1111(b) is that a class of creditors can elect to have its entire claim considered secured. A class of creditors will normally be only one creditor. Multiple-member classes may, however, exist where there are publicly issued debentures, where an indenture trustee holds a lien on behalf of the debenture holders, or when there is a group of creditors that have the same type of liens, such as mechanics' liens. If there is more than one creditor in a class, the class can exercise the option only if two-thirds in amount and a majority in number of allowed claims vote for such an election.[21] For example, in chapter 11 cases where most of the assets are pledged, very little may be available for unsecured creditors after administrative expenses are paid. Thus, the creditor might find it advisable to make the section 1111(b)(2) election. On the other hand, if there will be a payment to unsecured creditors of approximately 75 cents per dollar of debt, the creditor may not want to make this election. Note that the election is based on claims allowed, not just those voting. To be eligible for this election, the creditors must have allowed claims that are secured by a lien on property of the estate and their interest in such property as holders of secured claims must not be of inconsequential value (chapter 10, paragraphs 38–39). The election cannot be made if the holder has recourse against the debtor and the property is sold under section 363 or is to be sold under the plan.

43 The purpose of this election is to provide adequate protection to holders of secured claims where the holder is of the opinion that the collateral is undervalued. Also, if the treatment of the part of the debt that is accorded unsecured status is so unattractive, the holder may be willing to waive his unsecured deficiency claim.[22] The class of creditors that makes this election has the right to receive full payment for its claims over time. If the members of the class do not approve the plan, the court may confirm the plan as long as the plan provides that each member of the class receives deferred cash payments totaling at least the allowed amount of the claim. However, the present value of these payments as of the effective date of the plan must be at least equal to the value of the creditors' interest in the collateral.[23] Thus, while a creditor who makes the election under section 1111(b)(2) has the right to receive full payment over time, the value of that

---

[21] Ibid., Sec. 1111(b)(1)(A)(i).
[22] *Collier Bankruptcy Manual*, 3rd ed., para. 1111.03[5].
[23] 11 U.S.C. Sec. 1129(b)(2).

payment is required to only equal the value of the creditor's interest in the collateral.

44 Section 1111(b) does not specify when the election must be made. It should not, however, be required before the property is valued under section 506(a). Bankruptcy Rule 3014 provides that the election may be made at any time prior to the conclusion of the hearing on the disclosure statement, or within such later time as the court may fix. The election is to be made in writing and signed unless made at the hearing on the disclosure statement. Also, Bankruptcy Rule 3014 states that if the election, where there is more than one creditor, is made by the majority, it "shall be binding on all members of the class with respect to the plan." The Advisory Committee Notes to Bankruptcy Rule 3014 suggest that this election, once made and the disclosure statement approved, cannot be revoked unless the plan is not confirmed.

DEVELOPING THE PLAN

45 In cases where the debtor is allowed to operate the business as debtor in possession, the debtor has 120 days after the order for relief to file a plan and 180 days after the order of relief to obtain acceptance before others can file a plan.[24] The court may extend (or reduce) both time periods on request of any party after notice and hearing. For the average case the time periods may be adequate, but for larger cases it will take more than 120 days to develop a plan. Even if a plan is put together in 120 days, it will take more than sixty days to obtain approval. After these time periods have expired, any party (debtor, creditor, creditors' committee, equity security holder, and so forth) may file a plan. If a trustee has been appointed, the time restrictions do not apply and any party in interest may file a plan.

Classification of Claims

46 Section 1122 provides that claims or interests can be divided into classes provided each claim or interest is substantially similar to the others of such class. In addition, a separate class of unsecured claims may be established consisting of claims that are below or reduced to an amount the court approves as reasonable and necessary for administrative convenience. For example, claims of less than $1000, or those creditors who will accept $1000 as payment in full of their claim, may be placed in one class and the claimants will receive the lesser of $1000 or the amount of their claim. All creditors or equity holders in the same class are treated the same, but separate classes may be treated differently.

47 Generally, all unsecured claims, including claims arising from rejec-

[24] Ibid., Sec. 1121.

tion of executory contracts or unexpired leases, will be placed in the same class except for administrative expenses. They may, however, be divided into different classes if separate classification is justified. The Bankruptcy Code does not require that all claims that are substantially the same be placed in the same class. In *Barnes v. Whelan,*[25] the court stated that section 1122(a) "does not require that similar claims must be grouped together, but merely that any group created must be homogeneous." However, in *In re Mastercraft Record Plating, Inc.,* the court would not allow similar claims to be divided "to create a consenting class so as to permit confirmation."[26] If a group of unsecured claims was subordinated in favor of the other unsecured creditors and the holders of subordinated claims would receive less if the case were liquidated under chapter 7, the court would be required to consider the effect of this subordination and classify them separately.[27]

48 Subordination could occur by agreement or by order of the court. In fact there are at least four types of subordination[28] that require consideration in developing a plan:

1 Constructural Subordination—An agreement where a creditor agrees to give another superior rights to collect the debt. Some agreements forbid the subordination creditor from receiving any payment until the senior creditor is paid in full. For example, the bank may require this type— complete forbearance—where loans from the owner are subordinated. The more common type is "inchoate" forbearance where payments can be made to the subordinated creditor unless the debtor is in default on the senior debt.

2 Codebtor Claims Subordination—Under section 509 the codebtor who pays part of the claim of the primary creditor may have his or her claim against the debtor due to this payment subordinated to that of the primary creditor.

3 Securities Fraud Claims Subordination—Under section 510(b) claims for fraud in the purchase of a security are subordinated to all claims or interests superior or equal to the security, except that if such claim is common stock, it has the same priority as common stock. For example, defrauded purchasers of common stock will have the same priority as other common stockholders but will be subordinated to all preferred stockholders and to general unsecured creditors.

4 Equitable Subordination—Section 510(c) provides that the court, after notice and a hearing, may apply principles of equitable subordination.

---

[25] 689 F.2d 193 (D.C. Cir. 1982).
[26] 8 C.B.C.2d 1268 at 1270 (B. Ct. S.D.N.Y. 1983).
[27] Collier, para. 1122.04[4].
[28] Daniel C. Cohn, "Subordinated Claims: Their Classification and Voting under Chapter 11 of the Bankruptcy Code," *American Bankruptcy Law Journal,* Vol. 56 (October 1982), pp. 295–301.

Cohn suggests that courts have relied upon three basic kinds of unfairness as grounds for equitable subordination. The first is fraud, illegality, breach of fiduciary relationships, or other blatant wrongdoing. A second reason is undercapitalization.[29] It is not unusual for creditors to insist that insiders' claims be subordinated under the plan, or to object to insiders' claims on equitable grounds. For example, if the officers of an undercapitalized, closely held corporation made loans to the debtor and then sought to be paid on a par with other unsecured creditors, a court might be persuaded (on proper facts) that the funds should be deemed "capital contributions." Many factors might be considered, such as whether notes were executed under proper corporate authority and other aspects of how the debtor and the insider treated the transaction. A third ground for subordination, related to the second, relates to control over the debtor's operations. For example, in cases where a creditor controls another creditor for its own purposes and without regard to the debtor, the claim will most likely be subordinated.

49 Generally, each secured claim with an interest in specific property will be in a separate class. However, the court has allowed creditors holding purchase money mortgages on different parcels of real property in a similar location to be placed in the same class.[30] Collier suggests that the classification of secured claims is determined on the basis of priority under state law, nature of the collateral, and agreement among creditors with respect to subordination.[31]

50 Interests will also be classified separately if the securities have different rights. For example, preferred stock is in a separate class from common stock, and one issue of preferred stock may be in a separate class from another if the rights are not the same.

Content of the Plan

51 The items that may be included in the plan are listed in section 1123. The provisions are almost identical to those under Chapter X of prior law. Certain items are listed as mandatory and others are discretionary. The mandatory provisions are:

1 Designate classes of claims and interests.
2 Specify any class of claims or interests that is not impaired under the plan.

---

[29] Ibid., pp. 299–301.
[30] See *In re Palisades-on-the-Desplaines,* 89 F.2d 214 (7th Cir. 1937).
[31] Collier, para. 1122.04[6]. Rather than classify the subordinated debt separately, it is possible, but not common, to assign the subordinated claim to the holder of the senior claims, who then votes the subordinated claim and receives all payments attributed to it until the senior claim is paid in full and the balance received is then attributed to the subordinated claim. See *In re Itemlab, Inc.,* 197 F. Supp. 194, 198 (E.D.N.Y. 1961).

3   Specify the treatment of any class of claims or interests that is impaired under the plan.

4   Provide the same treatment for each claim or interest in a particular class unless the holders agree to less favorable treatment.

5   Provide adequate means for the plan's implementation, such as:

Retention by the debtor of all or any part of the property of the estate.

Transfer of all or any part of the property of the estate to one or more entities.

Merger or consolidation of the debtor with one or more persons.

Sale of all or any part of the property of the estate, either subject to or free of any lien, or the distribution of all or any part of the property of the estate among those having an interest in such property of the estate.

Satisfaction or modification of any lien.

Cancellation or modification of any indenture or similar instrument.

Curing or waiving any default.

Extension of a maturity date or a change in an interest rate or other term of outstanding securities.

Amendment of the debtor's charter.

Issuance of securities of the debtor, or of any entity involved in a merger or transfer of the debtor's business for cash, for property, for existing securities, or in exchange for claims or interests, or for any other appropriate purpose.

6   Provide for the inclusion in the charter of the debtor, if the debtor is a corporation, or of any corporation referred to in (5) above, of a provision prohibiting the issuance of nonvoting equity securities, and providing, as to the several classes of securities possessing voting power, an appropriate distribution of such power among such classes, including, in the case of any class of equity securities having a preference over another class of equity securities with respect to dividends, adequate provisions for the election of directors representing such preferred class in the event of default in the payment of such dividends.

7   Contain only provisions that are consistent with the interests of creditors and stockholders and with public policy with respect to the selection of officers, directors, or trustee under the plan.

Section 1124 describes what is meant by the impairment of a class of claims or interests (paragraphs 54–55).

Permissible Provisions

  52   In addition to the requirements listed above, the plan may also

1   Impair or leave unimpaired any class of unsecured or secured claims or interests.

2   Provide for the assumption, rejection, or assignment of executory contracts or leases.

3   Provide for settlement or adjustment of any claim or interest of the debtor or provide for the retention and enforcement by the debtor of any claim or interest.

4   Provide for the sale of all of the property of the debtor and the distribution of the proceeds to the creditors and stockholders.

5   Include any other provision not inconsistent with the provisions of the Bankruptcy Code.

Not covered in these requirements are the provisions for priority claims and administrative expenses. They are covered in the confirmation section of the Code beginning at paragraph 82. Exhibit 5-1 contains a copy of the plan developed by the Mansfield Tire and Rubber Company, along with Form 8-K which was used to submit the plan to the SEC.

53   The provision that the debtor can arrange for the sale of all of the property and distribute the proceeds to the creditors and stockholders generally was not available under Chapter XI of prior law.[32] In fact, several large as well as small companies have decided in recent years to use chapter 11 for this purpose because of some of the advantages it offers. It is often easier to collect receivables when a company is in a chapter 11 proceeding rather than in chapter 7, resulting in a higher realization on these accounts. The debtor may avoid the appointment of a trustee and the related costs. The debtor knows the business and may be in a position to liquidate the business in a more orderly fashion than a trustee that is not familiar with the debtor's operations. The court may allow more time for the debtor to operate the business since it is possible that the creditors might not be placing as much pressure on the debtor to liquidate the business. It is easier, too, for a firm undergoing a chapter 11 liquidation to obtain going concern values upon disposition of assets because management is in a better position to negotiate the sales transactions, if at least some of the current management is able to stay with the firm. Officers of the company will usually not receive salaries from a trustee unless they are retained as consultants, whereas they could be paid as employees of the debtor in possession in a chapter 11 proceeding. Also, the debtor has more flexibility in chapter 11. If a decision is made to continue the business, this may be easier to do if the debtor is already in a chapter 11 proceeding. The major advantage to the debtor of a chapter 11 liquidation plan over a liquidation under chapter 7 is that the debtor is able to maintain its control over the business, whereas in chapter 7, the debtor would not have any control. There may also be tax benefits, although a liquidating corporation is ineligible for a discharge under section 1141(d)(3). The creditors may not always accept a liquidating chapter 11 proceeding,

---

[32] *In re Pure Penn Petroleum Co.*, 188 F.2d 851 (2d Cir. 1951).

because they may have reservations about the debtor's management conducting a total liquidation without a trustee looking after the creditors' interest. Often when a trustee is not appointed there will be a change in management, or a professional liquidator will be retained to assist with the development of a plan of liquidation and with the eventual liquidation of the business.

Impairment of Claims

54 In determining which classes of creditors' claims or stockholders' interests must approve the plan, it is first necessary to determine if the class

Exhibit 5-1 Example of Plan and Form 8-K Used to Transmit a Copy of Plan to the SEC

SECURITIES AND EXCHANGE COMMISSION
WASHINGTON, D.C. 20549

FORM 8-K
CURRENT REPORT
Pursuant to Section 13 or 15(d) of the
Securities Exchange Act of 1934

Dated: April 21, 1980

The Mansfield Tire & Rubber Company

(Exact name of Registrant as specified in its charter)

Ohio	1-3961	34-0376390
(State or other jurisdiction of incorporation)	(Commission File Number)	(IRS Employer Identification No.)

515 Newman Street, Mansfield, Ohio	44901
(Address of principal executive offices)	Zip Code

Registrant's telephone number, including area code	(419) 522-4111

No Change

(Former name or former address, if changed since last report)

Item 5. Other Materially Important Events

On April 14, 1980 the Registrant and each of its active subsidiaries filed their reorganization plan in the cases they filed last Fall under chapter 11 of the Bankruptcy Code. In general, the plan proposes that the Registrant and each of these subsidiaries continue to collect outstanding accounts receivable and proceed to sell

Exhibit 5-1 *(Continued)*

their other assets. The plan classifies creditors of all three companies by type of claim as contemplated by the Bankruptcy Code. It also provides that the proceeds realized by the companies, net of costs of sale and collection and, in the case of sale of an asset, net of payment of any obligation secured by that asset, will be paid into a common fund and thereafter distributed to the classes of creditors in the order set forth in the plan. The plan also contemplates that the companies will hold back a certain portion of the common fund for a specified period of time as a reserve for product service, with any balance remaining to be subsequently distributed. The plan is to be voted upon by creditors holding impaired claims and is subject to confirmation by the Bankruptcy Court. Amounts to be paid out under the plan cannot be presently determined since they will depend on the proceeds realized upon the sale and collection of the assets involved.

As presently proposed, the plan is not subject to approval by shareholders of the Registrant since it does not alter their legal, equitable and contractual rights. Under its terms, the Registrant will not retain any proceeds which will benefit its shareholders, as such, unless a total amount substantially in excess of the aggregate consolidated book value of its assets and the assets of its subsidiaries can be realized. Management believes such a result is not likely to be achieved, particularly in view of prevailing economic conditions in the tire and automotive industries.

The Registrant, as debtor in possession, is continuing to operate its molded wood fiber products division in Springfield, Tennessee where it also manufactures mechanical rubber goods. This division has continued to operate at a loss since December 31, 1979 and, given the present conditions in the automotive industry, this division is not expected to become profitable within the foreseeable future. Accordingly, management does not presently anticipate being able to reorganize the Registrant around the division.

A copy of the abovementioned reorganization plan is filed as Exhibit I hereto.

Item 7. Financial Statements and Exhibits

(b) *Exhibits*
  I. Combined Reorganization Plan filed in the United States Bankruptcy Court, Northern District of Ohio, Eastern Division, at Canton, Ohio, by The Mansfield Tire & Rubber Company (Case No. 679-01238), Pennsylvania Tire and Rubber Company of Mississippi, Inc. (Case No. 679-01239) and Pennsylvania Tire Company (Case No. 679-01333).

SIGNATURES

Pursuant to the requirements of the Securities Exchange Act of 1934, the Registrant has duly caused this Report to be signed on its behalf by the undersigned thereunto duly authorized.

THE MANSFIELD TIRE & RUBBER COMPANY

By _____

Wm. M. Kochheiser, Secretary

Dated: April 21, 1980

Exhibit 5-1 *(Continued)*

UNITED STATES BANKRUPTCY COURT
NORTHERN DISTRICT OF OHIO
EASTERN DIVISION

In re:
THE MANSFIELD TIRE &
  RUBBER COMPANY,
  Debtor,

PENNSYLVANIA TIRE AND
  RUBBER COMPANY OF
  MISSISSIPPI, INC.,
  Debtor,

PENNSYLVANIA TIRE
  COMPANY,
  Debtor.

Case Nos. 679-01238
          679-01239
          679-01333
United States Bankruptcy Judge
James H. Williams

COMBINED REORGANIZATION PLAN

The Mansfield Tire & Rubber Company, an Ohio corporation ("MTR"), Pennsylvania Tire and Rubber Company of Mississippi, Inc., a Mississippi corporation ("Penn-Miss"), and Pennsylvania Tire Company, an Ohio corporation ("Penn-Ohio") (collectively the "Companies"), each hereby proposes the following combined reorganization Plan.

I. SUMMARY OF PLAN

This document sets forth in an integrated format the combined reorganization plan for the Debtors named above. Upon Confirmation, the provisions of the Plan will be binding upon all secured and unsecured creditors of the Companies. Chapter 11 proceedings provide an appropriate vehicle to maintain the going concern value inherent in the Companies' assets, especially the Fibrit division of MTR, and to maximize accounts receivable collections. In addition, the Plan permits the sale of assets of the Companies in an orderly manner, thereby realizing the highest market price possible.

The Plan divides creditors of the Companies into a number of classes with unsecured creditors of the Companies receiving payment from a Common Fund realized from the assets of the Companies. Certain creditors holding administrative, post-petition, and priority claims will be paid in full. Unsecured creditors of each of the Companies with claims of $500 or less and creditors electing to receive $500 in full satisfaction of their claims will be paid in full. Thereafter, unsecured Trade Creditors with claims exceeding $500 are to be paid as a class up to 100% of their claims from the Common Fund up to $9,500,000. Insurance Creditors will then receive payment from the Common Fund after net proceeds paid into the Fund exceed $9,500,000 up to 100% of their Claims. The Plan also establishes Product Reserves considered necessary for maintaining the quality of accounts receivable.

· II. DEFINITIONS

For purposes of the Plan, the following definitions shall apply with respect to each Plan and each Debtor, unless the context otherwise requires:

Exhibit 5-1 *(Continued)*

1. "Aetna" shall mean Aetna Life Insurance Company.

2. "Claim" shall mean, as the same is duly scheduled, listed, or timely filed and is allowed, approved, and ordered paid by the Court (or agreed to be assumed by a purchaser from the Debtor) any right to payment from a Debtor, whether or not such right is reduced to judgment, liquidated, unliquidated, fixed, contingent, matured, unmatured, disputed, undisputed, secured, or unsecured, or any right to an equitable remedy for breach of performance if such breach gives rise to a right to payment from such Debtor, whether or not such right to an equitable remedy is reduced to judgment, fixed, contingent, matured, unmatured, disputed, undisputed, secured or unsecured.

3. "Code" shall mean the Bankruptcy Code of 1978, effective October 1, 1979, as set forth in Title 11 of the United States Code.

4. "Chapter 11" shall mean Chapter 11 of the Code.

5. "Common Fund" shall mean the fund of proceeds from the sale of assets and collection of accounts receivable of the Debtors or from any source whatever.

6. "Confirmation" shall mean the entry by the Court of final orders confirming the Plans of MTR, Penn-Miss, and Penn-Ohio under Chapter 11.

7. "Consummation of the Plan" shall mean the accomplishment of all things contained or provided for in the Plan and the entry of an order by the Court finally closing the cases of the Debtors.

8. "Court" shall mean the United States Bankruptcy Court for the Northern District of Ohio, Eastern Division.

9. "Costs and Expenses of Administration" shall mean those claims defined as costs and expenses of administration in §507 of the Code from and after October 1, 1979, in the case of MTR and Penn-Miss, and November 1, 1979, in the case of Penn-Ohio.

10. "Debtor" shall mean MTR, Penn-Miss, or Penn-Ohio, as the case may be.

11. "Effective Date" shall mean that date on which the Confirmation becomes final and nonappealable.

12. "Equitable" shall mean the Equitable Life Assurance Society of the United States.

13. "Insurance Creditors" shall mean the Pension Benefit Guaranty Corporation, the Internal Revenue Service with respect to penalties imposed in regard to pension plan funding, Workman's Compensation Claimants, claimants asserting Claims for group health and life insurance, and claimants asserting Claims arising from product liability or breach of warranties.

14. "IRBs" shall mean Industrial Revenue Bondholders.

15. "Prepetition" shall mean arising or occurring prior to October 1, 1979, in the case of MTR and Penn-Miss, and November 1, 1979, in the case of Penn-Ohio.

16. "Priority Claims" shall mean those Claims which qualify as such under §507 of the Code.

17. "Product Reserve" shall mean funds retained for a period of 36 months after Confirmation to defray costs for product liability expenses and insurance, and product servicing costs (including a service department) and expenses related thereto, for which an annual accounting will be provided to the Court. At the end of the 36 month period, any remaining amounts in the Product Reserve will be distributed in accordance with the Plan.

Exhibit 5-1 *(Continued)*

18. "Secured Creditors" shall mean all creditors of the Debtors which hold a lien, security interest, or other encumbrance that has been properly perfected as required by law, with respect to property or assets of such Debtor.

19. "Trade Creditors" shall mean holders of unsecured Claims other than Priority Claims, Claims of Insurance Creditors, and Costs and Expenses of Administration, including, without limitation, any such Claim arising out of the rejection of an executory contract or lease.

20. "Value of a Secured Claim" shall mean value as determined in accordance with §506 of the Code.

21. "Workmen's Compensation Claimants" shall mean Ohio Workers' Compensation Coverage claimants, Mississippi Workmen's Compensation claimants, and Tennessee Workmen's Compensation claimants.

III. CLASSIFICATION OF CLAIMS

Claims are classified with respect to each Debtor as follows:

Class A-1:	Costs and Expenses of Administration, other than those included in Class A-2, for which an application for allowance or a claim is filed prior to the Effective Date.
Class A-2:	Costs and Expenses of Administration consisting of unpaid obligations incurred by the Debtors in Possession.
Class A-3:	Priority Claims.
Class B-1:	All Claims of Trade Creditors of $500 or less or Claims held by creditors electing to receive $500 in full satisfaction of their Claims.
Class B-2:	All Claims of Trade Creditors other than those Trade Creditors whose Claims fall within Class B-1.
Class B-3:	All Claims of Insurance Creditors.
Class C-1:	All Claims of IRBs, as Secured Creditors, as such Claims existed on October 1, 1979, to the extent that any such Claim is not greater than the value of each Debtor's assets which the Court finds are collateral for each such Claim.
Class C-2:	All Claims of Aetna and Equitable, as such Claims existed on October 1, 1979.
Class D:	Interests of shareholders of MTR.

IV. CLASSES OF CLAIMS NOT IMPAIRED

The following classes of claims are not impaired under the Plan of a designated Debtor:

Class A-1: (Costs and expenses of administration)	All Claims in Class A-1 shall be paid in full after Confirmation of the Plan, unless the holder of any such Claim agrees that payment of all, or any portion thereof, may be deferred.

Exhibit 5-1 *(Continued)*

Class A-2:
(Costs and administration expenses of Debtor in Possession)

All Claims included in Class A-2 shall be paid in full as they become due, unless the holder of any such Claim agrees that payment of all, or any portion thereof, may be deferred.

Class A-3:
(Priority Claims)

All Claims included in Class A-3 shall be paid in full after Confirmation of the Plan, unless the holder of any such Claim agrees that payment of all, or any portion thereof, may be deferred.

Class B-1:
(Trade Creditors —$500 or less)

All Claims included in Class B-1 (either in the full amount thereof or as reduced to $500 by the Creditor) shall be paid in full after Confirmation of the Plan.

Class C-1:
(Industrial Revenue Bondholders)

Any Claim included in Class C-1 shall be paid from the net proceeds of the sale or collection of the collateral securing the same to the extent such Claim is not greater than the value of the respective Debtor's assets which the Court finds are collateral therefor.

Class D:
(MTR)

All interests of MTR shareholders remain unaltered.

V. CLASSES OF IMPAIRED CLAIMS

The following classes of Claims are impaired and will be treated as follows:

Class B-2:
(Trade Creditors—more than $500)

All claims included in Class B-2 shall be paid after Confirmation, up to 100% of the claims.

Class B-3:
(Insurance Creditors)

All Claims included in Class B-3 shall be paid after Confirmation up to 100% of Claims from the Common Fund remaining after payment to Class B-2 Creditors and from the proceeds of the sale of the Company's real estate in Tupelo, Mississippi.

Class C-2:
(Aetna and Equitable)

Class C-2 Claims will be satisfied in accordance with the provisions of Part VI, paragraph B, of the Plan.

VI. DISTRIBUTION

A. Priority and Unsecured Creditors

After distribution to Class A Creditors, which will receive payment in numerical order, a Product Reserve fund of $550,000 will be set aside for the purposes specified in the definition thereof. Thereafter, Classes B-1, B-2, and B-3 Creditors, in that order, will be paid from the Common Fund up to $9,500,000. Net proceeds in the Common Fund in excess of $9,500,000 are designated for Classes B-3 and B-2 in that order.

Exhibit 5-1 *(Continued)*

B. Secured Creditors

Class C-1 Creditors, as first lien holders, will be paid from the proceeds of sale of the particular properties which are subject to their security interests. Payments of principal and interest due and owing to IRBs may be made from the Common Fund prior to sale of property subject to the security interests of IRBs.

At their option, Class C-2 Creditors are to receive either:

1. Annual cash payments in accordance with the notes heretofore executed by MTR; or
2. An amount equal to their claims discounted to their present value as of the Effective Date of the Plan; or
3. The amount of their Claims in accordance with their election under §1111(b) of the Code to convert to a nonrecourse loan and rely solely upon the proceeds of their collateral; or
4. An amount equal to the lesser of $3,000,000 or 50% of their allowed Claims and a lien upon all unencumbered real estate of MTR located in Mansfield, Ohio, for any excess amount of their Claims over $3,000,000.

Class C-2 Creditors must select one of the foregoing options, including without limitation a §1111(b) election, at least 14 days prior to the first date set for acceptance of the Plan, and failure to so elect will result in a waiver of Class C-2 Creditors' §1111(b) election.

Aetna and Equitable have received payments on their Claims since filing of the Debtor's case. Such payments shall be credited to any payments due them under the foregoing options or as otherwise directed by the Court.

C. Shareholders of MTR

After all other classes of Creditors are paid 100% of their Claims, the balance of any funds and assets will remain with MTR for the benefit of its shareholders.

VII. EXECUTION OF THE PLAN

The Companies are to proceed with the collection of their accounts receivable and the negotiation and sale of all or substantially all of their remaining assets. Upon the sale of any of the assets of the Companies, the net proceeds therefrom, after payment of costs of sale and any prior obligations encumbering such property, shall be retained by the Companies, which shall disburse the same in accordance with the foregoing.

The Companies shall have the right, but not the obligation, to withhold the making of a disbursement of any part of said net proceeds to the extent the same may be required to pay obligations to its Secured Creditors holding prior liens and security interests encumbering the remaining property of such Debtor.

VIII. COMBINED CREDITORS' COMMITTEE

The Court shall appoint a representative Combined Committee of Creditors of the Debtors. The Committee shall consult with and advise the Debtors on matters concerning the ongoing administration of the Plan and the preservation and disposition of assets.

Exhibit 5-1 *(Continued)*

IX. REJECTION OF EXECUTORY CONTRACTS AND LEASE

Upon the expiration of ninety (90) days after the entry of the order confirming the Plan, each and every executory contract and unexpired lease of personal and real property to which a Debtor was a party at the time of the commencement of this Chapter 11 case shall be deemed rejected, except those executory contracts and unexpired leases specifically affirmed by order of the Court prior to or within ninety (90) days after Confirmation of the Plan.

X. CONFIRMATION OF THE PLAN

The Plan which is set forth herein is conditioned upon its contemporaneous confirmation in each Debtor's case or an order of court substantively consolidating the Debtor's cases.

XI. JURISDICTION OF THE COURT

Upon entry of the Order of Confirmation, MTR will manage the Companies' business and property without further supervision of the Court, except as provided in this paragraph. After Confirmation and until Consummation of the Plan, the Court shall retain jurisdiction to insure that the purpose and intent of the Plan is carried out; to select and appoint members of the Combined Creditors' Committee; to hear and determine all claims against a Debtor and to enforce all causes of action which may exist on behalf of a Debtor; to hear and determine controversies concerning, and to adjudicate interests in and to, all property of a Debtor, including the Product Reserve, in proceedings arising in or related to cases under the Code involving a Debtor; to fix allowances of compensation; to hear and determine any requests for the rejection of executory contracts and leases.

Respectfully submitted,

THE MANSFIELD TIRE & RUBBER
COMPANY

By: _____/s/ Joseph Patchan_____
Title: Attorney For Debtor_____

PENNSYLVANIA TIRE AND RUBBER
COMPANY OF MISSISSIPPI, INC.

By: _____/s/ Joseph Patchan_____
Title: Attorney For Debtor_____

PENNSYLVANIA TIRE COMPANY
By: _____/s/ Joseph Patchan_____
Title: Attorney For Debtor_____

OF COUNSEL:

Baker & Hostetler
1956 Union Commerce Building
Cleveland, Ohio 44115

is impaired.[33] Section 1124 states that a class of claims or interests is impaired under the plan, unless the plan

1   Leaves unaltered the legal, equitable, and contractual rights to which such claim or interest entitles the holder of such claim or interest.

2   Notwithstanding any contractual provision or applicable law that entitles the holder of such claim or interest to demand or receive accelerated payment of such claim or interest after the occurrence of a default—

    A   cures any such default that occurred before or after the commencement of the case under this title, other than a default of a kind specified in section 365(b)(2) of this title [such as a bankruptcy or insolvency clause that would make the entire debt due];

    B   reinstates the maturity of such claim or interest as such maturity existed before such default;

    C   compensates the holder of such claim or interest for any damages incurred as a result of any reasonable reliance by such holder on such contractual provision or such applicable law; and

    D   does not otherwise alter the legal, equitable, or contractual rights to which such claim or interest entitles the holder of such claim or interest; or

3   provides that, on the effective date of the plan, the holder of such claim or interest receives, on account of such claim or interest, cash equal to—

    A   with respect to a claim, the allowed amount of such claim; or

    B   with respect to an interest, if applicable, the greater of—

       i   any fixed liquidation preference to which the terms of any security representing such interest entitle the holder of such interest; or

       ii   any fixed price at which the debtor, under the terms of such security, may redeem such security from such holder.

55   Thus, for a plan to leave unimpaired a class of claims or interests, the plan must leave unaltered the legal, equitable, and contractual rights of a class, cure defaults that led to acceleration of debts, or pay in cash the full amount of their claims.

Disclosure Statement

56   A party cannot solicit the acceptance or rejection of a plan from creditors and stockholders affected by the plan unless they are given a written disclosure statement containing adequate information as approved by the court. Section 1125(b) requires that this disclosure statement must be

---

[33] 11 U.S.C. Sec. 1129(a)(8).

provided prior to or at the time of the solicitation. The disclosure statement must be approved by the court, after notice and a hearing, as containing adequate information.

Adequate Information

57   Section 1125(a) states that adequate information means information of a kind, and in sufficient detail, as far as is reasonably practicable in light of the nature and history of the debtor and the condition of the debtor's books and records, that would enable a hypothetical reasonable investor typical of holders of claims or interests of the relevant class to make an informed judgment about the plan. This definition contains two parts. First it defines adequate information and then it sets a standard against which the information is measured. It must be the kind of information that a typical investor of the relevant class, not one that has special information, would need to make an informed judgment about the plan. Section 1125(a)(1) provides that adequate information need not include information about other possible proposed plans.

Objectives of Statement

58   The disclosure requirement is new under chapter 11 and the House Committee Report believed it to be the heart of the consolidation of Chapters X, XI, and XIII of prior law. Chapter XI did not contain any required disclosure. Chapter X, on the other hand, required the plan, once developed, to be sent to the SEC. The SEC would within a few months prepare an advisory report on the plan to inform the creditors and stockholders of the content of the plan and of the SEC's evaluation of its terms.

59   The objective of the disclosure statement provision is to require reasonable disclosure in all cases, but not necessarily to the extent required under Chapter X of prior law. While the new law does provide for considerable flexibility in the content of the disclosure statement, it seems clear that Congress wanted to end the highly informal disclosure practices followed in Chapter XI proceedings under prior law while avoiding the delay caused in obtaining SEC approval in Chapter X.

60   The disclosure statement must be approved by the court, after notice and hearing, before transmission to creditors or stockholders. The content of the disclosure statement is to be decided solely by the bankruptcy judge, and is not governed by any nonbankruptcy law, including the Securities Acts of 1933 and 1934. Any governmental agency, including the SEC, may be heard regarding the adequacy of the information disclosed, but such agency cannot appeal an order of the court approving the statement.[34] In cases where a large number of public security holders are affected by the proposed plan, it can be anticipated that the SEC will present its objection to any disclosure

---

[34] Ibid., Sec. 1125(d).

statements it believes do not contain adequate information or do contain misleading statements.

61 According to the House Committee Report, it was expected that the courts would take a practical approach to the question of what type of disclosure is necessary, taking into consideration the cost of preparing the statements, the need for speed in soliciting votes and confirming the plan, and the need for investor protection. Thus, precisely what constitutes adequate information in any given situation will develop on a case-by-case basis.

62 The act provides that the same disclosure statement must go to all members of a particular class, but it does allow different disclosures for different classes of creditors or stockholders.[35] This provision allows for flexibility in the preparation and distribution of statements based on the needs of the various interest groups and should provide for less printing and distribution costs. It is hoped that the information contained in the disclosure statement will in most corporate cases be based on an examination by an independent accountant. The Bankruptcy Code does, however, give the court the right to approve a disclosure statement without a valuation of the debtor or without an appraisal of the debtor's assets.[36]

Prepetition Solicitation

63 Before filing a petition under chapter 11 some debtors may have already acquired the necessary votes to obtain approval of the plan. The information disclosure requirement of section 1125 will not apply if the solicitation of such acceptance or rejection was in compliance with any applicable nonbankruptcy law, rule, or regulation governing the adequacy of disclosure in connection with the solicitation.[37] If no nonbankruptcy law is applicable, then the solicitation must have occurred after the holder received adequate information as required under section 1125. The creditors' acceptance of an out-of-court agreement that would also carry over to a chapter 11 reorganization if a petition is filed should follow the provisions of section 1125 to avoid subsequent problems if the debtor ends up in chapter 11. (See chapter 4, paragraph 31.)

Content of Disclosure Statement

64 As noticed in paragraph 57 the information disclosed in the statement should be adequate to allow the creditor or stockholder to make an informed judgment about the plan. An example of a disclosure statement issued by a small company is shown in chapter 9. Considerable difference in opinion exists as to the type of information that should be included in the disclosure statement. Phelan and Cheatham, for example, suggest that the best guides

---

[35] Ibid., Sec. 1125(c).
[36] Ibid., Sec. 1125(b).
[37] Ibid., Sec. 1126(b).

for drafting a disclosure statement are Form S-1 (used in connection with registration of securities under the 1933 Act), Form S-2 (used to register securities of new companies), and Form 10 (used for registration of securities under the 1934 Act.)[38] They also suggest that some of the items required in these forms are not relevant to a bankruptcy proceeding, but that the forms do constitute excellent evidence of the information the SEC believes to be the minimum required for the protection of the investors, and suggest that to vary widely from such information may affect the ability of a person to satisfy the good faith requirement (paragraph 79) of section 1125(e).[39]

65   Others feel that these requirements are more than would be necessary under most bankruptcy situations.[40] The Bankruptcy Code states in section 1125(d) that the requirements of the SEC are not applicable to reorganizations; indeed that was one of the reasons to avoid the need to file the detailed information required by the securities laws.

66   It should also be remembered that the amount of disclosure required under Chapter X proceedings of prior law varied from one district to another, and there will most probably be some differences in the amount of information that must be included in the disclosure statement. Information that might be included in the disclosure statement is discussed in paragraphs 67–76.

Introduction

67   The first part states that the proposed plan is enclosed, defines the classes that must vote and the percentage of acceptance needed for approval. There should be a statement to the effect that no representations concerning the debtor, particularly regarding future operations, value of property, or value of securities to be issued under the plan, are authorized by the debtor other than as set forth in this disclosure statement. The introduction also indicates which information presented has been audited by a certified public accountant. Also included is a brief description of the company and the nature of its operations. Other information presented by the debtor should be designated as not warranted to be without any inaccuracies, although every effort has been made to see that it is accurate.[41]

Management

68   In order to evaluate the ability of the firm to continue as a going concern, the creditors need to know about the management of the company. If existing management is to be replaced, the disclosure statement should

---

[38] Robin E. Phelan and Bruce A. Cheatham, "Issuing Securities Under the New Bankruptcy Code: More Magic for the Cryptic Kingdom," *St. Mary's Law Journal,* Vol. 11 (Number 2, 1979), p. 426.

[39] Ibid.

[40] See, for example, the disclosure statements filed in the central district of California.

[41] *Collier Forms Manual,* Form 11–721.

identify the new management. This is true even if a trustee is currently running the business. Included should be the list of all directors and key officers, including their ages, tenure with the company, and prior business experience.

Comments About the Plan of Reorganization

69 The objective of this section of the disclosure statement is for the debtor to present the reasons why the creditors could expect more from the plan than from a liquidation of the business. It sets forth in summary form the major parts of the plan, including a description of the various classes of creditors and stockholders. In a sample form presented by Collier, the following paragraph was included in the disclosure statement:

> The Plan is based upon the Debtor's belief that the present forced liquidation value of his principal assets is so small as to offer the potential of only a minimal recovery to creditors. The Debtor believes that it is possible that some of his properties to be retained pursuant to the Plan will appreciate in value in the future, and debts secured by liens on certain of these properties will be reduced by sales of the properties and future earnings, thus permitting a more substantial recovery to creditors and thus offer the possibility that creditors will receive payment in full by way of extension. Further, certain obligations undertaken by the Debtor in the Plan will be guaranteed by trusts created some years ago for the benefit of his children.[42]

70 Phelan and Cheatham indicate that the condition of the books and records of the debtor, the funds available for preparation of the disclosure statement, and other circumstances surrounding the rehabilitation may limit the amount of information that can reasonably be presented in the disclosure statement.[43] They recommend that the following should be included if the plan requires the issuance of securities:

1 A complete description of the capital structure of the rehabilitated debtor (including new infusions of capital and new funding agreements) and use of proceeds (if any).

2 A history of the business activities of the debtor (and the issuer in the case of a nondebtor issuer).

3 A list of parents, controlling persons, and subsidiaries of the issuer.

4 A complete description of the issuer's business, including, but not limited to, the following:

    a The competitive conditions in the industry or industries in which the issuer competes, and the issuer's competitive position in such industries.

---

[42] Ibid.
[43] Phelan and Cheatham, p. 426.

b The dependence of the issuer upon one or more customers.

c The principal products produced or services rendered by the issuer and the methods of distribution of such product or services.

d The current backlog of the issuer and comparable figures for the previous year.

e The course and availability of raw materials essential to the issuer's business.

f The importance of all patents, trademarks, licenses, franchises, and concessions held by the issuer.

g Information regarding research and development.

h The number of persons employed by the issuer.

i Information regarding the seasonal nature of the issuer's business.

j Information regarding foreign operations, regulatory problems, and working capital position. In addition, sales and revenue figures for each industry segment of the issuer and each class of similar products or services are required.

5 A description of all physical properties held by the issuer.

6 A complete description of major litigation involving the issuer.

7 Descriptions of each of the securities being issued.

8 Complete information regarding the officers and directors of the rehabilitated debtor.

9 Complete information regarding all remuneration to be paid or other transactions with insiders and controlling persons of the issuer or debtor.

10 A description of the major shareholders and controlling persons after the reorganization.

11 A description of any options or warrants to purchase securities of the issuer which remain outstanding.

12 A description of any pledges or other financing arrangements which conceivably could change control of the issuer at such date.

13 A complete description of the tax ramifications of the transaction.

14 Any attorneys' fees to be paid in connection with the proceeding.

15 The anticipated liquidity of the reorganized debtor.

The elimination of any one of the above items from the disclosure memorandum may constitute a material nondisclosure and subject all parties to securities law liabilities.[44]

Financial Information

71 There are several types of information that could be of considerable benefit to the creditors and stockholders in assessing the potential of the

---

[44] Ibid., pp. 426–428.

debtor's business. Some of these are: audited reports of the financial position as of the date the petition was filed or as of the end of a recent fiscal year and the results of operations for the past year; a more detailed analysis by the debtor of its properties, including a description of the properties, the current values, and other relevant information; and a description of the obligations outstanding with the material claims in dispute being identified. If the nature of the company's operations is going to change significantly as a result of the reorganization, historical financial statements for the past two to five years are of limited value.

72   In addition to the historical financial statements, the presentation of a pro forma balance sheet showing the impact the proposed plan, if accepted, will have on the financial condition of the company may be included. Included should be the source of new capital and how the proceeds will be used, the postpetition interest obligation, lease commitments, financing arrangements, and so forth.

73   If the plan calls for future cash payments, the inclusion of projections of future operations will help the affected creditors make a decision as to whether or not they believe the debtor will be able to make the required payments. Even if no future cash payments are called for in the plan, it may still be advisable to include the financial information in the disclosure statement that will allow the creditors and stockholders to see the potential the business has to operate profitably in the future. These projections must, of course, be based on reasonable assumptions and the assumptions must be clearly set forth in the projections accompanying the disclosure statement.[45]

Liquidation

74   Included in the disclosure statement should be an analysis of the amount that creditors and equity holders would receive if the debtor was liquidated under chapter 7. In order to effectively evaluate the reorganization alternative, the creditor and equity holders must know what they would receive through liquidation. Also, the court, in order to confirm the plan, must ascertain, according to section 1129(a)(7), that each holder of a claim or interest who does not vote in favor of the plan must receive at least an amount that is equal to the amount that would be received in a chapter 7 liquidation.

75   Generally, it is not acceptable to state that the amount provided for in the plan exceeds the liquidation amount. Data must be presented to support this type of statement.

Special Risk Factors

76   In any securities that are issued pursuant to a plan in a chapter 11 proceeding there are certain substantial risk factors that are inherent in the

---

[45] *Collier Forms Manual,* Form 11–721.

issue. It may be advisable to include a description of some of the factors in the disclosure statement.[46]

77 The U.S. Trustee's office for the Central District of California has issued a checklist of items it believes should appear in the disclosure statement. While issuing the checklist, the U.S. Trustee for this district indicates that this list is neither exclusive nor exhaustive and, depending on the desire and nature of the debtor, the plan may vary considerably. The checklist of 13 items is presented in Exhibit 5-2.

Exhibit 5-2 Disclosure Statement Review Checklist

1. *Purpose of the disclosure statement.* The statement should indicate that the purpose of the disclosure statement is to provide "adequate information" of a kind, and in sufficient detail, as far as is reasonably practicable in light of the nature and history of the debtor and the condition of the debtor's books and records, that would enable a hypothetical reasonable investor typical of holders of claims (creditors) or interests (shareholders) of the relevant class to make an informed judgment concerning the plan. See 11 U.S.C. §1125(a). The statement should not resort wholly to "boilerplate" language found in Colliers that disclaims all the numbers and assumptions found in the disclosure statement. Such a disclaimer is not only confusing, but makes the statement rather meaningless.

2. *Vote required for approval.* The statement should briefly indicate the vote required for approval, and should clearly indicate that creditors or interest holders have a choice: they can either vote for *or* against the plan. Creditors and interest holders have accepted a plan if those holding at least two-thirds in amount and more than one-half in number of the allowed claims or interests that have accepted or rejected the plan have voted for the plan. See 11 U.S.C. §1126(c) and (d).

3. *Liquidation analysis.* The disclosure statement should clearly indicate the difference between treatment accorded in the plan, and what creditors would receive under a chapter 7 liquidation alternative. Such comparison might be by way of percentage return to creditors under each alternative, and might include assumptions regarding liquidation values, administrative costs and the like. A disclosure of any assumptions utilized by management in formulating a liquidation alternative should be disclosed. See 11 U.S.C. §1129(a)(7)(A)(ii). It is generally insufficient to merely indicate that the plan would provide a better return than liquidation without any supporting information, that would justify that conclusion.

4. *Description of the plan.* The disclosure statement should give a description of the major provisions of the plan, including an estimated date by which creditors could expect to receive payment, an expected percentage return on their claim, a summary of the treatment of various classes under the plan, and the like. Generally, the description does not have to be intricate in detail, and a referral to the plan, which contains such detail, is appropriate.

5. *Means of effectuating the plan.* The statement should indicate how the debtor intends to accomplish the goals of the plan, i.e.: whether by infusion of cash

---

[46] Ibid.

Exhibit 5-2 (*Continued*)

by an investor, sale of real or personal property, continued business operations, issuance of stock or the like:

A. *Projections*. If the debtor is operating a business, and intends to repay creditors over time out of profits generated by the business, the statement should include projections as far into the future as is practicable, including assumptions used by management in formulating such projections, such as expected sales levels, gross and net profit levels, inventory acquisition, etc.

B. *Cash requirements*. The disclosure statement should indicate the amount of cash to be paid upon confirmation to administrative and other creditors to be paid at that date, and the expected source of such cash. If the debtor expects a cash infusion from an outside source, or from principals, which is to be repaid in the future, then the identity of the source, as well as the repayment terms should be disclosed. Similarly, the effect of such infusions (i.e.: principal and interest payments) should be reflected in the projections.

6. *Legal proceedings*. The disclosure statement should reflect the existence, if any, of any proceedings to which the debtor is either a plaintiff or defendant, either in the Bankruptcy or another court, and the effect, if any, of either a favorable or unfavorable judgment upon the plan. If possible, a status report of the litigation and a summary of the issues should be presented.

7. *Description of the business*. The statement should describe the debtor's business, including those things which may be unusual or peculiar to the business, such as seasonal cycles, unique product lines, etc. Such a description should indicate the reasons for the filing of the case, and what steps have been taken since the filing to cure, remedy, or otherwise deal with those factors.

8. *Valuation of assets*. In conjunction with projections and liquidation analysis the disclosure statement should contain as recent as is possible financial information about the debtor, including a balance sheet and profit and loss statement. The balance sheet should indicate whether or not such statement was audited, and the basis for the valuation of items indicated therein. Further, the disclosure statement should indicate, possibly in a separate statement, the debtor's estimate of current values of assets, and the source of such estimated values (such as cost, appraisals, etc.).

9. *Marketing efforts*. The statement should indicate what efforts the debtor has made since the filing to market any properties which are currently for sale. (Most appropriate to real estate cases). Such a description should include the identity of the listing agent, the listing price, any offers received or anticipated, or litigation existing which might affect the sale of the property.

10. *Administrative expenses*. The disclosure statement should indicate whether any administrative expenses have accrued which must be paid at the time of confirmation, unless such party to whom the expenses are owed consents to alternative treatment. See 11 U.S.C. §1129(a)(9)(A). Such disclosure should include the expected amounts owed, and the identity of the claimants.

11. *Post-petition events*. The disclosure statement should indicate whether any major postpetition events have occurred which might effect the case, such as the appointment of a creditors' committee, a trustee, an examiner, or the existence of litigation with significant consequences to the ability of the debtor to meet the plan requirements.

12. *Management compensation*. The statement should disclose the identities of top management, a description of their qualifications and their salary levels, if the plan contemplates that the debtor will continue to operate its business after confirma-

Exhibit 5-2   *(Continued)*

tion. Further, the statement should disclose the existence of insiders, as defined by 11 U.S.C. §101(25), and the amount of any claims they are asserting as creditors, and/or whether any or all of their claims have been subordinated.

13.   *Stock issued for debt.* If the debtor issues stock for all or part of its debt, the statement should indicate if such stock is exempt from securities laws under 11 U.S.C. §1145, and should describe the nature of the stock or securities, such as voting rights, interest rate, cumulation of dividends, liquidation preference, potential markets and market values after confirmation, and the existence of other classes of stock.

Source: U.S. Trustee's Office, Central District of California.

U.S. Trustee Evaluation

78   In districts where U.S. trustees are appointed, the disclosure statement will be studied and analyzed by the U.S. trustee and his or her staff. Their objective is not to take a substantive legal position, but to point out at the hearing any discrepancies between the operating data and the data in the disclosure statements. For example, if the U.S. trustee believes that the projections of future operations in the disclosure statement are too high based on prior operating statements issued, this will be pointed out in the hearings. The U.S. trustee will not, most likely, take the position that a disclosure statement is not adequate or misleading. Once the statement is approved by the court, the U.S. trustee will not comment further on it.

Safe Harbor Rule

79   Section 1125(e) provides that a person soliciting acceptance of a plan "in good faith" is not liable for violation of any applicable law, rule, or regulation governing the offer, issuance, sale, or purchase of securities. This provision codified the holdings in the *Ernst and Ernst* v. *Hochfelder*[47] case. The safe harbor rule provides that if the court has approved a disclosure statement indicating that it contains adequate information and meets the requirements of chapter 11, then the creditors, creditors' committee, counsel for committees, and others involved in the case are protected from potential civil and injunctive liability under the securities laws as a result of using the approved statement.

Modification of Plan

80   Only the proponent of a plan may modify the plan at any time before confirmation, provided the plan as modified meets the plan content requirements of sections 1122 and 1123. The modified plan becomes the plan after it

[47] 425 U.S. 185 (1976).

is filed with the court by the proponent. Also, section 1127(c) provides that the proponent of a plan must comply with the disclosure requirement of section 1125. As part of the bargaining process by which the debtor and various classes of creditors reach agreement on the terms of a plan, changes may be made affecting, for example, certain secured classes of claims. It is not uncommon for the holders of unsecured claims and interests to accept the terms of the proposed plan and any modifications that may be made thereafter, as long as the court determines that the rights of these classes are not materially and adversely affected by the modifications.

81 After confirmation, but before substantial consummation (see section 1101(2)), the plan may also be modified by the proponent or the reorganized debtor. The plan as modified must satisfy all of the statutory requirements and be confirmed by the court after notice and hearing.

CONFIRMATION OF PLAN

82 Prior to the confirmation hearing on the proposed plan, the proponents of the plan will seek its acceptance. Once the results of the vote are known, the debtor or other proponent of the plan will request confirmation of the plan.

Acceptance of the Plan

83 The holder of a claim or interest, as defined under section 502, is permitted to vote on the proposed plan. Voting is based on the classification of claims and interests. A major change from prior law is that the acceptance requirements are based on those actually voting and not the total value or number of claims or interests allowed in a particular class. The Secretary of the Treasury is authorized to vote on behalf of the United States when the United States is a creditor or equity security holder.

84 A class of claim holders has accepted a plan if at least two-thirds in amount and more than one-half in number of the allowed claims for that class that are voted are cast in favor of the plan. For equity interests it is only necessary that votes totaling at least two-thirds in amount of the outstanding securities in a particular class that voted are cast for the plan. The majority in number requirement is not applicable to equity interests.[48]

85 Section 1126(e) excludes from the voting results computation any entity whose acceptance or rejection of a plan was not in good faith or was not solicited or procured in good faith. Subsection (f) provides that a class that is not impaired under the plan is presumed to have accepted the plan and solicitation of acceptance is not required.

---

[48] II U.S.C. Sec. 1126(c) and (d).

Confirmation Hearing

86 After notice the court will hold a hearing on confirmation of the plan. A party in interest may object to the confirmation.[49] It is also possible that the SEC may object to a plan's confirmation even though not a party in interest, because the SEC has the right to appear and be heard on any issue in a case under chapter 11.

Confirmation Requirements

87 The requirements that must be satisfied before the court will confirm a plan under chapter 11 are based partly on the requirements of prior law Chapters X and XI; the balance is new. Chapter XI required that the plan be in the best interest of creditors; namely, the creditors had to receive at least as much under the plan of arrangement as they would in liquidation. Chapter X required that the plan observe the "absolute priority" rule: all members of the senior class of creditors must have been satisfied in full before members of the next senior class could receive anything, and the satisfaction of that class before the third senior class, and so on. This meant, of course, that if the corporation was insolvent in the bankruptcy sense, the plan of reorganization did not have to make provision for the stockholders.

88 The new law partially codifies the absolute priority doctrine, but the rest of the test under section 1129(b) is new. In the same manner, the best-interest-of-creditors test is retained, but applied in a different way.

Basic Requirements

89 Section 1129(a), which contains the requirements that must be satisfied before a plan can be confirmed, is one of the most significant sections of the new Code. The first six requirements that must be satisfied before the plan can be confirmed are taken from Chapter X. They insure, among other things, that the plan follows the plan requirements of sections 1122 and 1123 and that the court determines that disclosure was proper. Requirements 7, 8, and 9 are the provisions that require a valuation of the debtor's assets and business and determine how priority creditors are to be paid. They are described in more detail in paragraphs 90–108 along with the cram down provision of section 1129(b). Requirements 10 and 11 contain two additional general provisions. The provisions are listed below:

1 *The plan complies with the applicable provisions of title 11* Section 1122 concerning classification of claims and section 1123 on the content of the plan are two of the significant sections that must be followed.

---

[49] Ibid., Sec. 1128.

2 *The proponents of the plan comply with the applicable provisions of title 11*   Section 1125 on disclosure is an example of a section that is referred to by this requirement.

3 *The plan has been proposed in good faith and not by any means forbidden by law.*

4 *Payments are disclosed*   Any payment made or to be made for services, costs, and expenses in connection with the case or plan has been approved by, or is subject to the approval of the court as reasonable.

5 *Disclosure of officers*   The proponent of the plan must disclose those who are proposed to serve after confirmation as director, officer, or voting trustee of the reorganized debtor. Such employment must be consistent with the interests of creditors and equity security holders and with public policy. Also, names of insiders to be employed and the nature of their compensation must also be disclosed.

6 *Regulatory rate approval* Any governmental regulatory commission that will have jurisdiction over the debtor after confirmation of the plan must approve any rate changes provided for in the plan.

7 *Satisfies the best-interest-of-creditors test*   It is necessary for the creditors or stockholders who do not vote for the plan to receive as much as they would if the business were liquidated under chapter 7. This requirement is discussed in more detail in the "Financial Standards" section below (paragraphs 91–92).

8 *Acceptance by each class*   Each class of creditors or stockholders that is impaired under the plan must accept the plan. Section 1129(b) provides an exception to this requirement and is described in the "Cram Down" section below (paragraphs 96–108).

9 *Treatment of priority claims*   This requirement provides the manner in which priority claims must be satisfied unless the holders agree to a different treatment. (See "Financial Standards" section below, paragraphs 93–95).

10 *Acceptance by at least one class*   If a class of claims is impaired under the plan, at least one class that is impaired, other than a class of claims held by insiders, must accept the plan.

11 *Plan is feasible*   Confirmation of the plan is not likely to be followed by liquidation or the need for further financial reorganization unless such liquidation or reorganization is provided for in the plan. This requirement means that the court must ascertain that the debtor has a reasonable chance of surviving once the plan is confirmed and the debtor is out from under the protection of the court. A well prepared forecast of future operations based on reasonable assumptions, taking into consideration the changes expected as a result of the confirmation of the plan, is an example of the kind of information that can be very helpful to the court in reaching a decision on this requirement.

Financial Standards

90   The heart of section 1129, confirmation of the plan, is requirements 7, 8, and 9 (briefly mentioned above) of subsection (a) and subsection (b) which provide, for a "cram down." These requirements make it necessary under certain conditions to determine the value of the business, either liquidation or going concern values. Since these requirements involve an evaluation of the business, it is important that the accountant fully understand them and the impact they can have. The techniques for determining the value of the business are discussed in chapter 10.

Best Interest of Creditors

91   The first part of requirement 7 is that each holder of a claim or interest in each class must accept the plan or will receive, as of the effective date of the plan, a value that is not less than the amount the holder would receive in a chapter 7 liquidation.[50] Note that the first alternative is that each holder must accept the plan. Thus, if any holder does not vote or votes against acceptance, then it is necessary for the liquidation values to be ascertained. This requirement, in fact, makes it necessary for the court to have some understanding of the liquidation value of the business in practically all chapter 11 cases, since there will almost always be some creditors who do not vote. The extent to which the liquidation values will have to be applied to individual classes other than those of a large number of unsecured claims will depend on the manner in which the claims are divided into classes and whether there are any secured classes with a large number of claims.

92   The second part of the best interest test applies to those holders of secured claims that elected under section 1111(b)(2) to have their entire claim, even though undersecured, considered a secured claim and have not accepted the plan. The best interest test is satisfied here if the holder of such claim will receive under the plan property of value, as of the effective date of the plan, at least equal to the value of the creditor's interest in the debtor's property that secures the claim.[51]

Priority Treatment

93   Requirement 9 states that unless the holder of a priority claim agrees to different treatment, the plan of reorganization must provide:

1 *Administrative expenses and involuntary gap claims*   Cash equal to the allowed amount of the claim must be paid on the effective date of the plan

---

[50] 11 U.S.C. Sec. 1129(a)(7)(A).
[51] Ibid., Sec. 1129(a)(7)(B).

for administrative expenses and involuntary gap claims defined in section 507(a)(1) and (2). These claims are the first and second priorities under the Bankruptcy Code. (See chapter 3, paragraph 98.)

2 *Wages, employee benefits, and individual deposits* Claims of wages up to $2000 per employee, employee benefits up to the extent of the unused wage priority, and individual consumer deposits not to exceed $900 per individual as more specifically defined in section 507(a)(3–5) must receive deferred cash payments. These payments will have a present value as of the effective date of the plan equal to the allowed amount of the claim if the class has accepted the plan. If a class of these types of claims has not accepted the plan, they must receive cash on the effective date of the plan equal to the allowed amount of the claims. These claims are entitled to third, fourth, and sixth priority (fifth priority for petitions filed before October 8, 1984) under the Bankruptcy Code. (See chapter 3, paragraph 98.) The Bankruptcy Amendments and Federal Judgeship Act of 1984 added a priority number five for grain producers' and fishermen's claims (see chapter 3, paragraphs 98–99). The act, however, did not indicate how these claims were to be provided for in the plan. It is presumed that these claims must be provided for in the same manner as are priorities 3, 4, and 6.

3 *Taxes* Tax claims that are entitled to seventh priority (sixth priority for bankruptcy petitions filed before October 8, 1984) in section 507(a)(7) must receive deferred cash payments, over a period not to exceed six years from the date of assessment of the claim, of a value as of the effective date of the plan equal to the allowed amount of the claim. (See chapter 3, paragraph 98).

94 The effective date of the plan should be stated in the plan. The date most likely used is that which is an established number of days after the plan is confirmed, provided there are no appeals from the confirmation hearing. If a plan does not state the effective date and there are objections to the confirmation, confusion may exist as to what should be the effective date. The way to avoid this problem is to set forth clearly in the plan what the effective date will be.

95 These tax priority claim provisions represent a major change from prior law where deferred payments were allowed only if the taxing authority agreed to this provision. Under the Bankruptcy Code tax payments can automatically be deferred. This provision, along with other changes, will mean that less cash will have to be deposited at the time of the confirmation. More immediate cash will then be available to the debtor at a time when operating cash is critical to the ability of the debtor to continue operating the business.

Cram Down[52]

96　As noted in requirement 8, for a plan to be confirmed, a class of claims or interests must either accept the plan or not be impaired. However, subsection (b) of section 1129 allows the court under certain conditions to confirm a plan even though an impaired class has not accepted the plan. The plan must not discriminate unfairly, and must be fair and equitable, with respect to each class of claims or interest impaired under the plan that has not accepted it. The Code states conditions for secured claims, unsecured claims, and stockholder interests that would be included in the "fair and equitable" requirement. It should be noted that since the word "includes" is used, the meaning of fair and equitable is not restricted to these conditions.[53]

Modification of Secured Claims

97　The plan must provide for at least one of the following to be fair and equitable:

1　The holders of such claims must retain the lien securing such claims, whether the property subject to such lien is retained by the debtor or transferred to another entity, to the extent of the allowed amount of such claims (see chapter 10, paragraph 29). In addition each holder of a claim of such class must receive on account of such claim deferred cash payments totaling at least the allowed amount of such claim, of a value, as of the effective date of the plan, of at least the value of such holder's interest in the estate's interest in such property.

2　For the sale, subject to section 363(k), of any property that is subject to the lien securing such claims, free and clear of such lien, with such lien to attach to the proceeds of such sale, and the treatment of such lien on proceeds under clause (1) or (3) of this subparagraph. Or

3　For the realization by such holders of the indubitable equivalent of such claims.[54]

98　To illustrate the treatment of secured claims the following balance sheet based on going concern values is shown:

---

[52] The author acknowledges the contributions of Kenneth N. Klee, Stutman, Treister & Glatt, Los Angeles, California, to this section and chapter 10. For a more detailed discussion of the cram down provision, see Kenneth N. Klee, "All You Ever Wanted to Know About Cram Down Under the New Bankruptcy Code," *American Bankruptcy Law Journal,* Vol. 53 (Spring 1979), pp. 133–171.

[53] See 11 U.S.C. Sec. 102(3).

[54] 11 U.S.C. Sec. 1129(b)(2)(A).

X Corporation
Balance Sheet
Going Concern Values
(million dollars)

Current assets	$ 1	Trade debt (unsecured)	$ 1
Real estate	4	Subordinated notes	2
Other assets	5	Mortgage on real estate	6
		Stockholders' equity	1
Total	$10	Total	$10

99 All of the real estate is mortgaged. The plan proposes to pay the secured creditors $5 million in annual installments of $1 million per year at the beginning of each year. The holders of trade debt and the notes subordinated to trade debt have accepted the plan and the secured creditor has rejected the plan. The stockholders' interest was unaffected by the plan. The secured claim holder did not elect to have the provisions of section 1111(b)(2) apply. The court determined that 20 percent was the appropriate discount rate to use to determine the present value of the payments as of the effective date of the plan. The total present value of the payments is $3.6 million. The judge would not confirm the plan, since none of the three standards are satisfied. The first is not satisfied, even though the amount received is greater than the value of the claim, because the present value of the payments of $3.6 million is less than the value of the creditors' interest in the property of $4 million. If the discount rate were 12 percent, then this requirement would be satisfied since the present value of the payments would equal $4 million. The second requirement is not applicable, since the collateral is not going to be sold. The third requirement would not be satisfied since the value of the payments is less than the claim and could not, thus, be the "indubitable" equivalent.

100 If the interest rate is changed to 12 percent and the creditor has elected to have the provision of section 1111(b)(2) apply, the judge would still not confirm the plan. While the present value of the payments at the 12 percent rate does exceed the value of the property in which the creditor has an interest, the total amount to be received is only $5 million, which is less than the $6 million claim. The total allowed amount of the claim of $6 million is considered secured because of the section 1111(b)(2) election.

101 The third requirement states that the creditor must receive the indubitable equivalent.[55] Legislative history indicates that abandonment of the collateral to the creditor or accepting a lien on similar collateral would satisfy this requirement. However, the receipt of present cash payments less than the secured claims would not satisfy this standard because the creditor

---

[55] This last standard is derived from *In re Murel Holding Corp.*, 75 F.2d 941 (2d Cir. 1935).

is deprived of an opportunity to gain from a future increase in the value of the collateral. Unsecured notes or equity securities of the debtor are not sufficient to constitute the indubitable equivalent of secured claims.[56]

Unsecured Creditors Test

102   For holders of unsecured claims, the Code provides that one of the two following requirements must be satisfied for each class that is impaired and does not accept the plan:

1 The plan provides that each holder of a claim of such class receive or retain on account of such claim property of a value, as of the effective date of the plan, equal to the allowed amount of such claim.
2 The holder of any claim or interest that is junior to the claims of such class will not receive or retain on account of such junior claim or interest any property.[57]

Members of the class must, if they have not accepted the plan, receive or retain property that has a present value equal to the allowed amount of the claim. Alternatively, the plan can contain any provision for a distribution of less than full present value as long as no junior claim or interest will participate in the plan. Implicit in the concept of fairness is that senior classes will not receive more than 100 percent of their claims and any equal class will not receive preferential treatment.

Stockholders' Interest Test

103   The test for equity interests is very similar to the test for unsecured claims. Again, one of two standards must be satisfied for each class that is impaired and does not accept the plan:

1 The plan provides that each holder of an interest of such class receive, or retain on account of such interest, property of a value, as of the effective date of the plan, equal to the greatest of the allowed amount of any fixed liquidation preference to which such holder is entitled, any fixed redemption price to which such holder is entitled, and the value of such interest.
2 The holder of any interest that is junior to the interests of such class will not receive or retain under the plan on account of such junior interest any property.[58]

One major provision in the first standard is that the equity interest must receive the greatest of liquidation preference, fixed redemption price, or the value of its equity. Thus, a corporation could not file a chapter 11 petition

---

[56] 124 Cong. Rec. H 11,103 (September 28, 1978); S 17,420 (October 6, 1978).
[57] 11 U.S.C. Sec. 1129(b)(2)(B).
[58] Ibid., Sec. 1129(b)(2)(C).

just for the purpose of taking advantage of the low liquidation value of preferred stock.

Examples

104   In the example of X Corporation (paragraph 98), assume that the secured creditors have accepted a revised plan that provides for payments that have a present value of $5 million, and the holders of the subordinated notes agree to a settlement of 1.5 million. The trade creditors, who fare worse as the secured mortgagee renegotiated its position, now reject the revised plan as a class. They have to receive full payment of $1 million, since the holders of junior claims (subordinated notes) are receiving something in the plan, and in addition, the debtor is solvent and the stockholders will still have their interest in the corporation.

105   Consider another example with the following changes in the going concern values of the business.

Y Corporation
Balance Sheet
Going Concern Values
(million dollars)

Current assets	$0.5	Trade debt	$ 1.0
Real estate	4.0	Subordinated notes	2.0
Other assets	4.0	Mortgage on real estate	6.0
		Stockholders equity	(0.5)
Total	$8.5	Total	$ 8.5

The plan provided for (1) payment of $5.2 million ($5 million present value) to the secured claim holder that had made an election under section 1111(b)(2); (2) subordinated holders to receive 25 percent of the stock of the company plus cash payments with a present value of $1 million; (3) the trade creditors to receive $0.8 million; and (4) the common stockholders to retain a 75 percent equity. In all the plan provided for payments with a present value of $6.8 million plus 100 percent of the stock of the reorganized debtor.

106   Under these terms the secured claim, trade debt, and subordinated note holders classes must each approve the plan before the court could confirm the plan. Secured and trade creditors are receiving less than the value of their claim. Since the stockholders are retaining value (75 percent interest in the corporation), the subordinated note holders must assent or receive values in property equal to their claim of $2 million. They are receiving only $1.425 million according to the following calculations (in millions):

Present value of cash			$1.000
Value of equity interest:			
Total equity after confirmation:			
Total going concern value		$8.5	
Debt after confirmation			
Trade	$0.8		
Subordinated notes	1.0		
Mortgage	5.0	6.8	
Total equity		1.7	
Percent allocated to subordinated			
claim holders		×0.25	
Total value of equity			0.425
Total value of amount received by			
subordinated note holders			$1.425

Based on the above calculation it would be necessary for the holders of the subordinated notes to receive approximately 60 percent ownership of the stock to meet the cram down requirements.

107   Under the specified requirements for fair and equitable plan of reorganization, it is not necessary that the stockholders receive anything, but a class of creditors should not receive more than 100 percent. If the secured creditor and trade creditors accept the plan as proposed and receive property valued at $5.8 million, leaving the balance of property having a present value of $1 million and 100 percent stock for the holders of the subordinate notes the plan would not be confirmed. The subordinated note holders are receiving more than 100 percent, and this would not satisfy the general requirements of section 1129(b)(1), which states that the plan must not discriminate unfairly and must be fair and equitable. The court would most likely rule that granting the holders of subordinated claims more than 100 percent payment while giving stockholders nothing would not satisfy this requirement.[59]

108   Before any decision can be made about satisfying the cram down requirements, it is necessary to determine the value of the debtor's business. The process used to determine these values is discussed in chapter 10.

Required Deposits

109   Under Chapter XI of prior law it was necessary for the debtor to make a deposit equal to the amount of cash that was to be paid out under the

---

[59] If the stockholders retained the difference of the proposed consideration under the plan, namely 40 percent of their former interest in the corporation, of if they were given any interest and approved the plan, the court could confirm the plan. Section 1126(g) provides that a class receiving nothing cannot accept the plan.

plan of arrangement. The only claims that currently require cash payment at the date the plan of reorganization is confirmed are administrative expense and involuntary gap claims. Taxes (sixth priority) can be deferred, since the only requirement is that the present value of payments (not to exceed six years from date of assessment) must equal the amount of the claim (paragraph 93). The other priority claims can be deferred, although generally they are paid in full, provided the holders accept the plan; otherwise full cash payment at the effective date of the plan will be required. The amount of cash required to be deposited (or paid at the effective date of the plan) is generally less under the new law. Viable businesses that, under prior law, were required to be liquidated because they could not raise the cash required for the deposit may now be allowed to continue operating.[60] Bankruptcy Rule 3020(a) provides that the court may order the deposit of the consideration required to be distributed under the plan prior to the order confirming the plan. The money deposited is to be kept in a special account established for the purpose of making the distribution.

POST CONFIRMATION

110   The confirmation is binding on all creditors and stockholders, even though they did not accept the plan, were impaired under the plan, or were not dealt with in the plan. The confirmation of the plan, unless provided otherwise in the plan or order confirming the plan, vests all of the property of the estate in the debtor. All of the property is free and clear of all claims and interests of creditors, stockholders, general partners in the debtor, unless the plan or order confirming the plan provides differently.[61]

Distribution

111   Section 1143 provides that if a plan requires presentment or surrender of a security or the performance of any other act as a condition to participation in the distribution, such action must be taken within five years after the order for confirmation. Any entity that fails to follow this provision may not participate in the distribution. For example, if it is determined that a junior lienholder has no secured claim due to the low value of the property pledged, it may be required that the lienholder deliver a release of the lien before that lienholder can receive a distribution as an unsecured creditor. The lien must be released within the five-year period in order for the lienholder to receive the distribution.

112   Bankruptcy Rule 3021 states that the distribution to creditors whose claims are allowed and to holders of stock, bonds, debentures, notes, and

[60] Trost, p. 1343.
[61] 11 U.S.C. Sec. 1141.

other securities whose claims or equity interest security interest are allowed is to be made after the plan is confirmed.

Discharge of Debts

113   The new law provides for the discharge of debts in a manner similar to the provisions in Chapter X of prior law. Unless the plan is a liquidating plan, all claims and interests of the corporate debtor are discharged (unless provided otherwise in the plan) whether or not a proof of claim was filed, whether or not the claim is allowed, and whether or not the holder of the claim has accepted the plan. Thus, the obtaining of credit by a corporation through the use of false financial statements will not result in the denial of a discharge. If, on the other hand, the debtor is an individual, all the provisions of section 523, including the use of false financial statements, that can prevent the debtor from obtaining a discharge of certain types of claims, apply in a chapter 11 case (chapter 3, paragraphs 104–106).

Securities Law Exemption

114   Section 5 of the Securities Act of 1933 requires Securities of publicly held companies to be registered with the SEC prior to their sale or offer for sale. The Bankruptcy Code provides for exemptions from section 5 of the 1933 Act for chapter 11 companies. Section 1145(a) states:

a   Except with respect to an entity that is an underwriter as defined in subsection (b) of this section, section 5 of the Securities Act of 1933 (15 U.S.C. 77e) and any State or local law requiring registration for offer or sale of a security or registration or licensing of any issuer of, underwriter of, or broker or dealer in, a security does not apply to—

  1   the offer or sale under a plan of a security of the debtor, of an affiliate participating in a joint plan with the debtor, or of a successor to the debtor under the plan—

  A   in exchange for a claim against, an interest in, or a claim for an administrative expense in the case concerning, the debtor or such affiliate; or

  B   principally in such exchange and partly for cash or property;

  2   the offer of a security through any warrant, option, right to subscribe, or conversion privilege that was sold in the manner specified in paragraph (1) of this subsection, or the sale of a security upon the exercise of such a warrant, option, right, or privilege;

  3   the offer or sale, other than under a plan, of a security of an issuer other than the debtor or an affiliate, if—

  A   such security was owned by the debtor on the date of filing of the petition;

  B   the issuer of such security is—

    i   required to file reports under Section 13 or 15(d) of the Securities Exchange Act of 1934 (15 U.S.C. 78m or 780(d)); and

       ii   in compliance with the disclosure and reporting provision of such applicable section; and

   C   such offer or sale is of securities that do not exceed—

       i   during the two-year period immediately following the date of the filing of the petition, four percent of the securities of such class outstanding on such date; and

       ii   during any 180-day period following such two-year period, one percent of the securities outstanding at the beginning of such 180-day period; or

4   a transaction by a stockbroker in a security that is executed after a transaction of a kind specified in paragraph (1) or (2) of this subsection in such security and before the expiration of 40 days after the first date on which such security was bona fide offered to the public by the issuer or by or through an underwriter, if such stockbroker provides, at the time of or before such transaction by such stockbroker, a disclosure statement approved under section 1125 of this title, and, if the court orders, information supplementing such disclosure statement.

115   This exception is available only if the securities are not offered or sold by or through an underwriter. Note that the exchange must be *principally* for a claim against or an interest in the debtor or an affiliate. Thus, the issuance of securities in exchange for cash or some other form of consideration would not be exempted. The Code does, however, allow for securities to be issued for administrative expenses in the case. The exchange by an interest holder involving stock plus cash when the debtor is insolvent may still be opposed by the SEC.[62] Subsection (2) of 1145(a) also exempts the offering of a security through any warrant, option, right to subscribe, or conversion privilege sold in the manner described above. The Code also provides that the sale of a security upon the exercise of any warrant, option, right, or privilege is not subject to section 5 of the 1933 Act.

116   Section 1145(a)(3) also exempts from section 5 of the Securities Act of 1933 the sale of portfolio securities owned by the debtor on the date the petition was filed. To be exempted the distribution of securities within a two-year period subsequent to the date of the petition must not exceed 4 percent of the securities of that class outstanding at the date the petition was filed. Furthermore, subsequent distributions are allowed provided they do not exceed 1 percent during any 180-day period. The exemption is limited to securities of a company that is required to file reports under sections 13 and 15(d) of the 1934 Act and is in compliance with the disclosure and reporting provisions of the appropriate section. While SEC Rule 148 was issued prior

---

[62] Phelan and Cheatham, p. 418. See *SEC* v. *Bloomberg*, 229 F.2d 315, 319 (1st Cir. (1962); Comment, "The Issuance of Securities in Reorganizations and Arrangements Under the Bankruptcy Act and The Proposed Bankruptcy Act," *Ohio State Law Journal*, Vol. 36 (Number 2, 1975), pp. 380, 392.

to section 1145 becoming law, it still provides guidance on the issuance of portfolio securities in situations not covered by section 1145(a)(3).

117 Section 1145(a)(1) also provides that a successor to the debtor is exempted from the securities laws in the same manner that a debtor would be. Transactions of a stock during a forty-day period following the initial offer of the security under the plan are also exempt. Section 1145(a)(4) does provide that as a condition for the exemption the stockbroker must provide a copy of the disclosure statement required under section 1125 or other supplementary information that the court may require at the time of or before the transaction.

Resale of Securities

118 Section 1145(b) specifies the standards under which a creditor, equity security holder, or other entities acquiring the securities under the plan of reorganization may resell them. Since the 1933 Act limits the sales by underwriters, section 1145(b) exempts from the definition of an underwriter those who receive securities in a reorganization with four exceptions. A person who performs the following would be considered an underwriter:

1   Acquires a claim against, an interest in, or claim for an administrative expense in the case concerning the debtor with a view to distribution.

2   Offers to sell securities offered or sold under the plan for the holder of the securities.

3   Offers to buy securities offered or sold under the plan for the holder of the securities, if the offer to buy is made with a view to distribution and under an agreement made in connection with the plan.

4   Is an issuer within the meaning of section 2(11) of the 1933 Act.

Section 1145(b)(1) provides that an entity is not an underwriter with respect to ordinary trading transactions of an entity that is not an issuer. Also section 1145(b)(2) provides that an entity that issues stock for debt or for administrative expenses is not an underwriter.

119 Section 1145(c) makes an exempted offer or sale of securities under the chapter 11 plan a public offering to avoid its being characterized as a private placement that would result in restrictions under Rule 144 of the SEC on the resale of the securities.[63]

120 The last provision (subsection d) of section 1145, provides that the Trust Indenture Act of 1939 does not apply to a commercial note issued under the plan that matures within one year after the effective date of the plan.

---

[63] House Report No. 95–595, 95th Cong., 1st Sess. (1977) 421.

Final Decree

121   Bankruptcy Rule 3022 provides that after an estate is fully administered, including distribution of any deposit required by the plan, the court is to enter a final decree discharging the trustee, if appointed, and close the estate. The Advisory Committee Note indicates that the provision in section 1143 that places a five-year limitation on the surrender of securities when required for participation under a plan should not delay the entry of the final decree (see paragraph 111).

Conversion to Chapter 7

122   Section 112(a) provides that a debtor may voluntarily convert the chapter 11 case to chapter 7 unless a trustee has been appointed, the case originally was commenced as an involuntary chapter 11, or the case was converted to a chapter 11 other than on the debtor's request. The court may also convert the case to chapter 7 after notice and a hearing. Sections 1112(c) and (e) provide two exceptions to the general rule. Subsection (c) states that if the debtor is a farmer or a corporation that is not a moneyed, business, or commercial corporation, the debtor must consent to the conversion. Also, as provided in subsection (e), the court could not convert a case unless the debtor may be a debtor under chapter 7. Thus, a railroad case could not be converted since a railroad cannot file under chapter 7.

123   There are nine reasons stated in section 1112 that are given as reasons why a court may convert a chapter 11 case to chapter 7. They are:

1. Continuing loss to or diminution of the estate and absence of a reasonable likelihood of rehabilitation.
2. Inability to effectuate a plan.
3. Unreasonable delay by the debtor that is prejudicial to creditors.
4. Failure to propose a plan under section 1121 of title 11 within any time fixed by the court.
5. Denial of confirmation of every proposed plan and denial of *a request made for* additional time for filing another plan or a modification of a plan.
6. Revocation of an order of confirmation under section 1144 of title 11, and denial of confirmation of another plan or a modified plan under section 1129 of title 11.
7. Inability to effectuate substantial consummation of a confirmed plan.
8. Material default by the debtor with respect to a confirmed plan.
9. Termination of a plan by reason of the occurrence of a condition specified in the plan.

124   In addition to the above, a common ground for conversion is that there is a lack of good faith on the part of the debtor that constitutes an abuse of the court's jurisdiction.[64] There are also other grounds for conversion such as the failure of the debtor to maintain business records.[65]

125   Bankruptcy Rule 2002(a)(5) provides that all creditors, equity security holders, and indenture trustees must receive at least twenty days' notice by mail of a hearing to dismiss or to convert a chapter 11 case to chapter 7.

126   The conversion does not change the filing date of the bankruptcy case. The sixty-day period for the decision to assume or reject a lease in a chapter 7 case begins on the date the order transferring the case is entered. The services of a trustee or examiner are terminated prior to conversion.[66] Also, all claims incurred after the chapter 11 petition but before the conversion was filed that are not administrative expenses will be considered pre-petition claims. Administrative expenses, including accounting fees, incurred after the conversion to chapter 7 have priority over those incurred during the period the debtor operated under chapter 11.

ADVANTAGES AND DISADVANTAGES OF CHAPTER 11

127   Chapter 11 proceedings may be more appropriate under certain conditions than informal settlements made out of court:

Rather than near unanimous approval, majority approval in number and two-thirds in amount of allowed claims of creditors voting is sufficient to accept a plan of reorganization and bind dissenters.

Creditors bargain collectively with the debtor that may result in more equitable treatment of the members of each class of claims or interest.

The debtor's assets are in the custody of the court and safe from attack when the petition is filed.

Executory contracts and leases can be canceled when such action benefits the debtor and can be assumed or assigned when this action benefits the debtor.

The creditors have an opportunity to investigate the debtor and its business affairs.

Certain preferential and fraudulent transfers can be avoided by the debtor in possession or trustee.

Proper protection can be provided to holders of public securities.

Certain tax advantages are available under the Bankruptcy Code.

Creditors are additionally protected by the requirements that to be con-

---

[64] *Collier Bankruptcy Manual*, 3rd ed., para 1112.04[2][d][ix].
[65] *In re Larmar Estates, Inc.*, 3 C.B.C. 2d 218 (B. Ct. E.D.N.Y. 1980).
[66] 11 U.S.C. Sec. 348(e).

firmed by the court the plan must be in the best interests of creditors, be feasible, be fair and equitable to any impaired, dissenting classes, and provide for priority claims.

128 The major disadvantages of this method of rehabilitation are that it is more time-consuming and more costly, often resulting in smaller dividends to creditors.

CHAPTER 13: ADJUSTMENT OF DEBTS OF AN INDIVIDUAL WITH REGULAR INCOME

129 The Bankruptcy Reform Act of 1978 changed Chapter XIII of the Bankruptcy Act to make it more attractive for individual owners of small businesses. Prior to the new law only employees (wage earners) were allowed to file according to the provisions of the Bankruptcy Act. In addition, some courts allowed pension fund or Social Security recipients, and some self-employed individuals such as carpenters to seek relief under Chapter XIII while other courts interpreted the act very narrowly, allowing only employees to file a petition. The objective of chapter 13 is to provide individuals with some alternative other than liquidation when in financial trouble. Chapter 13 allows the individual, with court supervision, to work out a plan that can provide for full or partial payment of debts over an extended period of time similar in concept to a chapter 11 reorganization but on a less formalized and more practical scale.

Filing of Petition

130 Section 109(e) provides that only an individual with regular income that owes, at the time the petition is filed, noncontingent, liquidated, unsecured debts of less than $100,000 and noncontingent, liquidated, secured debts of less than $350,000 can file a petition under chapter 13. The definition of regular income requires that individuals filing the petition must have sufficient stable and reliable income to enable them to make payments under the chapter 13 plan. The limit on amount of indebtedness will prevent some wage earners from filing a petition. The purpose, however, of this limitation was to allow some small sole proprietors to file under this chapter, since the filing of a chapter 11 petition might be too cumbersome for them, and require the larger individually owned businesses to use chapter 11.

131 Stockbrokers and commodity brokers are prohibited from filing under this chapter, as are partnerships and corporations. Individual partners may, however, file a petition. Section 302(a) provides that joint petition can be filed by husband and wife. A small business owned by both husband and wife that is classified as a partnership would be excluded from filing a chapter 13 petition. It is also not necessary that there be a formal written partnership agreement between the husband and wife for the arrangement to be considered a partnership. The determination of the states of the husband and wife will to some extent depend on whether the assets of the business are for the benefit of all creditors of the debtor or only for business creditors. The mere fact that husband and wife are joint owners of property and joint obligers does not establish that they constitute a partnership.[67]

132   The debtor may voluntarily convert a case from chapter 13 to chapter 11 or chapter 7 and the creditors may petition a court to transfer a chapter 13 case to chapter 11 or chapter 7 for all businesses except for farmers.[68]

Operation of Business

133   Section 1304 provides that the debtor in a chapter 13 case will be allowed to continue to operate the business unless the court orders otherwise. In addition, the debtor has the responsibility of an operating trustee to file the necessary reports and other required information with the appropriate taxing authorities (see chapter 3, paragraph 148). To operate the business, it is necessary for the debtor to have control over its property. Section 1306(b) provides that the debtor remains in possession of all the property of the estate. The Bankruptcy Code also provides that the property of the estate includes, in addition to the property as of the date the petition was filed, all property acquired after the commencement of the case and earnings from services rendered before the case is closed.[69]

134   A trustee will be appointed in chapter 13 business cases. In districts which warrant it, a standing trustee may be appointed to handle all chapter 13 cases. Because of the amount of work that may be involved in the business cases, separate trustees may be appointed or the standing trustee may employ an accountant and attorney to assist in the performance of the required duties. As was mentioned above, the debtor remains in possession of the property and title is not transferred to the chapter 13 trustee. The principal function of the chapter 13 trustee is to collect payments under the plan and distribute them to the creditors. The duties were, however, expanded to include most of the functions of a trustee in a chapter 7 or 11 case except reporting to taxing authorities and taking possession of the debtor's assets. The trustee will conduct an investigation into the acts, conduct, assets, liabilities, and financial condition of a business debtor and file a report with the court regarding the result of the examination.[70]

The Plan

135   Only the debtor can file a plan in a chapter 13 case. The requirements for a plan in chapter 13 are much more flexible and lenient than those

---

[67] H.R. Rep. NO. 95–595, 95th Cong., 1st Sess. (1977) 198.
[68] 11 U.S.C. Sec. 1307.
[69] Ibid., 1306(a).
[70] Ibid., Sec. 1302(c).

in chapter 11. In fact, there are only three requirements set forth in the Code that must be met.[71] First, the debtor must submit to the supervision and control of the trustee all or such part of the debtor's future earnings as is necessary for the execution of the plan. Second, the plan must provide for full payment, in deferred cash payments, of all priority claims, unless the creditors agree to a different treatment. Third, where creditors are divided into classes, the same treatment must apply to all claims in a particular class.

136 The plan can alter the rights of secured creditors with an interest in real or personal property, but there are a few restrictions. A claim secured only by a security interest in real property that is the debtor's principal residence cannot be modified. Section 1325(a)(5) also provides that a lien secured by the debtor's property is to be retained by the holder of the secured claim in situations where the creditor does not approve the plan. Secured claims with liens on property of less value than the claim may be paid as a secured claim to the extent of the value of the property and as an unsecured claim for the balance. Once the amount set forth under the plan has been paid, it may be possible for the debtor to obtain an order from the court directing the lienholder to release the lien.[72] The Bankruptcy Code also permits the plan to provide for the curing of a default (such as payments on long-term mortgage debt) within a reasonable time and to make payments while the case is pending on any claim where the last payment is due after the date that the last payment under the plan is due.

137 The trustee has the power to assume or reject any executory contracts or unexpired leases under section 365(d)(2) and, if no action is taken by the trustee, the debtor may include a provision in the plan for the assumption or rejection of such contracts.[73]

138 The plan cannot provide for payments that exceed three years unless the court, for cause, approves for a longer time period. The court cannot, however, approve a time period for repayment that is longer than five years.[74] Section 1326(a) provides that unless the court orders otherwise the debtor is to start making payments under the proposed plan within thirty days after it is filed. The payments are to be retained by the trustee until the plan is confirmed. Upon confirmation, the trustee will distribute the payments in accordance with the plan. If the plan is not confirmed the trustee is to return the payments to the debtor after deducting all unpaid priority claims, including administrative expenses.

Confirmation of Plan

139 In order for the court to confirm the plan it must meet seven separate requirements.[75]

---

[71] Ibid., Sec. 1322(a).
[72] Joe Lee, "Chapter 13 née Chapter XIII," *American Bankruptcy Law Journal,* Vol. 53 (Fall 1979), p. 314.
[73] 11 U.S.C. Sec. 1322(b)(7).
[74] Ibid., 1322(c).
[75] Ibid., 1325.

1   Provisions must comply with chapter 13 and other applicable provisions of the Bankruptcy Code.

2   Required bankruptcy fees must be paid.

3   The plan must have been proposed in good faith.

4   Value, at the effective date, of property to be distributed under the plan to the unsecured creditors must not be less than the amount they would have received under a chapter 7 liquidation.

5   The holder of secured claims must (a) accept the plan or (b) must retain the lien securing the property and the value, as of the effective date of the plan, of property to be distributed on account of such claim must not be less than the allowed amount of the claim, or the debtor must surrender the property securing the claim to such holder.

6   The debtor must be able to make all payments under the plan and comply with the plan.

7   Section 1325(b) provides that if the trustee or a holder of an allowed unsecured claim objects to the confirmation of the plan, the court may not approve the plan unless, as of the effective date of the plan, the value of the property to be distributed to satisfy such claim is at least equal to the amount of this claim or the plan provides that the debtor's disposable income to be received during the three-year period following the due date of the first payment be applied to make payments under the plan. Disposable income includes income received by the debtor less the amount needed for the support of debtor and his or her dependents plus, if engaged in business, the amount necessary for the continuation, preservation, and operation of the business.

140   There are some major differences from chapter 11 in getting a plan confirmed under chapter 13. Note that the provisions above do not require that the creditors, either secured or unsecured, affirmatively approve the plan. Creditors may, however, object if their claim is not paid in full and the plan does not include disposable income of the debtor (see paragraph 141). The court must determine that the unsecured creditors will receive at least as much under the plan as they would in a chapter 7 liquidation. The unsecured creditors may, however, object to the confirmation of the plan under section 1324. Some possible reasons for their objection could be:

1   The plan was not proposed in good faith.

2   The plan as proposed is discriminatory in the way creditors' claims are classified.[76]

3   Creditors within the same class are unequally treated.

4   The plan does not satisfy the best-interest-of-creditors test.

---

[76] Lee, p. 319.

141 If the holders of secured claims do not accept the plan as required by section 1325(9)(5)(A), the court must see that the creditors retain a lien securing the property and the value to be distributed must be at least equal to the allowed claim, or that the debtor surrender the property as explained above. The amount of the allowed claim is determined as of the date of confirmation of the plan to insure that the creditor's claim will not be affected by a decline in the value of the collateral during the period of consummation of the plan. (See chapter 10 paragraph 19 for a discussion of the approaches used to value the property in a chapter 13 proceeding.)

Discharge of Debts

142 After completion of payments under the plan, the debtor is entitled to a discharge from all debts disallowed or provided for in the plan. The only exceptions are alimony, maintenance, or child support payments; certain long-term secured claims which will not be exhausted within the duration of the plan; and claims for postpetition consumer goods or services necessary for performance under the plan. This last exception would occur when the creditor failed to get prior approval of the trustee for the obligation and as a result it was disallowed.[77] Thus, the use of chapter 13 can result in the debtor obtaining discharge of debts that could not be obtained under a chapter 7 liquidation or a chapter 11 reorganization. (See chapter 3, paragraphs 104–106 and chapter 5, paragraph 113.) Under a chapter 11 plan the debtor is discharged upon confirmation, but under chapter 13 the debtor will not earn a discharge until all payments are made under the plan.

143 The debtor can apply for a hardship discharge under certain conditions where payments required under the plan cannot be made. However, any discharge obtained is subject to the same exceptions to discharge in section 523 that apply to a chapter 7 liquidation.[78] In order for a hardship discharge to be granted, the court must determine that the failure of the debtor to complete payments was due to circumstances arising after confirmation for which the debtor was not responsible, each unsecured claim holder received at least as much as would have been received under a chapter 7 liquidation as of the effective date of the plan, and modification of the plan is impracticable.[79]

Use of Chapter 13 by Business

144 Individuals owning businesses that can file in either chapter 13 or chapter 11 may find some advantages to using chapter 13. Merrick lists the following factors which might cause chapter 13 to be more appealing:

---

[77] 11 U.S.C. Sec. 1328.
[78] Ibid., Sec. 523.
[79] Ibid., Sec. 1328(b).

1 Chapter 13 has much less creditor involvement. In chapter 11, creditors' committees have the right to consult the debtor regarding the administration of the estate, the creditors have the right to participate in the formulation of the plan, they can request a trustee or examiner be appointed, and the creditors and their committee have the right to raise any issue and appear and be heard in regard to it.

2 In chapter 11, the debtor runs the risk of a trustee being appointed. In chapter 13, there is a standing trustee, but the debtor will operate the business.

3 A chapter 13 debtor must seek approval only from holders of secured claims while in chapter 11 approval from both secured and unsecured claim holders is necessary.

4 A disclosure statement containing adequate information is not required in chapter 13.

5 Confirmation of the plan may be more difficult in chapter 11. The section 1111(b) election is not available in chapter 13. Protection for unsecured creditors is not as inflexible in chapter 13 as in chapter 11 (section 1129(b)(2)).

6 Chapter 11 offers more opportunities for the debtor to find himself controlled by third parties. Under certain conditions, creditors can file plans in chapter 11 whereas only the debtor can file a chapter 13 plan. Chapter 13 offers greater opportunities for the debtor to make the critical decision to convert the case to liquidation and fewer reasons to allow a party in interest to request an involuntary dismissal of the case or conversion to liquidation.

7 Chapter 13 has a more comprehensive discharge provision (paragraphs 142–143).[80]

145 An analysis of the first years of the new law in one district indicates that most small businesses are not using chapter 13 to the extent visualized by some. One of the problems with a chapter 13 case is that a fee must be paid to the standing trustee, even though the debtor continues to operate the business. In chapter 11, this fee would not be required. In fact, some chapter 13 cases have been converted to chapter 11 to avoid these costs. Chapter 13 is, however, being used by small businesses where the unsecured creditors are not going to receive anything. In order to confirm a plan of this type, the judge needs only to ascertain that the creditors would not receive anything if the debtor were liquidated under chapter 7, providing it is determined that the plan was proposed in good faith. The Bankruptcy Amendments and Federal Judgeship Act of 1984 has made it more difficult for debtors to obtain a discharge in chapter 13 under these conditions, by allowing the creditors to

[80] Glenn Warren Merrick, "Chapter 13 of the Bankruptcy Reform Act of 1978," *Denver Law Journal,* Vol. 56 (1979), pp. 620–623.

object to the confirmation if the debtor's disposable income is not included in the plan (see paragraph 140). The extent, of course, to which bankruptcy judges continue to confirm plans where the unsecured creditors receive nothing will determine how much chapter 13 will be used by businesses. A majority of the bankruptcy courts that have considered the good faith requirement have concluded that chapter 13 plans must offer substantial and meaningful payments.[81]

[81] "News and Comments," *Bankruptcy Court Decisions,* Vol. 6 (July 17, 1980), p. A-65.

PART THREE

Accounting Services

Retention of the Accountant and Fees

1 Because there are several ways of coping with financial difficulties and many different parties are involved, accountants have many avenues by which they may become involved in bankruptcy and insolvency proceedings. This chapter sets forth the ways in which the accountant may be retained and describes the procedures related to retention and to the determination of fees.

2 The retention of an accountant by the bankruptcy court, trustee, creditors' committee, or debtor in possession must be by order of the court, which also issues notice on the amount of fees or the rate to be used. The accountant prepares an affidavit setting forth the scope of the services to be rendered and the estimated time and costs required for such services. Based on this affidavit, counsel for trustee, creditors' committee, or debtor in possession prepares an application for retention and submits it to the court. If the court approves the retention, it will enter an order, confirm the scope of the services to be performed, and set the compensation for such services. An accountant may also be retained to render services for a debtor company that has not formally petitioned the court. In this situation the accountant will obtain a signed engagement letter similar in format to that of the usual engagement letter; however, provision for a cash retainer and/or alternate sources of payment should be arranged if possible.

3 The accountant must keep adequate time and performance records while services are being rendered. Even in out-of-court settlements, the unexpected need to file a bankruptcy court proceeding should not find the accountant unprepared to justify his or her services. After the services have been rendered the accountant files a petition for compensation in affidavit form with the bankruptcy court. The petition should contain enough information about the services rendered so the court may evaluate and compare them with the services authorized in the order of retention. After the hearings, if required, the judge will fix the exact compensation which the accountant will receive.

RETENTION OF THE ACCOUNTANT

The Accountant's Role in the Proceedings

4 Usually the accountant becomes a party to the proceedings through retention by a creditors' committee, while serving a client who is headed for financial trouble, or through appointment by a trustee or assignee. In a voluntary reorganization under chapter 11 of the Bankruptcy Code, the debtor normally remains in possession and has the right to retain an accountant for necessary accounting functions. The creditors' committee may desire the services of an accountant, rather than using the information provided by the debtor's accountant, to inquire into the affairs of the debtor prior to insolvency and to aid the committee in developing a plan. In large cases where several committees are formed, each committee of creditors and/or stockholders may retain its own accountants. The trustee may also need the services of an accountant. (See chapter 1, paragraphs 9–14.)

Retention Procedure—Formal

5 The retention of an accountant for the trustee must be by order of the court and is granted upon the application of the trustee, which must show among other things the necessity for such retention.

6 Section 327(a) provides that the trustee "with the court's approval, may employ one or more attorneys, accountants, appraisers, auctioneers, or other professional persons . . . to represent or assist the trustee in carrying out the trustee's duties under this title." This requirement also applies to an accountant employed by a debtor in possession. An accountant who is not an employee cannot generally (see paragraph 8) be employed by a trustee or debtor in possession except upon an order of the court expressly fixing the amount of the compensation or the rate by which it is to be measured. Thus the accountant should not consider the engagement confirmed until the court has signed an order authorizing the retention, and since compensation must come from the debtor's estate, authorization must be in advance by written order of the court fixing the rate or measure of compensation. Section 1107(b) provides that accountants or other professionals are not disqualified for employment by a chapter 11 debtor solely because of such employment by or representation of the debtor prior to filing the petition.

7 Section 328(c) adds to the requirement by stating that the person must be a disinterested person and, under section 101(13), a creditor cannot be a disinterested person. This requirement might be interpreted to mean that if the accountant for the creditors' committee has unpaid fees as a result of rendering services for the debtor prior to the proceedings, such accountant is not disinterested and could be denied payment. In situations where this problem exists, the accountant should be sure the court is aware of the unpaid fees before the retention order is issued. In most bankruptcy courts, judges will not generally refuse to appoint the debtor's prior accountant solely because there are unpaid fees. There are, however, a few judges who do object.

8 The trustee or debtor in possession applies for the retention of an accountant by filing an application with the bankruptcy judge having jurisdiction. Included in the application are the facts of the case, reasons why an accountant is necessary, the name and address of the proposed accountant, a statement alleging that the particular accountant is qualified to perform such services and has no adverse interest in doing so, the hourly rates of the accountant and his or her associates, and an estimate of the total cost to the debtor's estate for his or her services.

9 Section 327(b) provides that if the trustee or debtor in possession is authorized to operate the business in a chapter 7 or chapter 11 proceeding and if the debtor has regularly employed attorneys, accountants, or other professional persons on salary, the trustee may retain or replace such professional persons if necessary to operate the business. The debtor in possession would also have this same right in a chapter 11 proceeding. While section 327(b) allows an accountant under restricted conditions to receive payments for services rendered without an order from the court, it is still advisable for the accountant to obtain court approval. The application for retention may state that the accountant is retained under the provision of section 327(b) to render periodic (monthly, quarterly, and so forth) accounting services. The application for retention may also request that the accountant be compensated at the firm's normal fee rates (current rates are then attached to the application) on completion of each periodic assignment. According to section 327(d), the court may also authorize the trustee to act as attorney or accountant for the estate if such action is in the best interest of the estate.

Creditor's Committee

10 Section 1103 grants the creditors' committee the right to employ, with court approval, accountants or other professionals to render services. This section does not require that the accountants or other professionals employed or retained by the creditors' committee be totally disinterested persons as defined by section 158 of Chapter X of the former Bankruptcy Act. However, if the person employed is to be compensated for the services rendered and reimbursed for expenses incurred, such person, according to section 328(c), must be a disinterested person as defined by section 101(13) and must not represent or hold an interest adverse to the interest of the estate during the period of employment. It was noted in paragraph 6 that section 1107(b) provides a limited exception to this policy by stating that a professional person is not disqualified from employment by a debtor simply because the person represented the debtor prior to the commencement of the case. In order to reduce the costs of having two accountants, under prior law the debtor's accountant was, at times, appointed to represent the creditors' committee. This practice has generally ceased under the Bankruptcy Code. Bankruptcy judges may, however, allow the debtor's accountant to provide information for the creditor's committee to avoid the cost of the committee having its own accountant, provided this procedure does not create a conflict of interest problem for the debtor's accountant. If a conflict of interest does arise, the court may at that time appoint an accountant for the creditor's committee. Section 1103(b) provides that a person appointed to represent a creditor's committee may not at the same time represent any other entity having an adverse interest in connection with the case. This section further provides that representation of one or more creditors of the same class as represented by the committee does not per se constitute the representation of an adverse interest. If the accountant for a creditor of the debtor is asked to become the accountant for the creditors' committee, care must be taken to disclose the prior representations and to consider if it is possible to serve as accountant to that creditor and comply with the requirement of section 1103(b) that the accountant for the creditors' committee may not represent any other entity having an adverse interest in connection with the case.

Affidavit of Proposed Accountant

11 Once the accountant is selected, it is then necessary to obtain authorization by the court through an order for retention. This requires that the accountant make a preliminary survey of the debtor's books, records, and affairs and use the survey's findings to compose a letter under oath addressed to the trustee or debtor in possession and containing the following information:

> The accounting firm's name and address, and, generally, the name of the specific accountant (normally a partner) asking to be retained.
>
> Nature of any relationship or business association of the accountant with the debtor, the creditors, the attorneys, or any other party to the proceedings (normally in the form of a disclaimer of any type of business association).
>
> The qualifications of the accountant, including any indication of past experience in bankruptcy and insolvency proceedings.
>
> A statement as to whether the accountant has already rendered services to the debtor or trustee and whether he has a claim against the estate.
>
> A statement that a preliminary survey of the bankrupt's books and records has been completed and that the accountant is familiar with their general contents (not necessary in all cases, especially when the accountant is not required to estimate the total cost of the services).
>
> A description of the extent and nature of the services expected to be rendered.
>
> An estimate of the time to be expended on the audit, broken down by class of employee and hourly billing rate.
>
> A request for retention for a maximum amount based on the estimate of hours and the stated billing rates (some judges do not require a maximum amount.)
>
> The accountant's notarized signature (or executed under pains and penalty of perjury).

In addition to the above, some judges may require a statement that no other agreement exists between the accountant and any other party to share compensation awarded to the accountant. The information described above is the type of information normally found in the affidavit. It should, however, be realized that some judges will not require all of the information. For example, some judges will authorize the retention based on the billing rates only, without requiring a maximum amount. However, the Administrative

Office of the United States Courts has requested that all orders authorizing the employment of accountants specifically state the hourly rates to be charged and a maximum allowance. The accountant should check with the debtor's counsel (or creditors' committee) if there is some question about the practices in the district where the retention is being requested.

12 An example of the type of information generally presented in the affidavit is shown in Exhibit 6-1. Again, it should be realized that this example includes much more detail than is required by many bankruptcy courts. In some cases judges do not require a detailed list of the services to be rendered, but only a general statement that the accountant will render normal accounting services, including the preparation of tax returns. Exhibit 6-2 contains a much shorter declaration that was filed in the Central District of California.

Exhibit 6-1 Accountant's Affidavit Describing Services to Be Performed in Proceedings for a Reorganization

UNITED STATES BANKRUPTCY COURT
EASTERN DISTRICT OF NEW YORK

In re
TOM CORPORATION } In Proceedings for Reorganization
Debtor   Case No. 85-16666 (NY)

AFFIDAVIT OF PROPOSED ACCOUNTANT

State of *New York*
County of *New York:* } SS.:
City of *New York*

JOHN X. DOE, JR., being duly sworn, deposes and says:

1. He is a partner of the accounting firm of John X. Doe & Co., and he is duly authorized to make this affidavit for and on its behalf.

2. The business addresses of said firm include its office at 90 Maple Street, New York, New York 10005.

3. John X. Doe & Co. is a firm of certified public accountants and has been in existence for over fifty years. The Firm operates through offices located in 20 cities in the United States and in a number of offices located overseas. He has been a Certified Public Accountant, licensed under the laws of the State of New York, for over 15 years and his firm has been retained as accountants in numerous matters to examine the books and records of debtors in bankruptcy court proceedings.

4. To the best of his knowledge, information and belief, neither he nor the members of the firm of John X. Doe & Co. have any business association with nor are related to any attorney, creditor, debtor in possession, or any party to the proceedings.

5. He has made an examination of the books and records of the debtor in possession in order to determine the services which must be rendered herein. Such examination indicates that it would be necessary to perform the following services.

Exhibit 6-1 (*Continued*)

a) Supervise and assist in the summarization of the books of account and posting to the general ledger in order to close the books for the period up to the date of the filing of the petition.

b) Prepare consolidated financial statements, including a consolidated balance sheet, consolidated statement of income and expense, consolidated statement of changes in financial position, and consolidated statement of affairs as of the date of the filing of the petition, May 31, 19X1, encompassing the operation of the debtor in possession and its subsidiary, TIM CORPORATION.

c) Reconciliation of cash balances to amounts confirmed by depositories and analysis of outstanding checks.

d) Prepare schedules, review and analyze trade accounts receivable, including confirmation of certain accounts by direct correspondence. Confirmation of other receivables as may be considered necessary.

e) Review of adequacy of provision for bad debts.

f) Examination of the inventory of the debtor in possession's stock in trade, and review of the valuation and mathematical accuracy.

g) Review of prepared expenses, supplies, unexpired insurance, etc.

h) Review of transactions relating to investments and acquisitions, if any.

i) Review of additions and dispositions to the fixed assets and to the related allowances for depreciation.

j) Confirmation of secured liabilities, if any, by direct correspondence with the creditors, and determination of the extent of collateral against each such liability.

k) Review of amounts of unsecured liabilities, including debts for merchandise, expenses, taxes, etc. Determination of adjustments that may be required to reflect such liabilities in the books of the Company. The scope of this work would recognize that creditors are to be notified to report directly to the Court the amount of such unsecured claims as of May 31, 19X1. Assist counsel to the Creditors' Committee in resolving differences between amounts shown on the books and records of the debtor in possession as compared with claims filed by various creditors.

l) Examine all other material assets and liabilities reflected on the books and records of the debtor in possession to determine fair and reasonable balance sheet values.

m) Examine into the transactions of the corporation for the twelve months preceding the petition filing date to determine the existence of any possible insider preferences and for the ninety days preceding the petition filing date to determine the existence of any other possible preferences.

n) Review the claims filed by the various taxing authorities in order to determine the propriety and accuracy of said claims, including attendance at meetings with representatives of these agencies where necessary.

o) Attend meetings with the counsel to the Creditors' Committee, as well as attend examinations of the principal officers of the debtor in possession.

p) Examine into and review the transactions of the debtor in possession with its subsidiary, TIM CORPORATION, to determine the proper classification of all amounts; the validity of all intercompany charges; the existence of any preferential

Exhibit 6-1 *(Continued)*

payments or other transactions which would be detrimental to creditors; and the proper financial statement presentation of the amount owing between companies.

q) Examine the books and records of TIM CORPORATION in order to prepare consolidated financial statements as of the petition filing date.

r) The affairs of the debtor in possession are in a considerably confused state and a substantial portion of the time required for analysis of the affairs of the debtor in possession will be expended in attempting to clarify the operations for the most recent fiscal period.

s) Furthermore, there are innumerable services which he and his firm will be required to render in relation to the aforesaid in order that a complete and proper understanding of the affairs of the debtor in possession may be presented.

6. The estimated charge for the accounting services proposed to be rendered is $28,850 plus actual out-of-pocket expenses for postage, telephone, etc. Such fee is based upon the regular standard hourly charges of the Firm for various categories of accountants and their assistants, as follows:

Assistant, typists, and clerks	80 hrs.	@	$ 15	$ 1,200
Junior accountants	150	@	30	4,500
Semi-senior accountants	150	@	40	6,000
Senior accountants	70	@	45	3,150
Supervisors and managers	90	@	80	7,200
Partners	40	@	170	6,800
Total				$28,850

7. The foregoing estimate has been prepared on the basis of our familiarity with accounting practices and procedures of the Company and presumes the reasonable continuity of the Company's activities in maintaining its own accounting records, under the direction of knowledgeable personnel.

JOHN X. DOE, JR.

Sworn to before me this
_____ day of June, 19X1

13 It is possible for an accounting partnership, corporation, or professional association authorized under applicable law to practice public accounting, to be retained to render services in bankruptcy cases without identifying the particular accountants who will actually be working on the assignment. Even in cases where a particular individual is identified in the order, Bankruptcy Rule 2014(b) allows for another partner, member, or associate to act as the accountant without further order of the court.

Survey of Work To Be Performed

14 As mentioned in paragraph 12, the accountant generally makes a preliminary survey of the work that is to be performed in order to include in

Exhibit 6-2   Declaration of Accountant

DECLARATION OF (NAME OF CPA)

I, (name of CPA), declare:

1.   I am a Certified Public Accountant, and I have been practicing, consulting, and teaching in the field of tax and financial accounting for approximately 13 years. My qualifications are fully set forth in the attached resume which I incorporate herein by reference as though set forth in full.

2.   I am not, nor have I ever been, a creditor, security holder, insider, investment banker for any of Debtor's securities, or a director, officer or employee of the Debtors, or of either Debtor, or of any investment banker for any of the Debtor's securities, or for an attorney for such investment banker.

3.   I hold no interest, either directly or indirectly, which is materially adverse to the interest of the estate or any class of creditors or equity holders thereof in connection with the Debtors or an investment banker for the Debtors' securities.

4.   I charge most of my clients $150 per hour when I am consulted regarding tax matters, such as the effects of transactions upon existing net operating losses, analysis of the tax ramifications of various structures of property transfers, and determining when taxes will become due for cash flow analysis purposes described in the Application of the Debtors in possession to employ me. I am willing to perform such services for the Debtors in possession at the same $150 hourly rate.

I declare under penalty of perjury that the foregoing is true and correct.

Executed at _____ , California this _____ day of September, 19X0.

_____
(Name of CPA)

---

the affidavit the scope of the services to be rendered. If the accountant has performed audits for the debtor in the past, the condition of the records will be known and very little new information will be needed in order to prepare the affidavit.

15   When a new accountant is selected, frequently at the request of the creditors or their committee, as much information as possible about the company must be gained in a very short time period. For example, the accountant may receive a call from one of the attorneys representing the creditors' committee, requesting services for the engagement. The attorney will then describe some of the background information about the debtor. After providing the accountant with this information the attorney arranges, often the same day, to accompany the accountant to the office of the company to determine the nature of the debtor's operations. At the premises of the debtor the accountant will make an inspection of the facilities, very briefly examine the records, and obtain copies of the most recent financial statements the company has issued. The accountant should ascertain directly from the controller whether the records are current, whether major impediments exist, and whether the key accounting personnel plan to stay with the company. The examination is very limited, with the accountant usually spending only part of a day at the debtor company. The accountant may be able to contact the debtor's independent accountant and obtain additional information.

16 It should be realized that the extent to which the accountant needs to investigate the nature of the debtor's operations depends on the type of information that must be included in the affidavit or declaration of the accountant. For example, if the court allows a general statement about the nature of the services and does not require a statement as to the maximum amount of fees necessary to perform the services specified, the preliminary survey of the debtor's books and records is not necessary. Accountants may still want to complete limited inquiries to be sure they want to be associated with this particular debtor.

Application for Retention

17 Counsel for the trustee, debtor in possession, or creditors' committee uses the information in the accountant's affidavit on proposed services to prepare an application for retention of the accountant, to be submitted to the bankruptcy court for its approval. If the court approves the retention of the accountant, it will enter the order, confirm the scope of the services to be performed, and set the rate or maximum compensation to be allowed for such services. A sample of an application filed by counsel for retention of an accountant is shown in Exhibit 6-3. As with the affidavit of the accountant, the amount of detail in the application for retention will vary depending on the requirements of the court or judge where the petition is filed. The format of a court order authorizing the retention of an accountant appears in Exhibit 6-4. The application must be made by either the trustee (debtor in possession) or committee and, according to Bankruptcy Rule 2014(a), include the necessity for the employment, the name of the person to be employed, the reason for his or her selection, the professional services to be rendered, any proposed arrangement for compensation, and the applicant's connections with the debtor, creditors, or any other party in interest.

Retention Order on a Retainer Basis

18 A retention order authorizing the accountant to render continuing accounting services is often required if the independent accountant assists the trustee, receiver, or debtor in possession in normal accounting duties, including the preparation of monthly, and sometimes weekly, operating statements for the court. This type of order is advantageous if the time period between commencement of the case and the confirmation of a plan is of considerable length, in that payment for services is normally monthly under a retainer of this nature. In many chapter 11 proceedings the time span covers several years. Accountants rendering normal periodic accounting services that would qualify under section 327(b) (see paragraph 9) may state this in their affidavit or declaration. This procedure may increase the ability of the accountant to receive payments on a monthly or other periodic basis. A sample of the accountant's affidavit requesting retention on a retainer basis as accountant for the debtor is shown in Exhibit 6-5.

Deviations from Retention Order

19 The accountant should pay close attention to the scope of the accounting services to be rendered as they are described in the order for retention entered by the court. Deviation from the stated services will be closely scrutinized by the court and may not be included in the accountant's

Exhibit 6-3   Application for Retention of Accountant

UNITED STATES BANKRUPTCY COURT
DISTRICT OF CONNECTICUT

In re	⎫	In Proceedings for a Reorganization
TERRY CORPORATION	⎬	Under Chapter 11
Debtor	⎭	Case No. 85-16666

APPLICATION FOR RETENTION OF ACCOUNTANT

TO THE HONORABLE_____, Bankruptcy Judge:

The application of *William Roberts,* by *John Green,* his attorney, respectfully represents:

1. That he is the trustee herein, duly qualified and acting as such trustee.

2. The debtor was engaged in the business of [*state business*] with a place of business at (address).

3. The assets, after sale of the debtor's property and effects, amount to (amount) while the liabilities exceed (amount).

4. Applicant believes that it is necessary in the best interest of the estate to have a complete audit and examination of the books of account of the debtor for the following reasons:

(a) *Books of Account:* The debtor has turned over *ten* books of account. A preliminary survey by applicant discloses that these books of account are involved, and contain entries covering a period of several years. In addition, there are numerous cancelled vouchers which it will be necessary to check with the entries in the books.

(b) *Preliminary Survey:* A preliminary survey of the books of account discloses that said books were not kept in an orderly fashion, and it appears that certain entries are obviously incorrect and that entries have been made without proper explanatory detail. To determine accurately the condition of the debtor's affairs, a complete analysis of the books of account will be necessary.

Source: Adapted from Asa A. Herzog, Sheldon Lowe, and Joel B. Zweibel, *Herzog's Bankruptcy Forms and Practice* (New York: Clark Boardman Co., Ltd., 1971).

Exhibit 6-3   *(Continued)*

(c) *Discrepancy Between Assets and Liabilities:* The debtor has failed to account for the discrepancy between his assets and his liabilities, nor do the books disclose the reason for the deficiency of assets.

(d) *Accounts Receivable:* Applicant is advised that there are numerous large outstanding accounts receivable, according to the records of the debtor, and that in order to determine the status of these accounts, an examination of the books of the debtor will be necessary.

(e) [*State any further reasons why applicant believes retention of accountants to be necessary.*]

5. That by reason of the premises aforesaid, applicant desires to retain the services of accountants to make the necessary examination and audit of the books of the debtor and applicant desires to retain the services of *Leon Robbin,* Certified Public Accountant, of (address). [*State reasons for selection.*] Said accountant has advised applicant that the cost of the proposed services will approximate (amount) which applicant verily believes to be a proper and reasonable charge.

WHEREFORE, applicant prays for an order authorizing the employment of *Leon Robbin* as accountant at a maximum compensation of (amount), the exact amount thereof to be fixed by this court upon the filing of a proper application for all of which no previous application has been made herein.

(Dated)

Signed _____

                Attorney for Trustee
                [Applicant signs where not
                represented by Attorney]
                (Address)

Exhibit 6-4   Order Authorizing the Retention of an Accountant

UNITED STATES BANKRUPTCY COURT
DISTRICT OF CONNECTICUT

In re
BANKRUPTCY, INC.   In Proceeding for a Reorganization
INSOLVENCY, INC.   Under Chapter 11
Debtors   Case No. 85-16666

ORDER AUTHORIZING DEBTOR TO EMPLOY ACCOUNTANT

At Hartford, in said District, on the _____ day of _____ 19X1.

This matter having come on before me on the above petition of the debtor herein to employ John Smith & Co. as its accountant, and no notice being necessary and due cause appearing to me therefor, it is hereby

ORDERED that the above petition be, and it hereby is allowed.

_____
                Bankruptcy Judge

Exhibit 6-5　Accountant's Affidavit Requesting Retention on a Retainer as Accountant for the Debtor

UNITED STATES BANKRUPTCY COURT
EASTERN DISTRICT OF NEW YORK

In re
TOM CORPORATION,　　In Proceedings for a Reorganization
Debtor　　　　　　　　Case No. 85-16666 (NY)

AFFIDAVIT OF PROPOSED ACCOUNTANT
FOR RETENTION AS ACCOUNTANT
FOR THE DEBTOR IN POSSESSION

State of *New York*　⎱ SS.:
County of *New York*　⎰

JOHN X. DOE, JR., being duly sworn, deposes and says

1. He is a partner of the accounting firm of John X. Doe & Co., and he is duly authorized to make this affidavit for and on its behalf.

2. The business addresses of said firm include its office at 90 Maple Street, New York, New York 10005.

3. John X. Doe & Co. is a firm of certified public accountants and has been in existence for over fifty years. The Firm operates through offices located in 20 cities in the United States and in a number of offices located overseas. He has been a Certified Public Accountant, licensed under the laws of the State of New York, for over 15 years and his firm has been retained as accountants in numerous matters to examine the books and records of debtors in bankruptcy court proceedings.

4. To the best of his knowledge, information, and belief, neither he nor the members of the firm of John X. Doe & Co. have any business association with nor are related to any attorney, creditor, debtor in possession, or any party to the proceedings.

5. He has made an examination of the books and records of the debtor in possession and has discussed the services required with officers of the debtor, counsel for the debtor, and counsel for the Creditors' Committee which consist of the following:

   a) The preparation of monthly statements to be submitted to the court.

   b) Review of the accounting records as deemed necessary.

6. He estimates that the cost of the foregoing services will be Nine Hundred Fifty Dollars ($950.00) per month payable upon completion of each monthly review.

7. WHEREFORE your deponent asks for the making of an appropriate order of employment.

　　　　　　　　　　　　　　　　　　　　　　———————————————
　　　　　　　　　　　　　　　　　　　　　　JOHN X. DOE, JR.

Sworn to before me this
———————— day of June, 19X1

———————————————————

allowance for compensation. Likewise, if more time than the original estimate will be needed by the accountant, a supplemental court order must be obtained allowing additional compensation.

20   Once the retention orders are entered by the court, the accountant may begin rendering compensable services.

Prepetition Retention

21   The debtor may need the services of an accountant just prior to filing the petition. For example, an accountant may be retained to help the debtor evaluate the alternatives that are available to pursue (for example, out-of-court settlement, chapter 11, find a buyer for business, and so forth) or to assist the debtor's counsel in gathering the information needed to file the petition. When engaged under these conditions, it is advisable for the accountant to obtain a retainer before rendering the services. If the accountant renders these services without a retainer and the debtor subsequently files a petition, the fees for these unpaid services will be considered a prepetition unsecured debt. It is customary practice for the debtor's counsel to receive a retainer and there is no reason why the accountant for the debtor could not also receive such a retainer.

Retention Procedure—Informal

22   An accountant engaged to render services for a company in financial difficulty who has not formally petitioned the court should obtain a signed engagement letter before any work is initiated. The format for the engagement letter is similar to that of the usual engagement letter; however, provision for alternate sources of payment should be arranged, in case the client elects to file a bankruptcy petition. Through this procedure the accountant may avoid becoming a general creditor with a consequent reduction in claims. The alternate sources may consist of a guarantee of payment by one or more of the larger creditors or a personal guarantee by the principal officer or officers of the company.

23   In many cases, it is advisable for the accountant to obtain an advance before beginning the engagement. A large number of accounting firms have seen their claims for prepetition accounting services rendered for the debtor reduced to almost nothing since this claim is considered along with all of the other unsecured claims in bankruptcy proceedings. Obtaining an advance before starting the assignment would have eliminated this problem. The extent to which advances are obtained by accounting firms depends upon the type of services being rendered, prior relationships with the client, the entity (for example, debtor or creditors' committee) that the accountant represents, and the policy and nature of the creditor community in the location where services are being rendered. Some firms will not start an engagement for a financially troubled debtor unless an advance is obtained and one New York accounting firm actively involved in bankruptcy audits receives advance payment on about 10 percent of its audits. Advances are more common where certain types of wrongdoing are suspected and the accountant is engaged to do a special investigation. It is also a good policy to have the client–debtor sign the engagement letter even though the creditors may be the party requesting the services of the accountant. If the insolvent firm has other affiliates that are solvent, it is desirable to have them sign the engagement letter, deposit funds for the payment of fees, or guarantee payment.

Accountants as Quasi-Officers of the Court

24 Appointment by order for retention through the bankruptcy court makes the accountant a quasi-officer of the court, owing a primary duty to the court. Normally this duty involves reporting to and discussing problems with the trustee in the proceedings. Further, in all cases where persons seek compensation for services or reimbursement for expenses, they shall be held to fiduciary standards.[1] Such standards mean a special confidence has been imposed on the accountant who, in equity and good conscience, is bound to act in good faith and with due regard to the interest of the one imposing the confidence.[2]

DETERMINATION OF ACCOUNTANT'S FEES

25 The accountant's fees are considered an administrative expense and receive first priority in payment. If the estate is not large enough to pay the administrative claims in full, the accountant shares in the balance available with others having administrative claims.

26 Even though the services of the accountant when retained by the court are a part of the cost of administering the estate, this priority may be reduced somewhat if the debtor is converted from chapter 11 or 13 to a chapter 7. If a company that originally filed under chapter 11 is subsequently converted to a chapter 7, the cost of administrative expenses claimed under the provisions of chapter 11 is secondary to administrative expense claims incurred under chapter 7.[3] A separate claim must be filed for the services rendered in each phase of bankruptcy proceedings. In order to protect the fees involved, it is, however, still important for the accountant to determine the condition of the debtor and the potential size of the debtor's estate.

---

[1] *Brown* v. *Gerdes,* 321 U.S. 178, 182 (1944).
[2] Chauncey Levy, "Creditors' Committees and Their Responsibilities," *Commercial Law Journal,* Vol. 74 (December 1969), p. 356n.
[3] 11 U.S.C. Sec. 726(b).

SEC May Object to Fees

27 Under prior law the SEC was considered a party in interest under Chapter X and under some Chapter XI proceedings. In Chapter X or other proceedings where the SEC was involved, the judge was required to get an advisory report from the Washington office regarding fees. Under these conditions it was an advisable practice for the accounting firm to review with district representatives of the SEC the entire application for fees before the time records were sent to the Washington office so that the SEC was aware of the type of work performed, the time worked, and the quality of the work. The SEC often determined the average hourly rate for the entire engagement. As a result it may not only object to the hourly rates as established for partners, managers, seniors, and juniors, but may claim that partners and managers devoted too much time to the engagement. For example, the nature of the engagement may require that a considerable amount of time be spent on tax matters and settling litigation, and partners and managers may have to do most of the work. This should be pointed out to the SEC at the local level; a realistic awareness of some of the work involved and of the level of services required may prevent future reductions in the fees allowed. It is to the accountant's advantage to find out the SEC's views regarding the fees before the report is written. If the SEC evaluation is in error, the accountant then has an opportunity to try to answer its objections.

28 The SEC's role under the Bankruptcy Code has been altered. The SEC may appear and be heard on any issue arising in the case but may not appeal (section 1109) as it could under prior law. While the SEC still has the right to be heard regarding fees, it may be that the SEC will prefer to direct most of its efforts toward the appointment of a trustee when needed, an assessment of the adequacy of the disclosure statement, and the process confirming the plan. In fact, the SEC recently indicated that it will devote more attention to policy matters and less to specific aspects of a case (see chapter 7, paragraphs 62–74). This does not, however, suggest that the accountant should ignore the SEC in filing for compensation. The precautionary steps described in paragraph 27 should continue to be followed. The SEC will continue to receive copies of business petitions under the Bankruptcy Rules referred to in chapter 3, paragraph 16.

Compensation Must Be Approved by the Court

29 When retained by a trustee or debtor in possession or the creditors' committee, the accountant's remuneration must come from the debtor's estate. Payment can be made only when the accountant is engaged upon an order of the court that expressly fixes the amount or rate of compensation.

30 If an accountant renders services in bankruptcy cases without having a retention order, it is possible for the court to grant approval *nunc pro tunc*.

The fifth circuit surveyed the case law and adopted the position that except in special circumstances *nunc pro tunc* relief would be allowed if a properly timed application would have been approved.[4] In another case the bankruptcy court refused to approve the appointment of any accountant because the application was not submitted until almost a year had passed since the services were completed and there had been no prior communication with the court.[5] While it is possible to find examples where the court has approved an order for the accountant to be engaged prior to the actual date the order is submitted and to receive payments for services rendered, it is advisable for the accountant to adopt the policy of obtaining the order before rendering services. For example, one bankruptcy judge requires the following be attached to any retention order:

The order authorizing employment of the professional person to which this supplement is attached is granted upon the following conditions:

(1) that the appointee shall receive no compensation from the debtor in possession until an application is filed requesting the same under Bankruptcy Rule 2016(a) and notice has been given to creditors as required by Bankruptcy Rule 2002,

(2) that if the net income of the debtor in possession is insufficient to pay administrative costs, including fees to professional persons appointed by court order, interim payments on said fees will not be allowed unless it can be shown that there is a reasonable likelihood that the business will in the future generate sufficient income to pay all administrative expenses in full on the confirmation of a plan,

(3) that all fee arrangements are subject to the provisions of 11 U.S.C. 328(a) stating, in part, . . . the court may allow compensation different from the compensation provided under the agreement and/or order after conclusion of such employment, if such terms and conditions prove to have been improvident . . . .

31 To aid the court in setting the amount of compensation where the court requires that the application for retention contain a maximum amount, the accountant is required to make a preliminary survey of the debtor's books and records to estimate the extent of the services it will be necessary to perform (see paragraph 14). The amount then fixed by the court is the maximum compensation the accountant will be given for services in the proceedings. Thus, if the accountant believes the value of these services will exceed the maximum amount provided for, there should be an immediate attempt to obtain an additional order increasing the maximum.

---

[4] *Fanelli* v. *Hensley,* 697 F.2d 1280 (5th Cir. 1983).
[5] *In re Mork,* 6 C.B.C.2d 1334 (B.Ct. D. Minn. 1982).

Factors To Consider When Estimating Fees

32   The criteria most often used in setting reasonable fees are those given by the court in its decision concerning *Owl Drug Company*.[6] The factors to be weighed are:

The time spent in the proceedings.

The complexity of the problems which arose.

The relative size of the estate and the amount which is available for distribution.

The quality of any opposition met.

The results achieved, otherwise known as the *salvage theory* (rather than letting the time involved determine the remuneration, the fees are measured by the extent of success or accomplishments and benefits to the estate).[7]

The experience and standing of the accountant.

The quality of skill necessary in the situation, and the amount of care and professional skill used.

The fee schedule in the area.

The ethics of the profession.

The accountant should be aware when estimating fees that because of the nature of a bankruptcy court engagement more seasoned personnel will be needed for this work than for a normal audit.

Compensation Based on Comparable Services

33   The court in the *Owl Drug* proceedings went on to note that any consideration of fee allowances must be according to the economy of administration principle, which requires that all unnecessary expenses be curtailed to a minimum in bankruptcy court proceedings. Thus the courts should attempt to set the fees at the lowest amount which is reasonable in order to maximize the distribution to creditors. Several accounting firms with considerable experience in bankruptcy proceedings estimate that under the Bankruptcy Act, the accountant normally received about 75 percent of the "going rate" for services rendered under prior law Chapter XI arrangements and less than 50 percent in straight bankruptcy cases. In addition, the accountant often found it necessary to work a greater number of hours than is stipulated in the order of retention, for which no compensation is received.

---

[6] 16 F. Supp. 142 (1936).

[7] William J. Rudin, "Fees and Allowances to Attorneys in Bankruptcy and Chapter XI Proceedings," *Fordham Law Review*, Vol. 34 (March 1966), p. 399.

34 In another case[8] the judge set an arbitrary limit on fees payable, based on the amount of a district judge's salary. Other cases in addition to this and the *Owl Drug* case indicated that fees under the Bankruptcy Act were determined on the notions of conservation of the estate and economy of administration.

35 To overrule these standards developed from case law, Congress passed section 330 which provides that reasonable compensation to professionals is to be paid based on the time, the nature, the extent, and the value of such services, and the cost of comparable services other than in a case under the Code. Legislative history indicates that if cases like these are allowed to stand, bankruptcy specialists, who enable the system to operate smoothly, efficiently, and expeditiously, will find higher income in other fields and will leave the bankruptcy field to those who cannot find other work or those who practice occasionally as a public service.[9] Thus, the policy of this section is to compensate accountants and other professionals serving in a bankruptcy proceeding at the same rate professionals would be compensated for performing comparable services other than in a bankruptcy case. Even with this law change, because of the nature of selected cases, the attitude of the bankruptcy judge, and the size of the estate, fees will not always be at normal private rates.

36 Reimbursement for actual, necessary expenses is also allowed under section 330.

Prepetition Fees

37 Accounting fees for services rendered on behalf of the debtor prior to the filing of the petition are generally not subject to priority, as an administrative expense, in bankruptcy court proceedings. Thus, if the accountant wants to be assured of receiving compensation for work performed, payments should be received from financially troubled debtors promptly upon the conclusion of the job. If the work extends over a fairly long time period, installment payments should be obtained. It may also be advisable to obtain an advance prior to starting the job. The timing of the payments, the nature of the services rendered, and the manner in which the payment process is handled may be crucial. The accountant does not want the payment made by the debtor to be considered a preferential payment under section 547. If the payment is considered preferential, then the trustee or debtor in possession has the right to recover all or part of the amount paid. For example, payments that are received subsequent to the time the services are rendered are payments on an antecedent debt. For these payments to be exempt, they must be for a debt incurred in the ordinary cause of business and made in the

[8] *In re Beverly Crest Convalescent Hospital, Inc.*, 548 F.2d 817 (9th Cir. 1976, as amended 1977).
[9] House Report No. 95–595, 95th Cong., 1st Sess. (1977), 329–330.

ordinary course of business according to ordinary business terms. See chapter 3, paragraphs 115–128. To prevent at least some of the prepetition fees from being a preference, it is a good policy to make arrangements for the payments, as they are received, to be credited to one of the more recent bills.

Compensation When Retained by Creditors' Committee

38 When engaged by a creditor or some party other than the trustee or debtor, the accountant must rely on that person rather than on the debtor's estate for compensation if a bankruptcy court petition is filed (see paragraphs 22–23). Section 503(b)(4) does, however, provide for the allowance of prepetition accountant's fees by stating that reasonable compensation for professional services rendered by an attorney or an accountant of an entity described in subsection (3) of section 503(b) based on the time, the nature, the extent, and the value of such services, and the cost of comparable services. Also included would be reimbursement for actual, necessary expenses incurred by the attorney or accountant. The entities described in subsection (3) for whom the accountant may render services and possibly be reimbursed include a creditor that files an involuntary petition, a creditor that recovers property for the benefit of the estate, or a creditor, indenture trustee, equity security holder, or a committee representing creditors or equity security holders (other than a committee appointed in a chapter 11 case under the provisions of section 1102), that makes a substantial contribution in a chapter 9 or 11 case. Thus, for an accountant to be reimbursed by the bankruptcy court for services rendered for a creditors' committee prior to the date of the petition, it will be necessary to show that the committee's prepetition work made a substantial contribution to the case. If it can be shown that the actions of this committee led to a confirmation of the plan, this would be an example of a substantial contribution. It is not required, however, for the actions of the committee to lead to a confirmation. A substantial contribution may be made if the accountant discovers fraud which leads to a denial of confirmation of the plan.

TIME RECORDS

39 It is important that the accountant keep adequate time and performance records while rendering services. When petitioning the court for a fee allowance, should the amount of the compensation be contested, such records would be vital. At the very least, the accountant should record the following information:

The date and a description of the work which has been done.
The time spent in the performance of the work.

The name, classification, and per-diem billing rate of each staff member performing the work.[10]

40   Many accounting firms used computerized forms for allocating time to their clients for services rendered. The court may not accept the computer runs unless there are authoritative records that support the work performed by the accountant. Computer records are often standardized and generally show only a minimum amount of information, usually including only the client's code number and time. In any accounting work performed for the court, it is advisable for the accounting firm to keep a hard set of records which clearly show in detail the nature of the work performed. In awarding fees the court also takes into consideration the quality of the services rendered by the accountant and the amount and types of reports issued. The accountant may need to spend a great deal of time looking for preferential payments and other types of irregularities. If none are discovered, the court may not understand the reason for the fees charged by the accountant. Thus, the accountant may need these detailed records to support the request for payment.

PETITION FOR FEE ALLOWANCE

Court Discretion in Ruling on Fees

41   The requirement that the level of compensation be fixed in the court order of appointment has been held to be directory and not mandatory.[11] This means that when ruling on fees the court may exercise its discretion in light of all the circumstances surrounding the case.

42   The court also makes the final decision concerning compensation and the time when services were rendered. An accountant on loan to perform bookkeeping services for a debtor both before and after bankruptcy court proceedings can be allowed to recover for postpetition costs under an order continuing the debtor in possession and allowing employment of outside help. On the other hand, an accountant completing a special examination of the debtor's financial position which was begun before bankruptcy was not entitled to first priority for the expenses of the work done after bankruptcy because an order of the court had not been obtained at the time of the commencement of the services[12] (see paragraphs 29–31). Section 327(b) allows the trustee or debtor in possession to engage an accountant as a salaried employee, if necessary in the operation of the business.

[10] Harold Gelb and Irving Goldberger, "Retention Order of the Accountant in Insolvencies and Bankruptcies and Petition for Compensation," *The New York Certified Public Accountant,* Vol. 23 (October 1953), p. 634.

[11] *Littleton* v. *Kincaid,* 179 F.2d 848 (1950).

[12] *Century Chemical Corp.,* 192 F. Supp. 205 (1961).

Procedure for Filing the Petition

43   When the accountant has completed the engagement, a petition for compensation should be filed in affidavit form with the bankruptcy court having jurisdiction over the proceedings. The petition should contain enough information about the services the accountant has rendered so that the court may evaluate and compare them with the services authorized in the order of retention. The application for compensation may include the following data:

The accountant's name, address, and firm affiliation.

The source of the accountant's authorization to perform the services.

Date the accountant began the engagement.

List of the services the accountant rendered and the exhibits and schedules presented in the report.

Total amount of compensation the accountant is requesting, accompanied by a schedule of the hours worked classified by the grade of accountant and the per-diem billing rate.

The accomplishments believed to have resulted from the accountant's services, in light of the benefits that the estate has obtained from such services.[13]

Sworn statement by the accountant concerning knowledge of the contents of the petition.

Notarized signature of the accountant or signature under pains and penalty of perjury.

44   An example of an affidavit applying for compensation is presented in Exhibit 6-6. The detail included in this example may not be required by some judges. In fact, in some districts the affidavit consists of only a reference to the retention order, a brief summary of the services rendered, and the total amount of fees requested based on the hours worked and the approved billing rates for the various level of services. While this brief form may be acceptable for some bankruptcy judges, the SEC has on occasion required the standard forms shown in Exhibit 6-6.

45   Bankruptcy Rule 2016 provides that a person seeking interim or final compensation for services or for reimbursement of expenses should include the following in the application:

1   The services rendered, time expended, and the expenses incurred.

2   The amount requested.

3   Statement as to what payments have previously been made or promised to the applicant for services rendered in connection with the case.

---

[13] Gelb and Goldberger, p. 634.

Exhibit 6-6   Accountant's Affidavit Requesting Compensation for
Services Rendered

UNITED STATES BANKRUPTCY COURT
EASTERN DISTRICT OF NEW YORK

In re TOM CORPORATION, Debtor	In Proceedings for a Reorganization Case No. 85-16666 (NY)

AFFIDAVIT FOR PETITION
FOR COMPENSATION OF ACCOUNTANTS

State of *New York* ⎱ SS.:
County of *New York* ⎰

JOHN X. DOE, JR., being duly sworn, deposes and says:

1. That he is a certified public accountant and a member of the accounting firm of John X. Doe & Co., with offices at 90 Maple Street, New York, New York 10005.

2. That his firm is well versed and experienced in the auditing of books and records of assignors, bankrupts, debtors, and others involved in insolvency proceedings;

3. That neither he, nor any member of his firm, is related to or has had business association with any attorney, creditor, debtor or any other party to these proceedings;

4. That in accordance with an order signed by the Honorable Herbert Robertson dated June 15, 19X1, the accounting firm of John X. Doe & Co. was retained to perform an audit and examine the books and records of the debtor in possession herein, and to render other miscellaneous services in connection with said audit and examination;

5. That pursuant to said retention, your petitioner rendered the following services:

1) Prepared an inventory of the books and records of the debtor in possession and its subsidiary, TIM CORPORATION.

2) Supervised and assisted in the summarization of the books of account and posting to the general ledgers of the debtor in possession and its subsidiary in order to close the books for the period up to the date of the filing of the petition.

3) Met with representatives of the debtor's former accountant, John Jones & Co., and obtained information as to the debtor's financial history, and photocopies of essential workpapers, tax returns, and documents contained in their files.

4) Examined the corporate minutes, resolutions, and stock records of the debtor and its subsidiary in order to determine their corporate history and ownership, and the existence and pertinent provisions of any significant contractual arrangements. In this connection, all significant contracts were examined and their pertinent provisions abstracted.

Exhibit 6-6   (*Continued*)

5) Assisted the debtor in planning and arranging for the taking of an inventory as at May 31, 19X1.

6) Supervised and observed a portion of the inventory taken by the debtor as at May 31, 19X1. In this connection, extensive tests of listed items were performed as to quantity, description, and physical existence.

7) Verified the mathematical accuracy of the May 31, 19X1, inventory by checking all multiplication and addition on the final listings.

8) Determined that the inventory at May 31, 19X1, was valued at the lower of cost or market values of each major category of items by extensive tests of the unit prices used therein against recent purchase and sales invoices, and internal cost records.

9) Examined into the relationships and transactions of the debtor with its subsidiary, TIM CORPORATION.

The intercompany account between TOM CORPORATION and TIM CORPORATION was examined and found to consist primarily of intercompany charges for expenses and purchases, payments made by the parent to creditors of its subsidiary, and cash advances for operations. It was also found that $96,000 of these advances were capitalized to pay for the debtor's investment in the subsidiary.

10) Examined into the transactions of the debtor and its subsidiary for the twelve months preceding the petition filing date to determine the existence of any possible insider preferences and for the ninety days preceding the petition filing date to determine the existence of any other possible preferences.

11) Prepared financial statements for the debtor and its subsidiary as of the petition filing date including:

a) Statement of Financial Position at May 31, 19X1.

b) Statement of Loss for the five months ended May 31, 19X1.

c) Statement of Changes in Financial Position for five months ending May 31, 19X1.

d) Schedules of operating expenses for the five months ended May 31, 19X1.

e) Statement of Affairs at May 31, 19X1. Copies of these statements are annexed hereto.

   [See chapter 12 for examples of the above statements.]

12) Reviewed the financial history of the debtor and its subsidiary to determine the existence and extent of any possible tax refund claims.

13) Reviewed the prior financial statements prepared by the debtor's former accountants.

14) Examined and reconciled the most recent statements for all bank accounts of the debtor and its subsidiary. In the process thereof, checks made payable to cash were reviewed to determine their purpose and authenticity.

15) Examined into the position of TED CORPORATION as relates to its financing transactions with the debtor and its subsidiary.

16) Prepared schedules of accounts receivable at May 31, 19X1, showing names and amounts due from the various customers of the debtor and its subsidiary.

Exhibit 6-6   *(Continued)*

17) Reviewed the status of the accounts receivable of the debtor and its subsidiary and provided for possible bad debts thereon.

18) Analyzed the security deposits of the debtor and its subsidiary to determine any possible recoveries.

19) Reviewed the recent acquisitions of fixtures and equipment by the debtor and its subsidiary to determine their propriety and the existence of any liens or encumbrances.

20) Examined into the debtor's loan transactions with its officers and employees to determine the existence of any possible recoveries or preferential payments.

21) Prepared schedules of accounts payable at May 31, 19X1, showing names and amounts due to the various trade creditors of the debtor and its subsidiary.

22) Prepared schedules of royalty and commission advances at May 31, 19X1, showing names and amounts owing to the debtor and its subsidiary.

23) Reviewed the prepaid project development costs expended by the debtor and its subsidiary to determine any possible recoveries thereof.

24) Determined the amounts of unpaid wages of the debtor at May 31, 19X1.

25) Reviewed the advances received by the debtor and its subsidiary from several of their distributors to determine the liability therefor.

26) Examined into amounts received by the debtor from various customers in advance of shipments, for which refunds are to be made.

27) Analyzed the debtor's insurance in force to determine any possible recoveries for unearned premiums and cash surrender values.

28) Prepared a schedule of royalties payable at May 31, 19X1, showing names and amounts owing.

29) Determined the extent to which assets were security for loans received by the debtor, and the approximate amounts of any equity therein available to general creditors.

30) Reviewed the liabilities of the debtor and its subsidiary for payroll taxes owing to the various tax authorities.

31) Examined into the status of the debtor's debenture bonds payable.

32) Examined the ledgers and journals and prepared analyses of all other significant balance sheets, income and expense accounts.

33) In addition to the foregoing, your deponent attended court [in pilot program districts, U.S. trustee] and creditors' meetings and conferred with counsel to the creditors' committee and counsel to the debtor on numerous occasions in order to resolve the various problems which arose during the administration period.

6. In order for your petitioner to render the aforementioned services, it was necessary to expend approximately 550.8 working hours. Based upon the time expended, the reasonable value of the services rendered by petitioner is the sum of $26,813.95, computed on the expenditure of 38.8 hours of partners' time at an average of $171 an hour, 70.7 hours of supervisors' time at an average rate of $79.50 an hour, 71.3 hours of senior accountants' time at a rate of $45.00 an

Exhibit 6-6 (*Continued*)

hour, 160 hours of semi-senior accountants' time at a rate of $40 an hour, 120 hours of time of junior accountants at a rate of $30 an hour, and 90 hours of assistant, typists, and clerks at a rate of $15.00 an hour, and out-of-pocket expenditures of $623.00.

_____

JOHN X. DOE, JR.

Sworn to before me this
_____ day of October, 19X1

_____

4 Source of the compensation paid or promised.
5 Nature of any sharing of compensation except with an associate or member of an accounting or legal firm.

Payment for Services Rendered

46 The court will award compensation after notice and a hearing, pursuant to bankruptcy code section 330(a). The time the accountant will receive payment for the services rendered depends on the type of retention order. An accountant working under a retention order for special services normally receives payment at the time the case is completed. However, under some conditions, especially where the time period before a plan of arrangement or reorganization is accepted is of considerable length, the court may allow the accountant to receive payment, or at least partial payment, for services rendered. Section 331 provides that professionals, including accountants, may apply for interim compensation. Application can be submitted not more than once every 120 days, unless the court permits more frequent requests. The application must be for services rendered or expenses incurred prior to the date of the interim request and cannot pertain to future services or expenses. This section formalized the existing practice followed in some districts which allowed accountants to apply for and receive interim compensation for services and expenses. Interim compensation may not be allowed where it appears that secured claims may cover all of the debtor's assets, when a case is converted to a chapter 7 case since administrative expenses in chapter 7 have priority over those previously incurred in chapter 11, when there exists a cash shortage, or when large retainers were received before the petition was filed.

47 Accountants who are retained to perform accounting and management advisory services on a monthly basis should consider requesting at the time of their retention that they be allowed to apply monthly for compensation for these services once rendered.

CHAPTER SEVEN

Accounting Services for the Debtor in Possession or Trustee: Part 1

1 Bankruptcy proceedings are filled with various types of reports, emanating from the debtor in possession or trustee to the bankruptcy judge, the creditors, and finally the Administrative Office of the U.S. courts in Washington. Since many of these reports deal with accounting information concerning the financial position of the debtor or estate, the projected profit or loss if the business continues, and other financial aspects of the debtor's operations, it is self-evident that the services of an accountant are essential in many of today's business reorganizations. This is especially true because of the complexities of modern business operations.

2 The unusual situations encountered in performing accounting services for a business involved in reorganization (chapter 11) or liquidation (chapter 7) often present several practical problems for the accountant. The unique aspects of this type of assignment require the accountant to be very resourceful in providing the additional information needed by the interested parties. This chapter and the next describe the nature of services that may be rendered by the accountant for the debtor in possession and the trustee. Chapter 9 discusses the services of the accountant as they relate to the creditors' committee and equity holders' committee. The services rendered for the debtor in possession and the trustee in a chapter 11 case are similar to those performed for the debtor in possession. The major difference is that the trustee may have a need for more investigative services. But even in a chapter 11 case where new management has been appointed, extensive investigative service may be performed for the debtor to determine—among other things—the extent to which possible preferential payments and fraudulent transfers were made.

3 An accountant may be engaged by any one of several parties in a chapter 11 case. The accountant may be retained:

1   By the debtor in possession. The debtor in a chapter 11 proceeding will continue to require the same accounting and auditing services that were provided prior to the financial difficulties. Special services are also required. Examples of these services include:

Preparation of information included in a bankruptcy petition.

Preparation of operating statements.

Assistance in developing a business plan determining the future direction of the company.

Assistance in formulating a plan and evaluating the tax impact of the plan.

2   By the trustee. In chapter 11 cases in which a trustee is appointed, an accountant may be retained by the trustee to provide any of the services that the debtor in possession may require.

3   As the examiner. Accountants can serve as examiners. Thus an accountant could be appointed to perform the investigative role of the examiner. Accountants may also render services for the examiner. This is normally the result of appointment as accountant for either the debtor or the creditors' committee.

4   By the creditors' committee. Accountants are engaged by the creditors' committee to perform whatever services the committee feels are necessary to protect the creditors' interests. Some of the services commonly rendered include:

Assisting the committee in exercising adequate supervision over the debtor's activities.

Performing an investigation and audit of the operations of the business.

Assisting the committee in evaluating the proposed plan of reorganization.

Accountants may also be retained by a committee of secured creditors or equity holders.

5   By the secured creditors. Accountants may be retained by a major secured creditor to help that creditor evaluate the debtor's operations and financial condition and to provide advice on the course of action that should be pursued.

6   By the stockholders. Accountants may be engaged by a major stockholder to perform services similar to those for secured creditors.

   4   The term ''accountant'' is used in this chapter to refer to both the independent accountant engaged by the debtor and the internal accountant of the debtor. Many accounting services in a bankruptcy proceeding may be performed by the debtor's internal accountant, and the debtor's accounting staff often assists the independent accountant. Auditing services and the preparation of certain schedules and reports for the court require the engage-

ment of an independent accountant. Under these circumstances the accountant must refer to an independent accountant. There may be some advantages in having most of the services involved in the proceedings performed by an independent accountant; however, a discussion of this point is beyond the scope of this chapter.

5   Accountants may render services in both chapter 11 and chapter 7 cases as well as in out-of-court situations. However, accountants have been more actively involved in chapter 11 cases than in chapter 7 cases. Most of the discussion in this chapter will relate to the work of the accountant in chapter 11 cases. At the end of the next chapter a brief summary will describe how services rendered in a chapter 7 case and in an out-of-court engagement might differ from those in chapter 11.

PREFILING STAGE OF REORGANIZATION PROCEEDINGS

6   The accountant will often be the first to become aware that a client is headed toward financial difficulties and will be unable to continue profitable operations or pay liabilities as they become due. With accountants' knowledge and experience, they can render valuable services for clients during this difficult period.

Importance of Early Meeting

7   It is difficult for debtors to admit that they cannot pay their debts and continue profitable operations. As a result, decisions to call a meeting of creditors or to file a petition under the Bankruptcy Code often are postponed until the last minute. This delay benefits no one, including the debtor. There are several reasons why it is advisable to take action as soon as it becomes obvious that some type of relief is necessary. First, the debtor still has a considerable asset base. There also is a tendency for many of the key employees to leave when they see unhealthy conditions developing; early corrective action may encourage them to stay. In addition, prompt action may make it possible for the debtor to maintain some of the goodwill that was developed during successful operating periods. The fact remains that in many cases no kind of action is taken, and it is the creditors that force the debtor to call an informal meeting or file a bankruptcy petition.

Advice on Selection of Counsel

8   One of the first steps of a debtor faced with financial difficulties is the employment of legal counsel. When a company realizes that it will be unable to continue profitable operations or pay liabilities as they become due, it should quickly seek a lawyer to help effect a compromise or extension of the indebtedness, or file a bankruptcy petition. The accountant should advise the debtor to select counsel who is qualified and who has considerable experience in bankruptcy work.

Conference with Attorney

9   Once the bankruptcy attorney has been selected, a meeting should be arranged with the debtor, the financial officer, the accountant and the attorney. The accountant plays an important role in this conference. If the company's situation has not been closely followed, the accountant should determine the basic facts and gain a sound knowledge of the business, its history, and the causes of its present difficulties so that at this meeting the attorney can be given an overall view of the debtor's financial condition and the events which preceded it. In order to provide the attorney with this information it will be necessary for the accountant to analyze the activities of the debtor, to compare the financial statements for the last three or four years, and to determine what caused the cash shortage. For example, a comparison of the income statements for the last four years may show that for the first three years the gross profit percentage was fairly constant; however, during the last year it dropped 10 percent. What caused the change? This is the type of analysis that the accountant must make so that the major causes of the financial problem can be identified and possible corrective action can be discussed with the attorney. (See chapter 2 for a discussion of the causes of business failure.) An independent accountant should discuss the company's financial condition with the members of the internal accounting staff. It is advisable to have the financial officer of the company present at this conference. In many initial conferences the debtor's internal accountants are intimately involved.

Information Required

10   The attorney will request certain information from the accountant, including the most recent balance sheet, an income statement, and an extensive list of the debtor's creditors. Each individual asset will be examined and an attempt made to determine the property's value. The nature and extent of the liabilities will be discussed, and it should be indicated whether they are secured, unsecured, contingent, or unliquidated. In order to initiate the reorganization proceedings the attorney must have a complete and exact list of all creditors including their addresses, the amounts due, the date incurred, the consideration for the debt, whether any security was given and, if so, its nature and value.

11   Under chapter 11 proceedings the debtor is permitted to reject any executory contracts that will be burdensome. Therefore the accountant should furnish the debtor's attorney with a list of all executory contracts including any contract which leaves something to be performed by either party, other than the obligation to pay money. Executory contracts may consist of employment contracts, long-term leases, commitments the company has made to produce goods for a specific customer at a set price over a long time period, construction contracts to expand the facilities, or agreements the company has signed for the purchase of a certain quantity of raw material. The accountant may also give an opinion as to which contracts will most likely be unprofitable and should be rejected.

12   It is also important to discuss at this prefiling conference what caused the debtor's current problems, whether the company will be able to overcome its difficulties, and if so, what measures will be necessary. The accountant may be asked to explain how the losses occurred and what can be done to avoid them in the future. To help with this determination, the accountant should project the operations for a thirty-day period over at least the next three to six months and indicate the areas where steps will be necessary in order to earn a profit (see paragraphs 44–47).

13   Discussion of the debtor's past history, including a thorough examination of its business conduct, is essential. The attorney will want to know whether any financial statements have been issued, the nature of such statements, whether they can be substantiated, and whether they might be construed to be deceptive. Also investigated will be any preferential payments made to favored creditors or other transfers of property that are not in the regular course of business. Any unusually large purchases should be closely scrutinized, and the debtor should be able to account for all of the assets. Any other information concerning the debtor's activities which the attorney should be aware of to determine some of the problems which may arise in the course of the proceedings should also be supplied. It is necessary that the debtor's counsel have complete knowledge of the situation in order to decide what course of action it will be best to pursue. Obviously, the accountant plays a crucial role in obtaining this information.

14   One other area where the independent accountant's services are indispensable is in the determination of insolvency and the exact date at which it occurred. The lawyer may be required to prove insolvency. But the independent accountant must determine the debtor's financial condition by an audit (chapter 11), prepare worksheets, and compile supporting documents and records necessary to prove the client's condition. Under prior law, it was necessary for the debtor to commit an act of bankruptcy before the creditors could force the debtor into bankruptcy. Most of these acts required that the debtor be insolvent at the time the act was committed. The new law eliminated these acts as a condition for involuntary bankruptcy. The proof of insolvency may still be necessary where preferential payments or fraudulent transfers are involved (chapter 3, paragraphs 20–22).

15   If at this preliminary meeting it is decided to file a petition to initiate formal reorganization proceedings, all parties involved must act quickly because a tax lien may be impending or a judgment sale or foreclosure of a mortgage may be threatening. This emphasizes the necessity for the accountant to have complete knowledge in advance of the accounting functions that must be performed.[1]

Determine Alternatives

16 One of the first decisions that must be made at an early meeting of the debtor with bankruptcy counsel and accountants is whether it is best to liquidate (under provisions of state law or Bankruptcy Code), to attempt an out-of-court settlement, to seek an outside buyer, or to file a chapter 11 petition. To decide which course of action to take, it is also important to ascertain what caused the debtor's current problems, whether the company will be able to overcome its difficulties and, if so, what measures will be necessary. Accountants may be asked to explain how the losses occurred and what can be done to avoid them in the future. To help with this determination, it may be necessary to project the operations for a thirty-day period over at least the next three to six months, and indicate the areas where steps will be necessary in order to earn a profit.

17 For existing clients, the information needed to make a decision about the course of action to take may be obtained with limited additional work; however, for a new client, it will be necessary to perform a review of the client's operations to determine the condition of the business. Once the review has been completed, the client must normally decide to liquidate the business, attempt an informal settlement with creditors, or file a chapter 11 petition, unless additional funds can be obtained or a buyer for the business is located. For example, where the product is inferior, the demand for the product is declining, the distribution channels are inadequate, or other similar problems exist that cannot be corrected, either because of the economic environment or management's lack of ability, it is normally best to liquidate the company immediately.

18 The decision whether a business should immediately file a chapter 11 petition or attempt an out-of-court settlement depends on several factors. Among them are the following:

1 Size of company.
>   Public.
>   Private.

2 Number of creditors.
>   Secured.
>   Unsecured.
>   Public.
>   Private.

---

[1] Harris Levin, "Accounting Aspects of Arrangement Proceedings," *New York Certified Public Accountant,* Vol. 28 (June 1958), p. 430.

3 Complexity of matter.
   Nature of debt.
   Prior relationships with creditors.
4 Pending lawsuits.
5 Executory contracts, especially leases.
6 Tax impact of alternative selected.
7 Nature of management.
   Mismanagement.
   Irregularities.

Other Prebankruptcy Services

19 There are several other services that the accountant may render for the debtor prior to the filing of the petition. The extent to which the accountant does additional work depends partly on the amount of time left before the debtor must file the petition. Often there is very little time left because the attorneys and accountants are not consulted until the debtor's operations have deteriorated to the point where a petition must be filed. In fact, in many bankruptcy engagements the CPA is consulted only after the petition is filed. Ideally, the accountant might assist the debtor in the following ways before a petition is filed, but as indicated above assistance might be postpetition:

1 Assemble data on loan agreements, requirements, defaults, encumbrances, and so forth to help the debtor evaluate the courses of action to take.
2 Assemble creditor data by priority.
3 Prepare a list of executory contracts and leases with an indication of those that should probably be rejected or assigned.
4 Prepare an analysis of intercompany debt and other arrangements.
5 Prepare cash projections for the immediate short term of four to six weeks and for the next year or so.
6 Prepare pro forma statements based on the changes management plans to make.
7 Prepare data necessary for the debtor to file the bankruptcy petition.
8 Perform an audit or other special investigative services including an analysis of selected transactions.
9 Reconcile and evaluate creditor's proofs of claims.
10 Assist in determining the value of the business. (Chapter 10 contains a discussion of the approaches used in determining the value of a business.)
11 Provide tax advice on several issues including the impact which debt discharge and the terms of the plan will have on the debtor's tax liability. (Chapter 14 discusses these factors.)

NATURE OF ACCOUNTING SERVICES

20   The services rendered by the accountant in bankruptcy and insolvency proceedings can be divided into over a dozen categories. The accountant:

1   Provides the debtor's counsel with the information needed to prepare the schedules, statement of affairs, and other forms necessary to file a petition.

2   Prepares special financial statements, including a balance sheet as of the date the petition is filed. (See Chapter 12.)

3   Provides the usual accounting services for the client.

4   Assists the client in formulating a plan that will meet with the approval of creditors and at the same time allow the debtor to operate the business successfully.

5   Develops the disclosure statement that must be issued prior to or at the time acceptance of the plan is solicited.

6   May be appointed as an examiner by the court.

7   Assists in the preparation of operating statements to be filed with the court.

8   May be asked to perform several different types of consulting activities (management advisory services) that provide information that assists the debtor in making decisions necessary to see that successful operations can be resumed.

9   Performs an audit or other special investigative services, including an analysis of selected transactions.

10   Reconciles and evaluates creditors' proofs of claims. After establishing the book balances for the unsecured creditors, these balances should be compared with the claims filed. If a claim has not been filed, the book balance is compared with the amount admitted on the debtor's Schedules of Liabilities to determine its accuracy. Discrepancies are analyzed, and if they are not reconcilable, this information is communicated to the trustee or counsel as well as to the creditors' committee. A proof of claim is filed on Bankruptcy Form 19. (A copy of Form 19 can be found in Appendix B. The procedures to evaluate the proof of claims are discussed in chapter 11.)

11   Assists in determining the value of the business. (Chapter 10 contains a discussion of the approaches used in determining the value of a business.)

12   Provides tax advice on several issues including the impact which debt discharge and the terms of the plan will have on the debtor's tax liability. (Chapter 14 discusses these factors.)

13   Renders other services including assistance in finding sources of credit.

21   The functions relating to preparation of operating statements and the rendering of management advisory services are discussed in chapter 8.

ACCOUNTING DATA RELATIVE TO THE PETITION

22   The accountant must supply the attorney with certain information necessary for a chapter 11 petition to be filed. This would normally include the following:[2]

1   *List of twenty largest creditors*   A list containing the names and addresses of the twenty largest unsecured creditors, excluding insiders, must be filed with the petition in a voluntary case. In an involuntary situation, the list must be submitted after an order of relief is entered. See Bankruptcy Rule 1007 and Bankruptcy Form 9.

2   *List of creditors*   The debtor must file with the court a list of the debtor's creditors of each class, showing the amounts and character of their claims and securities and, so far as is known, the name and address or place of business of each creditor and a notation whether the claim is disputed, contingent, or unliquidated as to amount, when each claim was incurred and the consideration received, and related data.

3   *List of equity security holders*   A list of the debtor's equity security holders of each class showing the number and kind of interests registered in the name of each holder, and the last known address or place of business of each holder.

4   *Schedules of assets and liabilities*   See paragraphs 27–36.

5   *Statements of financial affairs*   See paragraph 37.

6   *Statement of executory contracts*   See paragraph 38.

7   *Exhibit "A" to the Petition*   This is a thumbnail sketch of the financial condition of the business listing total assets, total liabilities, secured claims, unsecured claims, information relating to public trading of the debtor's securities, and the identity of all insiders. See Exhibit 7-1 for an example of Exhibit "A" and Official Form 1 (Appendix B).

23   Often the petition must be filed quickly to avoid pending legal proceedings, and the debtor's books are seldom up to date. In some circumstances the accountant may be called upon to assist the attorney to prepare a petition with only a few hours' notice. A so-called skeletal petition may be filed consisting principally of the petition, the exhibit "A," corporate minutes authorizing the filing, the list of twenty largest creditors plus a list of all

---

[2] Bankruptcy Rule 1007 directs that the following lists and schedules mentioned be submitted. The required lists and schedules may change once permanent rules are adopted. See chapter 3, paragraphs 15–16.

Exhibit 7-1 Exhibit "A"

[If petitioner is a corporation, this Exhibit A shall be completed and attached to the petition pursuant to paragraph 7 thereof.]

[Caption, other than designation, as in Form No. 1.]

FOR COURT USE ONLY

Date Petition Filed

Case Number

Bankruptcy Judge

1. Petitioner's employer's identification number is _____.

2. If any of petitioner's securities are registered under section 12 of the Securities and Exchange Act of 1934, SEC file number is _____.

3. The following financial data is the latest available information and refers to petitioner's condition on _____.

    a. Total assets: $_____.

    b. Liabilities:

		Approximate number of holders
Secured debt, excluding that listed below	$_____	_____
Debt securities held by more than 100 holders:		
Secured	$_____	_____
Unsecured	$_____	_____
Other liabilities, excluding contingent or unliquidated claims	$_____	_____
Number of shares of common stock	$_____	_____

Comments, if any: _____

4. Brief description of petitioner's business: _____

5. The name of any person who directly or indirectly owns, controls, or holds, with power to vote, 20 percent or more of the voting securities of petitioner is

6. The names of all corporations 20 percent or more of the outstanding voting securities of which are directly or indirectly owned, controlled, or held, with power to vote, by petitioner are _____

claimants with addresses. The debtor has a brief automatic extension of time after the petition is filed for the preparation of the remaining schedules and statements. Any additional extension of time may be granted only on application, for cause shown, and on notice to any committee, trustee, examiner, or other party identified by the court.

24   The original and at least six copies of each of the lists and schedules must be filed with the court for chapter 11 petitions. An original and at least three copies are required for proceedings under chapter 7 or chapter 13. In pilot districts for the U.S. trustee program additional copies will be required and local bankruptcy rules for each district should be consulted.

Affidavit as to Projected Operations

25   Certain districts may require a sworn statement containing the data necessary to prove to the court that the debtor in possession will be able to operate the business at a profit. These projections, usually prepared in budget form and on a monthly basis, should be revised as new information becomes available and should indicate which areas, in the accountant's opinion, are unprofitable and which costs should be eliminated. The following data are illustrative of the type that may be included in the affidavit:

> The total amount of the payroll each week and the salaries paid to the officers of the corporation.
>
> All items which compose overhead.
>
> A statement of any litigation or levies pending upon the debtor's property.
>
> The reasons why it is in the best interests of the creditors that the debtor remain in possession of the property. (It is most important to show that they will receive more under reorganization proceedings than they would if the estate were to be liquidated.) (See chapter 5, paragraphs 91–92.)

26   If there is reason to believe that the firm will not be able at least to break even, the independent accountant should consult with the debtor or the trustee, citing the reasons for this suspicion. At the end of each operating period, a statement of operations should be prepared and compared with the projection so that those interested may come to their own decisions about the future of the business and that subsequent budgets may be modified. These budgets as prepared by the accountant serve the dual function of controlling operations while the debtor remains in possession and guiding the preparation of the plan. See paragraphs 44–47 for comments relating to the preparation of the forecasts.

Supporting Schedules

27   The schedules that must accompany the petition are sworn statements of the debtor's assets and liabilities as of the date the petition is filed under chapter 11. These schedules consist primarily of the debtor's balance sheet broken down into detail, and the accountant will be required to supply the information generated in the preparation of the normal balance sheet and its supporting schedules. The required information is supplied on Schedules A-1 and A-3 which include a complete statement of liabilities, and Schedules B-1 through B-4 which are a complete statement of assets. Exhibit 7-2 contains an example of a supporting schedule filed with a court that contains the information required in Form No. 6.

28   It is crucial that this information be accurate and complete because the omission or incorrect listing of a creditor might result in a failure to receive notice of the proceedings, and consequently the creditor's claim could be exempted from a discharge when the plan is later confirmed. Also, omission of material facts may be construed as a false statement or concealment.[3]

Priority Claims

29   All claims holding priority under the Bankruptcy Code must be listed on Schedule A-1. The most frequent of such claims are wages now including salaries, contributions to employee benefit plans, and taxes. For wages, the name and address of each claimant to whom the debtor owes wages, commissions, salary, vacation pay, sick pay, or severance pay when the petition is filed must be listed. Each taxing authority must be listed separately. For the Internal Revenue Service, the District Director of the office where the debtor files its returns should be listed, with a breakdown of all federal taxes which are due. All other taxing authorities must be listed, with the address of each agency and the amount owing. See chapter 3, paragraphs 93–94 for additional priority claims.

Secured Creditors

30   Schedule A-2 is provided for listing the holders of claims secured by a deposit or property of the debtor. Required on the schedule are the name and address of each creditor, a description of the security being held and the date it was obtained, specification as to when each claim was incurred and the consideration therefor, indication as to whether the claim is contingent, unliquidated or disputed, and the amount of the claim, and the market value, of the collateral.

Unsecured Creditors

31   A list of all unsecured creditors is required on Schedule A-3 and must include their names and mailing addresses, when claim was incurred and the consideration therefor, and the amount due each claimant. This information is generally taken from the books and records of the company. It is important to list all creditors and give the full name and correct address of each

---

[3] Levin, p. 432.

Exhibit 7-2   Supporting Schedules

UNITED STATES BANKRUPTCY COURT FOR THE
CENTRAL DISTRICT OF CALIFORNIA

In re
DEBTOR CORP.
Debtor*

Case No. LA-XO-04065-JD
SCHEDULES

SCHEDULE A—STATEMENT OF ALL LIABILITIES OF DEBTOR

Schedules A-1, A-2, and A-3 must include all the claims against the petitioner or his property as of the date of the filing of the petition by or against him.

SCHEDULE A-1—Creditors having priority

1 Nature of claim	2 Name of creditor and complete mailing address including zip code (if unknown, so state)	3 Specify when claim was incurred and the consideration therefore, when claim is contingent, unliquidated, disputed, or subject to setoff, evidenced by a judgment, negotiable instrument, or other writing, or incurred as partner or joint contractor, so indicate, specify name of any partner or joint contractor on any debt	4 Indicate if claim is contingent, unliquidated or disputed	5 Amount of Claim
a Wages, salaries and commissions, including vacation, severance and sick leave pay owing to workmen, servants, clerks, or traveling or city salesmen on salary or commission basis, whole or part time, whether or not selling exclusively for the debtor, not exceeding $2000 to each earned within 90 days before filing of petition or cessation of business, if earlier (specify date)		(SEE RIDER A-1-a)		$ 3,020.00
b Contributions to employee benefit plans for services rendered within 180 days before filing of petition or cessation of business, if earlier (specify date)				–0–
c Deposits by individuals, not exceeding $900 for each purchase, lease or rental of property or services for personal, family, or household use that were not delivered or provided				–0–
d Taxes owing (itemize by type of tax and taxing authority)		(See Schedule A-1 Supplement)		21,736.58
(1) To the United States		(See Schedule A-1 Supplement)		39,589.70
(2) To any state				–0–
(3) To any other taxing authority				

* Include here all names used by debtor within last 6 years.   Total $64,346.28

Exhibit 7-2 *(Continued)*

RIDER A-1-a

Tom Jones 6420 Lexington Ave. Cerritos, California 90701	Sales Commission	$ 500.00 (contingent and unliquidated)
Bill Thompson 1247 Main Street Hacienda Heights, California 91745	Sales Commission	500.00 (contingent and unliquidated)
William Robertson 4201 South Street Woodland Hills, California 91634	Sales Commission	200.00 (contingent and unliquidated)
Denise Blank 5891 Smith Street Huntington Beach, Calif. 92647	Salary	1,820.00 $3,020.00

SCHEDULE A-1 SUPPLEMENT

d

(1) Taxes owing to United States Internal Revenue Service

Federal withholding tax	$14,243.06
FICA	7,194,43
Federal Unemployment tax	299.09
	$21,736.58

(2) Taxes owing to State of California

(a) State Board of Equalization

Sales and use tax 1st quarter	16,965.20
April	16,901.06
May 1-7	3,215.95
	$37,082.21

(b) Employment Development Department

State withholding tax	$1,512.45
State Disability Insurance	183.21
State Unemployment tax	811.83
	$2,507.49

(3) To any other taxing agency   –0–

Addresses:

Internal Revenue Service, 300 N. Los Angeles St.,
Los Angeles, Ca. 90012, Attn: Chief Special Procedures

Exhibit 7-2   (*Continued*)

State Board of Equalization, 1020 "N" Street, P.O.B. 1799
Sacramento, Ca. 95808

Employment Development Department, 800 Capitol Mall
Sacramento, Ca. 95814

Los Angeles County Tax Collector, 225 N. Hill St.,
Los Angeles, Ca. 90012

SCHEDULE A-2—Creditors Holding Security

1. Name of creditor and complete mailing address including zip code (if unknown, so state)	2. Description of security and date when obtained by creditor	3. Specify when claim was incurred and the consideration therefor; when claim is contingent, unliquidated, disputed, subject to setoff, evidenced by a judgment, negotiable instrument, or other writing, or incurred as partner or joint contractor, so indicate; specify name of any partner or joint contractor on any debt	4. Indicate if claim is contingent, unliquidated or disputed	5. Market value	6. Amount of claim without deduction of value of security
1) Bank of America 102 E. Las Tunas San Gabriel, CA 91776		Trade accounts receivable of the Debtor Corp. Accounts receivable financing loan opened July, 1977, with daily activity since that date		$590,781.76	$419,540.91
2) Bank of America 102 E. Las Tunas San Gabriel, CA 91776		Equipment loan Loan date May 1, 1978 for purchase of film processing equipment which in turn is leased to customer, London Press Book Value		22,500.00	25,710.00
3) Bank of America 102 E. Las Tunas San Gabriel, CA 91776		Auto Loan Loan date October 3, 1979 1979 C-30 Chev. Van Book Value		4,750.00	5,213.80
			Total	$618,031.76	$450,464.71

Exhibit 7-2 *(Continued)*

SCHEDULE A-3—Creditors Having Unsecured Claims Without Priority

Name of creditor (including last known holder of any negotiable instrument) complete mailing address including zip code (if unknown, so state)	Specify when claim was incurred and the consideration therefor; when claim is contingent, unliquidated, disputed, subject to setoff, evidenced by a judgment, negotiable instrument, or other writing, or incurred as partner or joint contractor, so indicate; specify name of any partner or joint contractor on any debt	Amount of Claim
1. Trade accounts payable (See Schedule A-3 Supplement [Schedule not included in Figure] for detail)		$586,437.20
2. Note payable Nancy Southern P. O. Box 6005 Booker, Texas 79005 Note dated May 1, 1978 for purchase of stock of J. P. Harwood Company at book value. Evidenced by judgment for $95,625.04 Disputed and case appealed Attorney: Jerome L. Daniels, Esq. 900 North Flower Street Los Angeles, California 90017		86,673.04 (disputed)
3. Lease/purchase contract Daniel R. Mai, dba Jefferson Ltd. P. O. Box 73056 Los Angeles, California 90018		16,000.00 (disputed and unliquidated)
4. Consulting contract date October 26, 1979 Corporate Associates 1100 Fox Street Los Angeles, California 92660		Unknown
5. Gustav Thompson 22505 West 8th Los Angeles, California 90032	'Landlord	–0–
6. Gary Dodsman Insurance Agency 9567 Westwood Boulevard Los Angeles, California 90047	Note	1,418.50
7. American Corporation Route 6 Somerville, New Jersey 08892	Note	61,078.21
	Total	$751,606.95

STATEMENT OF ALL PROPERTY OF DEBTOR

Schedules B-1, B-2, and B-4 must include all property of the debtor as of the date of the filing of the petition by or against him.

SCHEDULE B-1—Real Property

Description and location of all real property in which debtor has an interest (including equitable and future interests, interests in estates by the entirety, community property, life estates, leaseholds, and rights and powers exercisable for his own benefit)	Nature of interest (specify all deeds and written instruments relating thereto)	Market value of debtor's interest without deduction for secured claims listed in Schedule A-2 or exemptions claimed in Schedule B-4
2404 5th Avenue South El Monte, California 91733 Leasehold interest in commercial building of approximately 8,000 sq. feet	Lease expires November 30, 1980	$ –0–
	Total	$ –0–

Exhibit 7-2 *(Continued)*

SCHEDULE B-2—Personal Property

Type of Property	Description and Location		Market value of debtor's interest without deduction for secured claims listed in Schedule A-2 or exemptions claimed in Schedule B-4
a. Cash on hand			$ 980.49
b. Deposits of money with banking institutions, savings and loan associations, credit unions, public utility companies, landlords, and others	Bank of America 102 E. Las Tunas San Gabriel, CA	General Account #953216	18.87
	Gustav Thompson 22505 West 8th Los Angeles, CA 90032	Rent deposit	1,700.00
c. Household goods, supplies, and furnishings			–0–
d. Books, pictures, and other art objects; stamp, coin, and other collections			–0–
e. Wearing apparel, jewelry, firearms, sports equipment, and other personal possessions			–0–
f. Automobiles, trucks, trailers, and other vehicles	See Schedule B-2 supplement	Book value	4,417.15
g. Boats, motors, and their accessories			–0–
h. Livestock, poultry, and other animals			–0–
i. Farming supplies and implements			–0–
j. Office equipment, furnishings, and supplies	Cost $9,748.59 Less depreciation 7,700.08		2,048.51
k. Machinery, fixtures, equipment, and supplies (other than those listed in items i and j) used in business	Fork lift Shelving Computer		500.00 1,000.00 4,000.00

Schedule B-2 Sub-Total	$14,665.02

SCHEDULE B-2 SUPPLEMENT

f. Automobiles, trucks, trailers, and other vehicles

Make	Type	Year	Purchased	License	Cost
Dodge	B300 Van	1977	5-2-77	1T95568	
Dodge	Van	1977	3-2-78	1T51194	
Chevrolet	16′ Flatbed	1974	1-28-77	53679T	
Chevrolet	C-30 Van	1979	9-27-79	1T62560	
Ford	Pinto S/W	1976	5-25-76	328T	

	$31,943.41
Less Depreciation	27,526.26
Book Value	$ 4,417.15

Exhibit 7-2 (*Continued*)

SCHEDULE B-2—Personal Property (Cont'd.)

Description and Location	Type of Property	Market value of debtor's interest without deduction for secured claims listed in Schedule A-2 or exemptions claimed in Schedule B-4
	Schedule B-2 Sub-Total Forward	$ 14,665.02
l. Inventory		250,000.00
m. Tangible personal property of any other description		–0–
n. Patents, copyrights, franchises, and other general intangibles (specify all documents and writings relating thereto)		–0–
o. Government and corporate bonds and other negotiable and nonnegotiable instruments		–0–
p. Other liquidated debts owing debtor	SEE RIDER [Not included in figure] Notes payable from employees	590,781.76 7,667.64
q. Contingent and unliquidated claims of every nature, including counter-claims of the debtor (give estimated value of each)	Causes of action against Nancy Southern to recover monies heretofore paid	Unknown
r. Interests in insurance policies (itemize surrender or refund values of each)		–0–
s. Annuities		–0–
t. Stock and interests in incorporated and unincorporated companies (itemize separately)		–0–
u. Interests in partnerships		–0–
v. Equitable and future interests, life estates, and rights or powers exercisable for the benefit of the debtor (other than those listed in Schedule B-1) (specify all written instruments relating thereto)		–0–
	Total	$863,114.42

Exhibit 7-2 *(Continued)*

SCHEDULE B-3—Property Not Otherwise Scheduled

Type of Property	Description and Location	Market value of debtor's interest without deduction for secured claims listed in Schedule A-2 or exemptions claimed in Schedule B-4
a. Property transferred under assignment for benefit of creditors, within 120 days prior to filing of petition (specify date of assignment, name and address of assignee, amount realized therefrom by the assignee, and disposition of proceeds so far as known to debtor)		$ −0−
b. Property of any kind not otherwise scheduled		
	Notes receivable (equipment sale) Graphic Reproductions 2424 So. San Gabriel Blvd. Los Angeles, CA 90001 Unpaid balance	9,231.22
	A & W Investments 5635 Palms Blvd. Los Angeles, CA 90029 Unpaid balance	7,900.31
	Lease-Sale Contract (equipment lease/sale) Surrey Press, Inc. 7311 Woodley Ave North Hollywood, CA 91605 Unpaid balance	43,204.30
	Total	$60,335.83

SCHEDULE B-4—Property claimed as exempt

Debtor selects the following property as exempt pursuant to 11 USC & 522(d) or the laws of the State of _____ .

Type of Property	Location, description and, if relevant, the present use of the property.	Statute and section creating the exemption.	VALUE CLAIMED EXEMPT Dollars Cents
None			−0−
		Total	$ −0−

Exhibit 7-2 *(Continued)*

SUMMARY OF DEBTS AND PROPERTY

(From the Statements of the Debtor in Schedules A and B)

Schedule	DEBTS	Dollars	Cents
A-1/a, b	Wages, contributions	$ 3,020.00	
A-1/c	Deposits of money	–0–	
A-1/d (1)	Taxes owing United States	21,736.58	
A-1/d (2)	Taxes owing States	39,589.70	
A-1/d (3)	Taxes owing other taxing authorities	–0–	
A-2	Secured claims	450,464.71	
A-3	Unsecured claims without priority	751,606.95	
	SCHEDULE A TOTAL	$1,266,417.94	

PROPERTY

Schedule		Dollars	Cents
B-1	Real property (total value)	$ –0–	
B-2/a	Cash on hand	980.49	
B-2/b	Deposits	1,718.87	
B-2/c	Household goods	–0–	
B-2/d	Books, pictures, and collections	–0–	
B-2/e	Wearing apparel and personal possessions	–0–	
B-2/f	Automobiles and other vehicles	4,417.15	
B-2/g	Boats, motors, and accessories	–0–	
B-2/h	Livestock and other animals	–0–	
B-2/i	Farming supplies and implements	–0–	
B-2/j	Office equipment and supplies	2,048.51	
B-2/k	Machinery, equipment, and supplies used in business	5,500.00	
B-2/l	Inventory	250,000.00	
B-2/m	Other tangible personal property	–0–	
B-2/n	Patents and other general intangibles	–0–	
B-2/o	Bonds and other instruments	–0–	
B-2/p	Other liquidated debts	598,449.40	
B-2/q	Contingent and unliquidated claims	–0–	
B-2/r	Interests in insurance policies	–0–	
B-2/s	Annuities	–0–	
B-2/t	Interests in corporations and unincorporated companies	–0–	
B-2/u	Interests in partnerships	–0–	
B-2/v	Equitable and future interests, rights, and powers in personality	–0–	
B-3/a	Property assigned for benefit of creditors	–0–	
B-3/b	Property not otherwise scheduled	60,335.83	
B-4	Amount of Property claimed as exempt $___–0–___		
	Total of Schedule B-1 thru B-3	$ 923,450.25	

Exhibit 7-2 *(Continued)*

OATH TO SCHEDULES A AND B

I, _____, the person who subscribed to the foregoing Schedules A and B, do hereby declare (or certify, verify or state), under penalty of perjury*, that I have read the foregoing Schedules consisting of _____ sheets, and that they are a true and correct statement of all the debts and all the property of Petitioner in accordance with Title 11, United State Code.

Executed this ____ day of _____, 19____ at _____, California.

_____
Petitioner

* This unsworn declaration authorized by 28 USC 1746.

person. The exact amount due each creditor should be determined and the books posted so there is no doubt as to how much is owing. Unsecured creditors include not only general creditors, but also those who hold promissory notes, creditors with debt subject to setoff, judgment creditors, liabilities on notes or bills discounted that are to be paid by the drawers, makers, acceptors, or endorsers, creditors to whom the debtor is liable on accommodation paper, and officers or directors of the debtor who have loaned money to the company. It is important to list all claims that are disputed, contingent, or unliquidated, and indicate their status.[4] Also listed should be claims incurred as partners or joint contractors and the partner or joint contractor should be specified.

32   When Schedules A-1 through A-3 have been completed, all creditors who have or may have any interest in connection with the debtor's estate should have been listed. The accuracy of these schedules must again be emphasized in reorganization proceedings since a claim admitted on the debtor's schedules is deemed filed under section 1111(a). See chapter 5, paragraph 39.

Assets of the Debtor

33   Information concerning all interests of the debtor in property is provided in Schedules B-1 to B-4. Schedule B indicates that the property is to be presented at market values. However, for most business reorganization, the property is shown at book value. While market value as well as liquidation value may be needed for all or some of the debtor's property, they are subsequently determined by investment bankers, appraisers, and so forth. A statement of the real estate owned by the debtor with an estimated value of its interest is found on Schedule B-1.

[4] Ibid., p. 433.

34   Schedule B-2 concerns goods or personal property, telling where located, and including cash, negotiable instruments and securities, stock in trade, all motor vehicles and machinery, fixtures, equipment, patents, copyrights, and trademarks. One of the most important sections of this schedule for many businesses is the information regarding the debtor's stock in trade, to be computed from the actual inventory with a disclosure of the method of valuation used. The method used to value the inventory should be consistent with prior periods and should be a method that is in accordance with generally accepted accounting principles. If the method used to value inventory differs significantly (such as when LIFO is used) from the going concern value of the inventory, the value of the inventory should be used instead of historical costs. The figures required in this schedule are totals for each classification, not individual values for each item. Information about accounts receivable, insurance policies, all unliquidated claims (such as from fire, storm damage, and water damage as well as claims against insiders and other legal causes of action), and deposits of money made by the debtor is also included in Schedule B-2.

35   Property in reversion, remainder, or expectancy, including property held in trust for the debtor or subject to any power or right to dispose of or to charge should be included as real property on Schedule B-1 or personal property on Schedule B-2. Schedule B-3 lists property not otherwise scheduled. Included in this schedule would be property transferred under assignment for benefit of creditors within 120 days prior to filing of the petition. Schedule B-4 applies only to an individual debtor filing a petition and concerns all property which is exempt from the proceedings, such as household furniture, clothing, and so on. See chapter 3, paragraphs 101–103.

36   A summary of debts and property taken from Schedules A and B is also included with the petition. A single oath for all of the schedules must be submitted specifying the number of sheets included in the schedules and acknowledging that the affiant has read them. Separate forms of oath are provided for individuals, corporations, and partnerships. Form No. 6 which explains the information required on the schedules, summary, and oath is shown in Appendix B.

Statement of Financial Affairs

37   The statement of affairs, not to be confused with an accountant's usual use of the term, is a series of detailed questions about the debtor's property and conduct. The general purpose of the statement of affairs is to give both the creditors and the court an overall view of the debtor's operations. It offers many avenues from which investigations into the debtor's conduct may be begun. The statement (Form No. 8, Appendix B) consists of twenty-one questions to be answered under oath concerning the following areas:

1   The nature, location, and name of the business, including the employer's identification number, when the business was begun, where else and under what other names the debtor has conducted business.

2   Books and records, with the name and address of each person who kept and audited them during the preceding two years and who has possession of them now.

3   All financial statements that were issued within the previous two years.

4   The total dollar value of the last two inventories taken of the debtor's property, the valuation method used, the person who conducted the inventory, and the location of the records.

5   Income received from sources other than business operations.

6   Where and when income tax returns were filed for the last three years, tax refunds received or entitled to be received for the last two years.

7   All bank accounts and safe deposit boxes, including closed accounts.

8   Property held in trust for another person.

9   Prior bankruptcy proceedings.

10   Prior receiverships, general assignments, and other modes of liquidation.

11   Property of the debtor in the hands of a third person.

12   Suits pending at the time of the filing of the original petition; suits terminated within one year; any property attached, garnished, or seized within the year immediately preceding the filing of the original petition.

13   Any loans and installment purchases repaid during the year before the filing of the petition. Sufficient information must be given so as to determine whether any preferences have been made that might be recovered. Related to this will be a determination of the exact date when the debtor was insolvent.

14   Property transferred especially other than in the ordinary course of business during the preceding year. This is important because the transfer might have been fraudulent.

15   Assignment of accounts or other receivables.

16   Property returned or repossessed by a seller or secured party during the preceding year.

17   Business leases and security deposits.

18   Losses from fire, theft, or gambling.

19   Personal withdrawals, including compensation, bonuses, and loans made by officers, directors, insiders, managing executives, or shareholders (partners).

20   Payments or transfers to attorneys.

21   Names and addresses of all officers, directors, insiders, managing executives, and principal stockholders (members of partnership).

Exhibit 7-3   Statement of Executory Contracts of Debtor

UNITED STATES BANKRUPTCY COURT
SOUTHERN DISTRICT OF NEW YORK

In re   ⎫   In Proceedings for
ROE HOSIERY COMPANY INC.,   ⎬   a Reorganization
Debtor.   ⎭   Case No. X1-B-10999

STATEMENT OF EXECUTORY CONTRACTS OF DEBTOR

The following are all of the executory contracts of debtor on the date of the filing of the petition herein:

1. Conditional bill of sale dated *March* 11, 19___, from *Jones Auto Company, Inc.* to the debtor, covering *one* (1) 1940 *two ton International Truck,* Engine No. 3329145, Serial No. 2KH4-15282. Contract price is *two thousand one hundred and fifty* ($2,150) Dollars, of which *five hundred* ($500) Dollars was paid at time of contract, and balance of which was payable in monthly installments of *fifty* ($50) Dollars each over a period of *two* (2) years and *nine* (9) months, evidenced by promissory notes. The total amount of all unpaid notes is *eight hundred* ($800) Dollars.

2. Agreement made in *January,* 19___, between debtor and *Henry Jones,* for the employment of the latter from week to week at a weekly salary of *seventy-five* ($75) Dollars; the agreement may be terminated by either party upon *one* (1) week's notice to the other.

3. Lease dated *March* 6, 19___, between *Brown Holding Corporation,* as landlord, and debtor, as tenant, for space on the *fifth* floor of premises, 845 *Bleeker* Street, *New York, New York,* for a term of *seven* (7) years and *two* (2) months, beginning *April* 1, 19___, and terminating *May* 31, 19___, at a rental of *four thousand eight hundred* ($4,800) Dollars per year, payable in equal monthly installments in advance.

[Set forth a similar statement of any other executory contract of the debtor.]

> (Signed)   *Arthur Smith*
> Attorney for Debtor.
> (Address)   *22 Broadway*
> *New York, New York 10005*

Source: Adapted from *Collier Forms Manual,* Form 3012.

The statement of financial affairs must conform to the requirements set forth in Form No. 8 designed to be used by businesses. (See Appendix B.) Note that the statement of affairs consists of a large number of questions that deal with accounting information. In most bankruptcies it is more appropriate for the accountant to answer these questions and complete the schedules than for this service to be performed by counsel. Often, the internal accountant and the debtor are too busy handling normal accounting problems to prepare this information. Thus, independent accountants are engaged to perform this function.

Statement of Executory Contracts

38   This listing of unexpired leases and other unperformed agreements is provided to permit the trustee (or the debtor) to consider which of its obligations are burdensome to the estate and should be rejected under section 365. Relevant particulars for each executory contract such as the following should be listed:

Party contracting with debtor.

Address of party.

Concise characterization of contract (employment agreement, equipment lease, and so on).

Date of contract.

Term of contract, expiration date, options, and so on.

Price or payment terms of contract.

Balance of any monies owed by the debtor or other condition(s) of default as of the petition date.

Executory contracts were discussed in chapter 3, paragraphs 83–89 and Exhibit 7-3 contains an example.

NORMAL ACCOUNTING SERVICES

39   It is still necessary for the accountant to render the usual services that would be given any other client, and normal accounting procedures will be followed. However, it is important to realize that the debtor in possession is a new legal entity that must be distinguished from the debtor. The accountant must close the debtor's books as of the date the petition is filed and open new books for the new entity. In the opening entry all of the prepetition liabilities are grouped into one account usually labelled "prepetition debt." (See chapter 12, paragraph 40.) This is because none of the debtor's liabilities that existed at the date of the filing may be paid by the debtor in possession except upon specific order of the court. Permission of the court can often be obtained to pay, on a date after the filing of the petition, employee's wages earned during the payroll period prior to the filing of the petition. The dichotomy of the prefiling debtor and the debtor in possession must not be underemphasized. The operating guidelines of the U.S. trustee for Maine, Massachusetts, New Hampshire, and Rhode Island for example require that all checking accounts of the debtor be closed upon the filing and that all outstanding checks be permitted to "bounce." Similar procedures are followed in California and other districts. In such cases where the debtor has certain flexibility in timing the filing of its petition, care may be taken to avoid such embarrassment.

ASSISTANCE IN FORMULATING PLAN

40 The accountant will be asked to advise and give suggestions to the debtor and attorney in drawing up a plan. See Exhibit 5-1 (pages 155–162) for any example of a plan filed under chapter 11. Section 1121 of the Bankruptcy Code provides that only the debtor may file a plan of reorganization during the first 120 days of the case (unless a trustee has been appointed). This breathing period is intended to permit the debtor to hold lawsuits and foreclosures in status quo, and to determine economic causes of its financial predicament while developing a plan. Using the schedules of assets and liabilities, statement of affairs, and post and projected financial statements, the debtor, and its accountant will examine the liabilities of the debtor and the value of the business. They will explore sources of funding the plan such as enhanced profitability, partial liquidation, issuing debt securities, or outside capitalization. They will outline the classes of debt that cannot be deferred or reduced and negotiate with the rest.

41 The most important requirements are that the plan be approved by each class of claims and equity holders and that it be feasible. If the creditors or stockholders in any given class have not approved the plan, the class must receive at least as much as would be received if the debtor were liquidated under chapter 7. (This is the best interest test discussed in chapter 5, paragraphs 91–92.) In situations where a class of creditors or stockholders has not approved the plan, the plan must also be fair and equitable with respect to each of the classes impaired as discussed in chapter 5, paragraphs 96–107. The accountant's help may also be essential to the preparation of an adequate disclosure statement that must be issued at the time or before acceptance of the plan is solicited. (See paragraph 51.)

Liquidating Value of Assets

42 Section 1129(a)(7) provides that each holder of a claim must either accept the plan or receive or retain interest in property of a value that is at least equal to the amount that would have been received or retained if the debtor were liquidated under chapter 7. See chapter 10, paragraphs 42–44 for a description of the approaches used to determine liquidation values.

43   The liquidation alternative often leaves the unsecured creditors with very little. For example, in one Chapter XI case under prior law, the debtor was a major retailer and had already closed several stores. An alternative was to close all of the stores and liquidate the business as was done with W. T. Grant. The accountant identified for the creditors the following reasons why liquidation value would be so low:

Adverse impact of environment where the store is being liquidated:

  Constrains selling prices.
  Increases landlord settlements.
  Leads to operating losses.
  Lessens realization from liquidation of other assets.

Administrative expenses unique to liquidation would be realized which had not been incurred in cities where stores were previously liquidated:

  Additional administrative costs.
  Breach of contract claims.
  Materially higher settlement on pension costs, including probable additional assessments on already closed operations.
  Higher landlord settlement costs because there would be no rehabilitation motive by the court.
  Damages from personal property lease rejections, for example, computers and automobiles.
  Operating losses for a minimum of sixty days until operational closing is complete.

Projection of Future Operations

44   Section 1129(a)(11) contains the feasibility standard of chapter 11 requiring that confirmation of the plan of reorganization is not likely to be followed by liquidation or further reorganization (unless contemplated). The accountant may assist the debtor or trustee to formulate an acceptable plan by projecting the ability of the debtor to carry out and perform the terms of the plan. To establish feasibility, the accountant must project the profitability potential of the business. Where the plan calls for installment payments, the accountant will be requested to prepare projected budgets, cash flow statements, and statements of financial position. The creditors must be assured by the projected income statement and cash flow statement that the debtor will be in a position to make the payments as they become due. The forecast of the results or operations and financial position should be prepared on the assumption that the proposed plan will be accepted and that the liability and asset accounts reflect the balance that would be shown after all adjustments are made relative to the debt forgiveness. Thus, interest expense is based on the liabilities that will exist after the discharge occurs. See the projected operating statement at the end of this chapter for an example of the type of information presented in a forecast.

45   Not only are projections needed for legal purposes as mentioned in the previous paragraph, but they are an important part of the negotiation process. The creditors want to receive the maximum amount possible in any chapter 11 plan and often they want the payment in cash as of the effective date of the plan. The creditors realize, however, that if their demands are beyond the ability of the debtor to make payments, the plan will not work and they will not receive the payments provided for in the plan. Both creditors and debtor realize that there must be an asset base left with the company if future operations are to be profitable. Projections assist both parties in developing reasonable conclusions regarding the terms of a proposed plan. In some reorganizations, there is considerable debate and discussion over the projections. Once the debtor and its creditors' committee agree on the projections, it is then easier to negotiate the terms of the plan. For example, in one fairly large reorganization the debtor and the committee accepted the fact that the company would not be able to obtain a bank credit line once the plan was confirmed. Thus, the working capital needed must come from the cash built up during bankruptcy. Projections help determine the amount of

Exhibit 7-4   Projected Pro Forma Consolidated Balance Sheet

The projected pro forma consolidated balance sheet set forth below presents the pro forma impact of consummation of the Trustees' Proposed Joint Plan of Reorganization ("the Plan") upon the projected historical consolidated balance sheet of X Company as of December 31, 19X9, assuming the Plan is consummated on that date. The projected historical consolidated balance sheet as of December 31, 19X9 is based upon assumptions as to future events and operating results and, accordingly, is not audited and is subject to change.

X Company's investment in discontinued operations (Seafood operations) are carried in the projected pro forma consolidated balance sheet at X Company equity in the net assets of these operations. In the opinion of management, the net recovery by X company from the intended disposition of the Seafood operations will exceed their indicated carrying amount ($14,171,000) and if such disposition occurs on or before December 31, 19X9, the amount of any such excess would increase projected pro forma common stockholders' equity of the reorganized company by a like amount. The net recovery from disposal of the Seafood operations may be in the form of both current and non-current assets, neither the amount nor proportion of which is presently determinable. Additionally, any differences between actual operating results for the year 19X9 and the projected operating results upon which the projected historical balance sheet as of December 31, 19X9 has been prepared, would increase or decrease projected pro forma common stockholders' equity of the reorganized company by a like amount.

Exhibit 7-4 *(Continued)*

X COMPANY
PROJECTED PRO FORMA CONSOLIDATED BALANCE SHEET
December 31, 19X9

(Giving Pro Forma Effect to Consummation of the Trustees'
Joint Plan of Reorganization As of That Date)
(Unaudited—$000 Omitted)

	Projected Historical December 31, 19X9 (prior to reorganization adjustments)	Reorganization adjustments	Projected Pro Forma December 31, 19X9 (after reorganization adjustments)
Assets			
Current assets			
Cash and cash equivalents	$15,977	$(5,000) (A)	$10,977
Receivables	5,374		5,374
Inventories	1,590		1,590
Prepaid expenses	1,029		1,029
Total current assets	23,970	(5,000)	18,970
Property and Equipment, net of accumulated amortization:			
Owned	18,896		18,896
Capital leases	10,441		10,441
Total property and equipment	29,337		29,337
Deposits on aircraft purchase and lease agreements	3,522		3,522
Other assets			
Excess paid for stock of consolidated subsidiary over equity in net assets acquired	3,559		3,559
Other	483		483
Total other assets	4,042		4,042
Investment in and advances to discontinued operations (Seafood operations)	14,171		14,171
	$75,042	$(5,000)	$70,042
Liabilities, Preferred Stocks and Common Stockholders' Equity			
Current Liabilities			
Accounts payable and accrued liabilities	$ 9,023		$ 9,023
Other current liabilities	1,186		1,186
Current portion of long-term debt	1,050		1,050
Current portion of capitalized lease obligations	2,256		2,256
Total current liabilities	13,515		13,515

Exhibit 7-4 *(Continued)*

	Projected Historical December 31, 19X9 (prior to reorganization adjustments)	Reorganization adjustments	Projected Pro Forma December 31, 19X9 (after reorganization adjustments)
Total current liabilities	$13,515		$13,515
Other liabilities	4		4
Deferred gain on sale and leaseback	1,232		1,232
Long-term debt and capitalized lease obligations			
Long-term debt	11,056		11,056
Capitalized lease obligations	9,289		9,289
Long-term debt and capitalized lease obligations	20,345		20,345
Prebankruptcy liabilities of Chapter X companies (Unsecured liabilities in Classes 5, 6 and 7)	39,299	$(39,299)(B)	
Stockholders' equity prior to reorganization	647	(647)(C)	
Series A preferred stock (Redeemable from available income, as defined, commencing in the fifth year following reorganization) at par, which equals liquidation preference		14,952 (D)	14,952
Series B convertible, preferred stock, at par, which equals liquidation preference		4,568 (D)	4,568
Common stockholders' equity:			
Common stock and additional paid-in-capital		15,426 (D)	15,426
Retained earnings (after reorganization adjustments)		—	—
Total common stockholders' equity		15,426	15,426
Total common stockholders' equity and preferred stocks		34,946	34,946
	$75,042	$(5,000)	$70,042

(A) Payment of estimated costs of the case.
(B) Close out of prebankruptcy liabilities of Chapter X companies.
(C) Close out of stockholders' equity prior to reorganization.
(D) Creation of new preferred and common stocks.

working capital needed and the type of payments that could be funded in the future.

46   The forecast and the assumptions on which it is based originate with the debtor or trustee, who assumes the responsibility for them. However, the accountant would not want to be associated with the forecast in any way if the assumptions are believed to be incomplete or unreasonable. The assumptions on which the forecast is based should be clearly stated in the report. An example of how the assumptions may be shown in the forecast is contained in the projected operating statement at the end of this chapter. Any major changes in the operations of the business, such as the elimination of a division or a given product line, should be clearly set forth. If the forecast depends on the success of new products or markets, this should be stated.

Pro Forma Balance Sheet

47   Also of considerable help in evaluating a plan is a pro forma balance sheet showing how the balance sheet will look if the plan is accepted and all provisions of the plan are carried out. Exhibit 7-4 contains an example of the pro forma balance sheet prepared in a Chapter X case under prior law.

Formulating an Amended Plan

48   When a petition was filed under Chapter XI of prior law, an actual plan of arrangement was included or it was stated that the plan would be proposed. If a plan was filed with the petition, it was often filed only to halt other legal proceedings that were pending and could prove damaging if consummated. Thus the plan most likely had to be amended, and the changes were usually generated from meetings of the debtor with the attorney and the creditors' committee.

49   Under the new law, there may be fewer debtors that submit a plan at the time the petition is filed because of the requirement for adequate information disclosure before votes can be solicited. There will still be a need for modified plans to be developed and submitted to the creditors in an attempt to gain their approval, of course, as part of the negotiating process. There are many factors that can cover the need for a modified plan, including the discovery of additional claims, tax requirement changes, changes in financial condition, delays in obtaining plan approval, and changes in economic conditions.

50   Any amended plan of reorganization must make provision for taxes due at the time the petition was filed. At the time the initial petition was filed, the amount and nature of taxes may not have been known. Generally, taxes will not be compromised by taxing authorities, but installment payments are permissible. Section 1129(a)(9) provides that tax claims qualifying for the sixth priority must be satisfied with cash payments over a period not to

Exhibit 7-5   Disclosure Statement and Plan for Chapter 11 Case

UNITED STATES BANKRUPTCY COURT
CENTRAL DISTRICT OF CALIFORNIA

In re
FABRATEX CORP.,   Debtor No. BK X9-22313 PE
Debtor

DISCLOSURE STATEMENT AND STATEMENT OF AFFAIRS

FABRATEX CORPORATION, Debtor in the above-entitled proceedings submits the following statement of facts and accompanying data as a companion document of its Reorganization Plan (which is being filed concurrently with this disclosure statement).

A. INTRODUCTION

Fabratex Corporation is a soft goods manufacturer which at present produces complex sewn assemblies for the aircraft and military markets. It has expanded its product lines to include seat covers, cushions, an assortment of reinforced container bags for parachutes or storage, and strap assemblies ranging from chin straps to runway barriers.

The Company is the successor to a business started over 30 years ago as a designer and manufacturer of aircraft seats and survival systems. This line was gradually enlarged to include a variety of aircraft-related soft goods.

Fabratex Corporation started originally as the John T. Toster Company. This Company built up a line or proprietary aircraft seats and personnel survival systems that was widely used by the Air Force and Naval services. After several years of growth it was acquired by Tool Research and Engineering Corp. (now Astech Industries), which continued its operations as a division.

Eight years ago the soft goods line was divested and became an independent company operating as E & E Fabratex. It retained the aircraft seat portion of the proprietary line and added other products such as protective body armor (bullet-proof vests).

The business was gradually rebuilt with several key people who stayed through portions of the transition and maintained the basic capabilities in soft goods for the Military which had been the primary product line. The type of experience served well in the addition of the bullet-proof vest business.

The company was incorporated as E & E Fabratex, Inc. in June 19X6 when Eddie Johnson and John Wright bought the company. The corporate name was shortened to Fabratex Corporation in May 19X8. The new owners and present management have a combined experience of over 30 years in the aircraft and aerospace field spread through the Marketing Engineering, Manufacturing, and Quality Assurance activities.

Eddie Johnson   Ten years' marketing-related experience consisting of:

Sales representative for five years for a supplier of parts (Hi-

Exhibit 7-5 (*Continued*)

Shear) to the military and commercial aircraft market. He contacted procurement and technical people at military bases and major aircraft companies on both a regional and national basis. He negotiated contracts and technical details with them. Has extensive direct contacts with these activities.

Field service engineer for five years for a parts supplier (Omark Industries) where experience was gained working with procurement and technical people in product usage and development. Provided considerable insight into the internal operations of customers behind the purchasing departments. This knowledge is quite helpful in developing anticipation to customer needs for marketing planning.

Graduated fourteenth in class from University of Missouri at Kansas City with a B.S. in General Engineering. Has pursued graduate studies toward M.S. in Business Administration.

John Wright Twenty years' marketing-related and customer contract experience:

Consultant for two years in military and commercial aircraft products marketing. Developed marketing plans by market surveys of existing and long-term business potential, assessing possibilities relative to competitors and market position.

Division officer (Vice-President of Omark Industries for five years) responsible for division business planning and development. This included short and long-term market projections, product development planning capital needs, personnel needs, and organizational needs. Established many personal contacts and knowledge of procurement groups, both military and commercial.

Company Executive (Director of Quality and Reliability for Hi-Shear Corp.) for ten years. Managed Quality and Reliability departments, which involved extensive dealings with customers at both technical and procurement levels. Negotiated complex technical contracts, which involved development and testing as well as simple contracts. Customers were both military and commercial.

Graduated from the University of Pittsburgh with M.B.A. in Industrial Management. Undergraduate studies were done at Carnegie-Mellon University, culminating in a B.S. in Metallurgy.

B. BUSINESS HISTORY

The products manufactured by the company in June 19X6 were military air equipment parts and bullet-proof vests. Most of the sales were made as a manufacturing subcontractor with only a few items sold directly to the government. This limited the marketing potential of the company to a much smaller segment of the total market.

The bullet-proof vests were built exclusively for one distributor, which handled all marketing and sales. The major sales volume of these items went where federal

Exhibit 7-5 *(Continued)*

grants were received by the local political constituency, both domestic and overseas. This factor made the market volatile and subject to highly cyclic conditions. There is also a high product-liability potential. For a period of time this part of the business was quite profitable and required low operating capital, since the distributor supplied most of the costly material used in manufacture.

The appeal of the bullet-proof vests as part of the business dropped considerably when the distributor demanded cheaper prices and more support in product liability backup. He viewed his business as dominant and necessary for Fabratex's survival. Conditions worsened further when accounts receivable with the distributor were stretched out over sixty to ninety days and required considerable follow-up to collect.

It was decided in the late fall of 19X6 to enter actively the direct military procurement market for the following reasons:

1. It was a sizable steady replacement market for the company's products, which have a limited use and cycle life.

2. Most of the company experience existed in these products, but business had not been sought directly.

3. From prior experience the company was familiar with this market area and knew the government procurement systems.

4. Business could be acquired in a few months to build up the declining backlog and insure steady work.

5. Government small-business preferences and fast payment procedures for them would be an advantage to a small company with limited resources.

This course of action was tried successfully for a few months and the bullet-proof vest business was gradually terminated. As evidenced by the following table, good progress was made by March 19X7 and considerable success was made by June 19X7.

BACKLOG TOTALS—HISTORICAL

Date	Vests	Com'l & Subcont.	Military	Total
June 19X6	$21,348	$99,212	–0–	$120,560
Sept. 19X6	20,966	90,908	–0–	111,875
Dec. 19X6	16,500	43,590	$ 27,531	87,621
Mar. 19X7	12,814	54,207	74,103	141,124
June 19X7	5,787	45,953	350,757	404,497
Sept. 19X7	335	40,876	426,582	467,793
Dec. 19X7	–0–	45,818	538,263	584,081
Mar. 19X8	–0–	42,875	682,250	725,125
June 19X8	–0–	40,795	621,452	662,247
Sept. 19X8	–0–	58,250	546,235	604,485
Dec. 19X8	–0–	51,186	495,721	546,907
Mar. 19X9	–0–	57,613	456,654	514,267
July 19X9	–0–	97,916	628,806	726,722
Aug. 19X9	–0–	67,270	675,796	743,066

In June of 19X7, Fabratex was advised that its annual lease would not be renewed. The news came as a shock, and an immediate search for another building was launched, using these factors as a guide:

Exhibit 7-5 (*Continued*)

1. 12,000 square feet minimum space.
2. Ample basic power service (a 50% savings for leasehold improvement).
3. Good open space for shop layout.
4. Restroom facilities ample for shop personnel (leasehold improvement saving).
5. Located within five miles of Santa Ana and convenient bus lines for workers. (The Santa Ana, Garden area is the main labor pool source.)
6. Fireproof type building with concrete floors desired but not mandatory.
7. Five year lease with option to buy.

An extensive search was made and many buildings were examined in Garden Grove, Santa Ana, Costa Mesa, Huntington Beach, and Anaheim. Site selection was narrowed to two buildings, one in Anaheim and one in Garden Grove. An offer was made on the building in Anaheim on September 22, 19X7 after considerable preliminary negotiations. This building was selected since it satisfied all the company's needs and provided extra space, 24,000 square feet total, at the best available price. During the period from June to September the company received several additional contracts which increased the needed shop space to at least 14,000 square feet. This extra space was not available at the existing facility, which totalled 7,500 square feet.

The first new government contracts received were small items which ran well in small assembly areas. These contracts carried them well through September and into December 19X7 with good shipping months and profit margins.

Meanwhile, it had placed orders and received large shipments of goods for subsequent contracts that required more space and facilities. Negotiations for another building were progressing well and the company expected to move by December 19X7. Plans at the time were to start manufacture of the small subassemblies at the old facility and be ready to proceed with final assembly at the new facility. The proposed new building would have adequate space to maintain the increased total production with provision for hiring more people to break in at the lesser skilled preliminary operations. The company planned to maintain good production output and cash flow by blending in the learning curve of new hires.

The deal for the new building suddenly fell through, creating serious problems. The planned production flow was now interrupted, with rapidly mounting inventories (see following table) and reduced cash flow. The firm maintained production at a somewhat reduced level while actively searching for another building. The suitable previous alternate building located in September was no longer available.

INVENTORY HISTORY

Date	Value
June 1, 19X6	$ 43,035
June 1, 19X7	55,403
December 1, 19X7	165,523
March 1, 19X8	182,390
June 1, 19X8	162,134
September 1, 19X8	177,340
March 1, 19X9	150,376

Exhibit 7-5 *(Continued)*

The search resumed immediately. The company was fortunate to locate its present facility in late December 19X7. It negotiated a five-year lease with option to buy in January 19X8 and was able to take possession by February 1, 19X8. This building satisfies all requirements and provides ample growth space for several years. The building has 19,800 square feet and is located in Santa Ana.

It took six weeks to prepare the new facility. The principal task was to provide the complete electrical power distribution for equipment. The other task was erecting long work tables which arrange the sewing area, and provide support for the electrical distribution system. This power system was set up in modular form so that it can be moved or rearranged in sections and thus provides flexibility at minimum cost for future needs or changes. The total layout put together at this time has worked out exceptionally well. It provided ample room for sewing operations and permits flexibility in operations as a contract manufacturing factory. The company can handle a wide variety of products in the shop with no change in layouts.

There is also ample room for setting up special lines for bulky or very small assemblies, which may be received on an occasional basis. This versatility enables the maintenance of a good spread of product capability, which blends out the peaks and valleys in various procurement lines.

The present building has enough space to handle all the growth projected for the next five years. The company will need more capital equipment with the growth of business, but additional power distribution growth can be made from the present system with modest expenditures for line extensions.

The slowdown in cash flow resulting from the facility relocation problem and the production bottleneck slowed accounts payable. They rapidly slipped from prompt payment and taking discounts to ninety days and longer. The resulting squeeze on cash credit made it difficult to support production needs. Some jobs were slowed down, and production schedules were difficult to predict and maintain.

The move to the new facility was made in March 19X8 with a host of production problems. The firm was in a low cash situation with large accumulated inventory and a doubling of the work force to fulfill the contractual obligations. It was faced with the task of acquiring and training an added work force in three months that had originally been scheduled for six months. This task had to be accomplished with limited supervision as well as a language barrier.

The success of the effort started to appear in June shipments and became apparent in July 19X8.

Through this tumultuous period scheduled deliveries on contracts became delinquent, and a series of negotiations had to be made with customers. The company renegotiated extended delivery schedules that have cost over $6,900.00 to date in penalty of tradeoff fees. A possible alternative to this would have been contract cancellation, which could have resulted in assessments to have the items rebid at costs up to 25% over the original contract values by another supplier and charged to Fabratex. Additionally, Fabratex would have been removed from the bidders' lists and lost future business.

Increased costs of materials and labor reflecting the inflationary economy have been a further burden. The rises in these costs with some examples shown below have greatly reduced profitability on recent business, since the company was working to two-year-old prices in completing many contracts.

Exhibit 7-5 (*Continued*)

MATERIAL PRICES

Item	Oct. 'X7	Jan. 'X9	Difference	% change
Hardware (fasteners)	$11,414.45	$13,598.91	$2,184.46	19.0
Cloth	14,636.94	16,774.92	2,137.98	14.6
Webbing*	16,536.84	17,850.54	1,043.70	6.3
Thread	4,030.99	4,455.84	424.85	10.5
Totals	$46,619.22	$52,390.21	$5,771.01	12.4

* Prices raised 6% effective March 1, 19X9.

Note: These items were taken from representative buys of materials for the De-ployment Bag product line which represents over 40% of the total sales volume. Contracts for these parts are a major portion of the old work being finished now at two-year-old prices.

C. POSTCONFIRMATION STRATEGY

Fabratex has developed a five-year marketing plan to provide broader product line and market segments to insure a stable work flow and production efficiency. Primary emphasis is on aircraft support market with emphasis on government ground and personnel support equipment in nonaircraft related areas and on in-creasing penetration in the commercial and industrial markets.

A. General Goals

1. Increase the product lines in terms of related product.

2. Expand the market segment by contacting new procurement bases and depots and subsequently bidding successfully.

3. Bid on related type products such as cushions, belts, straps, and containers for government ground and personnel support equipment of nonaircraft variety. This strategy is to utilize existing expertise, avoiding the costly implementing of new techniques and training.

4. Expand the marketing and production of commercial and industrial product lines in products utilizing the existing skills and capabilities. Proprietary products would be for use in sports, recreation, and travel fields such as fabric containers (tote bags, equipment bags, covers), straps (slings, carriers, tie downs, special harnesses) or unique combinations. Protective equipment such as bullet-proof vests are still being considered for an increased portion of the business again, without the limitations imposed by the distributor.

5. Maintain minimum inventory by negotiating partial shipments when prac-tical from suppliers.

6. Maintain high turnover of Work in Progress Inventory by close job sched-uling with fewer jobs active at a given time.

7. Material Procurement

a. Discount payables invoices at an average 1½% (composite of 1% and 2% terms). Savings estimates, based on $36,000 to $40,000 per month in pur-chases offer total savings possible of $2,160 to $2,400 per month.

b. Negotiation prices on fast-pay terms. Estimated to net 2.5%.

c. Negotiate FOB plant deliveries based on quantity buys and good pay. Esti-mated to be worth 2%.

Exhibit 7-5 *(Continued)*

8. Make capital equipment purchases on a fast rate of return, one year on small items, two years maximum on others.

The added capital equipment would increase production capability by increasing total output and broadening the ability to do more varied kinds of work where profitability may be better.

9. Keep overhead and other indirect expenses to a minimum with austere restrictions on purchases and hiring for the areas.

10. Keep receivables current. About 90% of the business is government, so careful preparation of paperwork is the key here.

D. MECHANICS OF REORGANIZATION PLAN

The proposed Reorganization Plan (which is being filed concurrently with this document) provides for the ingestion of personal loan funds which have been committed subject to the Plan's confirmation. The loan proceeds will provide sufficient capital to cover (a) administrative expenses; (b) initial payments on priority and secured claims; (c) lump sum settlements with unsecured credit choosing same. Any moneys left over shall be earmarked for operating capital.

The debtor corporation asserts that the provisions for payment of unsecured claims contained in the proposed Plan are greatly preferable to liquidation because said provisions would (a) provide a greater payoff than liquidation (cf. Accountant's report which follows) and (b) allow a continuing business relationship with Fabratex that could bring future profits to the supplying creditors.

The report that follows is submitted as support for the preceding assertions on behalf of confirmation. It should be noted that the appraisal figures used by the C.P.A. were supplied by the officers of Fabratex. It is submitted that a forced sale liquidation of the corporation's equipment and inventory would bring an amount substantially below the "book value" of these assets because of the following factors:

1. Because the contracts are mostly with government, there is a limited market for the material on hand; many items have been cut to order.

2. Auctions historically draw a limited crowd with competitors often purchasing equipment and inventory at 25-35% of "market value."

3. The apparel industry is currently a severely depressed industry.

Dated: January 8, 19Y0

_____

Attorney for Debtor

To the Board of Directors and Stockholders
Fabratex Corporation
Santa Ana, California

The accompanying statement of affairs of Fabratex Corporation as of November 30, 19X9 and the related statements of operations and deficit and changes in financial position for the six months then ended have been compiled by me.

A compilation is limited to presenting in the form of financial statements information that is the representation of management. I have not audited or reviewed the accompanying financial statements and, accordingly, do not express an opinion

Exhibit 7-5 *(Continued)*

or any other form of assurance on them. However, I did become aware of certain departures from generally accepted accounting principles that are described in the following paragraphs.

The Company has filed a petition for relief under Chapter 11 of the Bankruptcy Code. As discussed in Note 1, the continuation of the Company's operations, realization of its assets, and liquidation of its liabilities are dependent upon consummating a successful plan of reorganization with creditors, attaining sufficiently profitable operations, and adequate additional financing.

As discussed in Note 1, the amounts set forth in the appraisal column are management's appraisal of the amounts realizable under a forced liquidation. I do not express an opinion on the amounts shown in the appraisal column.

January 2, 19Y0

FABRATEX CORPORATION
STATEMENT OF OPERATIONS AND DEFICIT
SIX MONTHS ENDED NOVEMBER 30, 19X9

Sales—net of sales discounts of $11,154		$210,706
Cost of goods sold		
Labor	$71,688	
Materials	97,097	
Payroll taxes	7,536	
Repairs & Maintenance	904	
Employee benefits	3,006	
Operating supplies	1,031	
Depreciation	8,760	
Estimated loss on contracts	(23,917)	166,105
Gross profit		44,601
General and administrative expenses		
Taxes	3,306	
Salaries	17,509	
Rent	16,800	
Professional fees	3,255	
Insurance	1,497	
Interest	5,071	
Auto	1,106	
Office	1,390	
Freight	3,019	
Telephone	1,663	
Utilities	1,746	
Miscellaneous	428	
Amortization	2,420	59,210
Net loss		14,609
Deficit—beginning		132,630
Deficit—ending		$147,239

See accountant's compilation report.

Exhibit 7-5 (*Continued*)

FABRATEX CORPORATION
STATEMENT OF CHANGES IN FINANCIAL POSITION
FOR THE SIX MONTHS ENDED NOVEMBER 30, 19X9

Source of funds

Net loss	$ 14,609
Items not affecting working capital	
Depreciation	8,760
Amortization	2,420
Working capital used by operations	(3,429)
Loans from stockholders	9,295
Decrease in working capital	1,373
	$ 7,239

Application of funds

Purchases of equipment	$ 549
Deposits	4,075
Repayment of notes payable	2,615
	$ 7,239

Changes in working capital

Current assets—increase (decrease)	
Cash	$ 7,564
Accounts receivable	(21,574)
Inventory	(25,104)
Prepaid expenses	1,400
Current liabilities—decrease (increase)	
Bank note payable	2,000
Accounts payable	3,315
Accrued expenses	8,603
Payroll taxes payable	(20,098)
Unearned revenue	18,604
Reserve for estimated loss	23,917
Decrease in working capital	$ 1,373

See accountant's compilation report.

Exhibit 7-5 (*Continued*)

FABRATEX CORPORATION
STATEMENT OF AFFAIRS
NOVEMBER 30, 19X9

Book Value	Assets	Appraisal (Note 1)	Estimated Amount Available	Loss or (Gain) on Realization
(Note 1)	**Assets pledged with fully secured creditors**			
$ 23,904	Accounts receivable	$23,904		
123,117	Inventories	26,467		$ 96,650
37,901	Equipment	35,716		2,185
6,450	Covenant not to compete	6,450		
		92,537		
	Less: Fully Secured Claims	61,226	$ 31,311	
	Free Assets			
9,908	Cash	9,908	9,908	
1,400	Prepaid expense	1,400	1,400	
8,005	Deposits	8,005	8,005	
435	Organization expense	—		435
9,125	Excess of cost over acquired Net Assets	—		9,125
	Estimated amount available		50,624	
	Liabilities with priority		49,040	
	Estimated amount available for unsecured creditors		1,584	
	Estimated deficiency on unsecured liabilities		208,634	
$220,245	Totals		$210,218	$108,395

See accountant's compilation report.

Exhibit 7-5 (*Continued*)

Book Value	Liabilities and Stockholders' Equity		Amount Unsecured
	Liabilities with priority		
	Estimated liquidation cost	$13,000	
$ 30,846	Taxes payable	30,846	
516	Accrued payroll	516	
4,678	Accounts payable	4,678	
	Total liabilities with priority	$49,040	
	Fully secured liabilities		
32,257	Notes payable	$32,257	
28,969	Unearned income	28,226	
	Total fully secured liabilities	61,226	
	Unsecured liabilities		
131,986	Accounts payable		$131,986
28,138	Accrued expenses		28,138
6,000	Bank note payable		6,000
44,094	Loans from stockholders		44,094
	Stockholders' equity		
60,000	Common stock		
(147,239)	Deficit		
$220,245	Totals		$210,218

Exhibit 7-5   (*Continued*)

FABRATEX CORPORATION
NOTES TO FINANCIAL STATEMENTS
NOVEMBER 30, 19X9

NOTE 1—Basis of Presentation

Book Value—Fabratex Corporation has sustained losses from its operations during the two years and six months ended November 30, 19X9. The accompanying financial statements—book value column—have been prepared on a going-concern basis. Continuation of the Company's operations, realization of its assets, and liquidation of its liabilities are dependent upon the ability of the Company to consummate a successful plan of reorganization with creditors, a profitable level of operations, and adequate additional financing.

Appraisal—The accompanying statement of affairs—appraisal column—sets forth amounts that are management's appraisal of the amounts realizable under a forced liquidation of the Company.

NOTE 2—Accounting Policies

Inventories are carried at the lower of cost or market and consist of the following:

	Book Value	Appraisal
Raw materials	$ 45,136	$ 22,568
Work in process	77,981	3,899
	$123,117	$ 26,467

Depreciation is provided on 150% declining balance and straight-line bases over the estimated useful lives of the equipment and leasehold improvements ranging from 3 to 10 years.

Equipment is composed of the following:

	Book Value	Appraisal
Equipment—at cost	$ 71,432	$ 35,716
less: accumulated depreciation	33,531	—
	$ 37,901	$ 35,716

The convenant not to compete is being amortized over 5 years, the length of the covenant. Amortization of organization expense is taken over 5 years, and the excess cost over acquired net assets is amortized over 40 years.

Intangible assets consist of the following:

	Cost	Amortization	Book Value
Covenant not to compete	$ 21,500	$ 15,050	$ 6,450
Organization expense	1,454	1,019	435
Excess of cost over acquired net assets	10,000	875	9,125

Exhibit 7-5 *(Continued)*

NOTE 3—Notes payable

At November 30, 19X9, three notes were outstanding. One note, for $7,616.43 is payable in monthly installments of $282.09 until paid and bears no interest.

The second note is payable in monthly installments of $941.74, including interest at 8.5 percent; there are 27 installments left to pay. A portion of the equipment is pledged as sucurity for these notes.

The third note is payable in monthly installments of $57 and is secured by equipment.

NOTE 4—Common Stock

At May 31, 19X8 there were 10,000 shares of no par common stock authorized and 400 shares issued and outstanding. The stated value of the shares is $50.00 per share.

On November 1, 19X8, an additional 800 shares were issued to John Wright; payment for these shares was made by a reduction of the loan from Wright.

NOTE 5—Bank Note Payable

The bank note payable is due on demand and bears interest at 15.5 percent.

NOTE 7—Income Taxes

Since the Company has incurred losses in the preceding two years, no future tax benefits have been recognized. At November 30, 19X9 the Company has a net operating loss carryforward of $128,259, an investment tax credit carryforward of $1,132, and a new job credit carryforward of $20,585.

UNITED STATES BANKRUPTCY COURT
CENTRAL DISTRICT OF CALIFORNIA

In re:
FABRATEX CORP. ⎱ Debtor No. BK X9-22313 PE
Debtor.

REORGANIZATION PLAN

FABRATEX CORPORATION, Debtor in the above entitled proceedings, proposes the following plan of reorganization with its creditors:

I. INTRODUCTION

The Debtor was organized and operated as a manufacturer of soft goods; e.g. seat cushions, belts, harnesses, and straps (mostly military contracts) for three and one-half years before filing the Petition for Reorganization under chapter 11. Operations were financially successful until approximately September, 19X7 when

Exhibit 7-5   (*Continued*)

Debtor undertook work on four major government contracts. Losses on these four contracts totaled nearly $210,000.00. The failure of these contracts may reasonably be traced to (1) unrealistically low bids and (2) delays in execution of the orders caused by a forced move of operations to another manufacturing facility. While other orders during this period turned a profit the enormity of the losses from these four contracts kept the Debtor substantially in the red for the years 19X8 and 19X9. Business has been slowly improving since that time.

II. TREATMENT OF SECURED CREDITOR

The Debtor's lone secured creditor shall, within 30 days after confirmation of the plan, begin receiving her regular monthly payments per the terms of her secured note with Debtor. Past-due obligations on said note shall be completely repaid within 210 days after confirmation.

III. DIVISION OF CREDITORS INTO CLASSES

The unsecured creditors of the Debtor are divided into the following classes:

Class A: All creditors whose claims are entitled to priority under the Bankruptcy Code.

Class B: All general unsecured creditors, except those identified in Class C, whose claims are allowed within the time provided by law.

Class C: The unsecured claims of the principal shareholders of Debtor, that is John Wright and Eddie Johnson.

IV. PROVISIONS FOR CREDITORS

Compensation for creditors shall be as follows:

Debtor will deposit the sums necessary to put this plan into effect with the disbursing agent selected. When so ordered, the disbursing agent will pay the allowed claims to the classes in the following manner:

Class A: Payment in full will be made upon order as soon after confirmation as possible except that the tax claims of governmental units shall be paid as follows:

(1) Back taxes owing to the United States: $5,000 30 days after confirmation with payments of $5,000.00 on the 60th, 90th, and 120th day thereafter. The remaining balance due shall be paid on the 150th day after confirmation.

(2) Back taxes owing to the State of California: $1,000.00 30 days after confirmation with payments of $500.00 on the 60th, 90th, and 120th days thereafter. The remaining balance shall be paid on the 150th day after confirmation.

(3) Back taxes owing to the County of Orange: $500.00 30 days after confirmation with payments of $250.00 on the 60th, 90th, and 120th days thereafter. The remaining balance shall be paid on the 150th day after confirmation.

Exhibit 7-5   (*Continued*)

Class B: Maturity and enforceability of the claims will be extended until payment hereunder. Creditors of Class B may elect

    (1)   10 cents on the dollar 30 days after confirmation.

    (2)   5 cents on the dollar 30 days after confirmation and an additional 10 cents on the dollar 24 months after confirmation.

    (3)   5 cents on the dollar 30 days after confirmation and an additional 15 cents 36 months after confirmation.

    (4)   5 cents on the dollar 30 days after confirmation and an additional 20 cents 48 months after confirmation.

    (5)   10 cents on the dollar 48 months after confirmation and an additional 10 cents each year thereafter until debt principal paid in full.

Class C: Debtor's majority shareholders John Wright and Eddie Johnson shall receive no compensation whatsoever on their unsecured notes to Debtor corporation, in total amounts of $36,594.24 and $7,500.00 respectively.

V. SOURCE OF FUNDS

The loan funds necessary to furnish the deposit and to make payment hereunder will be obtained from the personal resources of Debtor's principal shareholders, that is John Wright and Eddie Johnson. The loan(s) shall be secured by a lien on the assets and inventory of Debtor not heretofore subject to a security interest, by way of UCC-1 filing.

VI. PRIORITY OF POSTFILING DEBTS
OVER PREFILING DEBTS

Debts incurred subsequent to the filing of the chapter 11 petition and during the pendency of the reorganization shall have priority over debts affected by the reorganization.

VII. RETENTION OF JURISDICTION

Upon confirmation, the court will retain jurisdiction to consider the allowance of claims and to entertain amendment and modification of the plan.

VIII. ELECTION OF CREDITORS

Election by Class B creditors of the options provided for them is to be made in writing by notification 5 days prior to confirmation in default of which creditors not electing will be compensated under the first option presented therein.

January 8, 19Y0

_____

Attorney for Debtor

exceed six years after the date of assessment of the claim. The cash payments must have a value as of the effective date of the plan equal to the allowed amount of the claim.

Disclosure Statement

51 Before a proponent of a plan can solicit votes, a statement must be issued that contains adequate information. A large part of the information in this disclosure statement will be financial. The content of the disclosure statement is covered in chapter 5 (paragraphs 64–77). An example of a disclosure statement issued in a chapter 11 proceeding not contemplating the issuance of securities is in Exhibit 7-5 (pages 257–271), along with the plan.

ACCOUNTANT AS EXAMINER

52 The Code provides for the appointment of an examiner to investigate the financial condition of the debtor, the operation of the business, and the potential for successful continuance of the business. This investigation will also include any allegations against the debtor of fraud, dishonesty, or mismanagement. Accountants are well equipped to perform this function and provide the necessary report. Since the Code, as originally passed, did not provide for the appointment of professionals to assist the examiner, accountants would be the most logical professionals to be retained where most of the investigation centers around the evaluation of financial information. In fact, a large number of accountants or other individuals with a business background have been appointed, but the majority have been attorneys. Some judges have authorized the examiner to use professional persons already employed by creditors' or other appointed committees in the case. Some judges have allowed the examiner to retain professionals, such as accountants, to assist in the examination. If the practice does not develop in all districts where bankruptcy judges retain professionals to assist the examiner, an effort may be made to correct this problem by modifying the Code. See chapter 5, paragraphs 23–27 for a more detailed explanation of the role of the examiner.

ADDITIONAL OR OTHER SERVICES

53 The independent accountant will normally expand an examination of a client with financial difficulties, ascertaining that all liabilities have been recorded, all requirements of loan agreements have been met, and any departures with their possible consequences have been disclosed. The accountant will also be concerned with determining that none of the assets has been stated at an amount exceeding its realizable value.[5]

---

[5] Paul Conner, "Financial Reporting for Companies in Financial Difficulty," *Oklahoma CPA*, Vol. 7 (October 1968), p. 22.

Special Investigation

54   In conducting an audit, the independent accountant will primarily examine the accounts and prepare the financial statements. This investigation will consist of examining any unusual transactions that occurred before bankruptcy proceedings were initiated, with utmost attention to any transactions that resulted in the dissipation of assets from factors other than losses in the ordinary course of the business. These normally include a transfer or concealment of assets; preferential payments to creditors; transactions with related parties not conducted at arm's length; major acquisitions, mergers, and investments that resulted in a loss; acquisitions of property at exorbitant prices; and any bulk sale of assets or of a part of the business. The independent accountant should describe these transactions in as much detail as is possible and analyze their effect on the financial position of the firm.[6] In many situations, the accountant is engaged to review selected aspects of the debtor's operation without performing an audit.

55   When retained by a trustee appointed in a chapter 11 reorganization, the accountant has the same responsibilities to the trustee as to a debtor in possession. When retained for the trustee, there is generally an audit and investigation of the debtor's activities. In fact, an investigation under these conditions is generally much more extensive than that required in a normal situation where the debtor retains possession. The extent of the examination depends on several factors, including the extent to which the debtor's management misused the company's assets. The independent accountant will generally conduct a thorough inquiry into the acts, conduct, property, financial condition, business transactions, history, and background of the debtor to determine whether the present management should be retained and whether a successful plan can be worked out. Everything that will help to establish the causes of the failure, including the conduct, attitudes, business judgment, and insight of the officers, directors, and managers, should be scrutinized. These audit and investigative services may also be needed by a nonaccountant examiner appointed by the court to perform an investigation. The extent to which an accountant can be retained by an examiner is uncertain (see paragraph 52). It is possible for the accountant to be retained as the examiner.

56   Special studies may be made by accountants to analyze all transactions between the debtor and related parties, such as companies controlled, officers and directors, relatives of principal officers' families and so on. Included in Exhibit 7-6 are some excerpts from a report issued by Price Waterhouse & Company on the "Investigation of Related Party Transactions and Perquisites" for the creditors' committee of Food Fair Inc. and J. M. Fields, Inc. The total report was over 600 pages.

---

[6] Edward A. Weinstein, "Accountant's Examinations and Reports in Bankruptcy Proceedings," *New York Certified Public Accountant*, Vol. 35 (January 1965), pp. 31, 38–39.

Exhibit 7-6   Excerpts from Report on "Investigation of Related Party Transactions and Perquisites"

October 15, 1979

The Official Creditors' Committees
Food Fair, Inc. and J. M. Fields, Inc.
Debtors in Possession
3175 John F. Kennedy Boulevard
Philadelphia, Pennsylvania 19101

Dear Sirs:

On December 8, 1978, by Order of the Bankruptcy Court in the Southern District of New York, signed by the Honorable John J. Galgay (the Court), Price Waterhouse & Co. was retained as the accountants to your Committees with the general charge "to conduct an investigation into the affairs, actions and conduct of the Debtors." On January 5, 1979, the Court, among other charges, specifically ordered Price Waterhouse & Co. to perform "a review and analysis of any and all transactions by, between or among the Debtor and companies controlled by or related to the Debtor or present and former officers or directors of the Debtor or in which such present and former officers or directors may have an interest or in which other members and relatives of the Friedland or Stein families may have an interest, as well as any and all transactions by, between or among the Debtor, its subsidiaries or affiliates and stockholders of the Debtor within the period of five years prior to the filing of the Chapter XI petitions and the continuing period subsequent thereto." This specific charge will in the accompanying report be referred to as the investigation of transactions with related parties.

This report on our investigation of transactions with related parties is comprised of three parts. The background to, general information about, and the procedures we employed in the investigation are described in Part I. Part II contains our findings concerning transactions with parties deemed to be related. The inclusion of a report on investigation of a related party transaction in Part II is not indicative that the transaction involved wrongdoing or resulted in detriment to the Debtor. Part III contains our findings on perquisites received by both related parties and prior management. The report should be read in its entirety. The procedures we followed did not constitute an examination in accordance with generally accepted auditing standards. The findings are derived from information obtained from many and varied sources which often were not, and could not, be subjected to independent audit and verification procedures.

Throughout the investigation, we made numerous requests for the help of the management and employees of the company and we are grateful for the cooperation received.

PRICE WATERHOUSE & CO.

Exhibit 7-6   (*Continued*)

PART I   BACKGROUND, GENERAL INFORMATION
AND PROCEDURES EMPLOYED

A. Events Leading to the Investigation of
Related Party Transactions at Food Fair:

The August 21, 1978, issue of Forbes magazine contained an article entitled "Is All Fair at Food Fair?" which contained allegations unfavorable to the then management of Food Fair (referred to hereafter as Food Fair, the Debtor or the Company—including J. M. Fields, Inc., and all subsidiaries and divisions). As a result of the Forbes article, the Audit Committee of the Board of Directors of the Company (comprised of Messrs. William P. Davis, III, Willard S. Boothby, Jr., and W. Paul Stillman) resolved to conduct an investigation into the matters set forth in the magazine article with the assistance of independent counsel and accountants. The Philadelphia law firm of Dechert, Price & Rhoads (DP&R) was selected by the Committee as its independent counsel and the accounting firm of Coopers & Lybrand (C&L) was selected as special accountants. On August 29, 1979, the Audit Committee resolved that the scope of the project included, among other things, "an investigation and analysis of all transactions during the last five years" with related parties. On September 27, 1978, DP&R was replaced as counsel by the Philadelphia law firm of Ballard, Spahr, Andrews & Ingersoll.

On October 2, 1978, Food Fair, Inc., J. M. Fields, Inc. and various other related companies filed petitions for an arrangement under Chapter XI of the Bankruptcy Act.

The three members of the Audit Committee resigned as Directors of the Company on October 4, 1978, "because of their inability to devote sufficient time to carry out their responsibilities as Directors of the Company under its present circumstances." At that time, the Audit Committee's investigation of related party transactions ceased. The Audit Committee was not reconstituted by the Debtor until the spring of 1979.

The October 30, 1978, issue of Forbes magazine contained another article concerning the Debtor entitled "A $2.5 Billion Tale of Woe" which made additional allegations unfavorable to the then management of the Company.

On November 13, 1978, Jack M. Friedland resigned as both an officer and a director of the Company, and Samuel Friedland, Louis Stein, Hess Kline and Herman Silver resigned as directors of the Company.

B. The Creditors' Committees' Investigation:

On November 29, 1978, Official Creditors' Committees (the Committees) of Food Fair, Inc. and J. M. Fields, Inc. were designated by the Court. In an application to the Court by the Committees on December 5, 1978, it was stated that "at consolidated meetings of the Official Creditors' Committees held on November 22, 1978, and December 1, 1978, it was determined that the Official Creditors' Committees' desire to employ Price Waterhouse & Co. . . . to assist the Official Credi-

Exhibit 7-6 *(Continued)*

tors' Committees in their proceedings, pursuant to Rule 11-22 of the Rules of Bankruptcy Procedures." The application further stated that "as a result of allegations made prior to the filing of the Petitions for Arrangement by the Debtors, and as a result of the apparent intertwined relationship between the Debtors, members of the Friedland family, and other companies associated with the Debtors and/or the Friedland family, the Official Creditors' Committees believe that a thorough investigation into the affairs, actions and conduct of the Debtors is required. In addition, the Official Creditors' Committees believe that the retention of an independent certified public accounting firm is necessary for the services that may be requested by the Official Creditors' Committees." The January 5, 1979, Order of the Court quoted in the cover letter appearing at the beginning of this report, generally describes our charge for the investigation.

The Audit Finance Subcommittee (the Subcommittee) of the Committees was established in January 1979 to, among other duties, advise and direct as necessary, the services being provided by us.

During the course of our investigation of transactions with related parties, we met frequently with the Subcommittee and presented reports on our progress as requested. The Subcommittee provided direction to the investigation as it became necessary and, from time to time, requested that specific tasks be performed. Copies of draft reports on investigation of individual related party transactions were distributed at the request and on the authorization of the Subcommittee to the members of the Committees, their counsel, the Court, the Debtor and the Debtor's counsel.

C. Retention of Special Counsel:

The complexities of the investigation resulted in our requesting the Committees to approve the retention of special counsel. After consultation with co-counsel to the Committees, Marcus & Angel, P.C. and Otterbourg, Steindler, Houston & Rosen, P.C. (hereafter referred to jointly as counsel), it was determined that separate and independent counsel should be chosen who would have no responsibilities for any matters in the proceeding other than those related solely to the investigation of related party transactions.

The Philadelphia law firm of Pepper, Hamilton & Scheetz (PH&S) was retained as our Special Counsel. By Court Order of March 22, 1979, PH&S was authorized "to render legal services to Price Waterhouse & Co. in its capacity as accountants for the Official Creditors' Committees herein in connection with the investigation of Price Waterhouse & Co. into the affairs, actions and conduct of the Debtors."

In the course of our investigation a number of matters arose where the aid of counsel for the Committees was requested. These included matters of liaison with the Committees, obtaining formal orders from the Court, the issuance of subpoenas and providing office space for the taking of depositions. We and our special counsel wish to express our appreciation to Messrs. Marcus & Angel and Otterbourg, Steindler, Houston & Rosen for their cooperation and help in these and other matters.

Exhibit 7-6   (*Continued*)

*D. The Securities and Exchange
Commission (SEC) Investigation:*

In January 1979, the staff of the SEC advised us, counsel to the Committees, and the Debtor, that they had opened an investigation of the Company pursuant to a formal order of the Commission and that they required current access to the information being obtained by us. On March 14, 1979, and again on May 29, 1979, the SEC served subpoenas duces tecum on us pursuant to Section 20(a) of the Securities Act of 1933 and Section 21(a) of the Securities Exchange Act of 1934 requiring us to produce "all information and documents received" pursuant to our investigation of related party transactions.

In compliance with the SEC subpoenas, our working papers, draft reports on investigation of individual related party transactions, and all other documents relating to our investigation were made available to the SEC staff for their review. The SEC requested and received copies of selected documents and working papers from our files. Requests by the SEC for copies of Company documents which were included in our files were relayed to the Company's house counsel for their compliance therewith, as agreed among Food Fair, the SEC and us.

On March 30, 1979, Special Counsel requested access to the files of the SEC relating to their investigation of the Company. The request was made in order to expedite and aid our investigation, eliminate duplication of effort, avoid current and future delays to the investigation, etc. We offered to maintain the confidentiality of the information obtained from the SEC. The SEC declined to grant the requested access.

The SEC has not issued any reports on the findings of its investigation. Information may subsequently be disclosed by the SEC which may affect the findings contained in Parts II and III of this report.

E. The Federal Grand Jury Subpoena:

In August 1979, we received a subpoena duces tecum from the United States District Court for the Eastern District of Pennsylvania in which we were ordered to testify before the Grand Jury and produce "all reports and/or memoranda prepared in connection with the reorganization proceedings filed on behalf of Food Fair, Inc., including any reports and/or memoranda regarding possible conflicts of interest by corporate officers and/or employees of Food Fair, Inc." In compliance therewith, we supplied the Grand Jury with copies of draft reports on investigation of individual related party transactions completed at that time.

F. The Company's Auditors:

Laventhol & Horwath (L&H) were the Company's independent accountants through the completion of the examination of the consolidated financial statements for the fifty-two week period ended July 29, 1978. In their March 9, 1979, report thereon, L&H disclaimed an opinion with respect to such financial statements be-

Exhibit 7-6   (*Continued*)

cause of, among other things, the significance of the restriction of the scope of their examination imposed by management regarding "application of all the audit procedures prescribed in Statement on Auditing Standards No. 6—Related Party Transactions," a publication of the American Institute of Certified Public Accountants.

L&H cooperated with our investigation and the investigation started, but not completed, by the Company's Audit Committee which employed C&L as special accountants. L&H provided access to the audit working papers relating to their examinations of the Company's financial statements for the five years from 1974 through 1978. The first four years were reviewed by C&L in connection with their investigation and we were given access to C&L's files pertaining to that work. We were given access to and reviewed the 1978 L&H working papers regarding the related party transaction work they performed. Our efforts in this regard were intended solely to seek information regarding known, alleged or suspected related party transactions.

G. Description of Related Parties:

For purposes of the investigation and this report, related parties are individuals or entities who did business with the Company (including any affiliate, joint venture or subsidiary thereof) and who were or might have been in a position (through directorships, officerships or employment with the Company, family relationships, business arrangements, stockholdings, personal relationships, etc.) to influence persons at the Company who were responsible for or had control over Company business arrangements and transactions during the period covered by the investigation. Except as specifically stated in this report, the inclusion of the name of any person or entity in this report is not intended to and should not give rise to any inference that such person could or did influence persons at the Company who were responsible for or had control over Company transactions.

H. Condition of the Records:

The firm of Touche Ross & Co. was retained by the Debtor to provide certain services to the Debtor including a request, as described in the Annual Report 1978, to "determine the effects of certain 1978 fiscal year adjusting journal entries on previously reported unaudited quarterly financial information." The Touche Ross & Co. report stated that there were "deficiencies in internal accounting control during 1978 . . ." and that "reconstruction of available records to appropriately restate previously reported financial results may be impossible."

We encountered deficiencies in the Debtor's records and internal controls during the entire period covered by our investigation.

I. Organization and Conduct of the Investigation:

The investigation was conducted in two phases. The initial phase involved a search to identify who the related parties were and what, if any, transactions be-

Exhibit 7-6   (*Continued*)

tween them and the Debtor had occurred. The second phase was the investigation of the related party transactions identified in the search phase. The two phases were being performed concurrently during most of the period during which the investigation was being conducted. The direction of the overall investigation, the procedures considered appropriate in the circumstances, the detailed scope of the investigation of each individual related party transaction, etc., were established by us with consultation at various stages of the process with the Subcommittee, the Committees, their counsel, the Debtor and its counsel, and the Court.

J. Search Phase:

The sole formal company procedure for identifying transactions with related parties during the period under investigation, was a questionnaire circulated to Company officers and directors by Stein Rosen and Ohrenstein (SRO), outside general counsel, in connection with the preparation of the Company's annual proxy material. The application of these procedures resulted in the disclosure of certain related party transactions in proxy material filed with the SEC during the years 1974 to 1977. The information requested in the questionnaires was limited in scope to information required to be disclosed in a proxy statement and did not supply company management or Board of Directors with comprehensive information on the existence of related party transactions or conflicts of interest situations.

Food Fair itself did not have a written comprehensive corporate conflicts of interest policy. J. M. Fields executives however were required annually to sign a conflicts of interest statement. A letter was sent to suppliers annually around Christmas time stating that employees were not permitted to accept gifts from vendors or suppliers.

In the absence of a record maintained by the Company of related party transactions and conflicts of interest situations identified and reported by a system of procedures or accounting controls designed for that purpose, we had to develop that record through our search effort. Among the procedures we performed during the search phase of our investigation were the distribution of questionnaires designed to gather information from current and former officers, directors and employees of the Company and current and former vendors and suppliers; and extensive reviews of large volumes of Company files and records including, but not limited to: (a) cash disbursement and receipt records; (b) personnel files; (c) legal department files; (d) purchasing department records; (e) vendor correspondence files; and (f) real estate department records and files. Our search efforts identified 115 transactions or relationships which warranted investigation because there was an appearance of a related party being involved.

K. Investigative Phase:

The investigation of each transaction identified in the search program as apparently being with a related party was generally performed in two stages. The first, or internal phase, involved gathering facts and documentation using resources available within the Company. The second, or external phase, involved gathering

Exhibit 7-6 (*Continued*)

facts and documentation from sources external to the Company including, but not limited to, records obtained by subpoena and the deposition under oath of current and former employees, officers and directors of the Company and current and former vendors and suppliers and other third parties.

In this process, of the 115 transactions or relationships identified in the search phase, 60 were found, in the investigative phase, not to involve transactions or relationships between related parties and the Company, and reports thereon are not included herein in Part II.

L. Distribution of Questionnaires:

Three different questionnaires were designed and distributed to individuals, suppliers and vendors, and banks.

A questionnaire requesting information concerning related party activities was distributed to 774 current and former officers, directors and employees of the Company. The questionnaire offered recipients the option of responding in writing, orally or by requesting a conference with us. On advice from their counsel, defendants in lawsuits instituted prior to the filing for protection under Chapter XI declined to cooperate with the investigation by not completing, in whole or in part, the questionnaire. In addition, counsel for these individuals informed us that they had advised their clients not to discuss any matters with us which might relate to pending litigation.

A questionnaire was developed and sent to 228 vendors who did business with the company during the period under investigation. The primary purpose of this questionnaire was to obtain information concerning the relationships between vendors and the brokers representing them on sales to the Company. Distribution of the questionnaire was made to all vendors who used the brokerage companies identified as related parties in our search program and to a number of vendors selected at random.

Another questionnaire was developed and distributed to 82 banks in connection with the review for perquisites. The banks were requested to provide information regarding loans made to current and former Company directors, officers, and employees or members of their families.

M. Use of Subpoenas:

During the investigation, we made use of the subpoena power available under Section 205 of the Bankruptcy Act thirty-five (35) times in order to obtain access to individuals and/or records of former or current directors, officers, employees, vendors, suppliers or others.

N. Review of Board of Directors and Committee Minutes:

We reviewed the minutes of the Company's Board of Directors and Committees of the Board of Directors for the period October 1973 through October 1978 and

Exhibit 7-6   (*Continued*)

have included in the individual reports information as to whether a reference to the transaction discussed in such report appears in any of such minutes. The fact that a report does not contain a reference that a transaction or relationship appears in such minutes is not intended to imply and should not be taken to infer that there was any legal or ethical requirement that such transaction should have been considered by the Board of Directors or any such Committee of the Board of Directors. Additionally, it should be recognized that matters may have been considered by the Board or such Committees and not have been referred to in the minutes.

57   In performing an investigation of the acts and conduct of one company in a Chapter X corporate reorganization under prior law, the accounting firm looked at the following in examining the financial condition of the debtor:

1   *Return on equity and capital*   The debtor's operations were compared with other companies in the same industry and with all companies in a list prepared by *Forbes' Magazine* for a period of five years prior to the corporate reorganization.

2   *Sales performance*   Again, the debtor's record was compared with companies in the same industry and other public companies.

3   *Earnings performance*   The deteriorating trend in the debtor's earnings was emphasized by comparing it with companies in the same industry and other public companies. In this case the company was number seventeen of twenty-eight and 260 of 560. Four years later the company had the second lowest growth in earnings compared to other companies in the same industry.

4   *Business ratios and statistics*   The accountants determined the current ratio, quick ratio, and inventory/sales ratio for the year of the Chapter X petition and for the previous four years. These ratios were compared with composite financial data of seventeen leading competitors.

5   *Long term liquidity*   The accounting firm used a mathematical model to determine the nature of the year-to-year changes in liquidity of the debtor. The model computes the probability of the trend continuing until a point is reached where available resources will be depleted. In this model a ratio of 1 indicates that unless the trend is altered an illiquid position is probable within five years. The model indicated that this company was tending towad illiquidity during a year which ended four years prior to the date of the petition and continued to indicate this in each of the subsequent years prior to bankruptcy.

6   *Trade credit*   The percent of payables to inventory was calculated for the fourth, fifth, and sixth years prior to bankruptcy to show that during this period an unfavorable trend was developing. Compounding the effect

during this time period were the increases in inventory with the increase in sales.

7 *Other analysis* Both long-term and short-term bank indebtedness was analyzed for the prior six years to detect the trends that developed. In addition, the growth in off-balance-sheet financing arrangements along with the dividends paid was disclosed and evaluated. See the ratio analysis discussion in chapter 2, paragraphs 48–60.

58   In all bankruptcy proceedings, the independent accountant's primary duty is to indicate the areas where there may have been wrongdoing, misconduct, or misappropriation. It is then the attorney's job to determine whether there has been a violation of the law.

Accounting Services and the Granting of New Credit

59   The accountant may also assist the debtor in acquiring additional credit. Special schedules are prepared for the debtor in order to provide the credit grantors with the desired information.

60   Apart from the desire of the credit community to aid in the rehabilitation of a debtor, there are several business reasons for granting credit during a period of reorganization:

Assets are unencumbered by old liabilities during this period and hence there is a substantial asset value as a basis for the granting of new credit. This is true for all credit grantors, not only members of the creditors' committee and "prepetition" creditors.

Many creditors have obligations on bill-and-hold goods and on commitments. With proper credit lines, the liquidation of bill-and-hold goods and commitment position can be accomplished with minimum losses.

Many creditors may be dealing with the debtor as an important customer and hence it is essential to keep this concern functioning as a user of their goods.

A proper credit line will provide for earlier distributions to the creditors without undue risk. Controls will prevent a distribution if it is felt that it would have a detrimental effect in any way on new creditors.

A debtor with credit lines should be able to operate the business in a more efficient fashion and thus maximize the payment to general creditors.

61   The debtor must not emerge from the reorganization as a credit risk. The company must be able to go to its creditors in the early stages of the reorganization period and receive the assistance it needs to reestablish itself in the business community and come out of the reorganization with the confidence of its creditors. During the reorganization period the accountant can be of valuable assistance by helping the creditors understand the problem areas and the financial statements so that the groundwork for future credit granting can be established.

ROLE OF THE SEC

62 Under prior law the SEC had an interest in all Chapter X proceedings and an interest under other chapter proceedings if a public company was involved or if a considerable public interest was served by the company. Very frequently, the proceeding would be instigated as a result of an action brought by the SEC. The SEC has recently adopted a policy of examining with greater scrutiny financial reports which contain qualified statements as to viability or uncertainties involving the determination of financial position and the results of operations. A flood of letters to the SEC from dissatisfied shareholders, or volatility in the stock—primarily declines where shareholders may be hurt—might create immediate action from the SEC. Under these conditions, the SEC would hold an inquiry and often invite the accountant to explain the accounting treatment and position as to the statements. As a result of these hearings the stock might drop even further and the debtor might then become aware of the need to file a petition in the bankruptcy court.

63 Procedurally, once the company filed the petition, the SEC's reorganization division would step in and assign an attorney and an analyst, who is often an accountant, to work on the case. If the company was a broker or dealer in securities, the SEC might assign someone from the broker-dealer section to the case. As a party to the proceedings the SEC must be served with copies of all motions and all papers filed with the court. From a practical standpoint, if the case were one of significance, the SEC would work very closely with the other parties to the proceedings. Representatives might attend meetings held among counsel, trustees, and accountants, and participate in the discussion, at times almost to the point of making management decisions.

64 The SEC also determined whether the action taken by the debtor in possession or the trustee was within what it believed to be the interpretation of the law. It would see that proper notices were given for property sales, payments to creditors, or payments to shareholders. The SEC is also a source of background information for the accountant, since it retains copies of all public documents filed. The accountants in an initial audit of a public company often spend the first week reviewing the documents that have been filed, collecting all published financial data, and obtaining copies of the statements filed with the SEC as a means of trying to determine what has happened. Also, the SEC might have subpoenaed records which the accountant needs to review. There is a need for close rapport and participation between the SEC and the accountants involved in the proceeding.

65 The SEC's chief role was to protect the public's interest. As a result the accounting firm might find that, even though the payment of its fees was a priority item, it often came out second best. On the other hand, the SEC may not object to the principals' satisfying the demands of customers in order to avoid any criminal actions brought about the dissatisfied customers.

66   The SEC played another role in keeping the proceedings moving. Very often, the attorneys for the debtor and creditors have a backlog of cases they are attempting to resolve. Consequently, after the initial impact a slowdown of activities will occur. The SEC acted as a very welcomed motivating influence to move things along.

Bankruptcy Code Provisions

67   Section 1109 states:

a   The Securities and Exchange Commission may raise and may appear and be heard on any issue in a case under this chapter, but the Securities and Exchange Commission may not appeal from any judgment, order, or decree entered in the case.

b   A party in interest, including the debtor, the trustee, a creditors' committee, an equity security holders' committee, a creditor, an equity security holder, or any indenture trustee, may raise and may appear and be heard on any issue in a case under this chapter.

68   This section limits the extent to which the SEC can directly participate in the proceedings under chapter 11. The SEC may raise, appear, and be heard on any issue but does not have the right to appeal. The SEC is not considered a party in interest. The significance of the "party in interest" is summarized in Collier:

> . . . a party in interest may request an appointment of a trustee or examiner under section 1104(a) and (b); may request termination in a trustee's appointment under section 1105; may request conversion of the chapter 11 case to a case under chapter 7 or 13 of the Code pursuant to section 1112(b); may file a plan under section 1121(c) and may request an extension of the debtor's time to file a plan under section 1121(d); may object to confirmation of a plan under section 1128(b); and may request revocation of confirmation under section 1144 of the Code[7]

SEC Policy

69   The Bankruptcy Code does not contain any provisions that direct the SEC to perform any particular function in bankruptcy proceedings. Thus, the role of the SEC in bankruptcy cases is, in the opinion of some, optional

---

[7] *Collier Bankruptcy Manual*, 3rd ed., para. 1109.03[3]n.

rather than mandatory. The SEC, however, stated in Corporate Reorganization Release No. 331 (February 2, 1984) that the tradition of active SEC participation is almost as old as the agency itself. The release further stated that in cases involving significant public investor interest, the SEC has a commitment to the protection of public investors. In this release, the SEC stated that reorganization cases will have a new focus, based on three major concerns:

1   Less day-to-day Commission participation in reorganization cases, provided public investors are adequately represented by the committee process.
2   The SEC should work closely with the U.S. trustees.
3   The Commission should avoid partisan involvement in negotiations for a plan of reorganization.

70   Thus, as a general matter, the SEC will focus its participation in chapter 11 on legal and policy issues which are of concern to public investors generally and which may have an impact beyond the facts of the particular case.

71   The SEC stated that it would continue to address matters of traditional Commission expertise and interest relating to securities. For example, the SEC may comment, where appropriate, on the adequacy of the disclosure statement and participate where the SEC has a law enforcement interest.

72   The SEC has been primarily involved with five major issues (excluding enforcement issues) in chapter 11 cases:

1   Fee allowances.
2   Appointment of shareholders, creditors, or other committees.
3   Appointment of examiners or trustees.
4   Loan, sale, or lease of property prior to confirmation of a plan.
5   Adequacy of disclosure.

73   Corporate Reorganization Release No. 331 indicates that the SEC will be less concerned in the future about the first four issues unless they involve public policy in general. The SEC's role, according to the Bankruptcy Code and Release No. 331, is not to be determined by the size of the assets or liabilities' balances in the case. However, by the nature of the SEC's role, it will appear in the larger cases. During the first four years following the adoption of the Bankruptcy Code, the SEC appeared in seventyfive cases where debtor assets totaled almost $14 billion.

74   Since the issuance of this release, the SEC has remained fairly active in bankruptcy cases, but, as suggested by the release, it is directing its attention primarily to the significant issues in the cases that affect investors. While its activity in cases has changed focus and may have declined, its appearance in cases to see that public investors are adequately represented has, in fact, increased. The future role of the SEC may depend to some extent on whether the U.S. Trustee system is expanded to all districts.

75 The Bankruptcy Code does not alter the continuing disclosure requirements of a publicly held debtor. The SEC has maintained for some time that the reporting obligations under the Securities Exchange Act of 1934 are not suspended by the filing of a bankruptcy court petition. It is not anticipated that the SEC will change its position. Reporting provisions may, however, be relaxed, as they were under the Bankruptcy Act, for trustees or debtors in possession while operating during the bankruptcy proceeding, but as soon as the conditions merit, the full requirements of the reporting procedures will apply. The reason for the SEC's relaxing the requirements is that formal compliance may result in inordinate expense to the debtor. Modification by the SEC of its requirements will generally be made only if such modifications are consistent with the public protection purposes of federal securities laws.

76 The staff of the SEC has a high level of technical knowledge. They can very frequently offer the attorneys, and to some extent the accountants, guides as to how procedural problems may be resolved. They are a fertile source of information.

PROFESSIONAL CONDUCT OF ACCOUNTANTS

77 As in any engagement, the accountant must be competent and ethical. The role of the accountant is crucial in the proceedings, especially to the bankruptcy judge, who must preserve and restore the business, protect the rights of creditors and decide between rehabilitation or liquidation. In making these decisions, the bankruptcy judge relies on the accountant for objective and unbiased opinions. It is important to remember that the accountant is a quasi-officer of the court and owes primary responsibility to it. All of the accountants' findings must be disclosed to the court.

Personal Liability—Preparation of Financial Statements

78 The accountant should strictly adhere to generally accepted auditing standards and procedures and statement presentation. Full disclosure is required, as well as clear and unambiguous language, in the report relating to any auditing procedures not undertaken by the debtor's independent accountant. These may include observation of physical inventory, confirmation of accounts receivable or cash in banks, verification of potential or present legal liabilities of the debtor, or verification of security arrangements. Generous use of footnotes and comments to the financial statements is advisable.

79 Where the practice has been to issue unaudited financial statements for the use of management only, particular care must be given by the debtor's independent accountant in the preparation of these financial statements as well as those submitted to a creditors' committee or other interested third parties. The accountant should follow the appropriate guidelines in Statements on Standards for Accounting and Review Services or Statements on Auditing Standards in issuing any statement even though it may be intended for use primarily by management.

80 Since the report of the debtor's accountant is being examined by and relied upon by third parties, the accountant must be extremely careful about reliance upon management's oral representations as to various transactions, and must insist on written documentation. This danger often lurks in non-cash transactions such as the following:

Accounts receivable—accounts payable setoffs where the same party is a customer and a creditor.

Satisfaction of a trade liability by the transfer of fixed assets.

Private arrangement involving the collection of a customer's account but an oral representation that the account is uncollectible.

Professional Conduct of Debtor's Accountant—Toward Client

81 At the time the client recognizes that a bankruptcy petition is imminent, there often exist unpaid bills for services rendered by the accountant. The decision as to whether to liquidate or reorganize will depend to a great extent on the information which the debtor's accountant prepares for review by the client and the attorney. The accountant must decide whether these additional, usually time-consuming, services should be rendered when payment for them is very doubtful. Both ethical and practical considerations are involved. The resolution of the ethical aspects depends on the standards and the subjective motives of the individual practitioner. Some aspects of the practical side of this question that have bearing on the ethical issues should be considered.

82 The withdrawal of the accountant's services at this time will not prevent allegations from arising, however unjustified, regarding the failure of the accountant to exercise professional judgment prior to the withdrawal. It may be easier for the accountant to explain the basis of professional acts as an actively participating party in contact with the debtor's attorney, incoming creditors' accountant, or the creditors' committee, rather than as an outsider looking in while unjustified assumptions are being made. The creditors' committee is interested in finding as many recoveries as possible. One source is from the legal and professional staff of the debtor. If there is any indication, whether justified or unjustified, that the accountants of the debtor failed to exercise due care, this is often pursued by the legal staff of the committee.

83 Withdrawal at this time subjects the accountant's client to the findings of the accountant for the creditors' committee and to the assumptions drawn in the course of that review. The presence of the debtor's accountant and personal contact with the accountant representing the creditors' committee can explain or document various transactions that otherwise might be damaging to the client in negotiations with the creditors. If the debtor's accountant withdraws before the books and records are completed, treatment of individual items is left to the accountant for the creditors' committee. An example of this occurred where an accountant for a trustee in bankruptcy, working on the uncompleted books and records of a bankruptcy partnership, treated bank debit memos entered on the bank statements as an item of cost of goods sold. This resulted in a deficit gross profit on sales, which the trustee successfully used in court to deny the discharge in bankruptcy of the partnership and the individual partners on the basis of fraud. In reality, the debit memos represented insufficient-funds checks of customers; however, the damage had been done and no amount of oral testimony could correct the matter. Premature withdrawal of accounting services from an ailing business operation may result in a disservice not only to the client but to the accountant as well.

84 The debtor's accountant should appraise the client of what the creditors expect and what the debtor should or should not do during the interim period from the time of determination of an imminent bankruptcy proceeding to the actual negotiations with creditors. The accountant will want to identify for the client the prepetition acts that can result in criminal fraud charges, obviate the cooperation of creditors, or prevent a discharge of debts. The client should be aware of the fact that if the company's integrity is questioned very little cooperation can be expected from the creditors.

Professional Conduct of Debtor's Accountant— Toward Creditors' Accountant

85 One of the most frequent complaints of incoming independent accountants for creditors is the difficulties encountered in obtaining the necessary books of account of the debtor and various documentary evidence as the investigation proceeds. The duty of the incoming accountant is to the creditors and to the court. There is no room here for camaraderie between accountants but only for the fulfillment of professional, legal, and ethical responsibilities. The debtor's accountant, therefore, should undertake to do the following in order to facilitate the work of the accountant for the creditors' committee:

Assist in locating all books of accounts and records.

Explain the debtor's accounting system.

Aid in obtaining documents requested by the creditors' committee accountant.

Permit the accountant for the creditors' committee to review the debtor's accountant's workpapers as they relate to specific questions raised. There would appear to be no obligation for the debtor's accountant to release possession of his workpapers for a general review by the creditors' accountant.

Make available copies of all requested tax returns of the debtor and discuss potential trouble areas in the event of an audit by a taxing agency. Any records or information that is given to the creditors' committee by the debtors' accountant should first be cleared by the debtor unless, of course, the debtors' accountant is directed by the court to provide such information. Even under these conditions, it may be advisable to review with the debtor the information that is being submitted.

86 In one instance, an arrangement with creditors failed because of a New York City business tax audit assessment which reduced the available assets below the agreed settlement percentage. The reason for this unnecessary occurrence was the debtor's accountant's failure to forward copies of the debtor's tax returns as requested by the creditors' accountant. These returns revealed that the debtor had used an incorrect gross sales base in calculating the New York City business tax. If the creditors' accountant had been aware of this error, the potential audit assessment would have been considered in determining the percentage creditors would receive.

87 A question frequently asked the creditors' accountant by the creditors' committee is, "Did the debtor's accountant fully cooperate with you?" A negative answer will often result in the adoption of a poor attitude by the creditors' committee toward the debtor.

Direct Liability to Third Parties

88 The degeneration of the financial condition of a client's business operation creates natural alarm among creditors, credit agencies, bank loan officers, and various other financial institutions dealing with the debtor. The debtor's accountant, who previously had no direct contact with third parties, becomes very popular with them as they search for additional financial information relating to the debtor. The general integrity of the independent accountant will, no doubt, cause these very same third parties to rely upon any oral assertions made by the debtor's accountant. With complete awareness of professional status as it relates to conduct and to personal legal liability under these conditions, the accountant:

Should not engage in off-the-record conversation or written communication with third parties.

Should, officially and on the record, discuss the debtor's financial position when called upon by a proper third party, but only as to information reflected on the books and records of the client. It is advisable not to give personal opinions as to the future prospects of the client, whether they be good or poor, regardless of the sincerity of a personal opinion.

Should not submit a tentative financial statement to any third party unless all the required auditing standards and procedures and statement presentation standards have been followed.

Should seriously weigh the advisability of extending good offices in securing additional financing for the client where, in the accountant's judgment, repayment is highly doubtful.

Should avoid unofficial or informal contact with the various national and local credit reporting agencies but submit, as requested, financial statements fully documented and prepared in accordance with generally accepted accounting principles.

Other Professional Ethical Factors

89   Many ethical questions are raised when the accountant is involved in bankruptcy and insolvency proceedings. One question that deserves careful consideration arises when the accountant serves both the debtor and the creditors. As discussed in chapter 6, the accountant may not be engaged by both the debtor and the creditors' committee, but in order to keep accountants' fees as low as possible, the creditors' committee may use the debtor's accountant. This situation gives rise to some possible conflicts of interest, one of the largest involving the level of disclosure for which the accountant is responsible. The creditors will want to know as much as possible about the operations of the debtor. However, to reveal everything may prove misleading and unduly detrimental to the debtor. In this position the accountant must find the correct point between adequate disclosure so that creditors may protect their interests and avoidance of excess disclosure that may injure the debtor. Another area of potential conflict is in evaluating the plan proposed by the debtor. If the services of an accountant are needed by the creditors' committee to assist in the evaluation of the debtor's plan, the debtor's accountant will most likely be unable to assist the committee and it will be necessary for the committee to retain its own accountant at this point. This issue is discussed more fully in chapter 6, paragraphs 4–10.

90   The accountant is often required to assist the creditors' committee in exercising control over the assets of the debtor. The accountant's independence would appear to be impaired by performance of functions for the debtor that are generally performed by management. The Ethics Division of the AICPA has ruled that the following functions cannot be performed if the accountant is to remain independent:

Cosign checks issued by the debtor corporation.

Cosign purchase orders in excess of established minimum amounts.

Exercise general supervision to insure compliance with the budgetary controls and pricing formulas established by management, with the consent of the creditors, as part of an overall program aimed at the liquidation of deferred indebtedness.

See the discussion of creditors' committee and their accountants in chapter 4, paragraphs 20–27.

EXAMPLE OF PROJECTED OPERATING RESULTS

91   The preparation of projected financial statements to assist the debtor, creditors, and the court in working out a plan that will provide for the debtor to continue in business constitutes an important part of the accountant's function in the reorganization proceedings. Text discussion of the forecast or projection of operating results and the conditions surrounding their use can be found in paragraphs 44–47 of this chapter.

Exhibit 7-7   Projections of Operating Results

NO NAME INCORPORATED

PROJECTED OPERATING RESULTS

November 1, 19X1, Through October 31, 19X2

NO NAME INCORPORATED

COMMENTS ON MANAGEMENT ASSUMPTIONS
INCLUDED IN ACCOMPANYING PROJECTIONS

1. The Balance Sheet as of October 31, 19X2, as shown in Exhibit I, has been adjusted to reflect the conditions set forth in the plan of reorganization. The adjustment is as follows:

Notes Payable—Unsecured	$89,592	
Accounts Payable	183,055	
Retained Earnings		$152,547
Goodwill		62,600
Leasehold Improvements		52,400
Additional Paid-In Capital		5,100

All unsecured debt as of October 30, 19X1, the date the petition was filed under chapter 11, has been reduced by 60 percent for a total of $272,647. The deficit in Retained Earnings of $152,547 has been eliminated as a result of the anticipated debt forgiveness. The Goodwill account was completely written off

Exhibit 7-7   (*Continued*)

and the Leasehold Improvements account was reduced by $52,400. The balance of the anticipated benefit from debt forgiveness of $5,100 has been credited to the Additional Paid-In Capital account.

2. Exhibit I reflects the Company's actual Balance Sheet after adjustments as of October 31, 19X1, and the projected balance sheet as of October 31, 19X2, after giving consideration to the projected operating results and changes in cash flow reflected in the remaining Exhibits.

3. Exhibits II and III reflect projected operating results for the year ending October 31, 19X2, and are based on the following major assumptions:

   a. Sales are projected at $1,250,000 annual volume, and are based upon present backlog data as well as historical seasonal patterns.

   b. Cost of sales is projected as 73 percent of sales.

   c. Purchase costs are assumed to be 46 percent of sales, and purchase requirements are assumed to be three months prior to shipment.

   d. Payroll taxes are projected at 5.2 percent of payroll costs.

   e. Building rent is anticipated to increase from $2,000 per month to approximately $3,000 per month in April, 19X5, upon moving the Company's operations to new facilities. As of September 30, 19X2, the lease agreement would have required payments of $5,000 per month. The lessor has agreed to reduce the payments to $2,000 per month until the expiration of the lease, March 30, 19X2. At this time the debtor will be required to vacate the facilities.

   f. The officers of the Company have agreed to a 15 percent reduction in salary. This reduction is reflected in the Exhibits.

4. Exhibit IV reflects the projected cash flow for the year ending October 31, 19X2, and is based on the following major assumptions:

   a. Collections of Accounts Receivable are assumed to be as follows:

10%	of current month's sales
80	of previous month's sales
10	of second previous month's sales
100%	

   b. Additional long-term financing of $100,000 is anticipated. $38,000 will be used to acquire new equipment, which is essential if the company is to continue operating.

   c. All purchases are assumed to be paid for within 30 days of receipt of goods. Substantially all other creditors are paid within the same month of receipt of goods and services, except the ABC Advertising Company which has agreed to delay for one year the billings for advertising services rendered.

5. The forecast is based on the assumption that the plan of reorganization will be accepted.

Exhibit 7-7 *(Continued)*

NO NAME INCORPORATED

BALANCE SHEETS

For the Year Ending October 31, 19X2

(Based Upon Management Assumptions as Set Forth in
Accompanying Comments)

	October 31	
	19X2 (Projected)	19X1 (Actual)
Assets		
Current Assets:		
Cash (Exhibit IV)	$ 14,690	$ 33,545
Accounts Receivable	114,000	48,799
Inventory	258,049	254,875
Prepaid Expenses	3,388	3,388
Total Current Assets	390,127	340,607
Fixed Assets:		
Machinery and Equipment	119,874	81,874
Leasehold Improvements	28,974	28,974
Furniture and Fixtures	13,058	13,058
	161,906	123,906
Less: Accumulated Depreciation	65,118	47,118
	96,788	76,788
Other Assets:		
Deposits	2,636	2,636
Cash Surrender Value of Life Insurance	2,594	2,594
	5,230	5,230
Total Assets	$492,145	$422,625

	October 31	
	19X2 (Projected)	19X1 (Actual)
Liabilities		
Current Liabilities:		
Current Notes Payable—Unsecured	$ 59,727	$ 59,727
Current Notes Payable—Secured	–0–	33,748
Accounts Payable	52,844	122,038
Accrued Expenses	88,496	10,740
Estimated Income Taxes Payable	16,033	–0–
Total Current Liabilities	217,100	226,253
Long-Term Debt	95,823	48,061
	95,823	48,061
Owners' Equity:		
Common Stock—$10 Par Value— 8,000 Shares	80,000	80,000
Additional Paid-In Capital	68,311	68,311
Retained Earnings	30,911	–0–
	179,222	148,311
Total Liabilities and Owners' Equity	$492,145	$422,625

Exhibit 7-7   (*Continued*)

NO NAME INCORPORATED

PROJECTED STATEMENT OF OPERATIONS

For the Year Ending October 31, 19X2
(Based Upon Management Assumptions As Set Forth in Accompanying Comments)

	Actual	Total	Period 1	Period 2	Period 3	Period 4
Net Sales, All Products	$ 0	$1,250,000	$ 85,000	$120,000	$ 90,000	$190,000
Cost of Sales:						
Beginning Inventory	0	254,875	254,875	304,719	280,703	258,754
Purchases	0	598,000	87,400	41,400	18,400	41,400
Direct Labor	0	141,920	11,700	9,360	12,350	9,880
Manufacturing Burden	0	175,754	12,794	12,824	13,001	14,281
	0	1,170,549	366,769	368,303	324,454	324,315
Less: Ending Inventory	0	258,049	304,719	280,703	258,754	185,615
Cost of Sales	0	912,500	62,050	87,600	65,700	138,700
Gross Profit	0	337,500	22,950	32,400	24,300	51,300
Selling, General and Adm.	0	282,333	23,885	22,595	23,764	22,664
Operating Income	0	55,167	(935)	9,805	536	28,636
Interest Expense	0	8,823	547	660	660	797
Other Income	0	600	50	50	50	50
Income Before Tax	0	46,944	$ (1,432)	$ 9,195	$ (74)	$ 27,889
Provision for Tax	0	16,033				
Net Income	0	30,911				
Retained Earnings (Beg.)	0	0				
Retained Earnings (End)	$ 0	$ 30,911				

Period 5	Period 6	Period 7	Period 8	Period 9	Period 10	Period 11	Period 12
$ 90,000	$ 40,000	$ 90,000	$110,000	$115,000	$100,000	$105,000	$115,000
185,615	195,706	245,455	254,584	249,163	247,622	254,711	258,200
50,600	52,900	46,000	48,300	52,900	52,900	52,900	52,900
9,880	9,880	13,650	11,400	14,300	11,960	11,960	15,600
15,311	16,169	15,179	15,179	15,209	15,229	15,279	15,299
261,406	274,655	320,284	329,463	331,572	327,711	334,850	341,999
195,706	245,455	254,584	249,163	247,622	254,711	258,200	258,049
65,700	29,200	65,700	80,300	83,950	73,000	76,650	83,950
24,300	10,800	24,300	29,700	31,050	27,000	28,350	31,050
23,074	23,656	24,236	23,106	24,236	23,300	23,310	24,507
1,226	(12,856)	64	6,594	6,814	3,700	5,040	6,543
797	798	798	798	742	742	742	742
50	50	50	50	50	50	50	50
$ 479	$(13,604)	$ (684)	$ 5,846	$ 6,122	$ 3,008	$ 4,348	$ 5,851

Exhibit 7-7 (*Continued*)

NO NAME INCORPORATED

PROJECTED STATEMENT OF OPERATING EXPENSES

For the Year Ending October 31, 19X2

(Based Upon Management Assumptions As Set Forth in Accompanying Comments)

	Actual	Total	Period 1	Period 2	Period 3	Period 4
Manufacturing Burden						
Salaries and Wages:						
Engineering	$ 0	$ 66,450	$ 4,600	$ 4,600	$ 4,600	$ 5,850
Indirect Labor	0	14,000	1,000	1,000	1,000	1,000
	0	80,450	5,600	5,600	5,600	6,850
Payroll Taxes	0	11,556	963	963	963	963
Building Rent	0	26,802	1,613	1,613	1,750	1,750
Heat, Light, and Power	0	10,140	660	670	680	690
Small Tools and Shop	0	1,500	100	100	110	110
Depreciation	0	14,000	1,050	1,050	1,050	1,050
Insurance	0	2,200	160	160	160	160
Property Taxes	0	2,000	400	400	400	400
Maintenance and Repairs	0	3,400	400	400	400	400
Engineering Supplies	0	2,400	200	200	200	200
Employee Benefits	0	7,200	490	510	530	550
Equipment Rental	0	5,550	445	445	445	445
Accrued Vacations	0	8,556	713	713	713	713
Total (Exhibit II)	$ 0	$175,754	$ 12,794	$ 12,824	$ 13,001	$ 14,281
Selling, General and Adm.						
Salaries and Wages:						
Officers	$ 0	$ 87,000	$ 7,250	$ 7,250	$ 7,250	$ 7,250
Office	0	57,015	5,325	4,260	5,325	4,260
	0	144,015	12,575	11,510	12,575	11,510
Payroll Taxes	0	7,492	654	599	654	599
Employee Benefits	0	3,640	270	280	290	300
Accrued Vacations	0	7,200	600	600	600	600
Building Rent	0	4,096	231	231	250	250
Utilities	0	2,220	150	160	170	170
Depreciation	0	4,000	200	200	200	200
Telephone and Telegraph	0	9,410	700	710	720	730
Professional Fees	0	8,000	667	667	667	667
Freight-Out	0	600	50	50	50	50
Office Supplies	0	3,900	325	325	325	325
Travel and Entertainment	0	7,560	630	630	630	630
Insurance	0	2,800	233	233	233	233
Overtime Premium	0	600	200	0	0	0
Advertising	0	72,000	6,000	6,000	6,000	6,000
Equipment Rental	0	1,200	100	100	100	100
Miscellaneous	0	3,600	300	300	300	300
Total (Exhibit II)	$ 0	$282,333	$ 23,885	$ 22,595	$ 23,764	$ 22,664

Period 5	Period 6	Period 7	Period 8	Period 9	Period 10	Period 11	Period 12
$ 5,850	$ 5,850	$ 5,850	$ 5,850	$ 5,850	$ 5,850	$ 5,850	$ 5,850
2,000	2,000	1,000	1,000	1,000	1,000	1,000	1,000
7,850	7,850	6,850	6,850	6,850	6,850	6,850	6,850
963	963	963	963	963	963	963	963
1,750	2,618	2,618	2,618	2,618	2,618	2,618	2,618
690	990	970	950	950	950	970	970
120	120	130	130	140	140	150	150
1,050	1,250	1,250	1,250	1,250	1,250	1,250	1,250
160	200	200	200	200	200	200	200
400	0	0	0	0	0	0	0
400	200	200	200	200	200	200	200
200	200	200	200	200	200	200	200
570	590	610	630	650	670	690	710
445	475	475	475	475	475	475	475
713	713	713	713	713	713	713	713
$ 15,311	$ 16,169	$ 15,179	$ 15,179	$ 15,209	$ 15,229	$ 15,279	$ 15,299
$ 7,250	$ 7,250	$ 7,250	$ 7,250	$ 7,250	$ 7,250	$ 7,250	$ 7,250
4,260	4,260	5,325	4,260	5,325	4,435	4,435	5,545
11,510	11,510	12,575	11,510	12,575	11,685	11,685	12,795
599	599	654	599	654	608	608	665
300	300	310	310	320	320	320	320
600	600	600	600	600	600	600	600
250	412	412	412	412	412	412	412
170	230	220	200	190	180	180	200
400	400	400	400	400	400	400	400
740	1,100	760	770	780	790	800	810
667	667	667	667	667	667	667	667
50	50	50	50	50	50	50	50
325	325	325	325	325	325	325	325
630	630	630	630	630	630	630	630
233	233	233	233	233	233	233	233
200	200	0	0	0	0	0	0
6,000	6,000	6,000	6,000	6,000	6,000	6,000	6,000
100	100	100	100	100	100	100	100
300	300	300	300	300	300	300	300
$ 23,074	$ 23,656	$ 24,236	$ 23,106	$ 24,236	$ 23,300	$ 23,310	$ 24,507

Exhibit 7-7 *(Continued)*

NO NAME INCORPORATED

PROJECTED STATEMENT OF CASH FLOW

For the Year Ending October 31, 19X2

(Based Upon Management Assumptions As Set Forth in Accompanying Comments)

	Actual	Total	Period 1	Period 2	· · ·	Period 12
Beginning Balance (Exh. 1)	$ 0	$ 33,545	$ 33,545	$ 5,636		$ 24,740
Add:						
Accounts Receivable	0	1,184,799	57,299	88,500		95,500
Other Income	0	600	100	100		100
Financing Proceeds	0	100,000	0	50,000		0
	0	1,285,399	57,399	138,600		95,600
Deduct:						
Accounts Payable	0	122,038	45,122	19,200		0
Purchases	0	545,100	0	87,400		52,900
Salaries and Wages	0	366,385	29,875	26,470		35,245
Payroll Taxes	0	19,048	1,617	1,562		1,628
Building Rent (Mfg.)	0	26,802	1,613	1,613		2,618
Heat, Light, and Power	0	10,140	660	670		970
Small Tools and Shop	0	1,500	100	100		150
Property Taxes	0	2,000	400	400		0
Maintenance and Repairs	0	3,400	400	400		200
Engineering Supplies	0	2,400	200	200		200
Employee Benefits (Mfg.)	0	7,200	490	510		710
Equipment Rental (Mfg.)	0	5,550	445	445		475
Employee Benefits (Non-Mfg.)	0	3,640	270	280		320
Building Rent (Non-Mfg.)	0	4,096	231	231		412
Utilities	0	2,220	150	160		200
Telephone and Telegraph	0	9,410	700	710		810
Freight-Out	0	600	50	50		50
Office Supplies	0	3,900	325	325		325
Travel and Entertainment	0	7,560	630	630		630
Overtime Premium	0	600	200	0		0
Advertising	0	10,000	0	0		1,000
Equipment Rental (Non-Mfg.)	0	1,200	100	100		100
Miscellaneous	0	3,600	300	300		300
	0	1,158,389	83,878	141,756		99,243
Insurance	0	5,000	0	0		2,500
Professional Fees	0	8,000	0	0		1,000
Capital Additions	0	38,000	0	0		0
Interest Expense	0	8,879	547	660		742
Notes Payable	0	52,238	883	882		2,165
Income Taxes	0	33,748	0	0		0
	0	1,304,254	85,308	143,298		105,650
Ending Balance (Exhibit 1)	$ 0	$ 14,690	$ 5,636	$ 938		$ 14,690

Accounting Services for the Debtor in Possession or Trustee: Part 2

1 The debtor in most bankruptcy proceedings needs assistance in order effectively to regain the position once occupied when operations were profitable. Many factors are responsible for business failures, but as noticed in chapter 2 the major cause is inefficient management. Management may lack training or experience in basic business methods, such as interpreting financial data, managing funds, scheduling production and shipping, coordinating departmental activities, and any other management functions. In a common situation, a manager may be an expert in a technical field, such as designing, but have little managerial ability for directing the activities of the business.

2   There are several ways in which accountants can help the debtor overcome financial problems caused by inefficient management or other factors and carry out some of the procedural steps that are necessary to see that an agreement is reached with creditors. These were mentioned in the previous chapter and two of them are described in more detail in this chapter—issuance of operating statements and management advisory services. Also described in this chapter are the services that an accountant may render in a chapter 7 case.

REPORTS ISSUED DURING CHAPTER 11 PROCEEDINGS

3   Several different types of reports are required while the debtor is operating the business in a chapter 11 reorganization proceeding. The nature of the reports and the time period in which they are issued depend to some extent on local rules and on the type of internal controls of the debtor and the extent to which large losses are anticipated.

4   Since local rules will have impact on the nature of the reports required, they will be described before discussing the actual statements.

Local Requirements

5   Exhibit 8-1 contains an example of the local requirements for the Central District of California. The accountant should check with the counsel for the debtor or the bankruptcy clerk (U.S. trustee, where appointed) for

Exhibit 8-1   Local Rules for the Central District of California.

RULE 906

USE, SALE, OR LEASE OF PROPERTY OF THE ESTATE BY TRUSTEE

A request by the trustee to use, sell, or lease property of the estate, other than in the ordinary course of business, pursuant to § 363(b) of the Bankruptcy Code shall be by written application, served and filed with the bankruptcy court clerk. The application shall identify the property of the estate which the trustee intends to use, sell, or lease, and the proposed disposition of the property.

Unless a hearing is requested by a party in interest within fifteen (15) days after the service of notice thereof upon him, or within a different time if the bankruptcy judge for good cause shortens or enlarges the time, the failure to request

Exhibit 8-1 *(Continued)*

such a hearing shall be deemed to constitute consent to the granting of the application and a waiver of objections to the proposed disposition of the property, permitting the trustee to use, sell, or lease the property, as requested in the application, without order of the court.

Any request for hearing shall be governed by motion practice under Local Rule 904.

RULE 918

DISBURSEMENTS

Unless the U.S. trustee otherwise directs:

Disbursements of an estate shall be by check. All checks shall contain a statement of the consideration for the same.

Contemporaneously with issuing the disbursement checks the issuer shall file a statement with the U.S. trustee and the creditors' committee, if there is one, showing the following information:

1   Opening balance or balance on hand from last statement;
2   Receipts since last statement and brief description of source or receipt, for example, "receivables," "tax refund," "sale of inventory," and so forth;
3   Total of (1) and (2);
4   A list of disbursements with each check number, name of payee, and purpose for which issued, and amount;
5   Remaining balance on hand after disbursements;
6   The amount and nature of cash held in other accounts or in other form, for example, passbook accounts, time certificates of deposit;
7   The name of the depository bank, and account number; and
8   The amount of the [issuer's] bond.

These statements should be complete enough to advise the U.S. trustee and any party in interest of the financial condition and status of the administration of the case.

RULE 919

REPORTS REQUIRED DURING OPERATION OF BUSINESS

Unless the U.S. trustee otherwise directs:

(a) In the event that it is intended to continue the operation of a business, the debtor in possession or the trustee shall meet with the U.S. trustee, and file with him, within two working days after the filing of a petition, a report containing the following information:

Exhibit 8-1   (*Continued*)

  i   The estimated costs of operation for the next succeeding thirty days;

 ii   The estimated profit or loss for said period;

iii   The amount of cash available for the operation;

 iv   How the applicant intends to fund the cost of operation for the next thirty days; and

  v   Such other and additional information as is pertinent to advise adequately the U.S. trustee as to the desirability of continuing the business.

(b) Every debtor in possession or trustee operating a business shall file in duplicate with the U.S. trustee verified operating statements by Thursday of each week covering the operation during the prior week ending on the prior Saturday unless the U.S. trustee directs that such statement cover longer periods of operation, which period may not exceed one month. The statements shall be of an accrual type reflecting the actual loss or profit of the operation for the period and shall show the income earned (even though not yet received) during the accounting period, together with any appropriate adjustment such as a reserve for bad debts, and should not show as income cash realized from prefiling assets, for example, collection of the debtor's prefiling receivables. There shall also be stated and deducted from the income earned the expenses of operation such as purchases, labor, and overhead as well as the accrued liabilities (even though unpaid) for such items as rent, utilities, real and personal property taxes, sales taxes, insurance, and so forth. There shall be entered in the statement under the heading "Cost of Goods Sold" the cost of the inventory used during the period (which is an estimate of the inventory used based on the sales for the period). This figure must be adjusted by taking a physical inventory at the beginning of the operation and every ninety days thereafter or such other reasonable period as determined by the U.S. trustee. In addition, the statement shall show the amounts carried forward from the last operating statement and cumulative totals for the operation from the filing of the case to date.

As a separate part of the report, a statement shall be made showing the cash on hand and in the bank at the commencement of the period, the receipts and disbursements for the period, the cash balance, and the bank balance at the end of the period. There shall also be stated the amounts deducted and deposited for withholding and other taxes during the period and where deposited, and that paragraph (c) of this rule has been complied with; an itemization of accrued but unpaid obligations of the operation; any significant change in status or amount of inventory; and the amount if any of the debtor's prefiling assets which have been reduced to cash and the disposition of that cash.

The above stated report shall be dated and signed by the reporting officer and verified and shall contain a statement that the bank accounts set up as trust accounts for taxes and payroll contain sufficient funds to pay in full all taxes and payroll due.

In a given case, the U.S. trustee may modify any of the provisions of this rule in such fashion as will not violate its spirit and intent.

(c) The debtor in possession or trustee when operating a business under any

Exhibit 8-1 (*Continued*)

provision or section of the Bankruptcy Code shall open a special tax account in one of the depositories on the designated and approved list of this court, in which he shall forthwith upon receipt deposit all withholding, social security, unemployment, excise, sales, use or other taxes collected or received or withheld for or on behalf of the United States, State of California or any political subdivision thereof.

RULE 920

EMPLOYMENT OF DEBTOR IN REORGANIZATION

No compensation or other remuneration shall be paid from the assets of the estate to the debtor, or if a partnership, to any of the partners, or if a corporation to any present or former officer, director or stockholder thereof, from the time of the filing of the petition until confirmation of a plan unless such employment and the basis of compensation have been first authorized by the U.S. trustee. Any application for such compensation shall disclose, under oath, all income from any source for compensation for services related to the debtor proceeding.

special rules in the district where the petition is filed. Note that these rules indicate that all reports go to the U.S. trustee, since this district is one of the pilot districts.

6 Local Rule 919 requires that the operating statement be issued weekly. For most large businesses with any type of fiscal controls the time period is changed to monthly. While the local rules have specific procedures that may differ from district to district, the districts with U.S. trustees should have similar operating requirements even though the local rules may have different requirements. Special efforts are being made by the U.S. trustees to be consistent. The following section describes the procedures followed for operating a business in the Central District of California. Other districts with pilot programs should be similar.

U.S. Trustee's Requirements

7 The U.S. trustee would like to meet with the debtor and its counsel within two days after the petition is filed. Frequently the attorney will call the U.S. trustee and set up an appointment on the same day the petition is filed. It might also be helpful if the debtor has his or her accountant or chief financial officer attend this first informal meeting. In addition to the U.S. trustee or the assistant U.S. trustee, a bankruptcy analyst with an accounting orientation will also be present.

8 At this meeting the debtor will describe the nature of the business and its problems to the U.S. trustee and the bankruptcy analyst, who are at-

tempting to learn as much about the business as possible. The U.S. trustee will find out about any filing problems and discuss certain procedures with the debtor. For example, provision will have to be made for wages earned during the payroll period just prior to the filing in order to encourage the employees to stay with the company. They will discuss the procedures to be followed in opening new bank accounts, closing prepetition records, and establishing new records. Another important problem that must be resolved is compensation for officers. The trustee will determine what he thinks is an appropriate salary and subsequently confirm by letter stating that the amount established is subject to review by the creditors' committee. The salary of officers is generally reduced and is determined after evaluating what the company can afford and what the individual officers need to survive. In establishing the salary, the U.S. trustee should also realize that it is important to keep the key personnel to provide for smoother operations during the rehabilitation period. The debtor, of course, has the right to contest the salary established for officers and let the court rule on the amount that should be paid.

9   Other topics discussed at this meeting center around the reasons for financial difficulty and the problem areas. The U.S. trustee will want to know if there are any cash collateral problems, if a prefiling creditors' committee was appointed, and any additional information about how the committee was formed. The U.S. trustee is interested in finding out the kind of steps the debtor plans to take to correct the financial problems.

10   The U.S. trustee will establish with the debtor the type of operating reports that should be filed and the timing of such reports. Also requested will be a report on the verification of insurance coverage.

11   Subsequent to the meeting with the debtor and its counsel, the U.S. trustee, one of the bankruptcy analysts, or both, may decide to visit the debtor's business premises to gain additional knowledge about the operation of the business, meet the people who manage the operation, and, in general, find out as much as possible about the operation so all parties can be better served in the proceedings.

12   In a notice mailed to all attorneys for chapter 11 cases filed in the Central District of California, the U.S. trustee sets forth the requirements expected during the period of bankruptcy. Timely compliance with each of the following requirements is expected by the U.S. trustee unless a supplemental notice modifying any of the requirements is executed and served upon the debtor by the U.S. trustee. A request for the modification of any of the requirements should be made by letter addressed to the U.S. trustee requesting in writing a modification and setting forth in detail the reasons for any requested modification.

1   *List of creditors*   A list of the debtor's *twenty largest unsecured* creditors must be filed with the clerk of the bankruptcy court at the time of the filing of the petition. The list shall contain the name, address and phone number of each such creditor. If any such creditor is not an individual, the list shall also state the name of an individual employed by or associated with said creditor who is familiar with the debtor's account.

2 *Meeting with the U.S. trustee*   Either before or within two working days after the filing of a chapter 11 case, counsel for the debtor must contact the office of the U.S. trustee for an appointment to discuss the debtor's particular financial situation and potential problems of administration. See Local Bankruptcy Rule 919 (Exhibit 8-1).

3 *Projected operating statement*   Within two working days after the filing of the petition, the debtor must file with the U.S. trustee a projected operating statement for the first thirty days of operation under chapter 11. See Local Bankruptcy Rule 919(a) (Exhibit 8-1) for required contents of the statement.

4 *Bank accounts; books and records*   All of debtor's bank accounts must be closed immediately upon the filing of the petition and new accounts opened. Said accounts shall consist of general, payroll, and tax accounts. The new bank signature cards shall clearly indicate that the debtor is a "chapter 11 debtor in possession." Bank accounts may be maintained only in those institutions presently designated as authorized depositories. If the debtor uses "cash collateral," separate "cash collateral" accounts must be established and maintained pursuant to section 363(c)(4). The books and records of the debtor should be closed as of the date of the filing of the petition and new books and records kept thereafter for the debtor in possession.

5 *Proof of insurance coverage*   Within five days of the filing of the petition, the debtor must provide to the U.S. trustee a *verified* statement or written evidence on the insurance carrier or brokers' letterhead that worker's compensation, general liability, fire, theft, and motor vehicle insurance are in full force and effect, together with all other insurance coverages normally used in the debtor's type of business.

6 *Inventory*   The debtor must procure a physical inventory upon the filing of the petition and submit the inventory to the U.S. trustee within two days after the filing of the petition.

7 *Interim statements*   Separate interim statements for each bank account must be prepared and filed with the U.S. trustee for each day in which checks are drawn on any of said accounts. See Local Bankruptcy Rule 918 (Exhibit 8-1). An original and one copy of each statement are required. Exhibit 8-2 contains a sample of an acceptable form for the interim statements for the general account. Similar forms would be used for the payroll and tax accounts.

8 *Operating reports*   The debtor shall file weekly operating reports with the U.S. trustee. See Local Bankruptcy Rule 919(b) (Exhibit 8-1). An original and one copy of each report are required. Exhibit 8-3 contains

Exhibit 8-2 Interim Statement: Cash Accounts

UNITED STATES BANKRUPTCY COURT
CENTRAL DISTRICT OF CALIFORNIA

In re   Case No.
                                                         Debtor in Possession
                                                         General Account
Debtor(s)   Interim Statement No. _____

1. Total Receipts Per Prior Interim Statement(s) $_____
2. Less: Total Disbursements Per Prior Interim Statement(s)   _____
3. Beginning Balance   _____
4. Receipts Since Prior Interim Statement
   Description   *Amount*

                                                         $_____
5. Balance Available $_____
6. Less: Disbursements Per This Interim Statement
   Date   Check No.   Payee and Purpose   Amount

   TOTAL $_____ $_____
7. Balance Remaining on _____(Date)
   (Line 5 less Line 6) $_____

8. Depository:
   Branch/Location:
   Account No.:
Other Moneys on Hand. (for example, Certificates of Deposit and
   Petty Cash): _____

   I declare under penalty of perjury that the information contained in the above
interim statement is true and complete to the best of my knowledge.

   DATED:

                                   _____
                                   Debtor in Possession

Exhibit 8-3 Operating Statements: Cash Receipts and Disbursements and
Statement of Aged Payables and Receivables

UNITED STATES BANKRUPTCY COURT
CENTRAL DISTRICT OF CALIFORNIA

In re

Debtor(s).

Case No.
Debtor in Possession Operating
Report—Summary of Cash Receipts
and Disbursements; Statements of
Aged Payables and Receivables

Report No. _____
(For the period ending
_____, 1980)

Beginning Cash Balance in General Account $_____

	CURRENT PERIOD (____ thru ____)	PREVIOUS REPORTING PERIOD (____ thru ____)	CUMU-LATIVE TOTALS (____ ____)

Receipts:
  [Itemized by major category—
     below for examples]
  Operating Receipts
  Loan Proceeds
  Miscellaneous

| | Total receipts: | $_____ | $_____ | $_____ |

Disbursements:
  [Itemized by major category—
     below for examples]
  Accounting Services
  Advertising
  Auto Leases
  Executive Compensation
  Insurance
  Payroll
  Payroll Taxes
  Property Taxes
  Rent
  Repairs and Maintenance
  Utilities

| Total disbursements: | $_____ | $_____ | $_____ |
| Cash increase (or decrease): | $_____ | $_____ | $_____ |

Exhibit 8-3 *(Continued)*

STATEMENT OF AGED RECEIVABLES

Name of Accounts	Total Due	Current (0-30 days)	Overdue (31-60 days)	Overdue (61-90 days)	Overdue (90-120 days)
TOTALS	$____	$_____	$_____	$_____	$_____

STATEMENT OF AGED PAYABLES

Creditor	Total Due	Current (0-30 days)	Overdue (31-60 days)	Overdue (61-90 days)	Overdue (90-120 days)
TOTALS	$____	$_____	$_____	$_____	$_____

STATEMENT OF STATUS OF PAYMENTS OF SECURED CREDITORS AND LESSORS

Creditor/ Lessor	When Payments Due	Amount of Each Regular Payment	Number of Post-Petition Payments Delinquent	Amount of Post-Petition Payments Delinquent	Next Payment Due
	(for example, Monthly, Quarterly)				

VERIFICATION:

I declare under penalty of perjury that the information contained in the foregoing Operating Report is true and correct to the best of my knowledge.

DATED:

_____
Debtor in Possession

an example of the operating statement. The sample form shows a cash receipts and disbursements statement with supplementary statements of aged receivables and payables. Complete accrued statements along with cash receipts and disbursements may be filed by larger businesses. See Exhibit 8-4.

9 *Employment of principals and professionals* The debtor may not, prior to confirmation of a plan of reorganization compensate or remunerate itself, or any of its partners, officers, directors or shareholders in any manner without prior written approval of the U.S. trustee. See Local Bankruptcy Rule 920 (Exhibit 8-1). The application should set forth the name and proposed position of the individual sought to be employed along with a detailed description of the duties said individual is to perform, the number of hours each week said individual will devote to those duties and the reasons why employment of said individual is necessary to the successful reorganization of the debtor. The application should also set forth the amount of compensation sought on a weekly or monthly basis and disclose all perquisites, benefits and consideration of any kind the individual is to receive, for example use of company vehicles, payment of life or health insurance premiums, reimbursement for expenses. The application should disclose the individual's salary history for the year immediately preceding the filing of the chapter 11 petition, and shall be under oath. See Exhibit 8-5 for an example of a form used to apply for compensation for officers.

The U.S. trustee requests that applications for the employment of professional persons (for example, attorneys, accountants, appraisers, auctioneers) pursuant to section 327, as well as any application for compensation of such persons, be served upon the U.S. trustee prior to seeking an order of the bankruptcy court.

10 *Notice to United States trustee of applications and of adversary proceedings* The debtor must serve the U.S. trustee with a copy of any application or request filed by the debtor with the bankruptcy court which seeks an order of any kind from the bankruptcy court. Additionally, debtors must serve the U.S. trustee with a copy of any pleading in any adversary proceeding or contested matter filed by or against the debtor, including but not limited to complaints, motions, answers, responses, stipulations, notices, proposed orders or judgments, and so on, whether or not the U.S. trustee is a party to the adversary proceeding or contested matter.

11 *Modification of requirements* Local Bankruptcy Rules 918 and 919 (Exhibit 8-1) provide for the discretion of the U.S. trustee with respect to modification of certain reporting requirements. The U.S. trustee may, at any time during the course of a case add or delete requirements providing the additions or deletions appear necessary in the course of the supervision of the chapter 11 case.

Exhibit 8-4 Operating Statements: Accrued Receipts and Disbursements

UNITED STATES BANKRUPTCY COURT
CENTRAL DISTRICT OF CALIFORNIA

In re

Debtor(s)

Case No.
Debtor in Possession
Operating Report No.
Summary of Accrued Receipts and
Disbursements
For the period from _____, 19
thru _____, 19
Statement No.

Income:	Cum. Total Start of Period	This Period Receipts & Disbmts.	Accrued & Unpaid Oblig.	Totals	Cumulative Total End of Period
Sales (NOTE)	$	$	$	$	$
Other Income					
Total	$	$	$	$	$
Begin Inventory	*				
Plus: Purchases	*				
Less: Ending Inventory	*				
Cost of goods sold	$	$	$	$	$
Gross Profit	$	$	$	$	$

Expenses:

(Illustrative Only)
Advertising
Auto Leases
Insurance:
  Fire
  Group
  Liability
  Theft
  Workmen's Compensation
  Other
Miscellaneous
Officers' Compensation
Payroll
Payroll Taxes
Penalty Taxes
Postage
Rent
Repairs and Maintenance
Rubbish Service
Telephone
Utilities

Total Expenses					
NET PROFIT	$	$ *	$ *	$	$

* For purposes of this schedule, the items asterisked should not be filled in.

Exhibit 8-5 Application for Employment of Principals (Officers and Stockholders)

TO: ————————————
   United States Trustee
   Central District of California
   ATTN:

Re:
   Debtor in Possession
   Case No.

APPLICATION FOR COMPENSATION (LOCAL RULE C-2)

Applicant _____ declares and requests the following:
   1. That he is the _____ (and shareholder) of the debtor corporation (partnership herein and has served in said capacity since _____ _____ 19_____.
   2. Applicant has the following sources of income from the debtor other than for services rendered: _____
_____.
   3. Prior to filing the petition herein, applicant was working for the debtor as the _____ with the following responsibilities:
_____
_____, receiving a salary of $_____ per month.
   4. Since the filing of the petition herein and to the date of this application, applicant has been and will continue to devote _____% of his full working time to this debtor as _____ with the following responsibilities:
_____
_____.
   5. Applicant hereby requests a salary of $_____ per month. Applicant also requests an allowance of $_____ per month as necessary for the following purpose: _____
_____.
   6. Applicant has the following sources and amounts of income separate and apart from those received from the debtor or as above applied for:
   a.
   b.
   7. Wherefore, applicant requests approval of the above requested compensation effective from the date of filing of the petition herein.

   I declare under penalty of perjury that the above statements are true and correct.

                                    _____
                                                       Applicant

This application is hereby granted and authorized.

_____, UNITED STATES TRUSTEE

By _____
      Bankruptcy Analyst

Dated: _____

13 In addition to the above listed requirements, the U.S. trustee in the central district of California notifies the debtor of the following provisions of the Bankruptcy Code and Local Bankruptcy Rules:

1 *Use of "cash collateral"*   Section 363(c)(2) provides that "cash collateral" may not be used by the debtor without first procuring the consent of the secured creditor or court authorization "after notice and a hearing." This section describes "cash collateral" as "cash, negotiable instruments, documents of title, securities, deposit accounts, or other cash equivalents in which the estate and an entity other than the estate have an interest." The U.S. trustee requires that he be served with any and all papers filed with the court in this regard and be provided with notice of any proposed stipulation or any hearing in this regard.

2 *Obtaining credit*   Section 364(b) provides that the debtor may not obtain credit or incur unsecured debt other than in the ordinary course of business without court authorization after notice and a hearing. Also, section 364(c) requires court authorization "after notice and a hearing" before the obtaining of credit or the incurring of debt with priority over certain administrative expenses and section 364(c) and (d) require court authorization after notice and a hearing before the obtaining of credit or the incurring of debt to be secured by a lien on property of the estate. The U.S. trustee requires that he be served with any and all papers filed with the court in this regard and be notified of any proposed stipulation or any hearing in this regard.

3 *Use, sale, or lease of property of estate*   Section 363(b) provides for the use, sale, or lease of property of the estate when such use, sale, or lease is not in the ordinary course of business only after notice and a hearing. See Local Bankruptcy Rule 906 (Exhibit 8-1) which prescribes the appropriate procedure as a written application to be filed with the clerk of the bankruptcy court and which provides for the use, sale or lease of property without an actual hearing or court order unless a hearing is timely requested by a party objecting to the proposed use, sale or lease.

Operating Statements

14 A complete periodic profit-and-loss statement and often a statement of cash receipts and disbursements must be filed with the court as required by the local rules or specific order of the court. The types of statements required by the central district of California were mentioned above and included in Exhibits 8-3 and 8-4. It is important that the operating statement be carefully prepared because it is the court's and the creditors' and their committees' major source of information concerning the financial operations of the debtor in possession. It should be prepared on an accrual basis and must be signed by the debtor or trustee. However, for many small businesses, a cash receipts and disbursement statement may be used with a separate schedule of receivables and payables.

15 The income statement filed with the court differs somewhat from the typical statement. The accountant generally prepares the report based on an estimated gross profit figure because it is highly unlikely that a physical inventory will be taken every month. It may be necessary to have a physical inventory taken every ninety days. This would, of course, depend on the type of internal accounting control the debtor has, the nature of the business, and materiality of the inventory. Depreciation and other expenditures that do not require future cash outlays should be clearly identified in the statements and, if practical, presented in a separate category. For manufacturing concerns it is important to identify the amount of depreciation and other noncash expenditures in the cost of goods sold. In some businesses depreciation expense can be viewed as a cash outlay as would be the case in businesses that lease out a large amount of equipment with a relatively short life, such as automobiles. Under these conditions depreciation expense is helpful in providing some indication of the future viability of the company. Also, nonrecurring expenses should be clearly labeled because the U.S. trustee and creditors' committee are primarily interested in the next period's projected income. All liabilities that become due after the petition is filed should be paid by the debtor in the regular course of the business, as should taxes which relate to the period after filing. However, taxes that accrued before the petition was filed should not be paid by the debtor as a normal business transaction.

16 There is no particular form required for the revenue and expense statements; they are typically presented in the normal income statement format. Exhibit 8-4 contains the format suggested by the U.S. trustee for the central district of California.

17 In addition to the revenue and expense statement that is usually required, local rules may necessitate that a cash receipts and disbursements statement be filed also. Again, the format is not generally specified, but the typical format for a cash statement can be used. Exhibit 8-3 illustrates one possible form.

18 The operational guidelines issued by the U.S. trustee for the districts of Maine, Massachusetts, New Hampshire, and Rhode Island are included in Exhibit 8-6. The district that always has a large number of business petitions filed is the Southern District of New York. Their requirements are

Exhibit 8-6 Operating Guidelines for Debtors in the District of Maine, Massachusetts, New Hampshire, and Rhode Island

In furtherance of the duties imposed on the United States trustee by 28 U.S.C. 586(3), as added by section 224(a) of the Bankruptcy Code, debtors in possession and appointed trustees who operate businesses are required, as of the date of the filing of a petition commencing a case under chapters 7, 11 or 13 where a business is operated, to adhere to the following guidelines relating to the opening and maintenance of bank accounts and the filing of financial statements.

Exhibit 8-6 *(Continued)*

BANK ACCOUNTS

A debtor in possession shall open (a) a new bank account to reflect postpetition operations of the business and (b) a separate tax account (as more fully described below) as of the date of the order for relief. A trustee appointed to operate a business also is required to open and maintain such accounts. In a case in which the trustee supersedes a debtor in possession, the trustee, upon ascertaining that such accounts previously had been opened and maintained, may continue such accounts.

Deposits to the separate tax account, together with any necessary federal depository receipts, shall be made as follows:

(1) Within two business days from the date on which salaries are paid to employees

    (a) that portion of such salaries as are required to be withheld for federal, state and local taxes and for social security, and

    (b) the employer's portion of social security and disability and unemployment insurances; and

(2) In those cases in which the operating business is required to collect sales taxes, such taxes must be deposited in this tax account each Monday as were required to be collected in the previous week; and

(3) Any other taxes which the debtor is required to collect or for which it incurs liability in the ordinary course of the operation of its business (such as federal excise taxes), must be deposited in this tax account no later than Wednesday of the week following the one in which they were collected or in which the liability was incurred.

    The debtor in possession or operating trustee shall within one calendar week after making any remittances to a depository on account of federal taxes furnish the District Director of Internal Revenue Service with evidence, on forms provided by the District Director and on such terms as the District Director may prescribe, that such deposits have been made on behalf of the debtor.

MONTHLY FINANCIAL STATEMENTS

A debtor in possession or a trustee appointed to operate a business is required to file verified financial statements (described below) in duplicate with the United States Trustee no later than the 15th of each month (commencing with the month following the filing of the petition) reflecting the operations of the debtor's business during the immediately preceding month.

1. A monthly profit and loss statement prepared on the accrual method, including appropriate adjustments to reflect real estate taxes, insurance, and other expenses which are paid annually.

2. A bi-weekly cash flow statement together with a copy of the cash disbursements and cash receipts journal.

3. If in the real estate business, a monthly profit and loss statement based on actual cash receipts and accrued disbursements. Such statement shall include the amount of tenants' rent, arrearages for each property, if any, and an

Exhibit 8-6 *(Continued)*

analysis of the occupancy rate of each property, and the rate of rental percentage delinquency.

4. A monthly list of accounts payable and dates that payables were incurred, specifically noting those accounts which are disputed and those which are not being paid in accordance with their terms.

5. A monthly reconciliation of the separate tax account, showing all deposits and withdrawals made during the period.

6. A monthly statement of accounts receivable. Such statement should set forth information related to the financing of such accounts, including the nature and amount of the collateral, the age of the accounts and whether they are eligible for financing, and a breakdown of prepetition and post-petition accounts. In addition, this statement should include a reconciliation of the lender's accounts, including the opening balance, amounts paid back to the lender, amounts taken down, charges against the accounts and a closing monthly balance.

7. Special reports may be required from time to time, such as Inventory Reports.

ANNUAL FINANCIAL STATEMENTS

A debtor in possession or a trustee appointed to operate a business is required to file with the United States trustee, no later than 90 days after the close of the debtor's fiscal year, the following annual financial statements, in duplicate, prepared, to the extent possible, in accordance with generally accepted accounting principles.

1. A balance sheet with comparative figures for the prior fiscal year.

2. A profit and loss statement with comparative figures for the prior fiscal year.

****

Should a debtor in possession or a trustee appointed to operate a business believe that any of the information requested to be included in monthly financial statements cannot be provided, the debtor in possession or trustee should contact the United States trustee immediately in writing to explain the circumstances as to why such financial information may not be available. In addition to the requirements above, the responsibilities of this office include complete administrative supervision of chapter 11 cases. Therefore, we are calling on the debtor's attorney to make certain that we are kept apprised of all matters pertaining to the case at all times. This includes the following additional requirements:

1. Furnish UST office with evidence of debtor in possession and tax account (copies of new checks will suffice); evidence of Workmen's Compensation, liability and fire insurance currently in effect; copies of tax depository receipts.

2. Furnish UST office with copies of all papers including but not limited to letters, pleadings, applications, requests and stipulations.

3. Advise UST office of all hearing and continuance dates.

Exhibit 8-7   Operating Guidelines and Financial Reporting Requirements for Debtors in the Southern District of New York

MONTHLY FINANCIAL STATEMENTS

All debtors in possession and trustees who operate a business are required to file verified financial statements (described below) in duplicate with the U.S. trustee, with a copy to the creditors' committee (if one has been appointed).

Reports shall be filed not later than the 15th calendar day following the end of each calendar month, covering all transactions by or for a debtor in possession or a trustee for the calendar month immediately preceding the due date.

1   A cover sheet showing the name of the debtor, case number, identifying the preparer of the report, with verification by the preparer, the debtor, and/or debtor's attorney. If the operating report is prepared by a party other than the debtor, or its principals or employees, there should also be included an opinion letter or report specifying audit or review standards employed, and any deviations from the consistent application of generally accepted accounting principles.

2   An Accrual Basis Profit and Loss Statement and Balance Sheet prepared in accordance with generally accepted accounting principles (GAAP) with all disclosure appropriate for interim reporting.

3   A Schedule of Cash Receipts and Disbursements, either listing each transaction classified by ledger account, of if over 50 transactions per month, grouped and categorized by ledger account. A Chart of Accounts should be provided with the first report.

4   A Schedule of Accounts Payable. This schedule should list each account (or group if more than 25) showing by columnar classification amounts which are:

   a   Prepetition
   b   Current/not yet due
   c   1–30 days past due
   d   31–60 days
   e   61–90 days
   f   91–180 days
   g   180 and over

   NOTE—Payable transactions, other than trade payables, i.e., with related parties, intercompany, and notes payable should be segregated. Any items which are disputed, or which have financially significant terms, conditions, or covenants should be explained by appropriate disclosure.

5   A Schedule of Accounts Receivable. This should list accounts as described in 4, above. Disclosure is required wherever accounts are subject to factoring, discounting, or other financing practice.

6   A Schedule of Federal State and Local Taxes Collected, Received, Due, or Withheld. For each month, this schedule should provide the following information:

Exhibit 8-7   (*Continued*)

a   All wages and salaries paid (gross) or incurred.
b   The amount of payroll taxes withheld.
c   The amount of employer payroll tax contributions incurred.
d   The gross taxable sales.
e   Sales taxes collected.
f   The date and amount paid over to each taxing agency for taxes identified in items b, c, and e above.

7   A Schedule of Cost of Goods Sold classifying inventory by manufacturing process (raw materials, component, goods-in-process, and finished goods) or by product line for a distributor-type business showing beginning inventory, purchases, and ending inventory. The Schedule should show by ledger account all other items incurred or "expensed" as a cost of product, i.e., labor, overhead, etc.

WAIVER OR MODIFICATION

The reporting requirements propounded by the U.S. trustee may be waived or modified only after a request in writing demonstrating both just cause for the requested action and specifying what alternative safeguard is to be provided for the protection of the estate. No waiver or modification shall be effective unless in writing and signed by the U.S. trustee or an authorized delegate.

Debtors should be advised that a request to modify the Profit and Loss Statements to "cash basis," if approved, only modifies the recognition of revenue, and *will not release* the debtor in possession or trustee of the duty to report all costs or liabilities incurred in operating the business of the debtor.

DISCLOSURE REQUIREMENTS

Interim financial reports (monthly operating reports) shall comply with at least the minimum disclosure requirements established in AICPA Accounting Principles Board Opinion #28 for interim reporting. Mere compilation reports do not comply with these operating report requirements.

ANNUAL FINANCIAL STATEMENTS

All debtors in possession and any trustee who operates a business are required to file in duplicate with the U.S. trustee, with a copy to the creditors' committee, if any, no later than 90 days after the close of the debtor's fiscal year, or each taxable year (if a short tax year election *is* made pursuant to tax code 1398(d)(2), the following annual financial statements prepared, to the extent possible, in accordance with generally accepted accounting principles (including GAAP disclosure requirements).

Exhibit 8-7   (*Continued*)

  1 A balance sheet with comparative figures for the prior fiscal year.
  2 A profit and loss statement with comparative figures for the prior fiscal year.
  3 A copy of the 10K for the period, for a publicly held corporation.

  We recognize that each debtor in possession is different and that the ability of a debtor in possession to comply with the monthly financial reporting also may vary. Thus, counsel or the debtor's chief financial officer should feel free to advise the U.S. trustee as to the circumstances making it burdensome or otherwise difficult to provide the requested information and to indicate, for example, the type of financial statements the debtor in possession can provide, the form of such reports, and the timing. While we are willing to consider, on the basis of the facts of each case, any reasonable alternative that the debtor in possession may wish to propose, we wish to receive at least as much information as the debtor in possession provides to a creditors' committee.

  A copy of any communication sent to this Office concerning compliance with the financial reporting requirements should be served on the creditors' committee, if any. Questions regarding these guidelines should be addressed to the Attorney handling the case, or to the Bankruptcy Analyst.

presented in Exhibit 8-7. (Information on closing and opening bank accounts is similar to that in Exhibit 8-6 and is omitted here). The Central District of California requirements were discussed in paragraphs 5–17.

19   Exhibit 8-8 contains an example of a recently filed operating statement in a chapter 11 proceeding. Note that the statements were compiled by an independent accountant and a compilation report is included. Also, a statement of changes in financial position was substituted for the cash receipts and disbursement statement. It should be noted, however, that in most situations the cash receipts and disbursement statement or the statement of changes in financial position based upon the direct cash approach is preferred by most creditors' committees, courts, and U.S. trustees' offices.

MANAGEMENT ADVISORY SERVICES

20   Until recently most accountants actively involved in bankruptcy proceedings were primarily performing auditing and investigative services. There are, however, many opportunities for accountants to serve in a consultant capacity that can be of considerable benefit to management. Because of the many day-to-day problems the debtor has faced in the last few months prior to the time the petition was filed, the debtor spends most of its time trying to solve these problems and attempting to keep the corporation out of bankruptcy court in the short run. As a result of this type of action, the management of the business finds it very difficult to evaluate objectively the long-term prospects for the company.

21 The debtor needs direction in clearly defining its objectives and in preparing forecasts of future operations. Not only must these kinds of decisions be made, but they must be made in a relatively short time period if the company expects to regroup and resume profitable operations. For example, in a retail operation, a large number of stores may have to be closed, inventory that is obsolete must be liquidated, and the shelves must be restocked with inventory items that will sell. To make these kinds of short-run decisions and to evaluate carefully the type of opportunities, if any, available, the debtor may find special studies and analyses made by accountants very helpful. Consultants may be retained by the debtor and/or creditors' committee to render services even before a decision is made as to whether the debtor can be rehabilitated. For example, in the W. T. Grant, Chapter XI case, the finding by the consultants of the advanced state of deterioration in the retailing operations was a primary reason for the decision of the creditors' committee to recommend liquidation rather than rehabilitation under

Exhibit 8-8   Monthly Operating Statements of a Company in Chapter 11 Proceedings

FASAR SYSTEMS, INC.

FINANCIAL STATEMENTS

Month Ended February 29, 19X0

———

The accompanying balance sheet of Fasar Systems, Inc. as of February 29, 19X0 and the related statement of income and statement of changes in financial position for the ten months then ended, have been compiled by us.

A compilation is limited to presenting in the form of financial statements information that is the representation of management. Except for inventories as of February 29, 19XO (refer to a separate report dated March 14, 19X0), we have not audited or reviewed the accompanying financial statements, and, accordingly, do not express an opinion or any other form of assurance on them.

Glendale, California
March 14, 19X0

Exhibit 8-8 (*Continued*)

Fasar Systems, Inc.
Balance Sheet
as of February 29, 19X0

See accountants' compilation report

Assets	2/29/X0	1/31/X0	Increase (Decrease)
Current assets			
Petty cash	$ 100.00	$ 300.00	$(200.00)
Cash in bank—general	31,859.38	8,829.32	23,030.06
Cash in bank—payroll	2,543.62	7,719.83	(5,176.21)
Cash in bank—special	688.34	688.34	.00
Cash in bank—savings	38.16	38.16	.00
Accounts receivable—trade	84,001.17	234,284.19	(150,283.02)
Accounts receivable—other	1,489.21	1,489.21	.00
Inventory—finished goods— Notes 1b and 2	15,665.49	.00	15,665.49
Inventory—work in progress— Notes 1b and 2	50,195.90	.00	50,195.90
Inventory—raw materials— Notes 1b and 2	316,468.35	.00	316,468.35
Inventory—Notes 1b and 2	.00	285,546.40	(285,546.40)
Inventory—rework— Notes 1b and 2	4,242.75	.00	4,242.75
Prepaid expenses—insurance	4,655.00	5,320.00	(665.00)
Prepaid expenses—interest	.00	245.84	(245.84)
Prepaid expenses—other	5,020.00	600.00	4,420.00
Total current assets	516,967.37	545,061.29	(28,093.92)
Fixed assets—Note 1c			
Machinery and equipment	14,781.51	13,098.51	1,683.00
Allow for depreciation	(5,962.73)	(5,655.85)	(306.88)
Transportation equipment	4,732.03	4,732.03	.00
Allow for depreciation	(2,783.04)	(2,685.16)	(97.88)
Furniture and fixtures	262.30	262.30	.00
Allow for depreciation	(53.06)	(49.94)	(3.12)
Total fixed assets	10,977.01	9,701.89	1,275.12
Other assets			
Cash surrender value of life insurance	2,250.00	2,250.00	.00
Plant rental deposits	7,840.00	7,840.00	.00
Customer deposits	2,937.23	2,937.23	.00
Organization costs	573.24	595.28	(22.04)
Total other assets	13,600.47	13,622.51	(22.04)
Total assets	$541,544.85	$568,385.69	$(26,840.84)

Note: The accompanying notes are an integral part of this statement.

Exhibit 8-8　*(Continued)*

Liabilities and Capital	2/29/X0	1/31/X0	Increase (Decrease)
Current liabilities			
Accounts payable—trade	$ 462,759.43	$ 371,626.48	$ 91,132.95
Commissions payable	2,533.35	2,533.35	.00
Accrued interest payable—Note 3	44,916.70	47,375.03	(2,458.33)
Accrued royalties—Note 4	55,277.53	56,828.98	(1,551.45)
Insurance loan payable	2,713.38	2,713.38	.00
Payroll taxes payable	2,015.77	1,892.69	123.08
Sales tax payable	3.75	3.75	.00
Notes payable—Valley—Note 3	150,000.00	150,000.00	.00
Notes payable—SPNB—Note 3	1,979.16	2,144.09	(164.93)
Notes payable—RCB Corp—Note 3	35,000.00	35,000.00	.00
Total current liabilities	757,199.07	670,117.75	87,081.32
Long-term liabilities—Note 5			
Note payable—R.J.C.	170,000.00	170,000.00	.00
Note payable—R.B.	40,000.00	40,000.00	.00
Total long term liabilities	210,000.00	210,000.00	.00
Capital			
Common stock—Note 8	20,000.00	20,000.00	.00
Retained earnings	(265,344.31)	(265,344.31)	.00
Net loss for the period	(180,309.91)	(66,387.75)	(113,922.16)
Total capital	(425,654.22)	(311,732.06)	(113,922.16)
Total liabilities/capital	$ 541,544.85	$ 568,385.69	$(26,840.84)

Note: The accompanying notes are an integral part of this statement.

Exhibit 8-8 *(Continued)*

Fasar Systems, Inc.
Income Statement
For current period and ten months ended February 29, 19X0

See accountants' compilation report

	Current Period	%	Year to Date	%
Sales				
Sales—stoves—f	$ 2,124.00	(6.55)	$ 218,670.00	21
Sales—stoves—u	10,200.00	(31.43)	762,807.45	75
Sales—tiles	7,710.30	(23.76)	26,517.30	2
Sales—parts	7,023.16	(21.64)	73,366.93	7
Sales—industrial	.00	.00	11,290.00	1
Sales—returns—Note 9	(59,713.94)	184.01	(100,167.44)	(9)
Sales—other	.00	.00	16,386.53	1
Sales—service	(32.06)	.10	4,402.75	
Sales discounts	(422.26)	1.30	(3,336.98)	( )
Sales—rework	660.00	(2.03)	660.00	
Total sales	(32,450.80)	100.00	1,010,596.54	100
Cost of sales				
Purchases	557.61	(1.72)	500,429.83	49
Direct labor	5,610.20	(17.29)	89,327.31	8
Discounts taken	.00	.00	753.90	
Freight-in	565.30	(1.74)	10,454.96	1
Mfg. overhead	15,778.16	(48.62)	145,198.32	14
Inventory change	(1,026.09)	3.16	41,174.87	4
Total cost of sales	21,485.18	(66.21)	787,339.19	77
Gross profit	(53,935.98)	166.21	223,257.35	22
Selling & admin. exp.				
See schedule 1	55,871.84	(172.17)	364,530.14	36
Operating profit	$(109,807.82)	338.38	$(141,272.79)	(13)
Other income & (expense)				
Interest-income	.00	.00	75.62	
Rental income	.00	.00	1,225.00	
Interest-expense	(4,112.34)	12.67	(40,918.63)	(4)
Miscellaneous	(2.00)	.01	780.89	
Total other income & (expense)	(4,114.34)	12.68	(38,837.12)	(3)
Profit before tax	(113,922.16)	351.06	(180,109.91)	(17)
Income tax provision				
Provision for state taxes—Note 7	.00	.00	200.00	
Total tax provision	.00	.00	200.00	
Net earnings or (loss)	$(113,922.16)	351.06	$(180,309.91)	(17)

Note: The accompanying notes are an integral part of this statement.

Exhibit 8-8   *(Continued)*

Fasar Systems, Inc.
Support Schedules: Income Statement
For current period and ten months ended February 29, 19X0

See accountants' compilation report

	Current Period	%	Year to Date	%
Mfg. overhead				
Depreciation	$ 382.50	1.18	$ 3,795.45	.38
Equipment rental	79.50	.24	722.59	.07
Engineering supplies	256.75	.79	2,882.26	.29
Insurance—general	.00	.00	479.68	.05
Insurance—group	911.83	2.81	5,523.04	.55
Insurance—w. comp.	399.00	1.23	6,314.00	.62
Maintenance—general	497.48	1.53	4,629.68	.46
Miscellaneous	.00	.00	126.78	.01
Outside services	5,925.00	18.26	12,025.41	1.19
Payroll—indirect labor	2,246.26	6.92	48,302.83	4.78
Payroll taxes	717.28	2.21	14,738.05	1.46
Plant protection	46.80	.14	212.87	.02
Rent	4,781.00	14.73	21,969.59	2.17
R & M—equipment	244.20	.75	1,688.44	.17
Shop supplies	159.45	.49	5,161.78	.51
Small tools	(1,354.52)	4.17	7,358.92	.73
Taxes & licenses	.00	.00	1,786.91	.18
Utilities	605.63	1.87	5,905.44	.58
Professional literature	(120.00)	.37	1,474.60	.15
Insurance recovery	.00	.00	100.00	.01
Total mfg. overhead	$ 15,778.16	48.62	$145,198.32	14.37

Note: The accompanying notes are an integral part of this statement.

Exhibit 8-8   *(Continued)*

Fasar Systems, Inc.
Selling and Administrative Expenses
For current period and ten months ended February 29, 19X0

See accountants' compilation report

	Current Period	%	Year to Date	%
Selling and administrative expenses				
Accounting & legal	$ 7,819.95	(24.10)	$ 33,448.25	3.34
Advertising & promotional	.00	.00	8,791.35	.88
Amortization	22.04	(.07)	220.40	.02
Auto expense	272.93	(.84)	4,701.86	.47
Bad debts	27,454.03	(84.60)	27,756.67	2.78
Bank charges	5.00	(.02)	11.20	.00
Commissions	.00	.00	2,533.35	.25
Delivery	.00	.00	370.88	.04
Depreciation	25.38	(.08)	327.40	.03
Dues & subscriptions	.00	.00	168.60	.02
Employee welfare	34.00	(.10)	415.21	.04
Entertainment	56.99	(.18)	1,081.25	.11
Equipment rental	16.50	(.05)	2,479.34	.25
Freight-out	29.69	(.09)	(76.12)	(.00)
Insurance—general	.00	.00	4,848.83	.48
Insurance—group	427.55	(1.32)	6,239.92	.62
Insurance—w. comp.	266.00	(.82)	3,624.24	.36
Maintenance—general	307.30	(.95)	3,133.70	.31
Miscellaneous	.00	.00	82.69	.00
Office expense	201.84	(.62)	2,831.91	.28
Outside services	6,807.94	(20.98)	11,613.13	1.16
Penalties	.00	.00	531.89	.05
Permits & testing	.00	.00	260.00	.03
Plant protection	31.20	(.10)	141.91	.01
Postage	100.00	(.31)	494.73	.05
Professional literature	.00	.00	908.78	.09
Rent	3,851.00	(11.87)	15,308.80	1.53
R & M—equipment	65.00	(.20)	107.00	.01
Royalty expense	(1,551.45)	4.78	46,077.53	4.61
Salaries—office	2,273.40	(7.01)	24,484.11	2.45
Salaries—officers	2,885.00	(8.89)	65,037.65	6.50
Salaries—sales	.00	.00	15,750.84	1.58
Salaries—product services	.00	.00	19,313.69	1.93
Sales expense	1,202.97	(3.71)	8,752.92	.88
Service department expense	15.95	(.05)	5,923.18	.59
Shop supplies	.00	.00	578.07	.06
Balance to page 301	$ 52,620.21	162.18	$ 318,225.16	31.81

Exhibit 8-8 *(Continued)*

Schedule 1 *(Continued)*

	Current Period	%	Year to Date	%
Balance from page 300	$ 52,620.21	162.18	$ 318,225.16	31.81
Taxes–licenses	.00	.00	341.66	.03
Taxes–payroll	436.45	(1.34)	8,476.53	.85
Telephone	446.44	(1.38)	5,729.08	.57
Travel	118.00	(.36)	18,928.78	1.89
Utilities	403.74	(1.24)	3,513.37	.35
Warranty expense	1,847.00	(5.69)	9,265.56	.93
Total selling & admin. exp.	$ 55,871.84	(172.17)	$ 364,530.14	36.45

Note: The accompanying notes are an integral part of this statement.

Fasar Systems, Inc.
Statement of Changes in Financial Position
as of February 29, 19X0

See accountants' compilation report

Source of funds		
Operations		
Net earnings		$(180,309.91)
Add–non working capital charges		
Depreciation	$4,122.85	
Amortization	220.40	
		4,343.25
Funds provided by operations		(175,966.66)
Other sources		
Refund of city bond		1,000.00
Total source of funds		(174,966.66)
Use of funds		
Purchase of equipment		5,233.48
Decrease in working capital		$(180,200.14)

Note: The accompanying notes are an integral part of this statement.

Exhibit 8-8   *(Continued)*

Fasar Systems, Inc.
Statement of Changes In Working Capital
as of February 29, 19X0

See accountants' compilation report

	Increase (Decrease)
Current assets	
Cash in bank—general	$ 30,567.56
Cash in bank—payroll	1,049.50
Cash in bank—special	688.34
Cash in bank—savings	37.16
Accounts receivable—trade	(6,147.59)
Accounts receivable—other	1,257.13
Inventory—finished goods—Notes 1b and 2	15,665.49
Inventory—work-in-process—Notes 1b and 2	50,195.90
Inventory—raw materials—Notes 1b and 2	316,468.35
Inventory—Notes 1b and 2	(327,848.08)
Inventory—rework—Notes 1b and 2	4,242.75
Prepaid expenses—insurance	4,655.00
Prepaid expenses—interest	(2,405.84)
Prepaid expenses—taxes	(798.10)
Prepaid expenses—other	5,020.00
	$ 92,647.57
Current liabilities	
Accounts payable—trade	$ 244,967.90
Commissions payable	2,533.35
Accrued interest pay—Note 3	17,423.39
Accrued royalties—Note 4	36,077.53
Accrued warranties—Note 5	(5,608.29)
Insurance loan payable	2,713.38
Payroll taxes payable	448.36
Sales tax payable	(3.41)
Notes pay—Valley—Note 3	(24,055.20)
Notes pay—SPNB—Note 3	(1,649.30)
	$ 272,847.71
Decrease in working capital	$(180,200.14)

Note: The accompanying notes are an integral part of this statement.

Exhibit 8-8   (*Continued*)

Fasar Systems, Inc.
Notes to Financial Statements
For current period and ten months ended February 29, 19X0

Note 1: Major accounting policies

The following describes the more significant accounting and reporting policies of the company:

a. Assets and liabilities, and revenues and expenses, are recognized on the accrual basis of accounting.

b. Inventories are valued at cost, not exceeding market values, under the first-in, first-out method.

c. Fixed assets are stated at cost, less allowances for depreciation computed on the straight-line method. Property and equipment are depreciated over their estimated useful lives of from three to seven years. The cost of ordinary maintenance and repairs is charged to operations.

d. Income tax credits are accounted for on the "flow-through" method, whereby they are applied as a reduction of the provision for federal income taxes in the year in which they are realized.

Note 2: Inventories

A physical inventory was taken on February 29, 19X0 and the separate components are reflected on the balance sheet under current assets.

Note 3: Notes payable to banks and other creditors

Notes payable to banks and other creditors are reflected as separated components on the balance sheet under current liabilities. Interest is accrued monthly and consists of the following:

a. Valley National Bank:	$ 0
b. R. C. Bacerra Corporation:	6,416.70
c. R. J. Cunningham, officer and stockholder:	31,166.70
d. R. Bacerra, officer and stockholder:	7,333.30
Total	$ 44,916.70

Note 4: Accrued royalties

Under certain licensing agreements, the company is obligated to pay royalties to R. C. Bacerra Corporation. The terms of the agreement include a 5% royalty per unit sold based on the manufacturer's net selling price.

Note 5: Long-term liabilities

The long-term liabilities as reflected on the balance sheet is renewable annually at 10% per annum and comprises of $170,000 to R. J. Cunningham and $40,000 to R. Bacerra. Both are officers and stockholders of the company.

Exhibit 8-8 *(Continued)*

Note 6: Leases

The company leases the premises from Dimensional Research, Inc., a California corporation, on a month-to-month basis at a net monthly rental of $6,641 which includes maintenance. The company is also obligated to pay certain carrying charges on the leased property.

Note 7: Income taxes

The company has not been examined by the Internal Revenue Service. Substantial net operating losses and income tax credits are available to offset against future federal taxable income. Such carry-forwards expire as follows:

	Net Operating Losses	Investment Credits	New Jobs Tax Credits
April 30, 1985	$164,661	$ 819	$ 7,200
April 30, 1986	100,683	192	22,492
	$265,344	$1,011	$29,692

Note 8: Common stock

Common stock of no par value, authorized 1,000,000 shares, issued and outstanding 200,000 shares at a stated value of $0.10 per share.

Note 9: Sales—returns

$59,713.94 represents sales returns for a period of approximately five months ended February 29, 19X0.

Chapter XI. Indeed, in this case consultants were retained by both the debtor and the creditors' committee.[1]

22 The two types of consulting activities discussed in this chapter are the business plan and forecast of future operations.

Business Plan

23 Often companies do not have any type of business or strategic plan at the time they attempt to work out some form of arrangement with creditors out of court or in a chapter 11 proceeding. Up until the date the petition is filed, management have devoted most of their time to day-to-day problems and have not analyzed the major financial problems faced by the business.

---

[1] See Bankruptcy Reform Act of 1978; Hearings on S. 2266 and H.R. 8200 before the Subcommittee on Improvements in Judicial Machinery, 95th Cong., 1st Sess. (1977) 587 (Statement of John J. Jerome).

They fail to ask questions that are most important for the survival of the business such as:

1 What products are most profitable?
2 What are strengths and weaknesses of the company?
3 What areas should be expanded? liquidated?
4 In what areas does the real potential for this business lie?
5 What direction should this business take?

The greater the financial problems, the more time management devotes to day-to-day details and thus, almost no time is spent on providing direction for the company. After the petition is filed, it is then frequently left up to the bankruptcy court and the creditors to make strategic decisions that significantly influence the future of the business. They may decide which operations to eliminate and which products to discontinue. These decisions are made on a quasi-intuitive basis. For example, selected equipment may be sold or retained based on the influence of particular creditors rather than on the basis of an overall business plan.

24 In rendering advisory services to help develop a business plan, the accountant examines all the information that is available, analyzes it taking into consideration the future prospects, and develops recommendations. These recommendations may involve closing unprofitable units, replacing poor management, changing the information system, and revising the marketing approach. Some of the recommendations are implemented while the company is in chapter 11 proceedings where the effect is known immediately, such as closing some unprofitable operating units. Other strategic plans have a long-range effect, but they still have an impact on the nature of the company that comes out of the proceedings. A business plan allows all interested parties to have a better idea of what part of the operations are salvageable and provides for better understanding of a plan proposed by the debtor.

25 The analysis required to make reasonable recommendations must involve an assessment of the environmental forces (past, present, and future) influencing the business and an evaluation of the strengths and weaknesses of the company.

Assessment of Environmental Forces

26 In analyzing the environment, questions similar to the following must be studied and answered.

1 The market—What is total demand? Is it increasing? Is it decreasing?
2 The customers—What are their needs, expectations, values, and resources?

3   The competition—Who? Where? What are their strengths and limitations?

4   Suppliers—Are they there? For example, sugar beet factories in Maine went bankrupt in part because farmers did not plant enough beets.

5   The industry—Is there surplus capacity? A shortage of capacity? What is the distribution system?

6   Capital market—How and at what costs and conditions can capital be raised?

7   Government and society—What demands are society and government making on the firm?[2]

27   The current answers to these questions can be obtained from historical data. However, trying to answer these same questions in terms of the situation five to ten years from now is extremely difficult. The techniques now used for forecasting environmental factors are extremely weak and thus not highly reliable in terms of accuracy. However, it is generally conceded that it is better to have a somewhat inaccurate prediction of the future environment than no prediction at all.

Evaluation of Strengths and Weaknesses

28   Determining the strengths and weaknesses of the company may appear to be a very simple task, but, in fact it needs careful analysis. The answer, according to Drucker, is usually anything but obvious.[3] The evaluation should include an analysis of, at least, some of the following:

Organizational Structure

What is the present structure?

Does this structure lend itself to the creation of new operating divisions and profit centers?

Is there sufficient depth in top management so that management of new facilities can come from within or will it be necessary to hire outside of the firm?

Has management policy on recruitment and development of new employees been successful?

Competitive Ability

Does the firm know what its actual competition is?

Has past forecasting of the competitors' likely market strategies been accurate?

---

[2] William E. Rothschild, "The C.A.S.E. Approach—A Valuable Aid for Management Development," *California Management Review,* Vol. 14 (Fall 1971), p. 34.
[3] Peter F. Drucker, *The Practice of Management* (New York: Harper & Row, 1954), p. 49.

How quickly has the firm been able to react to completely unexpected moves by competitors?

Market Capability

In what market (both geographical and product) has the firm been involved? Is there a pattern of success and failure?

What promotional activities does the firm utilize?

What channels of distribution does the firm use?

Production Facilities

What types of production processes have been used in the past?

Where are the facilities located?

Does surplus capacity exist in the firm?

What technical skills do the workers possess? Can these skills be applied to other products?

Are labor relations favorable?

Administration

Is management given the information it needs?

Could the present administration handle a major acquisition?

Are the lines of communication well defined and operational?

Does the company have a data processing system that is able to handle present needs?

What changes would be necessary to handle additional requirements?[4]

This list is not intended to be all encompassing, since each business in financial difficulty will have differing requirements. The important point is that questions such as those above must be answered in making decisions about the direction the company should take as it comes out of the reorganization.

Illustration of Business Plan

29 Exhibit 8-9 contains some excerpts from a business plan Touche Ross & Co. developed for Food Fair in a Chapter XI arrangement under prior law. Two business plans were prepared by this company—one for retail operations and the other for nonretail operations. Included in this example are management summary, three parts of operations review—introduction, manufacturing division summary, and analysis of the beverage company—and part of an analysis of a division that was liquidated while

---

[4] James McKinnon, "Corporate Planning," *The Accountants' Magazine*, Vol. 163 (November 1970), p. 539.

Exhibit 8-9   Business Plan

I. MANAGEMENT SUMMARY

Purpose and Scope

The attached Business Plan for the manufacturing and produce nonretail operations was prepared by Food Fair, Inc. management to:

- Present the decisions which management has made for restructuring the Company and creating a strong, viable, and profitable Food Fair.
- Provide financial projections for the nonretail business operations which management has decided to retain.
- Describe the decision making process and the rationale underlying each of management's decisions.
- Document the significant analyses which were undertaken as a part of the decision making process.

Management has completed its reviews of the manufacturing and produce operations and decided to retain all of the manufacturing operations and the produce operations in Florida as well as World Wide Produce and Klein Packing. The other produce operations were entirely dependent upon the New York and Philadelphia retail volumes. As a result of the recent retail dispositions, these operations have been discontinued. Their respective assets were relatively insignificant. Further, the potato farming operations are being discontinued. Its assets, primarily real estate, will be sold.

Management, as of this date, is not yet prepared to review its decisions with respect to the meat division and other nonretail operations. As decisions on these operations are made and related planning completed, management will make available comparable analyses and documentation supporting their decisions similar to that included in this document.

Planning Process

Initially two sets of projections of future operating results were prepared by division management in the two nonretail divisions. One set of projections, the expected projections, assumed a continuation of recent operating trends based upon the retail operations projections, inventory levels, cash availability, credit terms, and no additional financing. The alternative, or improved projections, assumed a return to normal service and inventory levels based upon the improved retail operations projections and outside sales programs. Projections were prepared by the respective company personnel and reviewed by division management. In each case, the detailed assumptions underlying each set of projections were subjected to review and challenge. After the projections had been reviewed and finalized, they were submitted to senior management for review. In each case, the projections were subsequently modified, as appropriate, to reflect the impact of any decisions made by senior management.

Exhibit 8-9 *(Continued)*

II. OPERATIONS REVIEW

INTRODUCTION

Purpose

The review of various Food Fair nonretail operating entities has been undertaken to:

- Assess the impact on these nonretail operations resulting from the recent retail dispositions
- Identify opportunities for short-term improvement, primarily in the areas of:
  Sales
  Marketing
  Cash flow
  Cost and expenses
  Overhead
  Management
- Quantify the prospects for short-term contribution to corporate profitability
- Assess the long-term fit and potential for these operations within the restructured company.

Scope

The nonretail operations for which reviews have been undertaken to date include:

- Manufacturing Division
- World Wide Produce Group
- Meat Processing Division (not completed)

Methodology

Reviews were conducted on-site with operating management and at corporate headquarters with Supermarket Division, nonretail and corporate management personnel. Areas of focus included:

- Historical and projected operating performance and results
- Sales mix and customers
- Marketplace and competition
- Operating capital requirements
- Business risks
- Other areas of importance to the operations.

The results of the operations reviews have been included in this section of this document.

Exhibit 8-9   *(Continued)*

MANUFACTURING DIVISION
SUMMARY

Overview

The Manufacturing Division is comprised of four major operating companies:

- Boulevard Beverage—Manufacturer of carbonated and noncarbonated beverages
- L. Resnick and Sons—Distributor of paper and packing material
- Rozenco Coffee—Manufacturer of roasted and ground coffee
- Waverly Tea—Manufacturer of tea bags.

In addition to these operating companies, the Manufacturing Division has a number of smaller active and inactive operations which have not been included in the scope of the review of the Division. Detailed reports for the four major companies follow this summary.

The Division is under the overall supervision of the Vice-President for Manufacturing.

Reporting to the Vice-President is a Director of Purchasing, a Sales Director, a Divisional Controller, and three Divisional Managers responsible for each of the operating entities. Accounting for the Division is performed by its own Accounting Group.

The companies currently sell and ship products to both Food Fair and several outside customers. The geographic market area serviced by the companies extends along the east coast from New England to Miami, Florida and as far west as Iowa.

The historical and projected percentage relationship of Food Fair and outside customer sales for the Division are as follows:

	Sales To:	
	Food Fair	Outside
	Actual percentage	
1974	71	29
1975	71	29
1976	69	31
1977	59	41
1978	51	49
	Projected percentage	
1979	43	57
1980	37	63

The primary reason for the reduction of the percent of sales to Food Fair is the recent retail dispositions and the projected increase of outside sales.

The Manufacturing Division has in the past placed little emphasis on the generation of outside business through the use of brokers. Until recently only six

Exhibit 8-9   (*Continued*)

brokers were being utilized by the Division. With the loss of Food Fair sales due
to recent retail dispositions, significant emphasis is now being placed on replacement of this business through outside accounts. This emphasis is being accomplished through the establishment of a broker network for the Division's key
marketing areas. It is expected that within three months a total of twenty brokers
will be representing the Division from as far south as Jacksonville, Fla. to as far
north as Buffalo, N.Y. and west to Chicago, Ill.

The Division has been affected negatively in two primary areas as a result of
Chapter XI:

- Sales

  The Division has lost a significant percent of Food Fair sales due to the
  dispositions as specified previously

  To date, two major outside accounts have been lost; indications are that the
  remainder of the outside business is stable

- Supply/Credit Impact

  Supply problems resulted in a one-week shutdown in the Boulevard Beverage
  Company in early October

  Cash/credit constraints have prohibited taking long positions in the coffee,
  tea, and sugar future markets. However, given present market conditions,
  management indicates no long positions are required, and potential exposure
  to future swings is not considered significant in the short term

  Credit terms have been restricted by many vendors and cash before delivery
  is being required in a number of cases. Raw material supplies are not significantly short at present; since future Food Fair sales are projected to
  decline the near-term demand for raw materials should not cause shortage
  problems.

Operating Results

The Manufacturing Division has been and is expected to continue to be a
profitable operating entity.

Pretax profits for Fiscal Years 1974 through 1978 are summarized below:

	1974	1975	1976	1977	1978	5 Year Total
Boulevard Beverage	$1,190	$1,670	$1,095	$ 659	$ 651	$ 5,265
L. Resnick and Sons	698	842	745	400	304	2,989
Rozenco Coffee	562	742	1,291	1,877	1,194	5,666
Waverly Tea	325	567	530	808	1,058	3,288
Division Total	$2,775	$3,821	$3,661	$3,744	$3,207	$17,208

For Fiscal Year 1979 unaudited net profit through January 13, 1979 was reported as $680,000 on sales of $18.0 million.

For the remainder of the fiscal year operating results have been projected on
two different projection methodologies:

Exhibit 8-9   *(Continued)*

- Expected—Assumes Supermarket Division expected projections and no improvement in outside sales. Additionally, Food Fair purchases of paper supplies presently not purchased through L. Resnick and Sons are assumed to be recaptured immediately.

- Improved—Assumes Supermarket Division improved projections and improvement in outside sales resulting from broker activity. Additionally, Food Fair purchases of paper supplies presently not purchased through L. Resnick and Sons are assumed to be recaptured immediately.

A summary of the Fiscal Year 1979 projected operating results are provided below (000's):

	Net Profit	
	Expected	Improved
Total fiscal year	$1,335	$1,381
% of sales	3.6	3.7

Fiscal Year 1980 operating results have been projected based upon:

- Supermarket Division projections for Fiscal Year 1980
- Improved Fiscal Year 1979 Manufacturing Division projections
- Increased outside sales through brokers.

Fiscal Year 1980 projected net profit for the Division is approximately two million dollars (4.3 percent) on sales of $47.5 million.

Operating statements for the Division for Fiscal Years 1979 (expected and improved) and 1980 are provided on the following pages.

MANUFACTURING DIVISION
BOULEVARD BEVERAGE COMPANY

Overview

The Boulevard Beverage Company is a manufacturer of a full line of carbonated and noncarbonated beverages. Additionally, the Company provides packing (tolling) services for various national brands such as A & W. The Company currently sells and ships products to both Food Fair and several outside customers. The geographic market area serviced by the company extends along the eastern seaboard from New England to as far south as Jacksonville, Florida.

Sales to Food Fair's Jacksonville region were added in December, 1978 providing a partial offset to business lost through the recent retail dispositions. The Miami region is presently not serviced by the Company due to unfavorable transportation rates which do not permit a competitive transfer price.

The historical and projected percentage relationship of Food Fair and outside customer sales are as follows:

Exhibit 8-9   (*Continued*)

| | Sales To: | |
	Food Fair	Outside
	Actual percentage	
1974	68	32
1975	68	32
1976	67	33
1977	68	32
1978	52	48
	Projected percentage	
1979	52	48
1980	38	62

As stated previously, the primary reason for the reduction of the percent of sales to Food Fair is the recent retail dispositions and projected increases in outside sales.

There has been little emphasis in the past on the generation of outside business through the use of brokers. Only two brokers were being used to represent the Company in obtaining outside sales. Other outside sales were obtained through in-house sales activity. With the net loss of approximately 69% of the plant's Food Fair volume through the retail dispositions, significant emphasis is now being placed on expanding business through outside accounts.

This emphasis is being accomplished through the establishment of a broker network for the plant's key marketing areas.

During January, four new brokers were added in Albany and Syracuse, New York; Buffalo and Rochester, New York; Northern New Jersey and Metropolitan New York.

Through the National Food Brokers Association, management is currently in the process of interviewing potential brokers for representation in key areas, such as Boston, Mass.; Pittsburgh, Pa.; Washington, D.C.; Richmond, Va.; Jacksonville, Fla.; Chicago, Ill.; and Atlanta, Ga. These are key areas where major supermarket chains, wholesalers, distributors, and food service operators are located.

It is expected that within three months, a total of twenty brokers will be representing the Company. In addition, negotiations are currently in effect with First National Stores, Staff Supermarkets, and Colonial Stores in Norfolk, Virginia.

Primary competitors in the geographic market area include both national bottlers (such as Coca-Cola Bottling Co.) and regional private label bottlers (such as Frank's in Philadelphia).

While the Company is presently one of the smaller regional bottlers in the market area it has a number of advantages which enable it to compete effectively. Primary competitive advantages include:

- Full line manufacturing/bottling operation
  - 4 sizes—12, 28 and 64 ounce bottles and 16 ounce cans
  - 10 flavors, 16 brands

Exhibit 8-9   *(Continued)*

- Good quality, competitively priced product
- Efficient/cost effective operations
  - Fully automated line operation from pallet unloading to pallet loading.
  - Capability of running 3 operation lines concurrently.
  - Utilizes one of the most efficient, lowest cost glass packaging systems available to the industry.
  - Modern, well maintained equipment.
- Available capacity to expand business and provide production/shipping flexibility.

The primary competitive disadvantages faced by the Company include:

- Significantly larger competitors with proven sales and marketing history
- The current lack of an established, effective broker network to develop outside sales
- Unfavorable trucking rates particularly to the Miami, Florida area.

The primary impact of Chapter XI on the Company has been in the areas of Food Fair sales and supply/credit disruptions:

- Sales impact
  - Loss of almost 69 percent of Food Fair sales as a result of retail dispositions
  - Addition of Jacksonville sales in December, 1978 to partially offset the sales loss
- Supply/credit impact
  - Inability to obtain glass due to payables problems resulted in one week shutdown in early October, 1978
  - Two of the three major glass suppliers continue to sell glass supplies only on a cash before delivery basis.

Operating Results

The Company has been and is expected to be a profitable operating entity though trending downward in recent years.

For the Fiscal Years 1974 through 1978, its sales and net profits were as follows (000's omitted):

Year	Sales	Net Profit	Percent of Sales
1974	$12,108	$1,190	9.8
1975	14,185	1,670	11.8
1976	10,964	1,095	10.0
1977	10,402	659(1)	6.3
1978	10,340	651(1)	6.3

Exhibit 8-9 (*Continued*)

(1) Key factors significantly affecting net profit in these years include transportation rate increases (impact of $200,000/yr) which could not be passed through if competitive prices were to be maintained, and loss of glass supplier rebates ($150,000/yr).

For Fiscal Year 1979, net profit for the 24 weeks ending January 13, 1979 was $185,000 on sales of $4.2 million.

For the remainder of the fiscal year, operating results have been projected by management, based upon two different projection methodologies:

- Expected projection methodology—assumes Supermarket Division expected projections for Fiscal Year 1979 and no additional outside sales, except those known at this time which include Grand Union and American Food Supply Corporation

- Improved projection methodology—assumes Supermarket Division improved projections for Fiscal Year 1979 and partial effect of broker sales efforts.

A summary of the Fiscal Year 1979 projected operating profits are provided below (000's omitted):

	Net Operating Profit	
	Expected	Improved
Total fiscal year 1979	$203	$218
(percentage of sales)	2.4%	2.5%
August 1, 1978–January 13, 1979		
(actual)	$185	$185
February 10, 1979–July 28, 1979		
(projected)	$ 18	$ 33

Fiscal Year 1980 operating results have been projected based upon:

- Supermarket projections for Fiscal Year 1980
- Improved Fiscal Year 1979 Boulevard projections
- A full year impact of Grand Union and American Food Supply Corporation sales
- An increase in sales of approximately 17 percent over Fiscal Year 1979 total sales due to additional broker efforts.

Fiscal Year 1980 projected net profit is $495,000 based on sales of $12.4 million.

Total assets on the Company's books as of January 13, 1979 were approximately $5.2 million including:

- Accounts receivable of $2.0 million
  - Outside customers receivables—$.8 million
  - Food Fair and Affiliates receivables—$1.2 million
- Inventory—$1.2 million
- Capital facilities and equipment (net)—$1.4 million

Exhibit 8-9 *(Continued)*

Based upon book assets as of July 29, 1978, the Fiscal Year 1978 return on assets was 15.8 percent; return on Food Fair investment for the same period was 23.6 percent. Intercompany payables and receivables were eliminated for these calculations.

Operating Capital Requirements

No incremental working capital or major capital improvement is required for 1979 or 1980.

Risks

Primary downside risks associated with the Company include:

- Potential inability of brokerage entities to obtain significant increase in outside volume
- Exposure to significant swings in sugar prices due to short commodity market position:
    - Management believes that exposure is minimal given current market conditions
    - Management is investigating the potential for new sugar formulation to reduce costs. Significant swings in the price of sugar could materially affect operating results, particularly if sugar substitution is not feasible
- Potential impact on profits from loss of key outside account(s) given relatively small number of existing outside customers
- Potential impact of environmental restrictions on certain packaging types.

Primary upside considerations include:

- Business fit with Food Fair
    - Vertical integration provides Food Fair with supply and capacity availability without credit restrictions; the Company is provided with a stable sales base and potential growth primarily through sales to Miami, should favorable trucking rates be negotiated
    - The Company is projected to continue to provide positive cash flow and net profits with minimal downside risk of loss and no significant capital requirements
    - The Company provides good quality, competitively priced products which can be used effectively for supermarket promotional purposes
    - The Company has experienced management, knowledgeable in the business Minimal dilution of corporate management time required to operate the business
- Growth and profit potential appears significant given plant capacity availability, operating efficiency, equipment conditions and the development of a broad based, experienced broker network to aggressively pursue outside sales
- Return on investment is reasonable.

Disposition considerations:

- Potential disposition value of the Company has not been quantified. Key disposition issues identified include:

Exhibit 8-9 *(Continued)*

- Elimination of supply/credit source for Food Fair stores
- Valuation basis—Current earnings stream vs. potential earnings stream at normal capacity or valuation based on new plant construction costs
- Timing/salability—Current profitability and projected continued improvement provides opportunity to optimize sale timing and sale price if disposition is considered.

Conclusions

Boulevard Beverage is a stable modern operating company with significant potential growth and profitability and minimal risk of significant loss in the future. The Company provides a good business fit with Food Fair:

- Vertical integration benefits
- Minimal capital required over next two years
- Minimal corporate management attention required
- Competitively priced, high quality product

Development of outside business should be aggressively pursued and monitored closely.

PRODUCE OPERATIONS DIVISIONS
WORLDWIDE PRODUCE GROUP

(only selected parts of the analysis for these divisions are included in this excerpt)

Risks and Alternatives

The following alternative courses of action with salient factor and con, have been identified for the produce operations:

- Closed tomato, spinach, and salad packing operations:
  - Establish a new customer base and reopen the operation
    - lack of expected success in soliciting former competitors in an ongoing mode
    - cost of implementation would be a substantial cash outflow
    - cost of supplying outside chains would be higher than for a related chain due to time and expense of dealing with a greater number of "customers" and the absence of customer "loyalty" in the face of temporary price or quality fluctuations
  - Hold the processing facility idle, but for sale at an attractive price
    - cost to hold estimated at $80,000 through July 28, 1979
    - idle state not conducive to high price
    - realizable proceeds estimated at $200,000
    - timing not known
  - Sell facility at auctions or at forced-sale price
    - timing not known

Exhibit 8-9 *(Continued)*

- realizable proceeds not known
- Ongoing farming and buying operations:
  - Potato farm
    - retain and operate with attendant logistical management difficulty subject to market fluctuations
    - lease to farm and plant operation
    - sell at auction (price not estimated)
    - sell through listing agent(s) (price estimated at $900,000 for both farm and pack house)
  - Buying function
    - maintain as a separate profit center (intercompany sales)
    - maintain as a cost center
    - combine with merchandising functions
      - at corporate level
      - at regional level
    - delegate duties to regional buyers.

The question of whether produce buying should continue to be a centralized or regional operation of the restructured company is central to the issue of whether any World Wide personnel will continue functioning as corporate buyers for the chain.

That produce operations can be considered to have been a successful aspect of the Company is evidenced by the perception of high quality that consumers had for the produce department of Pantry Pride stores and the reported profitability of the World Wide Produce segments. Produce operations management attributes a large measure of this success to centralized buying, which they feel is conducive to effective management of the complex produce supply network. Unlike groceries, produce buying involves the interaction of many independent entities handling a product with high perishability. Besides the produce shipper; brokers, specialized carriers, and government inspectors enter into most purchase transactions. These suppliers are generally smaller and a more fragmented supply source than those of the other supermarket lines. This has been confirmed by senior Supermarket Division management.

Other advantages to centralized produce procurement include:

- Facilitates maintenance of uniformly high quality standards throughout the chain
- Enforces maintenance of gross profit levels above supermarket averages
- Enhances communication of timely information from a variety of supply and industry sources
- Avoids possible competitive bidding in marketplace by various supermarket regions
- Maintains a high profile in the produce marketplace resulting in superior product quality—(the wholesaler image of the present operation communicates the

Exhibit 8-9 *(Continued)*

need for higher quality product more than does the chain-store image of decentralized buying).

Possible disadvantages to centralized produce buying include:

- Increased difficulty in quantifying the operation for:
  - goal setting
  - performance measurement
  - output per unit of cost
- Potential duplication of effort in dealing with local produce sources because local shippers frequently are best utilized with noncentralized or local buying.

Conclusion

As of February 8, 1979 World Wide management had reached the conclusion that obtaining a new customer base for resumption of packing operations was not feasible. Preparations were then begun to terminate all but three to four key buyers and to arrange for disposition of the business assets with corporate management. The remaining buyers would then be prepared to function at the corporate level in a centralized produce buying operation.

The concept of a three-or-four man centralized buying staff was independently discussed with the regional managers in Baltimore, Jacksonville, and Miami to assess both the necessity for centralization and impact on local produce buying. All agreed that a centralized operation was essential to the bulk of produce buying for the chain and that the proposed staffing would have no impact on their local buying operations.

The major points of resolution now include:

- Produce buying results depend on supermarket volume
- Liquidation proceeds yet to be determined
  - $500,000-$1,000,000 approximation of management (includes real estate carried in other divisions or entities)
  - Book values of real estate
  - Collateralization assets
- Corporate buying format for produce
  - Centralized
  - Cost center with some outside sales potential
  - Centralized control of:
    - Technical aspects
    - Quality control
    - Market information
  - No capital requirements
    - Cost probably lower than the alternatives
  - Minimal corporate management attention required.

keeping the centralized purchasing function for produce. The plan developed for each of the operating units consists of (1) an overview of the nature of this unit's activities, (2) past operating results, (3) operating capital requirement, (4) risks and alternatives, and (5) conclusions. The report issued by Touche Ross was the result of a top-down review of all operations performed early in the case to identify operations that should be terminated or those that represented the potential to be a part of a "New Food Fair." There were specific criteria developed that the operation review summary attempted to follow to make judgments about each operation. Subsequent studies would be necessary to demonstrate the feasibility of the plan eventually proposed by Food Fair.

30   These examples illustrate the kinds of services accountants can render for businesses in financial difficulty that provide for a more orderly rehabilitation of the business and result in benefit to all parties involved in the proceedings.

Financial Projections

31   In chapter 7, paragraphs 43 to 47, it was pointed out how important it is to prepare projections of future operations to show that the plan is feasible. Also shown at the end of the chapter was an example of a projection for a business in financial difficulty. The benefits gained from projection of future operations go beyond simply determining if the plan of reorganization is feasible. These projections are necessary to develop an effective business plan and are crucial in determining the long-run prospects for the company. These projections are used to determine the value of the business as a going concern and to help determine the interest creditors and stockholders have in the reorganized company. Accountants have only recently taken an active

Exhibit 8-10   Example of Financial Projections

INTERSTATE STORES, INC. AND SUBSIDIARIES	
INDEX TO PRO FORMA FINANCIAL PROTECTIONS	
	Page
Accountants' Report	322
Consolidated Pro Forma Projected Balance Sheet as of September 30, 1977	324
Consolidated Pro Forma Projected Statement of Operations for the Four Years Ending February 1, 1981	327
Consolidated Pro Forma Projected Balance Sheet	328
Schedule of Pro Forma Projected Repayments of 8% Senior Notes and Redemptions of Preferred Stocks	Not included

Exhibit 8-10 *(Continued)*

ACCOUNTANT'S REPORT

> October 6, 1976 (except as to the
> effect of the proposed Plan of
> Reorganization as described
> below, the date of which is
> March 11, 1977)

Mr. Joseph R. Crowley and Mr. Herbert B. Siegel
   as Trustees of Interstate Stores, Inc.
   Under Chapter X of the Federal Bankruptcy Act
New York, New York

    The accompanying consolidated pro forma projected balance sheets of Interstate Stores, Inc. and subsidiaries at September 30, 1977, January 29, 1978, January 28, 1979, February 3, 1980, and February 1, 1981, the related consolidated pro forma projected statements of operations and cash flow for the periods ending January 29, 1978, through February 1, 1981, the schedule of pro forma projected repayments of 8% senior notes and redemptions of preferred stocks and the schedule of pro forma projected net income per share of common stock and book values and market values per share of common stock were prepared to assist the trustees, their advisers and management in assessing the future profitability and working capital requirements of Interstate Stores, Inc. only for the purpose of proposing a plan of reorganization for the Company and its subsidiaries. We have previously reported on projected consolidated financial statements for these periods in our report dated October 6, 1976. Those projections have been updated to give effect to the Proposal of Joseph R. Crowley and Herbert B. Siegel, trustees in reorganization of Interstate Stores, Inc. and subsidiaries, for a Plan of Reorganization as filed with the United States District Court, Southern District of New York, on March 11, 1977. The proposal assumes that the plan will take effect on Septem-

Exhibit 8-10 *(Continued)*

ber 30, 1977. The proposed plan is appended hereto. [omitted] The pro forma projections are based on provisions for payment of claims and assumptions and rationale as set forth on pages 333-338. The assumptions and rationale as set forth in our report, dated October 6, 1976, have been summarized and condensed for the purposes of the pro forma projected financial statements.

We have reviewed the assumptions and rationale underlying the pro forma financial projections. Our review included the following procedures:

- Review of proposed Toys "R" Us store expansion program to evaluate the reasonableness of undertaking such a program
- Review of computations and historical data to project sales
- Review of computations and historical data for gross margin and operating expenses
- Review of computations and historical and projected data as basis for projecting major assets and liabilities
- Review of computation of interest income and other income
- Review of cash flow computations
- Read Proposal of Joseph R. Crowley and Herbert B. Siegel, Trustees in Reorganization of Interstate Stores, Inc. and subsidiaries, for a plan of reorganization.

Management's plan of operations, upon which the pro forma projections are based, assumes that additional Toys "R" Us stores will be opened in both existing and new markets during the period of the projections as follows:

	Fiscal Year Ending			
	January 29, 1978	January 28, 1979	February 3, 1980	February 1, 1981
Toys "R" Us stores opened	8	12	15	18

The pro forma projections assume, based on management's assumptions, that certain real estate not currently used for retail operations by the Company will not be liquidated and, therefore, will be held as a long-term income producing asset. As a result, the pro forma projections reflect the net revenue from the subleasing of such property as other income for the periods ending January 29, 1978 through February 1, 1981.

To the extent described above, the assumptions and rationale were developed using historical financial and statistical data taken from the accounting and other records of Interstate Stores, Inc. and subsidiaries. We have examined the consolidated financial statements of Interstate Stores, Inc. and subsidiary companies for the years ended February 1, 1976 and February 2, 1975 and have reported thereon under date of April 23, 1976. Because of material uncertainties, most of which resulted from the Company's status under the Federal Bankruptcy Act, including the continuation of the Company as a going concern, we were unable to and, therefore, did not express an opinion on the financial statements for the years ended February 1, 1976 and February 2, 1975. Our examination of these financial statements was intended primarily for the purpose of formulating an opinion on the consolidated financial statements taken as a whole; accordingly, we did not subject

Exhibit 8-10 (*Continued*)

the historical financial and statistical data to auditing procedures sufficient to enable us to express an opinion concerning the fairness of all the details of such data.

Based upon our review of the assumptions and rationale underlying these projections, we believe, subject to the confirmation of the plan of reorganization, that they are reasonable and appropriate for the purpose of the pro forma projections. We have not reviewed the unaudited pro forma projected net income per share of common stock and book values and market values per share of common stock for the fiscal year ended January 30, 1977 as set forth on page 330. Accordingly, we cannot comment on their reasonableness for the purpose of the pro forma projections.

Since pro forma projections are based on assumptions about circumstances and events that have not yet taken place, they are subject to variations that may arise as future operations actually occur. Accordingly, we cannot give assurance that the projected results will actually be attained. Also, it should be understood that the underlying assumptions are based on present circumstances and information currently available. Because circumstances may change and unanticipated events may occur subsequent to the date of this report, the reader must evaluate the assumptions and rationale in the light of circumstances then prevailing.

Touche Ross & Co.
Certified Public Accountants

INTERSTATE STORES, INC.
AND SUBSIDIARIES
CONSOLIDATED PRO FORMA PROJECTED BALANCE SHEET
AS OF SEPTEMBER 30, 1977

($000's omitted)

| Assets | Consolidated Projected Balance Sheet at September 30, 1977 before giving effect to the proposed Plan of Reorganization | Reorganization adjustments | | Consolidated Pro Forma Projected Balance Sheet at September 30, 1977 |
		Debt	Credit	
Current assets				
Cash	$ 63,479	$ —	$ 59,000 (5)	$ 4,479
Accounts receivable—net	5,985	—	—	5,985
Merchandise inventories	73,221	—	—	73,221
Prepaid expenses and other	4,652	—	—	4,652
Total current assets	147,337	—	59,000	88,337
Leased property	3,259	—	—	3,259
Property and equipment—net	32,065	—	—	32,065
Excess of cost over net assets of subsidiaries acquired	14,651	—	14,651 (4)	—
Other assets	1,183	—	250 (2)	933
	$198,495	$ —	$ 73,901	$124,594

Exhibit 8-10 (*Continued*)

CONSOLIDATED PRO FORMA PROJECTED BALANCE SHEET
AS OF SEPTEMBER 30, 1977
(*Continued*)

Liabilities and Stockholders' Equity	Consolidated Projected Balance Sheet at September 30, 1977 before giving effect to the proposed Plan of Reorganization	Reorganization adjustments Debt	Reorganization adjustments Credit	Consolidated Pro Forma Projected Balance Sheet at September 30, 1977
Current liabilities				
Accounts payable—trade	$ 37,970	$ —	$ —	$ 37,970
Accrued expenses, taxes other than federal income taxes and sundry liabilities	4,741	—	—	4,741
Current installment of mortgages payable	501	—	—	501
Estimated claims and other liabilities under Chapter X Reorganization Proceeding	139,486	175,906	(3,000) (3) (33,420) (1)	—
Current portion of 8% senior notes	—	—	9,161 (5)	9,161
Current portion of 8% five-year debt	—	—	478 (5)	478
Total current liabilities	182,698	175,906	46,059	52,851
8% Senior notes—excluding current portion	—	—	16,839 (5)	16,839
8% Five-year debt—excluding current portion	—	—	1,911 (5)	1,911
Mortgages payable	6,568	—	—	6,568
Deferred items	527	—	—	527
Total long-term liabilities	7,095	—	18,750	25,845
	189,793	175,906	64,809	78,696
Stockholders' equity:				
Senior 8¾% preferred stock—at redemption value	—	—	17,423 (5)	17,423
Junior 9% preferred stock—at redemption value	—	—	6,732 (5)	6,732
Common stock	6,722	6,722 (5)	953 (5)	953
Additional paid-in capital	48,970	28,180 (5)	—	20,790
(Deficit)	(46,990)	(3,000) (3) (33,420) (1) (14,651) (4) (250) (2)	98,311 (5)	—
	8,702	86,223	123,419	45,898
	$198,495	$262,129	$188,228	$124,594

The accompanying summary of provisions for payment of claims and assumptions and rationale are an integral part of this projection.

Exhibit 8-10 *(Continued)*

INTERSTATE STORES. INC.
AND SUBSIDIARIES
NOTES TO CONSOLIDATED PRO FORMA PROJECTED BALANCE
SHEET AS OF SEPTEMBER 30, 1977
REORGANIZATION ADJUSTMENTS REFLECTING
PLAN OF REORGANIZATION

($000's omitted)

	Debit	Credit
1. Retained earnings	$ 33,420	
Estimated claims and other liabilities under		
Chapter X Reorganization Proceeding		$ 33,420
Accrual of interest on prepetition debt		
through September 30, 1977.		
2. Retained earnings	250	
Other assets		250
To write off deferred financing costs on		
institutional loans and debentures.		
3. Retained earnings	3,000	
Prepetition liabilities		3,000
To record estimated administrative expenses		
relating to the Plan of Reorganization.		
4. Retained earnings	14,651	
Excess of cost over net assets of subsidiaries		
acquired		14,651
Write-off of intangibles arising from		
acquisition of toy subsidiaries.		
5. Estimated claims and other liabilities under		
Chapter X Reorganization Proceeding	175,906	
Additional paid-in capital	28,180	
Old common stock at $1.00 par value per share	6,722	
Cash		59,000
8% Senior notes—current portion		9,161
8% Senior notes—excluding current portion		16,839
8% Five-year debt—current portion		478
8% Five-year debt—excluding current portion		1,911
Senior 8¾% preferred stock—at redemption value		17,423
Junior 9% preferred stock—at redemption value		6,732
New common stock at $.10 par value per share		953
Retained earnings		98,311
To record initial distribution of cash to		
creditors and issuance of 8% senior notes,		
8% five-year debt, Senior 8¾% preferred		
stock, Junior 9% preferred		
stock and common stock and to adjust		
retained earnings and additional paid-in		
capital.		

Exhibit 8-10 (*Continued*)

INTERSTATE STORES, INC.
AND SUBSIDIARIES
CONSOLIDATED PRO FORMA PROJECTED STATEMENT OF OPERATIONS

($000's omitted)

	Fiscal Year Ending			
	January 29, 1978	January 28, 1979	February 3, 1980	February 1, 1981
Net sales including leased departments	$269,621	$318,349	$382,293	$462,224
Other income—net	423	423	423	423
	270,044	318,772	382,716	462,647
Costs and expenses				
Cost of sales including occupancy and buying costs	190,413	225,496	271,986	330,178
Selling, advertising, general and administrative	50,167	58,605	69,746	83,080
Depreciation and amortization	2,890	3,327	3,855	4,566
Interest on mortgages	510	476	443	409
	243,980	287,904	346,030	418,233
Earnings before other credits, interest on debt issued pursuant to Plan and taxes on income	26,064	30,868	36,686	44,414
Other credits				
Interest income	2,000	—	—	—
Interest on debt issued pursuant to Plan:				
8% senior notes	683	1,502	732	106
8% five-year debt	64	153	115	76
Earnings before taxes on income	27,317	29,213	35,839	44,232
Taxes on income				
Federal	12,494	13,161	16,080	19,751
State	2,330	2,890	3,680	4,730
	14,824	16,051	19,760	24,481
Net Earnings	$ 12,493	$ 13,162	$ 16,079	$ 19,751
Note: Tax benefits from utilization of net operating loss carryforwards have been credited directly to additional paid-in capital in the amounts of	$ 12,494	$ 13,161	$ 16,080	$ 15,992

The accompanying summary of provisions for payment of claims and assumptions and rationale are an integral part of this projection

Exhibit 8-10 *(Continued)*

INTERSTATE STORES, INC.
AND SUBSIDIARIES
CONSOLIDATED PRO FORMA BALANCE SHEET

($000's omitted)

	September 30, 1977	January 29, 1978	January 28, 1979	February 3, 1980	February 1, 1981
Assets					
Current assets					
Cash for operations	$ 4,479	$ 24,954	$ 27,271	$ 29,409	$ 30,298
Cash to be used for Plan payments based on earnings	—	6,161	6,828	9,746	14,538
Accounts receivable—net	5,985	5,590	6,092	6,660	7,293
Merchandise inventories	73,221	48,807	59,605	73,525	90,955
Prepaid expenses and other	4,652	1,399	1,605	1,882	2,251
Total current assets	88,337	86,911	101,401	121,222	145,335
Leased property	3,259	3,215	3,092	2,969	2,846
Property and equipment—net	32,065	30,994	33,964	38,035	43,306
Other assets	933	982	1,251	1,407	1,597
	$124,594	$122,102	$139,708	$163,633	$193,084

NOTE TO CONSOLIDATED PRO FORMA PROJECTED BALANCE SHEET

(A) Stockholders' equity at February 1, 1981, as originally reported in the projected financial statements dated October 6, 1976, is reconciled to the amount shown in the consolidated pro forma projected balance sheet as follows:

Stockholders' equity as originally reported		$135,025
Add/(deduct):		
Projected interest income on excess cash for the period January 31, 1977 to September 30, 1977	$ 2,000	
Adjustment to reflect trustee's estimate of additional Chapter X claims	(1,813)	
Reorganization adjustment at September 30, 1977—net	37,196	
Interest on debt issued pursuant to the Plan during the four-year period ending February 1, 1981	(3,431)	
Dividends on preferred stocks during the four-year period ending February 1, 1981	(6,219)	
Redemptions of preferred stocks during the fiscal year ending February 1, 1981	(5,735)	
Federal income tax provision in excess of tax benefit from utilization of net operating loss carryforwards in the fiscal year ending February 1, 1981	(3,759)	18,239
Stockholders' equity as presently reported		$153,264

351

Exhibit 8-10   (*Continued*)

INTERSTATE STORES, INC.
AND SUBSIDIARIES

CONSOLIDATED PRO FORMA BALANCE SHEET
(*Continued*)

$000's omitted)

	September 30, 1977	January 29, 1978	January 28, 1979	February 3, 1980	February 1, 1981
Liabilities and Stockholders' Equity					
Current liabilities					
Accounts payable—trade	$ 37,970	$ 10,785	$ 13,250	$ 16,433	$ 20,426
Federal income taxes payable	—	—	—	—	376
Accrued expenses, taxes other than federal income taxes and sundry liabilities	4,741	7,994	9,115	10,636	12,676
Current installment of mortgages	501	516	485	500	533
Current portion of 8% senior notes	9,161	9,161	9,828	4,011	—
Current portion of 8% five-year debt	478	478	478	478	477
Total current liabilities	52,851	28,934	33,156	32,058	34,488
8% Senior notes—excluding current portion	16,839	13,839	4,011	—	—
8% Five-year debt—excluding current portion	1,911	1,433	955	477	—
Mortgages payable	6,568	6,382	5,896	5,395	4,861
Deferred items	527	521	504	488	471
Total long-term liabilities	25,845	22,175	11,366	6,360	5,332
	78,696	51,109	44,522	38,418	39,820
Stockholders' equity					
Senior 8¾% preferred stock— at redemption value	17,423	17,423	17,423	17,423	13,286
Junior 9% preferred stock—at redemption value	6,732	6,732	6,732	6,732	5,134
Common stock—par value $.10 per share	953	953	953	953	953
Additional paid-in capital	20,790	33,284	46,445	62,525	78,517
Retained earnings	—	12,601	23,633	37,582	55,374
	45,898	70,993	95,186	125,215	153,264 (A)
	$124,594	$122,102	$139,708	$163,633	$193,084

The accompanying summary of provisions for payments of claims and assumptions and rationale are an integral part of this projection

(A) See note to consolidated pro forma projected balance sheet on page 328

Exhibit 8-10   (Continued)

INTERSTATE STORES, INC.
AND SUBSIDIARIES

SCHEDULE OF PRO FORMA PROJECTED NET INCOME PER SHARE OF
COMMON STOCK AND BOOK VALUES AND MARKET VALUES
PER SHARE OF COMMON STOCK

		Fiscal Year Ending			
	Unaudited January 30, 1977	Projected January 29, 1978	Projected January 28, 1979	Projected February 3, 1980	Projected February 1, 1981
I. Net income per share of common stock (Notes 1 and 2) (Based on 9,534,000 shares outstanding)	$ .75	$ .90	$ 1.16	$ 1.46	$ 1.87
Percent increase over prior year	—	20.0%	28.9%	25.9%	28.1%
II. Pro forma market values per share of common stock:					
at 5 P/E Multiple	$ 3.75	$ 4.50	$ 5.80	$ 7.30	$ 9.35
at 7.5 P/E Multiple	5.63	6.75	8.70	10.95	14.03
at 10 P/E Multiple	7.50	9.00	11.60	14.60	18.70
at 12.5 P/E Multiple	9.38	11.25	14.50	18.25	23.38
at 15 P/E Multiple	11.25	13.50	17.40	21.90	28.05
III. Pro forma book value per share of common stock (Note 3)	$ 2.29	$ 4.91	$ 7.45	$ 10.60	$ 14.14
IV. Calculation of net income available for common stockholders:					
Projected earnings before interest on Plan debt and federal income taxes (Note 1)	$20,887 (A)	$23,734	$27,978	$33,006	$39,684
Less interest on Plan debt (Note 2)	2,271	2,261	1,655	847	182

Exhibit 8-10 (Continued)

Earnings before federal income taxes	18,616	21,473	26,323	32,159	39,502
Less federal income taxes	9,308	10,737	13,161	16,080	19,751
Net earnings	9,308	10,736	13,162	16,079	19,751
Less dividends on preferred stocks (Note 2)	2,130	2,130	2,130	2,130	1,959
Net income available for common stockholders	$ 7,178	$ 8,606	$11,032	$13,949	$17,792

Note 1—For the purpose of these calculations, earnings for the years January 30, 1977 and January 29, 1978 exclude interest income on investment of excess cash, reorganization administrative expenses charged to operations and provision for loss on store closings.

Note 2—For the years January 30, 1977 and January 29, 1978, pro forma recognition is given to the annualized effect of interest and dividends applicable to securities to be issued based on the plan of reorganization.

Note 3—The book value per share at January 30, 1977 reflects the pro forma effect of the Plan of Reorganization.

Note 4—It is assumed that any exercise of stock options will not result in dilution.

(A)—Estimate

The accompanying summary of provisions for payment of claims and assumptions and rationale are an integral part of this projection.

Exhibit 8-10 *(Continued)*

INTERSTATE STORES, INC.
AND SUBSIDIARIES
CONSOLIDATED PRO FORMA PROJECTED STATEMENT
OF CASH FLOW

($000's omitted)

	Fiscal Year Ending			
	January 29, 1978	January 28, 1979	February 3, 1980	February 1, 1981
Cash—beginning of year	$ 74,576	$ 31,115	$ 34,099	$ 39,155
Cash provided by:				
Cash provided from operations:				
Earnings before interest on plan debt and federal income taxes	25,734	27,978	33,006	39,684
Depreciation and amortization	2,993	3,511	4,268	5,067
Federal income tax provision in excess of tax benefit from utilization of net operating loss carryforwards	—	—	—	(3,759)
	28,727	31,489	37,274	40,992
Increase in accrued expenses (excluding accrued interest on plan requirements)	384	1,365	1,784	2,216
Increase in federal income taxes payable	—	—	—	376
Total cash provided	29,111	32,854	39,058	43,584
Cash used for:				
Additions to merchandise inventories (net of increases in accounts payable)	5,793	8,333	10,737	13,437
Additions to property and equipment	5,120	6,174	7,803	9,714
Payment of mortgage payable	517	517	486	501
Increase in accounts receivable	(1,512)	502	568	633
Increase in other assets	171	453	569	691
Increase in prepaid expenses	(75)	206	277	369
Decrease in deferred items	16	17	16	17
Total cash used before Plan requirements	10,030	16,202	20,456	25,362
Cash provided during year before Plan requirements	19,081	16,652	18,602	18,222
Plan requirements:				
Cash payout	59,000	—	—	—
Senior notes —principal	3,000	9,161	9,828	4,011
–8% interest	—	1,746	995	282
Senior preferred –principal	—	—	—	4,137
–8¾% dividend	—	1,524	1,524	1,401
Junior preferred –principal	—	—	—	1,598
–9% dividend	—	606	606	558
Five-year debt —principal	478	478	478	478
–8% interest	64	153	115	76
Total Plan requirements	62,542	13,668	13,546	12,541
Cash provided/(used)	(43,461)	2,984	5,056	5,681
Cash—end of year	$ 31,115	$ 34,099	$ 39,155	$ 44,836

The accompanying summary of provisions for payment of claims and assumptions and rationale are an integral part of this projection

Exhibit 8-10   *(Continued)*

INTERSTATE STORES, INC.
AND SUBSIDIARIES
ASSUMPTIONS AND RATIONALE FOR PRO FORMA PROJECTED FINANCIAL STATEMENTS

I. GENERAL

Operations

The pro forma projected financial statements (the "pro forma projections") for the periods ending through February 1, 1981, are based on the proposal for a plan of reorganization filed by the trustees on March 11, 1977. It is assumed that the reorganized debtors (the "Company") (after confirmation of the plan of reorganization) will consist of two continuing operations—the Toys "R" Us and the conventional department stores operations. In addition, the Company will retain certain real estate interests not relating to the continuing operations. The pro forma projections also include an estimate of general corporate expenses.

Interest Income

Additional interest income on the excess cash generated during the reorganization period has been projected for the period January 31, 1977 to September 30, 1977, the estimated determination [confirmation] date.

Plan of Reorganization

The pro forma projections have been prepared on the assumption that a plan of reorganization (the "plan") will be confirmed as of September 30, 1977. Estimated additional administrative charges relating to the plan of reorganization are included in the reorganization entries reflecting the implementation of the plan and the capitalization of the reorganized Company.

The reorganization adjustments have been prepared based on the assumption that all Toys "R" Us trade creditors would elect to receive 8 percent five-year debt in lieu of new common stock.

Interest on debt and dividends on preferred stocks issued pursuant to the plan are based on the applicable provisions of the plan.

Interest due creditors accruing from May 22, 1974 to September 30, 1977 is similarly reflected as a reorganization entry.

Cash to be used for plan payments based on earnings represents the additional contingent payment for the 8 percent senior notes and/or the sinking fund provision of preferred stocks. These payments will be made each May 31st following the balance sheet date.

The pro forma projections assume that no stock options will be exercised prior to February 2, 1981.

Federal Income Taxes

As of February 1, 1976, the end of the last audited fiscal year, the Company had available:

a. Net operating loss carryforwards for financial reporting purposes of approximately $95 million.

Exhibit 8-10   *(Continued)*

b. Net operating loss carryforwards for income tax purposes or approximately $80 million.

The principal difference between the financial and tax net operating loss carryforwards results from the recognition of substantial charges for financial accounting purposes applicable to the store-closing program, which will result in tax deductions in fiscal 1978. The pro forma projections give effect to additional tax deductions that are expected to arise as a result of the plan for matters such as interest payable on allowed creditor claims.

There will be no federal income tax payable on a substantial portion of the Company's earnings during the projection period. The tax benefit of the net operating loss carryforward is reflected in the pro forma projections as a direct credit to additional paid-in capital in the year in which it is utilized for financial statement purposes.

The provision for federal income tax was estimated at the rate of 50 percent without consideration of investment and other tax credits.

II. TOYS "R" US ASSUMPTIONS

Operations

The pro forma projections were based on the following new store opening program:

Fiscal year ending	Number of projected store openings
January 29, 1978	8
January 28, 1979	12
February 3, 1980	15
February 1, 1981	18

At January 30, 1977, there were 57 Toys "R" Us stores in operation.

The following assumptions are integral to the expansion program:

- Continuing availability of store sites and associated real estate financing.

- Availability of store management personnel and continued emphasis on store management development programs.

- Continuing availability of working capital to finance investments in inventory and fixtures in new stores.

- Continued standardization of operating policies and procedures.

Sales

The Toys "R" Us sales projections reflect an expansion program with plans for additional stores as summarized in the previous section, as well as a moderate increase in sales of existing stores.

The pro forma projections assume that each new store will be opened on November 1 of each year. Sales for the new stores are projected at levels consistent with Toys "R" Us prior experience in opening new stores.

Exhibit 8-10 *(Continued)*

Cost of Sales, Including Occupancy and Buying Costs

The cost of sales projections reflect the maintenance of gross margin at a percentage consistent with the experience of recent years. Variable distribution costs have been projected to increase in proportion with sales volume.

Projected occupancy costs are based on current lease commitments and estimates for new stores are based on the experience for new stores opened in the year ended January 30, 1977.

Selling, Advertising, General and Administrative

The selling, advertising, promotion, and general and administrative expense projections reflect the continuation of the expense levels now being incurred for the existing stores, adjusted for inflation and new stores.

The operating expenses for the new stores are included at levels consistent with Toys "R" Us prior experience in opening new stores. Other expense categories for the new stores, such as preopening expense, real estate acquisition costs, and training expenses have been projected individually, since these costs occur prior to the new store sales. Preopening expense is amortized in the projections during the first 12 months of operation.

Central office and area management expenses reflect the continuation of the current expense levels plus reasonable annual increases. Additional support personnel for the expansion program is also projected based on similar positions which exist at the present time.

Depreciation and Amortization

The depreciation and amortization expense projections include the depreciation associated with the assets of the existing stores, the asset additions for the new stores and warehouses and the asset additions for maintaining the existing stores. Depreciation expense is calculated consistent with current policies and guidelines.

Interest on Mortgages

The projections for interest expense represent the existing outstanding mortgages on Toys "R" Us stores.

State Income Tax Provisions

The provision for state income taxes included in the projections reflects the year ended February 1, 1976 tax level, which assumes that no significant changes will occur in tax structures in the states where Toys "R" Us is currently operating. The projection also assumes that the states in which new stores are to be located will have substantially the same tax structure as the states in which Toys "R" Us currently operates.

Cash

This asset, as of January 30, 1977, and September 30, 1977, includes normal cash generated from operations and the excess cash generated during the reorganization period. No attempt has been made to distinguish between cash and certificates of deposit. The projections assume that the Company will have sufficient lines of credit throughout the projection period.

Exhibit 8-10 *(Continued)*

Accounts Receivable

The majority of receivables is the result of vendor exchanges and is projected on the basis of historical experience.

Merchandise Inventories

The inventory levels are projected at a rate per store consistent with prereorganization year-end inventory levels adjusted for an inflation factor and new stores.

Prepaid Expenses and Other

Prepaid expenses and other are composed of such items as insurance, rent, etc., and are projected consistent with previous year levels adjusted for increases in levels of expenditures.

Property and Equipment

Property and equipment are projected consistent with the previously described expansion program and normal additions to existing stores. No permanent building acquisitions are planned in the expansion program; all new buildings are leased.

These asset additions are projected based on previous experience adjusted for inflation.

Other Assets

Other assets consist of security deposits and pre-opening expenses.

Accounts Payable—Trade

Vendor terms experienced during the year ended January 30, 1977, are assumed to remain approximately the same during the projection period. Accounts payable levels are based on the historical relationship to purchase and inventory levels.

Accrued Expenses

The pro forma projections reflect maintaining the year ended January 30, 1977 accrual policies. Accrued expenses include such items as taxes, payroll, and profit sharing and were increased primarily in proportion to sales.

Mortgages Payable

The pro forma projections for both current and long-term mortgages payable reflect the payment of mortgages currently in existence.

Deferred Items

The pro forma projections reflect the amortization of the gain on the sale of one store location.

III. DEPARTMENT STORES ASSUMPTIONS

Operations

The pro forma projections assume that the 12 Department Stores open at January 30, 1977, will continue to operate.

Exhibit 8-10   *(Continued)*

Sales

Moderate comparable store sales increases are projected during the projection period. Included in the pro forma projections are leased department sales that represent approximately 6 percent of the total Department Stores' own sales.

Costs of Sales, Including Occupancy and Buying Costs

An increased annual growth of one-tenth of one percent in gross margin from the level estimated for the year ended January 30, 1977, is projected.

The occupancy costs are based on current lease commitments.

Selling, Advertising, General and Administrative

Selling, advertising, general and administrative expenses are based on historical experience adjusted for increases based on sales.

Depreciation and Amortization

Depreciation and amortization expense is projected based on the depreciation and amortization expense for the year ended February 1, 1976, adjusted for store closing, projected additions and retirements.

Provision for State Income Taxes

Department Stores state income taxes are increased from the year ended January 30, 1977, levels based on the percentage change in the division's operating profits.

Accounts Receivable—Net

Trade receivables are projected to increase consistent with projected sales growth.

Merchandise Inventories

Inventories for the projection period represent January 30, 1977 inventories, adjusted upward consistent with the projected annual rate of increase in sales.

Prepaid Expenses and Other

Prepaid expenses principally represent supplies inventory and are projected to increase consistent with sales.

Property and Equipment

Capital expenditures represent normal asset additions and replacements.

Other Assets

Other assets consist primarily of security deposits.

Accounts Payable—Trade

Purchases are projected to increase in the same relationship to sales as has been experienced historically. Accounts payable are projected based on the dating terms obtained in the previous year.

Exhibit 8-10   *(Continued)*

Accrued Expenses, Taxes, and Sundry Liabilities

Accrued expenses, taxes and sundry liabilities are based on historical experience adjusted for inflationary increases for the period of the projection.

IV. CORPORATE OVERHEAD

Corporate overhead reflects only those items of expenses and income which will be part of the continuing Company in effect after the confirmation of the plan and do not include any expenses applicable to reorganization matters.

The items included in the pro forma projections for the period after the plan are as follows:

a. The financial transactions of real estate leasing operation relating to properties that are not part of Toys "R" Us or Department Stores. The pro forma projections are based on the income and cash flow of the present properties without consideration of any possible addition or disposals.

b. Professional fees and expenses and other general corporate expenses were projected based on historical experience prior to the chapter proceeding plus an increase for inflation.

role in helping prepare financial projections and in evaluating the assumptions on which they are based. A forecast which Touche Ross & Co. helped prepare for the trustees to use in a Chapter X corporate reorganization proceeding under prior law is presented in Exhibit 8-10 (see pages 344–361). Note that the report of the accountants states that they have reviewed the assumptions and rationale underlying the financial projections and discusses the procedures they followed in their examination. In reaching a conclusion regarding the reasonableness of the assumptions, the accountant will, first, evaluate the business plan to ascertain if it appears reasonable. In making this assessment, historical financial data are examined and analyzed and significant ratios and relationships are studied. The projected statements then require taking the business plan and projecting what is expected from it for the next three to five years. In addition, the accountant will review all of the computations used to prepare the forecasts.

ACCOUNTING SERVICES—CHAPTERS 7 AND 11 LIQUIDATIONS

32   The following paragraphs of this chapter describe the procedures for liquidating a business under chapter 7. The services accountants render in a chapter 11 proceeding where a liquidation plan is adopted are similar to those in a chapter 7 liquidation case. Thus, the discussion here of services under chapter 7 is also applicable to a chapter 11 liquidation case.

Items Requiring Immediate Attention

33   The importance of taking early action in a liquidation is very similar to that in a chapter 11 case where the accountant represents the creditors' committee. Even though a trustee is appointed in a chapter 7 case, it is still important that the accountant work with the trustee to see that the debtor's assets are not concealed. Paragraphs 20–23 of chapter 9 discuss the types of items that need immediate attention. Among them are taking an inventory or obtaining possession of all of the debtor's books and records. Where fraud is suspected, the accountant may assist the trustee in securing all the debtor's books and records and transferring them to a suitable location. Speed is of the utmost importance in the removal process for several reasons. Such records often disappear with no explanation as to their whereabouts. They may be disposed of innocently by persons who have no idea of their value. The trustee normally wants to vacate the premises as quickly as possible, to minimize rental expense. Thus, quick removal means greater assurance that the records will be adequately safeguarded. It is highly desirable that the accountants supervise this activity, since they are best able to determine which books are most useful and therefore should be preserved.

34   The accountant may assist the trustee in establishing controls over cash and other assets. The accountant also may be engaged to take a physical inventory and to inventory the property, plant, and equipment of the debtor.

Performance of Audits and Other Special Investigations

35   The accountant may be engaged to investigate the past actions of the debtor. Transactions that could have resulted in the dissipation of the debtor's assets in a manner other than by loss in the ordinary course of business are examined closely. In the investigation the accountant must be alert for irregular transfers, improper transactions with related parties, concealment of assets, false entries and statements, financing irregularities, or preferential payments. A comparison of the statements filed by the debtor with the company's records may reveal deliberate discrepancies, missing books or records, alterations, or fraud, as indicated by an inconsistent age of the records. In the audit of a liquidating business, attention is focused on the balance sheet; the profit-and-loss statement is of very little importance (See chapter 11 for a more detailed discussion of investigative services in bankruptcy situations.)

Reconciliation of Debts with Proofs of Claims

36   Accountants frequently are engaged to reconcile the claims shown on the debtor's books with the proofs of claims that are filed with the court. This process can take considerable time.

SIPC Liquidation

37   Accountants may be engaged to render services for the trustee in the liquidation of a stockbroker. Fees for administrative expenses (including accounting services) are paid out of the general estate of the stockbroker. However, if funds are not available from the estate to cover administrative expenses, they are covered by SIPC.

38   In a SIPC liquidation, the accountant works directly with the trustee in helping to control the assets of the brokerage firm to satisfy customer accounts and to liquidate the brokerage firm. Accountants also prepare various types of financial statements, including liquidation statements for companies in chapter 7 and for SIPC liquidations. These statements are discussed in chapter 12.

Accounting Services for the Creditors' Committee

1   The creditors' committee is the representative and bargaining agent for the creditors. The committee often needs an accountant to assist them in protecting their interests. This chapter describes the aspects of the services rendered by the accountant as they relate to the creditors' committee. The auditing services performed for the committee will be only briefly mentioned because a later chapter will be devoted entirely to a discussion of the audit of the corporation involved in bankruptcy and insolvency proceedings. The accountant, in order to adequately represent the creditors, must be thoroughly familiar with the manner in which the creditors' committee works. The services rendered by the accountant include assisting the committee in exercising adequate control over the debtor's activities, completing an investigation and audit of the operations of the business, and assisting the committee in evaluating the proposed plan of out-of-court settlement or bankruptcy reorganization. Unless specified differently, the term "accountant" as used in this chapter refers to an independent accountant engaged by the creditors' committee.

NATURE OF CREDITORS' COMMITTEE

2   Section 1102 of the Bankruptcy Code provides that a committee of unsecured creditors is to be appointed in a chapter 11 case. In addition, the section also provides that other committees of creditors of other classes and committees of equity holders may be appointed. There may be a need for another committee where a large number of individual customers made deposits with the debtor as a sixth priority item or where there are creditors holding claims against a grain storage facility, claims which have a fifth priority. A committee in these two situations would generally be appointed only if payments to these creditors must be defined under the terms of the plan. Also, there may be appointed one or more committees of creditors holding a secured interest in the debtor's assets.

3   There has developed a need in several cases for the equity holders' interests to be represented through an equity holders' committee. Again, one committee might represent the interests of all equity holders or there may be a need for the appointment of two or more equity holders' committees. For example, one committee might represent the interests of preferred shareholders and the other common shareholders.

4   In a small chapter 11 case where there are no public debt or equity security holders and no large number of secured creditors, the court may not authorize the appointment of other committees. On the other hand, in larger cases with public debts and equity securities and with complicated secured debt structures where conflicting claims exist, other committees are likely to be appointed.

5   The creditors' committee may be an unofficial or official committee. It is known as an unofficial committee if it is formed to effect a voluntary agreement, out of court, between the debtor and creditor. If the committee is appointed under the provisions of the Bankruptcy Code, it is known as an official committee. As was discussed in chapter 4, there are no rigid rules governing the formation of the committee in out-of-court matters. However, the Bankruptcy Code (section 1102) provides that the court shall appoint the committee and it will ordinarily consist of the seven largest unsecured creditors willing to serve. If a committee was established before the bankruptcy petition was filed, this committee may be allowed to continue provided the committee was fairly chosen and is representative of the different kinds of claims to be represented. Although the functions performed by the committee may vary depending on the particular case, the circumstances surrounding the case, and the type of remedy sought, the objective is basically the same: to provide the supervision and control essential to protect the interests of the creditors.

6   The creditors' committee is the "watchdog" over the activities of the debtor. The committee examines all aspects of the firm's operations, including an evaluation of the assets and liabilities. During the period while a plan is being formalized and the period immediately following the acceptance, the committee should closely and constantly supervise the debtor's business, in order to be sure that the assets do not continue to be diminished, wasted, or diverted.

7   The importance of the creditors' committee in chapter 11 proceedings cannot be overemphasized. The objective of the committee is similar to the SEC in Chapter X proceedings under prior law in that it counterbalances the strong position of control given to the debtor by the Bankruptcy Act. Under prior law the debtor alone could seek relief under Chapter XI,[1] had the right to petition for continuation in possession,[2] could solicit for acceptance of a proposed plan either before or after filing,[3] and was able to offer amendments or modifications to the plan.[4] Under these conditions, complete dominance by the debtor could only be overcome by active participation of the creditors' committee throughout all stages of the proceedings.

8   The new chapter 11 provisions give the creditors more opportunity to participate in the proceedings in selected areas. For example, the creditors can force the debtor into a chapter 11 reorganization proceeding and can, under certain conditions, file a plan. The debtor will still, in most cases, continue to operate the business and actions of the creditors will be focused through the creditors' committee or committees. Thus, the importance of the creditors' committee has not been diminished by the new law. Large corporations that might have filed a Chapter X corporate reorganization under the old law will have much more participation by creditors' and

---

[1] Bankruptcy Act, Secs. 321–322.
[2] Ibid., Sec. 342.
[3] Ibid., Sec. 336.
[4] Ibid., Sec. 363.

equity security holders' committees now than there would have been in Chapter X.

9 The involvement of the bankruptcy judge has been changed by the Bankruptcy Code. Prior to this Code the judge performed both administrative and judicial functions. Now the judge is restricted to only judicial matters and will not be involved in the operations of the business except to resolve disputes in an adversary context. The judge will not preside over the meeting of creditors. In districts where U.S. trustees are appointed, they will be involved in the administration of the estate, but in the other districts the creditors' committee may have increased responsibility to see that the debtor's actions are in accordance with the law. Even in areas where a U.S. trustee is appointed, the creditors' committee has greater responsibility under the Bankruptcy Code. Section 1103(c) provides that the tasks of the creditors' committee are:

1　To conduct an investigation of the financial affairs of the debtor.

2　To determine whether the business should continue to operate.

3　To participate in the formulation and solicitation of a plan.

4　To request the appointment of a trustee or examiner if such appointment is considered necessary.

5　To consult with the trustee or debtor in possession concerning the administration of the case.

6　To perform other services that are in the best interest of the creditors represented by the committee.

Bargaining Process

10　One of the basic functions performed by the creditors' committee is to negotiate a settlement and then make its recommendation to the other creditors. The accountant should be familiar with the bargaining process that goes on between the debtor and the creditors' committee in trying to reach a settlement. Bargaining can be both vigorous and delicate. The debtor bargains, perhaps, for a settlement that consists of a small percentage of the debt, one that demands only a small cash outlay now with payments to be made in the future. The debtor may want the debts outstanding to be subordinated to new credit or may ask that the agreement call for partial payment in preferred stock. The creditors want a settlement that represents a high percentage of the debt and consists of a larger cash down payment with the balance to be paid as soon as possible. If the creditors demand too high a percentage, the company may be forced to liquidate, either immediately or at some future date, because it cannot make a large payment and still continue to operate. Creditors must not insist on more than the debtor has the ability to pay. However, creditors have refused to accept a reasonable settlement that is very low because it establishes a bad example in the industry. In some trade areas all parties involved are almost of one large fraternity. Rutberg suggests that

> A meeting of creditors is like old home week. Everyone seems to know every-one else and there is much shaking of hands and slapping of backs and general good fellowship. It's something like the funeral of a lady who died at ninety-five after a full life and who left a great fortune to be divided up among the surviving relatives.[5]

The creditors do not want to establish a precedent with a settlement which is too low. As a result, the creditors' committee may demand that the debtor be liquidated although they will receive less than would have been received from a low out-of-court settlement or a plan of reorganization.

11 Some basic guidelines may be applicable in certain situations in the bargaining process. First, if a cash payment is called for in the proposal in full or partial settlement, the down payment should at least be equal to the probable dividend to creditors if the business were liquidated. To offer this much is a strong selling point for the debtor. Also, creditors will probably not accept anything less. Second, when a settlement calls for future pay-ments, the creditors' committee often insists that the payments be secured. The security may be in the form of notes of the debtor endorsed by its officers or other individuals acceptable to the committee. The creditors may also desire a mortgage on the debtor's real estate,[6] pledge of stock of a subsidiary, or other forms of security. Third, when an out-of-court settle-ment includes installment payments over a period of time, Mulder suggests that creditors are likely to insist upon one or more of these safeguards:[7]

> The debtor must execute an assignment for the benefit of creditors. This will be held in escrow, by the creditors' committee, to become effective only if the debtor defaults in subsequent payment. In such an eventuality, the creditors can liquidate the debtor's assets through the assignment, or use the assignment as an act of bankruptcy.
>
> A corporate debtor must require all stockholders to endorse in blank all shares of stock to be held in escrow by the creditors' committee, to become effective only on default by the debtor.
>
> The directors and officers of a corporate debtor must tender resignations to the creditor's committee, to be held in escrow, to become effective only on default by the debtor.
>
> During any period when installment payments are pending, the creditors' com-mittee will exercise control over the operation of the business. The committee,

---

[5] Sidney Rutberg, *Ten Cents on the Dollar* (New York: Simon and Schuster, 1973), p. 45.
[6] John E. Mulder, "Rehabilitation of the Financially Distressed Small Business—Revisited," *The Practical Lawyer*, Vol. 11 (November 1965), p. 44.
[7] Ibid., pp. 43–44.

its counsel, its accountant, or a designated person will supervise or control purchases, credit sales, cash inflow and outflow, signing of checks, payrolls, etc.

As another alternative creditors may insist upon the execution of a trust indenture and security agreement giving them a lien on all assets of the business as security for the debtor's performance of the settlement or plan of reorganization.

12 In addition, the debtor may be required to reduce expenses that the creditors consider excessive, such as travel and entertainment and officers' salaries.

Role of Creditors' Accountant in the Bargaining Process

13 The services that the accountant may render for the creditors' committee in the negotiations with the debtor will vary significantly depending upon several factors including the size of the debtor, the experience of the members of the creditors' committee, the nature of the debtor's operations, and the confidence the creditors' committee has in the debtor and in the professionals—especially attorneys and accountants—who are helping the debtor. The committee in most cases will, to varying degrees, depend upon the accountant to help them evaluate the debtor's operations, the information provided about those operations, and the terms of a proposed plan. Often accountants may be engaged to perform an audit or to investigate selected aspects of the debtor's operation and to obtain an overall understanding of the debtor's problems and possible solutions. The following paragraphs present an example of the particular functions an accountant might perform for a committee of unsecured creditors of a relatively small company. It is assumed that the accountant was engaged to first do a special investigation of the debtor's operations. As you read through this example, remember that the nature of the committee's activities and the accountant's services may vary considerably.

14 A creditors' committee meeting may be called as soon as the accountant has completed the special investigation. If there is enough time, the report will be given in advance to all members of the committee. A copy may also be given to the debtor in advance; however, some committees request that the debtor not be given a copy of the report, other than the balance sheet, before the meeting. In an unofficial committee case, where time is crucial, especially in the textile industry, it is not unusual for the accountant to complete the special investigation only a day or two before the meeting. The first order of business is for the accountant to discuss the report orally with the committee. The highlights of the report should be pointed out, any irregularities discovered by the accountant should be described, and the reason for the debtor's financial difficulty should be discussed. The creditors will generally want to know the type of cooperation the accountant received from the debtor in the investigation and whether they are dealing with an "honest" debtor.

15 The accountant may at this meeting go over the statement of financial position in general. Then each item will be analyzed and liquidating values will be assigned on the assumption that the business will be liquidated. (For an example of the type of statement of financial position that is issued, see Exhibits 12-1 and 12-2, on pages 491–497. Normally the accountant does not use liquidation values in preparing this statement; it is based on the going concern assumption. See chapter 13, paragraphs 15–21.) Liquidating values are established on the basis of the information gained from the accountant's examination and inquiries, the knowledge of the creditors at the meeting, and any appraisals which have been made (see chapter 7, paragraphs 33–35). If the company is very large, the accountant may prepare for the committee a statement of affairs which would contain the liquidating values (chapter 12, paragraphs 24–33). The accountant may be reluctant to prepare a statement of affairs for this meeting without performing additional auditing procedures and inquiries, but there is usually not enough time or funds available for this additional work. If the accountant prepares the statement of financial position in accordance with the format in Exhibit 12-2, where the assets are reduced by the amount of the obligation for which they are pledged, it will facilitate the discussion.

16 The committee, with the assistance of the accountant, will determine the amount that will be available from the sale of the assets after all priorities are paid. The administrative fees are estimated, and the balance represents the amount that would be available to unsecured creditors, a year or two hence.

17 At this point, the debtor and debtor's counsel are brought into the meeting. The debtor's counsel will present the defense of the debtor's operations, and may point out the cause of the financial difficulty and the steps management is prepared to take to prevent the problem from recurring. The counsel then indicates, if the debtor is ready, the terms of the debtor's offer to the creditors. With the assistance of the accountant and the creditors' counsel, the committee will question the debtor about the plan. After considerable discussion about the proposed plan, the committee will send the debtor out of the room and discuss the plan with the accountant and counsel. The committee may reject the plan as it is and submit to the debtor a plan that is acceptable to them, or they may simply suggest that the plan be modified, such as by increasing the cash payment by $.15 per dollar of debt. The negotiations will continue until they come to a consensus, or until it is determined that a consensus cannot be obtained at this meeting. Quite often in a chapter 11 case, where time is not as critical, the committee will want additional time to study the plan and compare, with the assistance of the accountant, the settlement amount in the plan with the amount that would be received upon liquidation.

18 The accountant for the creditors' committee will go over the plan with the committee and its counsel, make suggestions as to how it should be modified, and answer any questions the committee has about the plan.

Importance of Cash Flow in the Bargaining Process

19 The emphasis throughout the negotiations is on cash flow. The creditors' committee, as mentioned above, will first determine the amount the creditors would receive upon liquidation. This amount is compared with the suggested settlement amount as shown in the proposed plan. If the plan calls for a future payment, the committee must consider their prospects for receiving the payments. Before the committee can evaluate the plan, it must analyze the projected cash inflow. Normally, the debtor, in presenting the plan, will supply statements of projected cash receipts and disbursements to support its claim that at some future date cash will be available to make these payments. The committee's accountant will examine these statements and assist the committee in evaluating the assumptions on which the statements were prepared. The accountant may, based upon the proposed changes suggested by management and the committee's evaluation of them and upon the audit and analysis of the debtor's past operations, prepare a cash flow statement which will be compared with the one prepared by the debtor (see paragraph 36).

AREAS REQUIRING IMMEDIATE ATTENTION

20 Services for the creditors' committee can be broken down into two categories. One is a situation where the creditors' committee needs the accountant to assist it with immediate action, and the other can be spread over several months.

21 The environment that the creditors' committee works under varies significantly. At one extreme, it is important in some cases that the creditors obtain control of the business as soon as possible, obtain all of the books and records, and take an inventory of the merchandise and other property. In other situations it is necessary for the creditors to only obtain an understanding of the nature of the business and its problem areas and to be able to effectively evaluate the actions proposed by the debtor. As soon as the accountant for the creditors' committee is appointed, an immediate assessment must be made of the environment and the approach that should be taken. To make this assessment, the accountant should discuss the situation generally with both a representative of the creditors' committee and its counsel. In this discussion, the accountant must be satisfied that the necessary controls are in place to prevent the asset base from continuing to deteriorate. Often it will be necessary for the accountant to make an immediate visit to the debtor's offices in order to observe the nature of the operations and the types of controls that exist for cash, inventory, and other property.

At times, it is also helpful for the accountant to meet with the debtor's prior accountant and its new accountant, if one has been appointed.

22   In one case, the creditors' committee took very little action to evaluate the activities of the debtor during the first two months after the petition was filed. The debtor failed to pay administrative expenses associated with the postbankruptcy operations, and cash from postbankruptcy activities was diverted to other uses. Eventually the creditors realized what was happening and petitioned the court for the appointment of a trustee. However, this action was not taken until the creditors had sustained additional material losses. Frequently, the smaller the case, the more important it will be for creditors to quickly insure that proper controls are in place. A small asset base can be dissipated very quickly.

23   It should be realized that members of the creditors' committee may not be experienced in serving in this capacity. They may not know the types of action they should take. Under these conditions, the accountant should provide guidance to the committee by helping it to ask the right kinds of questions and by steering its activities in the right direction.

IMPORTANCE OF SPEED

24   When the creditors' committee retains an accountant, even if the environment is such that immediate action is not necessary, as discussed above, it usually wants the audit and investigation and resulting statements and reports to be completed as soon as possible so that a plan may be agreed upon quickly. The committee asks for the accountant's report immediately because it is impossible for the committee to take any type of action until it has examined the report and discussed the operations of the debtor with the accountant. As soon as the accountant accepts the engagement, he or she must begin the audit or special investigation. Accountants who are experienced representatives of creditors can complete the examination and issue the report in a relatively short time. For example, a New York accounting firm frequently issues a detailed report on the financial position of a debtor within ten to fourteen days after the engagement is accepted, even though the companies involved have sales volumes in excess of several million dollars. However, in some complex circumstances, it takes months just to establish the financial position from the records and much longer to complete the audit.

25   It is advisable to seek a prompt settlement in order to halt the losses which the debtor may be incurring in the operation of its business and to block the possibility of misconduct by the debtor in the form of preferential payments, concealment of assets, or conversion of assets into property that is exempt from liquidation proceedings. Also, in an out-of-court settlement, if there is an extended delay, some of the creditors may file suit for their claims, eventually forcing the debtor to file a petition under chapter 11, or may actually file an involuntary petition putting the debtor into chapter 7 or 11.

CONTROLS

26   Supervision of the debtor and its activities is essential throughout the proceedings, beginning with negotiations concerning the settlement and ending only when the plan has been consummated. Control is normally aimed at conservation of the assets, and the creditors' committee holds an excellent position to perform such a function.

27   The importance of the supervisory function of the creditors' committee and of its representation of an unbiased viewpoint that protects the best interests of all the creditors was noted in the *Credit Service* case.[8] There the judge stated that a complete review of the debtor's conduct must be made to insure that the proposed arrangement is fair, equitable, and feasible, and this "should be made by a disinterested and competent committee for the information of and action thereon by the creditors."[9]

28   The two most crucial time periods during which control must be exercised are the period after the filing of the petition but before agreement on a plan, and the period when installment payments are pending if called for by the plan. One of the key functions performed by the accountant, once the engagement for the creditors' committee has been accepted, is to preserve the assets through performance of an audit (chapter 11). The first assignment of the accountant is to inventory the books and records (chapter 11, paragraphs 39–45) and count the physical inventory. Recently an accounting firm received a telephoned request for services from the attorney for a creditors' committee. The call came in the morning; that same afternoon the accountants began and completed an inventory of the merchandise on the debtor's premises. The owner, unaware that the inventory had been taken, removed part of the inventory from the warehouse a few days later, hoping to conceal it from the assets of the estate. Obviously, the owner was unsuccessful in the attempt. The accountant, at times, must move very fast in order to exercise adequate control. (See paragraphs 20–23.)

29   In addition to an audit, the accounting methods most frequently used to exercise control over the estate include some type of supervision or control over the receipts and disbursements and a statement of review of the debtor's operations. Whether such supervision is requested by the creditors' committee or mandated by local rules of the bankruptcy court or U.S. trustee (see chapter 8, paragraphs 1–19), the objectives are the same.

[8] 31 F. Supp. 979 (1940).
[9] Ibid.

Investigate Causes of Failure and Develop Controls to Limit Further Impairment of Assets

30   The creditors' committee needs to know as early as possible after the petition is filed what caused the debtor's current problems, whether the company will be able to overcome its difficulties, and, if so, what measures need to be taken in the future to avoid further losses. A brief review of the debtor's operations may not necessarily reveal the cause of failure. It is the cause that must be identified by the accountant and eventually corrected; it is not enough just to correct the symptoms.

31   Once the underlying cause of failure has been identified, the accountant for the creditors' committee should develop procedures that will limit further impairment of assets. It is important during the early stages of the case to determine that proper controls are established over receipts and disbursements. The company may have had an adequate system at one time. However, during periods of financial difficulty, divisions of responsibility and other internal controls are often not enforced. Key accounting and financial personnel of the company may resign. Responsibilities must be reestablished, and proper control must be exercised over all receipts and disbursements.

32   In the case of unprofitable segments or divisions of the debtor's operations, the creditors' committee may insist that immediate action be taken to eliminate these operations. The accountant may monitor the results of the liquidations of unprofitable operations for the committee.

Review of Receipts and Disbursements Control

33   Direct control can be exercised over all disbursements by having the accountant countersign all checks. It is not unusual for the creditors' committee to make such a request and it was common practice, at one time, for accountants to sign the checks as part of their services for the creditors' committee. This practice is undesirable because of the ethical and legal implications associated with the signature. The ethical aspects are discussed in chapter 7 (paragraphs 89–90). If the accountant's signature is on all checks, the inference may be made that the accountant is assuming responsibility for the disbursements. One accounting firm countersigned payroll checks for the debtor, but failed to make sure that the taxes withheld from employees were remitted to the Internal Revenue Service. The funds were used for other purposes for which the accountant countersigned the checks. Officers, debtors in possession, and trustees may be held personally liable for failure to remit these taxes. Section 6672 of the Internal Revenue Code imposes a 100 percent penalty upon a person required to collect and pay over taxes who willfully fails to do so. In this situation the Internal Revenue Service assumed that since the accountant was responsible for signing the checks, he was also responsible for remitting the taxes withheld. Since the debtor did not have any funds to cover the taxes, the accountant personally had to pay the amount due. Some accounting firms that formerly counter-signed checks when requested to do so by creditors' committees have, at times, initialed all or selected checks before they were issued. It should be realized that initialing all checks before they are issued still presents some legal and ethical problems associated with the cosigning of the checks.

Receipts

34 Adequate records of all sales must be maintained and the accountant must see that all cash received from sales and from collections of accounts receivable are deposited intact. Control must also be exercised over pur-chases, credit sales, returns, and payroll.

Disbursements

35 The extent to which the accountant gets involved in the control of disbursements will vary depending on the nature of the proceeding and the size of the debtor. In some cases, the accountant's involvement may be in the design of a system that will provide for control over the disbursements. In other situations, the account may review for the creditors' committee all disbursements in excess of a set dollar amount and advise the creditors' committee of any disbursements that are questionable as unusual. Examples of such disbursements are unauthorized postpetition payments and pay-ments of prepetition obligations that have not been expressly authorized by the court. Accountants may also review with the creditors' committee chair or counsel the reports filed with the court for expense disbursement ap-proval. At times, before any disbursement is made, the accountant may review all invoices supporting the disbursement and in fact try to justify the expenditure. Certain types of expenditures such as travel and entertainment, professional fees, and other expenses of a personal nature should be care-fully examined by the accountant. The accountant and the creditors' com-mittee must, however, be very careful in the way in which they exercise control over the debtor's operations (see paragraph 39). The accountant will see that only those liabilities are paid which were incurred, in an out-of-court settlement, after the initial creditors' meeting. It is also important to make sure that all liabilities incurred for new services are paid promptly. An im-portant part of the accountant's assistance in disbursement control is to evaluate the extent to which the debtor is enforcing and following the estab-lished controls.

Review of Cash Flow Reports

36 By establishing a proper system of control, constantly monitoring the system to see that it is functioning properly, and frequently evaluating the cash flow, the accountant observes the day-to-day operations of the business during the time a settlement is being arranged. Cash flow receives a great deal of attention, primarily because the creditors do not want to see the assets of the business continue to diminish. Normally, the debtor's accountant will develop, with the cooperation of the debtor in possession, a forecast of the anticipated receipts and disbursements on a periodic basis, usually weekly, for a period of four to six months. At the end of each period, the debtor will submit a report comparing the actual results with the projected estimates. Exhibit 9-1 illustrates a statement of cash flow, and Exhibit 9-2 shows the actual and projected activity of a merchandise inventory account. The accountants for the creditors' committee will normally review these reports and discuss their analysis with the committee.

37 The accountant for the creditors' committee must take whatever steps seem necessary to insure that the assets do not continue to diminish

Exhibit 9-1   Cash-Flow Statement

THOMAS MERCHANDISE, INC. (DEBTOR-IN-POSSESSION)
STATEMENT OF CASH FLOW

For the Week Ended August 28, 19X1

(In Thousands)

		Actual (Unaudited)		Projected
Receipts:				
Transferred from Stores		$ 814		$ 850
Income—Leased Departments		67		54
Miscellaneous		304		120
Adam Drugs, Inc.		930		—
		2,115		1,024
Disbursements:				
Merchandise	$242		$990	
Rents	22		—	
Payroll	136		139	
Other	263		155	
		663		1,284
Excess of Receipts over Disbursements		1,452		(260)
Cash—Beginning		2,793		2,793
Cash—End		$4,245		$2,533

Note: This statement is subject to the accompanying letter of transmittal.

JOHN X. DOE & COMPANY

THOMAS MERCHANDISE, INC. (DEBTOR IN POSSESSION)

MERCHANDISE DATA—APPAREL

Weekly—July–December, 19X1

(In Thousands)

Week Ended	Sales Planned	Sales Actual	Orders Placed Retail	Orders Placed Cost	Orders Received Retail	Orders Received Cost	Open Orders—Cost	Cash in Banks	Payments on Purchases	Outstanding Debts to Vendors
19X1										
July 31	$ 650	$764	$4,166.0	$2,249.8	$ 360	$ 194.6	$2,055.2	$2,102	—	$ 195
Aug. 7	800	869	2,666.0	1,439.5	1,276	689.1	2,805.6	1,936	$ 11	872
14	800	817	3,276.0	1,768.9	1,940	1,047.6	3,526.9	2,378	87	1,833
21	800	883	956.5	516.5	2,026	1,093.8	2,949.6	2,793	118	2,808
28	850	800*	(752.8)	(406.5)	1,907	1,030.0	1,513.1	4,245	242	3,596
Sept. 4	850		1,100.0	600.0						
11	900		1,100.0	600.0						
18	900		1,100.0	600.0						
25	950		1,100.0	600.0						
Oct. 2	950		1,100.0	600.0						
9	950		1,100.0	600.0						
16	950		1,100.0	600.0						
23	950		1,100.0	600.0						
30	850		1,200.0	650.0						
Nov. 6	1,000		1,200.0	650.0						
13	1,000		1,200.0	650.0						
20	1,000		—	—						
27	1,050		—	—						
Dec. 4	1,150		900.0	500.0						
11	1,250		900.0	500.0						
18	1,450		900.0	500.0						
24	2,350		900.0	500.0						
31	1,200		—	—						

* Estimated.

because of mismanagement, or suspiciously disappear. The amount of control that must be exercised by the committee depends upon such factors as its faith in the debtor's honesty and integrity and whether the debtor has an accountant.

Review of Debtor's Accounting System

38 In many bankruptcy cases, the amount of attention given to the accounting system and internal controls during the time that the debtor is facing financial difficulty is insignificant. Thus, while a good accounting system with proper controls may have existed a year or so prior to the filing of the petition, it may no longer be in place. Before placing any confidence in the reports issued by the debtor, the creditors' committee may ask its accountant to make a study of the accounting system. If it is inadequate, the accountant may be appointed by the court to devise an accounting system that would provide for the flow of accurate and timely financial information to the creditors' committee.

"Insider" Problem

39 An insider as defined by section 101(25) includes, among others, a person in control of the debtor. An insider can be in a disadvantageous position in relationship to other creditors regarding the content of the plan, avoidance of preferences, and other aspects of bankruptcy proceedings. Thus, in an attempted out-of-court settlement the creditors and their committee must be very careful that they do not exercise a direct influence over the debtor's business that could result in the court's considering them insiders in case the debtor files a bankruptcy court petition. Any action taken by the accountant and the creditors' committee involving control over the debtor's operations must be taken only after consulting with the counsel for the creditors' committee. See chapter 4, paragraphs 20–27.

REVIEW WEEKLY/MONTHLY REPORTING

40 A key service that the accountant can render for the creditors' committee is to review the weekly or monthly reports issued by the debtor. Under conditions in which the debtor was not authorized to retain an independent accountant, or in situations in which the creditors do not trust the debtor's accountant, the accountant for the creditors' committee may actually prepare these reports. These reports generally include cash, key operat-

Exhibit 9-2 Summary of Merchandise Inventory Account

ing statistics, and operating statements. As discussed in paragraph 36 the creditors' committee frequently requires cash-flow reports that compare actual with projected cash flows.

Key Statistics

41   Accountants may work with the creditors' committee to identify key data that will help the committee properly monitor the debtor's activities. The type of data that is key depends on the nature of the business. For example, in a retail operation the key data might include inventory balances by type of product, sales, orders placed, orders received, open orders, merchandise payments, and outstanding debts. The members of the creditors' committee may not know the type of data that should be requested to effectively monitor the debtor's activities. In such situations, the accountant for the creditors' committee should take the lead and recommend key indicators to the committee. By working with the committee and the debtor, the accountant can develop projections for key areas and can recommend to the committee the weekly or monthly reports to be prepared that will compare the actual results with the projections.

Operating Statements

42   As stated above, close supervision of the debtor's business operations is desirable to insure that the assets do not continue to be diminished because of the mismanagement that originally caused the debtor's difficulties. Such control is also necessary to prevent the wasting or diversion of assets. To this end, the creditors' committee may require the debtor to furnish, in addition to periodic statements of cash receipts and disbursements, a monthly operating statement so that the committee may review the administration of the business, whether by the debtor or a receiver. In a chapter 11 proceeding, monthly operating statements must be filed with the court or the U.S. trustee (chapter 8, paragraphs 1–19). These will also put the committee in a better position to reveal to the court what is actually occurring, as well as enabling it to halt any undesirable events much more quickly.

43   If the debtor attempts to prepare these statements, the reports may be inadequate and give a misleading impression of the company's profitability. Under these conditions, it is therefore desirable that the committee use its accountant to make an independent review of the debtor's records and prepare its own statements. Thus in some proceedings the accountant for the creditors—while not engaged directly by the debtor—may perform the necessary accounting services and prepare the required statements for the committee and the court. At other times the debtor may have its own independent accountant who will prepare the required operating statements. The accountant for the creditors' committee will review the statements and advise the committee of the status of the company's operations. The operating statements are described and illustrated in chapter 8 (paragraphs 14–19, and pages 319–328).

AUDIT AND/OR INVESTIGATION OF DEBTOR'S BOOKS AND RECORDS

44   An important function performed by the accountant for the creditors' committee is a thorough examination of the debtor's past business transactions. The primary purpose of such an investigation is to insure that all assets have been accounted for and any misconduct adequately explained. This work serves as a foundation from which the accountant will issue statements and reports and conduct any necessary investigations into the debtor's conduct. The creditors must have the results of any such examination to judge first whether a proposed plan is feasible and in their best interests as they decide whether or not to accept it, and second, whether it will satisfy the Bankruptcy Code's fair and equitable requirements if they do not accept it. (See chapter 11.)

Discovery of Assets

45   It is crucial that the creditors have a knowledge of all the debtor's assets and their value. This includes all property which may be recovered because it was involved in a preferential transfer, assets that were concealed, and the like. (See chapter 11, paragraphs 98–105.) The total assets available to creditors in liquidation must be determined, to ascertain the dividend the creditors would receive in a chapter 7 liquidation and to indicate whether a proposed plan is in their best interests.

Discovery of Malfeasance

46   During the audit and/or investigation of the debtor, the accountant will be on the alert for any transactions believed to be questionable, including dishonesty, issuance of false financial statements, concealments, preferential payments, fraudulent transfers, and so forth (chapter 11). Any misconduct even merely suspected by the accountant should be reported to the creditors' committee because it will be taken into consideration by them when deciding whether the debtor should be rehabilitated. Such behavior may also influence the court in deciding to appoint a trustee and not allow the debtor to remain in possession or in requiring that the debtor furnish indemnity to protect the assets of the estate.[10] The discovery of certain types

---

[10] Asa S. Herzog, "CPA's Role in Bankruptcy Proceeding," *The Journal of Accountancy*, Vol. 117 (January 1964), p. 68.

of transactions may cause the debtor to be barred from a discharge of all or part of its debts or may, in the case of an out-of-court settlement, precipitate the filing of an involuntary chapter 7 or 11 petition in order to further investigate the nature of the questionable transactions.

47 In chapter 7 liquidation proceedings, rather than emphasizing the future potential of the business as in a chapter 11 reorganization, creditors are concerned with the liquidation value of the debtor's assets and with discovery of any unusual transactions, including the transfer or concealment of assets. Examples of the types of unusual transactions the accountant would seek to discover through the audit are listed below:

> Preferential payments made within ninety days (one year for insiders) prior to the petition date.
>
> Sales of inventory to vendors or other creditors.
>
> Fixed assets sold to creditors or others for less than their full value, sold to creditors as an account offset, or resold to the manufacturer as an account offset.
>
> The misappropriation of receipts, especially advances from factors.
>
> Liens given creditors prior to bankruptcy to enable them to obtain a greater percentage distribution than other creditors.
>
> Any assets withdrawn by stockholders in the form of dividends, loans, transfer of assets, and so forth.
>
> Potential assets, such as pending lawsuits, which might enlarge the size of the estate.
>
> All other transactions which may have arisen outside of the ordinary course of the business.[11]

REVIEW OF DEBTOR'S TRANSACTIONS

48 To assist the creditors' committee in its supervisory functions, the accountant for the committee may be asked to review the debtor's operations during the period when a plan is being formalized and immediately following its acceptance. This review generally concentrates on the major transactions of the debtor between the date the petition is filed and the date of review. In reviewing these transactions, accountants are looking for any indication that a trustee should be appointed. Emphasis is not solely on the discovery of irregularities that would indicate dishonesty on the part of management. The accountant also looks for indications of mismanagement of company resources or that management is not taking the steps necessary to reverse the loss trend developed prior to the filing of the petition. Another purpose of this review is to identify any payments on prefiling obligations

---

[11] Edward A. Weinstein, "Examining a Company in Bankruptcy," *Quarterly* (Touche, Ross, Bailey and Smart), Vol. 9 (September 1963), p. 18.

that were made after the petition was filed and any other payments that were not authorized by the court.

EVALUATION OF DEBTOR'S PROJECTIONS

49   Of primary significance to a creditors' committee is how realistic the projections and forecasts that are submitted by the debtor are. The representatives of the largest unsecured creditors on the committee typically are attorneys. Therefore, their ability to evaluate financial data may be limited. The accountant for the creditors' committee may be in a strong position to evaluate the debtor's evaluations and to make recommendations.

50   The intention is not to perform an audit of such data but rather to review it to determine whether or not the data in the projections can be supported to some extent by hard evidence. The level of involvement by the accountant for the creditors' committee will vary, depending upon the sophistication of the company or of the financial people who prepared the data. The review of the data in some cases could be limited to a discussion with those who prepared the projections, to determine whether or not they seem to make sense. In other situations, however, the accountant may find that the preparation of this information has been somewhat loose or vague. In these circumstances, the accountant for the committee may need to get involved in the preparation or to perform a review of the appropriate accounting records to see whether or not the basic underlying data has some foundation in fact.

51   To a large extent, this kind of review is similar to what would be done in conjunction with reviewing quarterly unaudited financial statements of a business. The biggest difference is that in quarterly reviews the accountant is looking at a historical period only, whereas the projection data submitted by the debtor will involve future periods of time as well.

52   The most desirable way to communicate the results of the review to the creditors' committee is to discuss the projections with key members, in addition to submitting a written report. The accountant for the creditors' committee also may be asked to prepare projections for the committee. Frequently, creditors' committees will express concern over the level of the debtor's operations, the continuation of losses, and the required level of trade credit. To help the committee have a better understanding of the debtor's operations and the potential losses that could occur, comparative projections assuming varying levels of operation can be prepared.

REVIEW OF PLAN OF REORGANIZATION AND DISCLOSURE STATEMENT

53   As was noted in chapter 7, the accountant for the debtor provides advice and assistance in the formulation of a plan of reorganization in a chapter 11 proceeding and a plan of settlement in an agreement out of court. An important function of an accountant employed by the creditors is to help evaluate the proposed plan of action. In a chapter 11 case where the debtor has not proposed a plan within 120 days, a proposed plan has not been accepted within 180 days after the petition was filed, or where the trustee has been appointed, the accountant may assist the creditors in developing a plan to be submitted to the court. The accountant is able to provide valuable assistance to the committee because of the familiarity with the financial background, the nature of the operations, and the management of the company gained from the audit. In committee meetings a great deal of time is spent in discussions between the committee members and the accountant concerning the best settlement they can expect and how it compares with the amount they would receive if the business were liquidated. The accountant also gives an opinion as to the debtor's future prospects for profit, assuming the business was not liquidated. (See chapter 7, paragraphs 42–47.)

54 The creditors are interested in receiving as much as possible under any reorganization plan. The accountant may work with the creditors' committee to see that the amount proposed under the plan is reasonable and fair based on the nature of the debtor's business. First, it must be determined that the plan provides for at least as much as would be received in a chapter 7 liquidation. Second, the creditors must leave the debtor enough assets to operate the business after reorganization. If a reasonable basis does not exist for future operations, the judge may not confirm the plan because it is not feasible.

55 To help the creditors' committee with an evaluation of the plan, the accountant may need to perform an audit of the debtor's business or at least make a limited review of the debtor's operations and investigate any unusual transactions. Normally, the accountant focuses, at least in part, on the following areas in an evaluation of the plan:

1 Since an attempt is being made to rehabilitate the business, the creditors will be interested in both prior years' operations and the future potential of the business. The accountant should attempt to provide information regarding the projected volume of the business and estimated gross and net profits. To determine the future success of the business, comparisons should be made of these figures with those typical of the industry.

2 The causes of the debtor's past losses should be ascertained, and measures necessary to eliminate the problems must be determined to insure that the debtor will be able to earn a profit in the future.

3 The liquidating value of the debtor's assets should be fixed so that, while attempting to agree on a plan, creditors will know the smallest dividend acceptable to them and have a basis for judging a proposed plan.

4 To determine the size of the initial payment that it would be possible to make to creditors, it will be necessary to ascertain the status and extent of any liens existing on the debtor's property, any secured claims, and the amounts owed on priority claims.

56   In serving as the accountant for the creditors' committee, it would be necessary to rely on the information contained in the disclosure statement and in other reports issued, if an audit had not been performed. Thus, the content of the disclosure statement may be most important. Also, since the disclosure statement serves as the basic report used by the creditors to evaluate the plan, it is critical that it be properly prepared and contain the type of information that would allow the creditors to effectively evaluate the proposed plan.

57   The accountant for the creditors' committee may be asked to evaluate the disclosure statement. If, in the accountant's opinion, it does not contain adequate information, the deficiencies may be conveyed to the debtor informally (normally through creditors' committee counsel) prior to submission of the plan to the court, or an objection to the content of the statement may be raised at the disclosure hearing. If a trustee is appointed or if the 120-day period (including extensions) allowed for the debtor to develop a plan has expired, anyone may propose a plan. In this case, the accountant may assist the creditors' committee in developing a plan and in drafting the disclosure statement.

58   In evaluating the information in the disclosure statement, the accountant for the creditors' committee may be asked to review the financial statements contained in the disclosure statement or others that were issued by the debtor. Special consideration must be made in reviewing pro forma and liquidation statements of financial condition. The pro forma statement provides the creditors with an indication of what the financial condition of the debtor will look like if the plan is accepted. This statement should show that the creditors will receive more if they accept the plan than would be received if the debtor were liquidated. The pro forma statement also should demonstrate that the plan is feasible in that, after satisfying the provisions of the plan, the debtor retains an asset base with which to operate. In reviewing the pro forma statement prepared by the debtor, special consideration must be given to the analysis of the assumptions used to prepare it and to the evaluation of the value of the assets (which may differ from book values).

59   Liquidation statements are prepared to show what the unsecured creditors would receive if the business were liquidated. The assumptions used in the adjustments to book values must be evaluated carefully. The accountant for the creditors' committee may be asked to review statements of this nature and to provide advice as to the reasonableness of the analysis. There may be a tendency for the debtor to understate liquidation values in order to make the terms of the plan more appealing to the unsecured creditors.

ACCOUNTING SERVICES—SECURED CREDITOR AND STOCKHOLDER OR EQUITY COMMITTEE

60   An accountant may be retained by either a secured creditor or major stockholder or—under restricted conditions—may be retained by the court to render services for a committee of secured creditors or stockholders. Under the latter arrangement, the fees are generally authorized by the court and come out of the estate of the debtor. When engaged directly by the secured creditor or stockholder, the fees are normally paid by the client.

Secured Creditor

61 An accountant can be engaged by a secured creditor to serve as its advisor during the bankruptcy proceeding. Under this type of arrangement, the objective is to watch for anything that might be of interest to the secured creditor. Work done in this capacity includes:

Abstracting any financial data that could be related to the case.

Attending various creditor and other meetings with the secured creditors and providing them with information and insight during the meetings.

Reviewing reports issued by the debtor.

Helping the secured creditor make proposals for and evaluating the proposed plan.

Major Stockholder or Equity Committee

62 The nature of the services accountants can render to either a major stockholder or to an equity security holders' committee is similar to those performed for the creditors' committee or for a committee of secured creditors. The equity holders generally are interested in the recovery of preferential payments, fraudulent transfers, or other transfers that might increase the value of the estate. Action for the recovery of these transfers generally is left to the creditors' committee. However, if the creditors' committee is not taking necessary steps to preserve the estate for some reason, such as a conflict of interests by one of its members, the equity committee may take a more active role.

63 For a major stockholder or an equity committee to be effective, they must know what caused the debtor's financial difficulty and its current activities. The accountant can assist them in doing this by identifying the type of information which should be obtained from the debtor. The accountant may review operating reports and other financial information and advise the major stockholder or equity committee of any potential problems in addition to the general status of the debtor's operations.

64 A major area in which the accountant can assist the client is in the evaluation of the plan. The extent to which the stockholders share in the plan of reorganization will depend to some extent on the solvency of the debtor. Thus, the debtor needs assistance in estimating the prospects for successful future operations and the going concern value of the business. A major stockholder or equity committee is also interested in the tax consequences the plan may have on future operations, especially the extent to which the net operating loss can be preserved.

RESPONSIBILITIES OF CREDITORS' ACCOUNTANT

65   An accountant retained by the creditors has a primary duty to them and performs all work in their interest. One of the accountant's first concerns will be to inquire into the transactions which have occurred, which will require an audit of the debtor's books and records. One of the purposes of this investigation will be to determine whether there have been any preferential or fraudulent transfers, unexplained losses, or other unusual and suspicious transactions. The creditors' accountant should, however, first ask the debtor about any questionable items rather than indiscriminately making accusations. In the same manner, the accountant will seek to establish the debtor's integrity and the soundness of the debtor's records and statements.

66   Another important function of an accountant employed by the creditors is to help them reach a conclusion about the proposed out-of-court settlement or plan of reorganization. This involves advising them as to the best settlement they can expect and comparing this with the distribution to be received if the business were liquidated. To accomplish this, the forced sale value of the assets must be ascertained and the accountant must give an opinion as to the debtor's future earning power. Here the accountant should also contact the debtor to gain awareness of any situations that should be given consideration.

67   Finally, both the creditors and the accountant are concerned with closely supervising the debtor in order to be sure that the assets do not continue to be diminished, wasted, or diverted, either before a plan is effected or after a settlement is reached. This includes studying the financial statements issued by the debtor and being aware of all its actions.

68   The creditors' accountant is thus responsible to the creditors for making sure they know all the facts, investigating anything about which there may be a question, and helping them choose the most advantageous course of action. At the same time there is a responsibility to the debtor to conduct all inquiries in a fair manner and to make sure the information given to the creditors is correct.

CHAPTER TEN

Valuation of a Business in Bankruptcy Proceedings

1   An additional service the accountant may be requested to render for the court, trustee, or debtor in possession is to assist in determining the value of the business. To be able to provide assistance it is necessary to have some understanding of the various approaches that have been used in determining the value of businesses and some knowledge of the conditions that must exist before a particular approach can be used. As we noted in chapter 5, the liquidation value of the business must be determined to establish if the plan is in the best interests of the creditors. The business must be valued also under the fair and equitable standards to determine the extent to which a dissenting class will participate in a plan. In other words, before accepting a plan the creditors needed to have some understanding of the amount they would receive if the company should be liquidated and the amount they should receive for their claims if the company were valued as a going concern. Related is the need to determine liquidating values of specific assets of the business for dissenting creditors in a given class. Section 1129(a)(7) provides that, before the court can confirm the plan, it must be determined that these creditors will receive as much from the plan as they would receive if the business was liquidated under chapter 7.

2   It should be noted that the prior Chapter X law required that a going concern value be placed on the business before a plan of reorganization could be confirmed. Chapter 11 requires only that the business be valued on a going concern basis when an impaired class fails to approve a plan. This does not necessarily mean that few businesses will have to be valued under the new law, but rather that more emphasis will be placed on the going concern value outside of the court's activities to determine whether a class of creditors should accept or reject the plan. Some, in fact, believe that the importance of arriving at a fair going concern value for the business is even more important under the new law.

3   The objectives of this chapter are to summarize the situations mentioned in chapters 3 and 5 where there is a need to determine the value of the business or the value of individual assets and to describe the detailed procedures followed in determining the value of assets, individually and collectively.

IMPORTANCE OF VALUATION

4   Asset valuation is very critical in many chapter 11 proceedings and also in chapter 7 proceedings. The discussion in this chapter will deal primarily with chapter 11 proceedings, but many of the Code sections covered apply equally to chapter 7 proceedings and out-of-court settlements.

Adequate Protection Under Section 361

5   Section 361 provides that the holders of secured claims, lessors, co-owners, conditional vendors, consignors, and so forth, are entitled to adequate protection of their interest in the property when such holders request relief from the automatic stay. It is the value of the secured creditor's collateral and not the creditor's claim or even the creditor's rights in specific collateral that is protected.[1] Adequate protection is also required before the debtor or trustee can use, sell, or lease certain kinds of collateral or before a lien that is prior to or equal to the creditor's lien can be granted. The Code provides three standards that can be used to provide adequate protection.[2] One of these requires that if the value of the secured creditor's collateral will decrease during the proceedings, the debtor in possession or trustee may be required to make periodic cash payments to the secured creditor.

6 The Code does not specify the method that is to be used to determine the value of the creditors' interest in the property of the debtor, nor does it define the time at which the value is to be determined. The legislative history indicates that these matters are left to case-by-case interpretation and development. It was expected that the courts would apply the concept in light of facts in each case and generally equitable principles and that the court would not develop hard and fast rules that would apply in every case. Legislative history also indicates that there is an infinite number of variations possible in dealing with debtors and creditors, that the law is continually developing, and that new ideas are continually being implemented in this field. Thus, the drafters of the Bankruptcy Code felt that flexibility is important to permit the courts to adapt to varying circumstances and changing modes of financing.[3]

7 Legislative history also indicates that it is not expected that the courts will construe value to mean in every case forced liquidation value or full going concern value. There is wide latitude between these two extremes. In any particular case, especially in a reorganization proceeding, the determination of which entity should be entitled to the difference between the going concern value and the liquidation value must be based on equitable considerations based on the facts in the case. Negotiations between the parties will, in most cases, determine the value and only if the parties cannot agree will the court become involved.[4]

8 From the legislative history it can be seen that to determine adequately the value for section 361 in a chapter 11 proceeding, it is necessary to know both the liquidation value and the going concern value.

Classifying Undersecured Claims

9 Section 506 provides that if a creditor is undersecured, the claim will be divided into two parts. The first part is secured to the extent of the value of the collateral or to the extent of the amount of funds subject to setoff. The balance of the claim is considered unsecured. The value that is to be used to

---

[1] *Wright* v. *Union Central Life Insurance Co.*, 311 U.S. 273 (1940).
[2] 11 U.S.C. Sec. 361.
[3] House Report No. 95–595, 95th Cong., 1st Sess. (1977) 338–340.
[4] Ibid.

determine the amount of the claim that is secured is, according to section 506(a), to "be determined in light of the purpose of the valuation and of the proposed disposition or use of such property, and in conjunction with any hearing on such disposition or use or on a plan affecting such creditors' interest." Before a decision is made regarding the value of the security, the court held in *In re Hotel Associates, Inc.*[5] that prior to the determination of secured status the claim must first be allowed. Bankruptcy Rule 3012 provides that any party in interest may petition the court to determine the value of a secured claim.

10   Thus, the approach used to value property subject to a lien for a chapter 7 may be different from that for a chapter 11 proceeding. Even within a chapter 11 case, property may be valued differently. For example, fixed assets that are going to be sold because of the discontinuance of operations may be assigned liquidation values, while assets that will continue to be used by the debtor may be assigned going concern values. Furthermore, legislative history indicates that a valuation made early in a case under section 361 (paragraphs 5–8 above) would not be binding on the debtor or creditor at the time the plan is confirmed. While courts will have to determine value on a case-by-case basis, it is clear that the value is to be determined in light of the purpose of the valuation and the proposed disposition or use of the property.[6]

11   As an example, a machine that cost $10,000 two years ago could have several different values assigned depending on the use of the machine and the nature of the debtor's operations. If it is the only machine the debtor uses to manufacture the products the debtor sells, the value to the debtor might be fairly high. On the other hand, if the debtor plans to sell this machine, which was specially made just for the debtor's product, it may have only a very small scrap value. If the debtor has other machines similar to this particular one and plans to use the others and leave this one idle until volume increases, the machine probably has a lower value than the first illustration, but, hopefully, higher than the second. To take the example further, if the debtor opposes a secured claimant's efforts to foreclose upon the machine at the beginning of the case and later, after the development of a business plan, decides to develop other product lines and sells this machine, the court could assign two different values to the very same machine.[7]

12   Also important in valuing the asset may be its benefit to the creditor. Consider an example where the debtor owns property that is surrounded by other property owned by the creditor and the creditor would like to remove the debtor's building to build a new shopping center on this location. With-

---

[5] 1 C.B.C.2d 819 (B.Ct., E.D. Pa. 1980).
[6] Senate Report No. 95–989, 95th Cong., 2d Sess. (1978) 68; *see Barash* v. *Public Finance Corp.*, 658 F.2d 504, 511 (7th Cir. 1981).
[7] Kenneth N. Klee, "All You Ever Wanted to Know About Cram Down Under the New Bankruptcy Code," *American Bankruptcy Law Journal*, Vol. 53 (Spring 1979), p. 152.

out this property, the center could not be built. These two examples illustrate the problems with the determination of value of individual assets as collateral for secured claims.

13 When a chapter 11 reorganization will use the specific property being valued in its business, courts have determined the value by an archetypical valuation based on a simulated conversion into cash in the most commercially reasonable manner practicable in the circumstances.[8]

14 In a chapter 7 case under the Code, the debtors (husband and wife) sought a section 506 valuation of their home, which secured the claims of four creditors. A year before the filing of their petitions, the debtors bought the home in Pennsylvania for $172,500, to which they made $35,000 worth of improvements. The debtors sought in this proceeding to establish a sheriff's sale value of $180,000, whereas creditors urged a value higher than $235,000 provided that the property was advertised and if there was an indefinite period in which to sell the property to the right buyer. The bankruptcy judge searched for guidance in valuing the collateral and adopted from the Bankruptcy Act a standard of commercial reasonableness for valuation of collateral based on the Uniform Commercial Code. The value is the amount that would be obtained by "the most commercially reasonable disposition under the circumstances," quoting *In re American Kitchen Foods*.[9] He also quoted the Fifth Circuit Court of Appeals, which determined to value collateral under the Bankruptcy Act by "applying the norm that a prudent businessman would employ to dispose of an asset."[10] Applying these standards to the facts, the court considered the disparate appraisals, the inflationary spiral of our time, and the depressing effect of high interest rates on the real estate market; it concluded that the property is worth what they paid for it plus the improvements they made, totalling $207,500.[11]

Determining Insolvency

15 Under prior law Chapter X corporate reorganization proceedings it was mandatory, for several reasons, that assets be valued at the outset of the proceedings to determine if the corporation was insolvent. First, section 130(1) of the Bankruptcy Act required that the petitioning corporation allege and prove either insolvency (in the bankruptcy sense) or an inability to pay its debts as they mature before the case could proceed under Chapter X. Valuation of assets at the start of the bankruptcy proceedings was more critical if the petition was filed by creditors. In order to force the debtor into straight bankruptcy or Chapter X corporate reorganization, the creditors had

---

[8] *In re Davis,* 5 C.B.C.2d 381 (B.Ct., D. Maine 1981); *see Savloff* v. *Continental Bank* (In re Savloff), 2 C.B.C.2d 56 (B.Ct., E.D. Pa. 1980) and *In the Matter of Reynolds,* 5 C.B.C.2d 1578 (B.Ct., N.D. Ga. 1981).

[9] 2 Bankr. Ct. Dec. 715, 722 (N.D. Me. 1976).

[10] *In re Pennyrich, Inc. of Dallas,* 473 F.2d 417, 424 (5th Cir. 1973).

[11] *In re Continental Bank et al.,* 6 Bankr. Ct. Dec. 349–51 (E.D.Pa. May 16, 1980).

to prove that the debtor had committed at least one of the six acts of bankruptcy. For most of these acts insolvency must have existed at the time the act was committed.

16 The acts of bankruptcy were eliminated by the Bankruptcy Reform Act. Insolvency is still, however, required under the new law as a condition for selected actions. For example, in order for certain payments to creditors to be preferences and for some transfers to be fraudulent, it is necessary for the debtor to be or to be rendered insolvent. The insolvency requirement under the Bankruptcy Code is defined in section 101(26): the debtor's liabilities exceed its assets, at a fair valuation, exclusive of fraudulent transfers (and exempt property for individuals). Legislative history indicates that the meaning of insolvency is based on section 1(19) of the Bankruptcy Act. Thus, until the courts more clearly define the manner in which the property is valued, the case law supporting section 1(19) of the prior law will be the guide.

17 Case law indicates that in determining "fair valuation" for the insolvency test a debtor's property should not be given a "distress" valuation. Fair value refers to what a willing owner not compelled to sell would take and a willing purchaser would pay, when not compelled to buy.[12] In *Andrew Johnson Properties, Inc.,*[13] the court defined "fair valuation" as the fair market value of the property between willing buyers and sellers or the value that can be made available to creditors within a reasonable amount of time. Widely varying elements may be considered in appraising real property, including physical characteristics, type of business for which the premises are designed, age, condition, original costs, and past and prospective earnings. In *Johnson Properties* the court went on to state that if the bankrupt is a going concern at the time of the transfer of assets, the property must be valued as a going concern.[14]

18 In determining insolvency for chapter 11 proceedings, case law based on the Bankruptcy Act suggests that going concern values will still be used.

Chapter 13 Secured Claims

19 If the holder of a secured claim does not accept the plan in a chapter 13 proceeding under the Bankruptcy Code, section 1325(a)(5) provides that the value of the property to be distributed as of the effective date of the plan must be at least equal to the amount of the secured claim. The amount of the secured claim would be determined according to the provisions of section 506(a) which would involve an evaluation of the collateral. In a chapter 13 case it would be anticipated that going concern values would be a factor in valuing property of secured creditors (see paragraphs 9–14).

---

[12] *Masonite Corp.* v. *Robinson-Slagle Lumber Co.,* 3 F. Supp. 754, 23 (D.C. La. 1933).
[13] CCH Dec. para. 65,254. (D.C. Tenn. 1974).
[14] Ibid.

Determining if a Class of Claims Is Impaired Under Chapter 11

20   If a class of claims is unimpaired, it is not necessary for the creditors or stockholders to vote for approval of the plan. Section 1124 sets forth three ways in which a plan may leave a class of claims or interests unimpaired. They include (1) not altering the rights of the claimants, (2) curing any default and damages and reinstating the maturity date, or (3) paying cash equal to the amount of the claim or, in the case of equity interest, the greater of liquidation preference or redemption price of the preferred stock.

21   Common stockholders must either accept the plan or the plan must satisfy the fair and equitable requirement in section 1129(b)(2)(C). Also note that payment must be in cash. By not allowing payment to be made in equity securities of the debtor, section 1124 obviates determining the value of the business. The only valuation process needed here is to determine the value of the debt as of the effective date of the plan. As noted in chapter 5, paragraph 39 and chapter 3, paragraph 91, a proof of claim or interest is deemed filed in a chapter 11 case if admitted on the debtor's schedules of liabilities and is deemed allowed by the court unless a party in interest files an objection.

Determining the Best Interest of Creditors and Stockholders Under Chapter 11

22   Under section 1129(a)(7) each holder of a claim or interest must accept the plan or receive or retain under the plan property that is not less, as of the effective date of the plan, than the amount that would be received or retained if the debtor were liquidating under chapter 7. This protection is afforded to each member of a class of claims or interest in contrast to other confirmation standards. As such, it is meaningful to those members of a class who vote to reject the plan but were overruled by a majority of the other members of the class accepting the plan. If the claim is held by a secured creditor and an election is made by that class to have the entire claim secured under section 1111(b)(2) then the creditor must receive or retain property of a value, as of the effective date of the plan, that is at least equal to the value of the creditor's interest in the collateral.[15]

23   Section 1129(a)(7) incorporates the "best interest of creditors" test that was found in former section 366(2) of Chapter XI under prior law, but sets forth what is intended. The new law also covers secured creditors and stockholders.

24   Obviously, the amount to consider when determining the values under a chapter 7 liquidation are liquidating values. The values used would most likely assume an orderly liquidation and not an immediate forced sale.

---

[15] 11 U.S.C. Sec. 1129(a)(B). Note that the 1111(b)(2) election requires approval by a class (sec. 1111(b)(1)(A)), but generally each secured debt is in a separate class.

In determining these values, there must be an evaluation of causes of action, such as avoiding powers that would be pursued in chapter 7 and costs of administration expenses. The value assigned to property pledged under the section 1111(b)(2) election would not necessarily be restricted to liquidation values but may depend on the possible disposition or retention of the collateral (see paragraphs 9–14).

Determining If a Plan is Fair and Equitable to a Dissenting Class in Chapter 11

25   Section 1129(b) permits the court to confirm a plan where creditors have not accepted the plan, provided the plan meets certain standards of fairness to dissenting classes of creditors or equity security holders. See chapter 5, paragraphs 96–108. Since the court can confirm the plan without creditor approval if these standards are met, the process is referred to as the "cram down" provision. The standards of fairness to dissenting junior classes center around a modification of the "absolute priority" doctrine where the dissenting class of creditors must be paid in full before any junior classes may share under the plan.

Bankruptcy Act Provisions

26   As a basis for determining if stockholders would participate in a Chapter X corporate reorganization under prior law, the court had to value the business and establish whether the debtor corporation was solvent or insolvent. According to section 179 of the Bankruptcy Act, if the debtor were insolvent, the plan of corporate reorganization completely terminated the interests of the existing stockholders without their approval. On the other hand, if the debtor were solvent, the stockholders had a vote to determine how the reorganization would be conducted, since their interests would be materially affected. Dissenting classes of stockholders were entitled to protection of their interests.

27   Section 221 of the Bankruptcy Act was the forerunner of section 1129(b) of the Bankruptcy Code. It required that the Chapter X plan of corporate reorganization be "fair, equitable and feasible." For almost forty years, the words "fair and equitable" have been judicially interpreted to require the application of the "absolute priority" doctrine; that is, each class of creditors and stockholders is given its proper priority, and the legal and contractual rights of each party are considered. Essentially, the absolute priority doctrine requires a full realization of senior creditor claims before junior creditors are allowed to participate in the plan of reorganization; similarly, the claims of junior creditors must be satisfied before shareholders may participate. Given this requirement to satisfy all classes of creditors and stockholders strictly according to their order of priority, it is necessary to determine the amounts owed to each class and the value of the business. Thus, one of the purposes of the reorganization is to provide an equitable distribution of the debt claims (and equity claims, if there are any) to assets among both the creditors and shareholders of the corporation. For this to be done, the court must assign a value to the securities issued to participants in the reorganization. Nothing except a speculative value could be assigned to the newly issued securities if no valuation were made of the debtor's business on a going concern basis. Hence, the corporate reorganization could hardly be deemed to be fair and equitable to everyone without a valuation and an allocation of those values to each class of creditors and interests designated by the plan.

Bankruptcy Code Provisions

28 The relaxed absolute priority doctrine described in the following paragraphs requires valuation of a chapter 11 debtor's business if any class of secured creditors' claims, unsecured creditors' claims, or stockholders' interests does not approve the plan and is impaired under the plan.

Secured Claims

29 For the courts to force the acceptance of a plan upon the holders of secured claims according to section 1129, the plan must provide for at least one of the following:

1 The holder retains the lien on the property up to the allowed amount of the claim. If the debtor elects to have section 1111(b)(2) apply (under which the entire debt is considered secured even though it exceeds the value of the collateral), the creditor is entitled to have the entire allowed amount of the debt secured by a lien even if the value of the collateral is less than the debt. In addition, the holder receives, on account of the allowed secured claims, payments, either present or deferred, of a principal face amount equal to the amount of the debt and of a present value equal to the value of the collateral.

2 The sale, subject to section 363(k) of the Code, of any property that is subject to the claimants' lien securing such claims, free and clear of such lien, with the lien to attach to the proceeds of the sale and the subsequent treatment of the lien consistent with clause 1 or 3 of this paragraph.

3 Realization by the holder of indubitable equivalent of the claim.

30 Note that in condition one above, it is necessary to determine two values — one for the collateral and the other for the present value of future payments called for under the plan. To determine the value for this section of the Code it is generally not necessary to value the business, but rather the individual assets constituting the collateral. The approaches used to determine the value for secured creditors in section 506 would also apply here; however, the creditor is not bound by any value placed on the property for the purpose of determining secured claims. The present value of future payments is determined by discounting the value to be received in the future to the present. The Code does not provide any guidance as to what should be the basis for determining the rate to use in discounting future value. This does not, however, mean that the interest rate should be assumed to be the discount rate.

Unsecured Claims

31   One of two standards must be satisfied before the plan can be confirmed where there is a dissenting class of impaired unsecured creditors. First, the plan may provide that the dissenting class receive or retain property that has a present value equal to the allowed amount of the claim. Note that if the proposed property was a present cash payment, the claim would not be impaired under section 1124(3)(A). The value to be assigned to the property would, it appears, be based on the nature of the property (deferred cash, securities and so on) and the conditions surrounding the transfer. The second standard states that the plan can provide for any fair type of treatment as long as junior creditors or stockholders do not participate in the plan and will not retain any claim against or interest in the debtor. The dissenting class has the right to prevent senior classes from receiving more than full compensation and to prevent equal classes from receiving preferential treatment. To determine if any class has received more than full compensation, it will be necessary to determine the value of the consideration given. If any consideration is stock of the debtor corporation, it will be necessary to value the business on a going concern basis.

32   The significance of this relaxed absolute priority doctrine is the flexibility and the leverage it may provide to creditors in the formulation of a plan of reorganization. If the principal creditors of W Corp. have security interests in all the assets of the business, it is possible that trade creditors will receive little and stockholders will receive nothing under the plan. If W Corp. has publicly traded securities and management hopes to preserve an opportunity for future equity capitalization, management may want very much to give up a little something to the old stockholders; or it may have another motive to do so. The holders of secured claims may agree and be willing to give up some of their compensation to be on good terms with or to bargain for the acceptance of the stockholder class. Such a proposed plan, which does not satisfy the absolute priority rule of Chapter X (because the senior, trade creditors are impaired but are not paid in full while stockholders participate), could be confirmed if all classes accepted the plan. Hence chapter 11 is more flexible than former Chapter X. The ability of the impaired class of trade creditors to bar the payment (or retention) of any consideration to the stockholder class by invoking section 1129(b)(2)(B)(ii) may persuade the holders of secured claims against W Corp. to give up a little more to the trade creditors to bargain for their acceptance of the plan. Hence certain classes of creditors may obtain an element of leverage (if only equal to nuisance value) in chapter 11 reorganizations as a result of the fair and equitable confirmation standards.

Stockholders' Interest

33   As with unsecured creditors, one of two standards must be met before a plan can be confirmed with a dissenting class of stockholders. The first

standard states that each member of a class must receive or retain on account of such interest property of a value, as of the effective date of the plan, equal to the greatest of any liquidation preferences, redemption price, or the value of their interest. If the dissenting class consists of common stockholders, the plan must provide for them to receive property with a present value equal to the value of their ownership based on a going concern valuation because the stock will not have a liquidation or redemption value. If the debtor is insolvent, then the stockholders will not be entitled to any compensation. The second standard will allow any kind of fair treatment as long as junior interests do not receive any property or retain any interest in the debtor as analyzed above. This would appear to indicate that any kind of treatment for common stockholders would be acceptable since there are no interests junior to the common stockholder.

34 However, if there is any value, based on a going concern valuation, to the common stockholders and the plan does not provide for their interest and they dissent to the plan, it would not be confirmed because by necessity some senior class is being provided for more than in full.[16] Obviously, the approach used to determine the value of the business and the claims and interest of creditors and stockholders must be based on the assumption of the going concern.

35 Even if there seems to be no value for the common stockholders, the new chapter 11 is flexible enough to permit them to retain something under the plan of reorganization with everyone's acquiescence or approval. One practical reason for throwing a bone to the stockholders is explained by Klee. Stockholders whose equity interests are worthless cannot prevent the plan from providing that the stockholders will retain no property and that the creditors will receive all the debtor's stock. But the stockholders can insist on their day in court. Since the stock will be part of the consideration distributed under the plan, a costly valuation of the business will be required to demonstrate that the stockholders have no interest in the business and that the unsecured creditors will not be overcompensated. Stockholders may be able to trade in the nuisance value of their fair and equitable protections by bargaining to give their consent to a plan that permits them to retain something.[17] See chapter 5, paragraphs 98 and 104–108.

36 To sum up the cram down permutations:

1 A class may be unimpaired and be deemed to have accepted the plan (section 1126(f)).

2 A class may receive nothing and be deemed to have rejected the plan (section 1126(g)); see 6.

3 A holder may accept the plan but be overruled by a rejecting majority; see 6.

4 A holder may accept the plan with a majority of its class.

[16] Klee, p. 146.
[17] Ibid., p. 145.

5 A holder may reject the plan but be overruled by an assenting minority and either:

   a receive treatment in the best interest of holders; or

   b defeat confirmation.

6 A holder may reject the plan with a majority of its class and either:

   a receive fair and equitable treatment; or

   b defeat confirmation.

Determining Feasibility

37 Under prior law, it was necessary for both Chapter X corporate reorganization plans and Chapter XI arrangement plans to be feasible. This requirement also concerned the question of value since a condition of feasibility is equated to the soundness of the proposed capital structure and the assurance of adequate working capital. The SEC suggests that the enterprise must have sufficient cash, working assets, and earning power to assure ample coverage of all financial obligations, including required capital expenditures as well as interest and principal payments on its debt obligations when due.[18] The feasibility requirement thus necessitates that the newly created entity have a reasonable prospect for successful business operations in the future. Since a debtor that remains insolvent after the confirmation of the reorganization has very little opportunity for future success, a reasonable and equitable valuation of assets was absolutely essential to Chapter X and Chapter XI proceedings. Section 1129(a)(11) also contains a similar requirement stating that confirmation of the plan will not be approved if the plan is likely to be followed by the liquidation or the need for further financial reorganization of the business (unless the plan so proposes). Thus the feasibility requirement of Chapter X and XI of prior law extends to the new law.

Determining Inconsequential Value

38 The election for the holders of secured claims to consider all of the claims secured in a chapter 11 case is not available if their interest in the debtor's property is of inconsequential value (section 1111(b)). Consider a creditor with a third mortgage of $400,000 on real estate in an excellent location. Because of a general decline in real estate values the property is currently valued at $1 million with a first mortgage of $800,000 and a second of $200,000 outstanding. The value of the claim may appear to be inconsequential in this case; however, the creditor may want to make an election under section 1111(b), especially if the value is expected to go up and the amount to be paid to unsecured creditors is expected to be low. While the

---

[18] 35 SEC 290, 297–298 (1953). See also *Group of Institutional Investors* v. *Ch., M., St. P. & P.R. Co.,* 318 U.S. 523, 539–41 (1943).

courts will eventually determine, to some extent, the meaning of "inconsequential," the accountant can provide information that can assist the courts in determining if the value is significant in this context.

39 Other sections of the Code also use an inconsequential value standard such as sections 522 and 554.

Codification of Value

40 Many provisions of the case law under the Bankruptcy Act have been added to the statutory language of the Bankruptcy Code. Thus, value is mentioned more frequently there than in the prior Bankruptcy Act. Among the other Code sections where a valuation is required are the following:

Section 101(17)—Valuation problems may arise in determining if an entity qualifies as a farmer as defined in this subsection.

Section 363(n)—Trustee may avoid a sale if price was controlled (collusive bidding) and recover an amount to the extent that the *value* of the property sold exceeded the sales price.

Section 503(b)—Compensation to be paid accountants and other professionals depends, among other factors, on the *value* of such services.

Section 506(b)—To the extent that the *value* of property pledged as collateral exceeds the claim, prepetition interest, reasonable attorney's fees, and related costs may be allowed.

Section 506(c)—Here *value* is associated with benefit in that the trustee may recover from property securing an allowed secured claim the reasonable costs of preserving or disposing of such property to the extent that it benefits the holder of the claim.

Section 522—Subsection (a) states that *value* when used in determining the property to be exempted from the estate of an individual means "fair market *value* as of the date of filing of the petition."

Section 541(a)(6)—Earnings from services performed by an individual debtor after the petition is filed are exempt from the estate. In situations where the talents of the debtor represent the most important asset of the business, significant valuation problems can arise.

Section 542(a)—An entity must deliver to the trustee all property, or the *value* of such property, of the estate as of the date the petition was filed.

Section 547—Contemporaneous exchanges must be for new *value,* as defined in subsection (a), for the transfer not to be considered a preference.

Section 548—Subsection (a)(2) states that one possible condition for a fraudulent transfer is for the debtor to receive less than a reasonably equivalent *value* in exchange for such transfer. Subsection (d) defines *value* to mean "property, or satisfaction or securing of a present or antecedent debt of the debtor, but does not include an unperformed promise to furnish support to the debtor or to a relative of the debtor." Subsection (c) also requires the determination of *value*.

Section 549(b)—In an involuntary case, any transfer during the involuntary gap period is valid to the extent of *value* given for such transfer. Services are considered *value* given and will have to be valued.

Section 550(d)—A good faith transferee from whom the trustee may recover property transferred has a lien on the property to the extent of the lesser of the cost of any improvements made or the increase in *value* as a result of such improvements. The determination of value could be very difficult here. For example, if property goes down in value after the transfer is made but before improvements are made and improvements then increase the value, will the transferee have a lien on the total increase? The time period used to determine the increase in value is also very important.

Section 723—Valuation problems will arise in assessing general partners for any deficiency of the partnership's estate to pay in full all claims.

Section 761—*Net equity* and *value* are defined in subsection 17 for commodity broker liquidations and used in subsequent sections of the Code dealing with the liquidation of commodity brokers. *Net equity* is also used in section 741.

41   There are other sections of the code that deal with value. These are presented to give the accountant some indication of the number of times value must be assigned to assets, liabilities, services, or the entire business.

LIQUIDATION VALUES

42   Liquidation values may have to be determined for several reasons. As noticed in paragraph 22, in order to confirm a plan of reorganization the court must determine that each creditor or stockholder will receive an amount not less than the amount that would be received if the corporation was liquidated under chapter 7. Liquidation values do not necessarily mean the amount that would be obtained in a forced sale but most likely refers to that amount that could be obtained in an orderly liquidation. The liquidation values will, in most cases, be much less than going concern values. For example, inventory in the garment industry is often worth no more than one third of the cost in situations where the business is liquidated.

43   To determine the size of the payment that could be expected upon liquidation, the accountant must establish the value of all assets that remain in the estate. Several methods are used by accountants to determine the immediate market price for the assets. The accountant may have another client in the same type of business who may be able to supply information about the values of some of the assets, especially inventory. The accountant may be able to reasonably estimate the values of the assets through earlier experience with companies in the same industry. In order to determine the value of plant and equipment, the accountant may contact the manufacturer or a used-equipment dealer. It is often necessary for the court or the creditors' committee to employ an auctioneer or appraiser to evaluate the assets. The assets listed will include not only the property on hand but also whatever may be recovered, such as assets concealed by the debtor, voidable preferences, any questionable transactions involving payments to creditors, returns of merchandise to vendors, sales of fixed assets, and repayment of loans to owners.

44 In determining liquidation values, certain outlays that would be necessary if the debtor's estate was liquidated under chapter 7 must be considered. Examples include expense of administration, priority claims, and costs of avoiding certain transfers and related costs associated with the recovery of assets for the benefit of the estate. The liquidation value of the business, therefore, is a projected evaluation of asset recoveries net of estimated expenses.

GOING CONCERN VALUATION[19]

45 The balance of this chapter will be devoted to a discussion of the method used to value a business on a going concern basis. To establish the background for this approach, it is necessary to look at how the going concern value was established in Chapter X corporate reorganizations under the Bankruptcy Act

46 The appropriate method for valuing a business in Chapter X proceedings was established in 1941 by the U.S. Supreme Court's decision in *Consolidated Rock Products Company* v. *DuBois*. In regard to the importance of determining the value of the debtor's assets, the Court stated:

> A prediction as to what will occur in the future, an estimate, as distinguished from mathematical certitude, is all that can be made. But that estimate must be based on an informed judgment which embraces all facts relevant to future earning capacity and hence to present worth, including, of course, the nature and condition of the properties, the past earnings record and all circumstances which indicate whether or not that record is a reliable criterion of future performance.[20]

47 Thus, the proper method of valuation of the business as a going concern is the assessment based on future earnings, rather than the utilization of a procedure based on either the market value of outstanding stocks

[19] Part of this section is based on an article by Grant W. Newton and James J. Ward, Jr. which appeared in the *CPA Journal*, August 1976, pages 26–32. Reprinted with permission of *The CPA Journal*, © 1976, New York State Society of Certified Public Accountants.
[20] 312 U.S. 510, 526 (1941).

[handwritten annotation at top: going concern value is based upon (1) the prospective future earnings of the company and (2) the appropriate rate of capitalization.]

and bonds or on the book value of the corporation's assets. The two factors through which the going concern value is derived are the prospective future earnings of the company and the appropriate rate of capitalization.

48 Before discussing the factors, it is important to note several exceptions to going concern valuation principles based on earnings and a capitalization rate. First there may be some situations where an appraisal of the assets is the best way to value a company. For example, consider a nonprofit corporation where the principal assets owned by the debtor are the properties used by the debtor in rendering a service. Exhibit 10-1 contains a balance sheet and the related notes presented on this basis along with the auditor's report. Here Arthur Young & Co. was engaged to prepare a schedule of assets and liabilities with the value of the principal asset—properties—being based on an appraisal from two outside real estate consulting firms.

49 Second, despite the *Consolidated Rock Products* decision, the valuation of the holding or investment company at the time of reorganization is not based on the prospective future earnings of the entity, but on the present realizable market value of the securities on hand. This approach was selected even though the appellants argued that the "going concern" value should be used to include matters such as increases in the value of securities held, increases in dividends, and "restoration of 'leverage' through the borrowing of money and the earnings of skilled management in the purchase and sale of securities."[21] It should be noted, however, that the securities held by the company in question did not represent a controlling interest in any company.

50 The rationale for the market approach is logical. The investment company has no fixed assets oriented to a particular function as would an industrial business; moreover, a specialized service is rendered only in the sense that the company offers diversification of investment and management of assets.[22] The market value is the fundamental valuation criterion used in the investment field when the debtor's shares comprise only a noncontrolling interest in another entity. The situation, however, is substantially altered when the debtor's only assets consist of stock shares representing total control of other businesses. Under such circumstances, it is apparent that the debtor's financial outlook is completely dependent upon the financial success or failure of the wholly owned entities. Accordingly, the debtor's valuation is based on the future earnings of those entities capitalized at the appropriate rate.[23]

51 Third, as discussed above, liquidation values are used in the case of an individual holder of a claim or interest who does not accept the plan. A fourth exception to going concern valuation occurs when the liquidation value is higher than the going concern value. In this case, it is best to

---

[21] *Central States Electric Corp.* v. *Austrian*, 183 F.2d 879, 884 (4th Cir. 1950), *cert. denied*, 340 U.S. 917 (1951).

[22] Ibid.

[23] *In re Equity Funding Corporation of America*, 391 F. Supp. 768 (C.D. Cal. 1975).

Exhibit 10-1   Example of Value Determined by Appraisal

ARTHUR YOUNG & COMPANY

515 South Flower Street
Los Angeles, California 90071

Richard E. Matthews
Trustee—Pacific Homes

The accompanying schedule of assets at estimated values and liabilities of Richard E. Matthews, as Trustee of Pacific Homes (Debtor) under Chapter X at December 9, 1977 was not audited by us and accordingly we do not express an opinion on it.

The schedule mentioned above has been prepared on a basis which includes an estimate of the value of the assets that the Trustee may call upon to settle existing liabilities and future obligations as it goes forward in operating its home and hospital facilities. It is subject to the many uncertainties which are described in the notes to the schedule of assets at estimated values and liabilities. It neither purports to nor does it present the financial condition of the Trustee as of December 9, 1977 in accordance with generally accepted accounting principles on a historical cost/accrual basis of accounting.

Arthur Young & Company

February 14, 1978

RICHARD E. MATTHEWS AS TRUSTEE OF
PACIFIC HOMES (DEBTOR) UNDER CHAPTER X

NOTES TO SCHEDULE OF ASSETS AT ESTIMATED VALUES
AND LIABILITIES

December 9, 1977

(Unaudited)

1. General

The accompanying schedule of assets at estimated values and liabilities of Richard E. Matthews as Trustee of Pacific Homes (Debtor) under Chapter X of the Bankruptcy Act has been prepared without audit utilizing the books and records of the predecessor entity, Pacific Homes, a California nonprofit corporation, as of December 9, 1977 and other available data including the appraisals discussed in Note 2. On December 9, 1977, the Bankruptcy Court converted the Chapter XI proceedings of the Federal Bankruptcy Act of Pacific Homes to Chapter X proceedings.

Exhibit 10-1 (Continued)

RICHARD E. MATTHEWS AS TRUSTEE OF
PACIFIC HOMES (DEBTOR) UNDER CHAPTER X

SCHEDULE OF ASSETS AT ESTIMATED VALUES AND LIABILITIES

December 9, 1977

(Unaudited)

Assets		*Liabilities*	
Cash	$ 875,039	Chapter X liabilities	$ —
Accounts and notes receivable, less allowance for doubtful accounts of $100,000	203,387	Chapter XI liabilities:	
		Accounts payable	202,025
		Accrued payroll and taxes	290,198
Prepaid expenses and supplies	74,969	Accrued property taxes	39,287
Deposits with vendors	126,496	Accrued expenses	11,246
Trust deed receivable	23,834	Unearned care fees to December 31, 1977 (Note 4)	601,000
			1,143,756
Home and hospital properties, at appraised market values (Note 2)	53,555,000	Long-term secured debt (Note 5)	20,699,481
Other assets:		Accrued interest on long-term secured debt (Note 5)	1,688,000
Funds held in trust pending final order of Court (Note 3)	1,467,332	Resident drawing and deposit accounts	31,956
Funds held in trust for resident drawing and deposit accounts	31,956	Unexpended designated gifts	63,103
Other	210,104	Pre-Chapter XI liabilities (Note 6)	1,716,526
Total other assets	1,709,392	Commitments and contingencies:	
		Future obligations for the accommodation and care of residents and other claims (Note 7)	
	$56,568,117		$25,342,822

See accompanying notes.

Exhibit 10-1 *(Continued)*

The accompanying schedule of assets at estimated values and liabilities has been prepared on a basis which includes an estimate of the value of the assets that the Trustee may call upon to settle existing liabilities and future obligations as it goes forward in operating its home and hospital facilities. It neither purports to nor does it present the financial condition of the Company as of December 9, 1977, and the related results of operations for the period then ended in accordance with generally accepted accounting principles on an historical cost/accrual basis.

The Trustee is currently operating the homes and hospital facilities from funds provided by monthly billings to the residents at rates dependent upon type of accommodation and level of care provided. Until such time as a plan or reorganization can be developed the future operations are dependent upon receipt of funds from such billings. It is anticipated that a plan of reorganization can be developed and approved by the Court whereby the homes and hospital facilities can continue to operate as a nonprofit organization.

Although the Trustee believes the assumptions are reasonable in the circumstances, it can provide no assurance that a plan of reorganization will be developed that will permit the Company to operate as contemplated by the assumptions nor can management provide assurances that actual future events will not differ materially from those contemplated by the assumptions used herein.

2. *Valuation of Home and Hospital Properties*

The values of home and hospital properties as of December 9, 1977 represent appraised market values based on a going concern nonprofit operation. These appraisals are as of October 13, 1977 and have been prepared by two outside real estate consulting firms.

All of these properties are security for long-term indebtedness (See Note 5).

3. *Funds Held in Trust*

These funds represent the proceeds from the sale of certain land and office buildings owned by Pacific Homes. Litigation subsequent to the sale as to whether such properties were security for certain long-term indebtedness caused such funds to be held in trust (in an interest bearing savings account) until the Court could rule upon the disposition of such funds. On January 30, 1978 a preliminary judgement was reached to release the funds to the Trustee. Approximately $850,000 of the funds are to be used in refurbishing of facilities and the remainder for working capital. This judgment is subject to the final findings of the judge. An appeal of the final decision may be made within 10 days after the decision is reached.

4. *Unearned Care Fees*

Prior to December 9, 1977, Pacific Homes while operating under Chapter XI had billed fees for the accommodation and/or care of residents for the month of December, 1977. The amount reflected as a liability as of December 9, 1977 is the amount of these fees to be earned during the period December 10 to December 31, 1977. The residents, approximately 1,700, will continue to be billed monthly

Exhibit 10-1 *(Continued)*

in advance for their accommodations and/or care at rates which are dependent upon the level of care provided.

5. Long-Term Secured Debt

Long-term secured debt obligations and accrued interest thereon are as follows at December 9, 1977:

	Total Debt	Accrued Interest
6% notes with mortgages or trust deeds on specified home properties and furnishings as collateral	$ 3,398,318	$ 187,000
First mortgage bonds, date July 1, 1970, on specified home properties and furnishings:		
(1) Series B, Principal due serially from April 1, 1975 to April 1, 1988; 9% interest payable semiannually on April 1 and October 1	4,610,000	115,250
(2) Series C, principal due serially from February 1, 1977 to August 1, 1996; 10% interest payable semiannually on February 1 and August 1	6,000,000	799,800
10% first mortgage notes due $52,654 monthly	5,991,971	549,500
State of California Department of Health 5% loan to bring certain facilities up to required standards	699,192	36,450
	$20,699,481	$1,688,000

6. Pre-Chapter XI Liabilities

Pre-Chapter XI liabilities represent the liabilities and claims of unsecured creditors as of February 18, 1977, the date Pacific Homes entered Chapter XI proceedings, and consists of the following:

Trade creditors-moratorium	$ 399,524
Trade creditors	206,905
Prospective resident deposits and resident prepayments (a)	98,888
Resident loans and advances (b)	497,013
Refunds due residents who left facilities under terms of contractual agreements (c)	514,196
	$1,716,526

Exhibit 10-1   *(Continued)*

a. These amounts represent deposits of $76,180 made by prospective residents and prepayments for monthly care of $22,708 made by residents. If a prospective resident moves into a facility the deposits are offset against amounts due from the resident. For residents who have made prepayments of monthly care charges, such prepayments are offset against amounts due from the residents upon withdrawal from the facility.

b. These amounts represent loans and advances made by residents to Pacific Homes prior to Chapter XI proceedings.

c. Under terms of contractual agreements with residents, refunds are due for amounts prepaid for accommodation and/or care costs. The amounts of the refund are determined under the terms of each resident's agreement.

7. Commitments and Contingencies

Liability for future accommodation and care of residents:

Under various terms and conditions Pacific Homes had agreed to provide lifetime accommodation and care on a prepaid basis, a fixed monthly basis, or combination of both prepaid and fixed monthly amounts. It is not at present practicable to determine the amount of the future liability for accommodation and care, as it is dependent upon future events such as life expectancy, cost of care, and the rate of inflation for each major component making up the cost of future care. There are approximately 1,850 residents who entered into such contracts, some of whom are no longer residents of the facilities but may have claims against the estate. Pacific Homes has sustained significant operating losses over the past several years before entering Chapter XI proceedings on February 18, 1977.

Lien by State of California on California Facilities:

Due to deficiencies of Pacific Homes in meeting the requirements of Section 16304 of the California Welfare and Institutions Code, which were present in prior years, the State of California, in October 1972, filed a lien upon all real property in California owned by Pacific Homes having an appraisal market value, of approximately $41,425,000 December 9, 1977. This lien, required by the Code, is primarily for the purpose of securing the performance of the obligations of Pacific Homes to the holders of its continuing care agreements. The lien has been subordinated by the State to substantially all of Pacific Homes long-term secured debt (See Note 5).

liquidate the company. Fifth, companies whose revenue is dependent upon wasting assets use the discounted cash flow approach. Another exception, which will be discussed later, involves the valuation of nonproductive and nonoperating assets. Having recognized these exceptions to the general rule, we now turn to a discussion of the factors to be considered in determining future earnings and the appropriate rate of capitalization.

Prospective Earnings

52   No universal formula exists for a certain and accurate estimate of future earnings. Thus, courts have concluded that "valuation must be determined on a case-by-case basis, and all relevant factors must be taken into consideration in each case in determining going concern values."[24] A survey of the literature and case law, however, reveals recurring factors which, though incapable of statement in concise formula fashion, will nevertheless prove instrumental in establishing valuation guidelines.

53   The logical first step to determine prospective future earnings is to evaluate "projected future sales and the estimated profit margin on those sales."[25] This evaluation of future sales may well be accomplished by means of a detailed analysis of the debtor's past operating history, information which may be of particular relevance to the court in its consideration of a plan of reorganization. Of course, past history is relevant only insofar as it is indicative of the future earning power of the corporation. If it is shown that the record of past earnings is an unreliable criterion of future performance, the court must form an estimate of future performance by inquiring into all foreseeable factors which may affect future prospects.[26]

54   Section 172 of the Bankruptcy Act required the bankruptcy judge to submit any corporate reorganization plan of a debtor whose indebtedness exceeds $3 million to the SEC for examination and report. While the role of the SEC under the Bankruptcy Code has been reduced, its influence will be felt for some time. The Commission has taken the position that past records of earnings must be adjusted or weighted to take into account unusual past conditions and reasonably foreseeable changes in the future. As an example, adjustments have been made for expected surges of new business from customers who had previously been unwilling to deal with a debtor whose past operating losses failed to inspire confidence.[27] Other examples of unusual conditions for which adjustment must be made are: the stability and prospects of the industry, the rate of obsolescence of assets due to technical developments in the industry, the efficiency and integrity of future management, increased expenses and possible alteration in competition within the debtor's industry.[28]

55   Closely allied to the problem of the weight to be assigned to past earnings is the difficulty in determining what year's earnings should be used as a base period. The SEC, in its analysis of corporate reorganization plans, has usually been inclined to eliminate—rather than adjust—abnormal years in the concern or industry and it has preferred to use earning trends instead

---

[24] *Moulded Products, Inc.* v. *Barry,* 474 F.2d 220, 226 (8th Cir. 1973).

[25] *In re Muskegon Motor Specialties,* 366 F.2d 522, 526 (6th Cir. 1966).

[26] *Protective Committee for Independent Stockholders of the TMT Trailer Ferry, Inc.* v. *Anderson,* 390 U.S. 414, 452 (1968).

[27] *Yale Express System, Inc.,* 44 S.E.C. 772, 780 (1972).

[28] *In re Chicago Rys. Co.,* 160 F.2d 59 (7th Cir. 1947).

of earning averages. Likewise, courts have steadfastly rejected estimates of future earnings based on unusual occurrences of prior years. In the case of *In re Keeshin Freight Lines, Inc.,* the court rejected the principal witness's estimates of earning expectancies because the two years in question had been subject to unusual events. In one of the two years, the company had purchased new machinery, thus significantly lowering its maintenance costs; in the other year, the company had received a 10 percent rate hike four months before its employees obtained their corresponding wage increase.[29] Predictions of future earnings based upon war-year revenues have also been rejected by the courts,[30] as have estimates obtained by disregarding the high and low profit years when computing the average profits.[31]

56   In any given case it is uncertain what years may ultimately be used as the base years. The SEC has in one instance rejected a nine-year earnings period for a department store and in another accepted earnings for a one-year period, although the latter was the highest on record for department stores throughout the country.

57   Another litigious area concerns the appropriate interest payments, based on the corporate debt, to be deducted in estimating future earnings. In the case of *Moulded Products, Inc.* v. *Barry,* the shareholders contended that utilization of the interest figure was inappropriate because the decision by management as to whether to capitalize the corporation through equity or debt was arbitrary. The court stated that interest payments on debt were to be deducted; not to do so would be "directly contrary to the basic approach courts have taken in the past to valuation of debtor corporations in reorganization proceedings."[32] The deduction from the estimated future earnings of 8 percent interest payments based on the corporate debt was affirmed in the case of *In re Imperial "400" National Inc.*[33]

58   The accountant, while assisting a chapter 11 debtor or trustee in the preparation of forecasts of future profits, should insure that all assumptions used in preparing the projections are clearly set forth and that they appear reasonable. The trustee must be prepared to explain the logic of each assumption, and this is especially true for any assumption which causes the forecast to deviate from past results. Any changes being implemented that will cause revenue to increase should be clearly identified for the judge. In addition, the projections should be adjusted for any changes to be caused by implementation of the plan of reorganization. For example, if debt is going to be reduced by 50 percent because of debt forgiveness and the issuance of equity securities, only the interest cost related to the remaining debt would be included. And finally, adjustments should be made for expenditure reductions from implementing cost efficiency measures.

[29] 86 F. Supp. 439, 442 (N.D. Ill., 1949).
[30] *In re Barlum Realty Co.,* 62 F. Supp. 81 (E.D. Mich. 1945).
[31] Supra note 22.
[32] Supra note 21.
[33] 374 F. Supp. 949 (D.N.J. 1974).

59 It has been consistently recognized that nonproductive and nonoperating assets that do not contribute to earnings should be valued separately. This separate category includes excess cash or working capital, income tax loss carryover, excess plant and equipment, other nonproductive property held for liquidation, and investments that are not related to the business of the company.[34] In determining the value of the assets in the *Yale Express* Chapter X case, the court used four components: capitalized value of earnings, appraised value of buildings, excess working capital, and present value of tax loss carryover.[35]

The Appropriate Capitalization Rate

60 In general, deciding the appropriate rate of capitalization of future earnings and predicting future earnings both face the same problem: lack of mathematical certainty. Nevertheless, even though no precise formula has been developed to determine the rate, general agreement does exist concerning the basic principles of choosing an appropriate rate. Virtually all would agree that the capitalization rate should reflect the market free-interest rate (based upon long-term government paper), to which is added an interest component that reflects the risk inherent in the enterprise and the industry. Thus, the basis for disagreement and uncertainty is provided by the assessment of the various factors contributing to the industry and enterprise risk.

61 As in forecasting future expected earnings, setting the rate of capitalization is best determined on a case-by-case basis, and any factors that appear relevant to a specific company's risk evaluation may be utilized to determine the rate of capitalization. Thus, when determining the appropriate rate of capitalization, courts have considered the cyclical nature of the industry, the number and character of the debtor's customers, the possible uncertainties in management, expenses and operations, the age and condition of the debtor's plant and equipment,[36] and the rate of technological progress in the industry.

62 Courts have also displayed a tendency to utilize in their calculations figures obtained from other companies within the industry, provided these companies are similar in nature to the debtor corporation. However, where the debtor has been compared to other concerns substantially differing in character, the courts have rejected the rate of capitalization so determined. As an example, in the case of *In re Muskegon Motor Specialties,* the expert witness had calculated the capitalization rate through utilization of the price earnings ratio of thirty-six selected auto parts manufacturers listed on the stock exchange. Since the debtor was an unlisted company with no real

---

[34] Henry B. Gardner, Jr., "The SEC and Valuation under Chapter X," *University of Pennsylvania Law Review,* Vol. 91 (January 1943), p. 441.

[35] Supra note 27 at 784 and 44 S.E.C. 886, 867 (1972).

[36] Supra note 25 at 527.

market for its shares—and its sales varied from four times as great to only one one-hundredth as great as the sales of the companies whose capitalization rates had been computed—the court concluded that a comparison between such entities would yield little beneficial information.[37]

63   The estimated reorganized value of the company should be compared to the market value of the securities. Obviously, these values will not necessarily agree. As a general rule, the estimated reorganized values will usually be greater than the market values of the securities for a short time after confirmation of the plan. However, if the assumptions underlying the calculations of the reorganized value turn out to be close to reality, then the securities' prices should approximate the reorganized value. The difference between the value of securities and the reorganized value should be evaluated to see if it appears reasonable. Any party who advocates a value which differs materially should be prepared to justify the difference.

64   In summary, all factors that could conceivably be attributed to the riskiness of the company should be considered in determining the appropriate rate of capitalization.

65   While the courts and the SEC have consistently valued companies by estimating the average earnings and multiplying them times a capitalization rate, a strong argument can be made that the discounting of future earnings would be a better approach. The current approach can place a larger value on the company than is justified if the average earnings value used is much higher than the earnings in the first several years subsequent to the reorganization, as is typically the case. At other times the value based on the capitalization of earnings approach can be too low. The process of determining the value of a business in chapter 11 reorganization needs to be reexamined, based on the developments of corporate finance in the last thirty years.

Determining Value

66   Once the capitalization rate and average projected earnings have been determined, the value is assigned as follows:

$$V = \frac{E}{R}$$

where V = going concern value of business
   E = average projected earnings for an indefinite time period
   R = capitalization rate
Most of the court cases refer to the capitalization rate in terms of a multiple which is the reciprocal of the capitalization rate. The earnings normally represent the net income after tax; net income before taxes and interest have been used on occasions, but not in recent years.

[37] Supra note 25 at 528.

SEC's Modified Approach

67   In reports issued by the SEC on a large number of Chapter X cases under prior law, the approach used above was modified and the courts on occasion accepted this modification. The value is determined on the basis of net income before interest but after taxes.

68   The following illustration of the calculation of the value of future earnings explains the procedure followed by the SEC in the *Yale Express* Chapter X corporate reorganization. This procedure was also adopted by the court.

69   In the *Yale Express*[38] case, the trustee estimated—based on the results of the first nine months—that the 1971 revenue of Yale Transport, the principal subsidiary of Yale Express, should be $10,902,000—an annual growth rate increase of 18 percent. For 1972, he selected a growth rate of 20 percent, since an increase in new business was anticipated, assuming that the approval of the plan of corporate reorganization would encourage companies that had previously refused to deal with Yale Express to do so now. Since the SEC estimated that some of this increase would carry over into 1973, a 15 percent growth rate was selected for that year. For the year 1974, a rate of growth of 11 percent was selected. The 1974 estimate was based on an analysis of the growth in operating revenue for the region where Yale Transport operates and for 20 carriers comparable to Yale. The results of this analysis are shown in Exhibit 10-2.

70   The trustee estimated an operating profit of 8 percent for 1974, and this ratio was used by the SEC. The net profit from operations was reduced

Exhibit 10-2   Operating Revenues, 1966–1970

Year	New England Middle Atlantic* ($1,000)	Percent Increase	Trustee's Selected Carriers ($1,000)	Percent Increase
1966	$546,578	—	$246,985	—
1967	569,955	4.3	254,135	2.9
1968	606,812	6.5	297,783	17.2
1969	738,974	21.8	331,402	11.3
1970	806,352	9.1	375,433	13.3
		Avg. 10.4		*Avg.* 11.2

* **Source:** Trince's *Red Book of the Trucking Industry,* 1971 Edition.

[38] Supra note 27 at 780, 782, 967.

Exhibit 10-3   Income Projections for Yale Transport

						($1,000)		
Year	Projected Revenues ($1,000)	Percent Increase	Operating Profit	Projected Interest	Net Profit Before Income Taxes	Net Income After Income Taxes (48%)	Net Income Plus Interest
1971	$10,902						
1972	13,082	20	$ 785	$162	$ 623	$324	$486
1973	15,044	15	1,053	159	894	466	625
1974	16,699	11	1,336	157	1,179	613	770

Note: Earnings value is determined by multiplying the earnings before interest after taxes times the chosen multiple. For 1974, the equation would be: $770,000 × 13 = $10,010,000.

by the amount of income taxes at the rate of 48 percent. Although interest in this case was considered only to the extent that taxes were reduced, the court's decision in the previously noted case of *Moulded Products, Inc.* v. *Barry* requires that earnings be reduced by the interest. Exhibit 10-3 shows the calculations leading to the net amount that was to be capitalized. The 1974 projections were used as an estimated level of earnings on which to construct an approximate value for Yale Transport.

71   As a basis for determining an appropriate capitalization rate, the SEC analyzed six publicly held motor carriers that in 1970 had revenues ranging from $23 million to $55 million. The average multiple for these six companies (derived by dividing the total market value of the equity plus principal amount of debt by the income before interest and after taxes) was determined to be 13.9 for 1969–71, as shown in Exhibit 10-4. For Yale Transport, a multiple of 13 was selected, taking into account primarily the company's past history and the fact that the earnings on which the valuation was based were not expected until 1974. Using the multiple of 13, the earnings value was determined to be $10,010,000 (see Exhibit 10-3).

72   The method used by the SEC to value Yale Transport attempts to follow the net operating income approach suggested by Modigliani and Miller.[39] This theory implies that leverage can only distribute the business

---

[39] F. Modigliani and M. Miller, "The Cost of Capital, Corporate Finance, and the Theory of Investment," *American Economic Review*, Vol. 48 (June 1958), pp. 261–297, and "Corporate Income Taxes and the Cost of Capital: A Correction," *American Economic Review*, Vol. 53 (June 1963), pp. 433–443.

Exhibit 10-4 Capitalization Multiples for Six Comparative Companies

(000s omitted)

	Market Value of Capitalization[a] as of			Net Operating Profit After Income Taxes but Before Interest			Multiples		
	12–31–68[b]	12–31–69[c]	12–31–70[d]	1968	1969	1970	1968	1969	1970
Branch Motor Express Company	$15,119	$14,752	$28,015	$1,894	$1,251	$1,869	8.0	11.8	14.9
Eastern Freightways, Inc.	13,253	12,604	23,693	865	765	1,362	15.4	16.4	17.5
Halls Motor Express, Inc.	23,789	17,471	24,854	2,044	1,310	1,362	12.5	13.3	18.2
Preston Trucking Co., Inc.	24,277	18,270	36,298	1,562	1,792	2,010	15.6	10.2	18.2
Smiths Transfer Corp.	22,841	25,784	61,994	1,894	2,400	3,804	12.0	10.7	16.4
Overnite Trucking Co.	32,386	32,220	55,818	2,449	2,644	4,284	13.1	12.2	13.0
Averages per year[e]							12.8	12.4	16.4

[a] Mean between high and low sale or bid prices of common stocks and debt at each year end taken at principal amounts.
[b] For year 1969.
[c] For year 1970.
[d] For period Jan. 1 to Oct. 31, 1971.
[e] Average multiple is 13.9 ((12.8 + 12.4 + 16.4) ÷ 3)

416

risk differently among the creditors and stockholders and that increasing the amount of borrowed funds does not increase the total risk. However, since interest is deductible for tax purposes, the larger the debt of Yale as it comes out of bankruptcy, the higher the value that would be assigned to the transport division. A 100 percent increase in debt will result in an increased valuation of approximately $1 million.

73 Exhibit 10-5 contains the average price earnings ratios (PER) for 1968, 1969, and 1970 for the same six comparable companies used by the SEC. Courts have frequently used these ratios to multiply times the net income after tax to determine the value of the equity interest. Using this approach, the value of the business would be the value of the stockholders' equity plus debt. The earnings used to calculate the PER was net income after tax and interest but before extraordinary items. Note that the average PER was approximately thirteen, which is the multiple used by the SEC. Using the PER of thirteen, and including the debt, the value of Yale Transport would be reasonably close to the value assigned to the business by the SEC.

74 In determining a value for Four Seasons Nursing Center of America,[40] the trustee used a PER of six and the net income before taxes to determine the value in a prior law Chapter X proceeding. In reviewing the approach used by the trustee, the SEC reported that it preferred to use a single multiple to be applied to earnings after taxes but before interest. The SEC further noted that a multiple of 10.6 would yield approximately the same value as determined by the trustee. Since this multiple of 10.6 appeared

Exhibit 10-5   Price Earnings Ratios for Six Comparative Companies

	1968	1969	1970
Branch Motor Express Co.	7.3	10.9	14.5
Eastern Freightways, Inc.	13.8	15.7	17.6
Halls Motor Express, Inc.	11.9	11.6	31.7
Preston Trucking Co., Inc.	15.3	10.3	17.2
Smiths Transfer Corp.	9.8	8.3	6.3
Overnite Trucking Co.	10.3	11.6	18.8
Average per year	11.4	11.4	17.6
Average for three years			13.5

Value of stockholders' equity using multiple of 13 is $7,969,000 ($770,000 net income less interest of $157,000 times 13).

[40] 44 SEC 821 (1971).

to be reasonable, the SEC adopted it. One problem in selecting a multiple for Four Seasons was the great variability in multiples for other health care chains. For the eleven companies selected by the trustee, the price earnings ratios varied from fifty-seven to 700 in 1969. Four Seasons had a multiple of 184. For 1971 the range was from thirteen to ninety-three. The multiples were not available for two companies in 1969 or 1971. The SEC noted that the 1969 multiples did not reflect genuine investment values, but were symptoms of a dazzling euphoria that had gripped the market. The 1971 prices were some evidence of a return to some realism, although a skeptic may still discern some elements of lingering afterglow.[41]

75   The manner in which earnings and capitalization rate have been calculated and used by the SEC has varied from one case to another. For example, in some cases the next year's earnings were used to determine the net income to multiply times the capitalization multiple. In other cases the earnings expected in three or four years were used. An attempt was made, however, to justify each of these changes on the basis of economic conditions and other relevant environmental factors.

Discounting Cash Receipts or Profits

76   One method frequently suggested as a viable approach to value a firm in bankruptcy is to discount future receipts. To use this method, reasonable estimates of future cash receipts must be obtained along with the liquidation or residual value at the end of the investment period. Or, alternatively, a stable cash flow must be expected indefinitely. Under certain conditions it may be reasonable to substitute profit for cash flows. For many companies, the cash inflows will be less than earnings during growth periods and toward the end of the life cycle cash inflows would exceed the reported profits.

77   In *Equity Funding Corporation of America*[42] the court allowed the use of discounted future profit flows as a basis to value part of the company on the argument that special factors may make the usual approach using past earnings reports and future sales and expense projections an unreliable guide. The court concluded that since the insurance companies (Bankers and Northern) owned by Equity Funding reported their earnings on the basis of statutory accounting as prescribed by state insurance departments, these records are "particularly unreliable indicators of future earning expectancy because both companies have substantially increased their new business production and have made significant changes in the nature of their operations and types of insurance sold during the administration of the estate.[43]

78   The value for Northern and Bankers was then developed by looking at three separate income streams coming from their in-force business, their

---

[41] Ibid., pp. 839–841.
[42] 416 F. Supp. 132 (1975).
[43] Ibid., p. 142.

future sales capacity, and their income from assets not attributed to policy reserves. The court summarized the approach allowed as follows:

1   The value of each company's existing business was determined by projecting profit flow from that business for 30 years and then discounting to present value at 15%.

2   The value of each company's future sales capability was determined by capitalizing five times the present value of the future profits from one year's production of business.

3   The value of the assets not attributed to policy reserves was determined by adjusting these assets to their market value. These assets are stocks, bonds, mortgages, and/or other investments that have a readily determinable market value. That market value is the appropriate measure of their value for reorganization purposes, since the value determined by investors in the marketplace is the best indicator of the present value of the future earnings of the assets.[44]

79   While the court was very critical of the type of past earnings records made available by the companies, it is possible that the use of this data may provide for a more equitable valuation. Statutory accounting requires that one-time payments be expensed in the first year of the policy, rather than spreading it over the life of the policy as allowed by GAAP. This is actually the type of information needed to estimate future cash flows. Other accounting requirements by state regulatory commissions are not in line with the actual cash flows. For example, most states require the buildup of reserves for new policies at a rate that is higher than experience would indicate is necessary. Another interesting aspect of this case is that cash projections were made for thirteen years beyond the expected confirmation date. A period of thirty years was used to discount future "profit flows." It appears that the thirteen years of cash flow projections could have served as the basis for thirty years of cash flow projections, thus allowing for cash flows to be discounted rather than profits.

An Alternative Approach

80   The use of the price earnings ratio (PER) valuation approach has the advantage of being easily explained to those in court who are not well trained in finance. There are several problems associated with its use. For most firms in bankruptcy, prior ratios are often not a valid indication of future ratios. This is true for several reasons. Recent past years are not appropriate because the business sustained losses during this time period. Also, many business and operational changes may have been made resulting in a differ-

---

[44] Ibid., p. 144.

ent type of operation, or major segments of the business may have been eliminated.

81   The bankruptcy courts have consistently used the PER of comparable companies. The net result is an average rate that may have little value. The rate in Four Seasons as discussed above was from fifty-seven to 700. Many factors cause these ratios to be different among similar size firms in the same industry. There is no indication that the business emerging from bankruptcy will have the characteristics to cause the PER to be the average of that of other companies. The assumption is also made that these firms are properly priced. These ratios may contain temporary increases or decreases in earnings that distort the results. The PER for companies with the same type of operations and debt structure may differ because of the accounting methods used to report income. In pricing the stock the market took into consideration these accounting differences. Yet when the court simply uses the average PER it is ignoring the adjustments made by the market. Finally, historical PERs are used and the value of the business must be in terms of the future.

Estimating a Rate

82   An alternative to using PER to determine the capitalization rate would be to estimate directly a required rate of return and use this to value the firm. The rate of return might consist of the yields of long-term corporate bonds plus an adjustment for ownership that reflects the systematic risk of the company. Ibbotson and Sinquefield[45] indicate that from 1926 to 1976 the average annual geometric return for long-term corporate bonds was 4.1 percent and the ownership premium was 4.9 percent for a common stock value of 9 percent. The systematic risk, which refers to the average relationship between the company's stock price and the market price, is measured for publicly traded companies using a beta coefficient. If, for example, the beta coefficient for a company is 1.2, this value would be multiplied times the 4.9 average percent ownership premium to arrive at a premium to add to the corporate bond rate to determine the total return.

83   Other adjustments may be necessary. In bankruptcy cases when the plan calls for a debt/equity ratio that is higher than the industry average, an upward adjustment may be necessary to compensate for the high risk. For corporations privately held, a higher rate may be necessary to compensate for the lack of liquidity for owners. Likewise, adjustment must be made for situations where the corporation is controlled by owners and not diversified adequately.

84   The use of a rate developed apart from the PER of comparative companies may, in fact, accomplish the objective of selecting a rate that is

---

[45] Roger G. Ibbotson and Rex A. Sinquefield, *Stocks, Bonds, Bills and Inflation: The Past and the Future* (1982 Ed.) (Charlotte, Virginia: Financial Analysts Research Foundation, the University of Virginia, 1982).

representative of the risk inherent in a particular business. A rate based on risk identified by the beta coefficient should be as easily justified as using an average PER of companies in the same industry.

Using the Rate to Determine the Value

85 Once a decision has been made regarding a reasonable value for the rate of return, the next step is to use this rate to determine the value of the business. If the business has a limited life, the expected returns for the remaining life of the business could be discounted to the present as described earlier. For a business expected to last indefinitely, the reciprocal of the rate of return could be multiplied times the expected average annual earnings as used in most courts' decisions to date. Thus, the only change made is that the rate, rather than being determined by an average of comparable firms, is estimated directly.

Determining Assets

86 Section 101(26) of the Bankruptcy Code provides the balance sheet definition of insolvency: the debtor's assets at fair valuation are insufficient to pay his or her debts. The only assets exempt from valuation by this section are fraudulently transferred or concealed assets and, in the case of individuals, those assets exempted from creditors of the estate under section 522. Under prior law individual debtors were allowed to exempt these assets from the estate, but they were included in determining insolvency (except for purposes of fraudulent transfers). Fraudulent and concealed assets are excluded in the Bankruptcy Code definition even if they are discovered before insolvency or solvency is determined. For example, the cash surrender value of an insurance policy concealed by the debtor would be excluded.[46] Included in the property, however, would be intangibles such as patents, trade names, tort claims, and property rights.[47] Goodwill has generally been omitted from the assets, since it is considered in the accounting sense as the surplus arising from the difference between going concern value and cost value.[48]

Determination of Liabilities

87 The finding of insolvency is determined by a comparison of assets with liabilities. Thus, a proper determination of insolvency would depend upon the types of liabilities included. Under prior law, some uncertainty

[46] *Peterson* v. *Peterson,* 400 F.2d 336, 343 (8th Cir. 1968).

[47] Collier, 1 *Collier on Bankruptcy* (Moore, 14th ed., Matthew Bender & Co., Albany, N.Y., 1940 to 1975), Sec. 1.19(2).

[48] Thomas Burchfield, "The Balance Sheet Test of Insolvency," *University of Pittsburgh Law Review* (October 1961), p. 8n.

existed, however, as to the types to be included in the balance sheet test of insolvency because section 1(14) of the Bankruptcy Act stated that "debt" shall include any debt, demand, or claim provable in bankruptcy. On the other hand, section 63 of the act indicated that only provable debts share in the assets of the estate. The definition of debts as stated in section 1(14)— used in the determination of insolvency—conceivably extended the scope of potential beyond those listed in section 63. This is true because the use of the phrase "shall include" in section 1(14) suggested that liabilities other than provable claims could be included. This would mean that certain types of debts, such as contingent liabilities of guarantors and endorsers, could have been included for the purpose of determining the amount of liabilities even though a likely default was not proved and as a result the contingent liability was not a provable debt.

88   The Bankruptcy Code changed significantly the definition of liability. Section 101(11) defines a debt as a "liability or a claim." No reference is made in the Code to the concept of provability. A claim, as defined in section 101(4), means (1) right to payment, whether or not such right is reduced to judgment, liquidated, unliquidated, fixed, contingent, matured, unmatured, disputed, undisputed, legal, equitable, secured, or unsecured; or (2) right to an equitable remedy for breach of performance if such breach gives rise to a right to payment, whether or not such right to an equitable remedy is reduced to judgment, fixed, contingent, matured, unmatured, disputed, undisputed, secured, or unsecured.

89   A debt under the new law is broad enough to include all legal obligations of the debtor that give rise to payment no matter how remote or contingent. Thus, the bankruptcy court can now deal with practically all types of debts and provide for the broadest possible relief. Debts that are contingent or unliquidated must be estimated under section 502(c).

90   No doubt one of the major problems associated with liabilities will be the amounts that are secured and unsecured for undersecured claims. This determination, however, depends on the value assigned to the collateral (see paragraphs 9–14).

PART FOUR

Auditing Procedures and Reports

Audit Procedures and Special Areas of Inquiry

1 Reporting on insolvent companies requires the application of audit procedures that vary somewhat from those utilized under normal conditions. Much more emphasis is placed on the balance sheet. The audit of a company in financial difficulty is very similar in many respects to the audit of a company that is in the process of being acquired by another. Emphasis is placed on selected accounts and others are completely ignored. In a normal audit the accountant searches for unrecorded liabilities and uses great care to see that the assets are not overstated; however, in a bankruptcy audit the accountant must ascertain that there are no unrecorded or concealed assets.

2 The accountant must be on the alert for indications that occurrences out of the ordinary have taken place. Any transactions that could possibly result in the dissipation of the debtor's assets in a manner other than by loss in the ordinary course of business should be examined closely. These include irregular transfers, transactions with related parties, concealment of assets, false entries and statements, financing irregularities, or preferential payments. In the course of the investigation the accountant may discover a more serious type of irregularity that constitutes fraud. A comparison of the statements filed by the debtor with the company's records may reveal deliberate discrepancies, or missing books or records, erasures and alterations, or the age of the records may indicate that fraud exists.

3 The generally accepted standards and procedures that apply to the normal audit are also relevant to bankruptcy and insolvency proceedings. The financial statements should be presented in accordance with generally accepted principles of accounting.

4 Most of the emphasis in this chapter is on audit procedures that differ from those utilized under normal conditions. The term "accountant" as used in this chapter refers to an independent accountant for either the debtor (or trustee, if appointed) or the creditors' committee.

NATURE OF AUDIT

5   The steps performed in an audit or an investigation of a company in financial difficulty are somewhat different from the normal audit designed to render an opinion. There are aspects of the audit that are quite unique. Generally more emphasis is placed on the balance sheet and, as the audit or investigation progresses, more modifications of the assignment are required in bankruptcy engagements than in normal engagements.

Objectives

6   The purpose of the audit or investigation in most bankruptcy and insolvency cases is to assist interested parties in determining what should be done with the "financially troubled debtor." Should the debtor reorganize and continue operations or liquidate? Where this is the key issue the accountant may do a limited investigation of the major aspects of the debtor's operations to ascertain if the debtor can operate profitably again. In other cases, especially where there is an indication of possible fraud or mismanagement of the debtor's assets, there is a need for an audit or a complete investigation of the debtor's prior activities. Here the objective of an audit of the assets is to determine the existence and extent of understated or undisclosed assets. The accountant searches for hidden bank accounts, assets in the name of the owner that were purchased with the debtor's funds, preferential payments, valuable assets written off or sold without adequate consideration, and any other unrecorded or concealed assets. Emphasis in the liability accounts is placed on the discovery of transactions that resulted in the reduction or modification of liabilities. The debtor may have granted invalid liens to secured creditors or overstated obligations to related companies. The accountant will search for executory contracts that may have been incorrectly recorded as actual liabilities. The claims filed by creditors will be examined to see that they are not overstated. The equity accounts must be examined to determine whether there are any improprieties that would result in an increase in equity. The debtor may have purchased treasury stock illegally, received inadequate consideration for stock issues, or written off uncollected stock subscriptions.

7   In examining the income, the accountant looks for unrecorded sales, interest income, or other types of income where a failure to record may have resulted in an understatement of assets of considerable value. In the examination of the expense accounts, the accountant ascertains whether there were any payments for overstated or nonexistent expenses such as wage payments to fictitious employees or payments for purchases that were never delivered.

Balance Sheet Emphasis

8 In the audit of a liquidating business, all attention is focused on the balance sheet; the profit-and-loss statement is of very little importance. Even in a chapter 11 proceeding, less emphasis is placed on the income statement. The creditors want to know the amount they would receive if the debtor was liquidated, so that they can compare it with the amount promised under a plan. This does not, however, mean that the income statement is not important. In fact, not enough attention is given to the income statement, and especially to projected statements, in many reorganization cases. An analysis of the income statements for the past few years is helpful in predicting future profits, and the success of the business in the long run will depend on its ability to make a profit. Over several years, the income statements provide information about the types of expenses that should be eliminated. They pinpoint the time period when the profits began to decline and often give some indication as to the causes of the company's failure. In most proceedings, both the creditors and the stockholders would be better off if the company could be successfully rehabilitated. While the income statement does indicate areas where corrective action is needed, presenting historical statements is of little value if the nature of the debtor's operation has significantly changed. Of much more value are projected income statements and cash flows showing what future operations should look like with the debtor's changes.

9 The long-run profitability of the company often does not emerge clearly because long-range operating plans are not prepared or no analysis is made of the past operating results. One of the major reasons for this can be found in the background and attitude of the representatives of the creditors. Many banks, financial institutions, and other large credit grantors have a separate department that handles all accounts of debtors in financial difficulty. These specialists do not have the interest in the future of the company that the credit manager or a salesman for the firm would have. Their primary interest is in obtaining the maximum amount from a particular account. It is immaterial that they may be able to keep a debtor in business, even when this means that an account that may have represented a large amount of sales for ten or fifteen years will continue. The performance of these specialists is measured by the size of the cash settlement. The accountant is frequently in a position to be of considerable benefit to the debtor by using the income statement—historical and forecasted—to help all parties involved consider the long-term prospects for the company. However, as noted in the previous paragraph, the projected statements are often more helpful.

Modifications of Audit

10 Examinations of companies involved in bankruptcy and insolvency could be extended endlessly. Throughout the examination, a judgment has to be rendered by the accountant as to the extent of detailed work that must be performed. The accountant does not have a blank order to go in all directions and probe as deeply as seems necessary. If the accountant goes beyond the scope of the examination as set forth in the retention order, payment for the extra work may not be authorized. (See chapter 6, paragraph 19.)

11 If at any time major revisions in the scope of the examination are required, it is a good policy for the accountant to discuss the changes with the party or its counsel that the accountant represents, that is, creditors' committee, trustee, or debtor in possession. The accountant should point out the initial findings and give an opinion on the direction that the investigation or review should take. With a consensus from the interested parties the accountant will continue the audit. The accountant should be very careful when selecting one or two areas to concentrate on and consequently making a judgment on the other areas that are not feasible to cover. A year or two later the accountant may be open to criticism for not including certain areas that perhaps should have been examined. It takes a certain amount of experience and know-how to be able appropriately to tailor the scope of an audit to particular situations. Restriction of time, fees, and various other influences often limit the scope of the engagement.

12 The priority of work assignments can also be affected by outside influences. The debtor may be faced with imminent foreclosure, and the conditions under which certain debts arose may have to be determined immediately. Very often while the accountant is carrying out the work assignment in an orderly manner, the trustee may say, "Forget about everything else. Put four people on this problem and find out what happened." Or the trustee's attorney may demand that another problem area be examined. The interruptions may cause the progression of the scope of the audit to become disorderly, and as a consequence the same phase of the examination may be reperformed a second or third time. The accountant may become resentful of this type of pressure, but these are the realities of bankruptcy and insolvency engagements. They are *not* all conducted in an orderly manner, nor are they the traditional type of examination. Pressure upon the attorney for the debtor in possession or the trustee, or even the attorney for the creditors' committee is transferred to the accountant. The orderliness and scope of an examination sometimes become completely uncontrollable, especially in the initial stages.

13 Since the audit of a company involved in bankruptcy and insolvency proceedings is not the traditional type of audit, the accountant's effectiveness will be measured in terms of creativity, imagination, and resourcefulness in finding out what really happened.

Audit Program Guide

14 An audit program guide for bankruptcy and insolvency proceedings appears on pages 466–485, at the end of this chapter. It is presented to assist the accountant in developing a program related to the needs of a particular engagement.

INTRODUCTION TO THE SPECIAL AREAS OF INQUIRY

15   The opportunity for manipulation of the books and transactions by the debtor means that the accountant must be on the alert for indications that occurrences out of the ordinary have taken place. Several types of transactions commonly found in insolvency cases demand extra attention on the part of the accountant.

Irregularities

16   An irregularity is any transaction that is not in the ordinary course of business, and especially includes any transaction that results in the apparent dissipation of the debtor's assets in a manner other than by loss in the ordinary course of business. The period of time during which irregularities may have occurred is not limited to the ninety-day period prior to the filing of the petition or the initiation of the out-of-court settlement. Instead, the time period covered during the audit may extend to a year or more, depending on the circumstances. The time period covered by the avoiding powers of the trustee is generally one year; however, it may extend beyond one year under section 544(b) availing the trustees of remedies under state law.

17   Irregularities are of utmost importance in the accountant's audit or investigation. The fundamental concern is with discovering transactions on the part of the debtor company that may act to bar it from a discharge of its debts, result in the recovery of assets, or provide information for a case for criminal prosecution. Recovered assets would enlarge the debtor's estate and make available a greater amount for distribution to creditors.

18   There are several common types of transactions that the accountant should carefully scrutinize as being suspect of irregularities. These will be briefly described here and the important items more fully covered in the remainder of this chapter.

19   *Fraudulent transfers*   These primarily include transfers made or obligations incurred by the debtor company, without fair consideration and within one year prior to the bankruptcy petition, that render it insolvent, leave it with an unreasonably small amount of capital, or are accompanied by the intent to incur debts beyond the debtor's ability to pay such debts as they mature. Fraudulent transfers also include those transfers made with an actual intent to hinder, delay, or defraud the creditors. Thus, for sales of assets made within one year prior to the filing of a petition, the accountant must determine whether a reasonable equivalent value was received and the effect or intent of such transfer. See paragraphs 46–66.

20   *Transactions with related parties such as insiders, officers, employ-*

ees, and relatives   It is especially important to ascertain that such transactions were made at arm's length, that fair consideration was received for any transfer of assets, and that there are no paddings, incorrect cash expenses, misappropriated receipts, or improper purchases. The withdrawal of assets by stockholders as dividends, loans, transfers of assets, etc., should all be very carefully examined for any manipulation or bad intent. See paragraphs 53–66.

21   *Concealment of assets*   This category usually includes an attempt to misappropriate property and hide the shortage. This is often difficult to prove since investigation must rely on records previously kept by the debtor. If it seems possible to show a concealment, turnover proceedings can be attempted, to regain possession of the property. See paragraphs 67–81.

22   *False entries and statements*   Common examples of this irregularity are mutilation or alteration of the books, concealment or destruction of records, forgery of any document, and issuance of false statements. See paragraphs 82–86.

23   *Financing irregularities*   These include any schemes whereby the debtor attempts to obtain goods or money using methods outside the ordinary course of business. The most frequently manipulated accounts are receivables and inventory. See paragraphs 87–97.

24   *Preferential payments*   These are defined as an irregularity by the Bankruptcy Code. Included are any transfers of property made by the debtor while insolvent, within ninety days (one year for insiders) prior to the filing of a petition, and in payment of an antecedent debt, when the effect of such payment was to cause one creditor to receive a greater percentage of debt than would have been received if the debtor was liquidated under a chapter 7 proceeding. In order for the trustee or debtor in possession to recover preferential payments from insiders on bankruptcy petitions filed prior to October 8, 1984, the creditor receiving the payments must have had reasonable cause to believe that the debtor was insolvent at the time of the transfer. Transactions that should be carefully examined by the accountant include sales of inventory or other assets back to vendors as an account offset that would favor certain suppliers, liens given to creditors in contemplation of filing a petition, and repayment of loans to certain creditors in anticipation of filing a bankruptcy petition. See paragraphs 98–105.

25   *Other types of transactions*   The types of transactions listed below should also be carefully examined by the accountant:

Any major acquisition, merger, or investment that results in a loss.

Bulk sales of assets or portions of the debtor's business.

Indications that the debtor deliberately allowed liabilities to increase, causing hardship to the more recent creditors. An analysis of the accounts payable may indicate that for several months prior to the filing of the petition, no payments were made on accounts even though new orders were being placed and some cash was received from sales.

Attempts on the part of creditors to inflate their claims (paragraphs 106–108).

Any potential assets that may increase the size of the estate if settled favorably for the debtor, such as pending lawsuits or insurance claims.

All other transactions that may have arisen outside the normal course of business.

26   The above list does not purport to include every type of irregularity possible in an insolvency case, but mentions only those most frequently encountered. Regardless of the reasons for any suspicions, the accountant's report should include any and all recoverable assets such as assets involved in preferential payments, assets concealed by the debtor, certain assets that have been sold and are suspected of being involved in a fraudulent transfer, and any other assets relating to questionable transactions. It is also crucial that the trustee's attorney be aware of such irregularities, in order to initiate proceedings to recover such property for the estate.

Fraud

27   A specific and somewhat more serious irregularity sometimes found in bankruptcy cases is fraud, or intentional deception in relinquishing some property or lawful right. This usually relates to the debtor's books and records (paragraphs 82–86), and may include a false oath in the administration period, or the filing of false schedules and the giving of false testimony under oath.[1]

28   The accountant normally attempts to discover fraud by comparing the schedules which the debtor has filed and the company's statement of affairs with the amounts for assets and liabilities as found in the books. Indications that fraud may exist include missing books or records; erasures and alterations; computer runs without underlying support; and evidence that the books were written at one point in time—a uniform color of ink, one handwriting, or an apparent age of the books that does not support the stated age of the books.[2]

29   In addition to its own penalties under commercial law, fraud acts to bar an individual debtor from a discharge of all debts under chapter 7 according to section 727. Section 523(a)(2) of the Bankruptcy Code provides that a discharge for a debt shall be denied to an individual when it has been proven

[1] Robert Bronsteen, "The Accountant's Investigation of Bankruptcy Irregularities," *New York Certified Public Accountant,* Vol. 37 (December 1967), p. 941.

[2] Asa S. Herzog, "CPA's Role in Bankruptcy Proceeding," *The Journal of Accountancy,* Vol. 117 (January 1964), p. 62.

that the debtor obtained money or property on credit or as an extension, renewal, or refinance of credit by issuing a materially false statement, in writing, representing the financial condition of the debtor (or an insider of the debtor). It is also necessary for the creditor to have relied on the false statements and for the debtor to have issued the statements with the intent to deceive. This standard is strictly construed. Nevertheless, it may generally be stated that any attempt intentionally to deceive creditors and thereby gain money or property will mean that the debtor remains liable for the debts so incurred.

30   Section 523(a)(4) also provides that debts for embezzlement or larceny are exempted from discharge. Thus, a debt resulting from willfully and maliciously taking of property of the debtor with the intention of returning the property or replacing it with actual value in a short time period, but where injury is inflicted even though intent was not to do so, is nondischargeable.

Proof of Fraud

31   To prove misrepresentation and thereby block a discharge of debt, the creditor must show the existence of three basic elements:

A fraudulent misrepresentation that is material (any substantial variation from the truth is considered material).

Moral depravity by the debtor in making the representation with the intent that it be relied upon.

Reliance in fact by the creditor.

Auditor's Responsibility for the Detection of Irregularities

32   According to Statement on Auditing Standards (SAS) No. 16 (Section 327), errors are basically defined as unintentional mistakes, and the term irregularities refers to intentional distortions of financial statements. Under generally accepted auditing standards (GAAS), the independent auditor has the responsibility, within the inherent limitations of the auditing process, to plan the examination to search for errors or irregularities that would have a material effect on the financial statements, and exercise due skill and care in the conduct of that examination. In addition to the procedures that the auditor judges appropriate in order to form an opinion on financial statements, extended procedures are required if evidence indicates that material errors or irregularities might exist. The scope of the auditor's examination would be affected by consideration of internal accounting control, by results of substantive tests, and by circumstances that cause uncertainty about management's integrity.

33 SAS No. 1[3] suggests the following approach to the auditor's evaluation of internal accounting control:

1 Consider the types of errors and irregularities that could occur.
2 Determine the accounting control procedures that should prevent or detect such errors and irregularities.
3 Determine whether the necessary procedures are prescribed and are being followed satisfactorily.
4 Evaluate any weaknesses—that is, types of potential errors and irregularities not covered by existing control procedures—to determine their effect on (1) the nature, timing, or extent of auditing procedures to be applied and (2) suggestions to be made to the client.

34 The auditor's examination includes substantive tests that are designed to obtain evidential matter indicating the possibility of errors or irregularities even in the absence of the material weaknesses in internal accounting control. Examples of such circumstances could include the following:

1 Discrepancies within the accounting records, such as a difference between a control account and its supporting subsidiary records.
2 Differences disclosed by confirmations.
3 Significantly fewer responses to confirmation requests than expected.
4 Transactions not supported by proper documentation.
5 Transactions not recorded in accordance with management's general or specific authorization.
6 Completion of unusual transactions at or near year-end.

35 The auditor should be aware of the importance of management's integrity to the effective operation of the internal accounting control system. The following circumstances could cause the auditor to be concerned about the possibility that management may have made material misrepresentations or overridden internal control procedures:

1 The company does not correct material weaknesses in internal accounting control that are practicable to correct.
2 Key financial positions, such as controller, have a high turnover rate.
3 The accounting and financial functions appear to be understaffed, resulting in a constant crisis condition and related loss of controls.

[3] *Codification of Auditing Standards* (New York: American Institute of Certified Public Accountants, 1984), Sec. 320.65–66.

Methods of Discovering Irregularities and Fraud

36   The accountant's major source for the discovery of unusual transactions is the debtor's books and records. In a liquidation proceeding where it is believed that documents may be missing, the accountant may request the trustee to arrange to have all mail addressed to the debtor delivered to the trustee instead. In this manner, all checks received can be recorded and deposited, improprieties might be revealed by correspondence, and any gaps in the current records may be filled in.[4] An analysis of purchase returns may also reveal fraud.

37   The following is a list of schedules that, when prepared, may aid the accountant in the discovery of irregularities. Each worksheet includes those accounts most subject to manipulation:

A schedule of all payments made by the debtor preceding the filing of the petition, to determine whether any preferential payments were made to creditors. Such a schedule should include all major payments made during the period from insolvency or during the ninety days preceding the filing of the petition and all payments to insiders made during the twelve months preceding the filing of the petition.

A worksheet of changes in major creditors' accounts, to indicate whether any payments were made to certain creditors for current or prior purchases and whether certain suppliers were being favored through substantial returns or other offsets.

A report of all repayments of debt, to ascertain whether some creditors were paid in anticipation of the filing of the petition. Especially included should be repayments to officers, directors, stockholders, and other related parties.

A schedule of the sale of fixed assets, to reveal any sales to creditors for less than full value, to creditors as an account offset, or back to the manufacturer for cash or as an account offset.

A study of the trend of liabilities, purchases, and sales, to indicate the pattern by which debts grew, whether purchases were not being paid for even though sales were large, and whether this was occurring to the detriment of the debtor's more recent creditors. This report would be of value in establishing the intent of the debtor, always a difficult procedure.

A reconciliation of the creditors' account balances per the debtor's books with the creditors' claims filed, including, if possible, explanation of any differences between the creditors' claims and the debtor's books.[5]

---

[4] Bronsteen, p. 935.
[5] Edward A. Weinstein, "Accountants' Examination and Report in Bankruptcy Proceedings," *New York Certified Public Accountant*, Vol. 35 (January 1965), pp. 36–38.

38 Even if the accountant harbors no suspicions about the debtor's actions, all transactions should be described in as much detail as possible and their effect upon the financial position of the business should be analyzed. Two different approaches have most commonly been used in reporting the debtor's history. One approach is a chronological index which is simply a schedule including a monthly chronology of all major inflows and outflows of cash and all major unusual transactions. Another approach consists of a narrative description that outlines the sequence of events. Either approach, used as a normal audit procedure, would give indications of those areas where the accountant should conduct further inquiry.

AVAILABILITY OF BOOKS AND RECORDS

Locating and Obtaining Possession of the Records

39 After receiving the retention order, one of the first steps performed by the accountant is to take an inventory of the debtor's books and records and their condition. At the same time, examples of documents used by the business may be obtained. These are helpful in outlining the nature of the operations of the business, in determining how its systems operate and its procedures flow, and in identifying the responsible parties. For some types of audits—for example, where a broker or dealer in securities is involved— examination of documents is absolutely essential. Ideally, management should prepare for the accountant the list of books and records and certify that the list is complete. If the records are turned over to the accountant, the list should be signed indicating receipt of the records.

40 In a chapter 7 or other liquidation proceeding or a situation where fraud is suspected, the accountant will assist the trustee or creditors' committee in securing all the debtor's books and records and transferring them to the accountant's office. Speed is of the utmost importance in the removal process for several reasons. Such records often disappear with no explanation as to their whereabouts. They may be disposed of innocently by persons who have no idea of their value. The trustee normally wants to vacate the premises as quickly as possible, to minimize rental expense. Thus, quick removal means greater assurance that the records will be adequately safeguarded. It is highly desirable for the accountant to supervise this activity, since the accountant is best able to determine which books are most useful and therefore should be preserved.

41 In a proceeding where the debtor remains in possession, the debtor will retain the records but the auditor will ascertain that all records are accounted for. The books cannot be removed if the entity continues in existence. Even under these conditions it is good practice to have management prepare a list of the books and records. The list should be signed by management and placed in the auditor's file for future reference.

42 It is important to realize that, as an appointee of the court, the accountant is correspondingly entitled to see all of the debtor's books and records (paragraphs 43–45).

Scheduling the Books; Procedure
Followed for Missing Records

43 The accountant is responsible for preparing a list of all the books and records turned over by the debtor, and for ascertaining whether any records are missing. Any such findings must be reported to the trustee's attorney. It is then the duty of the attorney to establish the existence and location of the missing books and initiate proceedings to recover them if such action is deemed necessary.

44 Again, speed is crucial. The shorter the time period between possession of the books by the trustee and proceedings to obtain missing records, the higher the probability that the books will be successfully recovered.

45 The trustee's attorney may employ turnover proceedings to obtain the debtor's books and records. The accountant's role in this process would be to reconstruct the debtor's bookkeeping system in order to show what books were kept in the system and what books are therefore missing. Once the books and records have been successfully located and obtained, they should be very carefully stored and made available only to those persons who are authorized to have access to them.

FRAUDULENT TRANSFERS

Transfer of Assets Without Fair Consideration

46 Fraudulent transfers and obligations are defined in section 548 and include transfers that are presumed fraudulent regardless of whether the debtor's actual intent was to defraud creditors. A transfer may be avoided as fraudulent when made within one year prior to the filing of the bankruptcy petition, if the debtor made such transfer or incurred such obligation with actual intent to hinder, delay, or defraud existing or real or imagined future creditors. Also avoidable are constructively fraudulent transfers where the debtor received less than a reasonably equivalent value in exchange for such transfer or obligation and (1) was insolvent on the date that such transfer was made or such obligation was incurred, or became insolvent as a result of such transfer or obligation; (2) was engaged in business, or was about to engage in business or a transaction, for which any property remaining with the debtor was an unreasonably small capital; or (3) intended to incur, or believed that the debtor would incur, debts that would be beyond the debtor's ability to pay as such debts matured (see chapter 3, paragraphs 129–132).[6]

47   Section 548 of the Bankruptcy Code is based on section 67(d)(2) of the Bankruptcy Act. The trustee may avoid the transfers or obligations if they were made or incurred with the intent to hinder, delay, or defraud a past or future creditor. Transfers made without fair consideration are also avoidable if the debtor was or became insolvent, was engaged in business with an unreasonably small capital, or intended to incur debts beyond the ability to repay such debts even without proving the intent to defraud creditors.

48   Insolvency as employed in the determination of fraudulent transfers is defined in section 101(26) as occurring when the present fair salable value of the debtor's property is less than the amount required to pay its debts. The fair value of the debtor's property is also reduced by any fraudulently transferred property, and for an individual, the exempt property under section 522.

49   It is important to ascertain when a fradulent transfer has in fact occurred because it represents a possible recovery that could increase the value of the estate. It can, under certain conditions, prevent the debtor from obtaining a discharge. To be barred from a discharge as the result of a fraudulent transfer, the debtor must be an individual and the proceedings must be under chapter 7 liquidation or the trustee is liquidating the estate under a chapter 11 proceeding.

50   In ascertaining if there have been any fraudulent transfers made or fraudulent obligations incurred, the independent accountant would carefully examine transactions with related parties within the year prior to the petition or other required period, look for the sale of large amounts of fixed assets, review liens granted to creditors, and examine all other transactions that appear to have arisen outside of the ordinary course of the business.

Sales of Assets Below Market Values

51   Upon realization that a business is in financial difficulty, those who are involved may attempt to minimize their personal losses by removing the company's assets. Or the business may be a sham operation, meaning that the company was created solely for the purpose of obtaining personal gain at the expense of creditors. The methods used to accomplish such objectives normally involve the transfer of assets without fair consideration or for no consideration at all. The proceeds that are withheld from the business are kept by the owners and thereby concealed from the trustee.

52   The accountant should examine all sales of the debtor's assets for a period of at least one year before the petition was filed in order to determine whether any sales were made without adequate consideration. Any price

[6] 11 U.S. Code Sec. 548(a).

discounts that are recorded should be investigated, for these may have been paid in cash to the owners. The accountant should also be on the alert for any price variations and compare sales of merchandise made to various customers.[7]

Transfer of Assets to Insiders, Officers, Employees, Relatives, and Others

53 Any payments made to those with a close relationship to the business, such as the owners, their relatives, employees, or other businesses controlled by these parties, should be closely investigated by the accountant. The usual question is whether fair consideration was received for the assets transferred. Assets may also be given to companies controlled by the debtor's owners in payment of various goods and services at highly inflated prices.[8] For example, the owner of one corporation resolved to retire and sell his business to a senior employee. The amount received by the owner from the employee for the company's stock appeared to be reasonable. Upon closer inspection, however, the former owner (1) had substantially increased the rent which the business paid to an owner-controlled entity (2) was paid a hefty stipend by the business for unrendered consulting services and (3) received monthly payments from the business for a long term covenant not to compete. These hidden costs for the transfer of the business rendered it insolvent within 24 months, and the former owner was the largest creditor of the estate.

Audit Procedures for Related Party Transactions

54 The term "related parties" as defined in SAS No. 6 means the reporting entity; its affiliates; principal owners, management, and members of their immediate families; entities accounted for by equity method; and any other party with which the reporting entity deals where one party has the ability to significantly influence the other to the extent that one party might be prevented from fully pursuing its own separate interests. Transactions indicative of the existence of related parties include borrowing or lending at interest rates below or above current market, selling real estate at a price significantly different from its appraised value, exchanging property in a nonmonetary transaction, and making loans with no repayment specifications.

55 Generally accepted accounting principles ordinarily do not require transactions with related parties to be accounted for in a manner different from that which would be appropriate if the parties were not related. Thus, within the framework of existing pronouncements, primary emphasis is

---

[7] Bronsteen, pp. 935–936.
[8] Ibid., p. 939.

placed on the adequacy of disclosure of such transactions and their significance in the financial statements.

56 In determining the scope of work to be performed with related parties, the auditor should, according to SAS No. 6, obtain an understanding of management responsibilities and the relationship of each component to the total entity, evaluate internal accounting controls over management activities, and consider the business purpose served by each component of the business. Business structure and style of operating decisions should be based on management abilities and tax, legal, product, and geographical considerations, but are at times designed to obscure related party transactions. In auditing companies in financial difficulty, the auditor must carefully consider transactions with related parties. The following auditing procedures set forth in SAS No. 6 represent the type of work the auditor should perform with respect to related party transactions:

Procedures to Determine Existence of Related Parties

1 Evaluate the company's procedures for identifying and properly accounting for related party transactions.

2 Obtain from management the names of all related parties and inquire whether any related party transaction existed during the period.

3 Review filings with SEC and other regulatory agencies, record of pensions, other employee trusts, and prior years' workpapers for related parties.

4 Review stockholder listings of closely held companies to identify principal stockholders.

5 Inquire of predecessor, principal, or other auditors of related entities as to their knowledge of existing relationships and extent of management involvement in material transactions.

6 Review material investment transactions to determine whether the nature and extent of investment created related parties.

Procedures to Identify Transactions with Related Parties

1 Provide audit personnel with names of known related parties so that they may become aware of transactions with such parties during their examination.

2 Review minutes of meetings of board of directors and executive or operating committees for information.

3 Review proxy and other material filed with SEC and any other regulatory agencies.

4 Review "conflict-of-interests" statements obtained by the company from its management.

5 Review the extent and nature of business transacted with major customers, suppliers, borrowers, and lenders for indications of previously undisclosed relationships.

6 Consider whether transactions are occurring but are not being given accounting recognition, such as receiving or providing management, accounting, or other services at no charge.

7 Review accounting records for large, unusual, or nonrecurring transactions or balances, particularly those at or near the end of reporting periods.

8 Review confirmations of compensating balance arrangements for indications that balances are or were maintained for or by related parties.

9 Review invoices from client's law firms for indications of the existence of related party transactions.

10 Review confirmations of loans receivable and payable for indications of guarantees. When guarantees are indicated, determine their nature and the relationships, if any, of the guarantors to the reporting entity.

Procedures to Examine Identified Related Party Transactions

1 Obtain an understanding of the business purpose of the transaction.

2 Examine invoices, executed copies of agreements, contracts, and other pertinent documents.

3 Determine whether the transaction has been approved by the authorized party.

4 Test for reasonableness of the compilation of amounts to be disclosed in the financial statements.

5 Arrange for the audits of intercompany account balances and for the examination of related party transactions by the auditors for each of the parties.

6 Inspect or confirm and obtain satisfaction as to the transferability and value of collateral.

Additional Procedures to Fully Understand a Particular Transaction

1 Confirm transaction amount and terms with the other party.

2 Inspect evidence in possession of the other party.

3 Confirm or discuss significant information with intermediaries.

4 Refer to financial publications, trade journals, credit agencies, and other sources when doubtful of lack of substance in any material transaction with unfamiliar party.

5 Obtain information as to the financial capacity of the other party in cases of material uncollected balances, guarantees, and other obligations.

*Information to Be Disclosed Concerning Material
Related Party Transaction*

1 The nature of the relationship.

2 A description of the transactions for the reported period including any necessary information revealing the effects on the financial statements.

3 The dollar volume of transactions and the effects of any change in the method of establishing terms from that used in the preceding period.

4 Amounts due to or from related parties and, if not otherwise apparent, the terms and meaning of settlement.

57 The auditor will generally not be able to determine whether related party transactions are on a basis equivalent to that which would have occurred in the absence of the relationship. Accordingly, representations to the effect that the related party transaction was recorded on the same basis as an equivalent arm's length transaction are difficult to substantiate. If such a representation is included in the financial statements and the auditor is unable to reach a conclusion as to the propriety, he or she should include in the report a comment to that effect and express a qualified opinion or disclaim an opinion. If the auditor believes that the representation is misleading, he or she should express a qualified or adverse opinion, depending on materiality.

Padding

58 There are several ways the debtor can transfer assets to related parties. Included are padding, manipulation of cash expenses, abstracting cash, and improper purchases (inventory or equipment), loans, and sales.

59 Padding, a form of payment of cash without fair consideration, attempts to obtain funds from the business by adding fictitious claims to expense accounts and then retaining the extra payment. The most common example is payroll padding: checks are prepared for employees who have been terminated or for fictitious employees who have been added to the payroll. It is very difficult to detect payroll padding that occurred in prior periods. The payroll records can be compared with the salaries reported to the Internal Revenue Service, but the tax records may agree with the payroll records because they also have been padded. One of the first steps usually taken by accountants is to compare the payroll for the period audited with prior periods. If there are any differences, the auditor will then attempt to determine what caused them. The payroll records are also examined for unusual names, addresses, and amounts. Confirmation can be sent to past employees for verification that wages were actually received by the employee and that the employee really exists. The auditor should examine the files to see whether any W-2 mailings were returned. (See the audit program guide on page 485 at the end of this chapter for procedures related to the current period's payroll.) The supplies expense might be padded through the presentation of invoices for supplies that were never received. Or a repairs expense account could be enlarged by a claim for services never performed. The rent expense paid to a related party may be inflated by a substantial amount.

Cash Expenses

60   Manipulation of cash expenses may be accomplished in the same ways as in the padding schemes described above. Other abstractions may be accomplished through improper petty cash withdrawals by using fictitious vouchers or increasing the amount of valid claims. Checks may be drawn to cash without the proper documentation. Individuals may have the corporation pay for large personal expenses, such as travel and entertainment. The methods of obtaining funds from a business through improper cash expenses are unlimited.

Nondeposit or Diverting of Receipts

61   Individuals may abstract the cash from a sale or collection on an account and attempt to cover up the shortage in various ways. The sale may be recorded at less than is collected or unrecorded entirely.

Improper Purchases

62   Invoices for amounts greater than the actual purchase price may be submitted for payment of assets purchased. Employees may submit for payment by the firm bills pertaining to merchandise bought for their own personal use. Assets may be purchased from a supplier connected to the debtor by common ownership or some other arrangement for a price well in excess of the product's value. In completing a review of the financial statements, an independent accountant noticed that paid invoices for the same type of equipment purchased for a dealership owned by the largest shareholder of the debtor company were different depending upon who financed the equipment. The correct amount was paid for equipment financed by the manufacturer but for purchases financed by banks, the amount paid was much higher.

63   Purchase discounts may be unrecorded and the resulting overpayment retained by an owner. Again, the methods of manipulating purchases are numerous and similar to those found in a business not experiencing financial difficulties.

Improper Loans

64   Individuals may borrow funds in the company's name without recording the note on the books, and abstract the cash. During one audit, an independent accountant discovered sealed envelopes containing information about the notes the president had signed without authorization.

Improper Sales of Merchandise

65 A less obvious method of transferring or diverting assets out of the debtor corporation is by selling merchandise at ridiculously low prices to a newly formed corporation or to a relative or friend. To uncover this possibility, the accountant usually examines the sales invoices for the months immediately preceding the filing, compares the prices charged thereon with prices charged at least six months prior to filing, and attempts to establish whether any substantial reduction occurred in the selling price of the bankrupt's merchandise.

Sale and Leaseback Arrangements

66 Funds can be removed from the business in several different ways through the sale of assets under a sale and leaseback agreement with another company normally related in some manner. One company established an affiliate with all of the stock owned by the company's own major stockholders to purchase selected equipment and then lease it back to the company. The lease was then used by the new corporation as security to obtain funds from the bank to pay for the equipment. The lease was for a five-year term and was based on the value of the equipment and the amount of the payments; a provision in the lease that would allow the debtor to purchase the equipment for a nominal fee should have been added, but was not. Thus, after five years the value of the equipment had been fully paid but the debtor had to continue the lease payments in order to use the equipment, which had a useful life of at least ten years.

CONCEALMENT OF ASSETS

67 In an attempt to minimize their own personal losses, those involved with a debtor corporation may conceal the debtor's assets. Regardless of the type of assets involved, the basis for determining whether the assets on hand at the time of filing the petition were depleted by possible concealment is usually the financial statements as found in the debtor's files. The accountant should closely examine these statements and supplement them with statements from the files of the accountant who was retained by the debtor company before the petition was filed.[9]

Merchandise

68 Merchandise concealments or shortages must often be proven theoretically or technically, that is, through a reconstruction of the accounts

---

[9] Sydney Krause, "Accountant's Role in a Liquidation Proceeding," *New York Certified Public Accountant,* Vol. 28 (July 1958), p. 508.

rather than a physical count. The beginning inventory is ascertained from a financial statement or physical inventory and the purchases to the date of the petition are added to it. From this total, the cost of sales is subtracted, which should yield the value of the merchandise in inventory as of the date of the petition. After a physical inventory is taken, if a lower figure results, the difference represents the amount of inventory which has been lost or concealed.

69 As an illustration of transfers of inventory by the bankrupt in a fraudulent matter, it was reported to a trustee that trucks had been seen loading up at the doors of the bankrupt's stores within a few days preceding the bankruptcy. The trustee obtained a copy of the auction inventory sheets for the accountant, in the hope that the missing inventory could be established. Unfortunately, the bankrupt had been operating five-and-dime stores that stocked and sold hundreds, if not thousands, of different items. The accountant could not make an actual unit count. Although the number of units purchased within the short period of time the debtor was in business could be established, it was impossible to determine how many units were sold, since the sales records consisted of only the register tapes. However, the accountant did pursue the following approach:

Since the debtor was in business only a few months, the total amount of purchases made by the debtor for its stores was established from the paid and unpaid bills.

Since the debtor commenced its operations without any inventory, the only inventory available for sale was that which the purchase records clearly indicated had been procured.

The auctioneer indicated (on an overall basis) that the merchandise brought at auction approximately 50 percent of the cost. Accordingly, the accountant doubled the auction proceeds, that is, the gross auction proceeds, to arrive at the approximate cost of the inventory on hand at the bankruptcy date.

Therefore, the difference between the total purchases made and the inventory on hand for the auction at cost was the merchandise that had been used or consumed in the sales.

The records then indicated what the sales were—that is, what the debtor reported as its sales—and by deducting the normal mark-up for this type of store from the sales, the cost of sales was determined. As might be expected, the inventory that evidently was consumed for the sales was far in excess of the indicated cost value of the sales. As a matter of fact, even if it were assumed that all sales were made at cost and that there was no mark-up on the sales, the merchandise consumed still far exceeded the sales, a clear indication that inventory was missing.

Unrecorded Sales

70   Other assets may be concealed through unrecorded sales. Merchandise may be removed from the business with no consideration given or accounting entry made. The delivery of merchandise purchases may be diverted to the owners of the firm. Cash may be concealed by not recording the sale of scrap or waste or by recording a sale of good merchandise as a sale of scrap or waste with a lower value.[10]

71   Several methods may be employed to discover the diversion of assets by unrecorded sales. The gross profit earned in previous periods should be compared with that currently being received, and large drops in the amount should be investigated for possible uncompensated removal of merchandise. A schedule for the immediate period, including sales, purchases, and direct labor and production costs, should be prepared to uncover any unusual occurrences. Concealments might be discovered through a theoretical units merchandise audit, where a list is made by unit and dollar amount of the opening inventory, purchases, sales, and ending inventory. Individual, specific units of the merchandise might be traced through serial, style, or identification numbers. Purchase bills should be checked against receiving records. A schedule of all sales of scrap and waste materials should be prepared. And an analysis should be made of all the processing and contracting bills to establish that all raw material purchased and not now in inventory has been incorporated into the finished product and that all units that were processed were later accounted for either in sales or in the closing inventory.[11]

72   Merchandise may be held as collateral by creditors and not disclosed. Or, merchandise may never have been delivered by the supplier, although notes were issued in payment and the purchases are reflected on the books. Collateral may have been given for notes received by the debtor. The loans may have been entered on the books but the merchandise transferred or the collateral never recorded.

Cash Surrender Value of Officers' Life Insurance Policies

73   Although the purchase of life insurance policies on the lives of corporate officers is not a deductible tax expense for the corporation, it is often deemed advisable to obtain life insurance on the officers of the corporation in order to provide the cash funds necessary to repurchase their capital stock from the widow or estate. Consequently, a large number of corporations own such life insurance policies. The asset is the cash surrender value of the policy. Since the corporation normally is in dire need of cash funds prior to the filing of the petition, loans have usually been taken by the corporation

---

[10] Bronsteen, pp. 936–937.
[11] Ibid., pp. 937–938.

from the insurance company against the policies either for payment of the premiums due or for other working capital needs. The accountant can uncover the existence of these policies by finding proper entries on the corporate books of account, by the discovery of the policies themselves, by premium notices found among the paid or unpaid bills, or by entries made on the books such as payments to life insurance companies for premiums.

74 The cash value can be determined by an examination of the policy itself or by direct communication with the insurance broker or the life insurance company in question. At the same time, the accountant must ascertain the loan, if any, outstanding against the policy either from entries on the books or from information received from the insurance company. Also, the accountant must determine that all dividends receivable on the policies have been credited to the debtor corporation. Once this information is compiled, the equity in the policy is readily ascertainable. A judgment can then easily be made as to whether an offer made by a former officer of the debtor to repurchase the policy is equitable. It is interesting to note that most corporate officers are well aware that these policies are a good buy for themselves and their families and they quite often will make an offer to repurchase the policies for the equity therein, whereas they may not as anxiously provide other information having a bearing on the administration of the debtor corporation.[12]

Deposits and Security

75 Deposits and security are usually assets of the corporation arising from down payments made on the purchase of machinery or items of merchandise, or security left with landlords for the performance of the terms of a lease. Where a complete set of books is available, these items are self-evident and present no problems to the auditor. However, many examinations have not uncovered such assets until more detailed searches were made of the records.

76 Among the records the accountant seeks are leases and receipts for deposits left with utilities. Naturally, the leases clearly indicate the security left with the landlord and the utility receipts likewise provide the information on utility deposits. Down payments on the purchase of machinery or equipment are a little more difficult to uncover and the accountant often relies on information provided by creditors. A search of correspondence is often helpful in uncovering deposits of this nature. There can also be a corresponding liability for deposits or security, if the debtor was a landlord or manufacturer of equipment for which such deposits are usually required.

---

[12] Elliot G. Meisel, "Services Rendered by the Accountant to the Trustee" (accounting firm of Roberts & Leinwander Co.), p. 7 (mimeographed).

Investments and Real Estate

77 Investments in stocks or bonds can be uncovered from brokers' statements or payments to brokerage houses among the cash disbursements. Investments in real estate usually appear in the form of unusual cash disbursements, that is, disbursements that normally would not be made for the business under review. Again, examination of the correspondence files will often lead to the discovery of such investments, and a reading of the minute books of the corporation can be a lead to such assets. Included in this category is the ownership of subsidiary companies whose stock may have value (where the subsidiaries are solvent corporations). An abundance of transactions with another corporation, clearly not in the nature of normal purchases by the debtor corporation, usually indicates an affiliation with that corporation through holdings of common stock, or a relationship of parent and subsidiary companies. A debtor corporation is often found to be the parent company of a real estate corporation that owns the premises from which the debtor corporation had conducted its business. The real estate frequently turns out to be quite valuable, notwithstanding the fact that usually the mortgages are substantial in amount.[13] Ownership of real estate by a debtor corporation is apparent where tax payments are made to the local real-estate taxing authorities or where payments of similar amounts are made to banks on a monthly or quarterly basis, indicating mortgage payments.

Machinery and Equipment

78 The accountant's inventory or an auctioneer's report will show the machinery and equipment located at the premises of the debtor, but the accountant is more interested in reporting on the machinery and equipment *not* at the premises. The most common assets of this type are the automobiles used personally by the corporate officers. Though registered in the officers' own names, the cars are often purchased by the corporation, with all operating expenses completely paid by the corporation. Insurance brokers' bills will usually point out the existence of these assets as well as installment payments made on a monthly basis. Often a letter will arrive, or will be discovered in the company's files, from an irate bailee wanting to know when someone is going to remove machinery from a warehouse or premises or who is going to pay for its storage cost. A review of the contracts file may uncover some assets that do not appear on the books of the corporation. Machinery or equipment usually does appear (at least in summary form) and the corporate tax returns ordinarily will have detailed schedules of the items included in this category.

[13] Ibid., p. 9.

79 Assets may also be concealed by the withdrawal of unusual receipts such as recovery of bad debts or insurance recoveries.

80 These investigations and determinations become the basis for a turn-over proceeding to compel the debtor to surrender the property or its value that is unaccounted for and therefore presumably concealed by the debtor. Thus the challenge to the accountant is to prove that certain assets exist, even though their physical existence is not immediately evident.

81 The concealment of assets when intended to hinder, delay, or de-fraud creditors is grounds for barring an individual debtor from the discharge of debts under a chapter 7 liquidation as discussed in paragraph 49.

FALSE ENTRIES AND STATEMENTS

Mutilation and Alteration of Records

82 Any suspicion that the books have been tampered with should be quickly and carefully acted upon by the accountant and the trustee's attor-ney. There may be attempts on the part of the firm's owners or employees to conceal assets, make preferential payments, hide a fraudulent transfer, or effect some other irregularity. Indications of such activities include suspi-cious erasures, names or amounts that have been crossed out, and pages that have been rewritten. Documents that should receive the closest attention are checks, payroll records, deposit slips, and petty cash slips. The most reliable method of examining and investigating any unusual condition is to contact an independent third party to verify the debtor's records. An example of this procedure would be a comparison between the duplicate deposit tickets retained by the bank and the debtor's cash receipts journal. Other examples are given below:

> Examination of purchase bills and receiving records, to bring to light fictitious purchase bills used to siphon off business funds.
>
> Examination of sales invoices and shipping documents, to reveal fictitious invoices used to obtain loans.
>
> Review of loans received, to determine whether they were bona fide loans or disguised sales.
>
> Analysis of receivable and payable subsidiary accounts, to see whether nonexistent or unusual accounts appear.
>
> Audit of petty cash slips, to check for alterations.

Concealment and Destruction of Records

83 As previously discussed, locating and obtaining possession of the debtor's books and records is one of the accountant's first and most important tasks. Should the investigation reveal that the debtor is withholding records, the attorney may initiate turnover proceedings to obtain possession of them. Intentional destruction of records, if proven, may give the attorney grounds for further legal actions. Section 727(a)(3) of the Bankruptcy Code explicitly states that a discharge of debts of an individual in a chapter 7 liquidation will be denied when it is proven that the bankrupt destroyed, mutilated, falsified, concealed, or failed to keep or preserve books of account or records from which the financial condition and transactions of the business might be ascertained. There is no similar provision in a chapter 11 reorganization unless the records are falsified for the purpose of obtaining credit.

Forgery

84   Officers of the debtor may falsify a third party's signature for numerous reasons. The debtor may attempt to receive credit illegally by forging notes, mortgages, warehouse receipts, trust receipts, shipping documents, and other evidences often used as security. Forgery might also be used to endorse a check and divert the moneys to personal use. The proceeds from the sale of marketable securities might be misappropriated through forgery.[14] Forgery is a form of deception and as such carries its own punishment under the federal laws.

Issuance of False Statements

85   The following list explains how several accounts may be altered for financial statement purposes.

Cash:
    Kiting of receipts.
    Withdrawals not recorded.
    Deposits of worthless checks from insolvent affiliates.

Accounts receivable:
    Worthless accounts not written off.
    Insufficient reserve for bad debts.
    Large returns and allowances in subsequent period.
    Fictitious sales.
    Invoices billed in advance of shipping dates.
    Fictitious accounts created to cover withdrawals to officers, etc.
    Nondisclosure of hypothecation to banks or factors.

Notes receivable:
    Worthless notes not written off.

[14] Bronsteen, p. 941.

Insufficient reserve for bad debts.
Forging or fictitious notes created to cover withdrawals.
Contingent liability for discounted notes not shown.

Merchandise inventory:

Nondisclosure of liens.
Inflated values and quantities.
Items billed in advance of shipping dates included in inventory.
Old obsolete inventory not disclosed.

Cash value—officers' life insurance:

Liability for loans not shown.
Corporation not beneficiary.

Fixed and other assets:

Liens not disclosed.
Inflated values by reappraisals and not shown.
Inadequate reserve for depreciations.
Leased equipment recorded as fixed assets.
Personal assets (such as autos) not registered in corporate name but recorded as assets.
Capitalized expenses that have no value.

Intercompany receivables:

From affiliates to cover withdrawals of officers.
From affiliates that are insolvent.

Investments:

Worthless, but shown at original cost.
Pledged and not recorded.
Not registered in corporate name.
To cover withdrawals to insolvent affiliates.

Liabilities:

Not recorded.
Withdrawals of subordinated debts not shown.

Capital:

Notes and loans payable recorded as capital.
False subordinations.

86 The accountant discovers the issuance of false financial statements by comparing the statements the debtor has issued with the books and records. The comparison can be presented in schedule form, which explains the difference between the statements and the records. Exhibits 11-1 and 11-3 present the statement of financial position and statement of income and profit or loss, respectively, as originally issued by the debtor. Exhibits 11-2 and 11-4 show the statements prepared by the accountant, comparing the debtor's statements with the records.

Exhibit 11-1   Statement of Financial Position, as Prepared by Debtor

A RETAIL CORPORATION

STATEMENT OF FINANCIAL POSITION

At December 31, 19X5

Assets			
Current assets			
Cash in banks		$ 20,730	
Accounts receivable	$26,530		
Less: allowance for doubtful accounts	3,500	23,030	
Merchandise inventory		131,810	
Prepaid expenses		4,470	
Total current assets			$180,040
Investments			
Common stock—Jones & Co.		4,760	
Preferred stock—Smith, Inc.		5,000	
Total investments			9,760
Fixed assets		49,530	
Less: accumulated depreciation		22,720	
Net Fixed Assets			26,810
Other assets			
Deposits as security		8,500	
Goodwill		8,000	
Total other assets			16,500
Total assets			$233,110
Liabilities and Capital			
Current liabilities			
Loan payable—bank		$ 20,000	
Accounts payable		80,560	
Taxes and accrued expenses		7,960	
Total liabilities			$108,520
Capital			
Capital stock issued		75,000	
Additional paid-in capital		35,000	
Accumulated earnings, January 1, 19X5	$ 5,170		
Profit for period [Exhibit 11-3]	9,420	14,590	
Total capital			124,590
Total liabilities and capital			$233,110

Exhibit 11-2 Accountant's Comparative Statement of Financial Position, as Prepared from Debtor's Books

A RETAIL CORPORATION

COMPARISON OF ISSUED STATEMENT OF FINANCIAL POSITION WITH BOOKS OF ACCOUNT

At December 31, 19X5

	Per Books	Per Financial Statement	Apparent Errors Assets Over-stated	Apparent Errors Liabilities Under-stated
Assets				
Current assets				
Cash in banks	$ 2,730	$ 20,730	$18,000	
Accounts receivable—net	21,030	23,030	2,000	
Merchandise inventory	121,810	131,810	10,000	
Prepaid expenses	4,470	4,470		
Total current assets	150,040	180,040	30,000	
Investments				
Common stock—Jones & Co.	4,760	4,760		
Preferred stock—Smith, Inc.	–0–	5,000	5,000	
Total investments	4,760	9,760	5,000	
Fixed assets—net	26,810	26,810		
Other assets	16,500	16,500		
Total assets	$198,110	$233,110	$35,000	
Liabilities and Capital				
Current liabilities				
Loan payable—bank	$ 20,000	$ 20,000		
Notes payable—John Doe	6,000	–0–		$ 6,000
Accounts payable	103,560	80,560		23,000
Taxes and accrued expenses	7,960	7,960		
Total current liabilities	137,520	108,520		29,000
Due after one year				
Notes payable—John Doe	9,000	–0–		9,000
Total liabilities	146,520	108,520		$38,000
Capital				
Capital stock issued	75,000	75,000		
Additional paid-in capital	–0–	35,000		
Accumulated earnings (deficit)	(23,410)	14,590		
Total capital	51,590	124,590		
Total liabilities and capital	$198,110	$233,110		

Exhibit 11-2 *(Continued)*

COMPARISON OF ISSUED STATEMENT OF FINANCIAL POSITION
WITH BOOKS OF ACCOUNT
(Continued)

At December 31, 19X5

| | | | Apparent Errors | |
	Per Books	Per Financial Statement	Assets Over-stated	Liabilities Under-stated
Reconciliation of Capital				
Accumulated deficit per books		$ 23,410		
Accumulated earnings per statement		14,590	$38,000	
Paid-in capital per statement			35,000	
Total to be accounted for				$73,000
Assets apparently overstated			35,000	
Liabilities apparently understated			38,000	
Total accounted for				$73,000

FINANCING IRREGULARITIES

87 Many schemes have been devised whereby the debtor attempts to receive goods or money using very confusing methods so that payment is delayed or the amount received is more than is actually due. The most common accounts manipulated to accomplish these goals are accounts receivable and inventory.

Receivables

88 Many different types of abuses may be found in the financing of accounts receivable. Customers may be sent bills before the goods are shipped or the sale is consummated. Documents such as sales invoices or customers' signatures on financing agreements may be forged. Employees

Exhibit 11-3   Statement of Income and Profit or Loss, as Prepared by Debtor

A RETAIL CORPORATION

STATEMENT OF INCOME AND PROFIT OR LOSS

For the Period from January 1 to December 31, 19X5

Net sales		$592,010
Cost of goods sold		
Merchandise inventory, January 1, 19X5	$ 98,490	
Net purchase	364,230	
Freight-in and other costs	10,510	
Available for sale	473,230	
Less: merchandise inventory, December 31, 19X5	131,810	
Cost of goods sold		341,420
Gross profit		250,590
Expenses		
Sales salaries	101,790	
Administrative salaries	20,180	
Rent	53,890	
Advertising	19,850	
Taxes	8,790	
Utilities	10,040	
Depreciation	5,820	
Other expenses	20,810	
Total expenses		241,170
Net profit for period (Figure 11-1)		$ 9,420

may fail to record merchandise that has been returned, thus showing an inflated accounts receivable total. Invoices may be padded so that if the receivables were factored, the debtor would receive funds in excess of the actual costs.[15]

89   In analyzing the receivables of a paint company an auditor noticed that excessive amounts of returns were being made by customers, depreciating the value of the accounts receivable. Salesmen were inflating the receivables by making sales that would later be returned. This practice was encouraged because the plant producer paid commissions on acceptance of the order, rather than after payment. Further analysis indicated that the sales-

[15] Ibid.

Exhibit 11-4   Accountant's Comparative Statement of Income and Profit or Loss, as Prepared from Debtor's Books

A RETAIL CORPORATION

COMPARISON OF ISSUED STATEMENT OF INCOME AND PROFIT OR LOSS WITH BOOKS OF ACCOUNT

For the Period from January 1 to December 31, 19X5

	Per Books	Per Financial Statement
Net sales	$562,010	$592,010
Cost of goods sold		
Merchandise inventory,		
January 1, 19X5	$ 98,490	$ 98,490
Net purchases	340,230	364,230
Freight-in and other costs	10,510	10,510
Available for sale	449,230	473,230
Less: merchandise inventory,		
December 31, 19X5	121,810	131,810
Cost of goods sold	327,420	341,420
Gross profit	234,590	250,590
Expenses		
Sales salaries	111,790	101,790
Administrative salaries	20,180	20,180
Rent	53,890	53,890
Advertising	24,850	19,850
Taxes	8,790	8,790
Utilities	10,040	10,040
Depreciation	5,820	5,820
Other expenses	27,810	20,810
Total expenses	263,170	241,170
Net profit or (loss)	$(28,580)	$ 9,420

SUMMARY

	Sales	Gross Profit	Expenses	Net Profit
Per financial statement	$592,010	$250,590	$241,170	$ 9,420
Per books	562,010	234,590	263,170	(28,580)
Apparent misstatement	$ 30,000	$ 16,000	$ 22,000	$ 38,000

men were promising customers exclusive rights to the paint in their geographic area and then selling the same type of paint to a local competitor of the first customer. They camouflaged this action by placing a different trade name label on the cans of paint.

90   The business should have full ownership of its receivables, and there should be no liens outstanding against them or any contingent liabilities for receivables which have been discounted. The total shown for accounts receivable should be the realizable cash value. Items that should not be included in accounts receivable but would be presented separately are:

Shipments made on consignment.

Accounts for which there is indication that collection will not be possible because the customer was a bad credit risk.

Permanent investments of capital in or loans to affiliated or subsidiary businesses.

Receivables which resulted from transactions with officers, employees, or subsidiary companies.

Loans or advances to employees or officers.

Claims that will never be enforced, such as those resulting from transactions conducted under false pretenses.

Installment receivables.

Receivables arising from transactions other than the sale of merchandise—the sale of plant assets, insurance claims, and the like.

Credit balances in accounts receivable.

91   To discover any of these irregularities, the most reliable procedure would be for the accountant to confirm the transactions with the third party involved. If there is a suspicion that merchandise was returned but not recorded, the customer should be contacted. Confirmation of a certain number of receivables is a normal audit procedure. If the receivables have been factored, they should be directly confirmed with the customer and all shipping documents, receipts, and the method and means of payment should be carefully examined to insure the transactions are valid. If the accountant suspects that a shipment shown as a sale was actually made on consignment, the receiver of the goods should be contacted to see whether title did actually pass. Doubtful credit risks should be investigated and any transactions made with employees or officers should be carefully scrutinized. Many of the procedures followed in determining whether irregularities exist in accounts receivable are extensions of those found in a normal audit.

Inventory

92   Inventories, the methods of financing purchases, and the use of inventories to obtain further credit are also subject to manipulation by the debtor. Signatures may be forged on receiving reports attesting that material was received and payment is therefore due the vendor. Subsequent payment may then be abstracted by the officers or employees. Other documents may be falsified to record a higher inventory value, cover up a shortage, and so forth. As with receivables, these transactions may best be verified through confirmation with outside parties.

93 A company with warehouses on its premises had a substantial amount of inventory subject to warehouse liens that were held by Lexington Warehouse Company. The accountant's investigation disclosed that items were not properly recorded in the warehouse receipts issued by Lexington Warehouse. As a result, in the recorded contents of certain lots there were variances from the description in the warehouse receipts, and inventory was overstated. Lot number 5589, for example, was on warehouse receipt number 36673 as 17,425 pounds headless shrimp at $.80 per pound for a value of $13,796. This lot actually contained fish that was valued at $.38 per pound for a total value of $6621, for a difference of $7175. It was determined that when the inventory of shrimp came into the facilities of the company, it would be proper inventory. A warehouse receipt would be prepared that went to a New York bank for financing. The shrimp were then taken out the front door and a lesser quality of shrimp—and in some cases even catfish— was substituted. The higher-quality shrimp were then taken to the back door and processed again.

94 The discrepancies were discovered by taking a detailed inventory. Also, the auditor discovered two black books which the company used to keep up with the changes it had made in the inventory placed in the warehouse.

95 Inventories may be financed through a technique known as kiting. This scheme uses the float period, or the time it takes for a check to clear the bank on which it is drawn. It is an attempt to prevent an overdraft from being detected by the bank and in effect uses the bank's credit without authorization or payment of interest. Kiting may also be tied in directly with the inventory. In the example described above, the local warehouse was slow in notifying the Lexington Warehouse Company (Lexington, Ky.) that the items had been sold. The company used the proceeds, which should have been directly applied to the payment of the loan since the inventory had been sold, until the bank in New York received notice of the sale of the inventory. The company continued to list the item in inventory even though the sale was recorded.

96 Inventories may also be used as collateral to obtain credit. They may become security for new credit or outstanding obligations. If the debtor has inflated the inventory figure, the collateral is actually insufficient for the amount borrowed and the creditors have been deceived.

97 In a typical audit not involving insolvency the accountant attempts to establish the correct quantity of items in inventory and the proper valuation of the goods. These are very important aspects of an audit involving a debtor in bankruptcy court where it is necessary to ascertain whether the collateral is adequate and the amounts paid were for items that actually represented purchases. The correct quantity as shown in the inventory figure is determined through observation of a physical inventory and statistical sampling of the correspondence between the inventory records and actual goods. Valuation is tested by examining sales invoices, obtaining prices paid by other vendees, and questioning the seller as to how much was actually received. All these procedures must be conducted with a higher degree of suspicion on the part of the accountant than would normally be the case, because of the nature of the proceeding.

PREFERENTIAL PAYMENTS

98   A preferential payment as defined in section 547 of the Bankruptcy Code is a transfer of any of the property of a debtor to or for the benefit of a creditor, for or on account of an antecedent debt made or suffered by the debtor while insolvent and within ninety days before the filing of a petition initiating bankruptcy proceedings, when the effect of such transfer is to enable the creditor to receive a greater percentage of payment than would be received if the debtor were liquidated under chapter 7. Insolvency will be presumed during this ninety-day period. A transfer of property to an insider between ninety days and one year before the filing of the petition is also considered a preferential payment. Preferences include the payment of money, a transfer of property, assignment of accounts receivable, or a mortgage on real or personal property (see chapter 3, paragraphs 116–127).

99   A preferential payment is not a fraud but rather a legitimate and proper payment of a valid antecedent debt. The voidability of preferences is created by law to effect equality of distribution among all the creditors. The ninety-day period (one year for transactions with insiders) prior to filing the bankruptcy petition has been arbitrarily selected by Congress as the time period during which distributions to the debtor's creditors may be redistributed to all the creditors ratably. During this period, a creditor who accepts a payment is said to have been preferred and may be required to return the amount received and later participate in the enlarged estate to the pro rata extent of its unreduced claim.

Recovery of Preferential Payments

100   The trustee will attempt to recover preferential payments, but not all payments are voidable. For the payment to an insider made between ninety-one days and one year prior to the petition to be voidable the Bankruptcy Code, as originally passed, required that the insider who received payment had to have reasonable cause to believe that the debtor was insolvent at the time the transfer was made.[16] This requirement was eliminated by the Bankruptcy Amendments and Federal Judgeship Act of 1984 for petitions filed after October 8, 1984.

101 It should be noted that section 547(f) provides that the debtor is presumed to be insolvent during the ninety-day period prior to bankruptcy. This presumption does not apply to transfers to insiders between ninety-one days and one year prior to bankruptcy. This presumption requires the adverse party to come forth with some evidence to prove the presumption. The burden of proof, however, remains with the party in whose favor the presumption exists. Once this presumption is rebutted, insolvency at the time of payment is necessary and only someone with the training of an accountant is in a position to prove insolvency.[17] The accountant often assists the debtor or trustee in presenting evidence showing whether the debtor was solvent or insolvent at the time payment was made. In cases where new management is in charge of the business or where a trustee has been appointed, the emphasis is often on trying to show that the debtor was insolvent in order to obtain the recovery of the previous payments to increase the size of the estate. The creditors' committee likewise wants to show that the debtor was insolvent at the time of payment to provide a larger basis for payment to unsecured creditors. Of course, the specific creditor recovering the payment looks for evidence to indicate that the debtor was solvent at the time payment was made.

102 It is important that the accountant note exceptions to the trustee's avoiding power provided for in section 547. They are described in detail in chapter 3, paragraphs 105–127 and briefly mentioned here:

1 Transfers intended as a contemporaneous exchange for new value.

2 Transfers for business debts made in ordinary courses of business of both the debtor and creditor and made according to ordinary business terms.

3 Giving of security in connection with an enabling lien to acquire property to the extent that the transferred interest is perfected within ten days.

4 Giving in good faith future credit without security of any kind for property that becomes part of the debtor's estate when a preferential payment had previously been made. The amount of the new credit remaining unpaid at the time of the adjudication in bankruptcy may be set off against the amount that would otherwise be recoverable from the debtor. To establish the final amount of preferential payments to one creditor, it is necessary to set off all new credits against the prior preferential payments.[18]

5 Transfers where there is a perfected "floating" security interest in inventory or receivables or the proceeds of either, providing the creditors'

---

[16] U.S.C. Sec. 547(b)(4)(B).

[17] Krause, p. 505.

[18] Herzog, p. 62.

position does not realize net improvement during the ninety-day period (one year for insiders) prior to the petition date. Here, the accountant will be required to analyze the security interest and the account balance of each creditor in inventories and receivables ninety days prior to the petition date and compare the results with the condition existing at the date the petition was filed.

6 Fixing of a statutory lien that is not avoidable.

Search for Preferential Payments

103 Any payments made within the ninety days preceding the bankruptcy court filing and that are not in the ordinary course of business should be very carefully scrutinized. Additionally, transactions with insiders should be carefully reviewed to see if any payments were preferences. Suspicious transactions would include anticipations of debt obligations, repayment of officers' loans, repayment of loans that have been personally guaranteed by officers, repayment of loans made to personal friends and relatives, collateral given to lenders, and sales of merchandise made on a contraaccount basis.[19]

104 Sales that are unrecorded and result in the transfer and concealment of merchandise may result in benefit to preferred creditors in several ways. Collateral may be given to creditors but not recorded on the debtor's books. Merchandise may be concealed from the trustee by suppliers who send bills for undelivered merchandise under a "bill and hold" arrangement; or merchandise may be returned to creditors for a direct or indirect consideration. All these schemes are intended to prefer a certain creditor over another.

105 In seeking to find voidable preferences, the accountant has two crucial tasks: to determine the earliest date on which insolvency can be established within the ninety-day period (one year for insiders), and to report to the trustee's attorney all payments, transfers, or encumbrances that have been made by the debtor after that date. It is then the attorney's responsibility to determine which payments are voidable. However, the accountant's role should not be minimized, for it is the accountant who initially determines those payments that are suspect.

INFLATED CLAIMS

106 Just as it is important to minimize the priority and administration creditors in order to provide the maximum dividend to unsecured creditors, it is likewise important to limit the filing of the unsecured creditors to their proper amounts. Excessive amounts allowed for unsecured creditors will naturally diminish the dividend payable to those in that group.

[19] Bronsteen, p. 942.

107   After establishing the book balances for the unsecured creditors, the accountant compares these balances with the claims filed, or if a claim is not filed with the amount admitted on the debtor's schedules of liabilities, to determine their accuracy. Discrepancies are analyzed and, if they are not reconcilable, this information is communicated to the trustee or counsel and also to the creditors' committee. Where the supplier has not given credit for payments made or credits allowed, the accountant locates the checks proving payment or the paperwork substantiating the allowance. In an interesting Chapter XI proceeding under prior law, the debtor (prior to the Chapter XI proceeding) had settled a claim with a supplier for $9800, payable by adding $.10 to each item of goods purchased in the future until the $9800 had been paid. This settlement was for an original invoice of approximately $60,000; however, the accounts payable records showed no liability at all to the creditor. Although the settlement preceded the filing of the arrangement petition and although there had been partial performance on the settlement, the creditor nonetheless presented a confirmation to the accountant showing the $60,000 balance as still due. Fortunately, the accountant noticed the $.10 additional payments on the invoices of the supplier (which aroused the accountant's suspicions) and the true facts were then uncovered. Consequently, instead of allowing a claim for $60,000, the statement reflected the true liability of $9800 less partial payment thereon.

108   In any bankruptcy court proceeding the accountant determines (by date of delivery as compared to the filing date of the petition) whether a claim is properly classified as administrative or nonadministrative. All the above verification naturally requires examination of the original documents, including receiving reports, purchase orders, and the actual supplier's invoices.

APPLICABILITY OF GENERALLY ACCEPTED AUDITING STANDARDS

109   When the accountant states that an examination was conducted in accordance with generally accepted auditing standards, this normally means that the examination performed was adequate to support an opinion on the financial statements and that it was performed with professional competence by properly trained persons. Such standards are really measures of an acceptable level of quality and are judged by the "prudent-person standard," or what other competent auditors would conclude to be necessary if given the same set of facts.

110   Two broad classifications of auditing standards are universally referred to. One is termed personal or general standards and concerns the auditor's training and experience and the quality of the work done. The second is the field work and reporting standards and refers to the evidence to be obtained and the means of reporting the results of the audit.

111 These standards are obviously quite general in their applicability. This is necessary because no one set of auditing procedures can be applied in all situations. Therefore, the accountant must select and apply the appropriate auditing procedures as required in the particular circumstances.

112 Because of their generality, the auditing standards as set forth in Statement on Auditing Standards No. 1 certainly apply to the audit of a client involved in bankruptcy or insolvency proceedings. The auditor must obviously have adequate technical training, maintain an independent mental attitude, and exercise due professional care. The work must be planned and supervised, internal control must be studied and evaluated, and sufficient competent evidential matter must be obtained. Finally, the financial statements must be presented in accordance with generally accepted accounting principles, consistently applied. There must be adequate disclosures, and either an expression of an opinion or reasons why one cannot be given should be included in the report.

Auditing Procedures

113 The nature of the bankruptcy and insolvency proceedings determines the specific procedures which will be followed. A liquidation proceeding allows for greater manipulation of the books and transactions, so in many areas the accountant will need to scrutinize the records and supporting documents more closely than might otherwise be necessary. Special attention must be given to uncovering any irregularities such as fraudulent transfers, preferential payments, false entries, concealment of assets, and the like. These investigations may necessitate greater reliance on sources outside the debtor's records than is normal, including confirmation with third parties. It may be necessary to reconstruct some accounts because of a lack of adequate data or the dubious nature of the debtor's information.

114 Other considerations also arise because of the nature of the situation. For example, the question may be posed as to whether the auditor can represent the debtor and still be independent when supplying information for the creditors. Or, if the accountant helps devise a plan (settlement or reorganization) for rehabilitation and recommends its acceptance, can the same accountant later be independent when auditing the debtor's progress? Is it ever possible to rely on the system of internal control in insolvency proceedings, or should the examination be conducted as if there were no adequate safeguards? These and other specific questions arise when applying auditing standards to a bankruptcy court case.

115 The various audit steps that will be necessary must be individually determined for each case. Whether such procedures are adequate can only be measured by a consideration of what a reasonable person with the same training would do in a similar situation. But it still remains true that those standards that generally apply to all audit cases are also relevant to insolvency and bankruptcy proceedings.

116   The first generally accepted auditing standard of reporting requires that the auditor state whether the financial statements are presented in accordance with generally accepted principles of accounting. This means that any financial statements prepared by an accountant must not deviate from the standard presentation and treatment of accounts and transactions as commonly used by the profession.

117   There is no definitive list of accounting principles that has been written down and may be referred to by auditors. Rather, the accountant must have a sound and thorough knowledge of accounting theory. It is also necessary to be aware of the pronouncements of the AICPA, FASB, other areas of accounting literature, and current industry practice. Using these sources, the accountant must then apply personal judgment to determine whether a particular principle is generally accepted and appropriate in the circumstances.

118   The most common sources of accounting principles are the Accounting Research Bulletins and Opinions previously issued by the rule-making bodies of the AICPA, and Standards issued by the Financial Accounting Standards Board. The principles set forth in these publications are deemed to have substantial authoritative support and therefore are considered to be generally accepted accounting principles. Any departures in the financial statements from these pronouncements must be disclosed in a footnote to the statement or in a separate paragraph of the auditor's report. Such deviations are to be acceptable to the auditor only if they have substantial authoritative support and are acceptable practices. This decision is made by the accountant after examining all the relevant and authoritative sources of literature, and evaluating what is commonly done in such situations.

119   Chapter 13 presents a discussion of the application of the reporting standards to reports issued in bankruptcy and insolvency proceedings, and includes an analysis of the going concern concept as it relates to entities facing financial difficulties.

120   The art of accounting is composed of the talent, training, experience, and knowledge that result in the accountant's judgment as to which auditing standards are appropriate and which accounting principles are applicable to a particular circumstance. Overriding these specific decisions are the general standards that apply to all cases, including bankruptcy and insolvency proceedings.

Appendix:
Audit Program Guide

The following audit guide has been prepared for the purpose of assisting accountants who are conducting audits of companies involved in bankruptcy and insolvency proceedings. By definition, it is designed to guide the auditor in preparing a customized program for each individual engagement; it is not intended to be used as a final program. Modification should and must be made depending upon the nature and characteristics of each situation, including the purpose of the audit. Emphasis would be different for an audit designed to provide information to help management and the creditors in determining the type of corrective action needed for the company to be able to return to profitable operations than for an investigative audit to determine the extent to which management has misused the company's resources.

In conducting an investigative audit, special emphasis is placed on locating the property of the debtor. At times the auditor may be retained for the purpose of valuing the debtor's business. Here emphasis is placed on locating and properly valuing the remaining assets and liabilities of the debtor. Where going concern values must be determined, it is necessary to consider many factors, including the past operations of the debtor and the prospects for the future. The program will also change substantially depending on the type of entity—service, retail, manufacturing, and so forth.

Judgment on the part of the auditor is of paramount importance, as it will determine the total time consumed on the engagement and the relative value of such inputs to the creditors and debtor. The auditor must see that the efforts expended are efficient and in the proper area.

The procedures and responsibilities of the auditor may also vary depending on whether retention was by a creditors' committee for an out-of-court settlement or assignment under state law, or by the courts in a chapter 11 reorganization or chapter 7 liquidation proceeding.

In working with a company in financial difficulty, the accountant must at all times keep in mind what the objectives of the work are and design the audit accordingly. The items in this program should be used as a guide and modified according to the objective of each particular audit.

GENERAL PROCEDURES

1 Prepare memorandum outlining:

   a How the engagement was acquired. If by referral, give source and date of referral.

   b Principal creditors and members of creditors' committee.

   c Attorneys for creditors' committee and debtor.

   d Background information about the company, including type of business, locations of offices, and any other general information about the firm.

   e The estimated assets and liabilities of the company.

   f Any affiliates or subsidiaries.

2 Prepare an engagement letter or request for retention order. In an out-of-court committee case, the accounting firm should make sure the attorney for creditors and the chairman of the creditors' committee arrange for covering of all fees, especially if talks cease and court action occurs. In an assignment under state law (providing judicial supervision of the liquidation), chapter 11 (reorganization), or chapter 7 (liquidation), an order is generally required and always recommended if payment is expected from the funds of the estate. However, if the work is accepted because of the "credit body," the cooperation of the creditors' committee must also be obtained to protect the accounting firm in payment of fees. If there are affiliates or other related parties not involved in the "official" action, acquire an advance payment if at all possible, and have them sign the engagement letter.

3 Obtain copies or extract significant information and review the following in order to become familiar with the background and details of the firm's operations:

   a Recent reports issued to credit agencies.

   b Financial statements for the previous three to five years issued to stockholders, SEC, creditors, banks, and others.

   c Bank statements for the last year. (Review for activity in account and unusually large deposits or charges.)

   d Federal, state, and local income and franchise tax returns and revenue agents' reports for the last three years.

   e Copies of inventories for last tax return, last interim statement, and last issued statement.

   f Board of directors' and its executive committee's minutes for the last two years prior to the petition date or commencement of settlement negotiations.

   g Selected correspondence files for the last year prior to date proceedings initiated of (based on the nature of the case, select those files that are most important for background information):

  1 Attorneys.
  2 Independent accountants.
  3 Creditors' committee.
  4 Bankruptcy judge, assignee, or other custodian of assets.
  5 Banks and other major creditors.
  6 Insurance companies.
  7 SEC.
  8 Internal Revenue Service.
  9 Management consultants.
  10 Chief operating officers.

 h Bankruptcy files in federal court building.
 i Management letters and engagement letters for past two years of previous accountant.
 j Contracts and agreements relating to:

  1 Leases.
  2 Shareholders' buy/sell agreements.
  3 Retirement agreements.
  4 Insurance agreements.
  5 Employment contracts.
  6 Construction contracts.
  7 Other commitments.

4 Compare the current statement of financial position with those recently issued to creditors. Account for the differences during audit.

5 Determine if it will be necessary to have fixed assets and inventories appraised for liquidation value by an appraiser or auctioneer.

6 Prepare, or if possible have management prepare, a list for the following books and records and state location (on premises, in warehouse, attorney's office, or accountants' office):

 a General ledger.
 b Journals.
 c Subsidiary ledgers.
 d Supporting records, such as minutes of directors' meetings, perpetual inventory cards, production records, cost sheets, and stock records.

Management should sign the list stating that the list includes all of the company's books and records, to the best of their knowledge.

7 In order to identify related persons, insiders, and affiliated entities, prepare an analysis of key executives, major stockholders, affiliated companies, and other affiliations, such as joint ventures, in the following manner: (For public companies review 10K, S-1, proxy statements, and other statements filed with SEC or other regulatory agencies.)

a   KEY EXECUTIVES

Position	Name	Address	Office Telephone Extension	Period With Company

b   MAJOR STOCKHOLDERS

	Shares Owned									
	Date of Petition		Other Dates (list)							
Name	No.	%	No.	%	No.	%	No.	%	No.	%

c   AFFILIATED COMPANIES

Name	Address	Telephone Number	Owners

d   JOINT VENTURES

Participants	Address	Telephone Number	Description of Venture	% Participation

8   Obtain names, addresses, and telephone numbers of key bookkeeping personnel.

9   Review bankruptcy audit program considering the information determined from the analysis of the "general" procedures and modify accordingly.

10   Prepare or have client supply trial balance for year end audit date, date of bankruptcy court petition, and for first audits, trial balance as of the beginning of the period covered by audit.

11   Maintain a "time and expense" log showing the name of each person, hours expended, nature of function performed, and other expenses incurred.

12   Prepare petition for fee allowance in tentative form as soon as major part of work is complete, then update the petition before filing with bankruptcy court.

Review of Reports and Information Filed with Courts

1   On a test basis, trace to the books and records significant data on supporting schedules that were filed with the petition or subsequent to the petition as required by the Bankruptcy Code.

2   Agree financial statements and other information filed with the court subsequent to petition with company books of original entries.

Review of Reports and Information Filed with SEC and Released to Public Investors

1   Review annual reports for the past three to five years to determine:

   a   Unusual trends.
   b   Adequacy of disclosures.
   c   Identify unusual transactions requiring further investigation.

2   Review all unusual year-end transactions and adjustments for the prior two years (such transactions may be evidenced by quarterly results).

3   Review and reconcile quarterly reports (Form 10Q) Filed with the SEC with internally prepared financial reports. In connection therewith review:

   a   Unusual quarterly adjustments.
   b   Adequacy of assumptions and accounting controls.

4   Compare the information in the annual reports and in statements filed with the SEC for the past two years with books and records. Explain any material differences.

5   Review divisional operating results reported in the annual and quarterly reports to determine any unusual trends or relationship of revenues and/or expenses.

6   Review all press releases and published articles in possession of the debtor for the period from one year prior to the filing of the petition to the present.

Reasons for Financial Difficulty

1   Prepare comparative statements of financial position for the past three to five years and examine (it may also be advisable to discuss these with debtor) for the following failure tendencies:

   a   Weakening cash position.
   b   Insufficient working capital.
   c   Overinvestment in receivables or inventories.
   d   Overexpansion in fixed assets.
   e   Increasing bank loans or other current liabilities.
   f   Excessive funded debt and fixed liabilities.
   g   Overcapitalization.
   h   Subordination of loans to banks and creditors.

2 Prepare comparative income statements showing dollars and percentages for the past three to five years and examine for the following failure tendencies:

   a Declining sales.
   b Increasing operating costs and overhead.
   c Excessive interest and other fixed expenses.
   d Excessive dividends and withdrawals compared to earnings records.
   e Declining net profits and lower return on invested capital.
   f Increased sales with reduced mark-up.

3 Calculate the following ratios for the year being audited and the prior year. If possible, determine why the unfavorable ratio developed.

Current ratio.

Quick ratio.

Cash flow/total liabilities.

Retained earnings/total assets.

Inventory/sales.

Return on total assets.

Trade payables/inventory.

Percent increase in inventory/percent increase in sales.

Percent increase in off-balance sheet financing.

Fixed charge coverage.

After the ratios have been calculated, evaluate them for changes from the previous year to the current and for unusual results, and attempt to determine why the ratio is infavorable or different from the normal results. In making this assessment, the nature and size of the company, the type of industry, the nature of the examination, and the type of proceeding must be considered.

4 Review the method used to determine division profitability for:

   a Comparability among all segments.
   b Adequacy and/or reliability of results achieved.

5 Consider the impact that economic conditions had on the deterioration of the company's position. Evaluate the manner in which the debtor reacted to the economic climate.

6 Determine the efficiency and adequacy of the information system by reviewing the type of information available to the management where critical decisions are made. (For example, types of merchandising reports, nature of divisional performance reports, types of reports prepared when a product line was eliminated, and so forth.)

7   Compare the actual results for the past three years with the firm's forecasts. Attempt to find the reason for the difference.

8   Based on the above analysis, prepare a brief summary of the major reasons for the financial difficulty.

Date of Insolvency (Determination of)

1   Examine internal financial reports. Look for periods with large cash outflows and operating losses.

2   Examine reports issued to creditors.

3   Examine pending legal action for nonpayment of obligations.

4   Examine correspondence with lenders.

5   Prepare an aging schedule of vouchers payable.

6   Look for large unusual cash outlays such as settlement of legal matters and related attorneys' fees.

CASH

Cash on Deposit

1   Examine cancelled checks in excess of $_____ for _____ months (especially the ninety days prior to the date of the bankruptcy petition) for endorsement and cancellation dates. Be alert for endorsements indicating:

    a   Payments to owners, directors, and/or officers.

    b   Payments to affiliated companies.

    c   Loan and exchange transactions.

    d   Checks made payable to cash.

    e   Cashing by "check cashers" (numbered endorsements), multiple endorsements, or other unusual and suspicious endorsements that may indicate fraudulent payments.

2   Review bank reconciliations of all bank accounts for the last statement to verify balances and uncover unusual disbursements.

3   Request "cutoff" bank statements and reconcile.

4   Test duplicate deposit slips to entries in cash receipts journal and to remittance advices for _____ months.

5   Prepare a schedule of the reconciliation of sales to bank deposits from _____ to _____ to determine:

    a   The extent and disposition of cash holdbacks.

    b   The existence and degree of control over sales subsequent to the petition.

6 Verify all general journal entries affecting cash, including an examination of all debit and credit memos.

7 Prepare reversal entries for outstanding checks that are unissued and on hand or for which there are no funds in the bank account.

8 Confirm balances with bank.

9 Review the propriety of the handling of checks outstanding at the petition date.

10 Review interbank transfers for names of banks not reflected on books. Be alert during examination for checks made payable to banks (and bank accounts) other than those maintained by the company. Vouch transfers in excess of $_____ during the period from _____ to _____ to the recipient's statement.

11 Scan cash receipts records and returns and allowance registers for possible unwarranted credits.

12 Examine receipts for disclosure of unusual sources of income that may lead to otherwise unknown assets.

Cash on Hand

1 Determine existing funds and take possession and control.

2 Count and reconcile funds simultaneously.

3 Test vouchers for supporting documents, signatures, and approvals.

4 Note all vouchers relating to loans or any other unusual vouchers.

5 Return funds to custodians.

6 If funds include loans and vouchers not recorded, adjust account to actual cash balance.

ACCOUNTS AND NOTES RECEIVABLE

1 Test or prepare aged schedule showing:

    a Name and address.

    b Balance due.

    c Accounts that are assigned.

    d Aging based on invoice data as follows:

        1 Current month.

        2 First preceding month.

        3 Second preceding month.

        4 Third preceding month.

        5 Fourth preceding month and prior.

    e Test (d) above by examining shipping documents.

2 Review aged schedule and determine required allowance for uncollectible accounts.

3 Tie in supporting records with statement amount and receivables.

4 Calculate allowance for trade and cash discounts.

5 Determine existence and approximate amount of possible advertising or other types of allowances.

6 Determine possibility and approximate amount of recorded and unrecorded sales on consignment.

7 Review sales contracts for unrecorded contractual rights of a recoverable nature.

8 Determine method of recording sample lines in possession of sales representatives or agents.

9 Review propriety of recent write-offs, large returns, and compromises of receivables.

10 Request confirmation of receivable balances with customer or collection agent.

11 List subsequent collections of receivables on separate schedule indicating full details. (This will be required in final accounting for court.)

12 Determine that collection agents have turned over all accounts collected.

13 Compare list of receivables with accounts payable to determine whether the business is also obligated to any of its debtors. In preparing reports for the creditors' committee, it may be desirable to offset a customer's balance in accounts payable against the receivable. In all reports, the amounts and accounts should be disclosed.

INVENTORIES

General

1 Obtain copies of previous inventories for the past two years or statements from management as to their disposition.

2 Perform unit reconciliation from previous to current physical inventory date:

Item Identification _____

     Quantity in prior inventory   _____

     Add: Quantity purchased   _____

     Total to account for   _____

     Less: Quantity sold   _____

Total Quantity which should be on hand   _____

Quantity on hand (actual count)   _____

Discrepancy   _____

This step may be difficult to perform, depending on the type of inventory system.

If unit information is not available, dollar values can be used by removing the gross profit from sales.

3 Determine if there are merchandise liens outstanding and list them, giving detailed information.

4 List separately and evaluate "bill and hold" merchandise in hands of creditors (check with counsel).

5 Review pending merchandise and freight for possible refunds.

6 Review all material inventory transactions with owners, officers, and affiliated companies during the year prior to the petition to ascertain that they were "arm's length" transactions.

7 Schedule, for a test of adequate consideration, _____ (_____%) transactions selected on a random basis with each supplier during the year prior to the filing of the petition.

8 Examine any unusual transaction involving inventory, including any transaction where the method and/or time of payments are different from those customary for this industry. (Examples are over and under billing arrangements, rebates, use of inventory for payment of account, and so forth.)

9 Determine that there was a proper cutoff of purchases as of the date the petition was filed.

10 Review all inventory transactions in excess of $_____ subsequent to the date of the petition. Compare invoice with receiving documents and ascertain that the goods either were sold or are still on hand.

Observation

1 Observe physical inventory. If business has been closed and no employees are available, arrange to have inventory examined, listed, and valued by a public auction company. This expense should be authorized by the bankruptcy judge.

2 Establish tag control to ascertain that all items are counted and there are no double countings.

3 Make test counts of inventory items, tracing them to completed inventory records.

4 Confirm inventory at contractors, if material. Prepare separate schedule of this inventory and list related "liens" by contractors.

5 Inventory at contractors should be evaluated to determine advisability of paying off contractor and obtaining merchandise.
6 Review cutoffs on all merchandise—incoming, outgoing, and in process.

Pricing

1 Establish basis of valuation of prior inventories.
2 Obtain copies of insurance report forms reflecting inventory values and compare to recorded values.
3 Test-check pricing of:

  a Raw materials.
  b Work in process.
  c Finished goods.
  d Packing supplies.
  e Factory supplies.
  f Obsolete inventory.

4 For manufacturing operations:

  a Review internal procedures for recording flow of raw materials.
  b Review costing of product lines and verify existence of pricing by book and/or formula.
  c Compare the incremental cost required to complete the work in process with the amount to be realized on sale to determine if completion is advisable.

Curtailment of Operations

1 Ascertain the method utilized by the company to dispose of assets in divisions and/or product lines discontinued. At a minimum, determine:

  a The extent to which competitive bids were obtained.
  b The control system established to insure:

    1 That all funds were received by the company relative to the sale.
    2 That all assets available for sale were either sold or are still held and are available for sale (utilize historical records).

  c That there was proper authorization for the sale, when sales occurred after the petition was filed.

2 Evaluate the method(s) utilized by the debtor, and/or appraisers to value the asset to be sold.
3 Ascertain that approval was acquired for the sale of assets at amounts substantially less than appraised values.

PREPAID EXPENSES

Prepaid Insurance

1. Prepare detailed analysis of insurance accounts showing the prepaid amounts, the cash and loan values of life insurance, and the recoverable deposit premiums.
2. Obtain schedule of insurance in force from brokers and compare with records.
3. Review calculation of premium earned based on payroll figures. If the advance exceeds the amount determined from payroll, set it up as a prepaid expense. If the premium is greater than the deposit, show the difference as an accrued liability.
4. Determine the short-rate cancellation values of insurance in force.
5. Determine whether life insurance policies on the lives of corporate officers exist by examining entries on corporate books, by searching for the policies themselves, by analyzing the paid and unpaid bills, or by looking for entries on the books that represent payments to life insurance companies for premiums.
6. Confirm cash and loan values of life insurance with insurers.
7. Determine that all dividends received on the policies have been credited to the corporation.
8. Review insurance claims for possible refunds.

Deposits

1. Examine the correspondence file to see if there are any deposits or securities unrecorded.

PROPERTY, PLANT, AND EQUIPMENT

1. Review all purchases of property, plant, and equipment within the year prior to the petition to see that the amount paid was not in excess of the value of assets.
2. Prepare a schedule of and review all sales of property, plant, and equipment subsequent to the date of the bankruptcy petition and for one year prior to such date to ascertain that the amount received was not less than the fair value of the asset transferred.
3. Verify that there are no unrecorded retirements.
4. Establish the existence of plant assets by inspecting major items.
5. Inspect contracts, deeds, title guarantee policies, and other related documents to determine ownership.

6 Determine existence and extent to which property items are security for existing debts.

7 Determine potential loss on abandonment of leasehold improvements.

8 Determine status of real estate tax arrearages.

9 Obtain court authorized estimates of realizable value of fixed assets from approved appraisers or equipment manufacturers.

10 Review in detail all property, plant, and equipment transactions with owners, officers, and affiliated companies during two years prior to and the period subsequent to the filing of the petition.

11 Evaluate the adequacy of the allowance for depreciation.

12 Determine the existence and disposition of company cars needed by officers.

13 Ascertain, with counsel's assistance, potential rebates of personal property and real estate taxes paid under discriminatory tax rates.

14 To locate assets not recorded on the debtor's books, search county recorder's offices in counties in which the company is located or has done business.

INVESTMENTS AND OTHER ASSETS

1 Review _____ percent of the investment purchase transactions during the year prior to and the period subsequent to the petition to see that the consideration paid was not in excess of the value of the securities.

2 Review _____ percent of the sales of investments during the year prior to and the period subsequent to the petition to ascertain that the amount received was adequate.

3 Review in detail all investment and other assets transactions with owners, officers, and affiliated companies during _____ years prior to the petition and also during the period subsequent to the petition.

4 Carefully examine all charges and credits to investments and other assets during the year prior to the petition that did not arise from cash transactions to uncover a fraudulent transfer or a preferential payment.

ACCOUNTS PAYABLE

1 Prepare or obtain from the client a schedule of the accounts payable, including names and addresses of creditors, amount owed, and distribution by size of debt.

2 Examine and prepare a schedule of all material payments and debits (those in the aggregate which exceed $_____) within the ninety-day period (or longer) prior to the date of the petition to determine possible

preferential treatment to specific creditors and consider the necessity to investigate further the accounts of those where the balance decreased substantially during the period six months prior to the petition. List all payments made before the due date and material returns.

3   Prepare a worksheet of changes in major creditors' accounts for the period of at least ninety days prior to the petition to ascertain that certain suppliers are not being favored by substantial payments, returns, or offsets.

4   Scrutinize accounts payable for names of related companies or relatives and investigate the nature and circumstances of any such accounts for the year prior to the petition.

5   Prepare a list of major vendors (representing more than _____ percent of merchandise purchased in a particular department but not less than $_____) and dollar purchases from _____ to _____ and investigate:

   a   Interrelationships of any officers and directors.
   b   Mark-up on purchased products.

6   Compare balances shown on the books with any claims filed by creditors and reconcile significant differences.

7   Review the accounts payable as of the date the petition was filed to ascertain that the transaction activity cutoffs for prefiling obligations were properly made.

8   Ascertain that all payments on accounts made after the date the petition was filed are for obligations incurred subsequent to the petition date.

9   Group liabilities due to factors. If a supplier factors its accounts, the obligation is to the factor. Obligations to suppliers using the same factor should be shown under the factor's name.

ACCRUED EXPENSES AND OTHER CURRENT LIABILITIES

1   Review the account balances as of the date the petition was filed to ascertain that the transaction activity cutoffs for prefiling obligations were properly made.

Taxes Payable

1   Determine the amount of tax liability indicated in the records.

2   Examine the most recently filed returns and review all open years' returns.

3   Ascertain the unpaid balance of the following taxes:

   a   Federal, state, and local corporate tax returns.
   b   Federal, state, and local payroll tax returns.

 c State and local sales tax returns.

 d State and local property tax returns.

 e Commercial rent, gross receipts, or occupancy tax returns (usually of a local nature).

 f Truck mileage tax returns.

 g Capital stock franchise tax returns or stock transfer tax returns.

4 Compute accrued payroll taxes to the date of the petition or of the report if an out-of-court settlement is being considered.

5 Analyze expense accounts and establish relationship to payroll.

6 Reconcile tax claims filed by various government authorities to amounts determined from examination of returns and records. Notify counsel of any difference so that claims or records can be adjusted.

7 Verify that all tax claims are properly classified as administration or nonadministration claims.

8 Determine the nature, amount, and availability of net operating loss carry-forward that can be used by the reorganized debtor.

Wages Payable and Other Accrued Expenses

1 Prepare or have management prepare a schedule including name, address, Social Security number, gross wages due, period covered, and taxes to be withheld for each employee (on hourly wages, salary, or commissions).

2 Verify amounts due against payroll records to establish that the particular employee in question actually worked for the period claimed.

3 Where union contracts exist, scrutinize the contracts to determine how much severance, sick leave, or vacation pay employees are entitled to receive.

4 Segregate the wages and accrued vacation, sick leave, and severance pay into priority and nonpriority classifications.

5 Accrue other wage-related obligations such as union fund contributions and retirement fund contributions.

6 Schedule all other unpaid and unrecorded expenses.

7 Determine existence and terms of any employee benefit plans.

NOTES PAYABLE AND LONG-TERM DEBT

Notes Payable

1 Prepare schedule showing:

 a Creditor name and address.

 b Date of inception.

    c Original principal amount and unpaid balance.
    d Interest rate.
    e Due date.
    f Description of security given and date lien was granted.
    g Guarantors and extent of their obligation.
    h Restrictive clauses and breaches thereof.
    i Arrearages in principal and interest payments.

2 Review the timing and nature of all security given _____ (at least ninety) days prior to the petition.

3 Examine all material payments and other debits within a period of at least ninety days prior to the petition to determine possible preferential treatment of specific creditors. List details with respect to large returns of merchandise and payments before maturity.

4 Review all material payable transactions with owners, officers, and affiliated companies during the year prior to bankruptcy to ascertain that they were ''arm's length'' transactions.

5 Compare balances shown on books with any claims filed and reconcile significant differences.

6 Ascertain whether any personal guarantees were given to any creditors within one year prior to date of the petition.

7 Review the account transactions _____ days before the petition was filed and _____ days subsequent to the filing to ascertain that the cutoffs for prefiling obligations were properly made.

8 Ascertain that all payments on notes made after the date the petition was filed are for obligations incurred subsequent to the petition date.

Mortgages and Other Secured Debts

 1 Prepare schedule showing:

    a Creditor name and address.
    b Original principal amount and unpaid balance.
    c Arrearage, in number of payments and total amount.
    d Date of inception.
    e Interest rate.
    f Copy of amortization schedule, including any balloon payment.
    g Description of security given and date lien was granted.
    h Guarantors and extent of their obligation.
    i Restrictive clauses and indication of breaches.
    j Extent of real estate tax arrearages.
    k Assessed value of real estate given as security.

 2 Review the timing and nature of all security given for a period of at least ninety days (one year for insiders) prior to petition.

3 Where accounts receivable are financed or factored, obtain a copy of the agreement and list special terms. List monthly debits and credits for a minimum of twelve months showing:

   a Cash advances.
   b Factor charges.
   c Interest charges.
   d Chargebacks.

4 Determine for factored or financed accounts receivable:

   a That no improprieties exist.
   b If the lender has unreasonably improved its position by taking collateral for less than fair value.
   c That the lender has at all times maintained dominion and control over its collateral with particular emphasis on promptness of remittances to the debtor.
   d That chargebacks on factored accounts have not been duplicated.

5 Examine all material payments and other debits within a period of at least ninety days prior to the petition to determine possible preferential treatment to specific creditors. List details with respect to large returns of merchandise and payments before maturity.

6 Review all material payable transactions with owners, officers, and affiliated companies during the year prior to the petition to ascertain that they were "arm's length" transactions.

7 Compare balances shown on books with claims filed and reconcile significant differences.

8 Ascertain whether any personal guarantees were given to any creditors ninety days (one year for insiders) prior to the petition.

9 Review the account transactions fifteen days before the petition was filed and fifteen days subsequent to the filing to ascertain that the cutoffs for prefiling obligations were properly made.

10 Ascertain that all payments on notes made after the date the petition was filed are for obligations incurred subsequent to the petition date.

11 Obtain details of UCC filings from the secretary of state for each state where debtor had assets to verify collateral given for loans and advances.

STOCKHOLDERS' EQUITY

Contributed Capital

1 Obtain stock certificate book and prepare schedule indicating:

   a Certificate number.
   b Shareholder.

    c　Number of shares.
    d　Date issued.
    e　Date canceled.
    f　Restrictions noted in stubs (or obtain information from transfer agent).

2　List significant characteristics of each class of stock.
3　Determine consideration received for stock, noting:

    a　Whether cash, services, or tangible assets.
    b　Per-share amount.
    c　Total amount.
    d　Amount paid in excess of par.

4　Obtain details surrounding all stock redemptions and reacquisitions, with particular emphasis on legally defined capital of company at such times.
5　Determine valuation basis of treasury stock.
6　Determine status of stock subscriptions receivable.
7　Examine and abstract all available minutes and resolutions related to contributed capital.
8　Analyze stock option and warrant activity and determine status of those not exercised.

Retained Earnings

1　Analyze for previous four to five years, with full explanations for all debits and credits.
2　Establish propriety of all charges not arising from operations.
3　Segregate any amounts that would properly be classified as donated or arising from revaluation of assets.

REVENUE

Sales Revenue and Sales Deductions

1　Test the cutoff of sales transactions.
2　Check recent common carriers' receipts to determine unrecorded amounts.
3　Test check a period of at least the last six months for sales at less than customary or list prices. Also check for prices that, although customary, are generally below those of competitors. Compare the prices charged during the last six months with those of the prior six months.
4　Prepare a schedule showing, by month, comparative sales, sales returns, sales allowances, and net sales for the last three years and indicate customers constituting in excess of 10 percent of total volume.

5 Review sales, sales orders, and cancellations subsequent to the date of filing the petition.

6 Prepare a brief description of purchasing procedure.

7 Determine unfilled orders and management's plans for completing orders.

8 Determine the potential cost of fulfillment of product guarantees.

9 Prepare a schedule of sales of scrap and waste materials. Compare with previous periods.

10 Examine all sales transactions with owners, officers, and affiliated companies during the year prior to the petition for adequate consideration.

11 The above procedures are normally not performed in as much detail for liquidating concerns, such as assignments or chapter 7 cases, as they are for going concerns such as out-of-court settlement or chapter 11 reorganizations.

Other Revenue

1 Scan other revenue accounts for unusual items and make appropriate examinations where required.

COSTS AND EXPENSES

Disbursements in General

1 Review all disbursements exceeding $_____ and merchandise returns during the last six months or longer prior to the date of the filing to ascertain that:

 a The goods and/or services were actually received.
 b The goods and/or services were received during this time period.
 c The payment or return of merchandise to the vendor was made in a similar manner to all other payments and returns.

2 Review all disbursements in excess of $_____ made for sixty days subsequent to the petition date to verify that they represent payment for goods and services received or rendered subsequent to the date of the filing.

3 Carefully review the disbursement to officers, directors, affiliated companies, and to other related parties for the year prior to date of the petition.

Cost of Products Sold

1 Test the cutoff of cost of sales.

2 Test cost of goods sold entries against shipping records.

3 Prepare a schedule showing, by month, comparative purchases for the last three years.

4 Prepare a brief description of purchasing procedure.

5 Test-check purchases during the previous six to twelve months for adequacy of receiving documentation.

6 Prepare a schedule and analyze all returns in excess of $_____ within six months prior to the petition indicating the business reason for the return.

7 Examine all returns and allowances granted owners, officers, relatives, or related companies during the year prior to the petition.

8 Ascertain whether the debtor received credit for all customary purchase discounts, allowances, and rebates.

9 Review purchase commitments for potential losses or excessive commitments.

Payroll

1 Test selected payroll entries against time cards or piecework reports, union contracts, rate authorization, and deductions authorized.

2 Determine that payroll has been distributed to proper account classifications.

3 Compare recent payroll periods with those of the previous year. Justify any differences.

4 Prepare a comparative analysis for three years prior to the petition date of executives' salaries which exceeded $_____ for the year ended _____.

5 Observe a payoff. Compare payroll checks to be distributed with the payroll register and prove register totals.

6 Scrutinize (selected weeks) _____

_____

of payroll for payments to officers, relatives, or principals, for unusual payments of back wages and for inordinately high rates of pay.

7 Determine the date of the last union audit and potential additional liability over and above reported contributions.

Other Costs and Expenses

1 Investigate month-to-month and year-to-year changes in amounts of various costs and expenses.

2 Analyze rent expense and abstract pertinent lease terms.

3 Inquire as to the possibility of subleasing of all or part of leased premises.

4 Analyze professional fees and determine services rendered.

5 Analyze officers' salaries and expense accounts.

6 Search for unrecorded liabilities that may involve losses or expenses.

7 Analyze all other significant expense accounts.

CONTRACTS AND AGREEMENTS

1 Examine and obtain copies of:

  a Shareholders' buy/sell agreements.
  b Retirement agreements.
  c Employment contracts.
  d Insurance agreements.

2 Examine and abstract all other significant information in contracts and agreements.

Financial Statements

1 The accountant will prepare not only current financial statements but supplementary statements that are helpful in evaluating the future prospects of the business. Three important questions must be answered in order to determine the direction in which the company's future will lie:

What is the current financial position of the business?

If the current position looks financially feasible, what about the future?

If, after projecting the company's operations, the future looks fairly promising, what financial methods can be employed to pump new, healthy financial "blood" into the business?

The report issued by the accountant states the results of operations, and hopefully provides needed information about the possibility of the company's future existence.

2   Among the documents the accountant will submit, at the time the petition is filed or shortly thereafter, are the Statement of Affairs (sworn answers to twenty-one questions about the debtor's past operations; see chapter 7), recent financial statements, schedules with detailed information about the assets and liabilities of the debtor, including the amount due each creditor, and a statement of the executory contracts of the debtor. Also, the accountant may prepare a statement of affairs showing realizable values, and other special-purpose statements to assist the debtor in securing additional funds. These various statements are discussed in detail in paragraphs 4–38.

3   The accountant's report, since it contains an opinion on the statements submitted, is of great importance in bankruptcy court proceedings. Because of the nature of the proceedings, there are limitations on the scope of the accountant's examination, and any uncertainty concerning the ability of the company to continue operations may require the accountants to disclaim an opinion on the statements. The nature of the report is described in chapter 13. The last part of this chapter (beginning with paragraph 50) deals with the effect of settlements on future statements.

FORM AND SUBSTANCE OF FINANCIAL STATEMENTS

4   Many of the statements and schedules the accountant is required to prepare in bankruptcy or insolvency proceedings are the same as those used by companies not experiencing financial difficulty. But in insolvency proceedings these reports are used in specific ways to provide the information needed to effect a fair and equitable settlement to all those involved.

Financial Data Required at the Date of Filing of Petition in Chapter 11

5   When a petition is filed to initiate proceedings under chapter 11, certain documents must be filed at that time or shortly thereafter. Among the most important are the following:

1   Statement of Affairs. This consists of answers to twenty-one questions concerning the debtor's past operations, and should not be confused with the report titled "Statement of Affairs," to be discussed later, which shows the realizable value of the assets and the liabilities in the order in which they will be paid.

2   Recent financial statements including:

   a   Statements of financial position, statements of changes in financial position, and income statements issued during the two years prior to filing.

   b   Current statement of financial position.

    c Statement of operations covering the period from the date of the last balance sheet to the date of the petition.

    d Statement of capital deficiency as of date of petition.

3 Schedules with detailed information about the assets and liabilities of the debtor as of the date of the petition.

4 Schedule showing the summary of operations and the percentage relationship of each item to sales for each of the previous three to five years.

5 Correct statement of the amount due each creditor, including secured, unsecured, contingent, and unliquidated claims.

6 Correct statement of the number and kind of interests of each equity security holder.

7 Statement of all executory contracts.

    6 The accountant obviously plays a very valuable role in obtaining the information required in these statements, and any attempt to file a petition without the aid of an accountant would reduce the reliability of the data accompanying the petition. Chapter 7, paragraphs 22–38, contains a more detailed description of the schedules and other information filed with the petition.

Balance Sheets (Statements of "Condition") as of Petition Date

    7 It is important to determine the financial position of the debtor as of the date the petition was filed. This is necessary to determine the liabilities that should be classified as prepetition claims. Liabilities incurred operating the business in a chapter 11 case are considered administrative expenses, and those incurred prior to filing the petition, unless entitled to a priority or secured claim classification, will be general, unsecured claims.

    8 The assets as of the petition date must be determined for several reasons. For example, where a floating lien exists on inventory and/or receivables, the actual balance in these accounts must be determined to establish the amount of the claim that is secured. These balances are also necessary to evaluate if certain suppliers were given a preference over others. Preparation of a balance sheet as of the petition date may help discover assets that were concealed prior to the filing of a petition.

    9 One other area where accountants' services may be needed is assisting in the determination of insolvency and the exact date at which it occurred. While the proof of solvency or insolvency is a function of attorneys, accountants determine the debtor's financial condition, prepare worksheets, and compile other supporting documents and records necessary to prove the client's condition. The proof of insolvency is necessary where preferential payments or fraudulent transfers are involved. Also, in a "cram down" the extent to which the stockholders participate in the plan depends on the solvency of the debtor. Normally, the first step in the determination of the solvency or insolvency of the debtor is the preparation of a balance sheet as of the date the petition was filed.

10 Often, an income statement showing the operating results for the year up to the date the bankruptcy petition was filed is also prepared. To prepare the balance sheet as of the petition date and an income statement for the year up to the date the petition was filed, it may be necessary to use a cutoff date subsequent to the petition date and evaluate the transactions that occurred between the two dates to establish the balance in the debtor's accounts as of the date the bankruptcy petition was filed.

11 Exhibit 12-1 contains the balance sheet for Marin Motor Oil as of the date the petition was filed and an income statement (in abbreviated form) for January 1, 1981 to April 20, 1981 (date of petition).

12 While balance sheets are normally prepared in the conventional manner, alternative forms are sometimes used because of the doubts surrounding the balances as they are found in the accounts. Three columns might be presented, showing balances as per books, certain proposed corrections, and balances after certain proposed corrections, so that all those using the statement will be aware that the figures are tentative. Exhibit 12-2 shows this type of balance sheet.

13 Exhibit 12-3 shows the conventional balance sheet for the ABC Company as of December 31, 19X6, along with the notes to the statement. This balance sheet and other statements of the ABC Company will serve as the focal point of discussion throughout this chapter. Four months after the date of the balance sheet presented in Exhibit 12-3, the ABC Company appealed to its creditors for their assistance. Exhibit 12-4 shows the balance sheet as of April 28, 19X7, which is prepared in the normal manner except that all secured liabilities are subtracted from the assets to which they relate. In this balance sheet, the balance of accounts receivable is reduced to zero since they are pledged to the First National Bank in the amount of $600,000 and the net realizable value is only $584,800. Priority claims are subtracted from the total unpledged assets before arriving at the total book value of assets available to unsecured creditors. The general claim for the Employees' Profit Sharing Trust was for past benefits due more than 180 days prior to the date the petition was filed. If these benefits had been due within the 180-day period, it is possible that some part would have been considered a priority claim (chapter 3, paragraph 93). Also listed are factors that may create an increased capital deficit, such as additional losses that may be sustained on realization of assets, and administrative expenses or additional contingent or undisclosed liabilities.

14 This type of balance sheet is very useful in meetings with creditors' committees, in chapter 11 reorganization proceedings, or in out-of-court settlements. The final total represents the assets that are available for unsecured creditors. All assets are normally presented at book value less any necessary adjustments that should be made as a result of the audit. These are not liquidation values. It is assumed that the business will be rehabilitated

Exhibit 12-1   Financial Statements as of Petition Date

BALANCE SHEET
APRIL 20, 1981

ASSETS

CURRENT ASSETS:

Cash	$ 640,997	
Accounts receivable—trade, less allowance for		
doubtful accounts of $24,338	1,907,551	
Other receivables (Note 2)	2,592,562	
Due from stockholder	818,077	
Prepaid and refundable income taxes	54,606	
Other current assets (Note 3)	41,259	
Total Current Assets		$6,055,052
PROPERTY AND EQUIPMENT (Note 4)		731,940
LAND HELD FOR INVESTMENT,		
ACAPULCO, MEXICO		86,440
		$ 6,873,432

LIABILITIES AND STOCKHOLDERS' DEFICIENCY

CURRENT LIABILITIES:

Notes payable to banks (Note 5)	$4,355,330	
Accounts payable (Note 6)	6,333,873	
Other current liabilities (Note 7)	494,050	
Other payables (Note 8)	34,623	
Total Current Liabilities		$11,217,876

CONTINGENCY (Note 9)

STOCKHOLDERS' DEFICIENCY:

Common stock	4,882	
Paid-in capital	4,785	
Accumulated deficit	(4,354,111)	
Total Stockholders' Deficiency		(4,344,444)
		$ 6,873,432

Unaudited—see accountants' compilation report and notes to financial statements.

Exhibit 12-1   (*Continued*)

STATEMENTS OF OPERATIONS

	Year Ended December 31, 1980	January 1, 1981 to April 20, 1981	January 1, 1980 to April 20, 1981
SALES	$272,715,150	$229,079,991	$501,795,141
COST OF SALES	271,113,817	230,188,378	501,302,195
GROSS MARGIN (LOSS) ON SALES	1,601,333	(1,108,387)	492,946
LOSS FROM COMMODITY TRADING	(1,188,248)	(785,480)	(1,973,728)
GROSS INCOME (LOSS)	413,085	(1,893,867)	(1,480,782)
EXPENSES:			
Operating	623,806	334,446	958,252
Selling, general and administrative	1,300,163	882,080	2,182,243
	1,923,969	1,216,526	3,140,495
NET LOSS	$ (1,510,884)	$ (3,110,393)	$ (4,621,277)

STATEMENT OF ACCUMULATED DEFICIT

Retained earnings, January 1, 1980	$ 267,166
Loss for period January 1, 1980 to April 20, 1981	(4,621,277)
Accumulated deficit, April 20, 1981	$(4,354,111)

NOTES TO FINANCIAL STATEMENTS

Note 1   Proceedings under Chapter 11:

On April 20, 1981, the Company filed a petition for reorganization under chapter 11 of the Bankruptcy Reform Act, and continued operating as a debtor-in-possession. The financial statements have been prepared on a going concern basis. No consideration has been given to the effect, if any, that a plan of reorganization, if and when consummated, may have on the financial position of the Company.

Unaudited—see accountants' compilation report and notes to financial statements.

Exhibit 12-1 *(Continued)*

Note 2	Other Receivables:	
	Other receivables are due from the following:	
	Cargill Investor Services, Inc.	$ 62,035
	Note receivable, due April 10, 1981	25,000
	Automobile service stations	2,327
	Petrobras Co., Inc.	10,679
	Oil Company, Inc.	238,557
	Nick-O-Mar Realty Corp.	76,013
	Aviation, Inc.	2,176,000
	Miscellaneous	1,951
		$2,592,562
Note 3	Other Current Assets:	
	Other current assets consist of the following:	
	Prepaid insurance	$ 17,451
	Mobil Oil Co. credit cards	14,023
	Bid bond	5,903
	Miscellaneous	3,882
		$ 41,259
Note 4	Property and Equipment:	
	Property and equipment consists of the following:	
	Cost:	
	Furniture and fixtures	$ 35,685
	Automotive equipment	278,673
	Warehouse equipment	17,991
	Helicopter	613,800
	Service station equipment and improvements	164,856
		1,111,005
	Less: Accumulated depreciation	379,065
		$ 731,940

The helicopter collateralizes the note payable to the National Community Bank of N.J.

Note 5	Notes Payable to Banks:	
	Notes payable to banks are payable to the following:	
	National Community Bank of N.J.	$3,355,330
	Citizens First National Bank of N.J.	1,000,000
		$4,355,330

Unaudited—see accountants' compilation report and notes to financial statements.

Exhibit 12-1   (*Continued*)

Note 6   Accounts Payable:

Accounts payable consist of the following:

Trade creditors	$5,839,071
Inventory overdrawn	493,802
Bank overdraft	1,000
	$6,333,873

Note 7   Other Current Liabilities

Other current liabilities consist of:

New Jersey fuel tax	$ 392,778
Federal excise tax	37,836
Payroll	5,368
Security deposit	10,000
Other taxes principally payroll withholding	6,843
Interest on notes payable	41,225
	$ 494,050

Note 8   Other Payables:

Other payables are due to the following:

Fra Mar, Inc.	$ 17,623
Retail Gasoline Sales Company	17,000
	$ 34,623

Note 9   Contingency:

The Company's activities are being audited by the Department of Energy. The ultimate outcome of the audit cannot be determined at this time.

Note 10   Unrecorded Rental Charges:

The financial statements do not give effect to rental charges for 1981 and prior years from Oil Company, Inc. and Retail Gasoline Sales Company totalling $123,000 and $207,000 respectively.

Unaudited—see accountants' compilation report and notes to financial statements.

and continue operations. The balance sheet differs from the Statement of Affairs in that the balance sheet is not prepared on the assumption that the business will be liquidated. The Statement of Affairs is described in detail in a subsequent section (paragraphs 24–33).

Notes to Statements

15   The notes to the balance sheet should also receive greater attention than is conventional. They should explain the content of each account,

Exhibit 12-2 Balance Sheet Presentation Showing Proposed Corrections to Bankrupt's Books and Final Balances after Corrections

JIM STORES, INC. AND SUBSIDIARY COMPANIES

CONSOLIDATED BALANCE SHEET

October 14, 19X7

Assets	Balances, as Per Books	Certain Proposed Corrections— Increase/ (Decrease)	Balances, After Certain Proposed Corrections
Cash	$ (66,857)	$ 116,257	$ 59,953
		(42,899)	
		53,452	
Accounts receivable—trade	2,968,661	10	2,900,516
		(61,746)	
		(6,409)	
Less: allowance for doubtful account	829,765	5,584	1,300,000
		(475,829)	
		10	
	2,138,896		1,600,516
Notes and other accounts receivable— nontrade	591,536	6,000	597,536
Merchandise inventories	1,005,344	105,987	1,043,072
		(68,259)	
Prepaid expenses	27,261	(12,538)	14,723
Investments and advances	1,323,262	(10,235)	1,579,651
		11,127	
		292,997	
		(37,500)	
Deposits and other assets	134,878	(25,863)	109,015
Property and equipment Land	673,750	—	673,750
Furniture, fixtures, and leasehold improvements	667,760	(238,220)	429,540
Less: accumulated depreciation and amortization	491,630	197,909	293,721
	176,130		135,819
Construction in progress	615	(615,000)	—
Total assets	$6,619,200	$ (805,165)	$5,814,035

Exhibit 12-2 *(Continued)*

Liabilities and Stockholders' Equity	Balances, as Per Books	Certain Proposed Corrections— Increase/ (Decrease)	Balances, After Certain Proposed Corrections
Collateralized obligations			
Notes payable—GCA Company	$ 122,500	$ (4,756)	$ 117,744
Advances from Jones Company	1,226,771	(42,899)	1,183,872
Mortgage payable	73,750	—	73,750
Lorraine Co. Chapter XI notes	53,954	—	53,954
	1,476,975		1,429,320
Uncollateralized obligations			
Construction loan	615,000	(615,000)	—
5% debenture bonds, due 2/1/X9	800,000	—	800,000
Notes payable—banks	162,000	—	162,000
Notes payable—other	493,830	1,000	464,830
Checks written in excess of		(30,000)	
bank balances	—	116,257	116,257
Accounts payable and			
accrued liabilities	1,261,734	53,741	1,312,043
		(25,120)	
		4,617	
		2,071	
		15,000	
Affiliated companies	—	293,882	293,882
	3,332,564		3,149,012
Deferred income taxes	360,000	—	360,000
Deferred income	1,425	—	1,425
Ledger imbalance	94,347	(58,310)	5,060
		(44,503)	
		13,527	
Stockholders' equity			
Common stock (par value 50¢ per share; authorized 500,000 shares, plus 36,000 shares reserved for issuance pursuant to acquisition of subsidiary NPR Co., less 23,856 shares held in treasury)	240,283	750	231,033
		(10,000)	
Paid-in surplus	1,008,337	10,377	1,024,714
		6,000	
Retained earnings (deficit)	105,269	(13,527)	(386,529)
		87,021	
		(2,286)	
		(563,007)	
	1,353,889		869,218
Total liabilities and stockholders' equity	$6,619,200	$ (805,165)	$5,814,035

Exhibit 12-3 Example of Standard Balance Sheet with Explanatory Notes, Showing Financial Condition of ABC Company as of December 31, 19X6

ABC COMPANY, INC.

BALANCE SHEET

December 31, 19X6

Assets				
Current assets				
Cash				$ 35,295
Accounts receivable			$553,200	
Less: allowance for discounts		$ 40,200		
Allowance for uncollectibles		92,300	132,500	420,700
Inventories				650,000
Tax refund receivable				294,673
Total current assets				1,400,668
Fixed and other assets:				
Property, plant, and equipment				
(note 4)				
Land			22,000	
Building	$1,150,000			
Less: accumulated depreciation	510,000	640,000		
Fixtures and equipment	93,000			
Less: accumulated depreciation	22,000	71,000	733,000	
Investment in XYZ Company			20,000	
Goodwill (notes 1 and 5)			10,250	763,250
Total assets				$2,163,918

include some of the major audit steps that were performed, and discuss any information that was not available during the examination and any deficiencies in the books and records. For example, a physical inventory might not have been taken at the date the petition is filed and the accountant may wish to disclose the method used to satisfy the requirement that the inventory be correctly stated. The notes in support of accounts receivable and inventories, which are only two of the many that were needed to explain the accounts in the balance sheet of Jim Stores, Inc. (Exhibit 12-2) are shown in Exhibit 12-5 to illustrate how detailed the notes to the financial statements must typically be.

Exhibit 12-3 (*Continued*)

Liabilities and Stockholders' Equity		
Current liabilities		
Accounts payable		$ 511,618
Salaries payable		100,500
Commissions payable		10,000
Taxes payable		100,000
Notes payable (note 3)		570,000
Payable to contractors		125,000
Reserve for liquidation losses (note 2)		200,000
Total current liabilities		1,617,118
Long-term liabilities		
Mortgages payable (note 4)		487,500
Other liabilities		
Notes payable—officer		36,000
Total liabilities		2,140,618
Stockholders' equity		
Common stock ($10 par, 20,000 shares authorized,		
18,000 shares outstanding; see note 5)	$180,000	
Additional paid-in capital	100,000	
Deficit	(256,700)	23,300
Total liabilities and stockholders' equity		$2,163,918

16   The balance sheet becomes the basis for the schedules of assets and liabilities that the debtor must file. These schedules consist of sworn statements of the debtor's assets and liabilities as of the date of filing the petition and include the same basic information found in the debtor's balance sheet. (For detailed discussion, see chapter 7, paragraphs 22–36.)

17   Bankruptcy Rule 1007 requires that the debtor file its detailed schedules within fifteen days after entry of the order for relief for an involuntary petition or within fifteen days of filing a voluntary petition. An extension of time may be granted only on application for cause shown and after notice.

18   Quite clearly, in addition to its conventional significance as a statement of position at one point in time, the balance sheet prepared as of the date of the petition derives greater importance because of the schedules that are prepared from it.

Exhibit 12-3   (*Continued*)

ABC COMPANY, INC.

NOTES TO BALANCE SHEET

Note 1. Basis of Presentation and Summary of Significant Accounting Policies

Basis of Presentation:

ABC Company, Inc., had sustained losses from its operations during the four years ended December 31, 19X6, and based on subsequent unaudited financial information, losses have continued since December 31, 19X6. The accompanying financial statements have been prepared on a going-concern basis. Continuation of the Company's operations, realization of its assets, and liquidation of its liabilities are dependent upon the ability of the Company to achieve a profitable level of operations and to obtain additional financing.

Summary of Significant Accounting Policies:

Inventories—The total merchandise inventory at December 31, 19X6, is stated at the lower of cost or market, determined by the FIFO method.

Property, Plant, and Equipment—Property, plant, and equipment are carried at cost. Additions and improvements are capitalized; maintenance and repairs are charged to operations as incurred. Depreciation is calculated using the straight-line method over the estimated useful lives of the assets.

Goodwill—The goodwill was transferred to the Company in 19X0 (see Note 5) and is being amortized at the rate of $1,000 per year.

Note 2. Operations to Be Discontinued and Estimated Liquidation Losses

On October 29, 19X6, the Board of Directors resolved to discontinue the operations of one division. A summary of the assets of this division is as follows:

Accounts Receivable—Net	$100,000
Inventories	225,000
Property, Plant, and Equipment	130,000
	$455,000

The liquidation of this division will probably result in liquidation losses. The Company had provided a reserve for estimated losses of $200,000; however, no determination can be made at this time as to the total amount of such losses.

Note 3. Notes Payable

The Company entered into a financing agreement in 19X4 with the First National Bank of Boston wherein it applied for a revolving credit of $600,000. As security for the payment of the Company's debts to the bank, it granted and assigned to the bank a continuing security interest in all accounts receivable owned or created by the Company. The continuation of this agreement is conditioned

Exhibit 12-3 *(Continued)*

upon (1) a cash projection (unaudited) for the six months ending June 30, 19X7, furnished to the bank by the Company, (2) the ability of the Company to improve cash flow (including the program set forth in Note 2), and (3) the assumption that there will be no material adverse changes in the Company's financial plans and projection on an overall basis.

Note 4. Mortgage Payable

Property, plant, and equipment are collateral for mortgages payable of $487,500. The mortgages payable mature in varying amounts to January 31, fifteen years from now, bearing interest from 5 percent to 9 percent per annum.

Note 5. Stockholders' Equity

ABC Company, Inc., was incorporated under the laws of the State of New York on September 17, 19X0. Prior to that date, on April 6, 19X0, AB Company, Inc., a wholly owned subsidiary of AF Industries, Inc., transferred certain assets to the new company, ABC Company, Inc., as follows:

Merchandise inventory	$296,000
Fixed assets (net of accumulated depreciation)	22,306
Goodwill	17,000
Cash surrender value of life insurance (net of loans thereon of $42,670)	5,775
Prepaid expenses	12,600
Other assets	4,500
	$358,181
Represented by: Capital Stock (8,000 shares)	$ 80,000
Loans payable	278,181
	$358,181

On August 5, 19X1, ABC Company issued 10,000 shares of stock at $20 per share to the public. As of December 31, 19X6, AF Industries owned 30 percent of the outstanding stock and the President, Irving J. Stein, owned 10 percent.

Income Statements

19 The debtor is required to file with the court, usually on a monthly basis, a statement setting forth the results from operations. At times the court may require operating or cash flow statements more frequently. Because of the complexities involved in preparing such a statement, an accountant's services usually prove to be necessary. For example, some statements must be prepared on an accrual basis (chapter 8, paragraphs 14–19).

20 A detailed income statement or Statement of Operations is presented for the last complete year of operation and for the period subsequently to the

Exhibit 12-4 Balance Sheet, or Statement of Financial Condition, of the ABC Company as of April 28, 19X7, after it Had Appealed to its Creditors for Assistance

ABC COMPANY, INC.

STATEMENT OF FINANCIAL CONDITION

April 28, 19X7

Assets

Current assets			
Cash			$ 7,327
Accounts receivable—assigned		$710,100	
Less: allowance for discounts	$ 50,100		
Allowance for uncollectibles	75,200	125,300	
		584,800	
Less: due to First National Bank			
of Boston (see contra)		$600,000	
Inventories		$795,000	
Less: due to contractors		75,000	720,000
Tax refund receivable			7,673
Total unencumbered current assets			735,000
Fixed and other assets			
Property, plant, and equipment			
Land		22,000	
Building	$1,150,000		
Less: accumulated depreciation	550,000	600,000	
Fixtures and equipment	93,000		
Less: accumulated depreciation	25,000	68,000	
		690,000	
Less: mortgage payable		487,500	202,500
Investment in XYZ Company		20,000	
Goodwill		10,000	232,500
Total unencumbered assets			967,500
Less: priority claims			247,500
Total assets available to			
unsecured creditors			$720,000

Exhibit 12-4   (*Continued*)

Liabilities, Less Capital Deficiency			
Priority claims			
Taxes payable			$100,000
Salaries payable			127,500
Commissions payable			20,000
Total priority claims			$247,500
Fully collateralized claims			
Mortgages payable			$487,500
Contractors payable (see contra)			75,000
Total fully collateralized claims			$562,500
Partially collateralized claims			
First National Bank of Boston			
Notes payable		$500,000	
Accounts payable (see below)		100,000	
		600,000	
Less: accounts receivable—assigned			
(see contra)		584,800	$ 15,200
General claims			
Due to ABC Company, Inc.—Employees'			
Profit Sharing Trust		25,000	
Accounts payable	$682,000		
Less: accounts payable—First National			
Bank of Boston (see above)	100,000	582,000	607,000
Notes payable—officer			36,000
Total unsecured liabilities			658,200
Reserve for liquidation losses			200,000
Capital deficiency			(138,200)
Subject to:			
1. Additional losses that may be sustained on realization of assets and administrative expenses			
2. Contingent and undisclosed liabilities			
Total unsecured liabilities less capital deficiency			$720,000

date of filing the petition in bankruptcy court. In addition to the amount, the percentage of each item listed on the statement is given in relation to net sales. Exhibit 12-6 is an example of this type of statement for the ABC Company. Comparative incomes are often prepared in less detail, but percentages for the last three to five years are included, as shown in Exhibit 12-7.

Statement of Changes in Financial Position

21 To abide by the requirement of APB Opinion No. 19, it may be necessary for the accountant also to prepare the statement of changes in financial position. This statement was illustrated in the operating statements contained in chapter 8.

Cash Receipts and Disbursements Statement

22 In some instances the court may require that a Cash Receipts and Disbursements Statement be filed weekly or bimonthly, although an order may be secured deleting this requirement for cause. The preparation of cash receipts and disbursements statements becomes extremely important where the debtor's plan calls for installment payments and it is necessary for the accountant to show that such payments will be made. See chapter 9, paragraphs 19 and 36.

Statement of Capital Deficiency

23 A Statement of Capital Deficiency is often prepared, setting forth in summary form the changes in the capital accounts for the last few years. This statement indicates the time period when the losses began to occur, any withdrawals by the owners, and all other major transactions dealing with the capital accounts. The Statement of Capital Deficiency for the ABC Company as of April 28, 19X7, is presented in Exhibit 12-8.

Statement of Affairs

24 A Statement of Affairs is quite commonly prepared when a business is experiencing financial difficulty and considering initiation of some type of remedy. This statement should not be confused with the Statement of Affairs which must be filed under the Bankruptcy Code when a debtor files a petition, and consists merely of answers to questions regarding the debtor's past operations (chapter 7, paragraph 37). The statement of affairs is often prepared at the request of the bankruptcy judge or the creditors' committee in out-of-court proceedings and it provides information that assists the credi-

Exhibit 12-5   Selected Notes to the Balance Sheet for Jim Stores, Inc., Shown in Exhibit 12-2

JIM STORES, INC.

NOTES TO CONSOLIDATED BALANCE SHEET (PARTIAL)

Accounts Receivable, Trade—$2,900,516

The amount of accounts receivable shown in the accompanying balance sheet as of October 14, 19X7, represents the aggregate amount appearing in the general ledgers of the companies, less a correction for certain accounts receivable that had been sold. Prior to October 14, the companies had closed a number of stores and had sold the accounts receivable originating at these stores. However, such accounts had inadvertently not been eliminated from the books of the companies and we have made a correction for such sold accounts.

In addition, the accounts receivable are subject to the following comments:

1. The accounts receivable have been pledged as collateral under a financing agreement with Jones & Company, Inc. Prior to our engagement, Jones & Company had requested each of the stores to prepare trial balances of its accounts receivable on or about October 14, 19X7 (detailed accounts receivable information is available only at the stores). We have obtained such trial balances from Jones and have compared the totals thereon to the companies' general ledger control accounts as of October 14, taking into consideration intervening sales and collections in cases where the trial balances were prepared as of a date other than October 14. In making this comparison, we find that the trial balances do not agree with the general ledger control accounts by an aggregate of $3,460.80 (trial balance totals in excess of ledger balances). These differences range from one corporation in which trial balances exceed the ledger balance by $6,402.32 to another where the aggregate of individual store balances is $16,693.02 less than the corporate ledger balance. We have not corrected for these differences because we did not investigate them to the extent necessary to determine their origin and their effect on other accounts. To the extent that we did investigate, we noted that the following factors contributed to the differences:

   a. As described in the Cash section of this report, there was considerable confusion and erroneous handling of cash collections on or about October 14, 19X7.

   b. Customers occasionally make deposits for layaway purchases and these deposits are entered in the accounts receivable control accounts without further segregation or detailed accounting. The trial balances prepared on or about October 14 did not include the amounts of open customer deposits. Such deposits, which are not otherwise segregated in the companies' records, represent unsecured obligations of the companies to the customers and should be recognized as such.

2. Jones & Company maintains a record of the amount of accounts receivable representing its collateral. We requested that Jones report to us the balance as shown on its records, for comparison with the companies' ledgers. The amount

Exhibit 12-5 *(Continued)*

reported by Jones to us differs from the amount recorded on the companies' books. We understand that Jones has attempted to identify this difference.

3. In 19X6 the companies sold certain accounts receivable that had previously been written off as uncollectible. Approximately $2,400,000 of such receivables were sold for a consideration of $300,000. Subsequent to that time the companies have collected at least $140,000 on accounts receivable that had been written off, but these collections have not been segregated into sold accounts and unsold accounts. The collections have been taken into income on the companies' books.

The purchase price for the accounts sold had been received in the form of a five-year $300,000 note; to the extent that collections may have been made by the companies on sold accounts, the companies should apply such collections against the face amount of the note.

Inventories—$1,043,072

Physical inventories were taken by the companies on or about November 30, 19X7. We visited six stores during the inventory counts to observe the procedures in operation, and visited six other stores after the inventory counts to check the accuracy of the results. We are satisfied that a reasonably accurate inventory was taken on or about November 30, 19X7.

Such physical inventories, after compilation, were worked back to October 14, 19X7, at retail prices by taking into consideration intervening sales and transfers. The information for such sales and transfers was obtained from machine tabulations prepared by a machine accounting service agency affiliated with Smith & Company in Atlanta, Georgia. We found that these tabulations do not tie in to sales and transfer data developed by alternate sources. While we have made corrections for certain types of differences, we have not satisfied ourselves that the data used, after correction, are reliable. Furthermore, while we have been informed that purchases during this period were nominal and would not materially affect the reconstruction of October 14 inventory amounts, we have not been able to gather any acceptable data with respect to such purchases.

tors in deciding on the course of action they should take in their dealings with the insolvent debtor. The Statement of Affairs, developed from the balance sheet in Exhibit 12-4, for the ABC Company as of April 28, 19X7, is shown in Exhibit 12-9 (pages 510–511).

25 The report prepared by the accountant is a statement of the debtor's financial condition as of a certain date, and presents an analysis of its financial position and the status of the creditors with respect to the debtor's assets. It has been termed "a statement of position from a 'quitting concern' point of view."

Exhibit 12-6   Statement of Operations of ABC Company for Completed Calendar Year and for Subsequent Period to Date of Filing of Petition

ABC COMPANY, INC.

STATEMENT OF OPERATIONS

Prior Year and Current Year to Date of Filing

	January 1 to April 28, 19X7			For the Year Ended December 31, 19X6		
Sales	$1,050,000			$3,750,000		
Less: returns	100,000	(9.5% of gross sales)		250,000	(6.7% of gross sales)	
	950,000			3,500,000		
Less: discounts and allowances	75,000	(7.9% of sales, less returns)		160,000	(4.6% of sales, less returns)	
Net sales		$ 875,000	100.0%		$3,340,000	100.0%
Cost of goods sold:						
Inventories— beginning	650,000			840,000		
Raw materials	505,000			1,827,000		
Labor and factory overhead	427,500			600,000		
	1,582,500			3,267,000		
Inventories—end	795,000			650,000		
Cost of goods sold		787,500	90.0		2,617,000	78.4
Gross profit		87,500	10.0		723,000	21.6
Operating expenses [Figure 12-6]:						
Production and designing	52,000			310,000		
Selling and shipping	95,000			450,000		
General and administrative	102,000			300,000		
		249,000	28.5		1,060,000	(31.7)
Operating loss		(161,500)	(18.5)		(337,000)	(10.1)
Estimated liquidation losses		—			(200,000)	(6.0)
Federal income tax credit		—			(287,000)	(8.6)
Net loss		$ (161,500)	(18.5)		$ (250,000)	(7.5)

Exhibit 12-7 Summary of Statement of Operations of ABC Company for Three Completed Calendar Years and for Subsequent Period to Date of Filing of Petition

ABC COMPANY, INC.

SUMMARY OF STATEMENT OF OPERATIONS

Prior Three Years and Current Year to Date of Filing

	January 1 to April 28, 19X7		For the Years Ended					
			December 31, 19X6		December 31, 19X5		December 31, 19X4	
Net sales	$ 875,000	100.0%	$3,340,000	100.0%	$4,400,000	100.0%	$4,700,000	100.0%
Cost of sales	787,500	90.0	2,617,000	78.4	3,100,000	70.5	3,200,000	68.1
Gross profit	87,500	10.0	723,000	21.6	1,300,000	29.5	1,500,000	31.9
Operating expenses	249,000	28.5	1,260,000*	37.7	1,500,000	34.1	1,570,475	33.4
Loss from operations	(161,500)	(18.5)	(537,000)	(16.1)	(200,000)	(4.6)	(70,475)	(1.5)
Income tax credits	—		(287,000)	(8.6)	(100,000)	(2.3)	(40,475)	(.9)
Net loss	$ (161,500)	(18.5)	$ (250,000)	(7.5)	$ (100,000)	(2.3)	$ (30,000)	(.6)

* Includes liquidation losses estimated at $200,000.

Exhibit 12-8 Statement of Capital Deficiency of ABC Company as of April 28, 19X7, the Date of Filing of Petition

ABC COMPANY, INC.

STATEMENT OF CAPITAL DEFICIENCY

April 28, 19X7

Common stock ($10 par value; authorized, 20,000 shares; issued and outstanding, 18,000 shares)			$180,000
Additional paid-in capital			100,000
Retained earnings:			
Balance—January 1, 19X4		$ 123,300	
Net loss for the year ended:			
December 31, 19X4	$ (30,000)		
December 31, 19X5	(100,000)		
December 31, 19X6	(250,000)		
	(380,000)		
Net loss—January 1 to			
April 28, 19X7	(161,500)		
		(541,500)	
Deficit—April 28, 19X7			(418,200)
Capital deficiency—April 28, 19X7			$(138,200)

26 The Statement of Affairs is based on assumptions which differ quite clearly from those on which the balance sheet is based. Some of the major differences follow:

It is hypothetical or pro forma; that is, it is an estimate of the probable outcome if the debtor's business should be liquidated.

Liquidation is assumed to occur, and therefore it is necessary to establish a time period over which the assets will be sold so that their value may be estimated. The shorter the time period, the smaller the proceeds from sales which will be realized.

Correspondingly, the assumption of a going concern is abandoned and the emphasis is shifted from measuring periodic profit to establishing the debts and resources available to meet those obligations.

The form used for the statement of affairs is that which will reveal the legal status of the several groups of creditors.

Exhibit 12-9   Statement of Affairs of ABC Company as of April 28, 19X7, the Date of Filing of Petition

ABC COMPANY, INC.

STATEMENT OF AFFAIRS

April 28, 19X7

Book Value	Assets	Appraised	Estimated Amount Available	Loss or (Gain) on Realization
	Assets constituting collateral for holders of fully secured claims:			
$ 795,000	Inventories	$ 400,000		$395,000
22,000	Land	35,000		(13,000)
600,000	Building	650,000		(50,000)
68,000	Fixtures and equipment	20,000		48,000
	Total	1,105,000		
	Less: fully secured claims (see contra)	562,500	$542,500	
	Assets constituting collateral for holders of partly secured claims:			
584,800	Accounts receivable	450,000		134,800
	Total	$ 450,000		
	Free assets (unencumbered):			
7,327	Cash	$ 7,327	7,327	
7,673	Tax refund receivable	7,673	7,673	
20,000	Investment in XYZ Company	20,000	20,000	
10,000	Goodwill	–0–		10,000
	Trademarks	5,000	5,000	(5,000)
	Estimated amount available		582,500	
	Liabilities with priority (see contra)		257,500	
	Estimated amount available for unsecured creditors (approximately 33¢ per dollar)		325,000	
	Estimated deficiency on unsecured liabilities		468,000	
	Reserve for liquidation losses established December 31, 19X6 (see contra)			(200,000)
$2,114,800	Totals		$793,000	$319,800

Exhibit 12-9 (*Continued*)

Book Value	Liabilities and Stockholders' Equity		Amount Unsecured
	Liabilities with priority:		
$ –0–	Estimated liquidation costs	$ 10,000	
100,000	Taxes payable	100,000	
127,500	Salaries payable	127,500	
20,000	Commissions payable	20,000	
	Total liabilities with priority (deducted contra)	$257,500	
	Fully secured liabilities:		
75,000	Payable to contractors	$ 75,000	
487,500	Mortgages payable	487,500	
	Total fully secured liabilities (deducted contra)	$562,500	
	Partly secured liabilities: First National Bank of Boston:		
500,000	Notes payable	$500,000	
100,000	Accounts payable	100,000	
	Total partly secured liabilities	600,000	
	Less: accounts receivable assigned (see contra)	450,000	$150,000
	Unsecured liabilities: Due to ABC Company, Inc., Employees'		
25,000	Profit Sharing Trust		25,000
	Accounts payable	682,000	
582,000	Less: payable to First National Bank of Boston	100,000	582,000
36,000	Notes payable to officer		36,000
200,000	Reserve for liquidation losses (deducted contra)	$200,000	
	Stockholders' equity:		
180,000	Common stock		
100,000	Additional paid-in capital		
(418,200)	Deficit		
$2,114,800	Totals		$793,000

27   The normal procedure followed in constructing the Statement of Affairs consists of setting up the section headings; reporting each liability in the appropriate section, and, if the liability is secured, reporting the related asset in the appropriate section; listing all the remaining assets that should be the unencumbered assets; and summarizing the asset and liability data. Clearly, before the Statement of Affairs can be prepared a balance sheet must be drawn up and additional data secured. In addition to the balance sheet, the following information is needed:

> Reliable estimates of the amount that can be expected to be realized from the sale of each asset.
>
> All assets which are collateral for specific obligations.
>
> Any obligations that are expected to arise while liquidation is proceeding, but that are not currently found in the balance sheet.[1]

28   Several values may be shown on the Statement of Affairs for each asset, but the most important is the realizable value or the cash value of each asset in liquidation through forced sale. The columns normally found for assets on the Statement of Affairs are:

> Book Value—the balance of each asset as it is found in the debtor's books and would appear on a balance sheet at that date.
>
> Appraised Value—the amount of cash expected to be realized upon sale of the asset.
>
> Estimated Amount Available—the proceeds which will be available for unsecured creditors as a result of the sale of the asset; obtained by subtracting the fully and partially secured claims and liabilities with priority from the total appraised value of assets.
>
> Estimated Loss or Gain on Realization of the Asset.

29   The basis of the classification scheme used for assets in the Statement of Affairs is the availability of assets to unsecured creditors, and this form is related to the liability classifications. It is important that all those assets that will probably be accruing to the debtor also be included. The groups and the order in which they are usually found are as follows:

> Assets constituting collateral for holders of fully secured claims, including all those assets with a realizable value expected to be at least equal to the claims against them.

---

[1] Harry Simons and Wilbert E. Karrenbrock, *Advanced Accounting—Comprehensive Volume* (Cincinnati: Southwestern Publishing Co., 1968), p. 643.

Assets constituting collateral for holders of partly secured claims, including assets with a realizable value expected to be less than the claims against them.

Free assets, which are those available to meet the claims of general creditors.

30 Liabilities and owners' equity are shown in the Statement of Affairs in the order in which the claims against the assets will be liquidated. The accountant should be careful to include all those liabilities expected to be incurred. Two columns are normally found for the liability section, one giving the book value or balance sheet amount of the claim and a second indicating the amount of the liability that is unsecured. They are classified in terms of their legal priority and secured status, with the following groups most commonly used:

Liabilities with priority—creditors who, under the priority granted by the Bankruptcy Code, must be paid before anything is given to unsecured creditors.

Fully secured liabilities—claims for which the collateral has a realizable value equal to or greater than the debt which it is intended to secure.

Partly secured liabilities—claims for which the collateral has a realizable value less than the debt it is intended to secure.

Unsecured liabilities—liabilities with no legal priority and not secured by collateral; these claims must be satisfied by the unencumbered assets.

Capital accounts.

31 The foregoing information readily gives an estimate of the amount the unsecured creditors may expect to receive. The percentage of each claim that will be paid is equal to the total realizable value of the free assets divided by the total amount of unsecured claims.

32 Along with the Statement of Affairs, a deficiency statement is often prepared to show the source of the deficiency to unsecured creditors. Normally included are the estimated gain or loss on the realization of each asset and any additional costs associated with liabilities that have not been recorded, thus giving the total estimated loss from liquidation. The amount of this loss to be suffered by the owners and the deficiency to creditors are then shown. This statement is valuable in that it reveals how the capital contributed to the business was used and why it is not possible to pay all the creditors. Exhibit 12-10 presents the Statement of Deficiency to Unsecured Creditors for the ABC Company.

33 The preparation of a Statement of Affairs is virtually mandatory when a company is experiencing difficulty and attempting to decide which course of action it would be best to follow. Its main advantage to the credi-

Exhibit 12-10   Statement of Estimated Deficiency to Unsecured Creditors Filed by the ABC Company as of April 28, 19X7, the Date of Filing of Petition

ABC COMPANY, INC.

**STATEMENT OF ESTIMATED DEFICIENCY
TO UNSECURED CREDITORS**

April 28, 19X7

Estimated losses on realization		
On inventories	$395,000	
On fixtures and equipment	48,000	
On accounts receivable	134,800	
On goodwill	10,000	$587,800
Estimated gains on realization		
On land	13,000	
On buildings	50,000	
On trademarks	5,000	68,000
Net loss on realization		519,800
Unrecorded expenses		–0–
Liquidation expenses		
Legal fees and liquidation costs	7,000	
Accountants' liquidation fees	3,000	10,000
Total estimated losses and costs of liquidation		529,800
Less: stockholders' equity		
Common stock	180,000	
Additional paid-in capital	100,000	
Less: deficit	(418,200)	(138,200)
Estimated deficiency to unsecured creditors		
before adjustment		668,000
Less: reserve for liquidation losses		200,000
Estimated deficiency to unsecured creditors		$468,000

tors is that it assists them in ascertaining what actions should be taken by setting forth the probable results from alternative policies.

Special-Purpose Statements

34   If the accountant is conducting an investigation aimed at uncovering irregularities, the preparation of special schedules is crucial. It may be necessary to prepare a statement of all the payments made preceding the filing of the petition, to reveal any preferential payments; or a schedule of all sales of assets may have to be devised to uncover fraudulent transfers.

35   The accountant will normally be asked to prepare, for a given time period following the filing of the petition, statements projecting the profit expectations of future operations. These statements provide a tool for working out a plan of reorganization and an out-of-court settlement, and should include budgets, cash flow statements, and profit projections.[2]

36   It is usually necessary to show why it would be in the best interests of the creditors for the debtor to remain in operation of the business. This involves proving that creditors would profit more from a plan of reorganization than from liquidation, and is usually accomplished with a schedule estimating the size of the dividend creditors would receive if the business should be liquidated. To obtain such a figure, the forced-sale value of the assets must be determined and all those assets and causes of action that may be recovered for the debtor's estate must be included.

37   If a plan of reorganization providing for installment payments over a period of time is proposed, the accountant will be required to prepare a projected budget, a cash flow statement, and a balance sheet, to show that the debtor will be able to make the payments and that the plan is feasible.

38   Thus, the two main categories where special statements are found are in the search for irregular transactions and in drawing up a plan to effect rehabilitation. However, each insolvency proceeding is unique and the individual situation will govern what additional reports the accountant must prepare so that the proceeding will provide complete and accurate information to all involved.

ACCOUNTING FOR A REORGANIZATION

39   The standard practice in a chapter 11 reorganization under the Bankruptcy Code will be for the debtor to remain in control of the business. The debtor's books and records retain their present form; however, some accounts will be closed and new ones added. Even where a trustee is appointed in a chapter 11 proceeding, the same books and records may be utilized.

Use of New Accounts

40   The debtor cannot make payments on prefiling liabilities unless special approval is obtained from the court. Thus, it is necessary for the debtor's accountant to see that the liabilities prior to petition are clearly identified so they will not be paid during the normal course of business. One approach would be to transfer the prefiling unsecured debts to a separate account as of the date of the petition, and then all liabilities incurred subse-

---

[2] Edward A. Weinstein, "Accountants' Examinations and Reports in Bankruptcy Proceedings," *New York Certified Public Accountant*, Vol. 35 (January 1965), p. 35.

quent to the petition would be recorded and paid in the normal manner. Generally, secured liabilities are not transferred but rather are left in the account and clearly identified as a prepetition debt. If there are current liabilities such as accounts payable when inventory or other assets were given as collateral, it may be best to transfer these liabilities to a separate account to avoid confusion. Also, if the creditor has an undersecured debt and does not elect under section 1111(b)(2) to have the entire claim considered secured, once the amount that is unsecured is determined it must be transferred to the prepetition unsecured debts account.

41   Another approach that could be used in accounting for the liabilities would be not to make any formal entries in the accounts. Establish controls so that no debt incurred prior to the petition date can be paid without prior approval and make a memorandum adjustment on all statements issued subsequent to the petition date so that the prepetition debts are presented separately. For large companies or companies with an extensive computerized system, this may be the best approach to take. Once the plan of reorganization has been confirmed, the debt will be reduced by the amount of forgiveness called for in the plan and by payments made under the provisions of the plan. One advantage of following this approach is that it reduces the future adjustments that have to be made in the accounts. Because of the section 1111(b)(2) election the amount of the claims that are unsecured is not known. Problems, such as whether this is a pre- or postpetition debt or whether it is secured or unsecured, will have to be resolved during the proceedings. Thus, it may be best to keep supplementary records regarding the prepetition liabilities. Once the issues are resolved and the plan is confirmed, the accounts can be properly adjusted.

42   It may also be desirable to establish new asset accounts. As of the petition date, it is necessary to establish the assets that existed and the extent to which they were pledged (see paragraph 8). For example, in the case of pledged accounts receivable it is not only necessary to know the balance of accounts receivable as of the petition date, but the individual accounts that make up this total. A common practice, however, is not to open new asset accounts but to prepare trial balances, as of the petition date, of both control and subsidiary accounts and to continue to use the existing asset accounts. The trial balances generally contain the information needed for the debtor to properly account for prebankruptcy assets.

43   At the time the petition is filed, it is not necessary to make any adjustments to the stockholder equity accounts.

Illustration of Entries

44   To illustrate types of entries that might be made as a result of the filing of a chapter 11 petition, refer to the Statement of Financial Condition in Exhibit 12-4 and consider this additional information:

1 On April 28, 19X7, ABC Company, Inc. filed a voluntary petition under chapter 11. The accountant elected to establish separate accounts for unsecured prepetition debts.

2 On May 31, 19X7, the First National Bank of Boston filed a secured claim for $520,000 and unsecured claims of $80,000. The net realizable value of the receivables was determined to be $520,000.

3 Jones Company shipped $50,000 in inventory to ABC Company on April 20, and the invoice was received April 27. The liability was recorded on that date, but the goods did not arrive until May 1.

4 On July 1, the court confirmed a plan that provides for the following:

a Debtor deposits $350,000 with escrow agent to cover priority claims and administrative costs.

b All unsecured creditors except First National Bank receive $300,000. (Payment was subsequently made.) First National Bank receives 2000 shares of common stock with an assigned value of $10 per share.

c First National Bank agrees to extend the Notes Payable for two years. The interest rate is changed from 12 to 15 percent.

d Debtor continues making normal payments on the mortgage.

45 During the period in which the debtor operates the business there would be many more activities that were not mentioned, including the discontinuance of operations of selected unprofitable parts of the business. The entries that would be made to record the facts mentioned above follow:

1	Taxes payable	100,000	
	Salaries payable	127,500	
	Commissions payable	20,000	
	Priority claims		247,500
	Due to ABC Company, Inc., Employees'		
	Profit Sharing Trust	25,000	
	Accounts payable	682,000	
	Notes payable to officer	36,000	
	Prepetition unsecured claims		643,000
	Prepetition secured accounts payable		100,000

To transfer priority claims, unsecured claims, and secured accounts payable to the separate accounts.

2	Prepetition secured accounts payable	80,000	
	Prepetition unsecured claims		80,000

To transfer the undersecured part of secured accounts payable to prebankruptcy unsecured claims since the value of the collateral of First National Bank was only $520,000 and the value of their claims was $600,000 ($500,000 notes payable and $100,000 accounts payable).

3	Prepetition unsecured claims	50,000	
	Accounts payable		50,000

To correct an error where inventory purchased was recorded as a prebankruptcy debt incorrectly.

4a	Escrow cash deposit	350,000	
	Cash		350,000

To record deposit with escrow agent according to terms of plan

4b	Prepetition unsecured claims	593,000	
	Cash		300,000
	Gain on debt forgiveness		293,000

To record payment to unsecured creditors except First National Bank according to terms of plan.

	Prepetition unsecured claims	80,000	
	Common stock		20,000
	Gain on debt forgiveness		60,000

To record exchange of stock for unsecured debt of First National Bank according to terms of plan.

4c	12 percent Notes payable, due December 1, 19Y7	500,000	
	15 percent Notes payable, due December 1, 19Y9		500,000

4d No entry required.

46 Note that entry (1) assumed that the accountant transferred the prepetition debts to a separate account. According to FASB No. 15, the gain on debt foregiveness is an extraordinary item (see paragraphs 56–78). If, however, the debtor elects (with proper approval) to eliminate the deficit through a quasi-reorganization or "mini" quasi-reorganization, the gain would be transferred to the paid-in capital account (see paragraphs 142–152). The entry, if an election is made just to eliminate the deficit, would be as follows:

Additional paid-in capital	65,200	
Gain on debt forgiveness	353,000	
Retained earnings		418,200

To eliminate the deficit in retained earnings (Exhibit 12-8).

Accrued Interest

47   Accrued interest on a secured debt continues to run during the bankruptcy period when the assets securing the debt have a value greater than the amount of the debt. Technically, interest should not be accrued beyond the point where the accrued interest causes the amount of the debt to exceed the value of the assets. Any other reasonable fees, costs, or charges provided under the agreement should also be accrued according to section 506(b) of the Bankruptcy Code.

48   For an unsecured debt and the amount of debt classified as unsecured because it is undersecured, interest should be accrued to the date the petition was filed. Interest accruing subsequent to this date will not be allowed as a claim unless there is a surplus. SFAS No. 15 (paragraph 13) states that the carrying amount of the payable is equal to the face amount, increased or decreased by applicable accrued interest and applicable unamortized premium, discount, finance charges, or issue costs. It has been suggested by some accountants that the carrying amount of the debt should include the accrued interest up to the effective date of the plan. Thus, the interest expense would be accrued during the proceedings and, since it would be disallowed by the bankruptcy court, the amount accrued (previously deducted as interest expense) would be reported as a gain on debt forgiveness along with the amount of debt and prebankruptcy accrued interest forgiven. This treatment is, however, questionable since the Bankruptcy Code (section 502) specifically disallows accrued postpetition interest on unsecured debt. It would appear that the applicable interest would include only that amount that could be paid under bankruptcy law. It should be realized that if the debtor's petition is subsequently dismissed, accrued postpetition interest would be an obligation of the debtor as it would be if there were a surplus. In most situations, these two contingencies would not be sufficient to justify accruing the interest.

49   The fact that interest is not accrued during bankruptcy can have a significant impact on the results of operation. Often companies in bankruptcy have a high debt-to-equity ratio with a large interest expense. Then the elimination of the interest payments and accruals can cause the company to report a profit. Thus many companies do report profits during bankruptcy and then show losses for the first full year of operations afterward, primarily due to interest payments on debt that was not paid or discharged. To keep the financial statements from being misleading, the interest that would have been accrued except for the bankruptcy petition should be at least disclosed. However, if the debtor has reached tentative agreement on a plan, disclosure of the interest associated with the debt existing after the confirmation of the plan is more meaningful.

EFFECT OF SETTLEMENTS ON FUTURE STATEMENTS

Accounting for Income from Debt Discharge

50 FASB Statement No. 15 provides that income arises when the carrying amount, including accrued interest before restructuring, is greater than the total future cash payments specified by the restructured liability terms. Total future cash payments include interest on the restructured debt. If the total future cash payments are greater than the carrying amount of debt before restructuring, no income is recorded, even if the revised interest rate is less than current market rates.

51 This statement clearly explains how to handle income from debt discharge when the transaction falls under its provisions. The problem faced is that in many bankruptcies FASB Statement No. 15 does not apply.

52 Footnote 4 to FASB Statement No. 15 states that this statement does not apply ". . . if, under provisions of those Federal statutes or in a quasi-reorganization or corporate readjustment with which a troubled debt restructuring coincides, the debtor *restates its liabilities generally*" (emphasis added).

53 Responding to a question as to how this footnote is to be interpreted, the FASB in Technical Bulletin 81–6 stated:

> This section (FASB 15) does not apply to debtors who, in connection with bankruptcy proceedings, enter into troubled debt restructurings that result in a general restatement of the debtor's liabilities, that is, when such restructurings or modifications accomplished under purview of the bankruptcy court encompass most of the amount of the debtor's liabilities.

> For example, enterprises involved with Chapter XI bankruptcy proceedings frequently reduce all or most of their indebtedness with the approval of their creditors and the court in order to provide an opportunity for the enterprise to have a fresh start. Such reductions are usually by a stated percentage so that, for example, the debtor owes only 60 cents on the dollar. Because the debtor would be restating its liabilities generally, this section would not apply to the debtor's accounting for such reduction of liabilities.

> On the other hand, this section would apply to an isolated troubled debt restructuring by a debtor involved in bankruptcy proceedings if such restructuring did not result in a general restatement of the debtor's liabilities.

54 It would appear that FASB Statement No. 15 is not applicable in many reorganizations under chapter 11. If FASB Statement No. 15 does not apply, there are two questions that remain unanswered. The first covers how to classify the income from debt discharge—extraordinary item or equity adjustment—and the second deals with how much income to recognize, as determined by the extent to which the issuing debt is discounted. Before looking at these two areas, the procedures to follow when FASB Statement No. 15 applies will be discussed.

Debt Discharge under FASB Statement No. 15

55   When a company is liquidated and all its assets are sold, the business is dissolved and the books are permanently closed. In a reorganization proceeding or an out-of-court settlement the debtor continues to use the same books and records, but the terms of the plan call for certain adjustments. The following sections discuss the most common entries made and the situations in which they are required under the assumption that FASB Statement No. 15 is applicable.

Debt Forgiveness as an Extraordinary Item

56   FASB Statement No. 15 established standards of financial accounting and reporting by debtors and creditors for a troubled debt restructuring. The statement supersedes FASB Interpretation No. 2, "Interpreting Interest on Debt Arrangements made under the Federal Bankruptcy Act," and amends APB Opinion No. 26, "Early Extinguishment of Debt." The statement applies to troubled debt restructurings consummated under reorganization or other provisions of the Bankruptcy Code but does not apply if the debtor restates its liabilities generally in a quasi reorganization or corporate readjustment.

57   A troubled debt restructuring may include, but is not necessarily limited to, one or a combination of the following:

1   Transfer from the debtor to the creditor of receivables from third parties, real estate, or other assets to satisfy fully or partially a debt (including a transfer resulting from foreclosure or repossession).

2   Issuance or other granting of an equity interest to the creditor by the debtor to satisfy fully or partially a debt unless the equity interest is granted pursuant to existing terms for converting the debt into an equity interest.

3   Modification of terms of a debt, such as one or a combination of:
  a   Reduction (absolute or contingent) of the stated interest rate for the remaining original life of the debt.
  b   Extension of the maturity date or dates at a stated interest rate lower than the current market rate for new debt with similar risk.
  c   Reduction (absolute or contingent) of the face amount or maturity amount of the debt as stated in the instrument or other agreement.
  d   Reduction (absolute or contingent) of accrued interest.[3]

58   A debt restructuring is not necessarily a troubled debt restructuring even if the debtor is experiencing some financial difficulties. For example, a troubled debt restructuring is not involved if:

---

[3] FASB, *Accounting Standards, Current Text* (Stamford, Ct.: FASB, 1984), Sec. D22.105.

1 The fair value of cash, other assets, or an equity interest accepted by a creditor from a debtor in full satisfaction of its receivable at least equals the creditor's recorded investment in the receivable as the debtor's carrying amount of the payable.

2 The creditor reduces the effective interest rate primarily to reflect a decrease in market interest rates in general or a decrease in the risk to maintain a relationship with a debtor that can readily obtain funds from other sources at the current interest rates.

3 The debtor issues in exchange for its debt new marketable debt having an effective interest rate based on its market price that is at or near the current market interest rates of debt with similar maturity dates and stated interest rates issued by nontroubled debtors.[4]

59 FASB Statement No. 15 (paragraph 21) states that the gains on restructuring of payables are to be aggregated, included in measuring net income for the period of restructuring, and if material, classified as an extraordinary item, net of related income tax effect.

Modification of Terms

60 When a restructuring involves only a modification of terms, the statement requires both the creditor and debtor to account for it on a prospective basis. No gain or loss would be recognized by debtors when only a modification of terms is involved unless the carrying amount of the debt exceeds the total future cash payments specified by the new terms. If the carrying amount of the debt exceeds future cash payments, the debtor reduces the carrying amount of the debt, and all cash payments are recorded as reductions in the debt. Thus, the debtor recognizes a gain equal to the excess of the carrying amount of the payable over future cash payments and no interest expended is recorded between the date of restructuring and the maturity date of the debt. The creditor recognizes an ordinary loss to the excess of the recorded investment in the receivable at the time of the restructuring over future cash receipts specified by the new terms, and such excess is not properly chargeable against a valuation allowance.

61 The following example illustrates the accounting for a debt restructuring as a result of a modification of terms.[5]

XYZ Company has the following debt at December 31, Year 10:

12% Note payable, due December 31, Year 10	$10,000,000
Accrued interest payable on the 12% note	1,200,000

---

[4] Ibid., Sec. D22.107.

[5] The examples in paragraphs 61–71 were adapted from Ernst & Ernst, *Financial Reporting Developments, FASB Statements* (1978), pp. 239–280. (Used by permission).

On December 31, Year 10, the debt is restructured as follows:

a $1,000,000 of the principal and $1,200,000 of accrued interest are forgiven by creditors.

b the maturity date is extended to December 31, Year 15.

c interest rate is reduced from 12% to 8%.

62 The total future cash receipts or payments under the new terms amount to $12,600,000 (principal of $9,000,000 and interest of $3,600,000) which exceeds the $11,200,000 carrying amount of the debt prior to the restructuring, and no gain or loss is recognized. The excess of the total payment over the carrying amount of the debt, $1,400,000 ($12,600,000 − 11,200,000 = 1,400,000) would be recognized as interest expense at a computed effective interest rate on the restructured amount of the debt. The computed interest rate will be 2.707 percent, the rate necessary to discount the future stream of cash payments to a present value equal to the remaining balance of the debt. The following amortization schedule shows the calculations:

Amortization Schedule

Date	Payment	Interest at Effective Rate of 2.707%	Payments of Principal	Bond Balance
12/13/Year 10				$11,200,000
12/31/Year 11	$ 720,000	$ 303,186	$ 416,814	10,783,186
12/31/Year 12	720,000	291,902	428,098	10,355,088
12/31/Year 13	720,000	280,314	439,686	9,915,402
12/31/Year 14	720,000	268,411	451,589	9,463,813
12/31/Year 15	9,720,000	256,187	9,463,813	-0-
	$12,600,000	$1,400,000	$11,200,000	

63 Excluding any related income tax effects, the creditor would record the debt restructuring and subsequent cash receipts as follows:

12/31/Year 11

Cash	720,000	
Receivable from XYZ Company		416,814
Interest Income		303,186

Similar journal entries would be made for each year up to 12/31/Year 15, and on 12/31/Year 15, the journal entry to record receipt of principal would be:

Cash	9,000,000	
Receivable from XYZ Company		9,000,000

64   For the debtors, using the similar amortization schedule, excluding any related income tax effects, the following journal entries summarize the accounting for future cash payments under the restructured terms:

12/31/Year 11

Payable to Creditors	416,814	
Interest Expense	303,186	
Cash		720,000

Similar entries would be made for each year up to 12/31 Year 15, and on 12/31/Year 15 the journal entry to record payment of principal would be:

Payable to Creditors	9,000,000	
Cash		9,000,000

65   However, assume the same facts as in the previous example, except that the interest rate is reduced to 3%, the total future cash payments under the new terms would be $10,350,000 (principal of $9,000,000 and interest of 270,000 for five years at 3%) which is $850,000 less than the $11,200,000 prerestructuring carrying amount of the debt. In this case, the recorded investment in the receivable and the carrying amount of the payable would have to be reduced by $850,000. The debtor would recognize an extraordinary gain of $850,000. The creditor normally would offset the reduction against an allowance for uncollectible amounts. No interest income or expense would be recognized.

66   The creditor would record the debt restructuring and subsequent receipts as follows:

12/31/Year 10

Allowance for Uncollectible Amounts	850,000	
Receivable from XYZ Company		850,000

To adjust recorded investment in receivable from XYZ Company due to modification of terms.

12/31/Years 11–15

Cash	270,000	
Receivable from Company		270,000

To record annual receipts as reductions to the recorded investment in the receivable.

12/31/Year 15

Cash	9,000,000	
Receivable from XYZ Company		9,000,000

To record receipt of payment for XYZ Company.

67   The debtor would record the debt restructuring and subsequent payments as follows:

12/31/Year 10

Payable to Creditors	850,000	
Gain on Restructuring of Debt		850,000

To adjust carrying amount of payable due to modification of terms.

12/31/Years 11–15

Payable to Creditors	270,000	
Cash		270,000

To record annual payment as reductions to carrying amount of payable.

12/31/Year 15

Payable to Creditors	9,000,000	
Cash		9,000,000

To record payment to creditors.

Full Satisfaction Through Transfer of Assets or Grant of Equity Interest

68   A debtor that transfers noncash assets (receivables, real estate, or other assets), or an equity interest to a creditor to settle fully a payable will recognize a gain on restructuring of payables. The gain is measured by the excess of the carrying value of the debt over the fair value of the assets or equity interest transferred.[6]

69   The fair value of the assets transferred is the amount upon which a willing buyer and a willing seller would agree in a current sale. If an active market exists, fair value shall be measured by the market value. If an active market does not exist, the selling prices for similar assets may be helpful in estimating fair value. If no market price is available, a forecast of expected cash flows may aid in estimating the fair value of assets transferred. The expected cash flows are to be discounted at a rate commensurate with the risk involved in holding that particular asset.[7]

70   For the creditors, the excess of the recorded investment in the receivable satisfied over the fair value of assets or equity interest transferred is a loss, and the creditors should normally charge the excess against an appro-

---

[6] FASB, *Accounting Standards, Current Text* (Stamford, Ct.: FASB, 1984), Sec. D22.109.
[7] Ibid.

priate allowance account. After a troubled debt restructuring, the creditor should account for assets received in satisfaction of a receivable the same as if the assets had been acquired for cash.

71 Two examples are used to illustrate the procedures described above.

EXAMPLE 1   Exchange of Debt for Real Estate Under Construction

On December 31, 19X1, X Company owes Y Bank a debt of $10,000,000. The debt is restructured as follows:

a   X Company transfers real estate under construction to Y Bank in full settlement of the debt.

b   The carrying value of the real estate is $9,000,000.

c   Current market prices are not available for either the real estate or similar real estate.

d   Both parties estimated that $6,000,000 incurred ratably over the next twelve months is required to complete construction.

e   The completed property will be sold immediately for $16,000,000.

Assuming a discount factor of 12 percent, the fair value based on discounted future cash flows would be estimated:

Estimated selling price of completed property	$16,000,000.0
Present value factor of 12 percent for 12 months	×0.892857
	$14,285,712.0
Less present value of cost to complete:	
Estimated monthly cost $6,000,000/12 = $500,000	
Present value of annuity factor of 1	
percent per month for 12 months ×11.255077	(5,627,538.5)
Estimated fair value	$ 8,658,173.5

X Company and Y Bank would make the following journal entries on December 31, 19X1:

X Company

Payable to bank	10,000,000.0	
Loss on disposition of assets	341,826.5	
Real estate under construction		9,000,000.0
Gain on restructuring		1,341,826.5

Y Bank

Real estate received in restructuring	8,658,173.5	
Allowance for loan losses	1,341,826.5	
Receivable from X Company		10,000,000.0

If at December 31, 19X2, the construction is completed at a cost of $6,500,000 and the property is appraised at an estimated current market value of $16,500,000, no adjustment should be made at December 31, 19X2, for the excess of market value of $16,500,000 over carrying value of $15,158,173.5 ($8,658,173.5 + $6,500,000).

EXAMPLE 2   Exchange of Equity for Debt

Debt between B Company and C Bank is restructured as follows:

a B Company issues 1,000,000 shares of its common stock with $1.00 par value to C Bank in full settlement of debt totalling $3,000,000.
b Market price of the common stock is $1.00 per share.
c The shares issued to C Bank are restricted shares and cannot be sold without filing a registration statement.
d A 20% reduction from market price is estimated to reflect the restricted nature of these shares.

In accounting for the debt restructuring, B Company would recognize an extraordinary gain of $2,200,000 ($3,000,000 less 800,000, the estimated fair value of the shares issued), and C Bank would charge $2,200,000 against its allowance for loan losses.

Partial Satisfaction

72 A troubled debt restructuring may involve receipt of assets or equity interests in partial satisfaction of a receivable and a modification of terms of the remaining receivable. Accounting for these restructurings should be the same as that for a modification of terms, and the fair value of assets transferred or equity interest granted should be accounted for as a partial cash payment.

73 The accounting required is as follows:

1 The recorded receivable or the carrying amount of the payable should be reduced by the fair value of the assets or equity interest transferred.
2 A debtor should recognize a gain or loss resulting from any disposition of assets.
3 No gain or loss on restructuring should be recognized unless the remaining balance of the debt exceeds future cash payments specified by the new terms.
4 Future interest income or expense should be determined using the interest method.[8]

---

[8] Ibid., Sec. D22.115 and D22.129.

Contingent Interest

74 If a troubled debt restructuring involves contingent payables, those contingent amounts shall be recognized as a payable and as interest expense in future periods in accordance with FASB Statement No. 5 "Accounting for Contingencies."[9] For the debtor, at the time of restructuring, contingent cash payments should be included in the total future cash payments specified by the new terms. A debtor should not recognize a gain on a restructured debt involving contingent cash payments as long as the total future payments exceed the carrying amount. After the time of restructuring, the debtor should recognize interest expense and a payable for contingent payments when it is probable that a liability has occurred and the amount can be reasonably estimated.

75 For the creditors, contingent cash receipts should not be included in the total future cash receipts specified by the new terms, and the creditor should recognize a loss on restructuring unless subsequent realization is probable and the amount can be reasonably estimated. After the time of restructuring, contingent cash receipts should not be recognized as interest income until they become unconditionally receivable.

Disclosure

76 A debtor should disclose the following information about troubled debt restructurings that have occurred as of the date of each balance sheet:

1 For each restructuring, a description of the principal change in terms, the major features of settlement, or both.

2 Aggregate gain on restructuring of payables and the related income tax effect.

3 Aggregate net gain or loss on transfers of assets recognized during the period.

4 Per-share amount of the aggregate gain on restructuring of payables, net of related income tax effect.[10]

77 For periods after a troubled debt restructuring, a debtor should disclose the extent to which amounts contingently payable are included in the carrying amount of restructured payables. Total amounts that are contingently payable on restructured payables and the conditions under which those amounts would become payable or would be forgiven should be disclosed when it is reasonably possible that a liability will be incurred.

78 A creditor should disclose the following information about troubled debt restructurings as of the date of each balance sheet:

[9] Ibid., Sec. D22.118.
[10] Ibid., Sec. D22.121.

1 For outstanding receivables whose terms have been modified in troubled debt restructuring by major category:

a The aggregate recorded investment.
b The gross interest income that would have been recorded in the period if those receivables had been current in accordance with the original terms and had been outstanding throughout the period or since origination, if held for part of the period.
c The amount of interest income on those receivables that was included in net income for that period. A receivable whose terms have been modified need not be included in the disclosure if, subsequent to the restructuring, its effective interest rate is equal to or greater than the rate that the creditor was willing to accept for a new receivable.

2 The amount of any commitments to lend additional funds to debtors owing receivables whose terms have been modified in troubled debt restructurings.[11]

Reporting of Income from Debt Discharge when FASB Statement No. 15 Is Not Applicable[12]

79 At least three alternatives are available as to how income from debt discharge is to be reported when there is a restructuring of liabilities and FASB Statement No. 15 does not govern the reporting procedure:

1 Extraordinary item.
2 Capital item (additional paid-in capital).
3 Income item—operating net income, one line below operating net income, or as an unusual item only.

80 The discussion of each of these procedures that follows is based on the assumption that the debtor did not report the gain from debt discharge as a part of a quasi reorganization. The procedures to follow when there is a quasi reorganization are discussed in paragraphs 142–152.

Extraordinary Item

81 A substantial amount of evidence exists to suggest that income from debts discharged should be classified as an extraordinary item even if FASB Statement No. 15 does not govern. First, it appears that in most chapter 11 reorganizations, the income from debts discharged would meet both the

---

[11] Ibid., Sec. D22.136.
[12] The author acknowledges the contributions of Donald E. Condit, Arthur Andersen & Co., to the bankruptcy accounting issues discussed in the balance of this chapter.

criteria of *unusual nature* and *infrequency of occurrence* as stated in APB Opinion No. 30. Also, FASB Statement No. 4 indicates in paragraph 8 that:

> Gains and losses from extinguishment of debt that are included in the determination of net income shall be aggregated and, if material, classified as an extraordinary item, net of related income tax effect. That conclusion shall apply whether an extinguishment is early or at scheduled maturity date or later. The conclusion does not apply, however, to gains or losses from cash purchases of debt made to satisfy current or future sinking-fund requirements. Those gains and losses shall be aggregated and the amount shall be identified as a separate item.

82 Paragraph 10 of this statement states that this classification shall be made without regard to the criteria of "unusual and infrequent" of APB Opinion No. 30. Additionally, the FASB used paragraph 8 of FASB Statement No. 4 as evidence that the income from debts discharged is an extraordinary item. Paragraph 21 of FASB Statement No. 15 states:

> Gains on restructuring of payables determined by applying the provisions of paragraphs 13–20 of this Statement shall be aggregated, included in measuring net income for the period of restructuring, and, if material, classified as an extraordinary item, net of related income tax effect, in accordance with paragraph 8 of FASB Statement No. 4 "Reporting Gains and Losses from Extinguishment of Debt."

83 In describing the basis for its conclusions, the Board further stated in paragraph 99 that ". . . a gain on restructuring of a payable in a troubled debt restructuring is indistinguishable from a gain or loss on other extinguishments of debt, and the same classification in financial statements is appropriate. Since FASB Statement No. 4 classifies a gain or loss on extinguishment of debt as an extraordinary item, the classification is appropriate for a gain on restructuring of a payable."

84 Based on the above analysis, it would appear that income from debts discharged could logically be classified as an extraordinary item.

Paid-In Capital

85 The difference between the amount of the liability and the amount that must be paid under the plan of reorganization is either a gift or an item of revenue. The definitions of revenue issued by authoritative bodies appear to indicate that income from debts discharged is a revenue item. In paragraph 12 of Statement No. 4, the APB defined revenue as:

> . . . a gross increase in assets or a gross decrease in liabilities recognized and measured in conformity with generally accepted accounting principles that results from those types of profit-directed activities of an enterprise that can change owners' equity. Revenue under present generally accepted accounting

principles is derived from three general activities: (a) selling products, (b) rendering services and permitting others to use enterprise resources, which result in interest, rent, royalties, fees, and the like, and (c) disposing of resources other than products—for example, plant and equipment or investments in other entities. Revenue does not include receipt of assets purchased, proceeds of borrowing, investments by owners, or adjustments of revenue of prior periods.

86 The FASB in Statement of Financial Accounting Concepts No. 3 stated:

Revenues are inflows or other enhancements of assets of an entity or *settlements of its liabilities* (or a combination of both) during a period from delivering or producing goods, rendering services, or other activities that constitute the entity's ongoing major or central operations.

Gains are increases in equity (net assets) from peripheral or incidental transactions of an entity and from all other transactions and other events and circumstances affecting the entity during a period except those that result from revenues or investments by owners.

Gains and losses may be described or classified according to sources. Some gains or losses are net results of comparing the proceeds and sacrifices (costs) in peripheral or incidental transactions with other entities—for example, from sales of investments in marketable securities, from dispositions of used equipment, or from *settlements of liabilities* at other than their carrying amounts.

87 The American Accounting Association in its 1948 statement dealing with concepts and standards stated that revenue represents an inflow of assets or net assets into the firm as a result of sales of goods or services, and that revenue also includes gains from the sale or exchange of assets other than stock in trade and gains from *advantageous settlement of liabilities*.[13]

88 A gift is a voluntary transfer of property without any consideration being given for the transfer. If a gift is made to a debtor, its debts are canceled without any consideration on the part of the debtor. Gifts to the enterprise may be classified as capital or revenue. If the contributions are in the form of "conscience payment," they are normally considered revenue. Otherwise, gifts are normally considered a contribution to capital. The criteria to be used in determining how to classify the gift are the intent of the donor and the events surrounding the contribution. The philosophy underlying the enactment of the Bankruptcy Act and Bankruptcy Code was to allow the debtor to have a new start. The debtor came out of the proceedings without any commitments of any type directly related to the amount of debt forgiven. The cancellation may be viewed as a type of gift, in part directly

---

[13] AAA Committee on Accounting Concepts and Standards, *Accounting and Reporting Standards for Corporate Financial Statements and Proceeding Statements and Supplements* (Columbus, Ohio: American Accounting Association, 1975), p. 15.

from the creditors who agreed to the settlement and in part from Congress, which has imposed the discharge of indebtedness. However, it should be pointed out that one of the main reasons why creditors accept a plan is that they believe they will receive a greater return under the plan than under complete liquidation. Thus, the handling of the cancellation as a gift is, it would appear, in most cases very questionable.

89   Under the additional paid-in capital approach, the accounting entries made when the amount of the liability is reduced and the debt is paid off are as follows: the liability is debited for the full amount of the original indebtedness, cash is reduced by the amount actually paid out, and paid-in capital is increased by the difference. If any of the assets are subsequently written down, the contributed capital account must also be reduced by this amount. (See paragraph 46.)

Income Item

90   Based on the evidence available that income from debts discharged (provided the gain is considered to be revenue and not a capital item) is an extraordinary item, the reporting of the gain as operating income, or just below operating income—before extraordinary items—has very little support.

Determining the Amount of Income from Debt Discharge when FASB Statement No. 15 Is Not Applicable

91   As noted in paragraph 50, FASB Statement No. 15 clearly indicates that debt issued in troubled debt restructuring is not discounted as long as the total amount to be paid (including interest) is less than the carrying value of the debt being restructured. However, the new debt will be discounted to the extent that the amount to be paid exceeds the carrying value of the old debt. If FASB Statement No. 15 does not apply, then can the above procedures be followed?

Arguments Against Discounting

92   In a large number of chapter 11 reorganizations, the liabilities are not discounted, even though there is a restructuring of liabilities in general. The bases for the Board's conclusions for limiting discounting, as set forth in FASB Statement No. 15, are as follows:

> The Board concluded that since a troubled debt restructuring involving modification of terms of debt does not involve transfers of resources or obligations (paragraph 77), restructured debt should continue to be accounted for in the existing accounting framework, on the basis of the recorded investment in the receivable or carrying amount of the payable before the restructuring.

> 147—The Board found persuasive the arguments that a creditor in a troubled debt restructuring is interested in protecting its unrecovered investment (repre-

sented in the accounts by the recorded investment in the receivable) and, if possible, obtaining a return. To the creditor, therefore, the effect of a restructuring that provides for recovery of the investment is to reduce the rate of return (the effective interest rate) between the restructuring and maturity. Similarly, the effect of that kind of restructuring to the debtor is to reduce the cost of credit (the effective interest rate) between the restructuring and maturity.

148—Thus, the Board concluded that no loss (creditor) or gain (debtor) should be recognized in a troubled debt restructuring if the total future cash receipts or payments (whether designated as interest or face amount) specified by the new terms at least equals the recorded investment or carrying amount of the debt before the restructuring.

93   The primary basis for the Board's conclusion appears to be that a modification of terms is not an exchange of resources or obligations, but rather is a continuation of an existing debt. Thus, in a chapter 11 reorganization where FASB Statement No. 15 does not apply and the transaction can be viewed as a modification of terms, it would appear that the new debt need not be discounted. The Board also found persuasive the arguments (see the quotation from paragraph 147 above) that the creditor is interested in protecting its unrecovered investment and the debtor in reducing the cost of debt between the restructuring and maturity. These same conditions exist in a chapter 11 reorganization in which FASB 15 does not apply.

94   It could also be argued that the principle of FASB 15—debt is not discounted—is clearly developed. FASB 15 was based on the assumption that a modification of terms does not involve an exchange. All exchanges of debt in a troubled debt restructuring in which FASB 15 applies must follow the provisions of the statement. This is true even though the opinion may exist that a modification of terms is in fact an exchange. The fact that FASB 15 does not apply because of footnote 4 (see paragraph 81) should not prevent accounting for the restructure in accordance with provisions of FASB 15 when debt is exchanged for debt. By definition, FASB 15 concludes that a modification of terms in a troubled debt restructuring is not an exchange. The restructuring should be accounted for in this manner even if liabilities are generally restated.

95   Those who favor not discounting also argue that if modification of terms that involve only 5 percent of the debt being discharged is not an exchange and FASB 15 applies, then why should the same kind of transaction, except that it involves 40 percent of the debt being canceled, be handled differently? The transaction is subject to different treatment only because FASB Technical Bulletin 81–6 states that FASB 15 would not apply to the latter modification.

Arguments for Discounting

96   In Chapter 11 cases in which FASB 15 does not apply, discounting may be considered appropriate for several reasons:

1 The reason FASB 15 does not apply is because there has been a major restructuring of the liabilities. The restructuring often involves much more than just a modification of terms. The underlying basis for not discounting—that an exchange of a resource or obligation has not occurred—is not applicable to a chapter 11 reorganization that involves a major restructuring of its liabilities. Under these conditions the discounting principles of APB Opinions No. 21 and No. 26 should apply. The Board stated in response to the suggestion that the content of the Exposure Draft conflicted with these opinions:

> . . . modifications of terms of continuing debt are different in substance from exchanges of resources or obligations and the Exposure Draft is consistent with the opinions.

It would thus appear that if the modifications are in fact an exchange, the FASB would take the position that APB Opinion 20 applies and that discounting is necessary.

2 The Board must have realized in adding footnote 4 that a restructuring of liabilities involves more than just a modification of terms and thus concluded that the provision for nondiscounting does not apply.

3 The major provision in FASB 15 that differs from prior practice or that is new is the provision for not discounting liabilities. Accounting for the issuance of stock or property, reporting gain on discharge, and disclosure requirements agree in general with prior practice. Thus, to claim that it is not necessary to discount liabilities has the effect of saying that the provisions of FASB 15 apply even though footnote 4 and Technical Bulletin 81–6 suggest otherwise.

4 FASB Statement No. 15 in general violates the provisions of APB Opinion No. 21. Most modifications of terms are in fact exchanges of obligations. The arguments made by the FASB to justify the conclusions reached are very weak and should be used only in the limited requirements of FASB 15. They should not be used in situations where FASB 15 does not apply.

5 Discounting is more in line with the economics of the transaction, and future balance sheets and income statements will more clearly reflect the financial position and results of operations.

97 An analysis of annual reports, issued in the year of the confirmation of the plan by companies in chapter 11, indicates that both approaches are used. It also reveals that the same accounting firm may account for the transaction for one client by discounting and for another client by not discounting. The SEC will accept financial statements using either approach. Because of the general acceptance of either approach, the CPA firm may receive considerable pressure from a client to either discount debt or not discount debt depending on the goals of that particular debtor. For example, if the debtor needs a balance sheet with an improved debt-to-equity ratio, a

position of discounting will be taken. On the other hand, if the debtor prefers to have future interest charges as low as possible, discounting will not be preferred.

98   The question still remains: which approach should be required? It appears that discounting should be used since it is more in line with the economics of the transaction. However, until the FASB or the SEC takes a position, accountants may find it difficult to advocate that only one method—discounting—should be used.

Accounting for Rejected Leases

99   According to FASB Statement No. 5, a claim must be "probable" and "reasonably estimable" before any amount is recorded. In this case, it would appear that almost all claims are probable. First, if the lease agreement was favorable to the debtor, it probably would not have been rejected. Generally, only the questionable or unfavorable agreements are rejected. Under these conditions, it generally can be assumed that there will be a legitimate claim. Of course, if that is not the case, there is no legitimate claim and no need to accrue a loss.

100   In considering accruals for rejected leases, there are three amounts to be concerned with:

1   The amount of the claim filed with the court. The claim for damages for rejection of leases of real property is limited to the rent reserved by such lease, without acceleration, for the greater of one year, or 15 percent, not to exceed three years, of the remaining term of such lease, following the earlier of (1) the date of the filing of the petition or (2) the date on which such lessor repossessed, or the lessee surrendered, the leased property, plus any unpaid rent due under such lease, without acceleration, on the earlier of such dates. The claim for damages due to the rejection of leases of personal property, it would appear, is limited to the payments required under the remaining term of the lease plus any unpaid rent due on the petition date.

2   The amount allowed by the court. The court, if the amount shown on the proof of claim is contested by the debtor, will fix the amount of the claim. Otherwise, the amount on the creditor's proof of claim stands.

3   The amount to be paid as provided for in the plan of reorganization. All claims for damages due to lease rejection are considered prepetition claims. The amount provided for in the plan may be less than the amount allowed by the court, as is the case with many unsecured claims.

101   Most liabilities that are on the books at the time the petition is filed are not reduced until the plan is approved even though, in most cases, the probability of 100 percent of the claims being paid is low. Thus, since damages from lease rejection are considered prepetition claims, it appears that they should be booked at the amount of the claim. That amount would be the amount of the claim that is filed by the lessor, or in the case where the debtor plans to challenge the claim, the amount management considers to be a reasonable estimate of the claim. If part of this claim is subsequently discharged, the amount of discharge is income due to debt discharge.

102   There is, however, one key factor that makes some people question the above reasoning. The amount eventually paid resulting from a rejected lease is an obligation that was incurred because of the special provisions of the Bankruptcy Code. From this it might be reasoned that the amount of obligation to be booked from a lease rejection is the amount that the debtor eventually has to pay, that is, the amount provided for in the plan. If the lease rejection occurred outside of bankruptcy proceedings, the debtor would accrue an amount that represents an estimate of the damages from the lease cancellation, providing the claim is probable and reasonably estimable. The amount to be accrued, based on the above reasoning, would be an estimate of the amount that the debtor would eventually pay.

103   The above discussion deals with the "problem" requirement that is necessary before a claim can be recorded. The next requirement of FASB Statement No. 5 is that the amount must be reasonably estimable. As noted in paragraph 100, the maximum amount that will be paid for real property is limited to three years' rent. Based on the remaining life of the lease, the market for rental property, and the financial condition of the debtor, a reasonable estimate could be made of the potential liability. For other lease agreements it would appear that the liability for damages could in most cases be estimated.

104   In summary, it appears that at the time leases are rejected, an amount should be accrued that is a reasonable estimate of the claim for damages due to the lease rejection.

Accounting for Warranty Reserves and Similar Liabilities

105   The discussion here will be restricted to warranty claims; however, the concepts should apply to other similar liabilities. There are two types of warranty claims to consider. One is those claims that have been made against the company prior to the petition data for faulty, damaged, and so forth, goods. The other is those claims that will be filed in the postpetition period for warranty guarantees on goods that were delivered prior to the filing of the petition. Both of these types of claims are prebankruptcy claims. All warranty claims arising from goods sold after the petition was filed are postpetition (administrative expense) claims. The first group of prepetition claims can generally be reasonably determined by reviewing all requests for refunds, exchanges, and other claims. However, the claims resulting from damages sustained by using the product are more difficult to estimate. An estimate of the prebankruptcy claims that will be filed during the proceeding may be even more difficult to determine. Prior experience can often provide the basis for a reasonable estimate. In fact, if the company has provided for this type of liability properly, the amount in the reserve account may be the most reasonable estimate of the potential liability available.

106   In estimating the amount to include in the prepetition liabilities, the FASB Statement No. 5 rules of "probable" and "reasonably estimable" apply. Thus it would appear that the warranty claims estimated in accordance with FASB Statement No. 5 should be included with other prepetition liabilities. Once all of the warranty claims have been filed and approved by the court, the amount of the warranty claims in the prepetition liabilities can be adjusted. The warranty claims may, however, be handled in a more practical manner. In a chapter 11 reorganization, the objective is to come out of the proceedings with a viable and profitable operation. Thus, customer goodwill is important. Debtor's counsel may petition the court for, and receive, permission to honor all reasonable warranty claims for faulty products, and so forth. Normally, a request of this nature would include authorization to cover refunds requested prior to, as well as those filed subsequent to, the petition date. The court may classify all of the payments of warranty claims as administrative expenses. Under these conditions it would appear that the debtor would leave the provision of warranty expense as a liability, but not prepetition. As these claims are paid, they would be charged against the reserve account as normally required by generally accepted accounting principles.

Accounting for Pension Costs

107   A claim is defined in the Bankruptcy Code (section 101(4)) as a:

Right to payment, whether or not such right is reduced to judgment, liquidated, unliquidated, contingent, matured, unmatured, disputed, undisputed, legal, equitable, secured or unsecured; or

Right to an equitable remedy for breach of performance if such breach gives rise to a right to payment, whether or not such right to an equitable remedy is reduced to judgment, fixed, contingent, matured, unmatured, disputed, undisputed, secured or unsecured.

108   It would appear that any liability associated with pension plans could be a prepetition debt. Thus, the debtor should consider estimating and classifying such debt as a prepetition obligation. The court and the other creditors may agree to an arrangement in which the company will assume any liability from the provisions of a pension plan and will continue to make payments as though the bankruptcy plan had not been filed. However, this type of arrangement does not alter the fact that the liability is a prepetition debt.

Nonvested Benefits

109 When a plan is terminated before or during bankruptcy and the conditions necessary for vesting—such as attainment of a specified age or minimum number of years of employment—have not occurred, claims for nonvested benefits are not allowed.

110 Under conditions where the plan is not terminated, it would appear that an employee with nonvested accrued benefits would have an allowable contingent claim for unfunded vested benefits.[14] The amount allowed would be the total amount of the employee's accrued benefits reduced by (1) the probability of such benefits vesting before the plan terminates and (2) the probability of the plan terminating with insufficient assets to pay benefits.[15] The allowance of a claim for these benefits conflicts with the provisions of ERISA[16] and with the encouragement of the IRC to defer pension payments until retirement. Thus, the extent to which a bankruptcy court will allow this claim is very questionable. The claim, if allowed, would be for third priority to the extent of the amount accrued during the ninety days prior to the filing of the petition. All other claims would be unsecured. The accrued amount that is based on prior services will be an unsecured claim.

Vested Benefits

111 At the time the plan is terminated, the employees have a claim only to the extent that the vested benefits are unfunded. The trust is responsible for the payment of benefits to the extent that they are funded. The amount of the claim will be the present value of the nonforfeitable deferred benefits less the amount of the trust fund assets allocable to the employee. Allocations are made according to the guidelines stipulated in ERISA, section 4044 (29 U.S.C. sec. 1344). A plan trustee may represent all prior claim holders and file a proof of multiple claims. Claims are unsecured except for the amount accrued within the ninety days prior to bankruptcy.

112 The liability to a plan trustee may be limited by contract to the amount of delinquent contributions. Thus, claims will be considered unsecured except for amounts that qualify as fourth priority. The fourth priority, consisting of contributions arising on account of service performed within 180 days prior to the filing of the petition, is limited to $2000 times the number of employees covered by the plan less the extent to which covered employees have a third priority for wages due within ninety days prior to bankruptcy.

---

[14] 11 U.S.C. Sec. 502(a).
[15] Sable, Eggertsen, and Bernstein, "Pension-Related Claims in Bankruptcy," *American Bankruptcy Law Journal* Vol. 56 (1982), p. 160.
[16] ERISA requires that pensions be administered strictly in accordance with the provisions of the plan (29 U.S.C. Sec. 1104(a)(1)(d)). Most plan agreements provide that payments are to be made only upon retirement or plan termination.

113   The Pension Benefit Guarantee Corporation (PBGC) is a guarantor of vested pension benefits. It may file a claim against the employer, since it must pay if the employer does not. It is not necessary for the PBGC to actually pay the benefits before it can file a claim. The PBGC guarantee is limited, however, to a maximum of $750 per month (adjusted annually in proportion to adjustments of the Social Security base). Benefit income made within the five-year period prior to termination of the plan is further limited. A claim can be filed for vested benefits to the extent that they are guaranteed and unfunded. PBGC can also file a claim for contributions that were not made under the plan. It has the power under ERISA to request a district court to appoint itself as trustee and to collect any amount due under the plan. Additionally, an employer can also be liable for up to 30 percent of its net worth to PBGC for unfunded guaranteed benefits. Net worth for a chapter 11 case is based on going concern concepts.

114   ERISA provides that the PBGC may place a lien upon all the property of the debtor when an employer terminates a pension plan that does not have the assets to pay guaranteed benefits. The lien is to be treated in the same manner as a tax lien. If the lien is not perfected, it would not be valid in the bankruptcy court. In most cases, the plan is terminated after the petition is filed, or if terminated earlier, notice may not have been filed.

115   Once it has been determined that all or part of the liability will be assumed by the PBGC, then the pension liability account should be reduced accordingly.

116   Generally, the only pension-related claim that is allowed when a plan is not terminated is a claim for delinquent contributions.

Accounting for Professional Fees

117   There are at least three methods that can be used to account for professional fees of a company in chapter 11.

Estimate Fees When Petition Is Filed

118   One might argue that all professional fees (current and future) associated with an event (that is, the filing of a bankruptcy petition) should be accrued as of the occurrence of the event (that is, the date the petition is filed). There are several problems with this interpretation. An assumption is being made that the filing of a petition is one event; all activities that are "probable" and "reasonably estimable" should be accounted for as of the date the petition is filed. Thus, not only should expenses associated with the bankruptcy be accrued, but income from debt discharge should also be estimated. Although the total income from debt discharge could not be booked, income could be used to the extent of the estimated professional fees. Also, it would appear that if professional fees are accrued, any other costs directly associated with the bankruptcy proceeding should also be accrued. Recording these fees before the services are rendered is in fact recording a nonexistent liability. Since the services have not been rendered a claim does not exist. Although a loss contingency may be established for certain transactions or events, it is questionable if this accrual would meet the requirements of FASB Statement No. 5.

Recognize Fees on Approval of Plan

119 Since there generally is a significant amount of debt forgiven in most reorganizations, the professional fees would not be expenses until the plan is approved and then they would be charged against the gain from debt discharge. In situations where there are no reported gains from debt discharge because stock was exchanged for prepetition debt, it would appear that the professional fees should be charged against capital.

120 There is an allocation problem associated with the accrual of professional fees and charging them as an expense when the plan is approved. Services provided in chapter 11 reorganizations can be classified in five separate but related areas. These are:

1 *Services Required Solely Because the Petition Is Filed.* Included would be the preparation of selected schedules that would not otherwise be prepared, such as the statement of affairs. Also included would be the time spent comparing proofs of claims with the debtor's records. It is difficult, however, to include in this category reports such as operating statements since they would be prepared even if the chapter 11 petition was not filed.

2 *Costs Associated with Discontinued Operations.* Any accounting services rendered to help the debtor dispose of unprofitable operations could—and would—logically be charged to the discontinued operations.

3 *Costs Associated with the Reorganization of the Ongoing Business.* Included here are the costs associated with identifying the problem that created the financial difficulty in the first place and developing a plan of action to correct the problem. Many of these costs are directly related to an analysis of business problems that, if addressed earlier, would have eliminated the need for the debtor to file a chapter 11 petition. The problem here is that the cost of professional fees necessary to correct the problem is much greater if the debtor did not take early action and—as a result—files a petition.

4 *Normal Legal and Accounting Services.* Certain professional services will continue during the proceedings. Included here might be some types of management advisory services or an audit. It should be realized, however, that the filing of a petition may change the focus of the audit and—to some extent—the nature of the assignment.

5 *Costs Associated with a Temporary Management Team of Workout Specialists.* Typically, in addition to salary and other costs, a large bonus might be paid at the conclusion of a successful reorganization of the company.

121   As can be seen, many of the expenditures for professional fees are related to ongoing operations, rather than to the legal, tax, and accounting aspects of the bankruptcy. Included are management consulting activities, including the development of a business plan, internal control evaluations, and assistance in developing a plan of reorganization. To illustrate the magnitude of the allocation problem, an accountant may spend a great deal of time helping the debtor evaluate possible alternatives associated with a plan. This would involve the evaluation of various projections as assumptions are changed or modified. Most of the work would be related to those operations that will continue. It would be very difficult to allocate these costs between the chapter 11 proceeding, the discontinuation effort, and ongoing operations.

122   In theory, it appears that the professional fees for direct bankruptcy services could be capitalized and charged against gain from debt discharge, assuming there is evidence to indicate that the gain from debt discharge will be large enough to offset the professional fees. The problem with this is that these costs are being capitalized as an asset on the books of a debtor whose prospects for successful future operations are highly questionable. In fact, the poorer the condition of the debtor the greater is the prospect that the administrative expenses can be offset against a gain from debt discharge. It should be realized that the debtor, however, is incurring an expenditure that will eventually be paid by the creditors through their debt reduction. That is to say, the expenditures of company assets to pay administrative expenses is ultimately a reduction of assets that otherwise might have been distributed to creditors.

Recognize Professional Fees as Services Are Performed

123   It would appear that the best alternative is to expense administrative expenses (professional fees) as they are incurred. This conclusion is based on the premise that this approach is the most theoretically viable alternative and that the allocation problem created by trying to separate costs between those purely related to bankruptcy and those related to ongoing operations are difficult to solve on a practical basis. If this approach is used, nonexistent liabilities will not appear on the balance sheet. The benefits for most of the professional expenditures relate to ongoing operations, and when they are expensed as incurred they are more clearly matched with revenue. Even when the policy is followed to expense items as incurred, specific costs related to the reorganization in the form of stock issuance costs and so forth would be charged against the proceeds or, in the case of stock, for debt against income from debt discharge.

Classification of Prepetition Liabilities

124   Because payment of pre–chapter 11 liabilities is postponed after the petition filing, such liabilities are classified in various ways until revised payment terms are accepted. Sample presentations follow (in millions):

EXAMPLE 1:

Current liabilities:

Notes payable	$ 900
Accounts payable	9,100
Accrued liabilities	500
Total current liabilities, excluding unsecured chapter 11 creditors' claims	$10,500
Unsecured chapter 11 creditors' claims not expected to require use of current assets	49,500
Total current liabilities	$60,000

EXAMPLE 2:

Current liabilities:

Notes payable	$ 900
Accounts payable	9,100
Accrued liabilities	500
Unsecured chapter 11 creditors' claims not expected to require use of current assets	49,500
Total current liabilities	$60,000

EXAMPLE 3:

Current liabilities:

Notes payable	$ 900
Accounts payable	9,100
Accrued liabilities	500
Total current liabilities	$10,500
Liabilities deferred pursuant to proceedings under chapter 11	$49,500
Long-term liabilities	$ 3,000

EXAMPLE 4:

Current liabilities:

Notes payable	$ 900
Accounts payable	9,100
Accrued liabilities	500
Total current liabilities	$10,500
Long-term liabilities:	
Liabilities deferred pursuant to proceedings under chapter 11	$49,500
Other long-term liabilities	3,000
Total long-term liabilities	$52,500

125 The decision as to which method of classification is most appropriate requires care and judgment on the part of the accountant. It probably will be desirable to include a footnote describing the composition of the chapter 11 creditors' claims by priority.

126   The first part of paragraph 7 of ARB No. 43, Chapter 3A, states:

> The term *current liabilities* is used principally to designate obligations whose liquidation is reasonably expected to require the use of existing resources properly classifiable as current assets, or the creation of other current liabilities. . . .

In all chapter 11 reorganization cases, it might be argued that all prepetition debts are not current liabilities because they are not going to be due within one year. At the time a chapter 11 petition is filed, there is an automatic stay that, with minor exceptions, prohibits any party from taking any action that will interfere with the debtor or its property until the stay is modified or removed. After a chapter 11 petition is filed, an unsecured creditor must generally wait until a plan has been developed in a chapter 11 case before any payment will be received on prepetition debt. The average time period for the development of a plan and obtaining its approval and confirmation is generally longer than one year. In answering the question as to how to classify prebankruptcy debt, our analysis will be divided into two categories—short-term obligations and long-term obligations.

Short-Term Obligations

127   As suggested above, most trade payables in a chapter 11 case will not be satisfied within a period of one year. Does this fact justify their classification as a noncurrent liability? FASB Statement No. 6, *Classification of Short-Term Obligations Expected to be Refinanced* was issued to attempt to eliminate the use of various ways to classify short-term obligations that will be refinanced. However, as with other FASB statements, the problems associated with chapter 11 reorganizations are not addressed. This statement provides that the refinancing of a short-term obligation on a long-term basis means either replacing it with a long-term obligation or with equity securities, or renewing, extending, or replacing it with short-term obligations for an uninterrupted period extending beyond one year. According to this statement, short-term obligations arising from transactions in the normal course of business that are due in customary terms (such as trade payables, advance collections, and accrued expenses) are to be classified as current liabilities in all instances. Other short-term obligations are excluded from current liabilities under that statement only if the enterprise intends to refinance the obligation on a long-term basis and such intent is supported by an ability to consummate the refinancing, as demonstrated by either a financing agreement or the post-balance-sheet-date issuance of a long-term obligation or equity securities. It might be argued that FASB Statement No. 6 suggests that current liabilities should remain as such until a plan is developed because the intent requirement is not satisfied. This statement, however, does not address what happens at the time the chapter 11 petition is filed.

128 Upon the filing of a chapter 11 petition, the liability, to some extent, loses its distinct character. For example, nonsecured trade payables, notes payables, and other unsecured claims (with some exceptions) are frequently grouped into one class—unsecured claims. Thus, obligations arising from transactions in the normal course of business no longer have that specific characteristic. Because of the nature of chapter 11 proceedings, it seems inappropriate to apply the distinction made in FASB Statement No. 6. Also, at the time the petition is filed, unsecured liabilities likewise lose their specific term distinction. Obligations due within one year are often grouped with those that have a longer due date. These changes are accounted for in this manner by most debtors, with all unsecured prepetition debt shown in one account on balance sheets issued subsequent to the filing of the chapter 11 petition.

129 As we noted above, most chapter 11 cases last longer than one year. Thus, the current assets on the balance sheet for the current year will not be used to pay off the prepetition debt. Furthermore, most reorganization plans use resources other than current assets to satisfy the debt that is not discharged. If the plan requires a partial cash settlement, the cash may come from a new investor or a new source of debt, which often is a long-term loan. Other plans may provide for future payments that would result in the debt being classified as long-term. Thus, there is considerable evidence available in many chapter 11 cases to suggest that prepetition debt should not be classified as current. However, it should be recognized that, if evidence is available to suggest that the chapter 11 case will last less than one year and/ or that current liabilities will be paid out of current assets, then the prepetition debt could logically be classified as a current liability.

Long-Term Obligations

130 Provisions that make long-term obligations callable because the debtor violated provisions of a loan agreement create difficulties in deciding if prepetition long-term liabilities should be reclassified. FASB Statement No. 78 amended paragraph 7 of ARB 43, Chapter 3A by adding the following:

> The current liability classification is also intended to include obligations that, by their terms, are due on demand or will be due on demand within one year (or operating cycle, if longer) from the balance sheet date, even though liquidation may not be expected within that period. It is also intended to include long-term obligations that are or will be callable by the creditor either because the debtor's violation of a provision of the debt agreement at the balance sheet date makes the obligation callable or because the violation, if not cured within a specified grace period, will make the obligation callable. Accordingly, such

callable obligations shall be classified as current liabilities unless one of the following conditions is met:

a. The creditor has waived* or subsequently lost† the right to demand repayment for more than one year (or operating cycle, if longer) from the balance sheet date.

b. For long-term obligations containing a grace period within which the debtor may cure the violation, it is probable‡ that the violation will be cured within that period, thus preventing the obligation from becoming callable.

If an obligation under (b) above is classified as a long-term liability (or, in the case of an unclassified balance sheet, is included as a long-term liability in the disclosure of debt maturities), the circumstances shall be disclosed. Short-term obligations that are expected to be refinanced on a long-term basis, including those callable obligations discussed herein, shall be classified in accordance with FASB Statement No. 6, *Classification of Short-Term Obligations Expected to Be Refinanced.*

* If the obligation is callable because of violations of certain provisions of the debt agreement, the creditor needs to waive its right with regard only to those violations.

† For example, the debtor has cured the violation after the balance sheet date and the obligation is not callable at the time the financial statements are issued.

‡ *Probable* is defined in FASB Statement No. 5, *Accounting for Contingencies,* as ''likely to occur'' and is used in the same sense in this paragraph.

131   Because of the automatic stay, the creditor loses the right to demand repayment until the plan has been confirmed by the court. Thus it would appear that long-term obligations need not be reclassified since one of the conditions (that is, the creditor has lost the right to demand payment for more than one year) necessary to prevent the reclassification of the callable obligations exists.

Summary

132   The following is a summary of the points made above.

1   Once a bankruptcy petition is filed, prebankruptcy debt loses some of its identity based on how the debt was initially incurred. The most important factor to consider is whether the debt is secured or unsecured. Since unsecured prepetition debt is considered as a separate class for bankruptcy purposes, it would appear that all of the prepetition unsecured debt—current and long-term—should have the same classification for accounting purposes unless evidence exists that the debt will be satisfied differently.

2   Most prepetition bankruptcy debt will not be paid or satisfied within a year (or operating cycle).

3 There is no specific generally accepted accounting principle that requires the debt to be classified as current or noncurrent. Thus, it appears that how debt is classified depends on the accountant's judgment, which is based on (among other factors):

    a The likelihood that payment will be made within one year (or operating cycle).

    b The terms of the proposed plan of reorganization.

Determining Nature of Security

133 A problem can arise as to whether a security is debt or preferred stock. The term preferred stock is used to refer to securities that are primarily subordinated debt, securities that have both equity and debt characteristics, and to securities that are very similar to preferred stock. Preferred stock which have all of the characteristics of debt should be accounted for as debt. Preferred stock with legal status of equity but with a mandatory redemption feature requires special handling. A mandatory redemption provision exists where the redemption by the issuer is specified as scheduled by the stipulated terms of the security or the redemption is outside the control of the issuer. Examples would include those securities with fixed or determinable redemption provisions, securities redeemable at the option of the holder, or securities redeemable under conditions outside of the control of the issuer such as when specified earnings levels are attained. Preferred stock redeemable at the option of the issuer would not be considered as containing a mandatory redemption feature.

134 For companies registered with the SEC, the guidelines set forth in ASR No. 268 (*Codification of Financial Reporting Policies,* Sec. 211) should be followed. This release requires that preferred stock with mandatory redemption features be disclosed separately on the face of the balance sheet, and not combined in a total with other preferred stock or common stock equity amounts or included under a general heading of stockholders' equity. Any changes in redeemable preferred stock must be disclosed in a note separate from the note discussing stockholders' equity. It would appear advisable to follow the same procedures for nonregistered companies.

Determining Value of Equity Securities

135 The value to be assigned to the common stock issued as part of the plan would normally be that value set by the bankruptcy court. If no value is assigned then the most appropriate method to follow would be to value the company according to the going concern value and then use this as the basis to assign values to the common stock after subtracting the value of the post-bankruptcy debt (see chapter 10). Where preferred stock or other classes of common stock are outstanding, the equity value must be allocated to the various classes of stock outstanding. Where preferred stock is involved, one alternative would be to use redemption value for these securities with the balance going to common stock. However, the SEC in SAB No. 40 (Topic 3C) states that the fair value can be used if more appropriate than redemption value. An example where market values might be more appropriate would be where the redemption feature is contingent upon future earnings and cash flow. Under this condition it may be that the debtor does not have the assets necessary to redeem any of the stock at the time stock is issued. Especially where the stock has a liquidation preference, it might be appropriately valued at the value per share left after subtracting the debt outstanding. The accountants in one case like this used net book values after giving effect in the accounts to the provisions of the plan. If this value exceeded the redemption value, then the redemption value would be used.

Assets—Write-Down to Realizable Values

136 Reduction in the book values of assets and the matter of when this is required for tax purposes are discussed more fully in chapter 14, "Tax Awareness." When a debtor company secures a reduction of its liabilities in a proceeding under the Bankruptcy Code, it is not held to have realized any income from the difference between the original debt and the actual payment. It is necessary under certain conditions, however, that the debtor's property be reduced in value by an amount equal to the amount of indebtedness that has been canceled. This reduction for tax purposes is not one that automatically should also be made in the financial records. It does, however, suggest that if the fair value of the asset is materially less than the book value, an adjustment may be necessary to account for this significant decline in value.

Subsequent Events

137 The acceptance by the creditors of an out-of-court settlement or plan of reorganization after the fiscal year's end but before the issuance of statements and the resulting cancellation of indebtedness is a subsequent event that requires recognition in the accounts. SAS No. 1, Section 560.03, states that the first type of subsequent event that requires adjustment to the accounts consists of "those events that provide additional evidence with respect to conditions that existed at the date of the balance sheet and affect the estimates inherent in the process of preparing financial statements." This statement suggests that as of the date of the balance sheet, liabilities are overstated. These liabilities had not been adjusted downward because of the uncertainty dealing with the actual amount to be paid. The liabilities should, however, be adjusted downward as soon as the amount that must be paid is known. Certainly, the events that require the need for debt forgiveness occurred prior to the balance sheet date, as a petition was filed before this date and these events led to the need to file the chapter 11 petition. Several examples of companies that have followed the practice of adjusting the accounts can be found in annual reports. For example, some comments relating to account adjustment are presented below.

> On March 24, 19X1, a plan of reorganization was confirmed and the Company deposited funds with the Court to be distributed in settlement of creditors' claims. Certain differences between claims filed with the court and the company's records have not as yet been resolved. The financial statements reflect the maximum liabilities to creditors under the chapter 11 proceedings and the plan of reorganization . . . As a result of the plan of reorganization $32,170,000 of indebtedness, net of administration expenses and the fair market value of the common stock issued, was forgiven and has been included as an extraordinary item in the accompanying financial statements (the fiscal year ended January 30, 19X1).
>
> The settlement of claims under the plan of reorganization, which is reflected in the financial statements, provided for the following distributions to be made subsequent to October 20, 19X1 (the date the plan was confirmed; fiscal year ended August 29, 19X1) . . .

138 An alternative to restating the accounts is to issue pro forma statements to show clearly those events that have occurred subsequent to year-end. For example, one company with a fiscal year ending June 30, 19X1, where a Chapter XI plan of arrangement was proposed on June 26, and confirmed by the court on August 31, issued the balance sheet presented in Exhibit 12-11 to reflect the acceptance of the plan and agreements with secured creditors to forgive significant debts. Note that the statement includes accrued interest up to June 30 on the secured debt. Most of this interest was forgiven by the creditors. The accrued interest from June 30 to September 10 (the effective settlement date) was not reported here as debt forgiven since the pro forma is presented as though the debt was canceled as of June 30. This accrued interest will be reflected in the statements for the year ending June 30, 19X2.

Effects of Plan of Reorganization on Statement of Changes in Financial Position

139 Generally, any transactions during the year that affect working capital should be disclosed in the Statement of Changes in Financial Position. Special problems can arise when stock is issued to satisfy all or part of the prepetition debt. One of the problems centers around the value to assign to the stock. Where it is difficult to assign value to the stock, to show the value of stock exchanged as a source of funds may lead to the interpretation that the stock had a value equal to the amount of the debt canceled. This would not be true in many situations. If fact, it is very difficult to estimate the value under the conditions of bankruptcy and insolvency proceedings. As a result, the exchange has been omitted in several situations from the statement on the basis that such disclosure would be misleading. Any omission of a change of this nature would have to be justified by the fact that the statements would be misleading if the value was included, since the omission is in violation of APB Opinion No. 9. Paragraph 14c states that the statement should clearly disclose the conversion of long-term debt or preferred stock to common stock.

Comparison with Prior Periods

140 In statements filed with the SEC, comparative statements are required. However, because of the reorganization, a comparison of the operations subsequent to confirmation with operations prior and during chapter 11 proceedings should be made with careful consideration. Several factors limit the benefits that can be derived from such a comparison. As a result of the reorganization, the capital structure may be totally changed. A large amount of debt may have been converted to stock. Overhead costs may have been reduced in several areas. Selected operations (including entire product lines or divisions) may have been discontinued. Thus, any comparison of post confirmation return on assets expressing per share or similar performance measuring devices with those of prepetition results will be of little value. The major benefit derived from the presentation of prepetition statements is that it serves as a historical record of what has happened and it gives the reader some indication of the changes that have been made in the asset and liability structure of the company. The problem the accountant faces in presenting these comparatives is caused by the fact that conventional accounting standards of disclosure and presentation do not deal with special problems encountered by bankruptcy and insolvency proceedings.

141 It is, however, common practice in most cases to present comparative data. For example, one auditor stated in the footnotes describing the reorganization proceedings that careful consideration was given as to whether last year's financial statements should be presented for comparative purposes since the adjustments in connection with the plan and related reorganization were material. The auditor concluded that it would be beneficial for a reader of the financial statements to have comparative data. In the middle paragraph, the auditor commented that although the reorganization adjustment materially affected the comparability of the balance sheets as of September 30, 19X1, and 19X2, accounting principles were consistently applied during the two years ending on those dates.

QUASI REORGANIZATION

142 A quasi reorganization occurs when a company restates its accounts to provide the same effect that would result if a new corporate entity were created and acquired the business of the existing corporation. Neither the FASB nor one of its predecessors has dealt with the question of what is a

Exhibit 12-11 Pro Forma Statement Describing Subsequent Events

CONSOLIDATED BALANCE SHEET
JUNE 30, 19X1

(Prepared from the accounts without audit)

Assets

	Historical	Pro Forma (Note 8)
Current assets		
Cash	$ 456,364	$ 1,409,364
Cash held in escrow	—	35,442
Accounts receivable, net of $90,000 allowance for doubtful accounts	1,256,005	1,256,005
Inventories (Note 1)	923,369	923,369
Investment in growing crops	340,000	340,000
Prepaid expenses	43,688	43,688
Total current assets	3,019,426	4,007,868
Plant, machinery, and equipment (Note 1)		
Machinery and equipment	7,734,748	7,902,956
Furniture and fixtures	105,064	105,064
Automobiles and trucks	666,772	671,072
Leasehold improvements	27,932	27,932
	8,534,516	8,707,024
Less—Accumulated depreciation and amortization	(3,077,735)	(3,111,667)
	5,456,781	5,595,357
Other assets		
Investment in and net advances to 50 percent-owned unconsolidated subsidiary, at cost	85,186	85,186
Other investments, at cost (Note 9)	15,650	30,500
Loan receivable from employee	26,400	26,400
Land purchase options (Note 6)	—	—
	127,236	142,086
	$ 8,603,443	$ 9,745,311

Exhibit 12-11   (*Continued*)

Liabilities		
	Historical	Pro Forma (Note 8)
Current liabilities		
Accounts payable, trade	$ 203,938	$ 203,938
Notes payable (Note 8d)	—	83,660
Accrued expenses—		
Payroll costs	231,921	231,921
Vacation pay	248,881	248,881
Other	97,978	97,978
Unsecured Chapter XI creditor claims (Note 2)	4,927,797	—
Obligations payable to secured creditors— pre-Chapter XI (Note 3)	9,858,126	—
Total current liabilities	15,568,641	866,378
Long-term liabilities		
Notes payable (Note 8a)	—	10,092,112
Obligation payable to affiliated entity (Note 9)	110,000	110,000
	110,000	10,202,112
Commitments and contingent liabilities (Notes 4, 8b and 9)		
Stockholders' equity		
Capital stock, $10 par value— Authorized—10,000 shares Outstanding—1,000 shares	10,000	10,000
Retained earnings (deficit)	(7,085,198)	(1,333,179)
	(7,075,198)	(1,323,179)
	$ 8,603,433	$ 9,745,311

Exhibit 12-11 *(Continued)*

8. *Subsequent Events and Pro Forma Balance Sheet*

Certain pro forma adjustments have been applied to the historical balance sheet at June 30, 19X1 to reflect the following events, which occurred after June 30, 19X1:

a. The Company obtained a $10,000,000 loan. In September, 19X1, the proceeds from the loan were disbursed as follows:

Secured creditors	$ 7,119,884
Unsecured creditors, including priority claims and costs of administration	1,873,500
Debtor Company	953,000
Escrow fees, closing costs, etc.	18,174
Balance held in escrow pending notification from Department of Motor Vehicles regarding transfer fees	35,442
Total	$10,000,000

The loan is guaranteed by the Company's principal stockholders and is secured by a first lien on growing crops, plant, machinery and equipment, inventory, and receivables. The Company has also agreed to certain other conditions that include, but are not limited to, restrictions on the sale and transfer of stock and purchase of fixed assets. The terms of the loan agreement require the payment of interest only on January 1, 19X2. Beginning on January 1, 19X3, interest and principal are payable annually. Other significant terms of the loan agreement are as follows:

Term of Loan (Years)	Interest Rate	Amount of Loan	Annual Principal Payments
7	9.5%	$ 5,610,630	$ 935,105
20	5.0	1,389,370	73,125
40	9.0	3,000,000	76,923
		$10,000,000	$1,085,153

quasi reorganization and what conditions are necessary for a company to go through a quasi reorganization. In 1953, the Committee on Accounting Procedures issued rules to be followed in making the adjustment and the procedures to follow after the adjustment is made. Paragraph 3 of ARB 43, Chapter 7A, indicates that the corporation should make a clear report to its shareholders of the restatements proposed to be made, and obtain their formal consent. Paragraph 4 indicates that in general ". . . assets should be carried forward as of the date of readjustment at fair and not unduly conservative amounts, determined with due regard for the accounting to be employed by the company thereafter. If the fair value of any asset is not readily determinable a conservative estimate may be made, but in that case the amount should be described as an estimate and any material difference arising through realization or otherwise and not attributable to events occurring or circumstances arising after that date should not be carried to income or earned surplus.''

143 Liabilities should also be restated to their value as a result of the readjustment. The other procedural requirement is that the retained earnings account should be dated after the quasi reorganization.

144 No reference is made in ARB 43 to an adjustment that only eliminates the deficit and does not result in the adjustment of asset and liability accounts. The APB in an interpretation relating to income taxes did, however, recognize this practice of only charging deficits against capital by stating, ''The concepts described in the preceding paragraphs relative to quasi-reorganization apply equally to reorganizations under the bankruptcy laws where a deficit is written off to capital.''

145 Several questions need to be analyzed when accounting for a quasi reorganization. The first deals with which accounts the debtor should adjust and the second with what conditions must exist before the debtor can elect a quasi reorganization. Quasi reorganizations can be roughly classified into two types—''mini quasi'' and ''regular quasi.''

Adjustment of Equity Section Only ("Mini Quasi")

146 Here the deficit in retained earnings is eliminated by reducing the paid-in capital by the amount of the deficit. The deficit that is eliminated is generally the amount that is left after income from debt discharge has been credited to the deficit account. An example of an adjustment of this type is presented in the statement of shareholders' equity that is on the next page as Exhibit 12-12. In this case, the adjustment was reflected as one arising out of a quasi reorganization. It appears from the notes that the only adjustment was to eliminate the deficit. The note to the financial statement is as follows:

Quasi-Reorganization:

In connection with the Plan of Arrangement and Asset Swap with its lending banks, the predecessor Trust effected a ''Quasi-Reorganization'' on May 31, 1979, resulting in a charge to shares of beneficial interest equal to the Trust's accumulated deficit. Net income since May 31, 1979 is reflected as retained earnings.

147 In Exhibit 12-13 is another example of the deficit being eliminated. However, in this case, the adjustment was not referred to as a quasi reorganization. The note to the financial statements states:

For financial reporting purposes, as a result of the reorganization and to reflect the reorganized status of Panex, the deficit as of June 4, 1981 has been extinguished by a charge to capital in excess of par and earnings for the period June

Exhibit 12-12 Mini Quasi Reorganization

CONSOLIDATED STATEMENTS OF SHAREHOLDERS' EQUITY (DEFICIT)
For the Years Ended November 30, 1981, 1980, and 1979

	Shares of Common Stock*		Capital in Excess of Par Value	Accumulated Deficit	Retained Earnings since May 31, 1979	Total Shareholders' Equity (Deficit)
	Number of Shares	Amount				
Balance at Nov. 30, 1978	1,330,454	$13,304	$21,621,954	($31,834,174)		($10,198,916)
Issuance of shares in connection with Plan of Arrangement (Note 2)	519,280	5,193	1,650,012			1,655,205
Loss before extraordinary items through May 31, 1979				(2,456,246)		(2,456,246)
Extraordinary items through May 31, 1979				18,282,108		18,282,108
Balance at May 31, 1979	1,849,734	18,497	23,271,966	(16,008,312)	—	7,282,151
Accumulated deficit charged to capital in excess of par value because of quasi reorganization (Note 2)			(16,008,312)	16,008,312		
Net income since May 31, 1979					2,175,322	2,175,322

554

	Shares	Common Stock	Additional Paid-in Capital		Retained Earnings	Total
Tax benefit of operating loss arising prior to May 31, 1979 quasi reorganization (Note 6)			1,000,648		(1,000,648)	
Issuance of shares at fair market value as additional compensation to Chairman of the Board of Trustees	10,000	100	37,400			37,500
Balance at November 30, 1979	1,859,734	18,597	8,301,702		1,174,674	9,494,973
Net income					1,748,033	1,748,033
Tax benefit of operating loss arising prior to May 31, 1979 quasi reorganization (Note 6)			1,399,144			1,399,144
Other			46,695			46,695
Balance at November 30, 1980	1,859,734	$18,597	$ 9,747,541		$2,922,707	$12,688,845
Net income					451,337	451,337
Issuance of shares in connection with conversion of 6% Debentures	3,500	35	28,420			28,455
Tax benefit of operating loss arising prior to May 31, 1979 quasi reorganization (Note 6)			380,315			380,315
Balance at November 30, 1981	1,863,234	$18,632	$10,156,276	$ ——	$3,374,044	$13,548,952

* 1978, 1979 and 1980 have been restated to conform with the 1981 presentation. Also, see notes to consolidated financial statements.

Exhibit 12-13   Elimination of Retained Earnings Deficit

CONSOLIDATED STATEMENTS OF STOCKHOLDERS' EQUITY (DEFICIENCY)
For the Years Ended September 27, 1981, September 28, 1980 and September 30, 1979

	Total Stockholders' Equity (Deficiency)	Common Stock $.10 Par Value	Preferred Stock Series B	Common Stock $.75 Par Value	Capital In Excess of Par	(Deficit)	Retained Earnings From June 4, 1981	Common Stock Held In Treasury
Balance at October 1, 1978	$(19,566,000)		$ 83,000	$ 2,599,000	$ 39,249,000	$(41,459,000)		$(20,038,000)
Retroactive adjustment for vacation pay—Note 10(g)	(156,000)					(156,000)		
Net income	7,382,000					7,382,000		
Balance at September 30, 1979	(12,340,000)		83,000	2,599,000	39,249,000	(34,233,000)		(20,038,000)
Net income	7,920,000					7,920,000		
Balance at September 28, 1980	(4,420,000)		83,000	2,599,000	39,249,000	(26,313,000)		(20,038,000)
Cancellation of issued shares pursuant to Plan of Reorganization—Note 1			(83,000)	(2,599,000)	(17,356,000)			20,038,000

Distribution of 2,714,861 shares of new common stock to creditors pursuant to Plan of Reorganization valued at $10 per share—Note 1	27,149,000	$271,000	26,878,000			
Net income—Note 1	20,195,000			17,952,000		$2,243,000
Elimination of deficit at June 4, 1981 against capital in excess of par in connection with reorganization—Note 1			(8,361,000)	8,361,000		
Benefit from use of net operating loss carryforward after reorganization—Note 1	2,000,000		2,000,000			
Balance at September 27, 1981	$ 44,924,000	$271,000	$ 42,410,000	$ —	$ —	$2,243,000

See notes to consolidated financial statements.

Exhibit 12-14 Quasi Reorganization Adjustments

PRO FORMA CONDENSED CONSOLIDATED BALANCE SHEET

July 31, 1978 (000's omitted)

	Historical	Pro Forma (Unaudited)				
		Assuming Confirmation of Chapter XI Plan and Quasi Reorganization		Assuming Conversion to Corporate Form		
		Adjustments (Note 1)	As Adjusted	Adjustments (Note 3)	As Adjusted	
ASSETS:						
Real estate investments—						
Operating properties to be held as long-term investments	$ —	{ $ 92,031 (E) 9,058 (F)	$101,089	$ —	$101,089	
	—	101,089	101,089	—	101,089	

Properties held for sale	257,746	{ (48,960) (D)
		  (92,031) (E)
		    (3,108) (F)
			113,647	—	113,647	

Mortgage loans, including accrued interest of $200,000	48,569	{ (4,134) (D) (7,903) (F)	36,532	—	36,532	
	306,315	(156,136)	150,179	—	150,179	
Less—allowance for possible losses	(53,094)	{ 53,094 (D) (34,122) (H)	(34,122)	—	(34,122)	
Total real estate investments	253,221	(36,075)	217,146	—	217,146	
Cash (Note 4)	15,801	—	15,801	—	15,801	
Other	5,286	(750) (F)	4,536	—	4,536	
	$274,308	$ 36,825	$237,483	$ —	$237,483	

LIABILITIES AND SHAREHOLDERS' INVESTMENT (DEFICIT):

Bank borrowings—					
Principal (Note 4)	$218,510	$(21,851) (A)	$196,659	$ —	$196,659
Interest notes	12,730	(12,730) (A)	—	—	—
Accrued interest	375	(375) (A)	—	—	—
Total	231,615	(34,956)	196,659	—	196,659
Subordinated debt—					
Principal (Note 4)	57,777	(27,505) (B)	30,272	—	30,272
Accrued interest	4,497	(4,497) (B)	—	—	—
Total	62,274	(32,002)	30,272	—	30,272
Debt discount	—	(75,065) (G)	(75,065)	—	(75,065)
Net unsecured debt	293,889	(142,023)	151,866	—	151,866
Mortgages payable	31,347	—	31,347	—	31,347
Other	5,231	2,500 (C)	7,731	—	7,731
Total liabilities	330,467	(139,523)	190,944	—	190,944
Shareholders' investment (deficit)—					
Shares of beneficial interest no par value, unlimited shares authorized	61,339	(14,800) (J)	46,539	(46,539)	—
Common stock, par value $.01, 10,000,000 shares authorized, 7,372,192 shares to be issued and outstanding	—	—	—	74	74
Additional paid-in capital	—	—	—	46,465	46,465
Accumulated deficit	(117,498)	{ 102,698 (I) 14,800 (J)	—	—	—
	(56,159)	102,698	46,539	—	46,539
Total shareholders' investment (deficit)	$274,308	$(36,825)	$237,483	$ —	$237,483

The accompanying notes are an integral part of this Pro Forma Condensed Consolidated Balance Sheet.

Exhibit 12-15   Quasi Reorganization: Direct Adjustment to Paid-In Capital

CONSOLIDATED STATEMENT OF SHAREHOLDERS' EQUITY (DEFICIENCY IN ASSETS)
YEARS ENDED SEPTEMBER 30, 1977, 1976, AND 1975
(In thousands of dollars, except share data)

	Common stock			Additional Paid-in Capital	Retained Earnings (Deficit)	Total
	Issued and Outstanding Shares	Issuable Shares	Amount			
Balance, September 30, 1974	1,997,452		$1,997	$ 803	$(14,187)	$(11,387)
Net loss for year					(25,492)	(25,492)
Exercise of employee stock options	1,500		2	3		5
Balance, September 30, 1975	1,998,952		1,999	806	(39,679)	(36,874)
Net loss for year					(173)	(173)
Balance, September 30, 1976	1,998,952		1,999	806	(39,852)	(37,047)
Net earnings through April 4, 1977					165	165
Effect of confirmation of plan and quasi reorganization (Note 1):						
Stock issued at date of confirmation	2,172,675		2,173			2,173

Stock issuable in lieu of cash payments on September 30, 1981	(173,814)	4,345,326	4,345			4,345
Less treasury stock issuable to Foreign Subsidiary		(347,626)	(521)			(521)
Settlement of liabilities on discharge from Chapter XI proceedings				31,829		31,829
Revaluation of property and plant				992		992
Change in stated value of common stock from $1.00 per share to $.10 per share			(7,196)	7,196		
Deficit charged to additional paid-in capital				(39,687)	39,687	
Net earnings subsequent to April 4, 1977					662	662
Tax benefit from use of net operating loss carryforward subsequent to April 4, 1977				602		602
Balance, September 30, 1977	3,997,813	3,997,700	$ 800	$ 1,738	$ 662	$ 3,200

See notes to consolidated financial statements

4, 1981 through September 27, 1981 have been shown as retained earnings arising after the date of reorganization. Tax benefit realized during such period from utilization of the net operating loss carry-forward has been credited to capital in excess of par and is not reflected as an extraordinary credit in the consolidated statement of income for the year ended September 27, 1981.

148 Based on these two exhibits and on other companies' annual reports, the procedure whereby only the deficit is adjusted appears to be an acceptable accounting practice. There is, however, no official statement issued by the FASB or its predecessor or the SEC that authorizes this practice. Additionally, there appears to be no general accounting standard that clearly justifies this practice.

Adjustment of All Accounts

149 Using this approach, assets and liabilities are adjusted to reflect market values and the retained earnings reflect only subsequent profit or loss. Excerpts from a prospectus showing how assets and liabilities were restated in the pro forma balance sheet to their estimated market values, and how shareholders' investment was restated to reflect those values, is presented in Exhibit 12-14.

150 Exhibit 12-15 contains another example of a quasi reorganization where assets and liabilities were restated. In this Chapter XI case, the gain from debt discharge was taken directly to the paid-in capital account, which differs from the practice followed by some accountants of reporting this gain as an extraordinary item when a quasi reorganization is adopted. The footnote describing the quasi reorganization follows:

As of the date of confirmation of Chapter XI proceedings, the Company has undergone a quasi-reorganization whereby:

a. The stated value per share of common stock was reduced from $1.00 to $.10.

b. The accumulated deficit of the Company was eliminated by a charge to additional paid-in capital

c. The net result of settling the liabilities incurred prior to the commencement of Chapter XI proceedings was credited to additional paid-in capital.

d. The fixed assets of the Company were increased by $992,000 to current fair market values and accumulated depreciation to the date of the quasi-reorganization was eliminated.

The issuance of shares of the Company's common stock has been recorded at the stated value of $.10 per share rather than the fair market value at the date of issuance. Any difference between the fair market value and the stated value would have no effect on shareholders' equity or the Company's results of operations

151 The theory of quasi reorganization should allow the assets to be revalued upward if they are stated below market values. The SEC did at one time generally oppose the procedure, but in one quasi reorganization it not only allowed but insisted that market values be used, even though they were greater than cost, for a given asset. In general, it appears that the practice of adjusting all accounts of the debtor is more in line with the purpose of a quasi reorganization.

Conditions Necessary for Quasi Reorganization

152 There appear to be more quasi reorganizations associated with companies that have not filed a bankruptcy petition than with those that have filed a petition. Thus, quasi reorganizations are not solely related to reorganization under bankruptcy law. A chapter 11 reorganization should, however, contain the necessary requirements for a quasi reorganization. Upon confirmation of the plan, the court grants the corporation the right to a "fresh start." In many cases, substantial amounts of debt are canceled. Also, the court will have determined that the new entity has the potential for successful future operations, that is, the plan is feasible. Since the court will have granted the corporation the right to a new start, it can be argued that we should account for the activities of the corporation from this day forward as a new entity—assets and liabilities should be stated at their market values and the retained earnings balance should be zero. If the creditors make the same type of concessions out of court, it could also be argued that a quasi reorganization is justified here also. The FASB (or its predecessors) has not decided to make the quasi reorganization a mandatory requirement. There is, however, ample evidence to suggest that a corporation that reorganizes under chapter 11 could account for the transaction as a quasi reorganization. The Accounting Standards Executive Committee of the AICPA is currently studying the issue of quasi reorganizations.

Reporting on an Insolvent Company

1   The report containing the accountant's opinion on the statements prepared and submitted has supreme importance in bankruptcy and insolvency
proceedings. It is the chief source of information for all those who are
interested in the debtor's affairs, and the degree of reliance placed on the
statements is dependent upon the accountant's opinion concerning them.
The objectives of this chapter are to describe several reports that are issued
in bankruptcy or insolvency proceedings and to identify some of the problems associated with the issuing of these reports.

ACCOUNTANT'S REPORT

2   It is first necessary to point out that the reports issued by accountants
concerning companies in liquidation or rehabilitation proceedings in or out
of court are very similar. The primary differences that arise relate mostly to
the material covered rather than to the basic format. It is crucial for the
accountant to realize, however, that liquidating proceedings involve audits
of companies being liquidated, while the various debtor rehabilitation devices involve reorganization audits of going concerns.

3   The reports issued in bankruptcy and insolvency proceedings do differ
significantly in certain respects from those issued as a result of a traditional
audit. When reporting on a going concern, the emphasis is on allocating
costs into expired and unexpired portions to determine the results of operations. However, when reporting on a firm involved in bankruptcy and insolvency proceedings, the concern shifts to the realizable value of the assets
and the legally enforceable obligations that have been incurred by the
debtor. Thus the emphasis completely shifts from the income statement to
the balance sheet in a chapter 7 case and partially shifts in a chapter 11 case.
It may become desirable to disclose the fair market value of certain assets,
when possible, and a comprehensive review of the assets is required to
assure that none is stated at a value significantly in excess of its realizable
value. The examination would also be expanded to insure that all liabilities
are recorded, the requirements of all loan agreements have been met, and
any deviations with their probable consequences have been disclosed. Included in the footnotes or elsewhere might also be management's appraisal
of the situation.

Limitations on Scope

4   The accountant's examination usually includes all the standard auditing procedures followed in a normal audit and conforms to generally accepted auditing standards. However, certain limitations do arise in the scope
of the accountant's examination. The accountant's report is usually needed
as soon as possible, to effect a plan, and the time necessary to perform the
audit procedures is therefore not available. Or the court or out-of-court

creditors' committee may attempt to keep administrative expenses to a minimum and accordingly may restrict professional services to those deemed absolutely essential. The most common limitations in scope include an inability to confirm accounts receivable, to request vendors' statements, and to confirm deposits, prepaid expenses, and the like.

5 The scope of the examination may be limited further by certain obstacles and unusual situations that emerge during bankruptcy and insolvency proceedings. Examples of problems that may be encountered include poor, incomplete, or missing books and records; lack of written explanation for occurrences such as major investments, loan repayments to insiders, and other transactions with parent companies or stockholders; absence of employees familiar with the books and records; major transactions that have not been recorded; and executives who refuse to cooperate or are not familiar with major financial transactions.[1]

6 When such situations arise, unusual audit procedures must frequently be employed. Alternative techniques, which are described in detail in chapter 11, paragraphs 5–108, include the following:

Interviews with those people who might have a knowledge of the unusual transactions being investigated.

Inspection of all available correspondence files.

Examination of the prior accountant's working papers.

Inspection of all documents held by the company's former attorneys.

Confirmation of transactions, either orally or in writing, with second parties.

Scheduling of all unusual transactions chronologically.

Extensive tracing and retracing.[2]

7 The obstacles and limitations in the scope of the examination and the subsequent employment of alternative procedures inevitably affects the type of report the accountant will be able to issue. Whether a qualified opinion or an actual disclaimer of opinion (compilation or review report for nonpublic company) should be given depends on the severity of the limitations. Other conditions prevalent in bankruptcy and insolvency proceedings must also be considered. These are discussed more fully in paragraphs 15–32.

8 Certain statements are normally found in an accountant's report concerning a company experiencing financial difficulty. Comparative balance sheets and income statements for a period of years may reveal the source of the debtor's problems. A statement of affairs, or a balance sheet with assets

---

[1] Edward A. Weinstein, "Accountants Examinations and Reports in Bankruptcy Proceedings," *New York Certified Public Accountant*, Vol. 35 (January 1965), p. 35.

[2] Edward A. Weinstein, "Examining a Company in Bankruptcy," *Quarterly* (Touche, Ross, Bailey and Smart), Vol. 9 (September 1963), p. 15.

classified as free or secured and liabilities shown as priority, secured, and unsecured may assist in deciding the best remedy to adopt. (See chapter 12, paragraphs 13–14.) It may also be advantageous to include a statement showing the debtor's capitalization with a schedule of all withdrawals of capital.[3] Of course, a statement of changes in financial position must be included where an opinion is being expressed on the financial statements as a whole, for the statements to be presented in accordance with generally accepted accounting principles.

Unique Disclosures in Report

9   The accountant's report covering these statements (and any additional ones prepared) contains some disclosures that are unique to bankruptcy and insolvency proceedings. Frequently the following items are found:

A brief history of the debtor, including a discussion of the reasons for filing a petition or seeking a settlement and any changes in management that have been made.

If the accountant has disclaimed an opinion, the reasons for so doing.

A discussion of any areas of the examination that were not completed and an indication as to why they were left undone. This includes disclosure of any books or records of the debtor that are withheld by an officer of the company.

Documentation of sources used to obtain information for the report other than the debtor's books and records.

Any corrections made to the book balances and the reasons for such changes.

A detailed description of all unusual transactions, including a schedule of all possible preferential payments and a list of all discrepancies found between the debtor's books and records and the financial statements issued to the trade, bank, and credit agencies.

An assessment of the probability of successfully continuing the business under a plan of settlement or a plan of reorganization.

10   The four standards of reporting established by the AICPA Committee on Auditing Procedures are to be followed by the auditor in presenting the report. The reporting standards are as follows:

The report shall state whether the financial statements are presented in accordance with generally accepted accounting principles.

The report shall state whether such principles have been consistently observed in the current period in relation to the preceding period.

---

[3] Chauncey Levy, "Creditors' Committees and Their Responsibilities," *Commercial Law Journal,* Vol. 74 (December 1969), p. 358.

Informative disclosures in the financial statements are to be regarded as reasonably adequate unless otherwise stated in the report.

The report shall either contain an expression of opinion regarding the financial
statements taken as a whole, or an assertion to the effect that an opinion
cannot be expressed. When an overall opinion cannot be expressed, the reasons therefor should be stated. In all cases where an auditor's name is associated with financial statements, the report should contain a clear-cut indication
of the character of the auditor's examination, if any, and the degree of responsibility being taken.[4]

Full Disclosure

11   When writing the report, the accountant must decide the necessary
and appropriate degree of disclosure about the debtor and its situation. In all
cases, the third standard of reporting, adequacy of informative disclosure,
must be followed. In order for the financial standards to be fairly presented
in accordance with generally accepted accounting principles, adequate disclosure is required of all material matters.[5] Strengthening this requirement
even further is the AICPA Code of Professional Ethics, Rule 202, which sets
forth that a member shall not permit his name to be associated with financial
statements in such a manner as to imply that he is acting as an independent
public accountant unless he has complied with the applicable generally accepted auditing standards promulgated by the Institute. Thus, the failure to
disclose adequate information violates the Code of Ethics.

12   The amount of disclosure required is more difficult for the accountant
to determine in a situation involving companies having financial problems
than in a normal audit. Thus, it might not be wise to reveal indiscriminately
that a company is experiencing financial trouble. Knowledge of this fact
might unjustifiably discourage customers from placing new orders, make
credit more difficult for the debtor to obtain, or provide important information to competitors. However, some disclosure is necessary for the benefit of
interested parties who lack the training to be able to discern the possibility of
financial difficulty from the statements or when this information is not readily apparent from a mere reading of the financial statements. The accountant
is again limited because the need to remain independent places a restraint on
any interpretation of the data or forecast of future events. Some suggestions
that have been made for more adequate disclosure involve a clear statement
in the footnotes that the company is headed toward financial trouble, and
disclosure of any recent appraisals or other special studies.[6] However, if the
enterprise is facing financial difficulty that may affect the continuance of

---

[4] *Codification of Auditing Standards and Procedures* (New York: American Institute of Certified Public Accountants, 1984), Secs. 410, 420, 430, and 450.

[5] Ibid., Sec. 430.02.

[6] Paul Conner, "Financial Reporting for Companies in Financial Difficulty," *Oklahoma CPA*,
Vol. 7 (October 1968), pp. 22 and 25.

general business operations, adequate disclosure of this fact is required in the opinion (paragraphs 15–32).

Accountant's Responsibility for Disclosure

13 The accountant's responsibility for disclosure in a bankruptcy proceeding is greater than in a normal audit because the accountant is an appointee of the court. In *Food Town, Inc.* it was ruled that when accountants are appointed by an order in such a proceeding, they become quasi-officers of the court and owe their primary duty to the court.[7] In *Brown* v. *Gerdes* the court further decided that, in all cases, persons who seek compensation for services or reimbursement for expenses are held to fiduciary standards.[8] These standards imply that a special confidence has been imposed in another who, in equity and good conscience, is bound to act in good faith and with due regard to the person granting the confidence. These relationships and requirements mean that accountants must include in their report all those facts that come to their attention during the examination, even if detrimental to the debtor or its management. Clearly then, when preparing a report, the accountant must realize that the special proceedings impose additional requirements and responsibilities, beyond the normal considerations, as to the facts that must be disclosed.

14 The type of opinion that the accountant issues on the financial statements submitted with the report has a strong effect on the degree of confidence that other interested parties place in the statements. This is important because the accountant's report is often the only source of information available to those who are trying to decide the relationship they wish to have with the debtor in the future.

GOING CONCERN CONCEPT

15 According to the first standard of reporting, "The report shall state whether the financial statements are presented in accordance with generally accepted accounting principles."[9] The accounting principle which presents the greatest obstacle for the accountant who is examining a company facing financial difficulty is the going concern concept. The concept is basic to accounting theory and was one of the first concepts to gain general acceptance. Hatfield called it in 1909 a "general principle which with various applications, is now universally accepted."[10]

---

[7] "Accountant's Role in a Bankruptcy Case," Statement in Quotes, *The Journal of Accountancy*, Vol. 115 (June 1963), p. 62n.
[8] 321 U.S. 178, 182 (1944).
[9] *Codification of Auditing Standards and Procedures*, Sec. 410.01.
[10] Henry Hatfield, *Modern Accounting* (New York: D. Appleton-Century Co., Inc., 1909), p. 80.

Going Concern Concept Defined

16 The going concern concept means continuance of a general enterprise situation. The assumption is made that assets are expected to have continuing usefulness for the general purposes for which they were acquired and that liabilities are expected to be paid at maturity. Statement No. 4 of the Accounting Principles Board (APB) recognizes the going concern concept as one of the basic features of financial accounting, determined by the characteristics of the environment in which financial accounting operates. It is described as follows: "Going concern—continuation of entity operations is usually assumed in financial accounting in the absence of evidence to the contrary."[11]

17 The APB recognizes the following elements of modern economic organization as helping to provide an underlying continuity and stability to some aspects of economic activity and hence to the task of measuring that activity:

1. Several forms of enterprise, especially the corporate form, continue to exist as legal entities for extended periods of time.

2. The framework of law, custom, and traditional patterns of action provides a significant degree of stability to many aspects of the economic environment. In a society in which property rights are protected, contracts fulfilled, debts paid, and credit banking and transfer operations efficiently performed, the degree of uncertainty is reduced and the predictability of the outcome of many types of economic activities is correspondingly increased.[12]

18 The going concern concept was recognized by Moonitz in Accounting Research Study No. 1, and by Grady in ARS No. 7. The American Accounting Association recognized "enterprise continuity" as an underlying concept in its 1957 publication:

The "going concern" concept assumes the continuance of the general enterprise situation. In the absence of evidence to the contrary, the entity is viewed as remaining in operation indefinitely. Although it is recognized that business activities and economic conditions are changing constantly, the concept assumes that controlling environmental circumstances will persist sufficiently far into the future to permit existing plans and programs to be carried to completion. Thus the assets of the enterprise are expected to have continuing usefulness for the general purpose for which they were acquired, and its liabilities are expected to be paid at maturity.

To the extent that termination of important activities can be predicted with assurance, a partial or complete abandonment of the assumption of continuity

---

[11] AICPA, *Accounting Principles* (Chicago: Commerce Clearing House, Inc., 1980), Sec. 1002.17(2).

[12] Ibid., Sec. 1023.16

is in order. Otherwise, the assumption provides a reasonable basis for presenting enterprise status and performance.[13]

Absence of Evidence to the Contrary

19   The assumption is made that the entity's operations will continue "in the absence of evidence to the contrary." The problem for the accountant is to determine what constitutes evidence to the contrary. A business that has had profits for several years and is expanding its operations is clearly a going concern. An entity that is in the process of liquidating its assets is clearly not a going concern. However, what assumption should the accountant make for a business that has had losses for the past three years, or for an entity that is in a chapter 11 reorganization or attempting to work out an agreement with creditors out of court?

Elements of Contrary Evidence

20   In the issuance of the report the accountant must be satisfied that evidence contrary to the going concern assumption does not exist. Carmichael classified the elements of contrary evidence in the following manner:

a. Financing problems—difficulty in meeting obligations.
   1. Liquidity deficiency—the company's current liabilities exceed its current assets, which results in difficulty in meeting current obligations.
   2. Equity deficiency—the company's solvency is questionable because of a retained earnings deficit or, in more extreme cases, an excess of total liabilities over total assets.
   3. Debt default—the company has been unable to meet debt payment schedules or has violated one or more other covenants of its loan agreements.
   4. Funds shortage—the company has either limited or no ability to obtain additional funds from various capital sources.

b. Operating problems—apparent lack of operating success.
   1. Continued operating losses—no net profit has been earned for more than one past period.
   2. Prospective revenues doubtful—revenue is insufficient for day-to-day operating needs, or there have been cut-backs in operations, such as personnel reductions.
   3. Ability to operate is jeopardized—legal proceedings related to operations may severely curtail operations, or suppliers of operating materials may refuse to transact with the company.

---

[13] AAA Committee on Accounting Concepts and Standards, *Accounting and Reporting Standards for Corporate Financial Statements and Preceding Statements and Supplements* (Columbus, Ohio: American Accounting Association, 1957), p. 2.

4. Poor control over operations—the company management has been unable to control operations, as evidenced by repetitive, uncorrected problems.[14]

21   The Auditing Standard Board approved SAS No. 34 on *The Auditor's Considerations when a Question Arises about an Entity's Continued Existence* during January, 1981. The opinion describes some factors the auditor should consider in evaluating any evidence that might indicate the inability of the business to continue as a going concern. A summary of the appropriate provisions is as follows:

1   Contrary information includes information that exists at the date of the financial statements or that comes to the auditor's attention from that date through the date of his report. The following examples of contrary information vary widely in importance and some have significance only when viewed in conjunction with others:

Information that may indicate solvency problems (negative trends such as working capital deficiencies and recurring operating losses and other indications such as default on loan agreements and denial of usual trade credit from suppliers).

Information that may raise a question about continued existence without necessarily indicating potential solvency problems (internal matters such as loss of key management and work stoppages and external matters such as legal proceedings and loss of a key franchise, license, or patent).

2   Factors tending to mitigate the significance of contrary information concerning solvency relate primarily to an entity's alternative means for maintaining adequate cash flows. Examples of such factors include the following.

Asset factors:

Disposability of assets that are not operationally interdependent.

Capability of delaying the replacement of assets consumed in operations or of leasing rather than purchasing certain assets.

Possibility of using assets for factoring, sale-leaseback, or similar arrangements.

Cost factors:

Separability of operations producing negative cash flows.

Capability of postponing expenditures for such matters as maintenance or research and development.

---

[14] D. R. Carmichael, *The Auditor's Reporting Obligation: Auditing Research Monograph* No. 1 (New York: American Institute of Certified Public Accountants, 1972), p. 94. Copyright © 1972 by the American Institute of Certified Public Accountants, Inc.

Possibility of reducing overhead and administrative expenditures.

Equity factors:

Variability of dividend requirements.

Capability of obtaining additional equity capital.

Possibility of increasing cash distributions from affiliates or other investees.

3 The auditor's initial consideration of mitigating factors is based primarily on (a) knowledge of matters that relate to the nature of the entity's business and its operating characteristics and of matters affecting the industry in which it operates, including an awareness of the specific effects and general influence of international, national, and local economic conditions and (b) discussions with principal officers having responsibility for administration, finance, operations, and accounting activities.

4 Additional considerations will generally focus on management's plans that are responsive to the observed conditions that resulted in the contrary information. The relevance of such plans to an auditor generally decreases as the time period for planned actions and anticipated events increases. Particular emphasis ordinarily is placed on plans that might have a significant effect on the entity's solvency within a period of one year following the date of the financial statements. The auditors will evaluate the impact of, for example, the following plans:

Plans to liquidate assets.

Plans to borrow money or restructure debt

Plans to reduce or delay expenditures

Plans to increase ownership equity.

5 The auditor also should discuss with management any forecasts, projections, budgets, or other prospective data, particularly data relating to cash flows, that are available or that can reasonably be developed and that are relevant in relation to the plans discussed above.

6 The auditor should consider the support for significant assumptions underlying the prospective data and should give particular attention to assumptions that are

Material to the relevant forecasts or projections.

Especially uncertain or sensitive to variations.

In deviation from historical trends.

TYPE OF OPINION

22 If any of the above problems or any of the difficulties described in chapter 2 exists in the entity, the accountant should clearly evaluate its consequences before issuing the report. The independent accountant may determine that it is best to qualify the report, disclaim an opinion, or issue an adverse report. The following discussion on the type of opinion is not restricted to reports issued under chapter 11, but applies to entities having any type of financial difficulty.

Qualified Opinion

23 A company experiencing financial difficulties is normally trying to correct the situation. If the accountant is of the opinion that evidence points to future operating success and if favorable financial arrangements are possible, a qualified or even an unqualified opinion may be issued. Many factors must be considered by the accountant before an opinion is expressed: the nature of the company's operations, the type of financial problem, the confidence that can be placed in the key personnel, and the manner in which the company has solved its problems in the past. In order to illustrate the nature of a qualified opinion it is assumed that there is a good possibility the ABC Company will have future operating success if the financial support it now receives continues and if the unprofitable division can be liquidated as planned. The qualified opinion based on the above assumptions for the ABC Company as of December 31, 19X1, is presented in Exhibit 13-1. The notes referred to in this qualified opinion are those illustrated in Exhibit 12-3.

Disclaimer of Opinion

24 If additional financial arrangements are uncertain and if the ability of the company to reverse the trend of unprofitable operations is in doubt, the auditor may disclaim an opinion in lieu of issuing an unqualified or qualified report. The fact that a company has a deficit in retained earnings does not necessarily mean that an unqualified report cannot be issued. The ability of the company to survive is the important factor that must be evaluated. Generally, for a company experiencing financial and operating difficulties, the first deviation from an unqualified report comes in the form of a qualified report. If corrective action is not taken, then the auditor, after studying and evaluating the operating and financial problems, may decide that an opinion cannot be expressed. The ABC Company has experienced three successive years of operating losses as stated in Exhibit 12-8. If there is very little possibility of reversing this loss trend and a good chance the financing agreement explained in Note 3 of Exhibit 12-3 will be canceled, the auditor for the ABC Company will find it necessary to issue a disclaimer of an opinion similar to the one illustrated in Exhibit 13-2.

Uncertainties of Future Operations

25 Quite often the accountant will disclaim an opinion on the statements issued in an insolvency proceeding. Usually this is because of the uncertain-

Exhibit 13-1 Qualified Opinion on the Financial Statements of the ABC Company as of December 31, 19X6. (the text of the notes referred to may be found in Exhibit 12-3).

To the Board of Directors and Stockholders
ABC Company, Inc.
New York, New York

We have examined the balance sheet of ABC Company, Inc., as of December 31, 19X6, and the related statements of income, retained earnings, and change in financial position for the year then ended. Our examination was made in accordance with generally accepted auditing standards, and accordingly included such tests of the accounting records and such other auditing procedures as we considered necessary in the circumstances.

As shown in the financial statements, the ABC Company incurred a net loss of $250,000 during the year ended December 31, 19X6 and, as of that date, the Company's current liabilities exceeded its current assets by $216,450 and its total assets exceeded its total liabilities by only $23,300. These factors among others, as discussed in Notes 2 and 3, indicate that the Company may be unable to continue in existence. The financial statements do not include any adjustments relating to the recoverability and classification of recorded asset amounts or the amounts and classification of liabilities that might be necessary should the Company be unable to continue in existence.

(Opinion Paragraph)

In our opinion, subject to the effects on the financial statements of such adjustments, if any, as might have been required had the outcome of the uncertainty about the recoverability and classification of recorded asset amounts and the amounts and classification of liabilities referred to in the preceding paragraph been known, the financial statements referred to above present fairly the financial position of ABC Company, Inc., as of December 31, 19X6 and the results of its operations and the changes in its financial position for the year then ended, in conformity with generally accepted accounting principles applied on a basis consistent with that of the preceding year.

New York, New York
February 15, 19X7

ties surrounding the entity's continuation or because the auditor is unable to obtain sufficient competent evidential matter during the course of the examination. Also, audit obstacles may have been encountered that resulted in incomplete field work, or the scope of the examination may have been limited by the engagement letter or retention order. These situations clearly require that the accountant deny an opinion so that third parties will not rely on the financial statements when such reliance is not warranted.

Exhibit 13-2   Disclaimer of Opinion on the Statements of the ABC Company, Issued Three Months after the Qualified Opinion (for the text of the notes referred to, see Exhibit 12-3).

ABC Company, Inc.
New York, New York

We have examined the consolidated balance sheet of ABC Company, Inc., as of December 31, 19X6, and the related consolidated statements of net loss and deficit, and changes in financial position for the year then ended. Our examination was made in accordance with generally accepted auditing standards, and accordingly included such tests of the accounting records and such other auditing procedures as we considered necessary in the circumstances.

The accompanying financial statements have been prepared in conformity with generally accepted accounting principles consistently applied on the basis of the continuation of the Company as a going concern. However, the Company has operated at a loss during the past three years, and its current liabilities exceed its current assets. The continuation of the business as a going concern is dependent upon the continued forbearance of certain creditors, the Company's ability to obtain additional working capital, and future profitable operations. Further, we are unable to evaluate the effect on the financial statements of the future outcome of the matters mentioned and described in Notes 2 and 3.

Because of the possible material effect on the financial statements of these uncertainties, we do not express an opinion on the financial statements referred to above.

New York, New York
March 30, 19X7

26   It is important that the accountant state all the reasons for disclaiming an opinion. These include disclosure of all areas of the examination that were not completed, any obstacles encountered, other limitations placed on the scope of the examination, and any sources of information other than the debtor's books and records.[15]

27   An example of the type of disclaimer often issued to creditors' committees and in chapter 11 reorganizations is shown in Exhibit 13-3. This is the type of disclaimer that would be issued with the statements as of April 28, 19X7 (see Exhibits 12-4 and 12-6), which the auditor prepared for the creditors' committee of the ABC Company. Note that this is the type of disclaimer for a public company. (See Exhibit 12-3.)

Adverse Opinion

28   The evidence to the contrary may be so convincing that the statements prepared on a going concern basis are not fairly presented. This type

---

[15]Weinstein, "Accountants' Examinations and Reports in Bankruptcy Proceedings," p. 33.

Exhibit 13-3 Sample of a Disclaimer of Opinion Issued to Creditors' Committees and in Chapter 11 Reorganizations

ABC Company, Inc.
New York, New York

We have examined the books and records of ABC Company, Inc., for the purpose of ascertaining its financial condition as of April 28, 19X7, as set forth in the accompanying report.

Our examination did not include the application of audit procedures sufficiently comprehensive to constitute an examination in accordance with generally accepted auditing standards. In accordance with prevailing standards of professional practice, the foregoing statements are deemed to be unaudited. We therefore do not express an opinion on the financial statements in the accompanying report.

The realization of asset values and the ability to continue as a going concern are dependent upon successful arrangement with creditors, attaining sufficiently profitable operations, and/or adequate additional financing.

New York, New York
May 14, 19X7

of situation may also arise when, even if the entity does continue, its assets are in such a condition that it is impossible for them to be worth their book values. If the statements are not corrected, the accountant would be required to issue an adverse opinion.

Reports Relating to the Results of Applying Agreed-Upon Procedures

29 In an audit of a debtor in a chapter 7, chapter 11, or an out-of-court proceeding, the accountant may be engaged to apply agreed-upon procedures to specific accounts or items in a financial statement. These procedures are generally not sufficient to enable the accountant to express an opinion on the specific accounts or items. Examples of this type of engagement would include the performance of selected procedures in connection with claims of creditors, or relating to inventory in a particular location. The standards that should be followed in an engagement of this nature were established in Statement on Auditing (SAS) Standard No. 35, *Special Reports*. Acceptance of an engagement of this nature is appropriate according to SAS No. 14 only if:

1 The parties involved have a clear understanding of the procedures to be performed.
2 Distribution of the report is to be restricted to named parties involved.

Exhibit 13-4   Report in Connection with Claims of Creditors

REPORT IN CONNECTION WITH CLAIMS OF CREDITORS

Trustee

XYZ Company

At your request, we have performed the procedures enumerated below with respect to the claims of creditors of XYZ Company as of May 31, 19XX, set forth in the accompanying schedules. Our review was made solely to assist you in evaluating the reasonableness of those claims, and our report is not to be used for any other purpose. The procedures we performed are summarized as follows:

a. We compared the total of the trial balance of accounts payable at May 31, 19XX, prepared by the company, to the balance in the company's related general ledger account.

b. We compared the claims received from creditors to the trial balance of accounts payable.

c. We examined documentation submitted by the creditors in support of their claims and compared it to documentation in the company's files, including invoices, receiving records, and other evidence of receipt of goods or services.

Our findings are presented in the accompanying schedules. Schedule A lists claims that are in agreement with the company's records. Schedule B lists claims that are not in agreement with the company's records and sets forth the differences in amounts.

Because the above procedures do not constitute an examination made in accordance with generally accepted auditing standards, we do not express an opinion on the accounts payable balance as of May 31, 19XX. In connection with the procedures referred to above, except as set forth in Schedule B, no matters came to our attention that caused us to believe that the accounts payable balance might require adjustment. Had we performed additional procedures or had we made an examination of the financial statements in accordance with generally accepted auditing standards, other matters might have come to our attention that would have been reported to you. This report relates only to the accounts and items specified above and does not extend to any financial statements of XYZ Company, taken as a whole.

(Source: *Codification of Statements on Auditing Standards,* New York: AICPA, 1984, Sec. 622.06)

3   Financial statements of the entity are not to accompany the report.[16]

The report issued by the accountant should

1   Indicate the specified elements, accounts, or items to which the agreed-upon procedures were applied.

2   Indicate the intended distribution of the report.

3   Enumerate the procedures performed.

[16]*Codification of Statements on Auditing Standards,* Sec. 622.01.

4 State the accountant's findings.

5 Disclaim an opinion with respect to the specified elements, accounts, or items.

6 State that the report should not be associated with the financial statements of the entity.[17]

30 If the accountant has no adjustments to propose to the specified elements, accounts, or items, he should include a comment to that effect in his report. He may also wish to indicate that had he performed additional procedures with respect to the specified elements, accounts, or items or had he made an examination of the financial statements in accordance with generally accepted auditing standards, other matters might have come to his attention that would have been reported.

31 The general standards and first standard of field work are applicable to such engagements; however, the second and third standards of field work and the standards of reporting do not apply.

32 An example of a report in connection with claims of creditors is found in Exhibit 13-4. Recall that the special provision for allowing claims without filing proofs of claim is discussed in chapter 5, paragraph 46.

UNAUDITED FINANCIAL STATEMENTS

33 Accountants may encounter situations where they are associated with statements of a firm involved in insolvency proceedings, but no audit of the company is conducted. If the company is a public company, Statement on Auditing Standards No. 26 applies. For nonpublic companies, the accountant would follow the guidelines set forth in statements issued by the Accounting and Review Services Committee. A public entity is defined as "any entity (a) whose securities trade in a public market either on a stock exchange (domestic or foreign) or in the over-the-counter market, including securities quoted only locally or regionally, (b) that makes a filing with a regulatory agency in preparation for the sale of any class of its securities in a public market, or (c) a subsidiary, corporate joint venture, or other entity controlled by an entity covered by (a) or (b)." [18]

Public Entity Report

34 It is first necessary to ascertain when financial statements are unaudited. In 1967, the Committee on Auditing Procedures issued Statement on Auditing Procedures No. 38. This statement was codified into Statement on

[17]Ibid., Sec. 622.04.
[18]Statement on Auditing Standards No. 26, Associated with Financial Statements (New York: AICPA, November 1979), para. 2n.

Auditing Standards (SAS) No. 1 and finally superseded by SAS No. 26. The second paragraph of Statement No. 38 stated that this situation arises if the accountant (a) has not applied any auditing procedures to them or (b) has not applied auditing procedures that are sufficient to permit the expression of an opinion concerning them. SAS No. 26 does not define unaudited financial statements, but states in the fourth paragraph that financial statements are audited if the accountant has applied auditing procedures sufficient to permit him to report on them. Financial statements that do not qualify for audited financial statements are presumed to be unaudited. According to SAS No. 26 (paragraph 3), accountants are considered to be associated with financial statements, first, when they consent to the use of their firm name in a report, document, or written communication setting forth or containing the statements, or second, when they submit to the client or others financial statements that they have prepared or assisted in preparing, even if the firm name is not appended to the financial statements.

35　Prior to the issuance of Statement on Auditing Procedures No. 38, the accountant could allow financial statements to be presented on plain paper without disclaiming an opinion. However, it is now required (SAS No. 26, paragraph 5) that whenever the accountant is associated with unaudited statements there must be a disclaimer of an opinion, making it clear that the accountant has not audited the statements and does not express an opinion on them. Furthermore, each page of the financial statements must be marked as unaudited. These steps are required so that anyone who becomes aware of the accountant's association with these statements will not place unwarranted reliance on them. See Exhibit 13-5 for the standard disclaimer report.

Required Procedures

36　Paragraph 5 of SAS No. 26 goes on to say that the accountant has no responsibility to apply any auditing procedures to unaudited financial statements beyond reading the statement for obvious material errors. But if the

Exhibit 13-5　Sample of Disclaimer of Opinion Issued with Unaudited Financial Statements of a Public Company

X Company, Inc.
New York, New York

The accompanying balance sheet of X Company as of December 31, 19X1, and the related statements of income and retained earnings and changes in financial position for the year then ended were not audited by us and accordingly we do not express an opinion on them.

New York, New York
May 14, 19X1

accountant concludes on the basis of known facts that the statements are not in conformity with generally accepted accounting principles, the following steps should be taken:

Insist upon appropriate revision; failing that

Set forth in the disclaimer the nature of the departure and, if practicable, state the effects on the financial statements or include the necessary information for adequate disclosures; failing that,

Refuse to be associated with the statements and, if necessary, withdraw from the engagement.[19]

37   In certain situations, it may be necessary for the accountant to prepare financial statements for the bankruptcy court or creditors' committees that are unaudited and do not contain the footnotes necessary to meet the standard of full disclosure. Paragraph 12 of SAS No. 26 allows the accountant to issue a disclaimer of opinion where substantially all disclosures have been omitted. It is not necessary for the accountant to include in his report the disclosures omitted under these conditions, but there should be a statement in the report that states that management has elected to omit substantially all of the disclosures. Since SAS No. 26 does not contain any suggestion as to how this statement should be worded, the accountant may refer to SSARS No. 1 for some guidance (see paragraph 50 in this chapter).

38   Furthermore, the accountant should refuse to be associated with any unaudited financial statements that are believed to be false or intended to mislead.

39   The case involving *1136 Tenants' Corporation v. Max Rothenberg & Co.*[20] clearly points out how important it is for the accountant to be very careful in the issuance of unaudited statements. The accountant should have a written agreement with the client as to the nature and scope of the engagement. In addition, the manner in which the statements are to be used should be understood by both the accountant and the client, and this understanding should be confirmed in writing and signed by both parties.

Comparative Statements

40   When unaudited statements for a prior year are presented with audited statements for the current year for comparative purposes, SAS No. 26 requires appropriate disclosure so that no opinion is expressed on the prior-year unaudited statements. When unaudited financial statements are presented in comparative form with audited financial statements in documents filed with the Securities and Exchange Commission, such statements should be clearly marked as "unaudited" but should not be referred to in the auditor's report. Paragraph 15 of SAS No. 26 states that when presented in any

---

[19]Ibid., para. 11–13.
[20]36 A.2d 802, 219 N.Y.S. 2d 1007 (1st Dept. 1971); *aff'd* Court of Appeals, March 15, 1972.

other document, the financial statements that have not been audited should be clearly marked to indicate their status, and either the report on the prior period should be reissued or the report on the current period should include as a separate paragraph an appropriate description of the responsibility assumed for the financial statements of the prior period. The accountant should also consider the current form and manner of presentation of the financial statements of the prior period in light of the information obtained during the current engagement.

41 An accountant for the creditors' committee may provide the committee with the necessary information so that it may reach an informed conclusion on the plan of settlement or reorganization. This normally requires only an investigatory audit, which does not constitute an examination sufficiently extensive to justify the accountant expressing an opinion on the statements. However, if any type of report is issued by the accountant, it must be accompanied by a disclaimer of opinion, making it clear that the accountant has not audited the statements and does not express an opinion on them. See Exhibit 13-5. While the examination of a public company in bankruptcy court may not be sufficient to express an opinion, the accountant may want to perform the necessary procedures to issue a review statement. Under these conditions, the auditor would follow the guidelines set forth in the standards issued by the Accounting and Review Services Committee for the review procedures and form of report applicable to such an engagement.

Nonpublic Entity Reports

42 Accountants are faced with new reporting procedures when issuing unaudited statements in bankruptcy and insolvency proceedings for nonpublic companies. In issuing financial statements, the accountant must either issue a compilation report or a review report, according to Statement on Standards for Accounting and Review Services (SSARS) No. 1 entitled *Compilation and Review of Financial Statements*. The accountant should not issue any report on unaudited financial statements of a nonpublic entity or submit such financial statements to his client unless the provisions of SSARS No. 1 are followed regarding a compilation or review report. Thus, it is important for the accountant to know the meaning of financial statements to determine the applicability of SSARS No. 1.

Financial Statements Defined

43 Financial statements are defined in paragraph 4 to consist of:

A presentation of financial data, including accompanying notes, derived from accounting records and intended to communicate an entity's economic resources or obligations at a point in time, or the changes therein for a period of time, in accordance with generally accepted accounting principles or a comprehensive basis of accounting other than generally accepted accounting principles.

Financial forecasts, projections and similar presentations, and financial presentations included in tax returns are not considered financial statements by SSARS No. 1. Tax returns, which are submitted to third parties in lieu of financial statements would, however, be considered financial statements. The following financial presentations were identified in SSARS No. 1 as being examples of financial statements:

Balance sheet.
Statement of income.
Statement of retained earnings.
Statement of changes in financial position.
Statement of changes in owners' equity.
Statement of assets and liabilities (with or without owners' equity accounts).
Statement of revenue and expenses.
Summary of operations.
Statement of operations by product lines.
Statement of cash receipts and disbursements.

44   Many of the statements containing financial information issued to the court, the U.S. trustee, creditors' committee, or the debtor by the accountant will be construed as financial statements and require that a compilation or review report be issued. This would include monthly cash receipts and disbursements reports or monthly operation statements. It would not, however, apply to any forecasts of future operations prepared or revised by the accountant and issued to the creditors' committee, debtor, U.S. trustee, or court or included in a disclosure statement issued prior to the solicitation of the acceptance of a proposed plan of chapter 11 reorganization.

Compilation of Financial Statements

45   A compilation of financial statements is defined as ''Presenting in the form of financial statements information that is the representation of management (owners) without undertaking to express any assurance on the statements.''

46   There are four general standards and three reporting standards that apply to the compilation of financial statements. The general standards are:

1 The accountant should possess a level of knowledge of the accounting principles and practices of the industry in which the entity operates that will enable him to compile financial statements that are appropriate in form for an entity operating in that industry.

2 To compile financial statements, the accountant should possess a general understanding of the nature of the entity's business transactions, the form of its accounting records, the stated qualifications of its accounting personnel, the accounting basis on which the financial statements are to be presented, and the form and content of the financial statements.

3   The accountant is not required to make inquiries or perform other procedures to verify, corroborate, or review information supplied by the entity.

4   Before issuing his report, the accountant should read the compiled financial statements and consider whether such financial statements appear to be appropriate in form and free from obvious material errors.

47   While the third standard suggests that it is not necessary for the accountant to make inquiries or perform other procedures, most accountants involved in rendering bankruptcy and insolvency services will have made inquiries or performed other procedures. This does not, of course, prevent the accountant from issuing a compilation report unless enough work was completed to issue a review or an audit report. In performing these inquiries and procedures, the accountant may become aware that information supplied by the entity is incorrect, incomplete, or misleading. Under these conditions, the accountant should see that the deficiency in the financial statements is corrected or that adequate disclosure, if appropriate, be made. Any other procedures performed before or during the compilation engagement should not be described in the reports.

48   The reporting standards require that when financial statements are compiled without audit or review they should be accompanied by a report stating that:

1   A compilation has been performed.

2   A compilation is limited to presenting in the form of financial statements information that is the representation of management (owners).

3   The financial statements have not been audited or reviewed and, accordingly, the accountant does not express an opinion or any other form of assurance on them.

49   The date of completion of the compilation should be used as the date of the accountant's report. Also, each page of the financial statement compiled by the accountant should include a reference such as "See Accountants' Compilation Report."

50   Paragraph 17 of SSARS No. 1 indicates that the following form of standard report is appropriate for a compilation:

We have compiled the accompanying balance sheet of XYZ Company as of December 31, 19XX, and the related statements of income, retained earnings, and changes in financial position for the year then ended, in accordance with standards established by the American Institute of Certified Public Accountants.

A compilation is limited to presenting in the form of financial statements information that is the representation of management (owners). We have not audited or reviewed the accompanying financial statements and, accordingly, do not express an opinion or any other form of assurance on them.

51 It is also possible to issue a report without all of the footnotes necessary for full disclosure. For example, the accountant may be requested to assist the client in the preparation of operating statements. These statements could be compiled for the client with substantially all disclosures omitted, provided the omission is clearly indicated in the report and the omission is not, to the accountant's knowledge, undertaken with the intention of misleading those who are expected to use the financial statements. The following paragraph, which would be added to the compilation report, is an illustration of the kind of explanation needed when substantially all disclosures are omitted:

Management has elected to omit substantially all of the disclosures (and the statement of changes in financial position) required by generally accepted accounting principles. If the omitted disclosures were included in the financial statements, they might influence the user's conclusions about the company's financial position, results of operations, and changes in financial position. Accordingly, these financial statements are not designed for those who are not informed about such matters.

52 While not required by SSARS No. 1, it is advisable for the accountant to maintain workpapers, which should describe, among other things, the steps taken by the client to insure that the compilation standards have been followed and the action taken to satisfy any questions raised during the engagement. The workpapers are especially needed in bankruptcy and insolvency proceedings because of the special procedures that may be performed in addition to compiling financial statements.

Review of Financial Statements

53 A review is defined as "Performing inquiry and analytical procedures that provide the accountant with a reasonable basis for expressing limited assurance that there are no material modifications that should be made to the statements in order for them to be in conformity with generally accepted accounting principles or, if applicable, with another comprehensive basis of accounting." A review differs significantly from a compilation in that inquiry and analytical procedures are performed to provide the accountant with a reasonable basis for expressing limited assurance that there are no material modifications that should be made to the financial statements. A review does not, however, provide the basis for the expression of an opinion in that it does not require a study and evaluation of internal accounting control or substantive testing.

54 The following guidelines (standards) apply to a review of financial statements:

1 The accountant should possess a level of knowledge of the accounting principles and practices of the industry in which the entity operates and an understanding of the entity's business that will provide him, through the performance of inquiry and analytical procedures, with a reasonable basis for expressing limited assurance that there are no material modifications that should be made to the financial statements in order for the statements to be in conformity with generally accepted accounting principles.

2 The requirement that the accountant possess a level of knowledge of the accounting principles and practices of the industry in which the entity operates does not prevent an accountant from accepting a review engagement for an entity in an industry with which the accountant has no previous experience. It does, however, place upon the accountant a responsibility to obtain the required level of knowledge.

3 The accountant's understanding of the entity's business should include a general understanding of the entity's organization, its operating characteristics, and the nature of its assets, liabilities, revenues, and expenses.

4 The accountant's inquiry and analytical procedures should ordinarily consist of the following:

a Inquiries concerning the entity's accounting principles and practices and the methods followed in applying them.

b Inquiries concerning the entity's procedures for recording, classifying, and summarizing transactions, and accumulating information for disclosure in the financial statements.

c Analytical procedures designed to identify relationships and individual items that appear to be unusual.

d Inquiries concerning actions taken at meetings of stockholders, board of directors, committees of the board of directors, or comparable meetings that may affect the financial statements.

e Reading the financial statements to consider, on the basis of information coming to the accountant's attention, whether the financial statements appear to conform with generally accepted accounting principles.

f Obtaining reports from other accountants, if any, who have been engaged to audit or review the financial statements of significant components of the reporting entity, its subsidiaries, and other investees.

g Inquiries of persons having responsibility for financial and accounting matters concerning (1) whether the financial statements have been prepared in conformity with generally accepted accounting principles consistently applied, (2) changes in the entity's business activities or accounting principles and practices, (3) matters as to which questions have arisen in the course of applying the foregoing procedures, and (4) events subsequent to the date of the financial statements that would have a material effect on the financial statements.

55   The Accounting and Review Services Committee did not specify the form or content of the workpapers that should be prepared in connection with a review of financial statements because of the different circumstances of individual engagements. In reviews where the client is in chapter 11, the workpapers will, in most cases, need to be more elaborate than in some other reviews because of the special demands placed on the accountant by the court or creditors' committee. As a minimum, paragraph 30 of SSARS No. 1 indicates that the workpapers should describe:

1   The matters covered in the accountant's inquiry and analytical procedures.

2   Unusual matters that the accountant considered during the performance of the review, including their disposition.

SSARS No. 1 also suggests that the accountant may wish to obtain a representation letter from the owner, manager, or chief executive officer and, if appropriate, the chief financial officer. In bankruptcy and insolvency reviews, a representation letter should, with rare exceptions, always be obtained.

56   The review of financial statements should be accompanied by a report which states that:

1   A review was performed in accordance with standards established by the American Institute of Certified Public Accountants.

2   All information included in the financial statements is the representation of the management of the entity.

3   A review consists principally of inquiries of company personnel and analytical procedures applied to financial data.

4   A review is substantially less in scope than an audit, the objective of which is the expression of an opinion regarding the financial statements taken as a whole and, accordingly, no such opinion is expressed.

5   The accountant is not aware of any material modifications that should be made to the financial statements in order for them to be in conformity with generally accepted accounting principles, other than those modifications, if any, indicated in his report.

57   The review report should be dated as of the date the inquiry and analytical procedures were completed and each page of the financial statements should include a reference such as "See Accountant's Review Report."

58   The standard review report follows:

> We have reviewed the accompanying balance sheet of XYZ Company as of December 31, 19XX, and the related statements of income, retained earnings, and changes in financial position for the year then ended, in accordance with standards established by the American Institute of Certified Public Accountants. All information included in these financial statements is the representation of the management (owners) of XYZ Company.
>
> A review consists principally of inquiries of company personnel and analytical procedures applied to financial data. It is substantially less in scope than an examination in accordance with generally accepted auditing standards, the objective of which is the expression of an opinion regarding the financial statements taken as a whole. Accordingly, we do not express such an opinion.
>
> Based on our review, we are not aware of any material modifications that should be made to the accompanying financial statements in order for them to be in conformity with generally accepted accounting principles.

59   The accountant should not issue a review report where substantially all disclosures are omitted from the financial statements. Any departures from generally accepted accounting principles should be disclosed in the report, including the effect of this departure if it has been determined. The accountant is not, however, required to determine the effects of a departure if management has not done so, provided the report discloses the fact that such determination has not been made.

60   In bankruptcy court proceedings, especially chapter 11, the basic financial statements may be accompanied by information presented for supplementary analysis purposes, such as a listing of general and administrative expenses or an analysis of the payroll and other taxes. (See chapter 12 of this book.) The accountant should clearly indicate the degree of responsibility being taken with respect to supplementary information. Two alternatives are available to the accountant. One involves subjecting the supplementary information to the inquiry and analytical procedures applied to the review and report of the supplementary information in the following manner:

> The other data accompanying the financial statements are presented only for supplementary analysis purposes and have been subjected to the inquiry and analytical procedures applied in the review of the basic financial statements, and the accountant did not become aware of any material modifications that should be made to such data.

Or, the accountant may elect not to assume any responsibility for the supplementary information and inform the user of the financial statements in the following way:

> The other data accompanying the financial statements are presented only for supplementary analysis purposes and have not been subjected to the inquiry and analytical procedures applied in the review of the basic financial statements, but were compiled from information that is the representation of management, without audit or review, and the accountant does not express an opinion or any other form of assurance on such data.

The accountants, in bankruptcy court proceedings, will most likely review the supplementary information presented because of the effect this information may have on the decisions of the court, the U.S. trustee, the creditors, or on the plan being formulated.

REPORTING ON A LIQUIDATION OF THE DEBTOR

61   A special type of report is required if the debtor has made a decision to file a plan of liquidation in chapter 11, has filed a chapter 7 petition, or has decided to liquidate the business without the assistance of the bankruptcy court. In an Interpretation of Statement on Auditing Standards No. 2, the staff of the Auditing Standards Board concluded that a liquidation basis of accounting may be considered generally accepted accounting principles if an entity is in liquidation or if liquidation appears imminent. Under these conditions the auditor would issue an unqualified opinion on the liquidation statements if

1   The liquidation basis of accounting has been properly applied
2   Adequate disclosures are made in the financial statements
3   The financial statements are not affected by a significant uncertainty

62   An assessment of the impact that uncertainty (see item 3 above) can have on the liquidation statements may be difficult to make in some bankruptcy proceedings because of the difficulty in valuing some of the debtor's assets or segments of the business that may be sold intact as a viable, ongoing business. If the liquidation basis financial statements are going to be affected by uncertainties as to the realizability of the amounts at which the assets are presented and the amounts that creditors will agree to accept in settlement of their obligations, the auditor should consider the need to modify the report due to the uncertainty as suggested in Section 509.21-26 of Auditing Standards. In addition to qualifying the report as discussed in paragraph 23 above, the auditor may want to add the following sentence to the explanatory paragraph found in the reports presented in paragraphs 64 and 65:

> It is not presently determinable whether the amounts realizable from the disposition of the remaining assets or the amounts that creditors agree to accept in settlement of the obligations due them will differ materially from the amounts shown in the accompanying financial statements.

63 Note that under these conditions the report would generally be qualified due to the uncertainty concerning liquidation value of assets or concerning the amounts creditors will accept as settlement of their claim.

Single-Year Report

64 The auditor may issue a single year's financial statement during the year the liquidation basis of accounting is adopted or the current year's liquidation basis statements may be presented in conjunction with the going concern statements of the prior year. The report for a single year should indicate, normally as a middle paragraph, that the debtor has changed its basis of accounting to the liquidation basis. An example of the report follows:

> We have examined the statement of net assets in liquidation of XYZ Company as of December 31, 19X2, and the related statement of changes in net assets in liquidation for the period from April 26, 19X2 to December 31, 19X2. In addition, we have examined the statements of income, retained earnings, and changes in financial position for the period from January 1, 19X2 to April 25, 19X2. Our examination was made in accordance with generally accepted auditing standards and, accordingly, included such tests of the accounting records and such other auditing procedures as we considered necessary in the circumstances.
>
> As described in Note X to the financial statements, the stockholders of XYZ Company approved a plan of liquidation on April 25, 19X2, and the company commenced liquidation shortly thereafter. As a result, the company has changed its basis of accounting for periods subsequent to April 25, 19X2 from the going-concern basis to a liquidation basis.
>
> In our opinion, the financial statements referred to above present fairly the net assets in liquidation of XYZ Company as of December 31, 19X2, the changes in its net assets in liquidation for the period from April 26, 19X2 to December 31, 19X2, and the results of its operations and the changes in its financial position for the period from January 1, 19X2 to April 25, 19X2, in conformity with generally accepted accounting principles applied on the bases described in the preceding paragraph.

Comparative Financial Statements

65 As mentioned in the above paragraph, the debtor may present comparative financial statements for the year prior to adoption of the liquidation basis with the year subsequent to such adoption. In the explanatory paragraph to the report, the audit should indicate the change in accounting basis of presenting financial statements. A sample report that was presented in the Interpretation to SAS No. 2 follows:

> We have examined the balance sheet of XYZ Company as of December 31, 19X1, the related statements of income, retained earnings, and changes in

financial position for the year then ended, and the statements of income, retained earnings, and changes in financial position for the period from January 1, 19X2 to April 25, 19X2. In addition, we have examined the statement of net assets in liquidation as of December 31, 19X2, and the related statement of changes in net assets in liquidation for the period from April 26, 19X2 to December 31, 19X2. Our examinations were made in accordance with generally accepted auditing standards and, accordingly, included such tests of the accounting records and such other auditing procedures as we considered necessary in the circumstances.

As described in Note X to the financial statements, the stockholders of XYZ Company approved a plan of liquidation on April 25, 19X2, and the company commenced liquidation shortly thereafter. As a result, the company has changed its basis of accounting for periods subsequent to April 25, 19X2 from the going-concern basis to a liquidation basis.

In our opinion, the financial statements referred to above present fairly the financial position of XYZ Company as of December 31, 19X1, the results of its operations and the changes in its financial position for the year then ended and for the period from January 1, 19X2 to April 25, 19X2, its net assets in liquidation as of December 31, 19X2, and the changes in its net assets in liquidation for the period from April 26, 19X2 to December 31, 19X2, in conformity with generally accepted accounting principles applied on the bases described in the preceding paragraph.

66   If the auditor issues subsequent year's statements on the liquidation basis, the auditor may want to continue to put an explanatory paragraph in the report to emphasize that the financial statements are presented on a liquidation basis.

PART FIVE

Taxes

Tax Awareness

1 The income tax effect of certain transactions during the administration period and of tax assessments related to prebankruptcy periods can impose undue hardship on the bankrupt, who is already in a tenuous financial position. It is not uncommon for a bankrupt to realize substantial taxable income during the administration period from the sale of all or part of the assets or from taxable recoveries. Net operating loss carryovers and other offsetting tax deductions are often unable to minimize the income tax effect. Therefore, in addition to ensuring that all statutory tax reporting and filing requirements are satisfied at the due dates, the accountant must be aware of those tax aspects that will permit the preservation and enlargement of the bankrupt's estate.

2 During the closing days of the 96th Congress, the Bankruptcy Tax Act of 1980 was passed as Public Law 96–589 and signed by President Carter on December 24, 1980. This bill eliminated a great deal of the uncertainty about handling debt forgiveness and other tax matters, since the Bankruptcy Code superseded the sections of the Bankruptcy Act that contained provisions for nonrecognition of gain from debt forgiveness along with other related tax items. The Bankruptcy Code does not contain the same type of federal tax provisions. The new tax law was passed after some last-minute compromises were made. Congress adopted an amendment that delayed until January 1, 1982, the requirement that net operating losses and other tax attributes must be reduced by the amount of debt that is forgiven. The Deficit Reduction Act of 1984 contained provisions that subsequently modified the income from debt discharge provisions of section 108 of the Internal Revenue Code.

3 The objective of this chapter is to identify items that the debtor, and to a limited extent creditors and other interested parties, should consider in developing a solution to problems faced by financially troubled companies. For a more detailed discussion of the tax issues raised here see Newton and Bloom's *Tax Planning for the Troubled Business*, published by Wiley and revised annually.

NOTIFICATION OF PROCEEDINGS AND FILING OF RETURNS

Notice to Governmental Agencies

4 Pursuant to section 6036 of the Internal Revenue Code (I.R.C.), every trustee in bankruptcy, assignee for the benefit of creditors, other fiduciary, and every executor must give notice of qualification to the Secretary of the Treasury or a delegated representative in the manner and within the time limit required by regulations of the Secretary or delegate.

5 Section 301.6036-1 of the Treasury Regulations requires that the individual in control of the assets of a debtor in any bankruptcy proceeding shall, within ten days of the date of an appointment or authorization to act, give notice in writing to the District Director of Internal Revenue for the district where the debtor is or was required to file returns. The notice shall not be required if, prior to or within ten days of the date of the fiduciary's appointment or authorization to act, any notice regarding the proceeding has been given under any provision of the Bankruptcy Code to the Secretary or other proper officer of the Treasury Department. The bankruptcy clerk generally gives notice in chapter 11 cases, but not in chapter 7 cases.

Form of Notice

6   Where written notice is required, it may be made on Treasury Form 56 (Notice Concerning Fiduciary Relationship) and should include:

The name and address of the person making such notice and the date of appointment or of taking possession of the assets.

The name, address, and employer identification number of the debtor or other person whose assets are controlled.

7   In the case of a court proceeding, the following additional information may be required in a supplementary schedule:

1   The name and location of the court in which the proceedings are pending.
2   The date on which the proceedings were instituted.
3   The number under which the proceedings are docketed.
4   The date, time, and place of any hearing, meeting of creditors, or other scheduled action with respect to the proceedings.

Similar notices may be required by other governmental taxing authorities and should be filed in accordance with their prescribed procedures.

8   The Internal Revenue Code (section 6903) requires that a fiduciary give to the Treasury Department a notice of relationship (a statement that any person is acting for another in a fiduciary capacity). This notice is filed on Treasury Form 56.

Failure to Give Notice

9   If notice is not given as required by I.R.C. section 6036 where notification is required, the period of limitations on the assessment of taxes is suspended from the date the proceeding is instituted to the date notice is received by the District Director and for an additional thirty days thereafter. However, the suspension in no case shall exceed two years.[1]

Responsibility for Filing Income Tax Returns—Corporations — *no separate entity created*

10   The receiver (under state law), trustee (under a title 11 case), or assignee having possession of or title to all or substantially all the property or

---

[1] I.R.C. Sec. 6872, and Treas. Reg. Sec. 301.6872–1.

business of a corporation shall file the income tax return for the corporation in the same manner and form as the corporation would be required to file the return.[2] The bankruptcy trustee, while acting on behalf of a bankrupt's estate, acts as a fiduciary. The trustee does not represent a separate taxable entity apart from the corporation. Regulations Section 1.641(b)-2(b) provides that in bankruptcy a corporation is not a taxable entity separate from the person for whom the fiduciary is acting. Hence income and expenses of a bankrupt corporation's trustee should be shown on the corporation's tax return. Also, the identification number of the bankrupt corporation should be used by the trustee.[3] Section 1399, which provides that no separate tax entity results from a corporation commencing a case under the Bankruptcy Code, was added to the Internal Revenue Code by the Bankruptcy Tax Act of 1980.

Responsibility for Payment of Tax

11   When a tax payment is due, the person who is required to file the return is also responsible for paying the tax.[4] Thus the trustee in bankruptcy, who is responsible for filing the corporate income tax return, must pay any tax that may be due. Failure to do so may result in personal liability on the part of the trustee. If a trustee has not been appointed, then the responsible official of the corporation operating as debtor in possession would be responsible.

12   When the bankruptcy estate is created, no tax is levied on the transfer of the debtor's assets to the estate, and there is no change in the tax basis of the assets transferred. Any gain realized on the disposition of the bankrupt's property results in an imposition of tax directly against the estate and indirectly against the creditors by the reduction of their bankruptcy dividend. Thus the effect of bankruptcy is to shift the tax burden from the debtor to the creditors.[5]

When to File a Corporate Tax Return

13   A corporate income tax return should be filed annually, regardless of whether the corporation has any income, as long as the corporation exists for tax purposes. A corporation in existence during any portion of the year must file a return. A corporation is not in existence after it ceases business and dissolves, retaining no assets, even though under state law it may thereafter be treated as continuing as a corporation for certain limited purposes connected with winding up its affairs, such as for purposes of suing and being sued.[6] If the corporation has valuable claims for which it will bring suit during this period, it has retained assets and therefore continues in exis-

---

[2] I.R.C. Sec. 6012(b)(3), and Treas. Reg. Sec. 1.6012–3(b)(4).
[3] Rev. Rul. 79–120, 1979–1 C.B. 382.
[4] I.R.C. Sec. 6151(a).
[5] Sidney Krause and Arnold Kapiloff, "The Bankrupt Estate, Taxable Income, and the Trustee in Bankruptcy," *Fordham Law Review*, Vol. 34 (March 1966), p. 417.
[6] Treas. Reg. Sec. 1.6012–5.

tence. A corporation does not go out of existence if it is turned over to receivers or trustees who continue operations.

Responsibility for Filing Income Tax Returns—
Individual and Partnership

14 Whereas the procedure for corporations is well established, much controversy existed in the past over the types of return to file for individuals and partnerships. To eliminate some of the uncertainty as to whether a separate entity was created, the Bankruptcy Tax Act added sections 1398 and 1399 to the Internal Revenue Code.

Partnerships   — *no new entity created*

15 Section 1399 of the Internal Revenue Code provides that no new entity is created when a case is filed by a partnership under the provisions of the Bankruptcy Code. The bankruptcy trustee would be required to file a partnership information return under section 6031 of the I.R.C. for the period(s) during which the trustee was operating the business. The Committee Reports indicate that it is the responsibility of the trustee to file the partnership return, although not specifically required by the statue.

Individuals   — *new entity created*

16 When bankruptcy proceedings intervene into the affairs of an individual, a separate taxable entity is created.[7] It is the estate consisting of the property belonging to the debtor before bankruptcy. After the petition has been filed, the bankruptcy estate can earn income and incur expenses. These transactions are administered by a trustee (or debtor-in possession) for the benefit of the creditors. Concurrently, the individual debtor can also earn income, incur expenses, and acquire property, which do not become part of the bankruptcy estate. The separate taxable entities for federal income tax purposes occur in bankruptcy cases under chapter 7 and 11 of title 11 of the U.S. Code. No new taxable entity is created, however, under chapter 13 of the U.S. Code. Also, when a bankruptcy case involving an individual is dismissed by the bankruptcy court, the estate is not deemed to have been a separate taxable entity.

17 In cases where the individual and bankruptcy estate are separate entities, they are required to file separate returns. The estate files Form 1041 for the period beginning with the filing of the petition or for any subsequent year if gross income is $2700 or more as required by I.R.C. section 6012(a)(9). The individual files Form 1040, as usual, and reports all income earned during the year. This includes income earned before bankruptcy proceedings, but not any income earned by the estate. I.R.C. section 6012(b)(4) requires that the fiduciary of the estate file the return. This would

[7] I.R.C. Sec. 1398.

be the trustee, if appointed; otherwise, the debtor in possession must file the estate's return.

18 The new act gives an individual debtor an election to close his taxable year as of the day before the date bankruptcy commences.[8] This election is available to individuals in either chapter 7 or 11 proceedings. If the taxpayer does make this election, his taxable year is divided into two "short" taxable years. The tax liability computed for the first short year is collectible from the bankruptcy estate. The tax is considered a liability before bankruptcy and thus payable by the estate. In the event the estate does not possess enough assets to pay the tax, the remaining liability is not discharged, but is collectible from the individual after the case.[9] This election must be made by the fifteenth day of the fourth month following bankruptcy, which is the due date for the return without an extension.

Effective Date

19 The effective date for sections 1398 and 1399 is March 25, 1981. Thus any bankruptcy case commenced prior to this date would follow the provisions in effect prior to the new law.

SPECIAL RULES FOR INDIVIDUALS

20 With the addition to the I.R.C. of section 1398, different considerations must be given to individuals because a new estate is created when a chapter 7 or 11 case is filed (see paragraph 16). Factors to be discussed include who—the individual or the estate—is required to report income and expense items in gross income, treatment of transfers between the debtor and the estate, carryover of the tax attribute to the estate and back to the debtor, and carryover and carryback of administration, liquidation, and reorganization expenses.

Income and Deductions

21 Section 1399 of the I.R.C. provides that the gross income of the estate for each taxable year includes the gross income of the debtor to which the estate is entitled under title 11 of the Bankruptcy Code. As noted in paragraph 20, this does not include any income earned by the individual prior to the commencement of the bankruptcy case. The gross income of the debtor (the individual as opposed to the estate) will include income earned prior to bankruptcy plus any item of income that is not included in the gross income of the estate.

---

[8] I.R.C. Sec. 1398(d)(3)(A).
[9] 11 U.S.C. Sec. 523(a)(1).

22 The original bill passed by the House contained rules for dividing deductions and credits between the debtor and the estate. These provisions were subsequently modified to provide that if any item of deduction or credit of the debtor is treated under I.R.C. section 1398(e)(3) as a deduction or credit of the bankruptcy estate, that item is not allowable to the debtor.[10]

Transfers Between Debtor and Estate

23 A transfer (other than by sale or exchange) of an asset from the debtor to the estate is not treated as a disposition that would give rise to recognition of gain or loss, recapture of deductions or credits, or acceleration of income. Thus, a transfer of an installment obligation is not treated as a disposition that would give rise to income under I.R.C. section 453(d).[11] The same provisions of nondisposition apply when assets are transferred (other than by sale or exchange) from the estate to the debtor.[12]

Attribute Carryover to Estate

24 The estate succeeds to the following income tax attributes of the debtor in a chapter 7 or 11 case[13]:

1 Net operating loss carryovers under I.R.C. section 172.

2 Capital loss carryovers under I.R.C. section 1212.

3 Recovery exclusion under I.R.C. section 111 (relating to bad debts, prior taxes, and delinquency amounts).

4 Credit carryovers and all other items that, except for the commencement of the case, the debtor would be required to take into account with respect to any credit.

5 Charitable contribution carryover under I.R.C. section 170(d)(1).

6 The debtor's basis in and holding period for and the character in the debtor's hand of any asset acquired (other than by sale or exchange) from the debtor.

7 The debtor's method of accounting.

8 Other tax attributes of the debtor to the extent provided by Treasury Regulations. For example, the regulations could allow the estate the benefit of I.R.C. section 341 if the estate repays income the debtor received under claim of right.[14]

---

[10] Senate Report No. 96–1035, 96th Cong. 2d Sess. (1980) 31.

[11] Ibid.

[12] I.R.C. Sec. 1398(f)(2).

[13] I.R.C. Sec. 1398(a).

[14] Senate Report No. 96–1035, 96th Cong., 2d Sess. (1980) 28.

Attribute Carryover to Debtor

25 Upon termination of the estate in a chapter 7 or 11 case, the debtor succeeds to the following:

1 Net operating loss carryover.

2 Capital loss carryover.

3 Recovery exclusion.

4 Credit carryover.

5 Charitable contribution carryover.

6 The estate's basis in and holding period for and the character in the estate's hand of any asset acquired (other than by sale or exchange) from the estate.

7 Other tax attributes to the extent provided by Treasury Regulations.[15]

Carryback of Net Operating Losses and Other Credits Incurred Subsequent to Commencement of Case

26 I.R.C. section 1398(j)(2)(A) provides that if the estate incurs a net operating loss (apart from the loss passing to the estate from the debor described in paragraph 28), the estate can carry back its net operating loss to taxable years of the individual debtor prior to the years in which the bankruptcy proceeding commenced, as well as to previous taxable years of the estate. An individual incurring net operating losses cannot carry back these losses to the years that preceded the year in which the chapter 7 or 11 case commenced. Similarly, the new law allows the bankruptcy estate to carry back excess credits, such as an investment tax credit, to the years prior to the commencement of the case; at the same time it prohibits the individual from carrying back these credits to the prebankruptcy time period.

Administrative Expenses

27 I.R.C. section 1398(h)(1) now provides that any administrative expense allowed under section 503 of the Bankruptcy Code and any fees or charges assessed under chapter 123 of title 28 of the U.S. Code (court fee and costs) are deductible expenses of the estate. These expenses are allowed even though some of them may not be considered trade or business expenses. Administrative expenses are, however, subject to disallowance under other provisions of the I.R.C., such as section 263 (capital expenditures), 265 (expenses relating to tax-exempt interest) or 275 (certain taxes).

[15] I.R.C. Sec. 1398(i).

28 A major addition to the new law is a provision that allows any amount of administrative, liquidation, and reorganization expenses not used in the current year to be carried back three years and carried forward seven years. The amount that is carried to any other taxable year is stacked after the net operating losses for that particular year. The unused administrative expenses can only be carried back or carried over to the taxable years of the estate. I.R.C. section 1398(h)(2)(D) also provides that expenses that are deductible solely because of the provision of section 1398(h)(1) are allowable only to the estate.

29 Often, administrative expenses are not paid until the end of bankruptcy proceedings, unless they were considered trade or business expenses. These costs are not deductible until paid and often there is no income during the last year of operating the estate to charge these expenses against, which means that no tax benefit is received from these expenses. To alleviate this problem the new law provided for the carryover and carryback provision.[16] Note that the restriction on carryback or carryover of administrative expenses to the estate applies only to those deductions that are allowed solely by reason of section 1398(h)(1) of the I.R.C. Thus it would appear that an expense (even though it is an administrative expense in a bankruptcy case) that would normally be classified as an operating cost could be carried forward to the debtor, once the estate is terminated, as an item in the net operating loss carryover.

Effective Date; Change in Accounting Period

30 The effective date of this provision is March 25, 1981, and the rules discussed for individuals apply only to cases filed under chapter 7 or 11. Section 1398(j)(1) allows the estate to change its accounting period (taxable year) once without obtaining approval of the IRS, as is normally required under I.R.C. section 442. This rule allows the trustee to effect an early closing of the estate's taxable year prior to the expected termination of the estate and then to submit a return for a "short year" for an expedited determination of tax liability as permitted under section 505 of the Bankruptcy Code.[17]

MINIMIZATION OF TAX AND RELATED PAYMENTS

31 There are several steps that a debtor in financial difficulty might take to reduce the cash outflow for taxes or to obtain tax refunds.

---

[16] Senate Report No. 96–1035, 96th Cong., 2nd Sess. (1980) 29.
[17] Ibid., p. 30.

Estimated Taxes

32   A company having financial problems may, after paying one or more installments of estimated taxes, determine that it should recompute its estimated tax liability. Downward recomputations may show that no additional payments are necessary. If it is determined that too much tax was paid, a quick refund can be obtained by filing Form 4466 immediately after the taxable year ends.

Prior Year Taxes

33   The Internal Revenue Service allows companies that owe taxes from the previous year to extend the time for payment to the extent that the tax will be reduced because of an expected net operating loss in the current year. This request is made on Form 1138. To obtain a quick refund of taxes previously paid, Form 1139 must be filed. This form must be filed within one year after the end of year in which the net operating loss occurred and can be filed only after Form 1120 for the loss year has been filed.

Pension Funding Requirements

34   An employer may be able to obtain a funding waiver if it can show that substantial business hardship exists and that funding the pension would be adverse to the interests of the plan's participants in the aggregate. If the funding cannot be waived, payments may be deferred under Rev. Rul. 66–144.[18]

TREATMENT OF INCOME DURING BANKRUPTCY PERIOD

Income Required to Be Reported

35   Generally, it is not thought that income would be a consideration during bankruptcy proceedings because insufficient profits have contributed to the insolvency. However, during the administration of the estate, transactions may occur that generate taxable income. Any income derived from the sale or operation of the debtor's assets must be reported as it is earned.

36   There may be many sources of income to a bankruptcy estate. Proceeds will be received from the sale or liquidation of assets. Rental income may be realized from real estate owned, royalties from patents, dividends from securities, and interest may be accumulated on savings and other de-

---

[18] 1966–1 C.B. 91. See Rev. Rul. 84–18, I.R.B. 1984–6,5.

posits of the debtor (or the trustee, who may deposit the bankruptcy estate's funds). In addition, if a debtor is solvent and not in a chapter 11 proceeding, then income will be recognized to the extent of the debts forgiven. However, even here an election can be made to reduce the basis of assets.

Deductions Allowed

37 In the determination of taxable net income, the trustee is allowed certain deductions. Most common are:

The costs of administration in general.

The costs of administration directly associated with the production of income by the estate, provided that they are construed as ordinary and necessary business expenses.

Payments made to priority and general unsecured creditors if such distributions are allocable to a debt associated with an item that would have been deductible by the bankrupt. It is necessary to realize, however, that debtors using an accrual basis may have already deducted the expense while actual payment is made by the trustee.

Payments for priority tax claims incurred before filing the petition, which therefore would have been deductible by the debtor if paid prior to bankruptcy.

Net operating loss carryovers.[19]

38 The taxpayer must, however, be very careful in deducting the general costs of administration. For example, the IRS stated in Rev. Rul. 77–204[20] that expenses connected with a reorganization are generally not deductible under I.R.C. section 162 because they are capital expenditures that will benefit the corporation in future years. However, all costs necessary to operate the business are deductible under I.R.C. section 162 in the same manner and to the extent they would have been had the bankruptcy proceeding not been instituted. It should be noted that a significant amount of professional fees is paid for professional help to operate the business profitably and not solely to reorganize the business. This ruling also held that in connection with a liquidation the expenses incurred in connection with the sale of assets are not deductible under I.R.C. section 162, but must be offset against the proceeds of the sale in determining the gain or loss on the transaction.

---

[19] P. B. Chabrow, "Estates in Bankruptcy: Return Requirements, Rules Concerning Income and Deductions," *Journal of Taxation*, Vol. 31 (December 1969), pp. 365–66.
[20] Rev. Rul. 77–204, 1977–C.B. 40.

Discharge of Debts

39   One major source of income in most insolvency and bankruptcy proceedings comes from debt cancellation. Section 61 lists discharge of debts as one of the items subject to tax, and Reg. 1.61–12(a) provides that the discharge of indebtedness may in whole or in part result in the realization of income. Taxable income, however, is not realized if a stockholder of a corporation cancels a debt owed to him without consideration. The amount cancelled results in an additional contribution to capital by the stockholder who cancelled the debt.

40   Clearly, in selecting the form of financial relief, a debtor should consider the tax factors related to a gain on debt forgiveness. The rules for out-of-court proceedings are different from those for proceedings under the Bankruptcy Code. Furthermore, with the passage of the new bankruptcy tax law, the cancellation of indebtedness in a chapter 11 proceeding may be subject to different treatment if the petition is filed after December 31, 1981.

41   In drafting the new bankruptcy tax law, one unresolved issue was how to handle the income from discharge of debt. If the income is taxed, it places a greater burden on the creditors who are already, in most cases, receiving less than 100 percent of their claims, since the amount going for taxes will reduce the amount creditors would receive. As initially passed by the House, H.R. 5043 provided that the gain from discharge of debt be used to offset net operating losses and other tax credit carryovers (including the reduction of basis). An option was available for the debtor to elect to reduce the basis of depreciable property rather than reduce net operating loss carryovers. A compromise was reached that will delay for one year the requirement to reduce net operating losses (see paragraphs 48–50).

42   The Bankruptcy Tax Act amended I.R.C. section 108 to apply to bankruptcy proceedings as well as to out-of-court debt settlements. Prior to this amendment, section 108, applied only to discharge of debt out of court, and discharge of debt in bankruptcy proceedings was a part of the Bankruptcy Act. The Bankruptcy Code, however, contained no federal tax provisions for discharge of debt.

43   The amended section 108 provides that income from discharge of debt can be excluded from gross income under any one of the following conditions:

1   The discharge occurs in a Bankruptcy Code case.

2   The discharge occurs when the taxpayer is insolvent.

3   The indebtedness discharged is qualified business indebtedness.[21]

---

[21] I.R.C. Sec. 108(a)(1).

44   A discharge in a bankruptcy case takes precedence over a discharge of debts of an insolvent debtor or of debts that qualify as business indebtedness. Also, the insolvency provisions take precedence over the qualified business indebtedness provisions. The amount excluded due to insolvency provisions, however, cannot exceed the amount by which the debtor is insolvent. Thus, in an out-of-court settlement where the debt outstanding is $10 million, the fair market value of the assets is $7 million, and $4 million of indebtedness is discharged, $3 million would fall under condition 2 (insolvent debtor) above and $1 million under condition 3 (business indebtedness).

Bankruptcy or Insolvency Cases

45   Although the amount of debt discharged is not considered income, I.R.C. section 108(b) provides that the following tax attributes are to be reduced in the order listed (but see paragraph 47):

1 *Net operating losses*   Any net operating loss for the taxable year of discharge and any net operating loss carryover to the year of discharge.

2 *Research credit and general business credit*   Any carryover to or from the taxable year of discharge of a credit under the following I.R.C. sections:

   Section 30 (relating to credit for increasing research activities).
   Section 38[22] (relating to general business credit).

3 *Capital loss carryovers*   Any capital loss for the taxable years of the discharge and any capital loss carryover to the year of discharge under I.R.C. section 1212.

4 *Basis reduction*   The debtor's property reduced according to the provisions of I.R.C. section 1017.

5 *Foreign tax credit carryovers*   Any carryover to or from the taxable year of discharge of the credit allowed under I.R.C. section 33.[23]

46   The foreign tax credit carryover was added by the Senate to H.R. 5043 as originally passed by the House. Notice that this credit is reduced only after the basis of property is reduced. Also, the foreign tax credit and other credit carryovers (item 2 above) are reduced 50 cents for each dollar of debt cancelled. All other reductions are dollar for dollar.[24] The reductions are to be made after the determination of the tax for the year of discharge. For net operating and capital losses, the reductions shall be made first from the losses for the taxable year and then from the loss carryovers in the order

[22] Any portion of a carryover that is attributable to the employee plan credit (within the meaning of section 48(o)(3) of the I.R.C.) is not considered in applying the provisions of section 108 of the I.R.C.

[23] I.R.C. Sec. 108(b)(2).

[24] I.R.C. Sec. 108(b)(3).

of the taxable years for which the losses arose. The reduction of tax credits
is to be made in the order the carryovers are considered for the taxable year
of the discharge.[25]

Election to Reduce Basis First

47   Section 108(b)(5) allows the debtor to elect to apply, first, any portion
of the reduction required due to debt discharge to the reduction of the basis
of depreciable property. The amount of the reduction cannot, however,
exceed the aggregate adjusted basis of depreciable property held by the
taxpayer as of the beginning of the first taxable year subsequent to the
taxable year of discharge. This eliminates the reduction in the basis of property that was sold during the year of the discharge, as was allowed under
prior law.

Special One-Year Delay Provision

48   The provisions of section 108(a) that require reduction of net operating losses, selected credits, capital losses, and basis due to discharge of debt
were quite controversial. To get some kind of bankruptcy tax law on the
books, section 7(a)(2) of the Bankruptcy Tax Act of 1980 provides that the
required reductions in tax attributes due to discharge of debt from a bankruptcy case or insolvent debtor (as defined in paragraphs 45 and 46 are not
required before January 1, 1982. The only requirement is that the basis of
property must be reduced to the extent of the debt discharged, but not below
the fair market value of the property as of the date the debt is discharged.

49   This provision applies to all debt discharged in cases under the Bankruptcy Code or similar judicial proceedings commencing between January 1,
1981, and December 31, 1981, and for all debt discharged between the same
dates for out-of-court proceedings where the debtor is insolvent. Also, section 7(f) of the Bankruptcy Tax Act of 1980 provides that for bankruptcy or
similar judicial proceedings, the debtor may elect to have the provisions of
debt discharge, including the modification discussed in paragraph 48, apply
to all cases commenced after September 30, 1979.

50   The net result of these modifications is to allow the debtor to handle
discharge of debt in the same manner as was available under the provisions
of the Bankruptcy Act.

Qualified Business Indebtedness

51   Indebtedness of the taxpayer will be treated as qualified business
indebtedness if the indebtedness was incurred or assumed by a corporation
or, in the case of an individual, in connection with property used in his trade
or business. The taxpayer may elect to exclude from gross income the gain
from discharge of debt to the extent the gain is applied to the reduction of the
taxpayer's depreciable property. The amount excluded cannot exceed the

---

[25] I.R.C. Sec. 108(b)(4).

aggregate adjusted basis of the depreciable property held by the taxpayer as of the beginning of the taxable year following the taxable year in which the discharge occurred.[26]

Basis Adjustment—Bankruptcy Tax Law

52   As noticed above, there are three conditions under which the debtor may elect or be required to reduce the basis in assets:

1   Under I.R.C. section 108(b)(5), the debtor can elect to apply the gain from discharge to depreciable property before reducing net operating losses, capital losses, or other credits.

2   Under I.R.C. section 108(b)(2)(D), the debtor (whether in bankruptcy or insolvent) is required to reduce the basis in property if net operating and capital loss carryovers and certain tax credits do not absorb these losses (paragraph 62).

3   Under I.R.C. section 108(c)(1)(A), an out-of-court solvent debtor may elect to reduce the basis of depreciable property in lieu of reporting income from the discharge.

53   The order of reduction of assets will be prescribed in Treasury Regulations to be issued. It is anticipated that the regulations will generally follow the procedure under Treas. Reg. sections 1.1016–7 and 1.1016–8 for proceedings under the Bankruptcy Code or for insolvent debtors and under Treas. Reg. sections 1.1017–1 and 1.1017–2 for solvent debtors. In all cases the reduction will take place on the first day of the taxable year following the year the discharge took place.

Limitation on Deduction

54   The basis reduction for a bankruptcy case or an insolvent debtor is limited in that the amount of reduction cannot exceed the total of basis of the debtor's property over the total liabilities immediately after the discharge. This limitation does not apply if the debtor elected to first reduce the basis in property under I.R.C. section 108(b)(5).

Recapture—Sections 1245 and 1250

55   Section 1017(d) provides that any gain on subsequent disposition of reduced-basis property is subject to the recapture provisions of I.R.C. sections 1245 and 1250 (depreciable real property). The amount of reduction is treated as depreciation for the purpose of these sections, and the straight-line depreciation calculation under section 1250 is made as if there had been no reduction in basis resulting from debt forgiveness.

---

[26] I.R.C. Sec. 108(c).

Recapture—Investment Tax Credit

56   Section 1017(c)(2) states that a reduction in basis is not considered a disposition of property. Thus it will now not be necessary to recapture investment credit due to basis reduction.

57   Under prior law, if the basis of property on which investment tax credit was claimed was reduced because of debt cancellation, the credit was recaptured as if part of the property were disposed.[27] In Rev. Rul. 74–184[28] the IRS held that a basis reduction, as a result of an election under sections 108 and 1017, amounted to the settlement of a claim for less than its fair value and in fact was a disposition of property to the extent of the reduction. The ruling was questioned, especially where the debt reduction was unrelated to the cost of property, because the reduction in basis served only as a way authorized by Congress to postpone the taxability of income.

Partnerships

58   I.R.C. section 108(d) provides that the provisions applicable to the discharge of debt in a bankruptcy case or a situation out of court involving either an insolvent debtor or solvent debtor (qualified business indebtedness provision) are to be applied at the partner level. The tax law in I.R.C. section 1017(b)(3)(c) provided that a partnership's interest in any partnership (whether or not that partnership's debt was discharged) may be treated as a depreciable asset only if there is a corresponding reduction in the partnership's basis in depreciable property with respect to such partner. The amount and nature of the reduction in the partner's basis in the partnership interest and in the assets of the partnership are to be determined by Treasury regulations.

Effective Date

59   The provisions of the Bankruptcy Tax Act of 1980 relating to the modifications of I.R.C. sections 108 and 1017 that require reduction of tax attributes and basis adjustment are effective for all bankruptcy proceedings and similar judicial proceedings commenced after December 31, 1981, and in nonbankruptcy or judicial proceedings for all transactions occurring after December 31, 1981. The other modifications contained in section 2 of the Bankruptcy Tax Act of 1980 dealing with tax treatment of discharge of indebtedness are effective for all bankruptcy or other judicial proceedings commenced after December 31, 1980 and in nonbankruptcy or judicial proceedings for all transactions occurring after December 31, 1980. The debtor may in bankruptcy or similar judicial proceedings elect to have the provision effective for all proceedings commenced after September 30, 1979—the effective date of the new Bankruptcy Code.

---

[27] Treas. Reg. 1.47–2(c)(1); Rev. Rul. 72–248, 1972–1 C.B. 16 and Rev. Rul. 74–184, 1974–1 C.B. 8.

[28] Ibid.

Exchange of Stock for Debt

60 The general rule developed by the courts where the exchange of stock for debt does not require the recognition of income was followed in I.R.C. section 108(e) of the revised Bankruptcy Tax Bill as it was finally approved. In addition to the fact that no income is recognized, the debtor will not be required to reduce attributes. Also, this provision applies to all debts even though not evidenced by a security. The Deficit Reduction Act of 1984 codified the general rules developed by case law and restricted the exclusion to title 11 cases and to insolvent debtors. Section 108(e) was amended to provide that for purposes of determining income of a debtor from discharge of indebtedness, if a debtor corporation transfers stock to a creditor in satisfaction of its indebtedness, such corporation shall be treated as having satisfied the indebtedness with an amount of money equal to the fair market value of the stock. This general rule shall not apply in the case of a debtor in a title 11 case or to the extent the debtor is insolvent. Thus, solvent corporations (fair market value of its assets exceed the amount of liabilities) will be required to recognize income from debt discharge on an exchange of stock for debt. Finally, section 108 as amended provides that a stock for debt does not give rise to income from debt discharge under a new workout exception. However, the effective date for the allowance of this exception is currently January 1, 1986, the date on which the amendments to section 382 by the Tax Reform Act of 1976 become effective.

61 Section 108 provides that if the creditor receives stock for debt that was previously written off as ordinary bad debt deduction, subsequent gain on the sale of the stock would be ordinary income to the extent of the loss previously taken. For example:

> Assume that corporation A made a $1,000 short-term loan to corporation B on July 1, 1980, and that corporation A, for its taxable year 1982, takes an $800 deduction for partially worthless bad debt under Code section 166(a). Assume further that on March 1, 1983, B satisfies the principal of the debt with B stock worth $500, resulting in a gain to A of $300. If A later disposes of the B stock for $1,500, $500 of A's gain will be treated as ordinary income ($800 bad debt deduction less $300 gain on receipt of the stock). In addition, if the stock is disposed of in a tax-free transaction (for example, by reasons of secs. 354 or 1306), the potential recapture will carry over to the stock received.[29]

62 If the taxpayer is on a cash basis, any amount not taken into account by the method of accounting used is to be handled as a bad debt deduction.

Limitations (De minimis *Cases*)

63 For purposes of determining income of the debtor from discharge of indebtedness, the stock for debt exception will not apply for the issuance of

---

[29] Senate Report No. 96–1035, 96th Cong., 2d Sess. (1980) 18.

nominal or token shares or with respect to the debt of an unsecured creditor if that creditor receives an amount of stock that is less than 50 percent of the amount of stock that such creditor would receive if all the corporation's unsecured creditors, to the extent their debts are either cancelled or satisfied with the debtor's stock, received a pro rata amount of the stock issued.[30]

64 For example:

> If creditor A held $1,000 of unsecured debt against a debtor corporation and if, in a workout, the debtor corporation fully satisfied $10,000 of its unsecured debt (including the debt to A) by the transfer of $6,000 of its stock, A must receive at least $300 of stock in satisfaction of its claim (assuming no other property is transferred) in order for the debtor to rely, with respect to the stock issued to A, on the general rule of present law that no debt discharge income is recognized and no attribute reduction is required when a corporation's debt is satisfied by the issuance of its own stock. If creditor A receives only $100 of stock for his $1,000 debt under these facts, then the debtor corporation will have a debt discharge amount of $900 with respect to issuance of stock to creditor A. If creditor A receives $300 or more of stock for his $1,000 debt under these facts, then the debtor corporation will not have any debt discharge amount with respect to issuance of stock to creditor A.[31]

65 Stock of a corporation in control of the debtor corporation is treated as stock of the debtor corporation. Regulations are to be prescribed by the Secretary similar to the ones for the exchange of debt for stock of a corporation with respect to the indebtedness of a partnership.

Purchase-Money Debt Reduction

66 When the debt arises out of the purchase of property, the discharge may be treated as a reduction of the purchase price. To be treated this way, the case must not be a chapter 11 case or the purchaser must not be insolvent; the reduction would otherwise be treated as income to the purchaser from a discharge of debt.

Tax Planning

67 Consideration should be given to the tax consequences of the decision made by the debtor to resolve its financial problems. A chapter 11 petition may be better for a company that will be solvent after debt discharge than an out-of-court agreement. Also, the tax advantages of issuing some stock to pay obligations as opposed to only cash or notes should not be ignored. These tax differences and others suggest that the tax consequences of various possible decisions should be considered throughout the case.

---

[30] Ibid., p. 17.
[31] Ibid.

CORPORATE REORGANIZATION

68   A corporation in bankruptcy or insolvency proceedings may find that one of the ways to provide for continued operations is to transfer all or part of its assets to another corporation. It is important for this transfer to be a tax-free exchange. To qualify for a tax-free exchange, the transfer must be made in connection with one of the types of tax-free reorganizations described in I.R.C. section 368(a)(1). For a transfer that qualifies as a tax-free reorganization, the new entity may be able to assume some of the tax attributes of the corporation in bankruptcy, such as unused net operating losses.

69   I.R.C. section 371, which provided for tax-free reorganization only for a Chapter X reorganization under the Bankruptcy Act or a receivership or similar proceeding, no longer applies, and corporate reorganizations must now qualify under section 368(a)(1).

Tax-Free, G Reorganization

70   The Bankruptcy Tax Act of 1980 adds a new category of tax-free reorganization to I.R.C. section 368(a)(1). The new G reorganization includes certain transfers of all or part of the debtor's assets to another corporation pursuant to a court-approved reorganization plan in a bankruptcy case under the new title 11 of the U.S. Code, or in a receivership, foreclosure, or similar proceeding in federal or state court.

71   This new provision is designed to eliminate many of the requirements that have prevented financially troubled companies from utilizing the tax-free reorganizations included under the current law. The new G reorganization does not require compliance with state merger laws (as in A reorganizations), does not require that the financially distressed corporation receive solely stock of the acquiring corporation in exchange for its assets (C reorganization), and does not require that the former shareholders of the financially distressed corporation control the corporation receiving the assets (D reorganization).

Requirements for G Reorganization

72   The G reorganization provision requires the transfer of assets by a corporation in a bankruptcy case and that the distribution of stock or securities of the acquiring corporation qualify under sections 354, 355, or 356 of the I.R.C.[32]

73   Under the general rule of section 354, stock or security holders recognize no gain or loss if stock or securities in a corporation in the reorganization are exchanged solely for stock or securities in that corporation or another corporation in the reorganization. Securities include stock and various

[32] I.R.C. Sec. 368(a)(1)(G).

long-term obligations such as bonds, debentures, and certain long-term notes. Section 354 will not apply if the principal amount of securities received exceeds the principal amount of securities surrendered. It will also not apply if securities are received and none is surrendered.

74 The general rule of section 354 will not apply unless (1) the corporation to which the assets are transferred acquires substantially all the assets of the distributing corporation *and* (2) the stock, securities, and other properties received by the distributing corporation are distributed in pursuance of the plan of reorganization.

75 The substantially-all test as indicated in the Senate report is to be interpreted in light of the underlying intent in adding the new G category. Thus, the need for the insolvent debtor to sell assets or divisions to raise cash or the need to pay off creditors is to be considered when determining whether a transaction qualified as a G reorganization. This liberal application of the "substantially all" test does not apply to other reorganizations. Although section 368(a)(1)(G) requires only part of the assets to be distributed in the plan of reorganization, the additional requirement of the provisions of sections 354, 355, or 356 may have the effect of reducing the flexibility of the intended liberal application of the "substantially all" test. For example, see the restrictions in I.R.C. section 354(b)(1) and (2) as discussed in paragraph 74. The extent to which section 354 will reduce the transfer of part of the assets is unclear. For example, if part of the assets are liquidated and distributed under section 363 of the Bankruptcy Code prior to the approval of a plan of reorganization, will a resulting reorganization qualify under the G reorganization?

Additional Rules for G Reorganization

76 The Bankruptcy Tax Act of 1980 added to I.R.C. section 368(a) a subsection (3) that contained additional requirements for a G reorganization. The G reorganization can be used only in a case under title 11 of the U.S. Code or in a receivership, foreclosure, or similar proceeding. A bankruptcy case under title 11 or similar cases will be treated as such only if the corporation is under the jurisdiction of the court and the transfer is pursuant to a plan of reorganization approved by the court. A proceeding before a federal or state agency involving a financial institution to which I.R.C. section 585 or 593 applies is to be treated as a court proceeding.

77 A transaction that qualifies as a G reorganization is not to be treated as also qualifying as a liquidation under I.R.C. section 332, an incorporation under I.R.C. section 351, or another type of reorganization under section 368(a)(1). An exception is made so that a transfer may require the recognition of gain under section 357(c) if the liabilities assumed exceed the basis. It is also not necessary for a reorganization in bankruptcy proceedings to qualify for a G reorganization to receive tax-free treatment. Thus, an acquisition of the stock of a company in a chapter 11 case not covered by the G type of reorganization can still, for example, qualify for the nonrecognition treatment under section 368(a)(1)(B) or E, for example.[33]

78   The continuity of interest requirement must be satisfied for the new G type of reorganization to qualify for nonrecognition treatment. Creditors receiving stock may be counted toward satisfying the continuity of interest rule.

Triangular Reorganizations

79   The new law permits a triangular reorganization where a corporation is allowed to acquire a debtor corporation in a G reorganization by using the stock of the parent rather than its own stock. Also allowed is the purchase of an insolvent corporation by a "reverse merger" if the former creditors of the surviving corporation exchange their claims for voting stock that has a value equal to at least 80 percent of the value of the debts of the insolvent corporation. The 80 percent requirement restricts the extent to which this type of reorganization could work. In addition, the new law permits a corporation to transfer the assets of a debtor corporation in a G reorganization by the acquiring corporation to a controlled subsidiary without affecting the tax-free status of this reorganization.

Transfer to Controlled Subsidiary

80   The new law allows a corporation that acquired in a G reorganization substantially all the assets of a debtor corporation to transfer the assets to a controlled subsidiary without endangering the nonrecognition status of the reorganization.

Treatment of Accrued Interest

81   Both the Senate and House reports indicate that a creditor exchanging securities in any corporate reorganization described in section 368 of the Code (including a G reorganization) is treated as receiving interest income on the exchange to the extent that the security holder receives new securities, stock, or any other property attributable to accrued but unpaid interest (including accrued original issue discount) on the securities surrendered. This provision, which reverses the so-called Carman rule,[34] applies regardless of whether the exchanging security holder realizes gain on the exchange overall. Under this provision, a security holder that had previously accrued the interest (including original issue discount) as income recognizes a loss to the extent that the interest is not paid in the exchange.[35]

---

[33] Senate Report No. 96–1035, 96th Cong., 2d Sess. (1980) 36.
[34] *Carman* v. *Commissioner,* 189 F.2d 363 (2nd Cir. 1951); Rev. Rul. 59–98, 1959–1 C.B. 76.
[35] Senate Report No. 96–1035, 96th Cong., 2d Sess. (1980) 37–38, and House Report No. 96–833, 96th Cong., 2d Sess. (1980) 33.

Personal Holding Company

82   The Bankruptcy Tax Act of 1980 exempts corporations in bankruptcy or similar proceedings from the personal holding company tax imposed by I.R.C. section 541. Section 5(a) of the Act provides a new paragraph (9) to I.R.C. section 542(c) that lists specific exemptions from personal holding company status. New I.R.C. section 542(c)(9) states that a corporation in a title 11 or similar case is not subject to personal holding company rules unless the primary purpose of instituting or continuing these proceedings was to avoid the personal holding company tax.

Liquidation Under I.R.C. Section 337

83   Under a section 337 liquidation, no gain or loss is recognized by a corporation when it sells its property and subsequently distributes all its assets according to a plan of a twelve-month liquidation. Property as defined under this Code section does not include installment notes receivable, accounts receivable, or inventory. There is an exception, however, regarding inventory. If the inventory is sold in a bulk sale to one individual, then it will qualify as property under this section and no gain or loss will be recognized on the sale.

84   It has been the position of the IRS that a section 337 liquidation does not apply to a liquidating corporation in bankruptcy or similar proceeding if the shareholders do not receive consideration in exchange for their shares. In this case, the IRS felt there was no distribution in liquidation in the meaning of section 337.[36]

85   Under the new Bankruptcy Tax Act of 1980, section 337 is now available to corporations in bankruptcy or similar proceedings regardless of whether the shareholders receive any consideration in exchange for their stock. The original bill that passed the House provided that shareholders could receive nothing as a result of the liquidation. Subsequent revisions were made to allow the shareholders to receive some consideration. The new law also modifies the time requirement imposed by section 337. No gain or loss is recognized by the liquidating corporation during the entire bankruptcy proceeding, even if it exceeds twelve months from the adoption of the plan.[37] To qualify under section 337, the property must be sold under a plan adopted in a title 11 or similar case. The period of nonrecognition begins on the date of the adoption of the plan and ends on the date the case is terminated. Property sold under section 363(b) of the Bankruptcy Code, rather than as part of a plan would not qualify.

---

[36] Rev. Rul. 73–364, 1973–1 C.B. 178; Rev. Rul. 56–387, 56–2 C.B. 189.
[37] I.R.C. Sec. 337(g)(2).

86   The new law provides further that for the purposes of section 337 the term *property* does not include items acquired, other than inventory sold in bulk, on or after the date the plan of liquidation was adopted. Sufficient assets may be retained to pay administrative claims after the case is closed.[38]

I.R.C. Section 351

87   The general rule of I.R.C. section 351 provides that no gain or loss is recognized when property is transferred to a corporation by one or more persons solely in exchange for stock or securities of that corporation and the person or persons are in control of the corporation immediately after this exchange. Under prior law, the term *property* for the purposes of this section included indebtedness of any kind.[39] Therefore, section 351 could be used by insolvent corporations because the transfer of unsecured debt was a tax-free exchange of property under section 351. The Bankruptcy Tax Act of 1980 changes the law in that indebtedness not evidenced by a security is no longer considered property for the purposes of section 351. Therefore, the transfer of unsecured debts may cause the recognition of gain or loss by the transferor.

AVAILABILITY OF NET OPERATING LOSSES

88   Section 172 provides for the carryback and carryforward of net operating losses. Under this provision a corporation is, in most cases, allowed to carry forward for up to fifteen years (nine years for regulated transportation companies) net operating losses sustained in a particular tax year and not carried back to prior years. The period was five years (seven for regulated transportation companies) for tax years ending before 1976. Beginning with tax years ending in 1976, the taxpayer can elect not to carry losses back (section 172(b)). Prior to that time, however, losses had to be carried back to the three preceding tax years first, and if all of the loss was not used against income in prior years it might then be carried forward. The extent, however, to which the net operating loss can be preserved in bankruptcy and insolvency proceedings depends on the manner in which the debt is restructured.

89   The net operating loss is generally presumed where there is no change in ownership, except that some of the creditors may become stockholders as a result of the debt discharge and restructuring. The forgiveness of indebtedness does not affect the ability of the corporation to carry forward prior net operating losses.[40] The loss carryover may, however, be

---

[38] I.R.C. Sec. 337(g)(1).
[39] Rev. Rul. 77–81, 1977–1 C.B. 97.
[40] Rev. Rul. 58–600, 1958–2 C.B. 29.

reduced to the extent of the discharge of debt. Special problems may arise when the debt restructuring involves the use of another corporation and special care must be exercised to assure the preservation of the net operating loss carryover.

Internal Restructuring

90   Generally, any internal restructuring of the debt and equity of the corporation does not affect the future use of net operating losses. However, in selecting the nature of the restructuring, the debtor must be aware of areas where potential problems can develop. For example, if the internal restructuring comes under the provisions of section 382, the net operating loss may be lost. This section applies to the purchase of stock. Generally, stock is said to be purchased "if its basis is determined by reference to cost." An exchange of bonds, debentures, or other debts evidenced by securities into stock in any type of internal restructure would normally qualify as a nontaxable recapitalization and would not be a purchase under section 382. However, the conversion of trade payables is not a tax-free transaction to creditors, and the stock going to these creditors would, prior to the Bankruptcy Tax Act of 1980, be considered purchased stock for the purpose of determining whether the debtor corporation undergoes a change of ownership under section 382(a) prior to the Tax Reform Act of 1976. A provision of the Tax Reform Act of 1976, effective January 1, 1986, provided that the purchase of stock by a security holder or creditor in exchange for debt of the corporation does not constitute a purchase unless the claim was acquired for the purpose of acquiring stock.[41] Prior to the Bankruptcy Tax Act of 1980, I.R.C. section 351 could be used to give the creditors tax-free treatment, but section 351(e)(2) eliminated this possibility (see paragraph 87).

91   If the internal restructuring falls under the provisions of section 382(a), in order to preserve the net operating losses, the debtor corporation must satisfy the business test (until January 1, 1986—see the next section, "Tax Reform Act of 1976") or avoid the change-in-ownership test. To satisfy the trade or business test the debtor must continue to carry on substantially the same trade or business that it conducted before the first purchase of stock under the change-in-ownership test. The determination of whether a corporation satisfies the trade or business test is based on all the relevant facts and circumstances including changes in employees, equipment, products, location, customers, and other items. Discontinuance of "more than minor" activities may not constitute carrying on substantially the same business; however, the addition of other business does not affect the business continuity requirement.

92   A change in ownership occurs if the ten largest stockholders at the end of any given year have increased their ownership of the debtor corpora-

---

[41] I.R.C. Sec. 382(a)(5)(c).

tion's stock by 50 percentage points or more by purchase in that year or the preceding year.

Tax Reform Act of 1976

93 Several changes were made by the Tax Reform Act of 1976 regarding the special limitations on net operating loss carryover of section 382(a). However, Congress decided that because the provision dealing with I.R.C. section 382 changed the basic concepts underlying these rules, an additional period of time was necessary to complete a review of the provisions. The effective date was changed to January 1, 1986. As a result, the new I.R.C. section 382 may be changed before it becomes effective.

94 First, the continuation of business rule is eliminated. The emphasis is now all on change of ownership. Second, the new law changes the increase in ownership of a buying group from 50 to 60 percentage points. Also, the number of stockholders in the buying group that is used to determine ownership change is increased from ten to fifteen. Thus, under the new section 382, the net operating loss will be limited if the fifteen largest stockholders have increased their ownership of the debtor corporation's stock by more than 60 percentage points, even though the new owners continue the same trade or business. The new law does not eliminate all the loss, but provides that the loss is to be reduced by 3.5 percentage points for each percentage point between 60 and 80 and by 1.5 percentage points for each percentage point in excess of 80.

95 To determine the percent changes, the new law requires the consideration of the first and second preceding taxable years. However, if the change in ownership takes place in one year and there are no further changes, losses in future years will not be reduced or eliminated. Section 351 exchanges are now under the provisions of section 382(a). *Purchase* has been redefined; it excludes stock given for valid debt unless debt was for the purpose of acquiring stock.

96 The revised I.R.C. section 382 is effective for all taxable years beginning after January 1, 1986. These revised rules have been delayed for almost ten years, and the effective date may be postponed again.

External Restructuring

97 Section 381 provides that in certain types of acquisitions of assets of a corporation by another corporation, the acquiring corporation inherits some of the tax attributes of the acquired entity. Net operating loss carryforwards is one of the specified tax attributes. The loss can be carried forward under the following acquisitions:

1 A distribution of subsidiaries' assets according to the complete liquidation requirements of section 332 (except in a case where basis is deter-

mined under section 334(b)(2)). Section 332 does not apply if the subsidiary is insolvent.

2   A transfer where property of one corporation is transferred in pursuance to a plan of reorganization, solely for stock and securities in another corporation (section 361), provided the transfer is in connection with the following types of tax-free reorganizations described in section 368(a)(1):

A reorganization   A statutory merger or consolidation under the laws of a state.

C reorganization   The acquisition by one corporation, in exchange for all or part of its voting stock, of substantially all the properties of another corporation.

D reorganization   A transfer by a corporation of all or part of its assets to another corporation where the transferor, or one or more of its shareholders or any combination thereof, is in control of the corporation to which the assets were transferred. For this transfer to be acceptable, the corporation to which the assets are transferred must acquire substantially all the assets, and, in addition, the stock, securities, and other properties received by the transferor must be distributed according to the plan of reorganization (section 354(b)).

F reorganization   A mere change in the identity, form, or plan of the organization.

G reorganization   A transfer by a corporation of all or part of its assets to another corporation in a bankruptcy case or similar case, but only if the plan provides that stock or securities of the corporation to which assets are transferred are distributed in a transaction that qualifies under section 354, 355, or 356.

Minimum Ownership

98   When a reorganization occurs (pursuant to plans adopted before January 1, 1982) as discussed above and described in section 381(a)(2), the net operating loss tax benefit must be reduced if the stockholders (immediately before reorganization) of the loss corporation own (immediately after reorganization) less than 20 percent of the fair market value of the outstanding stock of the acquiring corporation. The reductions amount to the percentage determined by subtracting from 100 percent the percentage of the fair market value of the outstanding stock of the acquired corporation owned by the stockholders of the loss corporation multiplied by 5.

99   For reorganization plans adopted on or after January 1, 1986, the Tax Reform Act of 1976 (if it ever becomes effective) increases the minimum ownership from 20 to 40 percent. If the stockholders own less than 40 percent but more than 20 percent, the loss carryover is reduced by 3.5 percent for each percentage point less than 40. If the stockholders own less than 20 percent, the loss carryover is reduced by 1.5 percent for each percentage point less than 20 percent. The change in I.R.C. section 382, in certain circumstances, eliminates the use of a stock-for-stock B reorganization or a triangular reorganization as a way to avoid the rules of this section.

100 The net operating loss of some financially troubled companies is quite significant, and every effort must be made to preserve the loss. There still exists some uncertainty as to when the loss can be carried forward. This uncertainty, of course, means that the debtor corporation must be exceptionally careful in devising any plan of reorganization so that as many potential problem areas as possible can be avoided.

EFFECTS ON EARNINGS AND PROFITS

101 The earnings and profits of a corporation determine the extent to which corporate distributions are taxable. Also, in determining the personal holding company tax and the accumulated earnings tax, the earnings and profits must be considered. Two factors must be considered in analyzing the impact bankruptcy proceedings have on the earnings and profits account of a corporation. The first deals with the need to adjust the earnings and profits account by the amount that the cancelled indebtedness exceeds the reduction in the basis of the assets. The second concerns the carryover of the earnings and profits balance, which is frequently a deficit to the reorganized corporation.

Account Adjustment

102 A corporation in a chapter 11 proceeding must adjust its earnings and profits. Generally, the determination of the earnings and profits of a corporation for dividend purposes is based on generally accepted accounting principles that take into consideration the economic realities of the transaction as well as the tax impact of a given transaction. Thus nontaxable income items, such as interest on state and municipal bonds, increase the earnings and profits available for dividends, and likewise losses and expenses that are disallowed for tax purposes reduce the earnings and profits.

103 I.R.C. section 312 is amended to provide that to the extent that the income from debt forgiveness is used to reduce the basis under I.R.C. section 1017, such basis reduction will not affect the earnings and profits account. Of course, this amount would eventually affect the earnings and profits account by reduced depreciation charges or an increase in the gain (reduction of the loss) when the asset is sold. The other income from debt forgiveness would be used to adjust the earnings and profits account.

104 The Senate added to the House bill a provision that would provide that any deficit in earnings and profits is reduced (but no provision made to increase positive earnings and profits balance) by the paid-in capital of any shareholder whose interest is terminated in a bankruptcy or similar case.

Earnings and Profits Carryover

105   In general, if the plan of settlement or reorganization provides for debt forgiveness where the existing stockholders' interests are not eliminated, the earnings and profits account is preserved. This would be true even if there were a contribution of new capital or if the stockholders who held debt transferred it for stock.

106   In the case of a tax-free reorganization, the earnings and profits or a deficit, as the case may be, will carry over. Section 381(c)(2) provides for the preservation of the earnings and profits account for those tax-free reorganizations specified in section 381(a)(2). Deficits of one corporation cannot be used to reduce the amount of prereorganization earnings that any other corporation brings to the combination, but may be used only to offset future earnings. Again, these provisions would apply to chapter 11 and out-of-court proceedings.

107   One major problem arises in interpreting how the provisions of section 381 can be applied. If the creditors receive stock in the acquiring corporation and the interests of original stockholders of the acquired corporation are eliminated, will section 381 provide for the preservation of the earnings and profits? Or should it be assumed that the earnings and profits were lost when the creditors, in fact, become the stockholders of the acquired corporation before the reorganization occurred? Revenue Ruling 77–204 might suggest that the earnings and profits are preserved, as would the amendment to section 382(b) provided by the Bankruptcy Tax Act, which provided that creditors receiving stock should be considered as stockholders before the reorganization. However, an amendment to section 312 (see paragraph 103) eliminates part or most of the carryover.

TAX PRIORITIES, PENALTIES, AND INTEREST

Tax Priorities

SEC. 507 of BANKRUPTCY CODE ~ PRIORITY

108   Normally secured debts are first satisfied and then unsecured debts are paid in the order of priority specified in section 507. For a general discussion of the order of priority see chapter 3, paragraphs 98–100. In this section the priorities are mentioned only to the extent they involve taxes.

Administration Expenses

109   First priority given to unsecured debts is allowed for administrative expenses. Included in these expenses is any tax incurred during the administration of the estate while bankruptcy proceedings are in progress (section 503(b)). Examples of taxes that would qualify for first priority are income tax liabilities, most employee's withholding taxes and the employer's share of employment taxes, property taxes, excise taxes, recapture of investment tax credit arising from property sales, and claims arising from excessive allowance of "quickie" refunds to the estate (such as the tentative net operating loss carrybacks allowed under section 6411 of the Code).[42] Taxes on post petition payment of prepetition wages would not be a first priority. Section 503(b)(1)(C) provides that any fine or penalty or reduction in credit relating to a tax classified as an administrative expense is also given first priority.

"Involuntary Gap" Claims

110   Creditors whose claims arise in the ordinary course of the debtor's business or financial affairs after any involuntary case is commenced, but before the appointment of a trustee or the order for relief is entered by the court, are granted second priority. Thus any taxes arising during this period would receive second priority.

Prepetition Wages

111   Claims for wages up to $2000 per employee earned within ninety days before the filing of the petition receive third priority. Any taxes withheld on these wages would receive the same priority according to section 346(f). Thus withholding taxes on wages earned prior to the ninety-day period and on wages earned by individuals in excess of the $2000 limit would not receive any priority. These claims would be classified with other general unsecured claims. Claims that fall within the ninety-day period and the $2000 limit would receive third priority.

Prepetition Taxes

112   Certain taxes are granted seventh priority. Thus the Bankruptcy Code continues the policy of requiring the creditors of a bankrupt to pay the taxes owed by the debtor, since the payment of this tax reduces the amount that general unsecured creditors would otherwise receive. The Code makes some modifications in the taxes that are granted priority status, and it attempts to solve some of the unresolved questions of the prior law.

Income and Gross Receipts Taxes

113   Section 507(a)(7)(A) contains several provisions granting priority to income and gross receipts taxes. First, any tax on income or gross receipts for a taxable year ending on or before the date of the filing of the petition is given seventh (sixth for petitions filed prior to October 8, 1984) priority provided the date the return was last due, including extensions, is within three years before the petition was filed. Thus any tax due for a taxable period that ended after the petition was filed is not granted seventh priority but would be considered an administrative expense (first priority). The date of the return test of the Reform Act replaces the section 17a(1) requirement

---

[42] Richard L. Bacon and James L. Billinger, "Analyzing the Operation and Tax Effects of the New Bankruptcy Act," *Journal of Taxation,* Vol. 41 (February 1979).

of the Bankruptcy Act of "legally due and owing," which was unclear and caused debate.

114   Second is any income or gross receipts tax assessed within 240 days before the petition was filed, even though the due date of the return does not fall within the three-year period discussed above. The purpose of the 240-day provision is to give the IRS time to take more drastic measures to collect the tax. If during this period an offer in compromise is made, the time from when the offer is made until it is accepted, rejected, or withdrawn is not counted. Furthermore, the tax will automatically be given priority if the petition is filed within thirty days after the offer was rejected or withdrawn or if the offer in compromise is still outstanding, provided the offer in compromise was made within 240 days after the assessment. If the petition is filed 240 days after the assessment, the tax does not have any priority unless it falls within the three-year period.

115   Third, any income or gross receipts tax that has not been assessed but that is assessable is granted priority. Thus, even though a tax was due more than three years ago, it is still granted priority provided the tax is assessable. Taxes that are nondischargeable under section 523a(1)(B) and (C) are excluded from this provision. Examples of taxes that qualify under this provision are claims still being negotiated at the date of petition, previous years' taxes for which the taxpayer has extended the statute of limitations period, taxes in litigation where the tax authority is prohibited from assessing the tax, or any other unassessed taxes that are still open under the statute of limitations.

116   A tax pending determination by the tax court at the date the petition is filed will be granted seventh priority. If the tax court has decided the issue against the taxpayer before a petition is filed and if no appeal is made, the tax will receive seventh priority even though no assessment has been made as of the petition date. The Bankruptcy Code ends the practice under prior law where once the case was resolved in tax court and the assessment restriction removed, the taxpayer could file a petition before the IRS could make the assessment and thus would avoid the tax being considered as a priority claim. If, of course, the assessment is made before the petition is filed, the 240-day rule is in effect. Thus tax claims due for petitions filed within 240 days after the assessment are seventh priority, and tax claims due where the petition is filed more than 240 days after would not receive priority unless the three-year period discussed above applies.[43]

Property Taxes

117   Property taxes assessed and last payable without penalty within one year before the petition is filed are granted seventh priority. Note that the time period here is one year rather than the three-year period that applies to income and gross receipts tax.

---

[43] Ibid., p. 77.

Withholding Taxes

118 Section 507(a)(7)(C) gives seventh priority to all taxes that the debtor was required to withhold and collect from others for which the debtor is liable in whatever capacity. There is no time limit on the age of these taxes. Included in this category would be income taxes, state sales taxes, excise taxes, and withholdings on interest and dividends of nonresidents. Taxes withheld on wages will receive seventh priority provided the wages were paid before the petition was filed. If not, then they will have the same priority as the wage claims. The part of the wages granted third priority will result in the related taxes being also granted third priority. Taxes that relate to the wages that are classified as unsecured claims (i.e., excess over $2000 for each employee or incurred more than ninety days before the petition was filed) will receive no priority.

119 To properly determine the priority of withholding taxes, the accountant must first determine when wages were paid (before or after petition date) for which withholdings were taken; if they were paid after the petition date, what is the priority of the wages? Withholding taxes on wages earned after the petition is filed are granted first priority.

120 Thus withholding taxes can have first, third, seventh, or general creditor priority depending on the status of the related payments.

Employer's Taxes

121 An employment tax on wages, salary, or commission earned before the petition was filed receives seventh priority provided the date the last return was due, including extensions, is within three years before the filing date. Taxes due beyond this date are considered general claims even though the individual responsible for submitting these taxes to the government is personally liable for these taxes under I.R.C. section 6672.

122 On wages not paid before the petition was filed, it was the intent of Congress to grant seventh priority only to the employer's share of the tax due on wages that receive third priority. The employee's tax on wages that are not granted priority would thus be a general claim, as would the wages. Section 507(a)(7)(D) does not state this, but it would be expected that a change would be made in a technical correction bill to reflect congressional intent.

Excise Taxes

123 For an excise tax to qualify as a tax priority, the transaction creating the tax must have occurred before the petition was filed. In addition, if the excise tax is of the type that requires a tax return, to receive seventh priority the day the return is last due (including extensions) must be within three years before the petition was filed. If no return is required, the three-year limitation begins on the date the transaction occurred (section 507(a)(7)(E)).

This group of taxes includes sales taxes, estate and gift taxes, gasoline taxes, and any other federal, state, or local taxes defined by statute as excise taxes.

Customs Duties

124   Section 507(a)(7)(F) provides that a customs duty arising from the importation of merchandise will receive priority if (1) entered for consumption within one year before the bankruptcy petition is filed, (2) covered by an entry liquidated or reliquidated within one year before the date the petition was filed, or (3) entered for consumption within four years before the petition date, but not liquidated by that date, if the Secretary of the Treasury certifies that the duties were not liquidated due to an investigation into assessment of antidumping or countervailing duties, fraud, or lack of information to properly appraise or classify such merchandise.

Tax Penalty

125   The priority granted a tax penalty depends on its nature. A tax liability that is called a penalty but in fact represents a tax to be collected is granted seventh priority. These penalties are referred to in section 507(a)(7)(G) as "compensation for actual pecuniary loss." Other prepetition penalties, including fines, forfeitures, and punitive damages, are not granted sixth priority, and in situations involving liquidations they are paid only after all unsecured debts have been satisfied [section 726(a)(4)]. Only amounts paid for postpetition interest and amounts paid to the debtor receive a lower priority in liquidation cases.

Interest

126   As under prior law, interest stops accruing when the petition is filed for purposes of determining prepetition liabilities. Interest that has accrued on prepetition taxes is considered part of the debt and would receive the same priority as the taxes received to which the interest applies. Interest that accrues during bankruptcy proceedings on a prepetition debt would, according to section 726(a)(5), receive payment only after all other creditors' claims have been satisfied.

Erroneous Refunds or Credits

127   Section 507 provides that a claim from an erroneous refund or credit of a tax will be treated in the same manner as the claim for the tax to which the refund or credit applied. Thus a refund received in error for income tax paid in 1977 will receive seventh priority if the tax liability incurred in 1977 would receive that priority. This provision would also apply to "quickie refunds" based on NOL carrybacks under section 6411 of the Code.[44]

Chapter 11 Reorganization

128   Section 1129(a)(9) states that a plan must provide for the payment of all taxes with priority before the plan will be confirmed. Taxes classified as administration expense and involuntary gap must be paid in full with cash on the effective date of the plan. Employees' withholding taxes on wages granted third priority are to be paid in full with cash on the effective date of the plan or, if the class has accepted the plan, with deferred cash payments that have a value equal to the claims. Claims for taxes granted seventh priority must be satisfied with deferred cash payment over a period not to exceed six years after the date of assessment of such claim; the value as of the effective date of the plan is equal to the allowed amount of the tax claims. These deferred payments include an amount for interest to cover the cost for not receiving payment as of the effective date of the plan. The Code does not state whether the tax rate, market rate, or some other rate should be used.

129   Other tax claims that do not qualify as a tax priority item would receive treatment similar to that for other unsecured claims. Furthermore, the Reform Act (section 322 of PL 95–598) contained a provision that exempts bankruptcy proceedings from Rev. Stat. section 3466. Section 3466 of the Revised Statutes of the United States (31 U.S.C. 191) provides that in case of insolvency, debts due to the U.S. government must be satisfied before others are paid. This section does, however, continue to apply to common law assignments for benefits of creditors and to equity receiverships under state laws.

Chapter 13 Adjustments

130   There is a provision that applies to chapter 13 proceedings similar to section 1129 (chapter 11 reorganization) requiring that priority items be provided for in the plan. Section 1322 states that the plan must provide for the full payment, in deferred cash payments of all claims entitled to priority under section 507, unless the holder of a claim agrees to different treatment. Thus all taxes with priority will be paid in full. Note that no interest is to be paid on these claims; it is not necessary that the present value of the future payments equal the claim, but only that the total future payments equal the debt. In chapter 11 proceedings the present value of future payments is compared with the value of the claim.

131   Section 1322 provides that the time period for future payments must not exceed three years, unless the court approves a longer period, and in no case will the period exceed five years.

---

[44] Ibid., p. 78.

TAX DISCHARGE

132   The extent to which a tax is discharged depends on (1) whether the debtor is an individual or corporation, (2) the chapter under which the petition is filed, and (3) the nature and priority of the tax.

Individual Debtors

133   Section 523(a) provides that in a chapter 7 or 11 proceeding involving an individual debt, all taxes that are entitled to priority (see chapter 3, paragraph 98) are exempt from a discharge. Also exempt from discharge are prepetition taxes due for a period when the debtor failed to file a return, filed the return late (exempt are late returns filed more than two years before petition date), and filed a fraudulent return or willfully attempted in any manner to evade or defeat the tax due. Any tax due that relates to the failure to file a return or to other misconduct of the debtor will automatically be considered nondischargeable if such tax qualifies for priority under section 507. Some question exists as to whether a return filed late due to a reasonable cause would be considered nondischargeable.

134   Taxes with priority are not exempt from a discharge under chapter 13, but section 1322 provides that a plan must provide for the full payment of all claims with priority under section 507. The net effect of this provision is that the government will still receive payment in full for taxes due. It would, however, appear that priority taxes due because of a late return, a fraudulent return, or a failure to file a return would be dischargeable.

135   Section 1328(b) provides for a later discharge of debts that were scheduled for payment in the plan if the debtor is, under certain conditions, unable to make these payments. The provisions of section 523(a) are fully applicable to this subsequent discharge, which means that taxes with priority are exempt from discharge, as are taxes resulting from the misconduct of the debtor.

Corporate Debtors

136   Section 727 prohibits the granting of a discharge to a corporation in a chapter 7 liquidation. Also, a corporation liquidating under a plan adopted in a chapter 11 case would not obtain a discharge. Since a corporation in effect goes out of business as a result of the liquidation, it might appear that the actual granting of a discharge is unimportant. A corporation, however, does not have to go out of existence, and shareholders have kept these shells alive so they could be reactivated at a later date for tax reasons or to avoid the costs of creating another corporation. A debtor will be reluctant to use these shells under the Reform Act because any assets owned by the corporation are subject to attachment by the creditors for prebankruptcy debts.

137   Section 1141(d) states that, unless otherwise provided, confirmation of the plan discharges the corporate debtor from any debt that arose before the date of confirmation. This would include all taxes that have not been paid, including taxes attributable to no return, late returns, or fraudulent returns. It should be noted, however, that before a plan will be confirmed, taxes with priority must be paid or provided for in full. Thus in reality the only taxes that can be discharged in corporate reorganization are those that do not have priority. It should be noted that section 1106(a)(6) provides that the trustee, in situations where the debtor did not file a tax return required by law, must furnish, without personal liability, the information that the government may require regarding prepetition liabilities arising from periods where the required returns were not filed. Also, the conference explanation indicates that the tax authority may disallow any tax benefit claimed subsequent to the reorganization if it results from a deduction, credit, or other item improperly reported prior to the filing of the petition.[45]

TAX PREFERENCES

138   The payment of a past due tax to a governmental unit can be considered a preferential payment under certain conditions. Section 547(b) provides that any transfer made within ninety days before the petition is filed of property of the debtor, while insolvent, in payment of an antecedent debt owed by the debtor to an undersecured creditor may be avoided. The avoidance is based on the assumption that the creditor received more as a result of the transfer than would have been received if the case were under chapter 7. A transfer is not, however, avoided if the payment was made within forty-five days after the debt was incurred in the ordinary course of business according to ordinary business terms. For tax purposes, the date the debt was incurred is, according to section 547(a)(4), the day when such tax is last payable, including any extensions, without penalty. Thus, the trustee or debtor in possession could recover a tax paid within the last ninety days that was due more than three years ago. In a chapter 11 reorganization the payment of a tax that has priority will for all practical purposes not be considered a preference, since the plan must provide for the payment of all priority debts.

139   Section 547(c)(6) provides that the fixing of a statutory lien is not a preference. Thus the creation of a tax lien is not a preference item unless the lien is not properly perfected (section 545).

TAX PROCEDURES

140   The provisions in the Bankruptcy Code changed the tax procedures to be followed in a bankruptcy case. The commencement of a bankruptcy

---

[45] 124 Cong. Rec. 5–17431. See Bacon, p. 79.

case automatically stays assessment and collection of prepetition tax liabilities of the debtor until the tax is determined by the bankruptcy court.[46] The IRS may, however, issue a notice of deficiency to the debtor while the debtor is in bankruptcy.[47] Section 362(a)(8) of the Bankruptcy Code also provides for a stay of the commencement or continuation of a proceeding before the tax court at the time the petition is filed.

STATE AND LOCAL TAX PROVISIONS

141   The Bankruptcy Reform Act of 1978 contained some tax provisions for state and local governments. This law differs in some respects from the provisions in the Bankruptcy Tax Act of 1980. Until these differences are reconciled by technical amendments, the taxpayer will be required to report selected items differently, such as gain due to debt discharge. Sections 346, 728, and 1146 of the Bankruptcy Code contain the provisions for state and local taxes. These provisions, along with other tax issues, are discussed in more detail in Newton and Bloom's *Tax Planning for the Troubled Business* which is also published by Wiley.

[46] 11 U.S.C. Sec. 362(a)(6) and Sec. 362(b)(8).
[47] 11 U.S.C. Sec. 362(b)(7).

Appendixes

Bankruptcy Rules

TABLE OF CONTENTS

PART III.
CLAIMS AND DISTRIBUTION TO CREDITORS AND EQUITY INTEREST HOLDERS; PLANS

PART IV.
THE DEBTOR: DUTIES AND BENEFITS

PART V.
BANKRUPTCY COURTS AND CLERKS

PART VI.
COLLECTION AND LIQUIDATION
OF THE ESTATE

PART VII.
ADVERSARY PROCEEDINGS

PART VIII.
APPEALS TO DISTRICT COURT OR
BANKRUPTCY APPELLATE PANEL

PART IX.
GENERAL PROVISIONS

PARTS V, VI, VII, VIII, AND IX, COVERING RULES 7001–9032 ARE
NOT INCLUDED IN THIS APPENDIX.

PART X.

UNITED STATES TRUSTEES

Rule 1001. Scope of Rules and Forms; Short Title

The Bankruptcy Rules and Forms govern procedure in United States Bankruptcy Courts in cases under chapters 7, 9, 11 and 13 of title 11 of the United States Code. The rules shall be cited as the Bankruptcy Rules and the forms as the Official Bankruptcy Forms. These rules shall be construed to secure the expeditious and economical administration of every case under the Code and the just, speedy, and inexpensive determination of every proceeding therein.

PART I

COMMENCEMENT OF CASE; PROCEEDINGS RELATING TO PETITION AND ORDER FOR RELIEF

Rule 1002. Voluntary Petition

(a) COMMENCEMENT. A debtor's petition commencing a voluntary case shall be filed with the bankruptcy court and shall conform substantially to Official Form No. 1.

(b) NUMBER OF COPIES.

(1) Chapter 7 Liquidation and Chapter 13 Adjustment of Debts of an Individual with Regular Income. An original and one copy of a petition requesting relief under chapter 7 or chapter 13 of the Code shall be filed, but additional copies may be required by local rule. If a stockbroker's petition for relief under subchapter III of chapter 7 is filed, an additional copy shall be filed and transmitted by the clerk to the Securities Investor Protection Corporation. If a commodity broker's petition for relief under subchapter IV of chapter 7 is filed, an additional copy shall be filed and transmitted by the clerk to the Commodity Futures Trading Commission.

(2) Chapter 9 Adjustment of Debts of a Municipality and Chapter 11 Reorganization. An original and five copies of a petition requesting relief under chapter 9 or chapter 11 of the Code shall be filed, but additional copies may be required by local rule. The clerk shall transmit one copy to the District Director of Internal Revenue for the district in which the case is filed, one copy of a chapter 9 petition to the Secretary of State of the state in which the debtor is located, two copies of a chapter 9 petition to the Securities and Exchange Commission and, if the debtor is a corporation, two copies of a chapter 11 petition to the Securities and Exchange Commission. If the petition requests relief for the reorganization of a railroad under subchapter IV of chapter 11 of the Code, two additional copies of the petition shall be filed, and the clerk shall transmit one copy to the Interstate Commerce Commission and one copy to the Secretary of Transportation.

Rule 1003. Involuntary Petition; Case Ancillary to Foreign Proceeding

(a) COMMENCEMENT. A petition commencing an involuntary case shall be filed with the bankruptcy court and shall conform substantially to Official Form No. 11.

(b) NUMBER OF COPIES. The number and distribution of copies shall be as specified in Rule 1002.

(c) TRANSFEROR OR TRANSFEREE OF CLAIM. A transferor or transferee of a claim shall annex to the original and each copy of the petition a copy of all documents evidencing the transfer, whether transferred unconditionally, for security, or otherwise, and a signed statement that the claim was not transferred for the purpose of commencing the case and setting forth the consideration for and terms of the transfer. A person who has transferred or acquired a claim for the purpose of commencing a case for liquidation under chapter 7 or for reorganization under chapter 11 shall not be a qualified petitioner.

(d) JOINDER OF PETITIONERS AFTER FILING. If the answer to an involuntary petition filed by fewer than three creditors avers the existence of 12 or more creditors, the debtor shall file with the answer a list of all creditors with their addresses, a brief statement of the nature of their claims, and the amounts thereof. If it appears that there are 12 or more creditors as provided in § 303(b) of the Code, the court shall afford a reasonable opportunity for other creditors to join in the petition before a hearing is held thereon.

(e) CASE ANCILLARY TO FOREIGN PROCEEDING.

(1) Petition; Number of Copies. An original and one copy of a petition commencing a case ancillary to a foreign proceeding shall be filed with the bankruptcy court.

(2) Service of Petition and Summons. On the filing of a petition pursuant to the preceding paragraph, the clerk shall forthwith issue a summons for service on all parties against whom relief is sought pursuant to § 304(b) of the Code and on such other parties as the court may direct. Rule 1010 applies to the manner of service of the summons and petition.

(3) Responsive Pleadings and Motions. Rule 1011(a), (b), (c) and (e) applies to responsibe pleadings and motions.

(4) Contested Petition. Rule 1018 applies when a petition filed under this rule is contested.

Rule 1004. Partnership Petition

(a) VOLUNTARY PETITION. A voluntary petition may be filed on behalf of the partnership by one or more general partners if all general partners consent to the petition.

(b) INVOLUNTARY PETITION; NOTICE AND SUMMONS. After filing of an involuntary petition under § 303(b)(3) of the Code, (1) the petitioning partners or other petitioners shall cause forthwith a copy of the petition to be sent to or served on each general partner who is not a petitioner; and (2) the clerk shall issue forthwith a summons for service on each general partner who is not a petitioner. Rule 1010 applies to the form and service of the summons.

Rule 1005. Caption of Petition

The caption of a petition commencing a case under the Code shall contain the name of the court, the title of the case, and the docket number. The title of the case shall include the name, social security number and employer's tax identification number of the debtor and all other names used by the debtor within six years before filing the petition. If the petition is not filed by the debtor, it shall include all names known to petitioners used by the debtor.

Rule 1006. Filing Fee

(a) GENERAL REQUIREMENT. Every petition shall be accompanied by the prescribed filing fee except as provided in subdivision (b) of this rule.

(b) PAYMENT OF FILING FEE IN INSTALLMENTS.

(1) Application for Permission to Pay Filing Fee in Installments. A voluntary petition by an individual shall be accepted for filing if accompanied by the debtor's signed application stating that he is unable to pay the filing fee except in installments. The application shall state the proposed terms of the installment payments and that the applicant has neither paid any money nor transferred any property to an attorney for services in connection with the case.

(2) Action on Application. Prior to the meeting of creditors, the court may order the filing fee paid to the clerk or grant leave to pay in installments and fix the number, amount and dates thereof. The number of installments shall not exceed four, and the final installment shall be payable not later than 120 days after filing the petition. For cause shown, the court may extend the time of any installment, provided the last installment is paid not later than 180 days after filing the petition.

(3) Postponement of Attorney's Fees. The filing fee must be paid in full before the debtor may pay an attorney for services in connection with the case.

Rule 1007. Lists, Schedules and Statements; Time Limits

(a) LIST OF CREDITORS AND EQUITY SECURITY HOLDERS.

(1) Voluntary Case. In a voluntary case, the debtor shall file with the petition a list containing the name and address of each creditor unless the petition is accompanied by a schedule of liabilities or a Chapter 13 Statement.

(2) Involuntary Case. In an involuntary case, the debtor shall file within 15 days after entry of the order for relief, a list containing the name and address of each creditor unless a schedule of liabilities has been filed.

(3) Equity Security Holders. In a chapter 11 reorganization case, a list of the debtor's equity security holders of each class showing the number and kind of interests registered in the name of each holder, and the last known address or place of business of each holder, shall be filed by the debtor within 15 days after entry of the order for relief unless the court orders otherwise.

(4) Extension of Time. Any extension of time for the filing of the lists required by this subdivision may be granted only on motion for cause shown and on notice to any trustee, committee appointed under the Code, or other party as the court may direct.

(b) SCHEDULES AND STATEMENTS REQUIRED. The debtor in a chapter 7 liquidation case or chapter 11 reorganization case shall file with the court schedules of assets and liabilities, a statement of financial affairs, and a statement of executory contracts, prepared as prescribed by Official Forms No. 6 and either No. 7 or No. 8, whichever is appropriate, unless the court orders otherwise. The debtor in a chapter 13 individual's debt adjustment case shall file with the court a Chapter 13 Statement conforming to Official Form No. 10 and, if the debtor is engaged in business, a statement of financial affairs prepared as prescribed by Official Form No. 8.

(c) TIME LIMITS. The schedule and statements, if not previously filed in a pending case, shall be filed with the petition in a voluntary case, or if the petition is accompanied by a list of all the debtor's creditors and their addresses, within 15 days thereafter, except as otherwise provided in subdivisions (d), (e) and (h) of this rule. In an involuntary case the schedules and statements shall be filed by the debtor within 15 days after entry of the order for relief. In a case converted from chapter 11 or chapter 13 to a chapter 7 case, the list of all the debtor's creditors, a schedule of assets and liabilities, a statement of financial affairs and a statement of executory contracts shall be filed by the debtor or other person directed by the court, within 15 days after the entry of the order of conversion. Any extension of time for the filing of the schedules and statements may be granted only on motion for cause shown and on notice to any committee, trustee, examiner or other party as the court may direct.

(d) LIST OF 20 LARGEST CREDITORS IN CHAPTER 9 MUNICIPALITY CASE OR CHAPTER 11 REORGANIZATION CASE. In addition to the list required by subdivision (a) of this rule, a debtor in a chapter 9 municipality case or a debtor in a voluntary chapter 11 reorganization case shall file with the petition a list containing the name, address and claim of the creditors that hold the 20 largest unsecured claims, excluding insiders, as prescribed by Official Form No. 9. In an involuntary chapter 11 reorganization case, such list shall be filed by the debtor within 2 days after entry of the order for relief under § 303(h) of the Code.

(e) LIST IN CHAPTER 9 MUNICIPALITY CASES. The list required by subdivision (a) of this rule shall be filed by the debtor in a chapter 9 municipality case within such time as the court shall fix. If a proposed plan requires a revision of assessments so that the proportion of special assessments or special taxes to be assessed against some real property will be different from the proportion in effect at the date the petition is filed, the debtor shall also file with the court a list showing the name and address of each known holder of title, legal or equitable, to real property adversely affected. On motion for cause shown, the court may modify the requirements of this subdivision and subdivision (a) of this rule.

(f) NUMBER OF COPIES. The number of copies of the schedules, statements and lists shall correspond to the number of copies of the petition required by Rules 1002 and 1003.

(g) PARTNERSHIP AND PARTNERS. The general partners of a debtor partnership shall prepare and file the schedules of the assets and liabilities, statement of financial affairs, and statement of executory contracts of the partnership. The court may order any general partner to file a statement of personal assets and liabilities with the court within such time as the court may fix.

(h) INTERESTS ACQUIRED OR ARISING AFTER PETITION. Within ten days after the information comes to the debtor's knowledge or within such further time as the court may allow, the debtor in a chapter 7 liquidation case, chapter 11 reorganization case, or chapter 13 individual debt adjustment case shall file a supplemental schedule with respect to any property that the debtor acquires or becomes entitled to acquire within 180 days after the date of the filing of the petition (1) by bequest, devise or inheritance; (2) as a result of a property settlement agreement with the debtor's spouse, or of an interlocutory or final divorce decree; or (3) as a beneficiary of a life insurance policy or of a death benefit plan. If any of the property required to be reported under this subdivision is claimed by the debtor as exempt, the debtor shall claim the exemptions in the supplemental schedule. The duty to file a supplemental schedule in accordance with this subdivision continues notwithstanding the closing of the case before the duty is or can be performed, except that the schedule need not be filed in a chapter 11 or chapter 13 case with respect to property acquired after entry of the order confirming the plan.

(i) DISCLOSURE OF LIST OF SECURITY HOLDERS. After notice and hearing and for cause shown, the court may direct an entity other than the debtor or trustee to disclose any list of security holders of the debtor in its possession or under its control, indicating the name, address and security held by any of them. The entity possessing this list may be required either to produce the list or a true copy thereof, or permit inspection or copying, or otherwise disclose the information contained on the list.

(j) IMPOUNDING OF LISTS. On motion of a party in interest and for cause shown the court may direct the impounding of the lists filed under this rule, and may refuse to permit inspection by any entity. The court may permit inspection or use of the lists, however, by any party in interest on terms prescribed by the court.

(k) PREPARATION OF LIST, SCHEDULES, OR STATEMENTS ON DEFAULT OF DEBTOR. If a list, schedule, or statement is not prepared and filed as required by this rule, the court may order the trustee, a petitioning creditor, committee, or other party to prepare and file any of these papers within a time fixed by the court. The court may approve reimbursement of the cost incurred in complying with such an order as an administrative expense.

Rule 1008. Verification of Petitions and Accompanying Papers

All petitions, lists, schedules, statements of financial affairs, statements of executory contracts, Chapter 13 Statements and amendments thereto shall be verified or contain an unsworn declaration as provided in 28 U.S.C. § 1746.

Rule 1009. Amendments of Voluntary Petitions, Lists, Schedules and Statements of Financial Affairs

A voluntary petition, list, schedule, statement of financial affairs, statement of executory contracts, or Chapter 13 Statement may be amended by the debtor as a matter of course at any time before the case is closed. The debtor shall give notice of the amendment to the trustee and to any entity affected thereby. On motion of a party in interest, the court may order any voluntary petition, list, schedule, statement of financial affairs, statement of executory contracts, or Chapter 13 Statement to be amended and the clerk shall give notice of the amendment to entities designated by the court. The amendment shall be filed in the same number as required of the original.

Rule 1010. Service of Involuntary Petition and Summons

On the filing of an involuntary petition, the clerk shall issue forthwith a summons for service on the debtor. The summons shall conform to Official Form No. 13 and a copy shall be served with a copy of the petition in the manner provided for service of a summons and complaint by Rule 7004(a) or (b). If service cannot be so made, the court may order the summons and petition to be served by mailing copies to the debtor's last known address, and by at least one publication in the manner and form directed by the court. The summons and petition may be served on the debtor anywhere. Rule 7004(f) and Rule 4(g) and (h) F. R. Civ. P. apply when service is made or attempted under this rule.

Rule 1011. Responsive Pleading or Motion in Involuntary Cases

(a) WHO MAY CONTEST PETITION. The debtor named in an involuntary petition may contest the petition. In the case of a petition against a partnership under Rule 1004(b), a nonpetitioning general partner, or alleged general partner, may contest the petition.

(b) DEFENSES AND OBJECTIONS; WHEN PRESENTED. Defenses and objections to the petition shall be presented in the manner prescribed by Rule 12 F.R. Civ. P. and shall be filed and served within 20 days after service of summons, except that if service is made by publication on a debtor or partner not residing or found within the state in which the bankruptcy court sits, the court shall prescribe the time for filing and serving the response.

(c) EFFECT OF MOTION. Service of a motion under Rule 12(b) F.R. Civ. P. shall extend the time for filing and serving a responsive pleading as permitted by Rule 12(a) F. R. Civ. P.

(d) CLAIMS AGAINST PETITIONERS. A claim against a petitioning creditor may not be asserted in the answer except for the purpose of defeating the petition.

(e) OTHER PLEADINGS. No other pleadings shall be permitted, except that the court may order a reply to an answer and prescribe the time for filing and service.

Rule 1012. Examination of Debtor, Including Discovery, on Issue of Nonpayment of Debts in Involuntary Cases

(a) DISCOVERY. When a petition commencing an involuntary case under § 303 of the Code alleges that the debtor is generally not paying its debts as they become due, and the debtor denies the allegation, discovery may be in accordance with Rules 26-37, F.R. Civ. P.

(b) SANCTIONS. If the debtor fails to appear, produce records, or submit to examination or deposition, the court may enter an order for relief or other appropriate order, in addition to the sanctions available under Rule 37 F.R. Civ. P.

(c) OTHER PROCEDURES. The examination or discovery provided in this rule does not preclude the procedures available under Rule 2004.

Rule 1013. Hearing and Disposition of Petition in Involuntary Cases

(a) CONTESTED PETITION. The court shall determine the issues of a contested petition at the earliest practicable time and forthwith enter an order for relief, dismiss the petition, or enter other appropriate orders.

(b) DEFAULT. If no pleading or other defense to a petition is filed within the time provided by Rule 1011, the court, on the next day, or as soon thereafter as practicable, shall enter an order for the relief prayed for in the petition.

(c) ORDER FOR RELIEF. An order for relief shall conform substantially to Official Form No. 14.

Rule 1014. Change of Venue

(a) TRANSFER OF CASES.

(1) *Cases Filed in Proper District.* If a petition is filed in a proper district, on

timely motion of a party in interest, and after hearing on notice to the petitioners and to other persons as directed by the court, the case may be transferred to any other district if the court determines that the transfer is for the convenience of the parties and witnesses in the interest of justice.

(2) *Cases Filed in Improper District.* If a petition is filed in an improper district, on timely motion of a party in interest and after hearing on notice to the petitioners and to other persons as directed by the court, the case may be retained or transferred to any other district if the court determines that the retention or transfer is for the convenience of the parties and witnesses in the interest of justice. Notwithstanding the foregoing, if no objection is raised, the court may, without a hearing, retain a case filed in an improper district.

(b) PROCEDURE WHEN PETITIONS INVOLVING THE SAME DEBTOR OR RELATED DEBTORS ARE FILED IN DIFFERENT COURTS. If petitions commencing cases under the Code are filed in different districts by or against (1) the same debtor, or (2) a partnership and one or more of its general partners, or (3) two or more general partners, or (4) a debtor and an affiliate, on motion filed in the court in which the first petition is filed and after hearing on notice to the petitioners and other persons as directed by the court, the court may determine, for the convenience of the parties and witnesses, in the interest of justice the court or courts in which the case or cases should proceed. Except as otherwise ordered by the court in which the first petition is filed, the proceedings on the other petitions shall be stayed by the courts in which the petitions have been filed until the determination is made. The courts in which petitions have been filed shall act in accordance with the determination.

Rule 1015. Consolidation or Joint Administration of Cases Pending in Same Court

(a) CASES INVOLVING SAME DEBTOR. If two or more petitions are pending in the same court by or against the same debtor, the court may order consolidation of the cases.

(b) CASES INVOLVING TWO OR MORE RELATED DEBTORS. If a joint petition or two or more petitions are pending in the same court by or against (1) a husband and wife, or (2) a partnership and one or more of its general partners, or (3) two or more general partners, or (4) a debtor and an affiliate, the court may order a joint administration of the estates. Prior to entering an order the court shall give consideration to protecting creditors of different estates against potential conflicts of interest.

(c) EXPEDITING AND PROTECTIVE ORDERS. When an order for consolidation or joint administration of a joint case or two or more cases is entered pursuant to this rule, while protecting the rights of the parties under the Code, the court may enter orders as may tend to avoid unnecessary costs and delay.

Rule 1016. Death or Insanity of Debtor

Death or insanity of the debtor shall not abate a liquidation case under chapter 7 of the Code. In such event the estate shall be administered and the case concluded in the same manner, so far as possible, as though the death or insanity had not occurred. If a reorganization or individual's debt adjustment case is pending under chapter 11 or chapter 13, the case may be dismissed; or if further administration is possible and in the best interest of the parties, the case may proceed and be concluded in the same manner, so far as possible, as though the death or insanity had not occurred.

Rule 1017. Dismissal of Case; Suspension

(a) VOLUNTARY DISMISSAL; DISMISSAL FOR WANT OF PROSECUTION. Except as provided in § 1307(b) of the Code, a petition shall not be dismissed on motion of the petitioner or for want of prosecution or other cause or by consent of the parties prior to a hearing on notice to all creditors as provided in Rule 2002(a). For such notice, the debtor shall file a list of all creditors with their addresses within the time fixed by the court unless the list was previously filed. If the debtor fails to file the list, the court may order the preparing and filing by the debtor or other person.

(b) DISMISSAL FOR FAILURE TO PAY FILING FEE.

(1) For failure to pay any installment of the filing fee the court may dismiss the petition after hearing on notice to the debtor and the trustee.

(2) If the petition is dismissed or the case closed without full payment of the filing fee, the installments collected shall be distributed in the same manner and proportions as if the filing fee had been paid in full.

(3) Notice of dismissal for failure to pay the filing fee shall be given within 30 days after the dismissal to creditors appearing on the list of creditors and to those who have filed claims, in the manner provided in Rule 2002.

(c) SUSPENSION. A petition shall not be dismissed or proceedings suspended pursuant to § 305 of the Code prior to a hearing on notice as provided in Rule 2002(a).

(d) PROCEDURE FOR DISMISSAL OR CONVERSION. A proceeding to dismiss a case or convert a case to another chapter is governed by Rule 9014.

Rule 1018. Contested Involuntary Petitions; Proceedings to Vacate Order for Relief; Applicability of Rules in Part VII Governing Adversary Proceedings

The following rules in Part VII apply in all proceedings relating to a contested involuntary petition and in all proceedings to vacate an order for relief: Rules 7005, 7008-7010, 7015, 7016, 7024-7026, 7028-7037, 7052, 7054, 7056, and 7062, except as otherwise provided in Part I of these rules and unless the court otherwise directs. The court may direct that other rules in Part VII shall also apply. For the purposes of this rule a reference in the Part VII rules to adversary proceedings shall be read as a reference to proceedings relating to a contested involuntary petition, or contested ancillary petition, or proceedings to vacate an order for relief. Reference in the Federal Rules of Civil Procedure to the complaint shall be read as a reference to the petition.

Rule 1019. Conversion of Chapter 11 Reorganization Case or Chapter 13 Individual's Debt Adjustment Case to Chapter 7 Liquidation Case

When a chapter 11 or chapter 13 case has been converted or reconverted to a chapter 7 case:

(1) *Filing of Lists, Inventories, Schedules, Statements.* Lists, inventories, schedules, statements of financial affairs, and statements of executory contracts theretofore filed shall be deemed to be filed in the chapter 7 case, unless the court directs otherwise. If they have not been previously filed, the debtor shall comply with Rule 1007 as if an order for relief had been entered on an involuntary petition on the date of the entry of the order directing that the case continue under chapter 7.

(2) *Notice of Order of Conversion.* Within 20 days after entry of the order

converting the case to a chapter 7 case, notice of the order shall be given to all creditors in the manner provided by Rule 2002 and shall be included in the notice of the meeting of creditors.

(3) *Reconversion to Chapter 7.* When a chapter 7 case had been converted to a chapter 11 or chapter 13 case and thereafter reconverted to a chapter 7 case, if the time for filing claims, a complaint objecting to discharge, or a complaint to obtain a determination of the dischargeability of any debt expired in the original chapter 7 case, the time shall not be revived or extended except as provided in Rule 4004 or 4007.

(4) *Claims Filed in Superseded Case.* All claims filed in the superseded case shall be deemed filed in the chapter 7 case.

(5) *Turnover of Records and Property.* After qualification of, or assumption of duties by the chapter 7 trustee, any debtor in possession or trustee previously acting in the chapter 11 or chapter 13 case shall, forthwith, unless otherwise ordered, turn over to the chapter 7 trustee all records and property of the estate in his possession or control.

(6) *Filing Final Report and Schedule of Postpetition Debts.* Each debtor in possession or trustee in the superseded case shall file with the court a final report and account within 30 days following the entry of the order of conversion, unless the court directs otherwise. The report shall include a schedule of unpaid debts incurred after commencement of the chapter 11 or chapter 13 case. If the conversion order is entered after confirmation of a plan, the debtor shall file with the court (A) a schedule of property not listed in the final report and account acquired after the filing of the original petition but before entry of the conversion order; (B) a schedule of unpaid debts not listed in the final report and account incurred after confirmation but before entry of the conversion order; and (C) a schedule of executory contracts entered into or assumed after the filing of the original petition but before entry of the conversion order.

(7) *Filing of Postpetition Claims; Notice.* On the filing of the schedule of unpaid debts, the court shall order that written notice be given to those entities, including the United States, any state, or any subdivision thereof, that their claims may be filed within 60 days from the entry of the order, pursuant to Rule 3001(a)-(d). The court shall fix the time for filing claims arising from debts not so scheduled or arising from rejection of executory contracts under § § 348(c) and 365(d) of the Code.

(8) *Extension of Time to File Claims Against Surplus.* Any extension of time for the filing of claims against a surplus granted pursuant to Rule 3002(c)(6), shall apply to holders of claims who failed to file their claims within the time prescribed, or fixed by the court pursuant to paragraph (7) of this rule, and notice shall be given as provided in Rule 2002.

PART II

OFFICERS AND ADMINISTRATION; NOTICES; MEETINGS; EXAMINATIONS; ELECTIONS; ATTORNEYS AND ACCOUNTANTS

Rule 2001. Appointment of Interim Trustee Before Order for Relief in a Chapter 7 Liquidation Case

(a) APPOINTMENT. At any time following the commencement of an involuntary liquidation case and before an order for relief, the court on written motion of a party in interest may appoint an interim trustee under § 303(g) of the Code. The motion shall set forth the necessity for the appointment and may be granted only after hearing on notice to the debtor, the petitioning creditors and other parties in interest as the court may designate.

(b) BOND OF MOVANT. An interim trustee may not be appointed under this rule unless the movant furnishes a bond in an amount approved by the court, conditioned to indemnify the debtor for costs, attorney's fee, expenses, and damages allowable under § 303(i) of the Code.

(c) ORDER OF APPOINTMENT. The order appointing the interim trustee shall state why the appointment is necessary and shall specify the trustee's duties.

(d) TURNOVER AND REPORT. Following qualification of the trustee selected under § 702 of the Code, the interim trustee, unless otherwise ordered, shall (1) forthwith turn over to the trustee all the records and property of the estate in possession or subject to control of the interim trustee and, (2) within 30 days thereafter file a final report and account.

Rule 2002. Notices to Creditors, Equity Security Holders, and United States

(a) TWENTY-DAY NOTICES TO PARTIES IN INTEREST. Except as provided in subdivisions (h), (i) and (k) of this rule, the clerk, or some other person as the court may direct, shall give the debtor, the trustee, all creditors and indenture trustees not less than 20 days notice by mail of (1) the meeting of creditors pursuant to § 341 of the Code; (2) a proposed use, sale, or lease of property other than in the ordinary course of business unless the court for cause shown shortens the time or directs another method of giving notice; (3) the hearing on approval of a compromise or settlement of a controversy, unless the court for cause shown directs that notice not be sent; (4) the date fixed for the filing of claims against a surplus in an estate as provided in Rule 3002(c)(6); (5) in a chapter 7 liquidation and a chapter 11 reorganization case, the hearing on the dismissal or conversion of a case to another chapter; (6) the time fixed to accept or reject a proposed modification of a plan; (7) hearings on all applications for compensation or reimbursement of expenses totalling in excess of $100; and (8) the time fixed for filing proofs of claims pursuant to Rule 3003(c).

(b) TWENTY-FIVE-DAY NOTICES TO PARTIES IN INTEREST. Except as provided in subdivisions (h), (i) and (k) of this rule, the clerk, or some other person as the court may direct, shall give the debtor, the trustee, all creditors and indenture trustees not less than 25 days notice by mail of (1) the time fixed for filing objections to and the hearing to consider approval of a disclosure statement; and (2) the time fixed for filing objections to and the hearing to consider confirmation of a plan.

(c) CONTENT OF NOTICE.

(1) *Proposed Use, Sale, or Lease of Property.* Subject to Rule 6004 the notice of a proposed use, sale, or lease of property required by subdivision (a)(2) of this rule shall include the time and place of any public sale, the terms and conditions of any private sale and the time fixed for filing objections. The notice of a proposed use, sale, or lease of property, including real estate, is sufficient if it generally describes the property.

(2) *Notice of Hearing on Compensation.* The notice of a hearing on an application for compensation or reimbursement of expenses required by subdivision (a)(7) of this rule shall identify the applicant and the amounts requested.

(d) NOTICE TO EQUITY SECURITY HOLDERS. In a chapter 11 reorganization case, unless otherwise ordered by the court, the clerk, or some other person as the court may direct, shall in the manner and form directed by the court give notice to all equity security holders of (1) the order for relief; (2) any meeting of equity security holders ordered by the court pursuant to § 341 of the Code; (3) the hearing on the dismissal or conversion of a case to another chapter; (4) the time fixed for filing objections to and the hearing to consider approval of a disclosure statement; (5) the time fixed for filing objections to and the hearing to consider confirmation of a plan; and (6) the time fixed to accept or reject a proposed modification of a plan.

(e) NOTICE OF NO DIVIDEND. In a chapter 7 liquidation case, if it appears from the schedules that there are no assets from which a dividend can be paid, the notice of the meeting of creditors may include a statement to that effect; that it is unnecessary to file claims; and that if sufficient assets become available for the payment of a dividend, further notice will be given for the filing of claims.

(f) OTHER NOTICES. Except as provided in subdivision (k) of this rule, the clerk shall give the debtor, all creditors and indenture trustees notice by mail of (1) the order for relief; (2) dismissal of the case; (3) the time allowed for filing claims pursuant to Rule 3002; (4) the entry of an order directing that the case be converted to a case under a different chapter; (5) the time fixed for filing a complaint objecting to the debtor's discharge pursuant to § 727 of the Code as provided in Rule 4004; (6) the time fixed for filing a complaint to determine the dischargeability of a debt pursuant to § 523 of the Code as provided in Rule 4007; (7) the order of discharge as provided in Rule 4004(g); (8) the waiver denial, or revocation or a discharge as provided in Rule 4006; (9) entry of an order confirming a chapter 9 or 11 plan; and (10) a summary of the trustee's final report and account in a chapter 7 case if the net proceeds realized exceed $250. Notice of the time fixed for accepting or rejecting a plan pursuant to Rule 3017(c) shall be given in accordance with Rule 3017(d).

(g) ADDRESSES OF NOTICES. All notices required to be mailed under this rule to a creditor, equity security holder, or indenture trustee shall be addressed as he or his authorized agent may direct in a request filed with the court; otherwise, to the address shown in the list of creditors or the schedule whichever is filed later, but if a different address is stated in a proof of claim duly filed, that address shall be used.

(h) NOTICES TO CREDITORS WHOSE CLAIMS ARE FILED. In a chapter 7 case, the court may, after 90 days following the first date set for the meeting of creditors pursuant to § 341 of the Code, direct that all notices required by subdivision (a) of this rule, except clause (4) thereof, be mailed only to creditors whose claims have been filed and creditors, if any, who are still permitted to file claims by reason of an extension granted under Rule 3002(c)(6).

(i) NOTICES TO COMMITTEES. Copies of all notices required to be mailed under this rule shall be mailed to the committees appointed pursuant to the Code or to their authorized agents. Notwithstanding the foregoing subdivisions, the court may order that notices required by subdivision (a) (2), (3) and (7) of this rule be mailed only to the committees or to their authorized agents and to the creditors and equity security holders who file with the court a request that all notices be mailed to them.

(j) NOTICES TO THE UNITED STATES. Copies of notices required to be mailed to all creditors under this rule shall be mailed (1) in a chapter 11 reorganization case to the Securities and Exchange Commission at Washington, D.C., and at any other place the Commission designates in writing filed with the court if the Commission has filed a notice of appearance in the case or has made a request in writing filed with the court; (2) in a commodity broker case, to the Commodity Futures Trading Commission at Washington, D.C.; (3) in a chapter 11 case to the District Director of Internal Revenue for the district in which the case is pending; (4) if the papers in the case disclose a debt to the United States other than for taxes, to the United States attorney for the district in which the case is pending and to the department, agency, or instrumentality of the United States through which the debtor became indebted; or if the filed papers disclose a stock interest of the United States, to the Secretary of the Treasury at Washington, D.C.

(k) NOTICE BY PUBLICATION. The court may order notice by publication if it finds that notice by mail as provided in this rule is impracticable or that it is desirable to supplement the notice.

(l) ORDERS DESIGNATING MATTER OF NOTICES. The court may from time to time enter orders designating the matters in respect to which, the person to whom, and the form and manner in which notices shall be sent except as otherwise provided by these rules.

(m) CAPTION. The caption of every notice given under this rule shall comply with Rule 1005.

Rule 2003. Meeting of Creditors or Equity Security Holders

(a) DATE AND PLACE. The court shall call a meeting of creditors to be held not less than 20 nor more than 40 days after the order for relief. If there is an appeal from or a motion to vacate the order for relief, or if there is a motion to dismiss the case, the court may set a later time for the meeting. The meeting may be held at a regular place for holding court or at any other place designated by the court within the district convenient for the parties in interest.

(b) ORDER OF MEETING.

(1) Meeting of Creditors. The clerk shall preside at the meeting of creditors unless (1) the court designates a different person, or (2) the creditors who may vote for a trustee under § 702(a) of the Code and who hold a majority in amount of claims that vote designate a presiding officer. In a chapter 11 reorganization case, if a chairman has been selected by a creditors' committee appointed pursuant to § 1102(a)(1), the chairman or his designee shall preside. The business of the meeting shall include the examination of the debtor under oath and, in a chapter 7 liquidation case, may include the election of a trustee or of a creditors' committee. The presiding officer shall have the authority to administer oaths. When a trustee is elected, the creditors may recommend the amount of the trustee's bond to be fixed by the court.

(2) Meeting of Equity Security Holders. If the court orders a meeting of equity security holders pursuant to § 341(b) of the Code, the clerk shall preside unless the holders of equity security interests present at the meeting who hold a majority in amount of the interests at the meeting designate a presiding officer.

(3) Right to Vote. In a chapter 7 liquidation case, a creditor is entitled to vote at a meeting if, at or before the meeting, he has filed a proof of claim or a writing

setting forth facts evidencing a right to vote pursuant to § 702(a) of the Code unless objection is made to the claim or the proof of claim is insufficient on its face. If the court orders an election of a separate trustee for a general partner's estate under Rule 2009(e)(1), a creditor of the partnership may file a proof of claim or writing evidencing a right to vote for that trustee notwithstanding that a trustee for the partnership has previously qualified. Notwithstanding objection to the amount or allowability of a claim for the purpose of voting, the court may, after such notice and hearing as it may direct, temporarily allow it for that purpose in an amount that seems proper to the court.

(c) MINUTES AND RECORD OF MEETING. Minutes of the meeting of creditors or equity security holders shall be prepared by the presiding officer. Any examination under oath shall be recorded verbatim by electronic sound recording equipment or other means of recording.

(d) REPORT OF THE COURT. The presiding officer shall transmit to the court the name and address of any person elected trustee or a member of a creditors' committee. If an election is disputed, the presiding officer shall promptly inform the court in writing that a dispute exists. Pending disposition by the court of a disputed election for trustee, the interim trustee shall continue in office. If no motion for the resolution of such election dispute is made to the court within 10 days after the date of the creditors' meeting, the interim trustee shall serve as trustee in the case.

(e) ADJOURNMENT. The meeting may be adjourned from time to time by announcement at the meeting of the adjourned date and time without further written notice.

Rule 2004. Examination

(a) EXAMINATION ON MOTION. On motion of any party in interest, the court may order the examination of any person.

(b) SCOPE OF EXAMINATION. The examination of any person under this rule or of the debtor under § 343 of the Code may relate only to the acts, conduct, or property or to the liabilities and financial condition of the debtor, or to any matter which may affect the administration of the debtor's estate, or to the debtor's right to a discharge. In an individual's debt adjustment case under chapter 13 or a reorganization case under chapter 11 of the Code, other than for the reorganization of a railroad, the examination may also relate to the operation of any business and the desirability of its continuance, the source of any money or property acquired or to be acquired by the debtor for purposes of consummating a plan and the consideration given or offered therefor, and any other matter relevant to the case or to the formulation of a plan.

(c) COMPELLING ATTENDANCE AND PRODUCTION OF DOCUMENTARY EVIDENCE. The attendance of any person for examination and the production of documentary evidence may be compelled in the manner provided in Rule 9016 for the attendance of witnesses at a hearing or trial.

(d) TIME AND PLACE OF EXAMINATION OF DEBTOR. The court may for cause shown and on terms as it may impose order the debtor to be examined under this rule at any time or place it designates, whether within or without the district wherein the case is pending.

(e) MILEAGE. A person other than a debtor shall not be required to attend as a witness unless lawful mileage and witness fee for one day's attendance shall be first tendered. If the debtor resides more than 100 miles from the place of examination when required to appear for an examination under this rule, the mileage allowed by law to a witness shall be tendered for any distance more than 100 miles from the debtor's residence at the date of the filing of the first petition commencing a case under the Code or the residence at the time the debtor is required to appear for the examination, whichever is the lesser.

Rule 2005. Apprehension and Removal of Debtor to Compel Attendance for Examination

(a) ORDER TO COMPEL ATTENDANCE FOR EXAMINATION. On motion of any party in interest supported by an affidavit alleging (1) that the examination of the debtor is necessary for the proper administration of the estate and that there is reasonable cause to believe that the debtor is about to leave or has left his residence or principal place of business to avoid examination, or (2) that the debtor has evaded service of a subpoena or of an order to attend for examination, or (3) that the debtor has willfully disobeyed a subpoena or order to attend for examination, duly served, the court may issue to the marshal, or some other officer authorized by law, an order directing the officer to bring the debtor before the court without unnecessary delay. If, after hearing, the court finds the allegations to be true, the court shall thereupon cause the debtor to be examined forthwith. If necessary, the court shall fix conditions for further examination and for the debtor's obedience to all orders made in reference thereto.

(b) REMOVAL. Whenever any order to bring the debtor before the court is issued under this rule and the debtor is found in a district other than that of the court issuing the order, the debtor may be taken into custody under the order and removed in accordance with the following rules:

(1) If taken at a place less than 100 miles from the place of issue of the order, the debtor shall be brought forthwith before the court that issued the order.

(2) If taken at a place 100 miles or more from the place of issue of the order, the debtor shall be brought without unnecessary delay before the nearest federal magistrate, bankruptcy judge, or district judge. If, after hearing, the magistrate, bankruptcy judge, or district judge finds that an order has issued under this rule and that the person in custody is the debtor, or if the person in custody waives a hearing, the magistrate, bankruptcy judge, or district judge shall issue an order of removal and the person in custody shall be released on conditions assuring prompt appearance before the court which issued the order to compel the attendance.

(c) CONDITIONS OF RELEASE. In determining what conditions will reasonably assure attendance or obedience under subdivision (a) of this rule or appearance under subdivision (b) of this rule, the court shall be governed by the provisions and policies of title 18, U.S.C., § 3146(a) and (b).

Rule 2006. Solicitation and Voting of Proxies in Chapter 7 Liquidation Cases

(a) APPLICABILITY. This rule applies only in a liquidation case pending under chapter 7 of the Code.

(b) DEFINITIONS.

(1) *Proxy.* A proxy is a written power of attorney authorizing any person to

vote the claim or otherwise act as the owner's attorney in fact in connection with the administration of the estate.

(2) *Solicitation of Proxy.* The solicitation of a proxy is any communication, other than one from an attorney to a regular client who owns a claim or from an attorney to the owner of a claim who has requested the attorney to represent the owner, by which a creditor is asked, directly or indirectly, to give a proxy after or in contemplation of the filing of a petition by or against the debtor.

(c) AUTHORIZED SOLICITATION.

(1) A proxy may be solicited only by (A) a creditor owning an allowable unsecured claim against the estate on the date of the filing of the petition; (B) a committee elected pursuant to § 705 of the Code; (C) a committee of creditors selected by a majority in number and amount of claims of creditors (i) whose claims are not contingent or unliquidated, (ii) who are not disqualified from voting under § 702(a) of the Code and (iii) who were present or represented at a meeting of which all creditors having claims of over $500 or the 100 creditors having the largest claims had at least five days notice in writing and of which meeting written minutes were kept and are available reporting the names of the creditors present or represented and voting and the amounts of their claims; or (D) a bona fide trade or credit association, but such association may solicit only creditors who were its members or subscribers in good standing and had allowable unsecured claims on the date of the filing of the petition.

(2) A proxy may be solicited only in writing.

(d) SOLICITATION NOT AUTHORIZED. This rule does not permit solicitation (1) in any interest other than that of general creditors; (2) by or on behalf of any custodian; (3) by the interim trustee or by or on behalf of any person not qualified to vote under § 702(a) of the Code; (4) by or on behalf of an attorney at law; or (5) by or on behalf of a transferee of a claim for collection only.

(e) DATA REQUIRED FROM HOLDERS OF MULTIPLE PROXIES. At any time before the voting commences at any meeting of creditors pursuant to Rule 2003, or at any other time as the court may direct, a holder of two or more proxies shall file with the clerk a verified list of the proxies to be voted and a verified statement of the pertinent facts and circumstances in connection with the execution and delivery of each proxy, including:

(1) a copy of the solicitation;

(2) identification of the solicitor, the forwarder, if he is neither the solicitor nor the owner of the claim, and the proxyholder, including their connections with the debtor and with each other. If the solicitor, forwarder, or proxyholder is an association, there shall also be included a statement that the creditors whose claims have been solicited and the creditors whose claims are to be voted were members or subscribers in good standing and had allowable unsecured claims on the date of the filing of the petition. If the solicitor, forwarder, or proxyholder is a committee of creditors, the statement shall also set forth the date and place the committee was organized, that the committee was organized in accordance with clause (B) or (C) of paragraph (c)(1) of this rule, the members of the committee, the amounts of their claims, when the claims were acquired, the amounts paid therefor, and the extent to which the claims of the committee members are secured or entitled to priority;

(3) a statement that no consideration has been paid or promised by the proxyholder for the proxy;

(4) a statement as to whether there is any agreement and, if so, the particulars thereof, between the proxyholder and any other person for the payment of any consideration in connection with voting the proxy, or for the sharing of compensation with any person, other than a member or regular associate of his law firm, which may be allowed the trustee or any person for services rendered in the case, or for the employment of any person as attorney, accountant, appraiser, auctioneer, or other employee for the estate;

(5) if the proxy was solicited by a person other than the proxyholder, or forwarded to the holder by a person who is neither a solicitor of the proxy nor the owner of the claim, a statement signed and verified by the solicitor or forwarder that no consideration has been paid or promised by him for the proxy, and whether there is any agreement, and, if so, the particulars thereof, between the solicitor or forwarder and any other person for the payment of any consideration in connection with voting the proxy, or for sharing compensation with any person other than a member or regular associate of his law firm which may be allowed the trustee or any person for services rendered in the case, or for the employment of any person as attorney, accountant, appraiser, auctioneer, or other employee for the estate;

(6) if the solicitor, forwarder, or proxyholder is a committee, a statement signed and verified by each member as to the amount and source of any consideration paid or to be paid to such member in connection with the case other than by way of dividend on his claim.

(f) ENFORCEMENT OF RESTRICTIONS ON SOLICITATION. On motion of any party in interest or on its own initiative, the court may determine whether there has been a failure to comply with the provisions of this rule or any other impropriety in connection with the solicitation or voting of a proxy. After notice and a hearing the court may reject any proxy for cause, vacate any order entered in consequence of the voting of any proxy which should have been rejected, or take any other appropriate action.

Rule 2007. Appointment of Creditors' Committee Organized Before Order for Relief

(a) APPOINTMENT. In a chapter 9 municipality or chapter 11 reorganization case, on application of a party in interest and after notice as the court may direct, the court may appoint as the committee of unsecured creditors required by § 1102(a) of the Code, members of a committee selected before the order for relief in accordance with subdivision (b) of this rule.

(b) SELECTION OF MEMBERS OF COMMITTEE. The court may find that a committee selected by unsecured creditors before the order for relief in a chapter 9 or chapter 11 case of the Code satisfies the requirements of § 1102(b)(1) of the Code if:

(1) it was selected by a majority in number and amount of claims of unsecured creditors who may vote under § 702(a) of the Code and were present in person or represented at a meeting of which all creditors having unsecured claims of over $1,000 or the 100 unsecured creditors having the largest claims had at least five days notice in writing, and of which meeting written minutes reporting the names of the creditors present or represented and voting and the amounts of their claims were kept and are available for inspection;

(2) all proxies voted at the meeting for the elected committee were solicited pursuant to Rule 2006 and the lists and statements required by subdivision (e)

thereof have been filed with the court; and

(3) the organization of the committee was in all other respects fair and proper.

Rule 2008. Notice to Trustee of Selection

The clerk shall immediately notify the trustee of his selection, how he may qualify and, if applicable, the amount of the bond. The trustee shall notify the court in writing of the acceptance or rejection of the office within five days after receipt of notice of selection.

Rule 2009. Trustees for Estates When Joint Administration Ordered

(a) ELECTION OF SINGLE TRUSTEE FOR ESTATES BEING JOINTLY ADMINISTERED. If the court orders a joint administration of two or more estates pursuant to Rule 1015(b), creditors may elect a single trustee for the estates being jointly administered.

(b) RIGHT OF CREDITORS TO ELECT SEPARATE TRUSTEE. Notwithstanding entry of an order for joint administration pursuant to Rule 1015(b) the creditors of any debtor may elect a separate trustee for the estate of the debtor as provided in § 702 of the Code.

(c) APPOINTMENT OF TRUSTEES FOR ESTATES BEING JOINTLY ADMINISTERED.

(1) Chapter 7 Liquidation Cases. The court may appoint one or more interim trustees for estates being jointly administered in chapter 7 cases.

(2) Chapter 11 Reorganization Cases. If a trustee is ordered, the court may appoint one or more trustees for estates being jointly administered in chapter 11 cases.

(3) Chapter 13 Individual's Debt Adjustment Cases. The court may appoint one or more trustees for estates being jointly administered in chapter 13 cases.

(d) POTENTIAL CONFLICTS OF INTEREST. On a showing that creditors or equity security holders of the different estates will be prejudiced by conflicts of interest of a common trustee, the court shall order separate trustees for estates being jointly administered.

(e) TRUSTEES FOR PARTNERSHIP AND PARTNERS' INDIVIDUAL ESTATES. Notwithstanding the foregoing provisions of this rule, the trustee of a partnership estate shall also be the trustee of the individual estate of any general partner if the estates are being jointly administered unless the court, for cause shown, either (1) permits the creditors of a general partner to elect a separate trustee or (2) appoints a separate trustee for the individual estate.

(f) SEPARATE ACCOUNTS. The trustee or trustees of estates being jointly administered shall keep separate accounts of the property and distribution of each estate.

Rule 2010. Qualification by Trustee; Proceeding on Bond

(a) BLANKET BOND. The court may authorize a blanket bond in favor of the United States conditioned on the faithful performance of official duties by the trustee or trustees to cover (1) a person who qualifies as trustee in a number of cases, and (2) a number of trustees each of whom qualifies in a different case.

(b) QUALIFICATION BY FILING ACCEPTANCE. A trustee for whom a blanket bond has been filed shall qualify by filing an acceptance of the election or appointment.

(c) EVIDENCE OF QUALIFICATION. A certified copy of the order approving the trustee's bond or of the acceptance filed under subdivision (b) of this rule shall constitute conclusive evidence of qualification.

(d) PROCEEDING ON BOND. A proceeding on the trustee's bond may be brought by any party in interest in the name of the United States for the use of the person injured by the breach of the condition.

Rule 2011. Evidence of Debtor in Possession

Whenever evidence is required that a debtor is a debtor in possession, the clerk may so certify and the certificate shall constitute conclusive evidence of that fact.

Rule 2012. Substitution of Successor Trustee; Accounting

When a trustee dies, resigns, is removed, or otherwise ceases to hold office during the pendency of a case under the Code:

(1) the successor is automatically substituted as a party in any pending action, proceeding, or matter; and

(2) within the time fixed by the court, the successor trustee shall prepare and file with the court an accounting of the prior administration of the estate.

Rule 2013. Limitations on Appointment or Employment of Trustees, Examiners, Appraisers and Auctioneers

(a) LIMITATION ON APPOINTMENTS. Appointments of trustees and examiners and employment of appraisers and auctioneers shall be made so that the annual aggregate compensation of any person shall not be disproportionate or excessive, giving proper regard to geographic constraints.

(b) RECORD TO BE KEPT. The clerk shall maintain a public record listing fees paid from estates (1) to trustees and attorneys, accountants, appraisers, auctioneers and other professional persons employed by trustees, and (2) to examiners appointed by the court. The record shall include the name and docket number of the case, the name of the individual or firm receiving the fee and the amount of the fee paid. The record shall be maintained chronologically and shall be kept current and open to examination by the public without charge.

(c) SUMMARY OF RECORD. At the close of each annual period, the clerk shall prepare a summary of the public record by individual or firm name, to reflect total fees paid during the preceding year. The summary shall be open to examination by the public without charge.

Rule 2014. Employment of Professional Persons

(a) APPLICATION FOR AND ORDER OF EMPLOYMENT. An order approving the employment of attorneys, accountants, appraisers, auctioneers, agents, or other professional persons pursuant to § 327 or § 1103 of the Code shall be made only on application of the trustee or committee, stating the specific facts showing the necessity for the employment, the name of the person to be employed, the reasons for his selection, the professional services to be rendered, any proposed arrangement for compensation, and, to the best of the applicant's knowledge, all of the person's connections with the debtor, creditors, or any other party in interest, their respective attorneys and accountants.

(b) SERVICES RENDERED BY MEMBER OR ASSOCIATE OF FIRM OF ATTORNEYS OR ACCOUNTANTS. If, under the Code and this rule, a law partnership or corporation is employed as an attorney, or an accounting partnership or corporation is employed as an accountant, or if a named attorney or accountant is employed, any partner, member, or regular associate of the partnership, corporation or individual may act as attorney or accountant so employed, without further order of the court.

Rule 2015. Duty of Trustee or Debtor in Possession to Keep Records, Make Reports, and Give Notice of Case

(a) TRUSTEE OR DEBTOR IN POSSESSION. A trustee or debtor in possession shall (1) in a chapter 7 liquidation and a chapter 11 reorganization case and if the court so directs within 30 days after entering on his duties file a complete inventory of the property of the debtor unless such an inventory has already been filed; (2) keep a record of receipts and the disposition of money and property received; (3) file the reports and summaries required by § 704(7) of the Code within the times fixed by the court and which shall include a statement, if payments are made to employees, of the amounts of deductions for all taxes required to be withheld or paid for and in behalf of employees and the place where these amounts are deposited; (4) as soon as possible after the commencement of the case, give notice of the case to every person known to be holding money or property subject to withdrawal or order of the debtor, including every bank, savings or building and loan association, public utility company, and landlord with whom the debtor has a deposit, and to every insurance company which has issued a policy having a cash surrender value payable to the debtor, except that notice need not be given to any entity who has knowledge or has previously been notified of the case; (5) within 30 days after the date of the order confirming a plan or within such other time as the court may fix, file a report with the court concerning the action taken by the trustee or debtor in possession and the progress made in the consummation of the plan and file further reports as the court may direct until the plan has been consummated; (6) after consummation of a plan, file an application for a final decree showing that the plan has been consummated, and the names and addresses, if known, of the holders of claims or interests which have not been surrendered or released in accordance with the provisions of the plan and the nature and amounts of claims or interests, and other facts as may be necessary to enable the court to pass on the provisions to be included in the final decree.

(b) CHAPTER 13 TRUSTEE AND DEBTOR

(1) *Business Cases.* In a chapter 13 individual's debt adjustment case, when the debtor is engaged in business, the debtor shall perform the duties prescribed by clauses (1) - (4) of subdivision (a) of this rule.

(2) *Nonbusiness Cases.* In a chapter 13 individual's debt adjustment case, when the debtor is not engaged in business, the trustee shall perform the duties

prescribed by clause (2) of subdivision (a) of this rule.

(c) TRANSMISSION OF REPORTS. In a chapter 11 case the court may direct that copies or summaries of annual reports and copies or summaries of other reports shall be mailed to the creditors, equity security holders, and indenture trustees. The court may also direct the publication of summaries of any such reports.

Rule 2016. Compensation for Services Rendered and Reimbursement of Expenses

(a) APPLICATION FOR COMPENSATION OR REIMBURSEMENT. A person seeking interim or final compensation for services, or reimbursement of necessary expenses, from the estate shall file with the court an application setting forth a detailed statement of (1) the services rendered, time expended and expenses incurred, and (2) the amounts requested. An application for compensation shall include a statement as to what payments have theretofore been made or promised to the applicant for services rendered or to be rendered in any capacity whatsoever in connection with the case, the source of the compensation so paid or promised, whether any compensation previously received has been shared and whether an agreement or understanding exists between the applicant and any other person for the sharing of compensation received or to be received for services rendered in or in connection with the case, and the particulars of any sharing of compensation or agreement or understanding therefor, except that details of any agreement by the applicant for the sharing of compensation as a member or regular associate of a firm of lawyers or accountants shall not be required. The requirements of this subdivision shall apply to an application for compensation for services rendered by an attorney or accountant even though the application is filed by a creditor or other person.

(b) DISCLOSURE OF COMPENSATION PAID OR PROMISED TO ATTORNEY FOR DEBTOR. Every attorney for a debtor, whether or not the attorney applies for compensation, shall file with the court on or before the first date set for the meeting of creditors, or at another time as the court may direct, the statement required by § 329 of the Code which shall also set forth whether the attorney has shared or agreed to share the compensation with any other person. The statement shall include the particulars of any such sharing or agreement to share by the attorney, but the details of any agreement for the sharing of the compensation with a member or regular associate of the attorney's law firm shall not be required.

Rule 2017. Examination of Debtor's Transactions with His Attorney

(a) PAYMENT OR TRANSFER TO ATTORNEY BEFORE COMMENCEMENT OF CASE. On motion by any party in interest or on the court's own initiative, the court after notice and a hearing may determine whether any payment of money or any transfer of property by the debtor, made directly or indirectly and in contemplation of the filing of a petition under the Code by or against the debtor, to an attorney for services rendered or to be rendered is excessive.

(b) PAYMENT OR TRANSFER TO ATTORNEY AFTER COMMENCEMENT OF CASE. On motion by the debtor or on the court's own initiative, the court after notice and a hearing may determine whether any payment of money or any transfer of property, or any agreement therefor, by the debtor to an attorney after the commencement of a case under the Code is excessive, whether the payment or transfer is made or is to be made directly or indirectly, if the payment, transfer, or agreement therefor is for services in any way related to the case.

Rule 2018. Intervention; Right to Be Heard

(a) PERMISSIVE INTERVENTION. In a case under the Code, after hearing on such notice as the court directs and for cause shown, the court may permit any interested entity to intervene generally or with respect to any specified matter.

(b) INTERVENTION BY ATTORNEY GENERAL OF A STATE. In a chapter 7, 11, or 13 case, the Attorney General of a State may appear and be heard on behalf of consumer creditors if the court determines the appearance is in the public interest, but the Attorney General may not appeal from any judgment, order, or decree in the case.

(c) CHAPTER 9 MUNICIPALITY CASE. The Secretary of the Treasury may, or if requested by the court shall, intervene in a chapter 9 case. Representatives of the state in which the debtor is located may intervene in a chapter 9 case with respect to matters specified by the court.

(d) LABOR UNIONS. In a chapter 9 or 11 case, a labor union or employees' association, representative of employees of the debtor, shall have the right to be heard on the economic soundness of a plan affecting the interests of the employees but it may not appeal from any judgment, order, or decree in the case unless otherwise permitted by law.

(e) SERVICE ON ENTITIES COVERED BY THIS RULE. The court may enter orders governing the service of notice and papers on entities permitted to intervene or be heard pursuant to this rule.

Rule 2019. Representation of Creditors and Equity Security Holders in Chapter 9 Municipality and Chapter 11 Reorganization Cases

(a) DATA REQUIRED. In a chapter 9 municipality or chapter 11 reorganization case, except with respect to a committee appointed pursuant to § 1102 of the Code, every person or committee representing more than one creditor or equity security holder and, unless otherwise directed by the court, every indenture trustee, shall file a verified statement with the clerk setting forth (1) the name and address of the creditor or equity security holder; (2) the nature and amount of the claim or interest and the time of acquisition thereof unless it is alleged to have been acquired more than one year prior to the filing of the petition; (3) a recital of the pertinent facts and circumstances in connection with the employment of the person or indenture trustee, and, in the case of a committee, the name or names of the person or persons at whose instance, directly or indirectly, the employment was arranged or the committee was organized or agreed to act; and (4) with reference to the time of the employment of the person, the organization or formation of the committee, or the appearance in the case of any indenture trustee, the amounts of claims or interests owned by the person, the members of the committee or the indenture trustee, the times when acquired, the amounts paid therefor, and any sales or other disposition thereof. The statement shall include a copy of the instrument, if any, whereby the person, committee, or indenture trustee is empowered to act on behalf of creditors or equity security holders. A supplemental statement shall be filed promptly, setting forth any material changes in the facts contained in the statement filed pursuant to this subdivision.

(b) FAILURE TO COMPLY; EFFECT. On motion of any party in interest or on its own initiative, the court may (1) determine whether there has been a failure to comply with the provisions of subdivision (a) of this rule or with any other applicable law regulating the activities and personnel of any person, committee, or indenture trustee or any other impropriety in connection with any solicitation and, if it so determines, the court may refuse to permit that person, committee, or indenture trustee to be heard further or to intervene in the case; (2) examine any representation provision of a deposit agreement, proxy, trust mortgage, trust indenture, or deed of trust, or committee or other authorization, and any claim or interest acquired by any person or committee in contemplation or in the course of a case under the Code and grant appropriate relief; and (3) hold invalid any authority, acceptance, rejection, or objection given, procured, or received by a person or committee who has not complied with this rule or with § 1125(b) of the Code.

PART III

CLAIMS AND DISTRIBUTION TO CREDITORS AND EQUITY INTEREST HOLDERS; PLANS

Rule 3001. Proof of Claim

(a) FORM AND CONTENT. A proof of claim is a written statement setting forth a creditor's claim. A proof of claim for wages, salary, or commissions shall conform substantially to Official Form No. 20 or No. 21; any other proof of claim shall conform substantially to Official Form No. 19.

(b) WHO MAY EXECUTE. A proof of claim shall be executed by the creditor or the creditor's authorized agent except as provided in Rules 3004 and 3005.

(c) CLAIM BASED ON A WRITING. When a claim, or an interest in property of the debtor securing the claim, is based on a writing, the original or a duplicate shall be filed with the proof of claim. If the writing has been lost or destroyed, a statement of the circumstances of the loss or destruction shall be filed with the claim.

(d) EVIDENCE OF PERFECTION OF SECURITY INTEREST. If a security interest in property of the debtor is claimed, the proof of claim shall be accompanied by evidence that the security interest has been perfected.

(e) TRANSFERRED CLAIM.

(1) Unconditional Transfer Before Proof Filed. If a claim other than one based on a bond or debenture has been unconditionally transferred before proof of the claim has been filed, the proof of claim may be filed only by the transferee. If the claim has been transferred after the filing of the petition, the proof of claim shall be supported by (A) a statement of the transferor acknowledging the transfer and stating the consideration therefor or (B) a statement of the transferee setting forth the consideration for the transfer and why the transferee is unable to obtain the statement from the transferor.

(2) Unconditional Transfer After Proof Filed. If a claim other than one based on a bond or debenture has been unconditionally transferred after the proof of

claim has been filed, evidence of the terms of the transfer shall be filed by the transferee. The clerk shall immediately notify the original claimant by mail of the filing of the evidence of transfer and that objection thereto, if any, must be filed with the clerk within 20 days of the mailing of the notice or within any additional time allowed by the court. If the court finds, after a hearing on notice, that the claim has been unconditionally transferred, it shall enter an order substituting the transferee for the original claimant, otherwise the court shall enter such order as may be appropriate.

(3) Transfer of Claim for Security Before Proof Filed. If a claim other than one based on a bond or debenture has been transferred for security before proof of the claim has been filed, the transferor or transferee or both may file a proof of claim for the full amount. The proof shall be supported by a statement setting forth the terms of the transfer. If the claim was transferred after the filing of the petition, the proof shall also be supported by (A) a statement of the transferor acknowledging the transfer and stating the consideration therefor, or (B) a statement of the transferee setting forth the consideration for the transfer and why the transferee is unable to obtain the statement from the transferor. If either the transferor or the transferee files a proof of claim, the clerk shall immediately notify the other by mail of the right to join in the filed claim. If both transferor and transferee file proof of the same claim, the proofs shall be consolidated. After a hearing on notice, the court shall enter such orders respecting allowance and voting of the claim, payment of dividends thereon, and participation in the administration of the estate as may be appropriate.

(4) Transfer of Claim for Security After Proof Filed. If a claim other than one based on a bond or debenture has been transferred for security after the proof of claim has been filed, evidence of the terms of the transfer shall be filed by the transferee. The clerk shall immediately notify the original claimant by mail of the filing of the evidence of transfer and that objection thereto, if any, must be filed with the clerk within 20 days of the mailing of the notice or within any additional time allowed by the court. After a hearing on notice, the court shall enter such orders respecting allowance and voting of the claim, payment of dividends thereon, and participation in the administration of the estate as may be appropriate.

(5) Service of Objection; Notice of Hearing. A copy of an objection to the evidence of transfer filed pursuant to paragraph (2) or (4) of this subdivision together with a notice of a hearing shall be mailed or otherwise delivered to the transferee at least 30 days prior to the hearing.

(f) EVIDENTIARY EFFECT. A proof of claim executed and filed in accordance with these rules shall constitute prima facie evidence of the validity and amount of the claim.

Rule 3002. Filing Proof of Claim or Interest

(a) NECESSITY FOR FILING. An unsecured creditor or an equity security holder must file a proof of claim or interest in accordance with this rule for the claim or interest to be allowed, except as provided in Rules 3003, 3004 and 3005.

(b) PLACE OF FILING. A proof of claim or interest shall be filed in accordance with Rule 5005.

(c) TIME FOR FILING. In a chapter 7 liquidation or chapter 13 individual's debt adjustment case, a proof of claim shall be filed within 90 days after the first date set for the meeting of creditors called pursuant to § 341(a) of the Code, except as follows:

(1) On motion of the United States, a state, or subdivision thereof before the expiration of such period and for cause shown, the court may extend the time for filing of a claim by the United States, a state, or subdivision thereof.

(2) In the interest of justice and if it will not unduly delay the administration of the case, the court may extend the time for filing a proof of claim by an infant or incompetent person or the representative of either.

(3) An unsecured claim which arises in favor of a person or becomes allowable as a result of a judgment may be filed within 30 days after the judgment becomes final if the judgment is for the recovery of money or property from that person or denies or avoids the person's interest in property. If the judgment imposes a liability which is not satisfied, or a duty which is not performed within such period or such further time as the court may permit, the claim shall not be allowed.

(4) A claim arising from the rejection of an executory contract of the debtor may be filed within the time as the court may direct.

(5) If notice of insufficient assets to pay a dividend was given to creditors pursuant to Rule 2002(e), and subsequently the trustee notifies the court that payment of a dividend appears possible, the clerk shall notify the creditors of that fact and that they may file proofs of claim within 90 days after the mailing of the notice.

(6) In a chapter 7 liquidation case, if a surplus remains after all claims allowed have been paid in full, the court may grant an extension of time for the filing of claims against the surplus not filed within the time hereinabove prescribed.

Rule 3003. Filing Proof of Claim or Equity Security Interest in Chapter 9 Municipality or Chapter 11 Reorganization Cases

(a) APPLICABILITY OF RULE. This rule applies in chapter 9 and 11 cases.

(b) SCHEDULE OF LIABILITIES AND LIST OF EQUITY SECURITY HOLDERS.

(1) Schedule of Liabilities. The schedule of liabilities filed pursuant to § 521(1) of the Code shall constitute prima facie evidence of the validity and amount of the claims of creditors, unless they are scheduled as disputed, contingent, or unliquidated. It shall not be necessary for a creditor or equity security holder to file a proof of claim or interest except as provided in subdivision (c)(2) of this rule.

(2) List of Equity Security Holders. The list of equity security holders filed pursuant to Rule 1007(a)(3) shall constitute prima facie evidence of the validity and amount of the equity security interests and it shall not be necessary for the holders of such interests to file a proof of interest.

(c) FILING PROOF OF CLAIM.

(1) Who May File. Any creditor or indenture trustee may file a proof of claim within the time prescribed by subdivision (c)(3) of this rule.

(2) Who Must File. Any creditor or equity security holder whose claim or interest is not scheduled or scheduled as disputed, contingent, or unliquidated shall file a proof of claim or interest within the time prescribed by subdivision (c)(3) of this rule; any creditor who fails to do so shall not be treated as a creditor with respect to such claim for the purposes of voting and distribution.

(3) Time for Filing. The court shall fix and for cause shown may extend the time within which proofs of claim or interest may be filed.

(4) Effect of Filing Claim. A proof of claim or interest executed and filed in accordance with this subdivision shall supersede any scheduling of that claim or interest pursuant to § 521(1) of the Code.

(5) Filing by Indenture Trustee. An indenture trustee may file a claim on behalf of all known or unknown holders of securities issued pursuant to the trust instrument under which it is trustee.

(d) PROOF OF RIGHT TO RECORD STATUS. For the purposes of Rules 3017, 3018 and 3021 and for receiving notices, a person who is not the record holder of a security may file a statement setting forth facts which entitle that person to be treated as the record holder. An objection to the statement may be filed by any party in interest.

Rule 3004. Filing of Claims by Debtor or Trustee

If a creditor fails to file a proof of claim on or before the first date set for the meeting of creditors called pursuant to § 341(a) of the Code, the debtor or trustee may do so in the name of the creditor. The clerk shall forthwith mail notice of the filing to the creditor, the debtor and the trustee. The creditor may thereafter file a proof of claim pursuant to Rule 3002 or Rule 3003, which proof when filed shall supersede the proof filed by the debtor or trustee.·

Rule 3005. Filing of Claim, Acceptance, or Rejection By Guarantor, Surety, Indorser, or Other Codebtor

(a) FILING OF CLAIM. If a creditor has not filed a proof of claim pursuant to Rule 3002(c) or 3003(c), one who is or may be liable with the debtor to that creditor, or who has secured that creditor, may, within 30 days after the expiration of the time for filing claims prescribed by Rule 3002(c) or 3003(c) whichever is applicable, execute and file a proof of claim in the name of the creditor, if known, or if unknown, in his own name. No distribution shall be made on the claim except on satisfactory proof that the original debt will be diminished by the amount of distribution. The creditor may thereafter file a proof of claim pursuant to Rule 3002(c) or 3003(c) and it shall supersede the proof of claim filed pursuant to the first sentence of this subdivision.

(b) FILING OF ACCEPTANCE OR REJECTION; SUBSTITUTION OF CREDITOR. One who has filed a claim pursuant to the first sentence of subdivision (a) of this rule may file an acceptance or rejection of a plan in the name of the creditor, if known, or if unknown, in his own name but if the creditor files a proof of claim within the time permitted by Rule 3003(c) or files a notice with the court prior to confirmation of a plan of his intention to act in his own behalf, the creditor shall be substituted for the obligor with respect to that claim.

Rule 3006. Withdrawal of Claim or Acceptance or Rejection of Plan

A creditor may withdraw a claim as of right by filing a notice of withdrawal, except as provided in this rule. If after a creditor has filed a proof of claim an objection is filed thereto or a complaint is filed against that creditor in an adversary proceeding, or the creditor has accepted or rejected the plan or otherwise has participated significantly in the case, the creditor may not withdraw the claim except on order of the court after a hearing on notice to the trustee or debtor in possession, and any creditors' committee selected pursuant to § § 705(a) or 1102 of the Code. The order of the court shall contain such terms and conditions as the court deems proper. Unless the court orders otherwise, an authorized withdrawal of a claim shall constitute withdrawal of any related acceptance or rejection of a plan.

Rule 3007. Objections to Claims

An objection to the allowance of a claim shall be in writing and filed with the court. A copy of the objection with notice of the hearing thereon shall be mailed or otherwise delivered to the claimant, the debtor or debtor in possession and the trustee at least 30 days prior to the hearing. If an objection to a claim is joined with a demand for relief of the kind specified in Rule 7001, it becomes an adversary proceeding.

Rule 3008. Reconsideration of Claims

A party in interest may move for reconsideration of an order allowing or disallowing a claim against the estate. The court after a hearing on notice shall enter an appropriate order.

Rule 3009. Declaration and Payment of Dividends in Chapter 7 Liquidation Cases

In chapter 7 cases, dividends to creditors shall be paid as promptly as practicable in the amounts and at the times as ordered by the court. Dividend checks shall be made payable and mailed to each creditor whose claim has been allowed, unless a power of attorney authorizing another person to receive dividends has been executed and filed in accordance with Rule 9010. In that event, dividend checks shall be made payable to the creditor and to the other person and shall be mailed to the other person.

Rule 3010. Small Dividends and Payments in Chapter 7 Liquidation and Chapter 13 Individual's Debt Adjustment Cases

(a) CHAPTER 7 CASES. In a chapter 7 case no dividend in an amount less than $5 shall be distributed by the trustee to any creditor unless authorized by local rule or order of the court. Any such dividend not distributed to a creditor shall be treated in the same manner as unclaimed funds as provided in § 347 of the Code.

(b) CHAPTER 13 CASES. In a chapter 13 case no payment in an amount less than $15 shall be distributed by the trustee to any creditor unless authorized by local rule or order of the court. Funds not distributed because of this subdivision shall accumulate and shall be paid whenever the accumulation aggregates $15. Any funds remaining shall be distributed with the final payment.

Rule 3011. Unclaimed Funds in Chapter 7 Liquidation and Chapter 13 Individual's Debt Adjustment Cases

The trustee shall file with the clerk a list of all known names and addresses of the persons and the amounts which they are entitled to be paid from remaining property of the estate that is paid into court pursuant to § 347(a) of the Code.

Rule 3012. Valuation of Security

The court may determine the value of a claim secured by a lien on property in which the estate has an interest on motion of any party in interest and after a hearing on notice to the holder of the secured claim and any other person as the court may direct.

Rule 3013. Classification of Claims and Interests

For the purposes of the plan and its acceptance, the court may, on motion after hearing on notice as the court may direct, determine classes of creditors and equity security holders pursuant to §§ 1122 and 1322(b)(1) of the Code.

Rule 3014. Election Pursuant to § 1111(b) by Secured Creditor in Chapter 9 Municipality and Chapter 11 Reorganization Cases

An election of application of § 1111(b)(2) of the Code by a class of secured creditors in a chapter 9 or 11 case may be made at any time prior to the conclusion of the hearing on the disclosure statement or within such later time as the court may fix. The election shall be in writing and signed unless made at the hearing on the disclosure statement. The election, if made by the majorities required by § 1111(b)(1)(A)(i), shall be binding on all members of the class with respect to the plan.

Rule 3015. Filing of Plan in Chapter 13 Individual's Debt Adjustment Cases

The debtor may file a chapter 13 plan with the petition. If a plan is not filed with the petition, it shall be filed within 15 days thereafter and such time shall not be further extended except for cause shown and on notice as the court may direct. Every proposed plan and any modification thereof shall be dated. The clerk shall include the plan or a summary of the plan with each notice of the hearing on confirmation pursuant to Rule 2002(b). If required by the court, the debtor shall furnish a sufficient number of copies to enable the clerk to include a copy of the plan with the notice of the hearing.

Rule 3016. Filing of Plan and Disclosure Statement in Chapter 9 Municipality and Chapter 11 Reorganization Cases

(a) TIME FOR FILING PLAN. A party in interest, other than the debtor, who is authorized to file a plan under § 1121(c) of the Code, may file a plan at any time before the conclusion of the hearing on the disclosure statement or thereafter with leave of court.

(b) IDENTIFICATION OF PLAN. Every proposed plan and any modification thereof shall be dated and, in a chapter 11 case, identified with the name of the person or persons submitting or filing it.

(c) DISCLOSURE STATEMENT. In a chapter 9 or 11 case, a disclosure statement pursuant to § 1125 or evidence showing compliance with § 1126(b) of the Code shall be filed with the plan or within a time fixed by the court.

Rule 3017. Court Consideration of Disclosure Statement in Chapter 9 Municipality and Chapter 11 Reorganization Cases

(a) HEARING ON DISCLOSURE STATEMENT AND OBJECTIONS THERETO. Following the filing of a disclosure statement as provided in Rule 3016(c), the court shall hold a hearing on not less than 25 days notice to the debtor, creditors, equity security holders and other parties in interest as provided in Rule 2002 to consider such statement and any objections or modifications thereto. The plan and the disclosure statement shall be mailed with the notice of the hearing only to the debtor, trustee, any committee appointed under the Code, the Securities and Exchange Commission and any party in interest who requests in writing a copy of the statement or plan. Objections to the disclosure statement shall be filed with the court and served on the debtor, the trustee, any committee appointed under the Code and such other entity as may be designated by the court, at any time prior to approval of the disclosure statement or by such earlier date as the court may fix.

(b) DETERMINATION ON DISCLOSURE STATEMENT. Following the hearing the court shall determine whether the disclosure statement should be approved.

(c) DATES FIXED FOR VOTING ON PLAN AND CONFIRMATION. On or before approval of the disclosure statement, the court shall fix a time within which the holders of claims and interests may accept or reject the plan and may fix a date for the hearing on confirmation.

(d) TRANSMISSION AND NOTICE TO CREDITORS AND EQUITY SECURITY HOLDERS. On approval of a disclosure statement, the debtor in possession, trustee, proponent of the plan, or clerk as ordered by the court shall mail to all creditors and equity security holders (1) the plan, or a court approved summary of the plan; (2) the disclosure statement approved by the court; (3) notice of the time within which acceptances and rejections of such plan may be filed; (4) notice of any date fixed for the hearing on confirmation; and (5) such other information as the court may direct including any opinion of the court approving the disclosure statement or a court approved summary of the opinion. In addition, a form of ballot conforming to Official Form No. 30 shall be mailed to creditors and equity security holders entitled to vote on the plan. In the event the opinion of the court is not transmitted or only a summary of the plan is transmitted, the opinion of the court or the plan shall be provided on request of a party in interest at the expense of the proponent of the plan. For the purposes of this subdivision, creditors and equity security holders shall include holders of stock, bonds, debentures, notes, and other securities of record at the date the order approving the disclosure statement was entered.

Rule 3018. Acceptance or Rejection of Plans

(a) PERSONS ENTITLED TO ACCEPT OR REJECT PLAN; TIME FOR ACCEPTANCE OR REJECTION. A plan may be accepted or rejected by the following entities within the time fixed by the court pursuant to Rule 3017: (1) any creditor whose claim is deemed allowed pursuant to § 502 of the Code or has been allowed by the court; (2) subject to subdivision (b) of this rule, any creditor who is a security holder of record at the date the order approving the disclosure statement is entered whose claim has not been disallowed; and, (3) an equity security holder of record at the date the order approving the disclosure statement is entered whose interest has not been disallowed. For cause shown and within the time fixed for acceptance or rejection of a plan, the court after notice and hearing may permit a creditor or equity security holder to change or withdraw an acceptance or rejection. Notwithstanding objection to a claim or interest, the court after notice and hearing may temporarily allow the claim or interest in an amount which the court deems proper for the purpose of accepting or rejecting a plan.

(b) ACCEPTANCES OR REJECTIONS OBTAINED BEFORE PETITION.

Acceptances or rejections of a plan may be obtained before the commencement of a case under the Code and may be filed with the court on behalf of (1) the holder of a claim or interest which is deemed allowed pursuant to § 502 of the Code or allowed by the court; (2) a creditor who is a security holder of record at the date specified in the solicitation for the purposes of such solicitation and whose claim has not been disallowed; and (3) an equity security holder of record at the date specified in the solicitation for the purposes of such solicitation and whose interest has not been disallowed. A holder of a claim or interest who has accepted or rejected a plan before the commencement of the case under the Code shall not be deemed to have accepted or rejected the plan if the court finds after notice and hearing that the plan was not transmitted to substantially all impaired creditors and impaired equity security holders, that an unreasonably short time was prescribed for such creditors and equity security holders to accept or reject the plan, or that the solicitation was not in compliance with § 1126(b) of the Code.

(c) FORM OF ACCEPTANCE OR REJECTION. An acceptance or rejection shall be in writing, identify the plan or plans accepted or rejected, be signed by the creditor or equity security holder or his authorized agent, and conform to Official Form No. 30. If more than one plan is transmitted pursuant to Rule 3017, an acceptance or rejection may be filed by each creditor or equity security holder for any number of plans transmitted and if acceptances are filed for more than one plan, the creditor or equity security holder may indicate his preferences among the plans so accepted.

(d) ACCEPTANCE OR REJECTION BY PARTIALLY SECURED CREDITOR. A creditor whose claim has been allowed in part as a secured claim and in part as an unsecured claim shall be entitled to accept or reject a plan in both capacities.

Rule 3019. Modification of Accepted Plan Before Confirmation

After a plan has been accepted and before its confirmation, the proponent may file a modification of the plan. If the court finds after hearing on notice to the trustee, any committee appointed under the Code and any other person designated by the court that the proposed modification does not adversely change the treatment of the claim of any creditor or the interest of any equity security holder who has not accepted in writing the modification, it shall be deemed accepted by all creditors and equity security holders who have previously accepted the plan.

Rule 3020. Deposit; Confirmation of Plan

(a) DEPOSIT. In a chapter 11 case, prior to entry of the order confirming the plan, the court may order the deposit with the trustee or debtor in possession of the consideration required by the plan to be distributed on confirmation. Any money deposited shall be kept in a special account established for the exclusive purpose of making the distribution.

(b) OBJECTIONS TO AND HEARING ON CONFIRMATION.

(1) Objections. Objections to confirmation of the plan shall be filed with the court and served on the debtor, the trustee, any committee appointed under the Code and on any other entity designated by the court, within a time fixed by the court. An objection to confirmation is govenred by Rule 9014.

(2) Hearing. The court shall rule on confirmation of the plan after notice and

hearing as provided in Rule 2002. If no objection is timely filed, the court may find, without receiving evidence, that the plan has been proposed in good faith and not by any means forbidden by law.

(c) Order of Confirmation. The order of confirmation shall conform to Official Form No. 31 and notice of entry thereof shall be mailed promptly by the clerk to the debtor, creditors, equity security holders and other parties in interest.

(d) Retained Power. Notwithstanding the entry of the order of confirmation, the court may enter all orders necessary to administer the estate.

Rule 3021. Distribution Under Plan

After confirmation of a plan, distribution shall be made to creditors whose claims have been allowed, to holders of stock, bonds, debentures, notes, and other securities of record at the time of commencement of distribution whose claims or equity security interests have not been disallowed and to indenture trustees who have filed claims pursuant to Rule 3003(c)(5) and which have been allowed.

Rule 3022. Final Decree

After an estate is fully administered, including distribution of any deposit required by the plan, the court shall enter a final decree (1) discharging any trustee if not previously discharged and cancelling his bond; (2) making provision by way of injunction or otherwise as may be equitable; and (3) closing the case.

Rule 4001. Relief from Automatic Stay; Use of Cash Collateral

(a) REQUEST FOR RELIEF FROM STAY OR TO USE CASH COLLATERAL. A request for relief from an automatic stay provided by the Code or for the use of cash collateral pursuant to § 363(c)(2) shall be made in accordance with Rule 9014.

(b) FINAL HEARING ON STAY. The stay of any act against property of the estate under § 362(a) of the Code expires 30 days after a final hearing is commenced pursuant to § 362(e)(2) unless within that time the court denies the motion for relief from the stay.

(c) EX PARTE RELIEF FROM STAY. Relief from a stay under § 362(a) may be granted without prior notice to the adverse party only if (1) it clearly appears from specific facts shown by affidavit or by a verified motion that immediate and irreparable injury, loss, or damage will result to the movant before the adverse party or his attorney can be heard in opposition, and (2) the movant's attorney certifies to the court in writing the efforts, if any, which have been made to give notice and the reasons why notice should not be required. The party obtaining relief under this subdivision and § 362(f) shall immediately give oral notice thereof to the trustee or debtor in possession and to the debtor and forthwith mail or otherwise transmit to such person or persons a copy of the order granting relief. On two days notice to the party who obtained relief from the stay without notice or on shorter notice to that party as the court may prescribe, the adverse party may appear and move reinstatement of the stay. In that event, the court shall proceed expeditiously to hear and determine the motion.

Rule 4002. Duties of Debtor

In addition to performing other duties prescribed by the Code and rules, the debtor shall (1) attend and submit to an examination at the times ordered by the court; (2) attend the hearing on a complaint objecting to discharge and testify, if called as a witness; (3) inform the trustee immediately in writing as to the location of real property in which the debtor has an interest and the name and address of every person holding money or property subject to the debtor's withdrawal or order if a schedule of property has not yet been filed pursuant to Rule 1007; and (4) cooperate with the trustee in the preparation of an inventory, the examination of proofs of claim, and the administration of the estate.

Rule 4003. Exemptions

(a) CLAIM OF EXEMPTIONS. A debtor shall list the property claimed as exempt under § 522 of the Code on the schedule of assets required to be filed by Rule 1007. If the debtor fails to claim exemptions or file the schedule within the time specified in Rule 1007, a dependent of the debtor may file the list within 30 days thereafter.

(b) OBJECTIONS TO CLAIM OF EXEMPTIONS. The trustee or any creditor may file objections to the list of property claimed as exempt within 30 days after the conclusion of the meeting of creditors held pursuant to Rule 2003(a) or the filing of any amendment to the list unless, within such period, further time is granted by the court. Copies of the objections shall be delivered or mailed to the trustee and to the person filing the list and his attorney.

(c) BURDEN OF PROOF. In any hearing under this rule, the objecting party has the burden of proving that the exemptions are not properly claimed. After hearing on notice, the court shall determine the issues presented by the objections.

(d) AVOIDANCE BY DEBTOR OF TRANSFERS OF EXEMPT PROPERTY. A proceeding by the debtor to avoid a lien or other transfer of property exempt under § 522(f) of the Code shall be by motion in accordance with Rule 9014.

Rule 4004. Grant Or Denial of Discharge

(a) TIME FOR FILING COMPLAINT OBJECTING TO DISCHARGE; NOTICE OF TIME FIXED. In a chapter 7 liquidation case a complaint objecting to the debtor's discharge under § 727(a) of the Code shall be filed not later than 60 days following the first date set for the meeting of creditors held pursuant to § 341(a). In a chapter 11 reorganization case, such complaint shall be filed not later than the first date set for the hearing on confirmation. The court shall give not less than 25 days notice of the time so fixed to all creditors in the manner provided in Rule 2002, and to the trustee and his attorney.

(b) EXTENSION OF TIME. On motion of any party in interest, after hearing on notice, the court may for cause extend the time for filing a complaint objecting to discharge. The motion shall be made before such time has expired.

(c) GRANT OF DISCHARGE. In a chapter 7 case, on expiration of the time fixed for filing a complaint objecting to discharge, the court shall forthwith grant the discharge unless (1) the debtor is not an individual, (2) a complaint objecting to the discharge has been filed, or (3) the debtor has filed a waiver under § 727(a)(10) of the

Code. Notwithstanding the foregoing, on motion of the debtor, the court may defer the entry of an order granting a discharge for 30 days and, on motion within such period, the court may defer entry of the order to a date certain.

(d) APPLICABILITY OF RULES IN PART VII. A proceeding commenced by a complaint objecting to discharge is governed by the rules in Part VII.

(e) ORDER OF DISCHARGE. An order of discharge shall conform to Official Form No. 27.

(f) REGISTRATION IN OTHER DISTRICTS. An order of discharge that has become final may be registered in any other district by filing a certified copy of the order in the office of the clerk of the bankruptcy court of that district. When so registered the order of discharge shall have the same effect as an order of the court of the district where registered.

(g) NOTICE OF DISCHARGE. The clerk shall promptly mail a copy of the final order of discharge to the persons specified in subdivision (a) of this rule.

Rule 4005. Burden of Proof in Objecting to Discharge

At the trial on a complaint objecting to a discharge, the plaintiff has the burden of proving his objection.

Rule 4006. Notice of No Discharge

If an order is entered denying or revoking a discharge or if a waiver of discharge is filed, after the order becomes final or the waiver is filed the clerk shall promptly give notice thereof to all creditors in the manner provided in Rule 2002.

Rule 4007. Determination of Dischargeability of a Debt

(a) PERSONS ENTITLED TO FILE COMPLAINT. A debtor or any creditor may file a complaint with the court to obtain a determination of the dischargeability of any debt.

(b) TIME FOR COMMENCING PROCEEDING OTHER THAN UNDER § 523(c) OF THE CODE. A complaint other than under § 523(c) may be filed at any time. A case may be reopened without payment of an additional filing fee for the purpose of filing a complaint to obtain a determination under this rule.

(c) TIME FOR FILING COMPLAINT UNDER § 523(c) IN CHAPTER 7 LIQUIDATION AND CHAPTER 11 REORGANIZATION CASES; NOTICE OF TIME FIXED. A complaint to determine the dischargeability of any debt pursuant to § 523(c) of the Code shall be filed not later than 60 days following the first date set for the meeting of creditors held pursuant to § 341(a). The court shall give all creditors not less than 30 days notice of the time so fixed in the manner provided in Rule 2002. On motion of any party in interest, after hearing on notice, the court may for cause extend the time fixed under this subdivision. The motion shall be made before the time has expired.

(d) TIME FOR FILING COMPLAINT UNDER § 523(c) IN CHAPTER 13 INDIVIDUAL'S DEBT ADJUSTMENT CASES; NOTICE OF TIME FIXED. On motion by a debtor for a discharge under § 1328(b), the court shall enter an order fixing a time for the filing of a complaint to determine the dischargeability of any debt pursuant to § 523(c) and shall give not less than 30 days notice of the time fixed to all creditors in the manner provided in Rule 2002. On motion of any party in interest after hearing on notice the court may for cause extend the time fixed under this subdivision. The motion shall be made before the time has expired.

(e) APPLICABILITY OF RULES IN PART VII. A proceeding commenced by a complaint filed under this rule is governed by the rules in Part VII.

Rule 4008. Discharge and Reaffirmation Hearing

Not more than 30 days following the entry of an order granting or denying a discharge, or confirming a plan in a chapter 11 reorganization case concerning an individual debtor and on not less than 10 days notice to the debtor and the trustee, the court shall hold a hearing as provided in § 524(d) of the Code. A motion by the debtor for approval of a reaffirmation agreement shall be filed before or at the hearing.

PART X

UNITED STATES TRUSTEES

Rule X-1001. Applicability of Rules

(a) PART X RULES. The rules in Part X apply to cases under the Code filed in or transferred to any district in which a United States trustee is authorized.

(b) INAPPLICABILITY OF RULES. The following rules do not apply in cases under the Code filed in or transferred to any district specified in subdivision (a) of this rule: 2001(a), (c), 2002(a)(1), 2003(a),(b)(1), (2), (d), 2007, 2008, 2009(c), (d), (e), 2010(a), 5008, and the second sentence of 6003.

Rule X-1002. Petitions, Lists, Schedules and Statements

(a) PETITIONS AND ACCOMPANYING MATERIALS.

(1) Number of Copies. In addition to the number of copies required to be filed pursuant to Rules 1002(b), 1003(b) and 1007(f), there shall be filed one copy of the petition, the list of creditors, the schedule of assets and liabilities, the statement of financial affairs, the statement of executory contracts, and the Chapter 13 Statement and any amendments thereto.

(2) Transmission to United States Trustee. The clerk shall forthwith transmit to the United States trustee the additional copies filed pursuant to this subdivision. Written notice of a hearing for an extension of time to file schedules, statements and lists pursuant to Rule 1007(a)(4) shall be given the United States trustee.

(b) FILING LISTS BY DEBTOR IN CHAPTER 11 REORGANIZATION CASES. In chapter 11 cases, the debtor shall file an additional copy of the lists of creditors and of the 20 largest unsecured creditors required by Rule 1007(a) and (d). The lists shall contain additional information as the United States trustee may require and one copy of each shall be transmitted forthwith by the clerk to the United States trustee.

Rule X-1003. Appointment of Interim Trustee before Order for Relief in a Chapter 7 Liquidation Case

(a) APPOINTMENT. At any time following the commencement of an involuntary liquidation case and before an order for relief, the court on written motion of a party in interest may order the appointment of an interim trustee under § 15303 of the Code. The motion shall set forth the necessity for the appointment and may be granted only after hearing on notice to the debtor, the United States trustee, and other parties in interest as the court may designate.

(b) FORM OF ORDER. The order directing the appointment of an interim trustee shall state why the appointment is necessary and shall specify the trustee's duties.

Rule X-1004. Notification to Trustee of Selection; Blanket Bond

(a) NOTIFICATION. The United States trustee shall immediately notify the trustee of his selection, how he may qualify, and, if applicable, the amount of the bond. The trustee shall give written notification to the court and the United States trustee of the acceptance or rejection of the office within five days after receipt of notice of selection.

(b) BLANKET BOND. The United States trustee may authorize a blanket bond in favor of the United States conditioned on the faithful performance of official duties by the trustee or trustees to cover (1) a person who qualifies as trustee in a number of cases, and (2) a number of trustees each of whom qualifies in a different case.

Rule X-1005. Trustees for Estates When Joint Administration Ordered

(a) APPOINTMENT OF TRUSTEES FOR ESTATES BEING JOINTLY ADMINISTERED.

(1) Chapter 7 Liquidation Cases. The United States trustee may appoint one or more interim trustees for estates being jointly administered in chapter 7 cases.

(2) Chapter 11 Reorganization Cases. If a trustee is ordered, the United States trustee may appoint one or more trustees for estates being jointly administered in chapter 11 cases.

(3) Chapter 13 Individual's Debt Adjustment Cases. The United States trustee may appoint one or more trustees for estates being jointly administered in chapter 13 cases.

(b) POTENTIAL CONFLICTS OF INTEREST. On a showing that creditors of the different estates will be prejudiced by conflicts of interest of a common trustee the court shall order the appointment of separate trustees for estates being jointly administered.

Rule X-1006. Meetings of Creditors or Equity Security Holders

(a) DATE AND PLACE. The United States trustee shall call a meeting of creditors to be held not less than 20 nor more than 40 days after the order for relief. If there is an appeal from or a motion to vacate the order for relief, or if there is a motion to dismiss the case, the United States trustee may set a later time for the meeting. The meeting may be held at a regular place for holding court or at any other place designated by the United States trustee within the district convenient for the parties in interest.

(b) ORDER OF MEETING.

(1) Meeting of Creditors. The United States trustee or his designee shall preside at the meeting of creditors. The business of the meeting shall include the examination of the debtor under oath and, in a chapter 7 liquidation case, may include the election of a trustee or of a creditors' committee. The presiding officer shall have the authority to administer oaths.

(2) Meeting of Equity Security Holders. If the court orders a meeting of equity security holders pursuant to § 341(b) of the Code, the United States trustee shall fix a date for the meeting and he or his designee shall preside.

(c) REPORT TO THE COURT. The United States trustee shall transmit to the court the name and address of any person elected trustee or a member of a creditors' committee. If an election is disputed, the presiding officer shall promptly inform the court in writing of the dispute. Pending disposition of the dispute by the court, the interim trustee shall continue in office. If no motion for the resolution of the election dispute is made to the court within ten days after the date of the creditors' meeting, the interim trustee shall serve as trustee in the case.

(d) SPECIAL MEETINGS. The United States trustee may call a special meeting of creditors on application or on his own initiative.

(e) FINAL MEETING. If the United States trustee calls a final meeting of creditors in a case in which the net proceeds realized exceed $250, the clerk of the bankruptcy court shall mail a summary of the trustee's final account to the creditors with the notice of the meeting, together with a statement of the amount of the claims allowed. The trustee or his designee shall attend the final meeting and shall, if requested, report on the administration of the estate.

Rule X-1007. Duty of Trustee or Debtor in Possession to Make Reports, Furnish Information, and Cooperate with United States Trustee

(a) DUTY TO FILE INVENTORY. A trustee or debtor in possession shall file the inventory required by Rule 2015(a)(1) with the United States trustee and with the court if the court so directs.

(b) DUTY TO FURNISH INFORMATION TO, AND COOPERATE WITH, UNITED STATES TRUSTEE. The trustee or debtor in possession shall cooperate with the United States trustee by furnishing such information as the United States trustee may reasonably require in supervising the administration of the estate. The trustee or debtor in possession in a chapter 11 reorganization case, and the debtor in a chapter 13 individual's debt adjustment case when the debtor is engaged in business, shall furnish the United States trustee and file with the clerk regular reports of operations as the United States trustee may reasonably require.

Rule X-1008. Notices to United States Trustee

(a) NOTICES TO BE FURNISHED TO UNITED STATES TRUSTEES. Unless the United States trustee otherwise requests, the United States trustee shall receive notice of and pleadings relating to:

(1) the matters described in Rule 2002(a)(2), (5), (7), 2002(b), and (f);

(2) applications for approval of the employment of professional persons under Rule 2014;

(3) applications for compensation of professional persons under Rule 2016;

(4) the hearing to consider a disclosure statement pursuant to Rule 3017;

(5) the hearing on the appointment of a trustee or examiner; and

(6) any other matter notice of which is requested by the United States trustee or ordered by the court.

(b) TIME FOR NOTICE TO UNITED STATES TRUSTEE. Subject to Rule 2002, the United States trustee shall receive notice within sufficient time to permit him to participate in the matter.

(c) UNITED STATES TRUSTEE NEED NOT FURNISH NOTICE. The United States trustee shall not be required to give any notice provided for in Rule 2002(a) or (b).

Rule X-1009. Right to be Heard; Filing Papers

(a) RIGHT TO BE HEARD. The United States trustee may raise and appear and be heard on any issue relating to his responsibilities in a case under the Code.

(b) FILING OF PAPERS. In the interest of effective administration, the court or the United States trustee may require a party in interest to file with the United States trustee a copy of any paper filed with the court.

Rule X-1010. Prohibition of Ex Parte Contacts

The United States trustee, his assistants, and agents shall refrain from ex parte meetings and communications with the bankruptcy judge concerning matters affecting a particular case or proceeding. This rule does not preclude communication with a bankruptcy judge to discuss general problems of administration and improvement of bankruptcy administration, including the operation of the United States trustee system.

Selected Official Forms and Advisory Committee Notes

Form 1.—Voluntary Petition

UNITED STATES BANKRUPTCY COURT FOR THE
. . . . DISTRICT OF . . . .

————————————————————————————————————x

In re   :

. . . . ,   :

Debtor [set forth here all names   :   Case No. . . . . .
including trade names used by   :
Debtor within last 6 years].   :
Social Security No. . . . .   :
and Debtor's Employer's Tax
Identification No. . . . .   :

————————————————————————————————————x

Voluntary Petition

1. Petitioner's mailing address, including county, is . . . .

. . . .

2. Petitioner has resided [or has had his domicile or has had his principal place of business or has had his principal assets] within this district for the preceding 180 days [or for a longer portion of the preceding 180 days than in any other district].

3. Petitioner is qualified to file this petition and is entitled to the benefits of title 11, United States Code as a voluntary debtor.

4. [If appropriate] A copy of petitioner's proposed plan, dated . . . . . , is attached [or Petitioner intends to file a plan pursuant to chapter 11 or chapter 13] of title 11, United States Code.

5. [If petitioner is a corporation] Exhibit "A" is attached to and made part of this petition.

WHEREFORE, petitioner prays for relief in accordance with chapter 7 [or chapter 11 or chapter 13] of title 11, United States Code.

Signed: . . . . ,
Attorney for Petitioner.

Address: . . . . ,
. . . .

[Petitioner signs if not represented by attorney.]

. . . . ,
Petitioner.

I, ... , the petitioner named in the foregoing petition, declare under penalty of perjury that the foregoing is true and correct.

Executed on . . . .

Signature: . . . .
Petitioner.

Exhibit "A"

[If petitioner is a corporation, this Exhibit "A" shall be completed and attached to the petition pursuant to paragraph 5 thereof.]

[Caption as in Form No. 1]

FOR COURT USE ONLY

. . . .
Date Petition Filed

. . . .
Case Number

. . . .
Bankruptcy Judge

1. Petitioner's employer identification number is . . . .

2. If any of petitioner's securities are registered under section 12 of the Securities and Exchange Act of 1934, SEC file number is . . . .

3. The following financial data is the latest available information and refers to petitioner's condition on . . . .

     a. Total assets: $ . . . .

     b. Total liabilities: $ . . . .

		Approximate number of holders
Secured debt, excluding that listed below	$	. . . .
Debt securities held by more than 100 holders	$	. . . .
Secured	$	. . . .
Unsecured	$	. . . .
Other liabilities, excluding contingent or unliquidated claims	$	. . . .
Number of shares of common stock	$	. . . .

Comments, if any: . . . .

. . . .

. . . .

4. Brief description of petitioner's business: . . . .

. . . .

. . . .

5. [If presently available, supply the following information] The name of any person who directly or indirectly owns, controls, or holds, with power to vote, 20% or more of the voting securities of petitioner is . . . . . .

. . . .

6.   [If presently available, supply the following information] The

names of all corporations 20% or more of the outstanding voting securities

of which are directly or indirectly owned, controlled, or held, with power to

vote, by petitioner are . . . .

. . . .

. . . .

ADVISORY COMMITTEE NOTE

This form may be used to commence a voluntary case under chapter 7, 11, or 13 of the Bankruptcy Code. A chapter 9 petition requires other allegations (see § 109(c) of the Code) but this form may be adapted for such use.

The title of the case, in the caption of the form, should include all names used by the debtor, such as trade names, names used in doing business, married names and maiden names. This will enable creditors to properly identify the debtor when they receive notices and orders.

A joint petition, available for an individual and spouse, may be filed under chapter 7, 11, or 13. See § 302 of the Code. This form may be adapted for such use.

The unsworn declaration at the end of the petition conforms with 28 U.S.C. § 1746 (1976) which permits the declaration to be made in the manner indicated with the same force and effect as a sworn statement. The form may be adapted for use outside of the United States by adding the words "under the laws of the United States" after the word "perjury.

"Exhibit "A" to be attached to the petition of a corporate debtor is for the purpose of supplying the Securities and Exchange Commission with the information it requires at the beginning stages of a chapter 11 case.

FORM 2.--Application to Pay Filing Fee in Installments

UNITED STATES BANKRUPTCY COURT FOR THE
.... DISTRICT OF ....

————————————————————————————x

In re   :

.............................., :

Debtor.   :   Case No. .....

                                          :

————————————————————————————x

Application to Pay Filing Fee in Installments

1. Applicant files herewith a petition commencing a voluntary [or joint] case under title 11, United States Code.

2. Applicant is unable to pay the filing fee except in installments.

3. Applicant proposes to pay such fee to the clerk of the bankruptcy court on the following terms: ....

....

4. Applicant has not paid any money or transferred any property to applicant's attorney for services in connection with this case or any pending case under title 11, United States Code, and applicant will not make any payment or transfer any property to his attorney for such services until the filing fee is paid in full.

WHEREFORE, applicant prays that he be permitted to pay the filing fee in installments.

Dated: ....

                              Signed: ....,
                                              Applicant.

                              Address: ....,
                                        ....

ADVISORY COMMITTEE NOTE

The application for permission to pay filing fees in installments may be filed in accordance with 28 U.S.C. § 1930(a), and Rule 1006. Only an individual debtor in a voluntary case, or individual debtors filing a joint petition may pay the fee in installments.

If a joint petition is filed, this form may be adapted for use by both petitioners.

FORM 4.—Unsworn Declaration under Penalty of Perjury
on Behalf of a Corporation or Partnership

I, ... , [the president or other officer or an

authorized agent of the corporation] [or a member or an authorized agent

of the partnership] named as petitioner in the foregoing petition, declare

under penalty of perjury that the foregoing is true and correct, and that the

filing of this petition on behalf of the [corporation] [or partnership] has

been authorized.

Executed on . . . .

Signature: . . . .

ADVISORY COMMITTEE NOTE

Rule 1008 requires all petitions to be verified. This form is to be used on behalf of a corporation or partnership. It may be adapted for use in connection with other papers required by these rules to be verified. See the Note to Rule 9011. 28 U.S.C. § 1746 permits an unsworn declaration to be used in lieu of a verification. See Advisory Committee Note to Form No. 1.

FORM 5.—Certificate of Commencement of Case

[Caption as in Form No. 1]

Certificate of Commencement of Case

I hereby certify that on . . . . , ... the above named

debtor filed a petition [or if applicable a petition was filed against the

above named debtor] requesting relief under chapter . . of title 11, United

States Code (the Bankruptcy Code).

Dated: . . . .

. . . .

Clerk of the Bankruptcy Court.

ADVISORY COMMITTEE NOTE

This form is adapted from certificates that have been in use in several
districts. The certificate may be used to alert persons dealing with the debtor or
property of the debtor of the pendency of a case under the Code before the notice
of the meeting of creditors is sent.

FORM 6.—Schedules of Assets and Liabilities

[Caption as in Form No. 1]

Schedule A. — Statement of All Liabilities of Debtor.

Schedules A-1, A-2 and A-3 must include all the claims against the debtor or his property as of the date of the filing of the petition by or against him.

Schedule A-1. — Creditors having priority.

(1)	(2)	(3)	(4)	(5)
Nature of claim	Name of creditor and complete mailing address including zip code	Specify when claim was incurred and the consideration therefor; when claim is subject to setoff, evidenced by a judgment, negotiable instrument, or other writing, or incurred as partner or joint contractor, so indicate; specify name of any partner or joint contractor on any debt	Indicate if claim is contingent, unliquidated, or disputed	Amount of claim

a. Wages, salary, and commissions, including vacation, severance and sick leave pay owing to employees not exceeding $2,000 to each, earned within 90 days before filing of petition or cessation of business (if earlier specify date). $ . . . . . .

b. Contributions to employee benefit plans for services rendered within 180 days before filing of petition or cessation of business (if earlier specify date). $ . . . . . .

c. Deposits by individuals, not exceeding $900 for each for purchase, lease, or rental of property or services for personal, family, or household use that were not delivered or provided. $ . . . . . .

d. Taxes owing [itemize by type of tax and taxing authority]

    (1) To the United States $ . . . . . .
    (2) To any state $ . . . . . .
    (3) To any other taxing authority $ . . . . . .

        Total . . . . $ . . . . . .

Schedule A-2. — Creditors holding security

(1)	(2)	(3)	(4)	(5)	(6)
Name of creditor and complete mailing address including zip code	Description of security and date when obtained by creditor	Specify when claim was incurred and the consideration therefor; when claim is subject to setoff, evidenced by a judgment, negotiable instrument, or other writing, or incurred as partner or joint contractor, so indicate; specify name of any partner or joint contractor on any debt	Indicate if claim is contingent, unliquidated, or disputed	Market Value	Amount of claim without deduction of value of security

Total $ . . . . . .

Schedule A-3. — Creditors having unsecured claims without priority.

(1)	(2)	(3)	(4)
Name of creditor [including last known holder of any negotiable instrument] and complete mailing address including zip code	Specify when claim was incurred and the consideration therefor; when claim is contingent, unliquidated, disputed, subject to setoff, evidenced by a judgment, negotiable instrument, or other writing, or incurred as partner or joint contractor, so indicate; specify name of any partner or joint contractor on any debt	Indicate if claim is contingent, unliquidated, or disputed	Amount of claim

Total $ . . . .

Schedule B — Statement of All Property of Debtor

Schedules B-1, B-2, B-3, and B-4 must include all property of the debtor as of the date of the filing of the petition by or against him.

Schedule B-1. — Real Property

Description and location of all real property in which debtor has an interest [including equitable and future interests, interests in estates by the entirety, community property, life estates, lease-holds, and rights and powers exercisable for his own benefit]	Nature of interest [specify all deeds and written instru-ments relating thereto]	Market value of debtor's interest without deduction for secured claims listed in Schedule A-2 or exemptions claimed in Schedule B-4
		Total $..........

Schedule B-2. — Personal Property

Type of Property	Description and Location	Market value of debtor's interest without deduc-tion for secured claims listed on Schedule A-2 or exemptions claimed in Schedule B-4
		Total $..........
a. Cash on hand		$..........
b. Deposits of money with banking institutions, savings and loan associations, brokerage houses, credit unions, public utility com-panies, landlords and others		....
c. Household goods, supplies and furnishings		....
d. Books, pictures, and other art objects; stamp, coin and other collections		....

e. Wearing apparel, jewelry, firearms, sports
    equipment and other personal possessions   . . . .

f. Automobiles, trucks, trailers and other
    vehicles   . . . .

g. Boats, motors and their accessories   . . . .

h. Livestock, poultry and other animals   . . . .

i. Farming equipment, supplies and implements   . . . .

j. Office equipment, furnishings and supplies   . . . .

k. Machinery, fixtures, equipment and supplies
    [other than those listed in Items j and l]
    used in business   . . . .

l. Inventory   . . . .

m. Tangible personal property of any other
    description   . . . .

n. Patents, copyrights, licenses, franchises
    and other general intangibles [specify all
    documents and writings relating thereto]   . . . .

o. Government and corporate bonds and other
    negotiable and nonnegotiable instruments   . . . .

p. Other liquidated debts owing debtor   . . . .

q. Contingent and unliquidated claims of every
    nature, including counterclaims of the
    debtor [give estimated value of each]   . . . .

r. Interests in insurance policies [name insurance
    company of each policy and itemize surrender or
    refund value of each]   . . . .

s. Annuities [itemize and name each issuer]   . . . .

t. Stock and interests in incorporated and un-
    incorporated companies [itemize separately]   . . . .

u. Interests in partnerships   . . . .

v.   Equitable and future interests, life estates,
     and rights or powers exercisable for the
     benefit of the debtor (other than those listed
     in schedule B-1) [specify all written instru-
     ments relating thereto]   . . . .

     _____

                                                    Total $ . . . .

Schedule B-3. — Property not otherwise scheduled

Type of Property	Description and Location	Market value of debtor's interest without deduction for secured claims listed in Schedule A-2 or exemption claimed in Schedule B-4

---

a.   Property transferred under assignment for
     benefit of creditors, within 120 days prior
     to filing of petition [specify date of
     assignment, name and address of assignee,
     amount realized therefrom by the assignee,
     and disposition of proceeds so far as known
     to debtor] $ . . . .

b.   Property of any kind not otherwise scheduled   . . . .

     _____

                                                    Total $ . . . .

Debtor selects the following property as exempt pursuant to 11 U.S.C.

§ 522(d) [or the laws of the State of . . . .]

Schedule B-4. — Property claimed as exempt

Type of Property	Location, description, and, so far as relevant to the claim of exemption, present use of property	Specify statute creating the exemption	Value claimed exempt
			$ . . . .
			. . . .
		Total	$ . . . .

Summary of debts and property.
[From the statements of the debtor in Schedules A and B]

Schedule		Total

Debts

A-1/a,b	Wages, etc. having priority	$ . . . .
A-1(c)	Deposits of money	. . . .
A-1/d(1)	Taxes owing United States	. . . .
A-1/d(2)	Taxes owing states	. . . .
A-1/d(3)	Taxes owing other taxing authorities	. . . .
A-2	Secured claims	. . . .
A-3	Unsecured claims without priority	. . . .
	Schedule A total	$ . . . .

Property

B-1	Real property [total value]	$ . . . .
B-2/a	Cash on hand	. . . .
B-2/b	Deposits	. . . .
B-2/c	Household goods	. . . .
B-2/d	Books, pictures, and collections	. . . .
B-2/e	Wearing apparel and personal possessions	. . . .
B-2/f	Automobiles and other vehicles	. . . .
B-2/g	Boats, motors, and accessories	. . . .
B-2/h	Livestock and other animals	. . . .
B-2/i	Farming supplies and implements	. . . .
B-2/j	Office equipment and supplies	. . . .
B-2/k	Machinery, equipment, and supplies used in business	. . . .
B-2/l	Inventory	. . . .

B-2/m	Other tangible personal property	. . . .
B-2/n	Patents and other general intangibles	. . . .
B-2/o	Bonds and other instruments	. . . .
B-2/p	Other liquidated debts	. . . .
B-2/q	Contingent and unliquidated claims	. . . .
B-2/r	Interests in insurance policies	. . . .
B-2/s	Annuities	. . . .
B-2/t	Interests in corporations and unincorporated companies	. . . .
B-2/u	Interests in partnerships	. . . .
B-2/v	Equitable and future interests, rights, and powers in personalty	. . . .
B-3/a	Property assigned for benefit of creditors	. . . .
B-3/b	Property not otherwise scheduled	. . . .

Schedule B total $ . . . .

Unsworn Declaration under Penalty of Perjury of Individual to Schedules A and B

I, ... , declare under penalty of perjury that I have read the foregoing schedules, consisting of . . . sheets, and that they are true and correct to the best of my knowledge, information and belief.

Executed on . . . .

Signature: . . . .

Unsworn Declaration under Penalty of Perjury
on Behalf of Corporation or Partnership
to Schedules A and B

I, ... , [the president <u>or other officer</u> or an

authorized agent of the corporation] [<u>or</u> a member <u>or</u> an authorized agent

of the partnership] named as debtor in this case, declare under penalty of

perjury that I have read the foregoing schedules, consisting of . . . sheets,

and that they are true and correct to the best of my knowledge,

information, and belief.

Executed on . . . .

Signature: . . . .

ADVISORY COMMITTEE NOTE

These schedules may be used pursuant to § 521(1) of the Code.

The unsworn declarations at the end of the form are in conformity with 28
U.S.C. § 1746. See Advisory Committee Note to Form No. 1

FORM 8.—Statement of Financial Affairs for
Debtor Engaged in Business.

[Caption as in Form No. 1]

Statement of Financial Affairs for Debtor Engaged in Business

[Each question shall be answered or the failure to answer explained.
If the answer is "none" or "not applicable," so state. If additional space is
needed for the answer to any question, a separate sheet properly identified
and made a part hereof, should be used and attached.

If the debtor is a partnership or a corporation, the questions shall be
deemed to be addressed to, and shall be answered on behalf of, the
partnership or corporation; and the statement shall be certified by a
member of the partnership or by a duly authorized officer of the
corporation.

The term, "original petition," used in the following questions, shall
mean the petition filed under Rule 1002, 1003, or 1004.]

1. Nature, location, and name of business.

    a.   Under what name and where do you carry on your business?

    b.   In what business are you engaged? (If business operations have
been terminated, give the date of termination.)

    c.   When did you commence the business?

    d.   Where else, and under what other names, have you carried on
business within the six years immediately preceding the filing of the
original petition herein? (Give street addresses, the names of any partners,
joint adventurers, or other associates, the nature of the business, and the
periods for which it was carried on.)

2. <u>Books and records.</u>

    a. By whom, or under whose supervision, have your books of account and records been kept during the six years immediately preceding the filing of the original petition herein? (Give names, addresses, and periods of time.)

    b. By whom have your books of account and records been audited during the six years immediately preceding the filing of the original petition herein? (Give names, addresses, and dates of audits.)

    c. In whose possession are your books of account and records? (Give names and addresses.)

    d. If any of these books or records are not available, explain.

    e. Have any books of account or records relating to your affairs been destroyed, lost, or otherwise disposed of within the two years immediately preceding the filing of the original petition herein? (If so, give particulars, including date of destruction, loss, or disposition, and reason therefor.)

3. <u>Financial statements.</u>

    Have you issued any written financial statements within the two years immediately preceding the filing of the original petition herein? (Give dates, and the name and addresses of the persons to whom issued, including mercantile and trade agencies.)

4. <u>Inventories.</u>

    a. When was the last inventory of your property taken?

    b. By whom, or under whose supervision, was this inventory taken?

    c. What was the amount, in dollars, of the inventory? (State whether the inventory was taken at cost, market, or otherwise.)

d. When was the next prior inventory of your property taken?

e. By whom, or under whose supervision, was this inventory taken?

f. What was the amount, in dollars, of the inventory? (State whether the inventory was taken at cost, market, or otherwise).

g. In whose possession are the records of the two inventories above referred to? (Give names and addresses.)

5. Income other than from operation of business.

What amount of income, other than from operation of your business, have you received during each of the two years immediately preceding the filing of the original petition herein? (Give particulars, including each source, and the amount received therefrom.)

6. Tax returns and refunds.

a. In whose possession are copies of your federal, state and municipal income tax returns for the three years immediately preceding the filing of the original petition herein?

b. What tax refunds (income or other) have you received during the two years immediately preceding the filing of the original petition herein?

c. To what tax refunds (income or other), if any, are you, or may you be, entitled? (Give particulars, including information as to any refund payable jointly to you and your spouse or any other person.)

7. Financial accounts, certificates of deposit and safe deposit boxes.

What accounts or certificates of deposit or shares in banks, savings and loan, thrift, building and loan and homestead associations, credit unions, brokerage houses, pension funds and the like have you maintained, alone or together with any other person, and in your own or any other name, within the two years immediately preceding the filing of the original petition herein? (Give the name and address of each institution, the name and number under which the account or certificate is maintained, and the name and address of every person authorized to make withdrawals from such account.)

b.   What safe deposit box or boxes or other depository or depositories have you kept or used for your securities, cash, or other valuables within the two years immediately preceding the filing of the original petition herein? (Give the name and address of the bank or other depository, the name in which each box or other depository was kept, the name and address of every person who had the right of access thereto, a description of the contents thereof, and, if the box has been surrendered, state when surrendered or, if transferred, when transferred and the name and address of the transferee.)

8. Property held for another person.

What property do you hold for any other person? (Give name and address of each person, and describe the property, the amount or value thereof and all writings relating thereto.)

9. Property held by another person.

Is any other person holding anything of value in which you have an interest? (Give name and address, location and description of the property, and circumstances of the holding.)

10. Prior bankruptcy proceedings.

What cases under the Bankruptcy Act or title 11, United States Code have previously been brought by or against you? (State the location of the bankruptcy court, the nature and number of the case, and whether a discharge was granted or denied, the case was dismissed, or a composition, arrangement, or plan was confirmed.)

11. Receiverships, general assignments, and other modes of liquidation.

a. Was any of your property, at the time of the filing of the original petition herein, in the hands of a receiver, trustee, or other liquidating agent? (If so, give a brief description of the property and the name and address of the receiver, trustee, or other agent, and, if the agent was appointed in a court proceeding, the name and location of the court, the title and number of the case, and the nature thereof.)

b. Have you made any assignment of your property for the benefit of your creditors, or any general settlement with your creditors, within the two years immediately preceding the filing of the original petition herein? (If so, give dates, the name and address of the assignee, and a brief statement of the terms of assignment or settlement.)

12. Suits, executions, and attachments.

a. Were you a party to any suit pending at the time of the filing of the original petition herein? (If so, give the name and location of the court and the title and nature of the proceeding.)

b. Were you a party to any suit terminated within the year immediately preceding the filing of the original petition herein? (If so, give the name and location of the court, the title and nature of the proceeding, and the result.)

c. Has any of your property been attached, garnished, or seized under any legal or equitable process within the year immediately preceding the filing of the original petition herein? (If so, describe the property seized or person garnished, and at whose suit.)

13. a. <u>Payments of loans, installment purchases and other debts.</u>

What payments in whole or in part have you made during the year immediately preceding the filing of the original petition herein on any of the following: (1) loans; (2) installment purchases of goods and services; and (3) other debts? (Give the names and addresses of the persons receiving payment, the amounts of the loans or other debts and of the purchase price of the goods and services, the dates of the original transactions, the amounts and dates of payments, and, if any of the payees are your relatives or insiders, the relationship; if the debtor is a partnership and any of the payees is or was a partner or a relative of a partner, state the relationship; if the debtor is a corporation and any of the payees is or was an officer, director, or stockholder, or a relative of an officer, director, or stockholder, state the relationship.)

b. <u>Setoffs.</u>

What debts have you owed to any creditor, including any bank, which were setoff by that creditor against a debt or deposit owing by the creditor to you during the year immediately preceding the filing of the original petition herein? (Give the names and addresses of the persons setting off such debts, the dates of the setoffs, the amounts of the debts owing by you and to you and, if any of the creditors are your relatives or insiders, the relationship.)

14. <u>Transfers of property.</u>

a. Have you made any gifts, other than ordinary and usual presents to family members and charitable donations during the year immediately preceding the filing of the original petition herein? (If so, give names and addresses of donees and dates, description, and value of gifts.)

b. Have you made any other transfer, absolute or for the purpose of security, or any other disposition which was not in the ordinary course of business during the year immediately preceding the filing of the original petition herein? (Give a description of the property, the date of the transfer or disposition, to whom transferred or how disposed of, and state whether the transferee is a relative, partner, shareholder, officer, director, or insider, the consideration, if any, received for the property, and the disposition of such consideration.)

15. Accounts and other receivables.

Have you assigned, either absolutely or as security, any of your accounts or other receivables during the year immediately preceding the filing of the original petition herein? (If so, give names and addresses of assignees.)

16. Repossessions and returns.

Has any property been returned to, or repossessed by, the seller, lessor, or a secured party during the year immediately preceding the filing of the original petition herein? (If so, give particulars, including the name and address of the party getting the property and its description and value.)

17. Business leases.

If you are a tenant of business property, what is the name and address of your landlord, the amount of your rental, the date to which rent had been paid at the time of the filing of the original petition herein, and the amount of security held by the landlord?

18. Losses.

a. Have you suffered any losses from fire, theft, or gambling during the year immediately preceding the filing of the original petition herein?

(If so, give particulars, including dates, names, and places, and the amounts of money or value and general description of property lost.)

b. Was the loss covered in whole or part by insurance? (If so, give particulars.)

19. Withdrawals.

a. If you are an individual proprietor of your business, what personal withdrawals of any kind have you made from the business during the year immediately preceding the filing of the original petition herein?

b. If the debtor is a partnership or corporation, what withdrawals, in any form (including compensation, bonuses or loans), have been made or received by any member of the partnership, or by any officer, director, insider, managing executive, or shareholder of the corporation, during the year immediately preceding the filing of the original petition herein? (Give the name and designation or relationship to the debtor of each person, the dates and amounts of withdrawals, and the nature or purpose thereof.)

20. Payments or transfers to attorneys.

a. Have you consulted an attorney during the year immediately preceding or since the filing of the original petition herein? (Give date, name, and address.)

b. Have you during the year immediately preceding or since the filing of the original petition herein paid any money or transferred any property to the attorney, or to any other person on his behalf? (If so, give particulars, including amount paid or value of property transferred and date of payment or transfer.)

c. Have you, either during the year immediately preceding or since the filing of the original petition herein, agreed to pay any money or transfer any property to an attorney at law, or to any other person on his behalf? (If so, give particulars, including amount and terms of obligation.)

(If the debtor is a partnership or corporation, the following additional questions should be answered.)

21. Members of partnership; officers, directors, managers, and principal stockholders of corporation.

a. What is the name and address of each member of the partnership, or the name, title, and address of each officer, director, insider, and managing executive, and of each stockholder holding 20 percent or more of the issued and outstanding stock, of the corporation?

b. During the year immediately preceding the filing of the original petition herein, has any member withdrawn from the partnership, or any officer, director, insider, or managing executive of the corporation terminated his relationship, or any stockholder holding 20 percent or more of the issued stock disposed of more than 50 percent of his holdings? (If so, give name and address and reason for withdrawal, termination, or disposition, if known.)

c. Has any person acquired or disposed of 20 percent or more of the stock of the corporation during the year immediately preceding the filing of the petition? (If so, give name and address and particulars.)

I, ... , declare under penalty of perjury that I
have read the answers contained in the foregoing statement of affairs and
that they are true and correct to the best of my knowledge, information,
and belief.

Executed on . . . .

Signature: . . . .

[Person declaring for partnership or corporation should indicate
position or relationship to debtor.]

ADVISORY COMMITTEE NOTE

Many of the questions on this form are the same as on Form No. 7,
Statement of Financial Affairs for Debtor Not Engaged in Business.

The question regarding loans repaid (#13) includes installment credit sales of
goods or services. The information is helpful with respect to possible preferences.

Information regarding leases (#17) may be helpful with respect to lease
termination or extension and whether the landlord may be holding a deposit.

FORM 9.--List of Creditors Holding 20 Largest
Unsecured Claims

[Caption as in Form No. 2]

List of Creditors Holding 20 Largest Unsecured Claims

Following is the list of the Debtor's creditors holding the 20 largest
unsecured claims which is prepared in accordance with Rule 1007(d) for
filing in this chapter 11 [or chapter 9] case. The list does not include (1)
those persons who come within the definition of insider set forth in 11
U.S.C. § 101(25), (2) secured creditors unless the value of the collateral is
such that the unsecured deficiency places the creditor among the holders of
the 20 largest unsecured claims, or (3) governmental units.

(1)	(2)	(3)	(4)	(5)
Name of creditor and complete mailing address including zip code	Name, telephone number and complete mailing address including zip code of employee, agent or department of creditor familiar with claim who may be contacted	Nature of claim (trade debt, bank loan, type of judgment, etc.)	Indicate if claim is contingent, unliquidated, disputed or subject to set-off	Amount of claim [if secured also state value of security]

Date: . . . .

. . . .

Debtor.

ADVISORY COMMITTEE NOTE

This form is for use in chapter 11 reorganization and chapter 9 municipality debt adjustment cases to enable the appointment, pursuant to §§ 1102 and 901 of the Code, of a committee of unsecured creditors. The information contained on the form is to assist in expediting the formation of the committee and to assure adequate creditor representation.

In accordance with § 1102 of the Code, the form indicates that insiders should not be listed. "Insiders" is defined in § 101(25) of the Code to include, inter alia, persons who are related to the debtor, are partners, officers, directors, affiliates as further defined in § 101(2) of the Code, or are otherwise in control of the debtor. Reference should be made to § 101 for the complete listing of insiders.

The nature of the claim should be specified to indicate whether it is an institutional debt, a trade debt for merchandise or supplies, a debt based on a judgment and the underlying basis for the judgment, or the like.

In column (2), it is important to provide specific information with respect to the person to be contacted. In order to form the committee it may be necessary to write or telephone the creditors. If the creditor company is a large organization individual contact may otherwise be difficult or impossible.

A secured creditor should be listed among the 20 largest unsecured creditors only if that creditor is sufficiently undersecured so as to fall within that category.

Form No. 11.—Involuntary Case: Creditors' Petition

[Caption as in Form No. 1]

Involuntary Case: Creditors' Petition

1. Petitioners, ..., of *

................., and ...., of *

................., and ...., of *

................., are creditors of ....,

of * .... [include county], holding claims against the

debtor, not contingent as to liability, amounting in the aggregate, in excess

of the value of any lien held by them on the debtor's property securing such

claims, to at least $5000. The nature and amount of petitioners' claims are

as follows: ....

....

....

2. The debtor's principal place of business [or principal assets or

domicile or residence] has been within this district for the 180 days

preceding the filing of this petition [or for a longer portion of the 180 days

preceding the filing of this petition than in any other district].

3. The debtor is a person against whom an order for relief may be

entered under title 11, United States Code.

4. [The debtor is generally not paying its debts as they become due as indicated by the following . . . `. . . . . . . . . . . . . . . . . . . . . . . . . . . . . . .`

. . . .]

or [Within 120 days preceding the filing of this petition, a custodian was appointed for or has taken possession of substantially all of the property of the debtor, as follows:

. . . .

. . . .]

WHEREFORE petitioners pray that an order of relief be entered against . . . . under chapter 7 [or 11] of title 11, United States Code.

Signed: . . . . ,
<u>Attorney for Petitioners.</u>
Address: . . . .
. . . .
[Petitioners sign if not
<u>represented by attorney]</u>
. . . . ,
. . . . ,
<u>Petitioners.</u>

I, ... , one of the petitioners named in the foregoing petition, declare under penalty of perjury that the foregoing is true and correct according to the best of my knowledge, information, and belief.

Executed on . . . .

Signature: . . . . ,
<u>Petitioner.</u>

ADVISORY COMMITTEE NOTE

The requisites for an involuntary petition are specified in § 303 of the Code.

28 U.S.C. § 1746 permits the unsworn declaration in lieu of a verification. See Advisory Committee Note to Form No. 1.

Form No. 12.--Involuntary Case Against Partnership:
Partner's Petition

[Caption as in Form No. 1]

Involuntary Case Against Partnership: Partner's Petition

1.   Petitioner, ... , of

* . . . . is one of the general partners

of . . . . , a partnership, of

* . . . . [include county]

2.   The other general partners of the debtor are

. . . . , of * . . . .

and . . . . of * . . . .

3.   The debtor has had its principal place of business [or its principal assets or its domicile or its residence] within this district for the 180 days preceding the filing of this petition [or for a longer portion of the 180 days preceding the filing of this petition than in any other district].

4.   The debtor is a person against whom an order for relief may be entered under title 11, United States Code.

5.   [The debtor is generally not paying its debts as they become due as indicated by the following . . . .] or [Within 120 days preceding the filing of this petition, a custodian was appointed for or has taken possession of substantially all of the property of the debtor, as follows:

---

*   State mailing address.

. . . .

. . . .]

WHEREFORE, petitioner prays that an order of relief be entered against . . . . under chapter 7 [or 11] of title 11, United States Code.

Signed: . . . . ,
<u>Attorney for Petitioner.</u>
Address: . . . . ,
. . . . ,
[Petitioner signs if not
<u>represented by attorney]</u>
. . . . ,
<u>Petitioner.</u>

I, ..., the petitioner named in the foregoing petition, declare under penalty of perjury that the foregoing is true and correct according to the best of my knowledge, information and belief.

Executed on . . . .

Signature: . . . . ,
<u>Petitioner.</u>

ADVISORY COMMITTEE NOTE

Pursuant to § 303(b)(3)(A) of the Code, a petition by fewer than all of the general partners seeking an order for relief with respect to the partnership is treated as an involuntary petition. It is adversarial in character because not all of the partners are joining in the petition.

Section 303(b)(3)(B) permits a petition against the partnership if relief has been ordered under the Code with respect to all of the general partners. In that event, the petition may be filed by a general partner, a trustee of a general partner's estate, or a creditor of the partnership. This form may be adapted for use in that type of case.

28 U.S.C. § 1472(1) specifies the proper venue alternatives for all persons, including partnerships, as domicile, residence, principal place of business or location of principal assets. These options are set forth in paragraph (3) of the form. The paragraph may be adapted for use when venue is based on a pending case commenced by an affiliate pursuant to 28 U.S.C. § 1472(2).

Form No. 13.—Summons to Debtor.

[Caption as in Form No. 1]

Summons

To the above-named debtor:

A petition under title 11, United States Code having been filed against you on . . . . , in this bankruptcy court, praying for an order for relief under 11 U.S.C. chapter 7 [or 11],

You are hereby summoned and required to file with this court and to serve upon . . . . , the petitioners' attorney, whose address is

. . . . , a motion or an answer* to the petition which is herewith served upon you, on or before . . . . If you fail to do so, the order for relief will be entered.

. . . . ,
Clerk of the Bankruptcy Court.

By: . . . .
Deputy Clerk.

[SEAL OF THE UNITED STATES BANKRUPTCY COURT]

Date of issuance: . . . .

ADVISORY COMMITTEE NOTE

This form is to be used as provided in Rule 1010.

---

* If you make a motion, Bankruptcy Rule 1011 governs the time within which your answer must be served.

Form No. 14.—Order for Relief

[Caption as in Form No. 1]

Order for Relief

On consideration of the petition filed on . . . . against the

above-named debtor, an order for relief under chapter 7 [or 11] of title 11

of the United States Code is GRANTED.

Dated: . . . .

BY THE COURT

. . . .
Bankruptcy Judge.

ADVISORY COMMITTEE NOTE

This form is an adaptation of former Official Form No. 11. It is appropriate for use when relief is ordered on an involuntary petition filed under § 303 of the Code with respect to chapter 7 (liquidation) or chapter 11 (reorganization).

If a contested petition is tried by the court without a jury (or with an advisory jury), the findings of fact and conclusions of law thereon must be stated separately. See Rule 7052(a), which is made applicable to proceedings on a contested petition by Rule 1018.

Form No. 15.—Appointment of Committee of Unsecured Creditors in a Chapter 9 Municipality or Chapter 11 Reorganization Case

[Caption as in Form No. 1]

Appointment of Committee of Unsecured Creditors in a Chapter 9 Municipality or Chapter 11 Reorganization Case

The following creditors of the above-named debtor holding the 7

largest unsecured claims [or who are members of a committee organized by

creditors before the order for relief under chapter 9 (or 11) of the

Bankruptcy Code which was fairly chosen and is representative of the different kinds of claims to be represented and who are willing to serve are appointed to the committee of unsecured creditors:

1. . . . . of * . . . .
. . . .

2. . . . . of * . . . .
. . . .

3. . . . . of * . . . .
. . . .

4. . . . . of * . . . .
. . . .

5. . . . . of * . . . .
. . . .

6. . . . . of * . . . .
. . . .

7. . . . . of * . . . .
. . . .

Dated: . . . .

                                        BY THE COURT

                                        . . . .
                                        Bankruptcy Judge.

ADVISORY COMMITTEE NOTE

This form is new. Pursuant to § 1102 of the Code the court is to appoint a committee of unsecured creditors which ordinarily is to consist of the creditors holding the 7 largest claims and who are willing to serve. If, however, a committee has been organized prior to the filing of the petition, is representative and was fairly chosen, that committee may be continued as the official or statutory committee.

This form can be adapted for use by the United States trustee who, pursuant to § 151102 of the Code, will appoint the committee. It may also be adapted for use if the court (or United States trustee on order of the court) appoints any other committee, e.g., of equity security holders.

Pursuant to § 901(a) of the Code, the provisions of § 1102, including subsection (a)(1) apply in a case under chapter 9, Adjustment of Debts of Municipality. In a chapter 9 case, only the court will appoint the committee. There is no provision in chapter 15 for a United States trustee to have any appointing function in that type of a case.

Subsection (a)(1) of § 1102 is not applicable in a railroad reorganization case and, therefore, the court will not appoint an unsecured creditors' committee.

Form No. 16.—Order for Meeting of Creditors and Related Orders, Combined with Notice Thereof and of Automatic Stay

[Caption as in Form No. 1]

Order for Meeting of Creditors and Fixing Times for Filing Objections to Discharge and for Filing Complaints to Determine Dischargeability of Certain Debts, Combined with Notice Thereof and of Automatic Stay

To the debtor, his creditors, and other parties in interest:

An order for relief under 11 U.S.C. chapter 7 [or, 11, or 13] having

been entered on a petition filed by [or against] . . . . of

* . . . . , on . . . .

it is ordered, and notice is hereby given, that:

[MEETING OF CREDITORS]

1. A meeting of creditors pursuant to 11 U.S.C. § 341(a) has been

scheduled for . . . . at

. . . . . . o'clock . . . .m. at . . . .

* State mailing address.

* State mailing address.

2. The debtor shall appear in person [or, if the debtor is a partnership, by a general partner, or, if the debtor is a corporation, by its president or other executive officer] at that time and place for the purpose of being examined.

[DEADLINE TO OBJECT TO DISCHARGE OR DETERMINE
NONDISCHARGEABILITY OF CERTAIN DEBTS]

3. [If the debtor is an individual] .... is fixed as the last day for the filing of objections to the discharge of the debtor pursuant to 11 U.S.C. § 727.

4. [If the debtor is an individual] .... is fixed as the last day for the filing of a complaint to determine the dischargeability of any debt pursuant to 11 U.S.C. § 523(c).

[ADDITIONAL INFORMATION CONCERNING THE MEETING,
THE AUTOMATIC STAY AND THE DISCHARGE]

You are further notified that:

The meeting may be continued or adjourned from time to time by notice at the meeting, without further written notice to creditors.

At the meeting the creditors may file their claims, [elect a trustee as permitted by law, designate a person to supervise the meeting, elect a committee of creditors,] examine the debtor, and transact such other business as may properly come before the meeting.

As a result of the filing of the petition, certain acts and proceedings against the debtor and his property are stayed as provided in 11 U.S.C. § 362(a).

[If the debtor is an individual] If no objection to the discharge of the debtor is filed on or before the last day fixed therefor as stated in subparagraph 3 above, the debtor will be granted his discharge. If no complaint to determine the dischargeability of a debt under clause (2), (4), or (6) of 11 U.S.C. § 523(a) is filed within the time fixed therefor as stated in subparagraph 4 above, the debt may be discharged.

[FILING OF CLAIMS]

[For a chapter 7 or 13 case] In order to have his claim allowed so that he may share in any distribution from the estate, a creditor must file a claim, whether or not he is included in the list of creditors filed by the debtor. Claims which are not filed within 90 days following the above date set for the meeting of creditors will not be allowed, except as otherwise provided by law. A claim may be filed in the office of the clerk of the bankruptcy court on an official form prescribed for a proof of claim.

[If a no-asset or nominal asset case, the following paragraph may be used in lieu of the preceding paragraph.] It appears from the schedules of the debtor that there are no assets from which any dividend can be paid to creditors. It is unnecessary for any creditor to file his claim at this time in order to share in any distribution from the estate. If it subsequently appears that there are assets from which a dividend may be paid, creditors will be so notified and given an opportunity to file their claims.

[For a chapter 11 case] The debtor [or trustee] has filed or will file a list of creditors and equity security holders pursuant to Rule 1007. Any creditor holding a listed claim which is not listed as disputed, contingent, or unliquidated as to amount, may, but need not, file a proof of claim in this case. Creditors whose claims are not listed or whose claims are listed as disputed, contingent, or unliquidated as to amount and who desire to participate in the case or share in any distribution must file their proofs of

claim on or before . . . . , which date is hereby fixed as the last

day for filing a proof of claim [or, if appropriate, on or before a date to be

later fixed of which you will be notified]. Any creditor who desires to rely

on the list has the responsibility for determining that he is accurately

listed.

[OBJECTION TO CLAIM OF EXEMPTIONS]

Unless the court extends the time, any objection to the debtor's claim

of exempt property (Schedule B-4) must be filed within 30 days after the

conclusion of the meeting of creditors.

[TRUSTEE]

[If appropriate] . . . . of*

. . . . has been appointed

[interim] trustee of the estate of the above-named debtor.

Dated: . . . .

BY THE COURT

. . . . ,
Bankruptcy Judge.

ADVISORY COMMITTEE NOTE

This form can be used for cases filed under chapter 7, 11, or 13. It conforms with Rule 2003 which specifies that the court is to call the meeting of creditors even though, under the Code, it may not preside at such meeting.

This form revises former Official Form No. 12. The alternative paragraph is to be used when the court exercises the option under Rule 2002(e) to notify the creditors that no dividends are to be anticipated and no claims need be filed.

---

*   State mailing address.

Form No. 19.--Proof of Claim

[Caption as in Form No. 2]

Proof of Claim

1. [If claimant is an individual claiming for himself] The undersigned, ... who is the claimant herein, resides at * . . . .

[If claimant is a partnership claiming through a member] The undersigned, ... , who resides at *. , is a member of . . . . , a partnership, composed of the undersigned and . . . . , of *. . . . ., and doing business at * . . . . , and is authorized to make this proof of claim in behalf of the partnership.

[If claimant is a corporation claiming through an authorized officer] The undersigned, ... , who resides at * . . . . , is the . . . . of . . . . , a corporation organized under the laws of . . . . and doing business at *. . . . . , and is authorized to make this proof of claim on behalf of the corporation.

[If claim is made by agent] The undersigned, ... , who resides at * . . . . , is the agent of . . . . , of *. . . . . , and is authorized to make this proof of claim on behalf of the claimant.

2. The debtor was, at the time of the filing of the petition initiating

---

* State mailing address.

this case, and still is indebted [or liable] to this claimant, in the sum of
$ . . . .

3. The consideration for this debt [or ground of liability] is as
follows: . . . .
. . . .

[If filed in a chapter 7 or 13 case] This claim consists of $ . . . .
in principal amount and $ . . . . in additional charges [or no additional
charges]. [Itemize all charges in addition to principal amount of debt, state
basis for inclusion and computation, and set forth any other consideration
relevant to the legality of the charge.] . . . .
. . . .
. . . .

4. [If the claim is founded on writing] The writing on which this
claim is founded (or a duplicate thereof) is attached hereto [or cannot be
attached for the reason set forth in the statement attached hereto].

5. [If appropriate] This claim is founded on an open account, which
became [or will become] due on . . . . , as shown by the itemized
statement attached hereto. Unless it is attached hereto or its absence is
explained in an attached statement, no note or other negotiable instrument
has been received for the account or any part of it.

6. No judgment has been rendered on the claim except . . . .
. . . .

7. The amount of all payments on this claim has been credited and
deducted for the purpose of making this proof of claim.

8. This claim is not subject to any setoff or counterclaim except . . .
. . . .

9. No security interest is held for this claim except . . . .

. . . . [If security interest in property of the debtor is claimed]
The undersigned claims the security interest under the writing referred to
in paragraph 4 hereof [or under a separate writing which (or a duplicate of
which) is attached hereto, or under a separate writing which cannot be
attached hereto for the reason set forth in the statement attached
hereto]. Evidence of perfection of such security interest is also attached
hereto.

10. This claim is a general unsecured claim, except to the extent that
the security interest, if any, described in paragraph 9 is sufficient to
satisfy the claim. [If priority is claimed, state the amount and basis
thereof.] . . . .

. . . .

Dated: . . . .

Signed: . . . .

Penalty for Presenting Fraudulent Claim. Fine of not more than
$5,000 or imprisonment for not more than 5 years or both — Title 18,
U.S.C., § 152.

ADVISORY COMMITTEE NOTE

This form is derived from former Official Form No. 15. It may be used by
any claimant, including a wage earner for whom alternative short forms have been
specially prepared (Form Nos. 20 and No. 21), or by an agent or attorney for any
claimant. Such a combined form is commonly used in practice.

If a security interest in the debtor's property is claimed, paragraph 9
requires that any security agreement (if not included in the writing on which the
claim is founded and which is required by paragraph 4 to be attached) be attached
to the proof of claim or that the reason why it cannot be attached be set forth.
Paragraph 9 further requires evidence of perfection of the security interest to be
attached to the proof of claim. See the Note to Rule 3001(d) as to what
constitutes satisfactory evidence of perfection. The information so required will

expedite determination of the validity of any claimed security interest as against the trustee.

Paragraph 10, requiring an explicit statement as to whether the claim is filed as a general, priority, or secured claim, will facilitate administration and minimize troublesome litigation over the question whether a proof of claim was intended as a waiver of security. See, e.g., United States National Bank v. Chase National Bank, 331 U.S. 28, 35–36 (1947); 3 Collier, Bankruptcy ¶ 57.07[3.1] (14th ed. 1961).

Form No. 20.--Proof of Claim for Wages, Salary, or Commissions

[Caption as in Form No. 2]

Proof of Claim for Wages, Salary, or Commissions

1.   The undersigned, ... , claimant herein resides

at . . . . and has

social security number . . . .

2.   The debtor owes the claimant

computed as follows: $ . . . .

(a) wages salary, or commissions for

services performed from . . . .

to . . . . , at the following rate

or rates of compensation . . . .

. . . . $ . . . .

[if appropriate]

(b) allowances and benefits, such as

vacation, severance and sick leave pay

[specify]

. . . .

. . . . $ . . . .

Total amount claimed $ . . . .

3. The claimant demands priority to the extent permitted by 11 U.S.C. § 507(a)(3).

4. The claimant has received no payment, no security, and no check or other evidence of this debt except as follows: ....

Dated: ....

Signed: ....
<u>Claimant.</u>

<u>Presenting Fraudulent Claim.</u> Fine of not more than $5,000 or imprisonment for not more than 5 years or both - Title 18, U.S.C., § 152.

ADVISORY COMMITTEE NOTE

This form is an adaptation of former Official Form No. 16 for the exclusive use of claimants for personal earnings in cases under the Code. Its limited purpose permits elimination of recitals that are appropriate for other classes of claimants. Most claimants using the form will be entitled to priority under § 507(a)(3) of the Code. If the claim as filed includes an amount not entitled to priority because, for example, not earned within the applicable 90 day period, reference to payroll records will ordinarily permit determination of the amount of the priority, if any, to which the claimant is entitled. If such records are unavailable, the claimant may be required to supply additional information as a condition to allowance of the claim with priority.

Form No. 21.—Proof of Multiple Claims for Wages,
Salary, or Commissions

[Caption as in Form No. 2]

<u>Proof of Multiple Claims for Wages, Salary, or Commissions</u>

1. The undersigned, ..., whose address is *......................., is the agent of the claimants listed in the statement appended to this proof of claim and is authorized to make this proof of claims on their behalf.

---

* State mailing address.

3.   The claimants demand priority to the extent permitted by 11
U.S.C. § 507(a)(3) and (4).

4.   The claimants have received no payment, no security, and no
check or other evidence of this debt except as follows: . . . .
. . . .
. . . .

   Dated: . . . .

                                Signed: . . . .

   Penalty for Presenting Fraudulent Claim.   Fine of not more than
$5,000 or imprisonment for not more than 5 years or both - Title 18,
U.S.C., § 152.

Statement of Wage Claims

Name, Address, & Social Security Numbers	Dates services rendered, rates of pay, and fringe benefits	Contributions to employee benefit plans	Amounts Claimed

ADVISORY COMMITTEE NOTE

This form is an alternative for Form No. 20 provided for use when there are
numerous claimants for wages, salary, or commissions against a debtor's estate
and they wish to have their proofs of claim executed and filed by a common
agent.   Use of the form should not only simplify the filing procedure for the
claimants but facilitate the handling of the claims by the court.

Form No. 22.—Order Appointing Interim Trustee and
Fixing Amount of Bond

[Caption às in Form No. 1]

Order Appointing Interim Trustee and Fixing Amount of Bond

(1) . . . ., of * . . . .,

is hereby appointed interim trustee of the estate of the above-named

debtor.

(2) [If blanket bond has not been authorized or filed] The amount of

the bond of the interim trustee is fixed at $ . . . .

Dated: . . . .

BY THE COURT

. . . .,
Bankruptcy Judge.

ADVISORY COMMITTEE NOTE

This form is for use only in a chapter 7 case. Pursuant to § 701 of the Code, the court is to appoint an interim trustee promptly after the order for relief. The interim trustee becomes the trustee if no trustee is elected. The interim trustee is to be disinterested as defined in § 101(13) and a member of the panel of private trustees established under 28 U.S.C. § 604(f). If the chapter 7 case was converted from chapter 11 or 13 the court may appoint as interim trustee the person serving as trustee in the prior case. Section 322(b) requires the court to determine the amount of the bond and sufficiency of the surety. See Form Nos. 23 and 25.

---

* State mailing address.

Form No. 23.—Order Approving Election of Trustee and
Fixing Amount of Bond

[Caption as in Form No. 2]

Order Approving Election of Trustee and Fixing Amount of Bond

(1) ...., of *..........................., is

hereby approved as the elected [or is hereby appointed] trustee of the

estate of the above-named debtor.

(2) The amount of the bond of the trustee is fixed at $ .... [or

A blanket bond has been authorized and filed].

Dated: ....

BY THE COURT

.................,
Bankruptcy Judge.

ADVISORY COMMITTEE NOTE

Creditors may elect a trustee pursuant to § 702 of the Code. If none is
elected the interim trustee becomes the trustee.

---

* State mailing address.

Form No. 24.--Notice to Trustee of Selection and of Time Fixed for Filing a Complaint Objecting to Discharge of Debtor

[Caption as in Form No. 2]

Notice to Trustee of Selection and of Time Fixed for
Filing a Complaint Objecting to Discharge of Debtor

To . . . ., of *. :

You are hereby notified of your election [or appointment] as trustee of the estate of the above-named debtor. The amount of your bond has been fixed at $ . . . . You are required to notify . . . ., Bankruptcy Judge, at . . . ., in writing within five days following receipt of this notice of your acceptance or rejection of the office. If you accept, your bond must be filed with the court on or before . . . .

[If appropriate] You are further notified that . . . . has been fixed as the last day for the filing by you or any other party in interest of a complaint objecting to the discharge of the debtor.

Dated: . . . .

. . . .
Clerk of the
Bankruptcy Court.

ADVISORY COMMITTEE NOTE

This form is to be used in giving the notice required by Rule 2008. If a blanket bond has been authorized pursuant to Rule 2010(a), the second sentence of the form and the last sentence of the first paragraph may be deleted.

---

* State mailing address.

Form No. 26.--Certificate of Retention of Debtor in Possession

[Caption as in Form No. 1]

Certificate of Retention of Debtor in Possession

I hereby certify that the above-named debtor continues in possession

of its estate as debtor in possession, no trustee having been appointed.

Dated: . . . .

. . . . ,
Clerk of the Bankruptcy Court.

ADVISORY COMMITTEE NOTE

This form may be used in chapter 11 reorganization cases. Usually, a trustee
will not be appointed in which event the debtor is automatically continued in
possession pursuant to § 1101(a) of the Code.

When evidence of debtor in possession status is required, this certificate may
be used in accordance with Rule 2011.

Form No. 27.--Discharge of Debtor

[Caption as in Form No. 1]

Discharge of Debtor

It appearing that the person named above has filed a petition

commencing a case under title 11, United States Code on . . . . , and

an order for relief was entered under chapter 7 and that no complaint

objecting to the discharge of the debtor was filed within the time fixed by

the court [or that a complaint objecting to discharge of the debtor was

filed and, after due notice and hearing, was not sustained]; it is ordered

that

1. The above-named debtor is released from all dischargeable debts.

2. Any judgment heretofore or hereafter obtained in any court other

than this court is null and void as a determination of the personal liability of the debtor with respect to any of the following:

(a)   debts dischargeable under 11 U.S.C. § 523;

(b)   unless heretofore or hereafter determined by order of this court to be nondischargeable, debts alleged to be excepted from discharge under clauses (2), (4) and (6) of 11 U.S.C. § 523(a);

(c)   debts determined by this court to be discharged.

3.   All creditors whose debts are discharged by this order and all creditors whose judgments are declared null and void by paragraph 2 above are enjoined from instituting or continuing any action or employing any process or engaging in any act to collect such debts as personal liabilities of the above-named debtor.

Dated: . . . .

BY THE COURT

. . . .
Bankruptcy Judge.

ADVISORY COMMITTEE NOTE

This form is a revision of former Official Form No. 24. It takes into account the features of § 523 of the Code which in turn, were derived from the 1970 amendments to the Bankruptcy Act.

Form No. 28.--Order and Notice for Hearing on
Disclosure Statement

[Caption as in Form No. 1]

Order and Notice for Hearing on Disclosure Statement

To the debtor, its creditors, and other parties in interest:

A disclosure statement and a plan under chapter 11 [or chapter 9] of

the Bankruptcy Code having been filed by . . . .

on . . . . ,

it is ordered and notice is hereby given, that:

1. The hearing to consider the approval of the disclosure statement

shall be held at . . . . ,

on . . . . , at . . . . . . o'clock . . . .m.

2. . . . . is fixed as the the last day for filing and serving

in accordance with Rule 3017(a) written objections to the disclosure

statement.

3. Within . . . . days after entry of this order, the debtor in

possession [or trustee or debtor or . . . . , proponent of the plan]

shall transmit the disclosure statement and plan to the debtor, trustee,

each committee appointed pursuant to § 1102 of the Code, the Securities

and Exchange Commission and any party in interest who has requested or

requests in writing a copy of the disclosure statement and plan.

4. Requests for copies of the disclosure statement and plan shall be

mailed to the debtor in possession [or trustee or debtor or . . . .]

at * . . . .

Dated: . . . .

_____
* State mailing address.

BY THE COURT

. . . .

<u>Bankruptcy Judge.</u>

ADVISORY COMMITTEE NOTE

This form is new and is related to Rule 3017(a). Section 1125 of the Code requires court approval of a disclosure statement before votes may be solicited for or against a plan in either chapter 11, reorganization or chapter 9, municipality cases. Before the court may approve a disclosure statement it must find that it contains adequate information to enable creditors whose votes will be solicited to be able to make an informed judgment about the plan.

Objections may be filed to the disclosure statement. Rule 3017(a) specifies that the court may fix a time for filing of objections or they can be filed at any time prior to approval of the statement.

Rule 3017(a) also specifies the persons who are to receive copies of the statement and plan prior to the hearing. These documents will not be sent to all parties in interest because at this stage of the case it could be unnecessarily expensive and confusing. However, any party in interest may request copies. The request should be made in writing (Rule 3017(a)), and sent to the person mailing the statement and plan which, as the form indicates, would usually be the proponent of the plan.

Form No. 29.--Order Approving Disclosure Statement and Fixing Time
for Filing Acceptances or Rejections of Plan,
Combined with Notice Thereof

[Caption as in Form No. 1]

<u>Order Approving Disclosure Statement and Fixing
Time for Filing Acceptances or Rejections
of Plan, Combined with Notice Thereof</u>

A disclosure statement under chapter 11 of the Bankruptcy Code

having been filed by . . . ., on . . . .

[if appropriate, and by . . . ., on . . . .],

referring to a plan under chapter 11 of the Code filed by . . . .,

on . . . . [if appropriate, and by . . . .,

on . . . . respectively] [if appropriate, as modified by a

modification filed on . . . .]; and

It having been determined after hearing on notice that the disclosure statement [or statements] contain [s] adequate information;

It is ordered, and notice is hereby given, that:

A.   The disclosure statement filed by . . . . dated . . . . [if appropriate, and by . . . . , dated . . . .] is [are] approved.

B.   . . . . is fixed as the last day for filing written acceptances or rejections of the plan [or plans] referred to above.

C.   Within . . . . days after the entry of this order, the plan [or plans] [or a summary or summaries thereof approved by the court], [if appropriate a summary approved by the court of its opinion, if any, dated . . . ., approving the disclosure statement [or statements]], the disclosure statement [or statements] and a ballot conforming to Official Form No. 29 shall be transmitted by mail to creditors, equity security holders and other parties in interest as provided in Rule 3017(d).

D.   If acceptances are filed for more than one plan, preferences among the plans so accepted may be indicated.

[If appropriate] E.   . . . . is fixed for the hearing on confirmation of the plan [or plans].

[If appropriate] F.   . . . . is fixed as the last day for filing and serving pursuant to Rule 3020(b)(1) written objections to confirmation of the plan.

Dated: . . . .

BY THE COURT

. . . .
Bankruptcy Judge.

[If the court directs that a copy of the opinion should be transmitted in lieu of or in addition to the summary thereof, the appropriate change should be made in paragraph C of this order.]

ADVISORY COMMITTEE NOTE

This form is new. As provided in § 1125 of the Code, a disclosure statement must be approved by the court prior to the solicitation of votes to a plan. This form may be used for such approval, to give notice of the time fixed for filing acceptances or rejections and the time fixed for the hearing on confirmation if such a time has been fixed.

Form No. 30.--Ballot for Accepting or Rejecting Plan

[Caption as in Form No. 1]

Ballot for Accepting or Rejecting Plan

Filed by . . . . on . . . .

The plan referred to in this ballot can be confirmed by the court and thereby made binding on you if it is accepted by the holders of two-thirds in amount and more than one-half in number of claims in each class and the holders of two-thirds in amount of equity security interests in each class voting on the plan. In the event the requisite acceptances are not obtained, the court may nevertheless confirm the plan if the court finds that the plan accords fair and equitable treatment to the class rejecting it. To have your vote count you must complete and return this ballot.

[If equity security holder] The undersigned, the holder of [state number] . . . . shares of [describe type] . . . . stock of the above-named debtor, represented by Certificate(s) No. . . . . , registered in the name of . . . .

[If bondholder, debenture holder, or other debt security holder] The undersigned, the holder of [state unpaid principal amount] $ . . . . of [describe security] . . . . of the above-named debtor, with a stated maturity date of . . . . [if applicable registered in the name of . . . .] [if applicable bearing serial number(s) . . . .]

[If holder of general claim] The undersigned, a creditor of the above-named debtor in the unpaid principal amount of $ . . . . ,

[Check One Box]

/_/   Accepts

/_/   Rejects

the plan for the reorganization of the above-named debtor.

[If more than one plan is accepted, the following may but need not be completed.] The undersigned prefers the plans accepted in the following order: [Identify plans]

1.   . . . .

2.   . . . .

Dated: . . . .

Print or type name: . . . .

Signed: . . . .

[If appropriate] By: . . . .

as: . . . .

Address: . . . .

. . . .

Return this ballot on or before ....

to:

Name: ....

Address: ....

ADVISORY COMMITTEE NOTE

This form may be modified as necessary to include identification of as many plans as may have been transmitted on which a vote will be taken.

The form can also be modified to take account of the types of parties who will vote as among equity security holders (see § 101(15) of the Code for definition of equity security), security holders (see § 101(35) for definition of security), secured creditors and unsecured creditors.

Before the form is transmitted, the blanks identifying the plan and the name and address of the person to whom it should be returned should be completed for the information of creditors and equity security holders.

Form No. 31.—Order Confirming Plan

[Caption as in Form No. 1]

Order Confirming Plan

The plan under chapter 11 of the Bankruptcy Code filed by ....

..............., on .... [if appropriate,

as modified by a modification filed on ....,] or a summary

thereof having been transmitted to creditors and equity security holders;

and

It having been determined after hearing on notice that:

1.   The plan has been accepted in writing by the creditors and equity security holders whose acceptance is required by law; and

2.   The provisions of chapter 11 of the Code have been complied with; that the plan has been proposed in good faith and not by any means forbidden by law; and

3.   Each holder of a claim or interest has accepted the plan [or will receive or retain under the plan property of a value, as of the effective date of the plan, that is not less than the amount that such holder would receive or retain if the debtor were liquidated under chapter 7 of the Code on such date] [or The plan does not discriminate unfairly, and is fair and equitable, with respect to each class of claims or interests that is impaired under, and has not accepted the plan]; and

4.   All payments made or promised by the debtor or by a person issuing securities or acquiring property under the plan or by any other person for services or for costs and expenses in, or in connection with, the plan and incident to the case, have been fully disclosed to the court and are reasonable or, if to be fixed after confirmation of the plan, will be subject to the approval of the court; and

5.   The identity, qualifications, and affiliations of the persons who are to be directors or officers, or voting trustees, if any, of the debtor [and an affiliate of the debtor participating in a joint plan with the debtor] [or a successor to the debtor under the plan], after confirmation of the plan, have been fully disclosed, and the appointment of such persons to such offices, or their continuance therein, is equitable, and consistent with the interests of the creditors and equity security holders and with public policy; and

6.   The identity of any insider that will be employed or retained by the debtor and his compensation have been fully disclosed; and

7.   [If applicable] Any regulatory commission with jurisdiction, after confirmation of the plan, over the rates of the debtor has approved any rate change provided for in the plan [or any rate change is expressly conditioned on approval of any regulatory agency having jurisdiction over the rates of the debtor; and]

8.   [If appropriate] Confirmation of the plan is not likely to be followed by the liquidation, or the need for further financial reorganization, of the debtor or any successor to the debtor under the plan;]:

It is ordered that:

The plan filed by . . . . ,

on . . . . , a copy of which plan is attached hereto, is confirmed.

Dated: . . . .

BY THE COURT

. . . .
Bankruptcy Judge.

ADVISORY COMMITTEE NOTE

The order of confirmation specifies those matters heard and determined by the court at the hearing on confirmation which are required by the Code in order for a plan to be confirmed.

In the case of an individual chapter 11 debtor, Form No. 27 may be adapted for use together with this form.

Form No. 32.—Notice of Filing Final Account

[Caption as in Form No. 1]

Notice of Filing Final Account[s] of Trustee,
of <u>Hearing on Applications for Compensation</u> [and
of <u>Hearing on Abandonment of Property by the Trustee</u>]

To the creditors:

The final report[s] and account[s] of the trustee in this case having

been filed,

Notice is hereby given, that there will be a hearing held at . . . . ,

. . . . , on . . . . , at . . . . ,

o'clock . . . .m., for the purpose [<u>as appropriate</u>] of examining and passing

on the report[s] and account[s], acting on applications for compensation,

and transacting such other business as may properly come before the

court. Attendance by creditors is welcomed but not required.

The following applications for compensation have been filed:

Applicants	Commission or Fees	Expenses
. . . . <u>Interim Trustee</u>	$	$ . . . . . .
. . . . <u>Trustee</u>	$	$ . . . . . .
. . . . <u>Attorney for debtor</u>	$	$ . . . . . .
. . . . <u>Attorney for interim trustee</u>	$	$. . . . . .
. . . . <u>Attorney for trustee</u>	$	$ . . . . . .
. . . . <u>Attorney for petitioning creditors</u>	$	$ . . . . . .
. . . .	$	$ . . . . . .

Creditors may be heard before the applications are determined.

The account of the trustee shows total receipts of $ . . . . and total disbursements of $ . . . . . . The balance on hand is $ . . . .

In addition to expenses of administration as may be allowed by the court, liens and priority claims totalling $ . . . . . . , must be paid in advance of any dividend to general creditors.

Claims of general creditors totalling $ . . . . . . have been allowed.

[If appropriate] The trustee's application to abandon the following property will be heard and acted on:

. . . .

. . . .

The debtor has [not] been discharged.

Dated: . . . .

BY THE COURT

. . . . ,
Bankruptcy Judge.

ADVISORY COMMITTEE NOTE

This form is adapted from former Official Form No. 29 which is an adaptation of a form which has been made available to bankruptcy judges by the Administrative Office of the United States Courts and used for a number of years.

Form No. 33.—Final Decree

[Caption as in Form No. 1]

Final Decree

The estate of the above-named debtor having been fully administered [if appropriate and the deposit required by the plan having been distributed] It is ordered that:

1.   [If applicable] ....

is hereby discharged as trustee of the estate of the above–named debtor

and the bond is cancelled.

2.   [Add provisions by way of injunction or otherwise as may be

equitable.]

3.   The chapter 7, [or 9 or 11 or 13] case of the above–named debtor

is closed.

Dated: ....

BY THE COURT

.................,
Bankruptcy Judge.

ADVISORY COMMITTEE NOTE

This form is to be used in conjunction with Rule 3022. The final decree may discharge the trustee if one was appointed and if the trustee had not been discharged at an earlier time.

Section 350 of the Code requires the court to close the case after an estate has been fully administered and the trustee discharged. That section is applicable to chapter 7, 9, 11 and 13 cases and this form may be adapted to the circumstances of the particular case.

Glossary

Accountant An accountant, as used in the Bankruptcy Code, means accountant authorized under applicable law to practice public accounting, and includes professional accounting association, corporation, or partnership, if so authorized.

Adjudication An order, whether by decree or operation of law in proceedings under the Bankruptcy Act (filed before October 1, 1979), declaring that a petitioner is bankrupt. The Bankruptcy Code replaces the term adjudication with "order for relief."

Administrative expenses The actual, necessary costs of preserving the estate, including wages, salaries, and commissions for services rendered after the commencement of the case, are considered administrative expenses. Compensation awarded a professional person, including accountants and attorneys, for postpetition services is an expense of administration.

Adequate protection Holders of secured claims, lessors, co-owners, conditional vendors, consignors, and so forth, are entitled to adequate protection of their interest in the property when such holders request relief from the automatic stay. Adequate protection is also required before the debtor or trustee can use, sell, or lease certain kinds of collateral or before a lien that is prior to or equal to the creditor's lien can be granted.

Arrangement An agreement between a debtor and its creditors, subject to court approval, wherein the debtor normally remains in business but secures an extension of time for payment, or a reduction in amount, or both, of all or part of its unsecured debts. Also was used to refer to the proceedings under Chapter XI of the Bankruptcy Act. (Filed before October 1, 1979).

Assignment A remedy available under state insolvency laws, many of which provide for judicial proceedings. The debtor voluntarily transfers title to assets to an assignee who then liquidates them and distributes the proceeds among the creditors. The debtor will not be discharged of any unpaid indebtedness.

Automatic Stay   A petition filed under the Bankruptcy Code automatically stays virtually all actions of creditors to collect prepetition debts. As a result of the stay, no party, with minor exceptions, having a security or adverse interest in the debtor's property can take any action that will interfere with the debtor or the debtor's property, regardless of where the property is located or who has possession, until the stay is modified or removed.

Bankruptcy   The proceedings initiated voluntarily by a financially troubled debtor, or involuntarily by creditors when the debtor is generally not paying debts as they become due, and involving the filing of a petition in a federal court under the Bankruptcy Code.

Bankruptcy Act   A federal statute enacted July 2, 1898, as Title 11 of the United States Code and amended more than ninety times, which is applicable to all cases filed before October 1, 1979, the date the Bankruptcy Reform Act of 1978 became law.

Bankruptcy Code   A federal statute, enacted October 1, 1979 as Title II of the United States Code by the Bankruptcy Reform Act of 1978 that is applicable to all cases filed on or after its enactment and that provides the basis for the federal bankruptcy system in effect today.

Bankruptcy Court   The United States Bankruptcy Court of trial jurisdiction. Responsible for all cases filed under chapters 7, 11, and 13 of the Bankruptcy Code.

Bankruptcy judge   The judge of the court of bankruptcy where a bankruptcy case is pending.

Bankruptcy Reform Act of 1978   The Act passed by and signed by the President on November 6, 1978, which provided for the new Bankruptcy Code, established the U.S. Trustee System in ten districts or groups of districts, and revised the bankruptcy court system.

Bankruptcy rules   Section 2075 of Title 28, chapter 131 provides that the Supreme Court shall have the power to prescribe the general rules, the forms to be used, and procedures to follow as long as these do not conflict with the provisions of the Bankruptcy Code. On April 25, 1983, the United States Supreme Court prescribed new Bankruptcy Rules that were reported to Congress and became effective on August 1, 1983.

Business bankrupt/debtor   A bankrupt/debtor whose financial problems result from some type of business activity.

Cash collateral   Cash collateral is cash, negotiable instruments, documents of title, securities, deposit accounts, or other cash equivalents where the estate and someone else have an interest in the property. Also included would be the proceeds of noncash collateral, such as inventory and accounts receivable, if converted to proceeds of the type defined as cash collateral, provided the proceeds are subject to the prepetition security interests.

Chapter X proceeding A corporate reorganization taken under Chapter X of the Bankruptcy Act (filed before October 1, 1979). Used mostly by large corporations with complex debt structures and with widely held public securities and replaced by chapter 11 of the Bankruptcy Code.

Chapter XI proceeding An arrangement under Chapter XI of the Bankruptcy Act was used mostly by businesses for the purpose of working out a settlement, with court approval, providing for creditors to agree to accept partial payment in satisfaction of their claims and/or an extension of the time for repayment. The provisions of Chapter XI applied only to unsecured creditors. Chapter XI was replaced with chapter 11 of the Bankruptcy Code.

Chapter 7 proceeding A liquidation voluntarily or involuntarily initiated under the provisions of the Bankruptcy Code on or after October 1, 1979 that provides for an orderly liquidation of the business or debtor's estate.

Chapter 11 proceeding A reorganization action, either voluntary or involuntary, initiated under the provisions of the Bankruptcy Code on or after October 1, 1979 that provides for a reorganization of the debt structure of the business and allows the business to continue operations.

Chapter 13 proceeding A voluntary action initiated under the provisions of the Bankruptcy Code on or after October 1, 1979 that provides for the settlement of debts of individuals with regular income. Some small individually owned businesses may also file a petition under chapter 13.

Claim Section 101(4) of the Bankruptcy Code defines claim as (A) right to payment, whether or not such right is reduced to judgment, liquidated, unliquidated, fixed, contingent, matured, unmatured, disputed, undisputed, legal, secured, or unsecured, or (B) right to an equitable remedy for breach of performance if such breach gives rise to a right to payment, whether or not such right to an equitable remedy is reduced to judgment, fixed, contingent, matured, unmatured, disputed, undisputed, secured, or unsecured.

Committee case A nonjudicial endeavor by the debtor and an unofficial creditors' committee to effect a voluntary agreement, out of court, wherein the debtor normally remains in business but secures an extension of time for payment, or a reduction in amount, or both, of all or part of its unsecured debts.

Composition (informal) An out-of-court agreement between a debtor and its creditors whereby the debtor normally remains in business but provides for full satisfaction of claims by partial payment, and for cancellation of remaining indebtedness.

Confirmation An official approval by the court of a plan of reorganization under chapter 11 proceedings that makes the plan binding upon the debtor and creditors. Before a plan is confirmed, it must satisfy eleven requirements in section 1129(a) of the Bankruptcy Code.

Corporate reorganization Used to refer to the proceedings under Chapter X of the Bankruptcy Act.

Cram down For a plan to be confirmed, a class of claims or interests must either accept the plan or not be impaired. However, the Bankruptcy Code allows the court under certain conditions to confirm a plan even though an impaired class has not accepted the plan. The plan must not discriminate unfairly, and must be fair and equitable, with respect to each class of claims or interests impaired under the plan that have not accepted it. The Code states conditions for secured claims, unsecured claims, and stockholder interests that would be included in the fair and equitable requirement. It should be noted that, since the word "includes" is used, the meaning of "fair and equitable" is not restricted to these conditions.

Creditors' committee In a chapter 11 case, a committee of creditors holding unsecured claims shall be appointed as soon as practicable after the order for relief is granted. In those districts where a U.S. Trustee exists, the Trustee has the responsibility for appointing the committee without any authorization from the court. The committee will ordinarily consist of the seven largest creditors willing to serve or, if a committee was organized before the order for relief, such committee may continue provided it was fairly chosen and is representative of the different kinds of claims to be represented.

Date of bankruptcy Date when a petition in bankruptcy is filed with the Bankruptcy Court.

Debt Defined in section 101(11) of the Bankruptcy Code to mean liability on a claim.

Discharge An order entered in a bankruptcy court proceeding which releases the debtor from all debts remaining due after nonexempt assets are distributed, or upon confirmation of a plan under chapter 11 or after payments agreed to under a chapter 11 plan are completed.

Disclosure of adequate information Disclosure of information of a kind, and in sufficient detail, as far as is reasonably practicable in light of the nature and history of the debtor and the condition of the debtor's books and records, that would enable a hypothetical reasonable investor typical of holders of claims or interests of the relevant class to make an informed judgment about a plan of reorganization under chapter 11 of the Bankruptcy Code.

Disinterested person A disinterested person is anyone other than a:

1 Creditor.
2 Stockholder.
3 Insider.
4 Investment banker for any outstanding security of the debtor.

5 Investment banker, or an attorney for the investment banker, in connection with the offer, sale or issuance of a security of the debtor within three years prior to filing of the petition.

6 Director, officer, or employee of the debtor or investment banker within two years prior to filing of the petition.

7 Person who has an interest adverse to the interest of the estate, creditors, or stockholders due to any direct or indirect relationship to the debtor or investment banker.

Accountants, attorneys or other professionals must be disinterested persons in order to be retained to render professional services in connection with the bankruptcy proceedings.

Estate   The commencement of a case under the Bankruptcy Code creates an estate comprised of the property of the debtor.

Examiner   An official appointed by the Bankruptcy Court in a chapter 11 reorganization if no trustee is serving, to conduct an investigation of the debtor as is appropriate, including an investigation of any allegations of fraud, dishonesty, incompetence, misconduct, mismanagement, or irregularity in the management of the affairs of the debtor of or by current or former management of the debtor, if (1) such appointment is in the interests of creditors, any equity security holders, and other interests of the estate, or (2) the debtor's fixed, liquidated, unsecured debts, other than debts for goods, services, or taxes, or owing to an insider, exceed $5 million.

Executory contract   A contract in which something other than payment itself must be performed wholly or in part to complete the original agreement. Unexpired leases or purchase commitments are examples of executory contracts typically found in cases under the Bankruptcy Code.

Exempt assets   Property of an estate which by federal or state laws is not liable for any debt of the debtor that arose before the commencement of the case. The debtor maintains possession of the assets.

Fraudulent transfer   A transfer of an interest or an obligation incurred by the debtor, within one year prior to the date the petition was filed, with the intent to hinder, delay, or defraud creditors or whereby the debtor received less than fair equivalent value and the debtor (1) was insolvent before or became insolvent as the result of such transfer, (2) was left with unreasonably small business capital, or (3) intended to incur debts beyond the ability to pay such debts as they matured. Fraudulent transfers may be voided.

Impairment of claims   In determining which classes of claims or stockholders' interest must approve the plan, it is first necessary to determine if the class is impaired. A class of claims or interest is impaired under the plan unless the plan provides for the following:

1 Leaves unaltered the legal, equitable, and contractual right of a class.

2 Cures defaults that led to acceleration of debts or equity interest.

3 Pays in cash the full amount of the claim or, in the case of equity interest, the greater of the fixed liquidation preference or redemption price.

Individual with regular income   An individual other than a stockbroker or a commodity broker whose income is sufficiently stable and regular to enable such individual to make payments under a plan under chapter 13 of the Bankruptcy Code (in a case filed on or after October 1, 1979).

Insider   Includes director, officer, person in control, relative, partner, affiliate, and managing agent.

Insolvency   (1) In the equity sense, the inability of the debtor to pay obligations as they mature. (2) In the bankruptcy sense, a condition where the liabilities of the debtor exceed the fair valuation of its assets.

Insolvency proceeding   Action undertaken in a state court or otherwise under state insolvency laws.

Interim Bankruptcy Rules   Rules, suggested by the Advisory Committee on Bankruptcy Rules of the Judicial Conference of the United States and adopted as local rules by all districts with various nonuniform changes, that provided guidance in meeting the substantive and procedural changes mandated by the Bankruptcy Code until the new bankruptcy rules became effective on August 1, 1983.

Involuntary petition   A petition filed under chapters 7 or 11 by creditors forcing the debtor into bankruptcy court.

Irregularities   Any transactions that are not in the ordinary course of business. Especially include those transactions that resulted in the apparent dissipation of the debtor's assets in a manner other than by loss in the ordinary course of business.

Judicial lien   A lien obtained by judgment, levy, sequestration, or other legal or equitable process or proceeding.

Lien   A charge against or interest in property to secure payment of a debt or performance of an obligation.

Liquidation   Used to refer to proceedings under chapter 7 of the Bankruptcy Code filed on or after October 1, 1979; also generally used to refer to the cessation of business and sale of all assets of the debtor.

Nonbusiness bankrupt/debtor   A bankrupt whose financial difficulties are unrelated to any type of business operations.

Order for relief   An order, whether by decree or by position of law in a case with the Bankruptcy Code (filed on or after October 1, 1979) granting relief to (or against) the debtor. In a voluntary case, the entry of the order for relief is the filing of the petition. The court must enter the order or relief in an involuntary case if the petition is uncontested or if the court determines that (1) the debtor is generally not paying debts as they become due or (2) within 120 days before the petition was filed, a custodian was appointed for substantially all of the debtor's property.

Person As defined by the Bankruptcy Code includes individual, partnership, and corporation, but does not include governmental unit.

Petition A document filed in a court of bankruptcy, initiating proceedings under the Bankruptcy Code.

Plan The creditors' agreement formulated in chapter 11 proceedings under the supervision of the bankruptcy court that allows the debtor to continue in business. The plan may affect secured creditors and stockholders as well as unsecured creditors' interests.

Preference A transfer of property on account of a past debt within ninety days (one year for insiders) prior to filing the petition, while the debtor is insolvent, to a creditor who receives more than would be received if the debtor's estate were liquidated under chapter 7. The Bankruptcy Code provides exceptions for certain transactions which are substantially contemporaneous or in the ordinary course of business.

Priority Claim A claim or expense which is paid after secured claims and before unsecured claims are satisfied, in accordance with statutory categories. The discharge is a privilege and the bankruptcy laws provide exceptions to discharge, in whole or in part, for certain wrongdoing, such as concealment of assets, or certain types of debt, such as alimony. Under the Bankruptcy Code (cases filed after October 1, 1979) a corporation which liquidates all (or substantially all) of its assets is ineligible for a discharge.

Proof of claim The Bankruptcy Code permits a creditor or indenture trustee to file a proof of claim and an equity holder to file a proof of interest. The filing of the proof is not mandatory in a chapter 11 case, and the debtor may obtain a discharge for debts that were listed on the schedules filed with the court, even though a proof of claim is not filed. The debtor or trustee has the power to file a claim on behalf of the creditor if the creditor did not file a timely claim. Thus, for debts that are nondischargeable, the debtor may file a proof of claim to cause the creditor to receive some payment from the estate and avoid having to pay all of the debt after the bankruptcy proceedings are over.

Receiver An individual appointed by the bankruptcy court under the Bankruptcy Act in cases filed before October 1, 1979 to receive and preserve the property of the estate, to operate its business legally or represent the estate until a trustee can be elected or appointed. Also, an official appointed by any court of equitable jurisdiction as its agent for most any proper purpose, which may include the liquidation of a business.

Relative An individual related by affinity or consanguinity within the third degree as determined by the common law, and includes individuals in a step or adoptive relationship. Included would be spouse, son, daughter, brother, sister, father, and mother.

Reorganization Proceedings under chapter 11 of the Bankruptcy Code (cases filed on or after October 1, 1979) where a debtor attempts to reach an agreement with creditors, secured and unsecured, and continue in business.

Schedules The detailed lists of debts and assets that the debtor is required to file with a petition in bankruptcy court or shortly thereafter.

Secured claim A claim against a debtor that is secured by collateral which may be used to satisfy the debt in the event the debtor defaults. Under the Bankruptcy Code a creditor's claim is secured only to the extent of the value of the collateral unless the creditor selects in a chapter 11 proceeding [section 1111(b)(2)] to have the entire debt considered secured.

Setoff Setoff is that right which exists between two parties to net their respective debts where each party, as a result of unrelated transactions, owes the other an ascertained amount. The creditor has the right to offset a mutual debt, providing both the debt and the credit arose before the commencement of the case.

Statement of Affairs A report filed with a petition under chapter 11 and consisting of answers to twenty-one questions concerning the debtor's past operations. Also used to refer to a statement of a debtor's financial condition as of a certain date, based on the assumption that the business will be liquidated. The statement consists of an analysis of the debtor's financial position and the status of the creditors with respect to the debtor's assets.

Straight Bankruptcy Proceedings under Sections 1 through 7 of the Bankruptcy Act (filed before October 1, 1979).

Trust Indenture and Security Agreement An agreement between the debtor and creditors, in the nature of an out-of-court extension agreement, that provides creditors with a lien on all the debtor's assets as security for the debtor's performance of its obligations to them under the agreement. Such agreements may also be used in connection with a chapter 11 case under the Bankruptcy Code.

Trustee The Bankruptcy Code refers to four categories of trustees—U.S. Trustee, interim trustee, trustee under a chapter 7 or 11 case, and standing trustee.

   U.S. Trustee—A trustee appointed by the Attorney General in ten pilot districts or groups of districts to establish, maintain, and supervise a panel of private trustees who are eligible and available to serve as trustees in a case under chapters 7 and 11.

Interim Trustee—As soon as the order for relief has been entered in a chapter 7 case, the court will appoint a disinterested person from a panel of private trustees to serve as the interim trustee.

Chapter 7 Trustee—At a meeting of creditors called under section 341, a trustee may be elected if an election is requested by at least 20 percent in amount of qualifying claims.

Chapter 11 Trustee—The Bankruptcy Code provides in chapter 11 cases that a trustee can be appointed in certain situations based on the facts of the case and not related to the size of the company or the amount of unsecured debt outstanding. The trustee is appointed only at the request of a party in interest after a notice and hearing.

Standing Trustee—In districts where warranted, the court may appoint one or more individuals to serve as standing trustees for cases filed under chapter 13. In addition to most of the duties of a trustee in a chapter 7 or 11 case, the standing trustee collects payments under the plan and distributes them to the creditors. A percentage fee based on payments under the plan will be collected by the standing trustee to cover trustee's costs.

Turnover order An order by a bankruptcy judge directing that property or proceeds from sale of property be turned over to a trustee as part of the debtor's estate.

Undersecured claim A secured claim where the value of the collateral is less than the amount of the claim.

Unsecured claim A claim that is not secured by any collateral. In the case of an undersecured creditor, the excess of the secured claim over the value of the collateral is an unsecured claim, unless the debtor elects in a chapter 11 proceeding to have the entire claim considered secured. The term is generally used in bankruptcy and insolvency proceedings to refer to unsecured claims that do not receive priority under the Bankruptcy Code.

U.S. Trustee A trustee appointed by the Attorney General in ten pilot districts or groups of districts to establish, maintain, and supervise a panel of private trustees that are eligible and available to serve as trustees in a case under chapters 7 and 11. The pilot program is effective for cases filed on or after October 1, 1979 through September 30, 1986, and Congress must pass legislation at that time if the U.S. trustee program is to be used beyond September 30, 1986.

Voluntary petition (bankruptcy) A petition filed by a debtor of its own free will, initiating proceedings under the Bankruptcy Code.

Bibliography

Aaron, Richard I. "The Bankruptcy Act of 1978: The Full Employment-for-Lawyers Bill, Part I: Overview and legislative History," *Utah Law Review* (1979, No. 1), pp. 1-28; "Part II: Consumer Bankruptcy" (1979, No. 2), pp. 175-229; "Part III: Business Bankruptcy" (1979, No. 3), pp. 405-469.

Abramson, Leslie W., Ed. *Basic Bankruptcy: Alternatives, Proceedings and Discharges.* Ann Arbor, Mich.: Institute of Continuing Legal Education, 1971.

"Accountant's Role in a Bankruptcy Case" (Statement in Quotes), *The Journal of Accountancy,* Vol. 115 (June 1963), pp. 59-63.

AICPA Professional Standards, Statement on Auditing Standards No. 1. New York: American Institute of Certified Public Accountants, 1980.

Altman, Edward I. "Bankrupt Firms' Equity Securities as an Investment Alternative," *Financial Analysts Journal,* Vol. 25 (July-August 1969), pp. 129-133.

―――. *Corporate Bankruptcy in America.* Lexington, Mass.: D. C. Heath and Co., 1971.

―――. "Corporate Bankruptcy Prediction and Its Implications for Commercial Loan Evaluation," *The Journal of Commercial Bank Lending,* Vol. 53 (December 1970), pp. 8-22.

―――. "Financial Ratios, Discriminant Analysis and the Prediction of Corporate Bankruptcy," *Journal of Finance,* Vol. 23 (September 1968), pp. 589-609.

Anderson, John C., and Peter G. Wright. "Liquidating Plans of Reorganization," *American Bankruptcy Law Journal,* Vol. 56 (Winter 1982), pp. 29-54.

Arner, Michael Reed. "The Worthier Creditors (and a Cheer for the King)—Revisited," *The American Bankruptcy Law Journal,* Vol. 53 (Fall 1979), pp. 389-397.

Arneson, George S. "Accounting for Inflation in Valuing Closely Held Companies," *TAXES—The Tax Magazine,* Vol. 59 (June 1981), pp. 391-398.

Ashe, George. "The Corporate Entity in Bankruptcy: Subordination—Consolidation—Mergers," *The American Bankruptcy Law Journal,* Vol. 46 (Fall 1972), pp. 291-304.

Baker, Erin Y. "The Automatic Stay in Bankruptcy: An Analysis of the Braniff Chapter 11 Proceeding," *Texas Tech Law Review*, Vol. 14 (1983), pp. 433-457.

Bankruptcy Law Reporter. Chicago: Commerce Clearing House. 1985.

"Bankruptcy—Tax Discharge—Tax Priority," *Southwestern Law Journal*, Vol. 25 (May 1971), pp. 326-330.

"Bankruptcy—Tax Liens—A Government Lien Securing Taxes Legally Due and Owing More Than Three Years Prior to Bankruptcy Does Not Attach to Property Acquired Subsequent to Discharge in Bankruptcy," *Texas Law Review*, Vol. 49 (March 1971), pp. 554-562.

Banks, Charles S. *Treatise on Bankruptcy for Accountants*. Chicago, Ill.: LaSalle Extension University, 1948.

Banks, Margaret A. "The Canada Act 1982—Some Facts and Comments," *University of Western Ontario Law Review*, Vol. 21 (May 1983), pp. 155-161.

Beaver, William H. "Alternative Accounting Measures as Predictors of Failure," *Accounting Review*, Vol. 43 (January 1968), pp. 113-122.

———. "Financial Ratios as Predictors of Failure," in *Empirical Research in Accounting: Selected Studies 1966*. First University of Chicago Conference (May 1966), pp. 71-127.

Bennett, Keith W. "Is There Life After Chapter 11?" *Iron Age* (November 1982), pp. 42-44.

Bergman, Bruce J. "Compensating the Receiver in Foreclosure Actions," *New York State Bar Journal*, Vol. 53 (June 1981), pp. 276-306.

Beyer, Robert. "Profitability Accounting: The Challenge and the Opportunity," *The Journal of Accountancy*, Vol. 117 (June 1964), pp. 33-36.

Binder Thomas M. "Bankruptcy—Preferences—Payment to Judgment Creditor Pursuant to an Income Execution," *Villanova Law Review*, Vol. 27 (Summer 1982), pp. 1286-1307.

Blum, Marc, "Failing Company Discriminant Analysis," *Journal of Accounting Research*, Vol. 12 (Spring 1974), pp. 1-25.

Blum, Walter J. "Corporate Reorganizations Based on Cash Flow Valuations," *The University of Chicago Law Review*, Vol. 38 (Fall 1970), pp. 173-183.

———. "Full Priority and Full Compensation in Corporate Reorganizations: A Reappraisal," *The University of Chicago Law Review*, Vol. 25 (Spring 1958), pp. 417-444.

Boshkoff, D. G. "The Bankrupt's Moral Obligation to Pay His Discharged Debts: A Conflict Between Contract Theory and Bankruptcy Policy," *Indiana Law Journal*, Vol. 47 (Fall 1971), pp. 36-69.

Bowman, Andrew S., and William M. Thompson. "Secured Claims Under Section 1325(a)(5)(B): Collateral Valuation, Present Value, and Adequate Protection," *Indiana Law Review*, Vol. 15 (1982), pp. 569-592.

Breitowitz, Irving A. "Article 9 Security Interests as Voidable Preferences," *Cardozo Law Review*, Vols. 3-4 (Spring, Fall 1982), pp. 357-429.

Bronsteen, Robert. "The Accountant's Investigation of Bankrupt Irregularities," *The New York Certified Public Accountant*, Vol. 37 (December 1967), pp. 935-943.

Broom, H. N., and J. G. Longenecker. *Small Business Management*. Cincinnati: Southwestern Publishing Co., 1971.

Brownstein, G. W. "Awarding Fair Fees in Bankruptcy: Recent Developments," *Connecticut Bar Journal*, Vol. 45 (March 1971), pp. 69-83.

Buchanan, Norman. *The Economics of Corporate Enterprise*. New York: Henry Holt & Co., 1940.

Burchfield, Thomas H. "The Balance Sheet Test of Insolvency," *University of Pittsburgh Law Review*, Vol. 23 (October 1961), pp. 5-15.

Burke, William M. "Consumer Credit and the New Bankruptcy Act," *The Business Lawyer*, Vol. 34 (April 1979), pp. 1467-1475.

Butenas, John P. "Establishing Attorney's Fees Under the New Bankruptcy Code," *Commercial Law Journal*, Vol. 87 (May 1982), pp. 237-243.

Carmichael, D. R. *The Auditor's Reporting Obligation: Auditing Research Monograph No. 1*. New York: American Institute of Certified Public Accountants, 1972.

Cavitch, Zolman. *Business Organizations with Tax Planning*, Vol. 7. New York: Matthew Bender & Co., Inc., 1965.

Cerf, Alan R. *Professional Responsibility of Certified Public Accountants*. California Certified Public Accountants Foundation for Education and Research, 1970.

"Certified Public Accountants Held to Fiduciary Standards," *Journal of the National Association of Referees in Bankruptcy*, Vol. 37 (January 1963), pp. 7-10.

Chabrow, P. B. "Estates in Bankruptcy: Return Requirements, Rules Concerning Income and Deductions," *The Journal of Taxation*, Vol. 31 (December 1969), pp. 362-368.

Chambers, Edward J., and Raymond L. Gold. "Factors in Small Business Success or Failure; Prepared for the Montana State Planning Board," *The National Public Accountant*, Vol. 8 (October 1963), pp. 8-9, 33.

Chatz, Robert B., John W. Costello, and Karen Gross. "An Overview of the Bankruptcy Code," *Uniform Commercial Code Law Journal*, Vol. 84 (August 1979), pp. 259-265.

Clark, Barkley. "Preferences Under the Old and New Bankruptcy Acts," *Uniform Commercial Code Law Journal*, Vol. 12 (Fall 1979), pp. 154-182.

Cohen, Neil B. "Value Judgments: Accounts Receivable Financing and Voidable Preferences Under the New Bankruptcy Code," *Minnesota Law Review* (April 1982), pp. 639-665.

Cohn, Daniel C. "Subordinated Claims: Their Classification and Voting Under Chapter 11 of the Bankruptcy Code," *American Bankruptcy Law Journal*, Vol. 56 (October 1982), pp. 293-324.

Conner, Paul. "Financial Reporting for Companies in Financial Difficulty," *Oklahoma CPA*, Vol. 7 (October 1968), pp. 21-25.

Connors, Pete. "Bankruptcy Reform: Relief for Individuals with Regular Income," *University of Richmond Law Review* (Winter 1979), pp. 219-246.

Constandse, William. "Why Companies Fail," *Business Management,* Vol. 39 (October 1970), pp. 13, 42.

Coogan, Peter F. "Confirmation of a Plan Under the Bankruptcy Code," *Case Western Reserve Law Review,* Vol. 32 (1982), pp. 301-363.

Coppel, Lawrence D., and Lewis A. Kann. "Defanging Durrett: The Established Law of 'Transfer,' " *Banking Law Journal,* Vol. 100 (October 1983), pp. 676-699.

Corkery, J. F. "Winding Up by the Court for Inability to Pay Debts: The Court's Exercise of Its Discretion," *Adelaide Law Review,* Vol. 8 (Fall 1982), pp. 61-94.

Costello, Michael J. "The Troubled Business Venture—Dealing with the New Bankruptcy Reorganization and Cancellation of Indebtedness Provisions," *40th Annual N.Y.U. Institute,* pp. 43-1–43-22.

Countryman, Vern. "Treatment of Secured Claims in Chapter Cases," *Commercial Law Journal,* Vol. 82 (October 1977), pp. 349-360.

Danehy, Maureen R. "Inequality or Equality Among Creditors? The Second Circuit Preserves the Right to Setoff: In re Applied Logic Corp," *Connecticut Law Review,* Vol. 11 (Spring 1979), pp. 601-613.

Dash, Lawrence J. "Equity Cushion Analysis in Bankruptcy," *Hofstra Law Review,* Vol. 10 (Summer 1982), pp. 1149-1192.

Davidson, Sheldon. "Schemes and Methods Used in Perpetrating Bankruptcy Frauds," *Commercial Law Journal,* Vol. 71 (December 1966), pp. 383-387.

Dobbs, C. E. "Reorganization Under the Bankruptcy Reform Act of 1978—An Overview (Part II)," *Georgia Small Business Journal,* Vol. 16 (August 1979), pp. 13-17.

Dolphin, Robert J. *An Analysis of Economic and Personal Factors Leading to Consumer Bankruptcy.* Occasional Paper No. 15. Flint, Mich.: Michigan State University Graduate School of Business Administration, Bureau of Business and Economic Research, 1965.

Donaldson, Elvin, John Pfahl, and Peter L. Mullins. *Corporate Finance,* Fourth Edition. New York: The Ronald Press Co., 1975.

Donnelly, R. A. "Alive and Kicking; Chapters X and XI Sometimes Have a Happy Ending," *Barron's,* May 26, 1969, p. 3f.

———. "Unhappy Ending? Chapters 10 and 11 of the Bankruptcy Act Don't Always Tell the Story," *Barron's,* July 12, 1971, p. 3f.

Douglas-Hamilton, Margaret Hambrecht. "Troubled Debtors: The Fine Line Between Counseling and Controlling," *Journal of Commercial Bank Lending,* Vol. 60 (October 1977), pp. 29-35.

Duncan, Richard F. "Preferential Transfers, the Floating Lien, and Section 547 (c)(5) of the Bankruptcy Reform Act of 1978," *Arkansas Law Review,* Vol. 36 (1983), pp. 1-46.

Duree, David M. "Effect on the Surety of Bankruptcy Reorganizations of Bond Principals, Obligees and Claimants Under the Bankruptcy Reform Act of 1978," *The Forum,* Vol. 17 (Fall 1981), pp. 360-373.

Ediger, Gerald. "Is There a Right to Reclaim Bailed Property from the Estate of a Debtor Under the Bankruptcy Code?," *Tulsa Law Journal,* Vol. 17 (Summer 1982), pp. 728-752.

Dun and Bradstreet, Inc. *Failure Record Through 1962: A Comprehensive Failure Study, by Location, by Industry, by Age, by Size, by Cause.* New York: Dun and Bradstreet, Inc., 1963.

————. *The Business Failure Record,* 1981. New York: Dun and Bradstreet, Inc., 1983.

Elliot, Milton. "What Taxes, If Any, Are Released by a Discharge in Bankruptcy?," *The Journal of the Oklahoma Bar Association,* Vol. 40 (March 29, 1969), pp. 683-689.

Epling, Richard L. "Cramdown Under the Bankruptcy Code of 1978: Effect upon the Soft Collateral Lender," *Loyola University Law Review,* Vol. 12 (Summer 1981), pp. 627-645.

————. "Treatment of Land Sale Contracts Under the New Bankruptcy Code," *Bankruptcy Law Journal,* Vol. 56 (Winter 1982), pp. 55-64.

Erbacher, Philip J. "Is the National Bankruptcy Act Paramount over the Internal Revenue Code in Federal Tax Matters?," *TAXES—The Tax Magazine,* Vol. 48 (March 1970), pp. 153-162.

Farrar, John H. "The Bankruptcy of the Law of Fraudulent Preference," *Journal of Business Law* (Spring 1983), pp. 390-408.

Fearon, Richard H., and Mitchell R. Julis. "The Role of Modern Finance in Bankruptcy Reorganizations," *Temple Law Quarterly,* Vol. 56 (1983), pp. 1-48.

Feldman, Franklin, and Judah C. Sommer. "The Special Commodity Provisions of the New Bankruptcy Code," *Special Commodity Provisions,* Vol. 37 (July 1982), pp. 1487-1519.

Flanagan, Harold T. "The Determination and Payment of Federal Taxes in Bankruptcy," *The American Bankruptcy Law Journal,* Vol. 47 (Spring 1973), pp. 81-100.

Foreman, Leon S. *Compositions, Bankruptcy, and Arrangements.* Philadelphia: The American Law Institute, 1971.

Fundamentals of Investment Banking. Sponsored by the Investment Bankers Association of America. Englewood Cliffs, N.J.: Prentice-Hall, Inc., 1949.

Gardner, Jr., Henry B. "The SEC and Valuation under Chapter X," *University of Pennsylvania Law Review,* Vol. 91 (January 1943), p. 441.

Gattuso, Christina Marie. "The Bankruptcy Reform Act of 1928: Dischargeability of Obligations Incurred under Property Settlements, Separation Agreements, and Divorce Decrees," *University of Baltimore Law Review,* Vol. 12 (Spring 1983), pp. 520-540.

Gelb, Harold, and Irving Goldberger. "Retention Order of the Accountant in Insolvencies and Bankruptcies and Petition for Compensation," *The New York Certified Public Accountant,* Vol. 23 (October 1953), pp. 632-634.

Gerstenberg, Charles. *Financial Organization and Management of Business.* Englewood Cliffs, N.J.: Prentice-Hall, Inc., 1959.

Given, Thomas C., and Linda J. Philipps. "Equality in the Eye of the Beholder—Classification of Claims and Interests in Chapter 11 Reorganizations," *Ohio State Law Journal,* Vol. 43 (1982), pp. 735-769.

Gordanier, Dean C. Jr. "The Indubitable Equivalent of Reclamation: Adequate Protection for Secured Creditors under the Bankruptcy Code," *American Bankruptcy Law Journal,* Vol. 54 (1980), pp. 299-337.

Gordon, Herbert G. "Operation of a Business in Bankruptcy," *The Canadian Chartered Accountant,* Vol. 76 (May 1960), pp. 454-458.

Grange, William J., et al. *Manual for Corporation Officers.* New York: The Ronald Press Co., 1967.

Green, Donald. "To Predict Failure," *Management Accounting* (NAA), Vol. 10 (July 1978), pp. 39-41, 45.

Greenfield, Robert A. "*Lines* v. *Frederick* (91 Sup. Ct. 113): The Effect of Bankruptcy on a Bankrupt's Accrued Vacation Pay and Other Forms of Deferred Compensation," *Los Angeles Bar Bulletin,* Vol. 47 (December 1971), pp. 67-73.

Greidinger, B. Bernard. "Responsibilities of Independent Accountants in Chapter X Proceedings," *The New York Certified Public Accountant,* Vol. 36 (April 1966), pp. 278-282.

Grindstaff, Michael J., and Thomas M. Hackle. "Involuntary Bankruptcy: The Generally Not Paying Standard," *Mercer Law Review,* Vol. 33 (Spring 1982), pp. 903-923.

Groschadl, Paul S. "Freezing the Debtor's Bank Account: A Violation of the Automatic Stay?," *American Bankruptcy Law Journal,* Vol. 57 (January 1983), pp. 75-81.

Hahn, George A., and Jeffery L. Schwartz. "Letters of Credit Under the Bankruptcy Code," *Uniform Commercial Code Law Journal,* Vol. 16 (1983), pp. 91-102.

Hammon, Carmelita J. "Setoff in Bankruptcy: Is the Creditor Preferred or Secured?," *University of Colorado Law Review,* Vol. 50 (Summer 1979), pp. 511-526.

Handlan, Allen L. "The Stampede to Chapter 11 Bankruptcy: Some Special Problems and Considerations Relating to Oil and Gas Workouts," *Eastern Mineral Law Institute,* Vol. 4 (1983), pp. 1-56.

Hanley, Jr., John W. "Partnership Bankruptcy Under the New Act," *Hastings Law Journal,* Vol. 31 (September 1979), pp. 149-182.

Harbeck, Stephen P. "Stockbroker Bankruptcy: The Role of the District Court and the Bankruptcy Court Under the Securities Investor Protection Act," *American Bankruptcy Law Journal,* Vol. 56 (July 82), pp. 277-288.

Harter, Robert J. Jr., and Kenneth N. Klee. "The Impact of the New Bankruptcy Code on the 'Bankruptcy Out' in Legal Opinions," *Fordham Law Review,* Vol. 48 (Dec. 1979), pp. 277-290.

Hatfield, Henry. *Modern Accounting*. New York: Appleton-Century Co. Inc., 1909.

Hazelett, John M. "Need for Investigation of Business Failures" (Letters), *The Journal of Accountancy*, Vol. 118 (August 1964).

Hellerstein, Jerome R., and Victor Brudney. "Tax Problems in Bankruptcy or Insolvency Reorganization," in *Lasser's Encyclopedia of Tax Procedures*, Second Edition. Englewood Cliffs, N.J.: Prentice-Hall, Inc., 1960.

Herzog, Asa S. "CPA's Role in Bankruptcy Proceeding," *The Journal of Accountancy*, Vol. 117 (January 1964), pp. 59-69.

———. "Referee in Bankruptcy—Mr., Master or Judge?," *Credit and Financial Management*, Vol. 72 (August 1970), pp.12-14.

Hillman, William C. "Keeping Track of Creditors in Bankruptcy Chapter Proceedings," *The Practical Lawyer*, Vol. 19 (January 1973), pp. 53-58.

Hoffman, Melvin S. "The Attorney-Client Privilege in Proceedings Under The Bankruptcy Act of 1898 and The Bankruptcy Reform Act of 1978," *The American Bankruptcy Law Journal*, Vol. 53 (Summer 1979), pp. 231-251.

Hogan, William E. "Games Lawyers Play with the Bankruptcy Preference Challenge to Accounts and Inventory Financing," *Cornell Law Review*, Vol. 53 (April 1968), pp. 553-574.

Hopper, Edward B. "Confirmation of a Plan Under Chapter 11 of the Bankruptcy Code and the Effect of Confirmation on Creditor's Rights," *Indiana Law Review*, Vol. II (1982), pp. 501-546.

Hoover, John Edgar. "Investigation of Fraudulent Bankruptcies by the Federal Bureau of Investigation," *The New York Certified Public Accountant*, Vol. 32 (March 1962), pp. 187-194.

Horvitz, Jerome S., and H. L. Jenson. "How Bankruptcy and Preexisting Obligations Affect Withholding Tax Liability," *Journal of Taxation*, Vol. 49 (August 1978), pp. 96-99.

Hughes, Hal. "Wavering Between the Profit and the Loss: Operating a Business During Reorganization Under Chapter 11 of the New Bankruptcy Code," *American Bankruptcy Law Journal*, Vol. 54 (1980), pp. 45-91.

Husband, William, and James Dockeray. *Modern Corporation Finance*. Homewood, Ill.: Richard D. Irwin, Inc., 1965.

Irish, R. A. "Should We Blame the Auditing Profession?," *Chartered Accountant in Australia*, Vol. 34 (August 1963), pp. 79-96.

Jones, Ida Mae. "The Automatic Stay and the Creditor Who Has Leased Consumer Goods," *Commercial Law Review*, Vol. 88 (March 1983), pp. 134-140.

Jones, J. Devereaux. "Rejection of Unexpired Oil and Gas Leases in Bankruptcy Proceedings: *In re J.H. Land and Cattle Co.*," *Tulsa Law Journal*, Vol. 19 (Fall 1983), pp. 68-99.

———. "Section 522(f): A Proposal for the Survival of Purchase Money Security Interests Following Refinancing," *Tulsa Law Journal*, Vol. 18 (Winter 1982), pp. 280-304.

Kaplan, Michael J. "Nonrecourse Undersecured Creditors Under New Chapter 11—The Section 1111 (b) Election: Already a Need for Change," *American Bankruptcy Law Journal,* Vol. 53 (Summer 1979), pp. 269-274.

Karlen, Andrew N. "Adequate Protection Under the Bankruptcy Code, Its Role in Business Reorganization," *Pace Law Review,* Vol. 2 (1982), pp. 1-33.

Katskee, Melvin. "The Calculus of Corporate Reorganization: Chapter X vs. Chapter XI and the Role of the SEC Assessed," *The American Bankruptcy Law Journal,* Vol. 45 (Spring, 1971), pp. 171-194.

Kauffman, David. "Procedures for Estimating Contingent or Unliquidated Claims in Bankruptcy," *Stanford Law Review,* Vol. 35 (November 1982), pp. 153-174.

Kaye, Richard A. "Federal Taxes, Bankruptcy and Assignments for the Benefit of Creditors—A Comparison," *Commercial Law Journal,* Vol. 73 (March 1968), pp. 78-80.

Keenan, James I., Jr., "Reformation or Consternation: The Effect of the Bankruptcy Reform Act of 1978 Upon Surety Underwriting," *Insurance Counsel Journal,* Vol. 50 (October 1983), pp. 599-608.

Kelly, James J. *Toward Increasing the Effectiveness of Creditors' Committees.* Hanover, N.H.: Dartmouth College, Amos Tuck School of Business Administration, 1966.

Kennedy, Frank R. "Automatic Stays Under the New Bankruptcy Law," *University of Michigan Journal of Law Reform,* Vol. 12 (Fall 1978), pp. 3-65.

———. "Secured Creditors Under the Bankruptcy Reform Act," *Indiana Law Review,* Vol. 15 (1982), pp. 477-500.

King, Lawrence P. "Chapter 11 of the 1978 Bankruptcy Code," *American Bankruptcy Law Journal,* Vol. 53 (1979), pp. 107-131.

———. Ed. *Collier on Bankruptcy.* 15th ed. New York: Matthew Bender, 1980.

———. Ed. *Collier Bankruptcy Manual.* 3rd ed. New York: Matthew Bender, 1980.

Kingsmill, T. H., Jr. "Bankruptcy and the Tax Law," *Tulane Tax Institute,* Vol. 18 (1969), p. 633.

———. "When and How Is a Bankrupt Discharged from Federal Tax Debt?," *Journal of Taxation,* Vol. 31 (September 1969), pp. 180-183.

Klee, Kenneth N. "A Lending Officer's Primer on the New Bankruptcy Code," *The Banking Law Journal,* Vol. 97 (May 1980), pp. 388-425.

———. "All You Ever Wanted to Know About CRAM Down Under the New Bankruptcy Code," *American Bankruptcy Law Journal,* Vol. 53 (Spring 1979), pp. 133-171.

———. "Legislative History of the New Bankruptcy Law," *De Paul Law Review,* Vol. 28 (Summer 1979), pp. 941-960.

———. "The New Bankruptcy Act of 1978," *American Bar Association Journal,* Vol. 64 (December 1978), pp. 1865-1867.

Klein, Martin I. "H. R. 8200—The Bankruptcy Act Comes of Age," *New York State Bar Journal* (December 1978), pp. 657-664.

————. "The Bankruptcy Reform Act of 1978," *American Bankruptcy Law Journal,* Vol. 53 (1979), pp. 1-33.

Kossack, Nathaniel E., and Sheldon Davidson. "Bankruptcy: Legal Problems and Fraud Schemes," *Credit and Financial Management,* Vol. 68 (May 1966), pp. 28-32.

————. "Bankruptcy Fraud: Alliance for Enforcement," *Journal of the National Conference of Referees in Bankruptcy,* Vol. 40 (January 1966), pp. 12-19.

————. "Bankruptcy Fraud: The Unholy Alliance Moves In," *Credit and Financial Management,* Vol. 68 (April 1966), pp. 20-24.

————. " 'Scam'—The Planned Bankruptcy Racket," *The New York Certified Public Accountant,* Vol. 35 (June 1965), pp. 417-423.

Krasnowiecki, Jan Z. "The Impact of the New Bankruptcy Reform Act on Real Estate Development and Financing," *American Bankruptcy Law Journal,* Vol. 53 (Fall 1979), pp. 363-388.

Krause, Sydney. "Accountant's Role in a Liquidation Proceeding," *The New York Certified Public Accountant,* Vol. 28 (July 1958), pp. 503-510.

————. "What Constitutes Insolvency?," *New York University Institute of Federal Taxation,* Vol. 27 (1969), pp. 1081-1093.

Krause, Sydney, and Arnold Kapiloff. "The Bankrupt Estate, Taxable Income, and the Trustee in Bankruptcy," *Fordham Law Review,* Vol. 34 (March 1966), pp. 401-418.

Labovitz, Irving D. "Outline of 'Cram Down' Provisions Under Chapter 11 of the Bankruptcy Reform Act of 1978," *Commercial Law Journal,* Vol. 86 (Fall 1981), pp. 51-56.

Lake, William H. "Chapter 13 of the New Bankruptcy Code," *Commercial Law Journal,* Vol. 84 (October 1979), pp. 365-371.

————. "Representing Secured Creditors under the Bankruptcy Code," *The Business Lawyer,* Vol. 37 (April 1982), pp. 1153-1183.

Lander, David A. "The Automatic Stay Provision of the Bankruptcy Reform Act," *Journal of the Missouri Bar,* Vol. 38 (April, May 1982), pp. 155-166.

Lavien, Harold. *Bankruptcy Forms,* 79-81. (West Publishing Co., 1979).

Lee, Joe. "Chapter 13 Nee Chapter XIII," *The American Bankruptcy Law Journal,* Vol. 53 (Fall 1979), pp. 303-326.

Lee, Rex E., Paul McGrath, Steven M. Shapiro, et al. "Brief for the United States of America in Support of the Constitutionality of the Provisions of 28 U.S.C. § 1471 Vesting in the United States District Courts and Delegating to Adjunct Bankruptcy Courts Jurisdiction Over All Bankruptcy-Related Controversies," *The American Bankruptcy Law Journal,* Vol. 56 (Spring 1982), pp. 97-120.

Levin, Harris. "Accounting Aspects of Arrangement Proceedings," *The New York Certified Public Accountant,* Vol. 28 (June 1958), pp. 429-438.

Levin, Richard B. "An Introduction to the Trustee's Avoiding Powers," *American Bankruptcy Law Journal,* Vol. 53 (1979), pp. 173-199.

Levinthal, Louis. "The Early History of Bankruptcy Law," *University of Pennsylvania Law Review,* Vol. 66 (1917-1918), pp. 223-250.

Levit, Louis W. "Use and Disposition of Property Under Chapter 11 of the Bankruptcy Code: Some Practical Concerns," *American Bankruptcy Law Journal,* Vol. 53 (Summer 1979), pp. 275-294.

Levy, Aaron. "The Role of the Securities and Exchange Commission and the Judicial Functions Under the Bankruptcy Reform Act of 1978," *American Bankruptcy Law Journal,* Vol. 54 (Winter 1980), pp. 29-42.

Levy, Chauncey. "Creditors' Committees and Their Responsibilities," *Commercial Law Journal,* Vol. 74 (December 1969), pp. 355-363.

———. "Customers' Rights in Stockbroker Insolvencies," *Commercial Law Journal,* Vol. 84 (May 1979), pp. 173-182.

Levy, Nathan Jr. "Impact of the New Bankruptcy Code on Article 2 Sales," *Uniform Commercial Code Law Journal,* Vol. 14 (Spring 1982), pp. 307-346.

Logan, Joseph P. III. "Federal Tax Liens in Bankruptcy," *Washington and Lee Law Review,* Vol. 23 (Fall 1966), pp. 370-384.

Luna, David, and John Frances Hilson. "Chapter 13 of the Bankruptcy Code: Law Made Simple, the Creditor Made Secure," *Los Angeles Lawyer,* Vol. 3 (January 1981), p. 34f.

Lutsky, Irwin. "Tax Services in Insolvency Proceedings," *The New York Certified Public Accountant,* Vol. 38 (June 1968), pp. 433-439.

Macey, Morris W. "Preferences and Fraudulent Transfers under the Bankruptcy Reform Act of 1978," *Emory Law Journal,* Vol. 28 (1979), pp. 683-702.

Machtinger, Sidney. "Dischargeability of Taxes in Bankruptcy," *Los Angeles Bar Bulletin,* Vol. 43 (March 1968), pp. 216-218.

Mann, Richmond A., and Michael J. Phillips. "The Timing of Perfection of Security Interests Under the Uniform Commercial Code and the Bankruptcy Reform Act," *Akron Law Review,* Vol. 15 (Fall 1981), pp. 369-382.

Mannix, Raymond R. "Analyzing the Financial Statement in a Bankruptcy Proceeding," *Commercial Law Journal,* Vol. 63 (September 1958), pp. 251-254, 257.

Mapother, William R. "Bankruptcy Strategies for Representing Creditors in Chapter 7 and Chapter 13 Cases," *Commercial Law Journal,* Vol. 86 (April 1981), pp. 133-137.

Marshack, Richard A. "Adequate Protection for the Undersecured Creditor Under the Bankruptcy Code," *Commercial Law Journal,* Vol. 88 (December 1983), pp. 621-629.

Mautz, Robert K. "Accounting and Business Ethics," *Florida Certified Public Accountant,* Vol. 4 (May 1964), pp. 12-20.

McLaughlin, Gerald T. "Letters of Credit as Preferential Transfers in Bankruptcy," *Fordham Law Review,* Vol. 50 (May 1982), pp. 1033-1084.

Meigs, Walter B., et al. *Advanced Accounting.* New York: McGraw-Hill Book Co., 1979.

Merrick, Glen Warren. "Chapter 13 of The Bankruptcy Act of 1978," *Denver Law Journal,* Vol. 56:4 (1979), pp. 585-624.

Miller, Walter W., Jr. "Bankruptcy Code Cramdown Under Chapter 11: New Threat to Shareholder Interests," *Boston University Law Review,* Vol. 62 (November 1982), pp. 1059-1113.

Mitchell, Clyde III. "Securities Regulation in Bankruptcy Reorganizations," *American Bankruptcy Law Journal,* Vol. 54 (Spring 1980), pp. 101-151.

Moss, Guy B. "Insolvency Alternatives in the United States," *Commercial Law Journal,* Vol. 87 (November 1982), pp. 567-572.

Mulder, John E. "A Problem: Time for Filing Involuntary Petitions," *The Practical Lawyer,* Vol. 3 (May 1957), pp. 25-35.

————. "Rehabilitation of the Financially Distressed Small Business—Revisited," *The Practical Lawyer,* Vol. 11 (November 1965), pp. 39-49.

Munson, Mark P. "Discharge of Post-Marital Support Obligations Under the New Bankruptcy Code," *Harvard Women's Law Journal,* Vol. 4 (Spring 1981), pp. 177-192.

New York State Bar Association Tax Section. "Report on the Ancillary Tax Effects of Different Forms of Reorganization," *Tax Law Review,* Vol. 34 (Summer 1979), pp. 475-538.

Nimmer, Raymond T. "Executory Contracts in Bankruptcy: Protecting the Fundamental Terms of the Bargain," *Colorado Law Review,* Vol. 54 (Summer 1983), pp. 507-555.

Novick, Lawrence G., and S. J. Seif. "Perfecting Security Interests in Federal Tax Refund Claims," *Uniform Commercial Code Law Journal,* Vol. 12 (Summer 1979), pp. 34-47.

O'Donovan, James. "The Duties and Liabilities of a Receiver and Manager Appointed Out of Court," *Melbourne University Law Review,* Vol. 12 (June 1979), pp. 52-79.

————. "The Interaction of Winding Up and Receivership," *The Australian Law Journal,* Vol. 53 (May 1979), pp. 264-269.

Orlanski, Leib. "The Resale of Securities Issued in Reorganization Proceedings and the Bankruptcy Reform Act of 1978," *American Bankruptcy Law Review,* Vol. 53 (Fall 1979), pp. 327-362.

Orr, Ronald S., and K. N. Klee. "Secured Creditors Under the New Bankruptcy Code," *Uniform Commercial Code Law Journal,* Vol. 11 (Spring 1979), pp. 312-345.

Ostow, Meir Jeremy. "Landlord's Bankruptcy: An Analysis of the Tenant's Rights and Remedies Under Bankruptcy Code 365(h)," *Rutgers Law Review,* Vol. 35 (Spring 1983), pp. 631-660.

O'Toole, Niall L. "Adequate Protection and Postpetition Interest in Chapter 11 Proceedings," *American Bankruptcy Law Journal,* Vol. 56 (July 1982), pp. 251-275.

Owens, Hubert F. "New Bankruptcy Acts," *Business Lawyer (Special Issue),* Vol. 36 (March 1981), pp. 721-725.

Paustian, Paul W., and John E. Lewis. *Small Business Instability and Failure in Alabama*. University, Alabama: Bureau of Business Research, University of Alabama, 1963.

Pearson, Roy. "The Fine Art of Failing in Business," *Personnel Journal,* Vol. 47 (March 1968), pp. 198-200.

Pennington, W. J. "Embezzling: Cases and Cautions," *The Journal of Accountancy,* Vol. 118 (July 1964), pp. 47-51.

Phelan, Marilyn. "Carryover of Tax Attributes," *TAXES—The Tax Magazine,* Vol. 51 (May 1973), pp. 273-293.

———. "Tax Proceeding in Bankruptcy: Normal Safeguards Are Denied Taxpayer," *The Journal of Taxation,* Vol. 38 (June 1973), pp. 336-340.

Phelan, Robin E., and Bruce A. Cheatham. "Issuing Securities Under the New Bankruptcy Code: More Magic for the Cryptic Kingdom," *St. Mary's Law Journal,* Vol. 11 (Number 2; 1979), pp. 393-436.

———. "The Issuance of Securities in Bankruptcy Proceeding: The Magic World Meets the Cryptic Kingdom," *American Bankruptcy Law Journal,* Vol. 51 (Spring 1977), pp. 99-125.

Phillips, Walter Ray. "Insider Provisions of the New Bankruptcy Code," *American Bankruptcy Law Journal* (October 1981), pp. 363-371.

Phipps, Patrick J. "Questional Constitutionality of Article I Bankruptcy Courts," *Creighton Law Review,* Vol. 15 (1981–1982), pp. 733-748.

Pitts, Thomas E., Jr. "Insider Guaranties and the Law of Preferences," *American Bankruptcy Law Journal,* Vol. 55 (October 1981), pp. 343-361.

Plumb, W. T., Jr. "Federal Priority in Insolvency: Proposals for Reform," *Michigan Law Review,* Vol. 70 (November 1971), pp. 1-108.

———. "Federal Tax Liens and Priorities in Bankruptcy—Recent Developments," *Journal of the National Conference of Referees in Bankruptcy,* Vol. 43 (April 1969), pp. 37-46; (July 1969), pp. 83-85.

Poe, Stephen L. "Automatic Stay of the 1978 Bankruptcy Code Versus the Norris La–Guardia Act: A Bankruptcy Court's Dilemma," *Texas Law Review,* Vol. 61 (October 1982), pp. 321-339.

Poorman, John Kevin. "Bankruptcy Reform Act of 1978," *Oklahoma Law Review,* Vol. 32 (Summer 1979), pp. 583-625.

Queenan, James F., Jr. "The Bankruptcy Code's Ethical Standards: A Current Controversy," *Massachusetts Law Review,* Vol. 67 (Fall, 1982), pp. 118-122.

Quittner, Arnold M. "Current Developments in Bankruptcy and Reorganization," *Commercial Law and Practice* (1980), pp. 429-450.

Rabinowitz, Martin J., and Kenneth A. Rubin. "The Bankruptcy Tax Act of 1979—H.R. 5043: Proposals for New Tax Treatment of Debtors and Creditors," *TAXES—The Tax Magazine* (December, 1979), pp. 911-917.

Ramanauskas, Helene M. A. "How Close to Bankruptcy Are You?," *Woman CPA,* Vol. 28 (October 1966), p. 3f.

Reed, Michael H., Barbara H. Sagar, and Gail P. Granoff. "Subject Matter Jurisdiction, Abstention and Removal Under the New Federal Bankruptcy Law," *American Bankruptcy Law Journal,* Vol. 56 (1982), pp. 121-153.

"Report of the Commission on the Bankruptcy Laws of the United States," *The Business Lawyer,* Vol. 29 (November 1973), pp. 75-116.

Resnick, Alan N. "Prudent Planning or Fraudulent Transfer: The Use of Non Exempt Assets to Purchase or Improve Exempt Property on the Eve of Bankruptcy," *Rutgers Law Reviews,* Vol. 31 (December 1978), pp. 615-654.

Resnick, Alan N., and Wendy Finkel. "A House May Not Be a Home: Liquidation Under the Bankruptcy Act," *New York State Bar Journal* (June, 1981), pp. 23-52.

Ring, L. S. "How to Fail in Business Without Half Trying," *Price Waterhouse Review,* Vol. 7 (Spring 1962), pp. 30-34.

Rochelle, William J., III, and Gwen L. Feder. "Unauthorized Sales of a Debtor's Property: The Rights of a Purchaser under Section 549 of the Bankruptcy Code," *American Bankruptcy Law Journal,* Vol. 57 (January 1983), pp. 23-52.

Romans, Thomas J. "Seller's Right of Reclamation Under the Bankruptcy Code," *Louisiana Law Review,* Vol. 41 (June 1981), pp. 1159-1176.

Rone, Donald Lee. "The New Bankruptcy Act and the Commercial Lender," *Banking Law Journal,* Vol. 96 (May 1979), pp. 389-417.

Rosen, Kenneth Alan, and Angel Ruiz Rodriguez. "Section 1121 and Non-Debtor Plans of Reorganization," *American Bankruptcy Law Journal,* Vol. 56 (October 1982), pp. 349-378.

Rosenfield, S. James, and Gregory Lee. "Bankruptcy: Business Reorganization Under the New Bankruptcy Code (Part I)," *Corporation Law Review,* Vol. 2 (Fall 1979), pp. 339-344.

Rudin, William J. "Allowances in Chapter XI Proceedings," *Journal of the National Conference of Referees in Bankruptcy,* Vol. 40 (January 1966), pp. 29-30; (July 1966), pp. 86-87.

Rutberg, Sidney. *Ten Cents on the Dollar.* New York: Simon and Schuster, Inc., 1973.

Sadd, Victor, and Robert Williams. *Causes of Commercial Bankruptcies.* U.S. Department of Commerce Domestic Commerce Series—No. 69, 1932.

Sauder, Scott. "Bankruptcy and Turnover Proceedings Against the IRS: A Path Toward Reorganization and Rehabilitation Fraught with Pitfalls," *Whittier Law Review,* Vol. 4 (1982), pp. 87-129.

Savage, Charles L., Ed. "Causes of Business Failures," *The New York Certified Public Accountant,* Vol. 34 (December 1964), p. 869.

Schwartz, Alan. "Security Interests and Bankruptcy Priorities: A Review of Current Theories," *The Journal of Legal Studies,* Vol. 10 (January 1981), pp. 1-37.

Schwartz, Elizabeth Jane. "Inflation and the Concept of Reorganization Value," *Vanderbilt Law Review,* Vol. 34 (1981), pp. 1727-1749.

Shanker, Morris G. "The Treatment of Executory Contracts and Leases in the 1978 Bankruptcy Code," *The Practical Lawyer,* Vol. 25 (October 1979), pp. 11-34.

Shapiro, Bernard. "A Composition or Extension Agreement," *The Practical Lawyer,* Vol. 23 (September 1977), pp. 28-40.

Shapiro, H. D. "Discharging Taxes in Bankruptcy: How It Works; The Problems Involved," *The Journal of Taxation,* Vol. 35 (September 1971), pp. 168-171.

Shuchman, Philip, and Thomas Rhorer. "Personal Bankruptcy Data for Opt-Out Hearings and Other Purposes," *American Bankruptcy Law Journal,* Vol. 56 (Winter 1982), pp. 1-28.

Simpson, David B. "Leases and the Bankruptcy Code: Tempering the Rigors of Strict Performance," *The Business Lawyer,* Vol. 38 (November 1982), pp. 61-89.

———. "Leases and the Bankruptcy Code: The Protean Concept of Adequate Assurance of Future Performance," *American Bankruptcy Law Journal,* Vol. 56 (July 1982), pp. 233-249.

Sishtla, P. V. "Financial Ratios as Detectors of Business Failure," *Management Accountant* (India), Vol. 3 (August 1968), pp. 373-378.

Sivertsen, Elmer T. "How To Prevent Credit Frauds," *Credit and Financial Management,* Vol. 69 (October 1967), pp. 30-33.

Smaha, John Lindon. "Automatic Stay Under the 1978 Bankruptcy Code: An Equitable Roadblock to Secured Creditor Relief," *San Diego Law Review,* Vol. 17 (August 1980), pp. 1113-1135.

Snedecor, Estes. "Fees and Allowances in Straight Bankruptcy," *Journal of the National Conference of Referees in Bankruptcy,* Vol. 40 (January 1966), pp. 26-29.

Stanley, David T., et al. *Bankruptcy: Problems, Process, Reform.* Washington, D.C.: The Brookings Institution, 1971.

Starkweather, Louis P. "Corporate Failure, Recapitalizations and Readjustments." *Fundamentals of Investment Banking.* Englewood Cliffs, N.J.: Prentice-Hall, Inc., 1949.

Stein, Jeffrey A. "Section 1111(b): Providing Undersecured Creditors with Postconfirmation Appreciation in the Value of the Collateral," *American Bankruptcy Law Journal,* Vol. 56 (July 1982), pp. 195-215.

Stiglitz, Joseph E. "Some Aspects of the Pure Theory of Corporate Finance: Bankruptcies and Takeovers," *Bell Journal of Economic and Management Science,* Vol. 3 (Autumn 1972), pp. 458-482.

Strischek, Dev. "Solvency: The Concept and an Approach for the Analysis of Long-Term Borrowers," *The Journal of Commercial Bank Lending,* Vol. 55 (February 1973), pp. 30-47.

Stubbs, Donald H. "Automatic Stays and Setoffs in Consumer Bankruptcies," *Ali-Aba Course Materials Journal,* Vol. 5 (December 1980), pp. 5-14.

Stutman, Jack, et al. "Your Corporate Client Is in Financial Difficulty and Solicits Your Advice," *The Business Lawyer,* Vol. 28 (November 1972), pp. 253-274.

Sullivan, George. *The Boom in Going Bust.* New York: The Macmillan Co., 1968.

Tait, N. Williams. "Bankruptcy Preference Laws: The Scope of Section 547(c)(2)," *Banking Law Journal,* Vol. 99 (January 1982), pp. 55-66.

Tamari, M. "Financial Ratios as a Means of Forecasting Bankruptcy," *Management International Review,* Vol. 4 (1966), pp. 15-21.

Teofan, Vernon O., and L. E. Creel, III. "The Trustee's Avoiding Power Under the Bankruptcy Act and the New Code: A Comparative Analysis," *St Mary's Law Journal,* Vol. 11 (Number 2; 1979), pp. 311-347.

Thimmig, Paul Joseph. "Adequate Disclosure Under Chapter 11 of the Bankruptcy Code," *Southern California Law Review,* Vol. 53, Part 2 (May/September 1980), pp. 1527-1562.

Tillinghast, David R., and Stephen D. Gardner. "Acquisitive Reorganizations and Chapters X and XI of the Bankruptcy Act," *Tax Law Review,* Vol. 26 (May 1971), pp. 663-723.

Trost, J. Ronald. "Business Reorganization Under Chapter 11 of the New Bankruptcy Code," *The Business Lawyer,* Vol. 34 (April 1979), pp. 1309-1346.

Trost, J. Ronald, Geo. M. Treister, Ken N. Klee, Richard Levin, and Leon S. Forman. "The Discharge of Debts Under the New Bankruptcy Code," *The Practical Lawyer,* Vol. 25 (June 1979), pp. 51-56.

Ulrich, Joseph E. "Comments on the Consumer Finance Industry's Proposals to Improve the Position of Secured Creditors in Consumer Bankruptcy Cases," *Washington & Lee Law Review,* Vol. 39 (Spring 1982), pp. 381-419.

————. "Fraudulent Conveyance and Preferences in Virginia," *Washington & Lee Law Review,* Vol. 36 (Winter 1979), pp. 51-81.

Ungerman, Jay. "The False Financial Statement: The Plague of Our Credit Economy," *Commercial Law Journal,* Vol. 68 (February 1963), pp. 39-40.

University of Michigan Law School. "Tort Claims Under the Present and Proposed Bankruptcy Acts," *University of Michigan Journal of Law Reform,* Vol. 11 (Spring 1978), pp. 417-442.

Vidmar, Stephan M. "Filing for Personal Bankruptcy: Adoption of a Bonafide Effort Test Under Chapter 13," *University of Michigan Journal of Law Reform,* Vol. 14 (Winter 1981), pp. 321-345.

Vihon, Charles F. "Classification of Unsecured Claims: Squaring a Circle?," *American Bankruptcy Law Journal,* Vol. 55 (April 1981), pp. 143-175.

Wahoff, William J. "Adequate Protection of Secured Creditors in Termination of Stay Litigation Under the Bankruptcy Code," *Ohio State Law Journal,* Vol. 43 (1982), pp. 715-734.

Waldrip, Stuart T. "Fraudulent Financial Statements and Section 17 of the Bankruptcy Act—The Creditor's Dilemma" (Notes), *Utah Law Review* (May 1967), pp. 281-296.

Walker, Ernest. *Essentials of Financial Management.* Englewood Cliffs, N.J.: Prentice-Hall, Inc., 1965.

Walker, John A., Jr. "Mineral Bankruptcies: Special Considerations," *Eastern Mineral Law Foundation Annual Institute,* Vol. 4 (1983), pp. 7.1-7.10.

Walter, James. "Determination of Technical Solvency," *The Journal of Business,* Vol. 30 (January 1957), pp. 30-43.

Ward, Larry D. "The TEFRA Amendments to Subchapter C: Corporate Distributions and Acquisitions," *The Journal of Corporation Law,* Vol. 8 (Winter 1983), pp. 277-336.

Warner, Elizabeth. "Consumer Warranty Claims Against Companies in Chapter 11 Reorganizations," *University of Michigan Journal of Law,* Vol. 14 (Winter 1981), pp. 347-369.

Warner, Sherman D. "CPA Services in Insolvency Trial Proceedings," *The New York Certified Public Accountant,* Vol. 28 (April 1958), pp. 262-267.

Warren, Charles. *Bankruptcies in United States History.* Cambridge, Mass: Harvard University Press, 1935.

Watkins, Charles E., Jr. "The Chapter 11 Plan," *Practical Lawyer,* Vol. 28 (December 1982), pp. 11-27.

Weingarten, Herbert N., and Leonard M. Salter. "The Internal Revenue Service in the Bankruptcy Court: Can Sovereign Immunity Be Eroded?," *The American Bankruptcy Law Journal,* Vol. 47 (Spring 1973), pp. 101-110.

Weinstein, Edward A. "Accountants' Examinations and Reports in Bankruptcy Proceedings," *The New York Certified Public Accountant,* Vol. 35 (January 1935), pp. 31-39.

———. "Examining a Company in Bankruptcy," *The Quarterly* (Touche, Ross, Bailey and Smart), Vol. 9 (September 1963), pp. 14-19.

Weintraub, Benjamin, Harris Levin, and Eugene Sosnoff. "Assignments for the Benefit of Creditors and Competitive Systems for Liquidation of Insolvent Estates," *Cornell Law Quarterly,* Vol. 39 (1953-1954), pp. 3-42.

Weintraub, Benjamin, and Alan N. Resnick. "Freezing the Debtor's Account—A Banker's Dilemma Under the Bankruptcy Code," *Banking Law Journal,* Vol. 100 (April 1983), pp. 316-324.

Weintraub, Charles. "Loss Carryback Tax Refund—Property of the Estate of the Bankrupt Within 70a of the Bankruptcy Act," *New York Law Forum,* Vol. 12 (Summer 1966), pp. 311-318.

Weston, Fred. *Managerial Finance.* New York: Holt, Rinehart and Winston, Inc., 1972.

Whelan, John G. "Analysis of Business Failures—Some Practices Under Scrutiny," *Chartered Secretary* (Australia), Vol. 16 (May 1964), pp. 110, 113, 115.

Whitehurst, Elmore. "How to Avoid Corporate Bankruptcy," *Texas Bar Journal,* Vol. 34 (February 22, 1971), pp. 143-146.

Williams, Donald B. "Liquidations Beware," *Accountant* (Eng.), Vol. 160 (June 21, 1969), pp. 890-891.

Williams, Elizabeth Y. "The New Bankruptcy Act—From a Creditor's Point of View," *Orange County Bar Journal,* Vol. 6 (Spring 1979), pp. 15-25.

Yerpe, A. J. "Getting the Most from Settlements," *Credit and Financial Management,* Vol. 70 (June 1968), pp. 18-22.

Yu, S. C. "A Reexamination of the Going Concern Postulate," *International Journal of Accountancy,* Vol. 6 (Spring 1971), pp. 37-58.

Zaretsky, Barry L. "The Fraud Exception to Discharge Under the New Bankruptcy Code," *American Bankruptcy Law Journal,* Vol. 53 (Summer 1979), pp. 253-268.

Statutes Citations

Bankruptcy Act:
Section 1(14), 10:71
Section 1(19), 3:25, 10:16
Section 3(a)(1–6), 3:25
Section 17(a)(1), 14:112
Section 63, 10:71
Section 67(d), 3:23, 3:129, 3:131
Section 67(d)(1)(d), 3:23
Section 67(d)(2), 11:47
Section 70(c), 3:110
Section 70(e), 3:113
Section 130(1), 10:15
Section 158, 6:10
Section 172, 10:54
Section 179, 10:26
Section 221, 10:27
Section 321, 9:7
Section 322, 9:7
Section 336, 9:7
Section 342, 9:7
Section 363, 9:7
Section 366(2), 10:23

Bankruptcy Code:
Section 101(4), 3:28, 10:72
Section 101(11), 3:28, 10:72
Section 101(13), 6:10
Section 101(17), 10:40
Section 101(25), 9:39
Section 101(26), 10:16, 11:48
Section 101(29), 3:28
Section 101(30), 3:142
Section 101(40), 3:116
Section 102(1), 5:35
Section 102(3), 5:96
Section 105(a), 4:8

Section 109(e), 5:130
Section 112(a), 5:122
Section 302, 3:101
Section 302(a), 5:131
Section 303(a), 3:63
Section 303(b)(3), 3:65
Section 303(f), 3:134
Section 303(h)(1), 3:44
Section 303(h)(2), 3:39
Section 303(i), 3:64
Section 305, 3:50
Section 321(b), 5:24
Section 325(b), 5:139
Section 327(a), 6:6
Section 327(b), 6:9, 6:18, 6:42
Section 327(d), 6:9
Section 327(f), 5:24
Section 328(a), 6:30
Section 328(c), 6:7, 6:8
Section 330, 5:28, 6:35
Section 330(a), 6:45
Section 331, 6:46
Section 341, 3:66, 3:67, 3:146
Section 341(a), 3:66, 3:67, 3:150
Section 341(b), 3:66, 3:68
Section 346, 14:140
Section 346(f), 14:110
Section 361, 3:73, 3:100, 10:5
Section 362, 3:72, 3:76, 3:77, 3:79, 3:137
Section 362(a), 3:69
Section 362(a)(6), 14:139
Section 362(a)(8), 14:139
Section 362(b), 3:70
Section 362(b)(7), 14:139
Section 362(b)(8), 14:139
Section 362(c), 3:71

References are given by chapter and paragraph numbers.

References are given by chapter and paragraph numbers.

Section 550(d), 10:40
Section 552, 3:134
Section 553, 3:95, 3:136, 3:137
Section 553(b), 3:138
Section 553(c), 3:136
Section 554, 10:39
Section 701(a), 3:145
Section 702, 3:146
Section 702(a), 3:66
Section 703, 3:146
Section 704, 3:148
Section 705(a), 3:150
Section 705(b), 3:150
Section 707, 3:165
Section 721, 3:149
Section 723, 10:40
Section 723(a), 3:151
Section 723(b), 3:151
Section 723(c), 3:153
Section 723(d), 3:155
Section 724(a), 3:160
Section 724(b), 3:159
Section 726(a), 3:153
Section 726(a)(4), 14:124
Section 726(a)(5), 14:125
Section 726(b), 3:162
Section 726(c), 3:163
Section 727, 3:157, 3:165, 11:29, 14:135
Section 727(a)(1), 3:42, 3:156
Section 727(a)(3), 11:83
Section 727(a)(7), 3:158
Section 728(c), 3:153
Section 741, 3:169, 10:40
Section 752, 3:169
Section 761(17), 10:40
Section 1101(2), 5:81
Section 1102, 5:13, 6:38, 9:2, 9:5
Section 1102(a)(1), 5:6
Section 1102(a)(2), 5:6
Section 1102(b), 5:6-15
Section 1103, 1:13, 6:10
Section 1103(b), 6:7, 6:10
Section 1103(c), 9:9
Section 1104(a), 5:6, 5:20
Section 1104(b), 5:23
Section 1106(a)(6), 14:136
Section 1107(a), 5:28, 5:30
Section 1107(b), 6:7, 6:10
Section 1108, 5:28
Section 1109, 6:28, 7:67
Section 1109(a), 5:19
Section 1109(b), 5:19

Section 1111(a), 7:32
Section 1111(b), 5:40-42, 5:44, 5:141, 10:38
Section 1111(b)(1)(A), 10:22
Section 1111(b)(1)(A)(i), 5:42
Section 1111(b)(2), 5:40, 5:42-44, 5:92, 5:99, 5:100, 10:22, 10:24, 10:29, 12:41
Section 1112, 5:123
Section 1112(c), 5:122
Section 1112(e), 5:122
Section 1121, 5:45, 5:123, 7:40
Section 1122, 5:46, 5:80, 5:89
Section 1123, 5:46, 5:80, 5:89
Section 1124, 5:51, 5:54, 10:20, 10:21
Section 1124(3)(A), 10:31
Section 1125, 5:63, 5:80, 5:89, 5:114, 5:117
Section 1125(a), 5:57
Section 1125(b), 5:56, 5:62
Section 1125(c), 5:62
Section 1125(d), 5:60, 5:65
Section 1125(e), 5:64, 5:79
Section 1126, Exhibit 4-1
Section 1126(b), 5:63
Section 1126(c), 5:84
Section 1126(d), 5:84
Section 1126(e), 5:85
Section 1126(f), 5:85, 5:89, 10:36
Section 1126(g), 5:107, 10:36
Section 1127(c), 5:80
Section 1128, 5:86
Section 1129, 5:123, 10:29, 14:129
Section 1129(a), 5:89, 5:90
Section 1129(a)(B), 10:22
Section 1129(a)(7), 7:42, 10:1
Section 1129(a)(7)(A), 5:91
Section 1129(a)(7)(B), 5:92
Section 1129(a)(8), 5:54
Section 1129(a)(9), 14:127
Section 1129(a)(11), 10:37
Section 1129(b), 5:88, 5:89, 5:96, 10:25, 10:27
Section 1129(b)(1), 5:107
Section 1129(b)(2), 5:43, 5:144
Section 1129(b)(2)(A), 5:97
Section 1129(b)(2)(B), 5:102
Section 1129(b)(2)(B)(ii), 10:32
Section 1129(b)(2)(C), 5:103, 10:21
Section 1141, 5:112
Section 1141(d), 14:136
Section 1141(d)(3), 5:53
Section 1143, 5:111, 5:120
Section 1144, 5:123
Section 1145, 5:116

References are given by chapter and paragraph numbers.

References are given by chapter and paragraph numbers.

References are given by chapter and paragraph numbers.

Name Index

References are given by chapter and paragraph numbers.

Subject Index

References are given by chapter and paragraph numbers.

References are given by chapter and paragraph numbers.

References are given by chapter and paragraph numbers.

geographic distribution, 2:10
size of, 2:9
stage of, 2:35
trend analysis, 2:46
underlying causes, 2:22
Business plan, Exhibit 8-2, Exhibit 8-4
Business ratios and statistics, 2:5–13, 7:57

California, 3:39, 3:47, 8:5
Capital:
insufficient, 2:32
unbalanced structure, 2:30
Capital deficiency, statement of, 12:5, 12:23
Capitalization rate, 10:47–48, 10:20–21, 10:60
Capital losses:
basis adjustment, 14:51–54
carryovers, 14:23–24, 14:44
reduction due to debt discharge, 14:46
Carman v. *Commissioner*, 14:80n
Cash:
audit procedures, 11:1–12
shortage as symptom, 2:40
weak position, 2:30
Cash collateral:
nature, 5:33, 8:13
problems, 8:9
use of, 5:34, 8:13
Cash expenses, manipulation of, 11:60
Cash flow:
importance of, 9:19
reports, 9:19–43
Cash inflow, projected, 9:19
Cash receipts, diverting of, 11:61
Cash receipts and disbursements statements,
Exhibit 8-3
required by court, 12:22
Cash surrender value of insurance policies,
11:73–74
Celler-Kefauver, 2:55
Central States Electric Corp. v. *Austrian*,
10:49, 10:50
Century Chemical Corp., 6:42n
Change in ownership, 14:91, 14:93
Changes in financial position, statement of,
12:21, 12:131
Chapter 7, defined, Glossary
Chapter X proceedings, defined, Glossary. *See
also* Bankruptcy Act
Chapter 11:
advantages, 5:127–128
consolidation, 5:8
conversion to chapter 7, 5:122
defined, Glossary

disadvantages, 5:127–128
operating under, 5:4–7
purpose of, 5:3
reports issued, 8:3
Chapter XI proceedings, defined, Glossary. *See
also* Bankruptcy Act
Chapter 13:
advantages over chapter 11, 5:145
defined, Glossary
nature of, 5:129–145
objective, 5:129
Charitable contribution carryovers, 14:23
Checks:
accountant's signature, 9:33–35
co-sign, 7:90
initialed by accountant, 9:33
Chicago, 4:1
In re Chicago Rys. Co., 10:54n
Civil War, 3:9
Claims:
administrative, 3:98, 5:52, 5:93, 11:108
chapter 13 secured, 10:19
classification, 5:46–50, 12:124–132
contingent, 3:93, 7:30, 12:5
defined, Glossary
disallowance of, 3:93–94
disputed, 7:30
dissenting class, 10:31
false, 3:168
fishermen, 3:99
grain producers, 3:99
impaired, 5:52, 5:54, 10:31–36
inflated, 11:106–108
involuntary gap, 5:93, 5:109, 14:109, 14:127
modification of secured, 5:97–99
postpetition, 3:136
priority, 3:161, 5:52
priority treatment, 5:93
proof of, 3:91, 3:93, 3:161, 5:39, 7:20
provable, 3:114
reconciled, 11:37
rejection of executory contracts, 3:94, 5:42,
5:52
secured, 3:95–96, 12:5
SIPC, 3:177
subordinated, 5:42
tax, *see* Tax claims
tax priority, 5:93
undersecured, 3:95, 10:9
unliquidated, 3:93, 7:30, 12:5
unsecured, 12:5
filed late, 3:161
wages, 5:93

References are given by chapter and paragraph numbers.

References are given by chapter and paragraph numbers.

References are given by chapter and paragraph numbers.

References are given by chapter and paragraph numbers.

References are given by chapter and paragraph numbers.

References are given by chapter and paragraph numbers.

References are given by chapter and paragraph numbers.